The American Senate

The American Senate

An Insider's History

Neil MacNeil and
Richard A. Baker

OXFORD
UNIVERSITY PRESS

Oxford University Press is a department of the University of Oxford.
It furthers the University's objective of excellence in research,
scholarship, and education by publishing worldwide.

Oxford   New York
Auckland   Cape Town   Dar es Salaam   Hong Kong   Karachi
Kuala Lumpur   Madrid   Melbourne   Mexico City   Nairobi
New Delhi   Shanghai   Taipei   Toronto

With offices in
Argentina   Austria   Brazil   Chile   Czech Republic   France   Greece
Guatemala   Hungary   Italy   Japan   Poland   Portugal   Singapore
South Korea   Switzerland   Thailand   Turkey   Ukraine   Vietnam

Oxford is a registered trade mark of Oxford University Press
in the UK and certain other countries.

Published in the United States of America by
Oxford University Press
198 Madison Avenue, New York, NY 10016

Library of Congress Cataloging-in-Publication Data
MacNeil, Neil, 1923–2008.
The American Senate : an insider's history / Neil MacNeil and Richard A. Baker.
pages cm
Includes bibliographical references and index.
ISBN 978-0-19-536761-4 (hardcover : alk. paper)
1. United States. Congress. Senate—History. I. Baker, Richard A. II. Title.
JK1161.M316   2013
328.73'071—dc23   2012046807

1 3 5 7 9 8 6 4 2

Printed in the United States of America
on acid-free paper

For my gallant daughter,
Tara MacNeil Veitch
NMN

For Pat
For a half-century of caring
RAB

The Senate was the home of compromise, the fount of compromise, the citadel of compromise. It wore down those who refused to compromise. With some, the process took longer than it did with others, but in time it conquered them all—if they wanted to stay, and if they really wanted to accomplish anything in the Senate.

—Allen Drury, *Mark Coffin, USS* (1979)

CONTENTS

Preface   ix

Acknowledgments   xiii

Prologue: Entering the Contemporary Senate   3

1. Money and Politics: Electing US Senators   14

2. The Collapse of Campaign Finance Reform   35

3. Dancing with Presidents: A Wary Embrace   53

4. Struggling for Primacy: From TR to FDR   84

5. Losing Ground to the Imperial Presidency   114

6. Living with the House of Representatives   149

7. The Center to Which Everyone Comes   168

8. Leadership Empowered: The Modern Era   197

9. The Senate Investigates   230

10. The Watchdogs   245

11. Debate, Deliberation, and Dispute   276

12. Dilatory Tactics   302

13. Reform and Reaction   335

To the Future   357

Notes   363

Selected Bibliography   421

Index   437

PREFACE

IN THE LIFE OF THE American republic, the Senate of the United States has played an extraordinary role. Unique among legislatures, the Senate over the past two centuries has developed in ways that would have surprised the framers of the Constitution. Yet it has also stayed true to their intention that it stand as a "necessary fence" against the "fickleness and passion" that drives popular pressure for hasty and ill-considered lawmaking. Today, the US Senate continues as the most powerful upper house of any legislative body in the world. Highly visible nationwide via cable television and twenty-four/seven news coverage, and immediately accessible through the Internet and e-mail, the Senate is more familiar to Americans than at any time in its history.

Ever since its creation, the Senate has been a source of national pride—and national frustration. It has risen to meet enormous challenges and, crippled by its inherent flaws, has fallen periodically to a state of functional paralysis. The current Senate is a legislative body in transition, as it has always been—from the framers' early pretensions; through its Golden Age of constitutional debates; and on to the corruption of the Gilded Age spoilsmen, the Millionaires' Club, the progressive reforms that followed in the 1910s, '30s, and '60s; and finally down to cacophony of our own times. Its nearly two thousand members since 1789 have included statesmen and politicos, brilliant legislative tacticians, fiery demagogues, time-servers, and lots of former high school class presidents—a genuine cross section of the nation's political class.

Most US senators have been conscientious individuals doing their best to meet the demands of their times; firm in their convictions, but also—among the best of them—individuals willing to seek compromise in preference to the gridlock that comes with the pursuit of rigid ideological orthodoxy. Media coverage, however, of a single recalcitrant senator or a small minority of senators, doggedly working to sabotage the legislative machinery of the great American government—a senator perhaps from one of the nation's more thinly populated states, or a small group of senators with a determined ideological purity—can render the Senate contemptible in the eyes of frustrated Americans.

At their best, senators have functioned with a live-and-let-live philosophy that was more than a vulgar or amoral indifference to ethical considerations. They have displayed a tolerance toward opposing views, a willingness to have those views voiced and voted, and recognition of the fundamental right of disagreement, which lies at the heart of a free society. For decades, senators, and House members, too, acted largely within those views, performing much like lawyers, as many of them were, representing their client constituencies as best they could but avoiding personal animosities with those in opposition. Of course, there have been periods of great one-sided bickering, as in the years before the Civil War, when pistol duels and physical and verbal abuse were not uncommon. In our own time, with the ugliness of election campaigns and the growth of bitter ideological commitments, much of the comity required of all legislative bodies—if they are to operate rationally—has been lost across the Senate chamber's ever-widening center aisle. This is clearly a low point within the broad historical cycles of boom and bust, growth and retrenchment that have defined the evolution of the Senate—and the nation.[1]

The history of the Senate demonstrates its fundamental power to respond to the never-ending problems and crises of government. That has been the history of the Senate from its beginning, a process of ceaseless change, not always obvious even to those making the changes. Most of the changes arrived at a glacial pace, measured in decades. Pick any major feature of today's Senate—committee operations, floor leadership, the manner in which members are elected, investigations, relations with the House of Representatives and the president, debate management, public access—and one will find the product of struggle; setbacks; and tireless, grinding, calculated determination.

This book explores areas, some scarcely touched by others, that give special meaning to the Senate's life. One book can hardly pretend to be a comprehensive history of a nearly two-and-one-quarter-century-old legislative body with many hundreds of members, past and present. What the authors hope it will do, however, is satisfy the reader's basic curiosity about what one astute observer called "the one touch of authentic genius in the American political system,"[2] whose actions—and inactions—shape the lives of countless millions at home and across the globe. We hope this work will also serve as a filter for the torrent of information and opinion about modern political and governmental affairs that cascades into the daily consciousness of discerning Americans.

We believe the Senate, from its start, has been under constant, if not always obvious, revision. Webster, Clay, and Calhoun, who dominated one phase of the Senate's life, could hardly have recognized the place a half century later and, needless to say, they certainly would not today.

—Neil MacNeil
—Richard A. Baker

ACKNOWLEDGMENTS

———————

THIS PROJECT EVOLVED AS A logical extension of Neil MacNeil's 1963 history of the US House of Representatives, *Forge of Democracy*. He spent seventeen years, until his death in 2008, pursuing his research like a bloodhound in search of a culprit. His work would have not made it this far without the tireless support of his daughter, Deirdre MacNeil. An attorney by day, she became his typist on evenings and weekends, transforming his virtually indecipherable scrawl into manageable documents.

US Senate historian Donald A. Ritchie is the godfather of this project. He convinced Neil and Oxford University Press executive editor Nancy Toff to begin a conversation. Neil, Deirdre, and Nancy convened for lunch at Washington's National Press Club and a contract soon followed. In 2008, Oxford sent MacNeil's preliminary manuscript to several reviewers. As one of them, I responded that there was a very good book lurking in the submitted document, but it needed to be carved out and reduced to a size that would appeal to general readers as well as congressional specialists. After Neil's death, Deirdre invited me to lunch and succeeded in convincing me to implement my own recommendations. None of that would have been possible without the guidance and sustained effort of Deirdre and Nancy Toff, and Nancy's colleague Sonia Tycko—a master of making the editorial trains run on time.

The timely completion of this project also owes much to a generous Robert H. Michel Special Project Grant from the Dirksen Congressional

Center in Pekin, Illinois. The Center had honored MacNeil in 1980 with its inaugural Everett McKinley Dirksen Prize for Distinguished Reporting of Congress and is now the repository of the papers documenting his nearly sixty years in political journalism.

I am particularly indebted to the deeply knowledgeable staff of the US Senate Historical Office, including Don Ritchie, Betty Koed, Karen Paul, Stephen Tull, Beth Hahn, and Mary Baumann. Senate photo historian Heather Moore worked her special magic to help select the illustrations in this volume. In the US Senate Library, truly one of the world's finest legislative research facilities, a talented team of reference librarians found constructive answers to even the vaguest of questions. Specifically helpful on this project were library director Leona Faust and librarians Brian McLaughlin, Zoe Davis, and Nancy Kervin, along with Meghan Dunn, Natalie Sager, Melanie Jacobs, and Tamara Elliott. My thanks also go to Secretary of the Senate Nancy Erickson and to Senate curator Diane Skvarla and her able colleagues Scott Strong and Rich Doerner. In College Park, Maryland, I spent countless hours in the stacks of the University of Maryland's McKeldin Library, a well-managed and richly stocked research facility, indispensable to my needs.

Had he lived to complete the project, Neil surely would have added names of family members and sources helpful to him over the decades. Any of those who read these pages will know who they are and should accept his silent appreciation.

My own family members have put up with my preoccupation with "the Senate book" for three intense years. Special thanks go to Chris, Dave, Michelle, Tony, Matt, Lauren, Drew, and Bob. Most of all, I extend my love and deepest appreciation to my alter ego for the past half century, Dr. Patricia K. S. Baker.

Richard A. Baker
Kensington, Maryland
January 2013

The American Senate

Prologue

Entering the Contemporary Senate

FRESH FROM THEIR VICTORIES IN the senatorial elections of 1996, fifteen very pleased women and men filed into the tightly secured chamber of the US Senate. Their purpose, on December 3, was to hear one of a dozen lectures in a three-day orientation program. Members of this largest freshman class in sixteen years were allowed to sit in the prime front-row, center-aisle locations usually occupied by senators heavy with seniority. Simultaneously gleeful and awe-stricken, these soon-to-be senators acted like third graders at the start of a new school year, impishly opening and closing the hinged tops and drawers of the highly polished mahogany desks. In those drawers, partially obscured by notepapers, documents of State, and candy wrappers, they saw the names—carved by penknife or written in ink—of a dozen or more senators who had once worked from that particular relic.

With the gallery doors bolted shut and the floor-level entrances carefully monitored against the intrusion of curious onlookers, a staff member introduced the coming hour's speaker. The Senate's most senior Democratic member, seventy-nine-year-old Robert C. Byrd, had represented West Virginia in this chamber for nearly four decades. Over that span, his party had awarded him every one of its elective offices: conference secretary, party whip, and floor leader—both in the majority and minority. Until recently, Byrd had also served as Senate president pro tempore—third in the line of presidential succession following the vice president and Speaker of the House. His immaculately styled silver-white hair, his dark blue three-piece suit framing a carefully chosen silk necktie, and his dignified bearing conveyed the modern image of an ancient Roman senator.

Over the previous quarter-century, Senator Byrd had spent countless hours educating himself on the Senate's procedural rules, parliamentary precedents, cultural traditions, and political history. To that end, he would take a fresh copy of the 1,500-page manual of Senate procedure, and with a yellow highlighter, note text that he intended to memorize. When he reached the concluding page, he would start over with a clean copy. (An autodidact, he gave the same treatment to dictionaries.) Throughout the 1980s, the West Virginia legislator had worked with Senate historians to prepare dozens of chapter-length research studies that explored the Senate's past with a view to understanding its contemporary operations. He then delivered each of these works as a floor speech—one hundred in all. In anticipation of the body's bicentennial, the Senate in 1988 voted to have Byrd's addresses published in two extensively illustrated volumes.[1] Successive classes of freshmen senators adopted his work as their textbook.

Senate insiders saw the aging Byrd, if perhaps a bit of a throwback to an earlier time, as a repository of wisdom and experience, an ideal mentor for freshly minted members. He gloried in the frequent compliment that he would surely have been at home in any session of the Senate—eighteenth, nineteenth, or twentieth century.

Byrd began his 1996 orientation remarks by welcoming senators to "what I consider to be 'hallowed ground.'" "Make no mistake about it," he said, "the office of United States Senator is the highest political calling in the land."[2] Some of his listeners appeared unsettled by his overly deliberate and occasionally grandiose speaking style. A rumble of nervous laughter, discretely muffled, annoyed attending Senate veterans, conditioned to respect through long observation of this institutional patriot.

Within minutes, however, the entire class of senators-elect sat transfixed. Here, they realized, were words to be written down, thoughts to be remembered. Forty-five minutes later, Byrd received a heartfelt standing ovation. Years later, those present recalled the event as a personally defining experience. So impressed was party elder Edward Kennedy that he obtained Byrd's permission to have these private remarks published in the *Congressional Record*, and successive freshmen classes received his text in pamphlet edition for leisurely study.[3]

Behind those closed doors, Byrd explained to his soon-to-be colleagues that although the "Senate is often soundly castigated for its inefficiency, but in fact, it was never intended to be efficient. Its purpose was and is to examine, consider, protect, and to be a totally independent source of wisdom and judgment on the actions of the lower house and on the executive. As such," he continued, "the Senate is the central pillar of our Constitutional system."[4] This member of the 1958 freshman class advised these incoming members to "study the Senate in its institutional context, because that is the best way to understand your personal role as a United States Senator." He followed with a prediction that engaged his audience, and resonated with seasoned senators who read it later:

> The pressures on you will, at times, be enormous. You will have to formulate policies, grapple with issues, serve [your] constituents, and cope with the media. A Senator's attention today is fractured beyond belief. Committee meetings, breaking news, fundraising, all of these will demand your attention, not to mention personal and family responsibilities. But, somehow, amidst all the noise and confusion, you must find the time to reflect, to study, to read, and, especially, to understand the absolutely critically important institutional role of the Senate.[5]

The fifteen senators-elect filed out of the chamber, most of them more somber and reflective than when they had entered, but soon to be diverted by more practical matters. "How do I get from the Capitol to my temporary office quarters?" "When can I start hiring staff?" "Why can't I use my cell phone in the Senate chamber?"

It is commonly observed that legislators tend to be either "workhorses" or "show horses." In the Senate, "workhorses" seek out companionable mentors, perhaps their state's other senator, a seasoned colleague of similar political orientation, or an elder in the style of Robert Byrd. They spend more time reading and listening than they do speaking. Those at the other end of the spectrum—the natural "show horses"—seek out media representatives and, continuing in campaign mode, quickly fill their schedules with public appearances. Active and restless by temperament, infused by the deep reservoirs of energy that promote success in modern-day electoral politics, they rarely have the time or inclination to master the Senate's complex floor procedures. Of course, most new senators fall somewhere between these extremes, but those seeking lengthy Senate careers and the incalculable benefits of rising seniority that come with several successful reelection campaigns—lifting them from the "baby senator" characterization reserved for first-term members—tend to cluster toward the "workhorse" regions on the spectrum.

Among the priorities facing newly arriving senators are assignment to desirable committees, selection of a competent staff, and a search for adequate working space in one of the three Senate office buildings. Committee assignments are subject to vast amounts of political log-rolling. The highest of all honors is a seat on the Appropriations Committee—a career-making gift forever cherished by its few fortunate first-year recipients. Close behind comes the Senate Committee on Finance. Committees closely identified with home-state constituency interests are especially prized. Committee service also awards senators coveted additional staff positions. In all cases, modern-era senators join committees far superior in technical proficiency to those that Senator Byrd found upon his arrival in 1959.

The title "chief of staff," unknown within the Senate until the 1980s, suggests military structure and discipline. Senators' personal office staffs, confronting tidal waves of paper and electronic communications from constituents and others, require effective management. Some staffs figure it out and some do not, but a poorly organized staff can surely pave a fast road to reelection defeat. Members' staffs, both in Washington and in the home state, range in combined size from thirty to sixty, depending on the state's population. As senators gain in seniority and committee responsibility, their staffs may increase to as many as one hundred individuals. Today's Senate experiences significant amounts of staff turnover, with younger employees—those in their twenties—tending to remain less than three years in what for many is a unique postgraduate educational experience.

Most new senators do not need to spend much time searching for an office suite; it is found for them. Very quickly, they comprehend the seniority ranking system that places them close to the dreaded number "one hundred." The fifteen new senators in the 1996 class, for example, took their place in line for office suite selection under a system that awarded priority to those with former congressional service, followed by previous presidential cabinet members, state elective officeholders, and then—the tiebreaker—by state-population rank. Many freshmen aim for accommodations in the Beaux-Arts-style Russell Building, opened in 1909, with its high ceilings and marble fire mantels. Less alluring is the Dirksen Building, with places for two dozen senators. Completed in 1958 and reflecting the functionalist architectural tastes of that era, it was intended principally for committees and the state constituency offices of their chairmen. That plan, however, did not count on the desire of many of those chairmen to keep their personal offices in the elegant Russell Building.

A major expansion in Senate staffs during the 1960s and '70s filled the Russell and Dirksen buildings beyond capacity—interior toilets became office cubicles—and caused staff to overflow into nearby former hotels, apartment buildings, and expensive commercial real estate. This compelled the Senate to plan for a third office building, and motivated the belated naming of the existing structures, previously known, unimaginatively, as the Old Senate Office Building and the New Senate Office Building. In 1972, the Senate selected for that honor two recently deceased senior members, Richard B. Russell, a Georgia Democrat, and Everett M. Dirksen, an Illinois Republican. (This began an epidemic of memorial space naming that had become so widespread that when Majority Leader Bob Dole departed in 1996, all that remained for him was a Capitol Building exterior balcony—but one with a great view.)

The third Senate office building, severely over budget upon completion in 1982, bears the name of the widely respected Michigan Democrat, Philip A. Hart. That building's starkly modern design and widely publicized excessive costs made senators reluctant to choose one of fifty office suites upon its opening, which was tactfully timed to occur several weeks after the 1982 senatorial elections.

New senators also learn the value of seniority, as determined by their respective Senate party organizations, for receiving attractive committee assignments and for the location of their desk in the Senate chamber. Those at the bottom of the seniority ladder sit in the farthest corner of the chamber's back row—a forsaken zone known to some as Dogpatch. Trent Lott complained in 1989 that he and his other freshmen colleagues had been placed "in storage" in "an aloof, sedate organization, set in its ways and distinctly unfriendly to the plebes who entered the chamber after their first election." He continued, "Slowly, though, I began to know and understand my fellow senators. Many of them were lone wolves—courteous enough in conversation, but hardly warm and personable."[6] Mitch McConnell, who had arrived four years earlier, peered out from his back-row perch at the multitudes before him and quietly lamented, "None of these people is ever going to die, retire, or be defeated."[7]

Standing in the chamber's center aisle for the first time, new members typically comment on how human-scale the rectangular room appears, compared with its televised image, or the cavernous House chamber. Measuring 114 feet by 80 feet, and rising more than two stories, the room accommodates one hundred mahogany desks, with armchairs upholstered in chestnut-brown leather, arranged in four concentric semicircles. These desks, organized since 1877 by political party, with Republicans on the presiding officer's left and Democrats to the right, offer an instant visual clue as to the chamber's current partisan makeup. At the start of the 107th Congress in January 2001, for the first time each party claimed an even fifty desks—a far cry from 1937 ratio of seventy-five Democratic seats to an anemic seventeen on the Republican side, or that of 1907 with sixty-one Republicans against twenty-nine Democrats.

As a consequence of the nation's mid-nineteenth-century population expansion and resulting new states, Congress in 1850 authorized a major extension of the Capitol to relieve pressure from its increasingly crowded legislative chambers. On January 4, 1859, the Senate's then sixty-four members, with mixed emotions, departed the semicircular room that had been its meeting place for the forty years that embraced the Golden Age of Henry Clay, Daniel Webster, and John C. Calhoun. They paraded the forty-five paces through a connecting corridor to the new quarters that a reporter for the *New York Herald* described as "finely proportioned" and "light and graceful." The arriving senators at once admired the room's Rococo and classical architectural themes, muted colors, deep-purple floral-patterned carpet, and galleries accommodating six hundred—instead of just a few dozen. Crowning it all was a grand ornamental skylight decorated with twenty-one stained-glass panels, each with a colored medallion containing such images as a printing press, a steam engine, a cornucopia, and other symbols of the nation's progress and abundance.

Many of those parading senators, however, soon came to despise their new quarters. Located at the center of the new wing without exterior windows, they found it dark, drafty, and noisy. Within months, some of the more aggrieved among them had introduced legislation to tear the place down. They proposed a reconstruction along the Capitol's exterior walls to admit longed-for natural lighting and ventilation. Only the emergency of the Civil War kept that plan from materializing.[8]

Ninety years passed before the chamber underwent major and long-desired reconstruction, inspired by the corroding iron supports that threatened to land the heavy glass ceiling onto senators' laps. During summer recesses in 1949 and 1950, the room got its makeover. Gone was the leaky and sound-amplifying glass ceiling and the Victorian ornamental detail in plaster and iron. In its place stood a more blandly functional chamber with floral-themed carpeting, which alternated in its replacements over the years from an aggressive burgundy to a washed-out blue. The 1986 advent of gavel-to-gavel television coverage finally infused the place with decorative vigor, introducing an outspoken dark blue carpet, unobtrusive damask-patterned wall coverings, and camera-friendly lighting that gave freshmen members a sense that they had truly arrived.

New members quickly learn, as Senator Byrd had promised in 1996, that "a senator's attention today is fractured beyond belief." The significance of that statement has only intensified over the intervening years. A memorable occasion for a visiting constituent—or even a journalist—is to find a senator riding alone on one of the subway cars that shuttle between the Capitol and the office buildings. For the three-minute duration of that trip, that visitor is likely to enjoy an animated conversation, until the doors spring open and the senator hurries off. (Such a memorable experience is not likely, however, when one encounters a senator being briefed by an aide, or engaged with other senators on their way to a vote. In such a setting, nonsenators would do well to keep a respectful distance.)

Whether on Capitol Hill or back in the home state, senators tend to be tightly scheduled and perpetually accompanied by hovering staffers. For those contemplating reelection, the need to raise millions of dollars for media campaigns and to remain publicly visible through cooperation with home-state media outlets can be thoroughly draining. Yet only a few decades separate the modern senator from such redoubtable members as Vermont's George Aiken, who, in 1968, reported total campaign expenditures of only $17.09. Members like Aiken, and those from states more distant than Vermont, in the Senate's earlier times, customarily traveled home just a few times during each session. Since the 1960s, with the greater availability of high-speed jet aircraft, senators have found it convenient—or politically necessary—to return home at least weekly. And, increasingly, that is where members will find their families. No longer is it common for a new member of Congress to resettle spouse and children in or near the District of Columbia.

Today's Senate, composed principally of white men, is mostly Protestant in religious affiliation, and its members' educational preparation and prior career experience tilt toward law and business. The ratio of women to men—in both the Senate and House—hovers around one-to-five, although this compares favorably with the mid-1970s, when the Senate had no women in office. Over the six decades from the election of the first woman member in 1932 to 1992, no more than two women served together at one time. Senators of African, Hispanic, and Asian ancestry occasionally win seats, but their numbers in the Senate, unlike the House, are vastly unrepresentative of their numbers among the nation's population. The average age of senators has risen in recent years from the upper fifties to the low- to mid-sixties. While 41 percent of those in the 112th Congress (2011–13) were serving their initial six-year term, 21 percent of their colleagues had held seats for at least twenty years. Close to half of that Congress's Senate membership had previously been House members, while many decades had passed since a former senator managed to secure a seat in the lower chamber.[9]

New senators learn quickly the role tradition plays in the institution's culture. Why, once a year, would a senator spend forty-five minutes in the Senate chamber listening to a specially anointed colleague read George Washington's 1796 farewell address to the nation? Not even Washington chose to read that speech aloud; he simply sent it to a newspaper for publication. Yet annually, since the late nineteenth century, senators have dutifully labored through Washington's late-eighteenth-century remarks in celebration of the first president's birthday. The House abandoned that tradition in the 1980s, but the Senate views it differently.

Each new senator focuses, perhaps nervously, on a Senate tradition that will never die—the "maiden speech." Prior to the 1960s, a freshman regularly waited up to a year or more before summoning the will to make his or her first substantive floor remarks. Many of them understood that more senior members expected them to be occasionally seen but rarely heard. In more recent times, however, with the noise of their campaign victory celebrations yet alive in their ears, freshmen are not well disposed to silence. And, of course, their constituents expect them to swing into action to immediately "clean up the mess in Washington." The pressures of full-time media coverage have pushed the silent freshman into extinction. Once the date and time have been set for this initial oration, family, staff, proud former schoolteachers, and other supporters take their seats in the galleries, just as at least a few of the new member's Senate colleagues loyally move to their desks. Party leaders offer their support, and all take note of a Senate career well launched.

All freshmen of the majority party learn quickly about "the roster." Someone needs to preside, especially during those long hours of quorum calls and desultory speeches to a nearly empty chamber. Do not expect the vice president of the United States—whose only constitutional duty is to preside over the Senate—to appear! (That essentially ended with Alben Barkley in the early 1950s.) Nor is one likely to find the president pro tempore—usually the Senate's most senior majority-party member—hastening to take up presiding duties. Freshmen members will hear repeatedly that presiding is good for them. It is a good way to learn the identities of their ninety-nine colleagues, who must be announced by the name of their states ("Was that North Dakota or South Dakota?"); a good way to learn the Senate's rules and procedures; or just a good way to catch up on office reading or letter signing. These temporary presiding officers learn to listen very carefully to an official Senate parliamentarian, one of whom will always be seated within convenient whispering distance. Second only to properly identifying a senator seeking recognition is the necessity of repeating exactly what the parliamentarian whispers in response to the procedural situation on the floor. As an incentive to enjoy this chore, senators who preside for a session-total of one hundred hours are presented with an ornate "golden gavel award"—worth at least a home-state press release to show that the new senator has been noticed in the Capitol.[10]

In the mid-1970s, when Senate Republicans had begun to think of themselves as a permanent minority party, members inaugurated weekly party luncheons to help boost morale and to discuss legislative strategy. Within several years, following the 1980 elections that unexpectedly dropped Senate Democrats into the minority for the first time in a quarter-century, that party initiated its own weekly luncheon meetings. Although conceived as opportunities for the minority to strengthen its internal cohesion, these weekly events continued even when a party regained majority status. Today, these Tuesday members-only sessions begin with a catered meal and then move to a discussion of current legislative business. They provide an effective means for new members to interact with colleagues in the low-key social setting of a table for eight. The greenest freshmen have ready access to battle-worn veterans. For a rare moment in the course of a hectic day, no one else is watching: no media, no staff, and no constituents. Briefly out of the spotlight, senators are free to be themselves. Yet in recent years, these politically one-sided sessions have erected unwelcome barriers to bipartisan cooperation. Former Senate Majority Leader Trent Lott observed that by meeting's end, "We would always come out on fire." His Democratic counterpart, Tom Daschle, characterized the sessions as "pep rallies" with a quest for "red meat." He noted that the resulting "emotional fervor has a profound effect on how the Senate operates." Both leaders agreed that it took an entire day to get those members "calmed down."[11]

Eventually, freshmen become sophomores, and then juniors and seniors: moving up the ladder of experience just as predictably as high school and college students. Committee work becomes more engrossing as senators focus more keenly on their legislative objectives. They tend to look back with fondness to their fellow class members and to their years of learning what Senator Byrd had in mind when he urged the newcomers to take the trouble "to understand the absolutely critically important institutional role of the Senate."

In 2011, one of the members of the 1996 class, Susan Collins of Maine, summarized what she had learned about trying to be effective in this complex legislative body. Her top recommendation was, "Don't surprise people. Be open and straightforward about what you want to do." She counseled flexibility. "It is like buying a plane ticket online. You can be flexible about the date and time, but your destination is the same." As a skilled negotiator, she advised those who would seek to be effective not to "make a concession unless you are getting something in return." She added, "It took me a while to learn that." Senator Collins's final guideline related to the unique definition of "friendship" in the Senate context.[12] "Your allies today may not be your allies tomorrow, but that doesn't mean you can't stay friends."[13]

Senator Christopher Dodd, a thirty-year Senate veteran and son of a former senator, received considerable attention for his 2010 farewell address. Directing his remarks to the incoming senators of the future, Dodd identified three troubling issues affecting the Senate's ability to function coherently. First, he articulated the widely shared view that the nation's system for electing members of Congress "is completely dysfunctional." "Powerful financial interests, free to throw money about with little transparency, have corrupted . . . the basic principles underlying our representative democracy. . . . Newly-elected Senators will learn that their every legislative maneuver, their every public utterance, and even some of their private deliberations will be fodder for a 24/7 political media industry that seems to favor speculation over analysis and conflict over consensus." Dodd went on to lament the shift in media coverage. "[W]hile the corridors of Congress are crowded with handheld video and cell phone cameras, there is a declining role for newspaper, radio, and network journalists reporting the routine deliberations that are taking place in our subcommittee hearings. Ten years ago, 11 or 12 reporters from Connecticut covered the delegation's legislative activities. Today, there is only one doing the same work." He concluded with regret for the "intense partisan polarization [that has] raised the stakes in every debate and on every vote, making it difficult to lose with grace and nearly impossible to compromise without cost. Americans' distrust of politicians provides compelling incentives for senators to distrust each other, to disparage this very institution, and to disengage from the policymaking process."[14]

New members entering today's Senate have much to be worried about. But the most challenged of all freshman classes was the one that arrived at the Senate's temporary quarters in the spring of 1789. They took up their duties without knowing exactly what those duties were beyond the brief sketches contained in the US Constitution. In the following two years, they established Senate precedents and procedures, and overcame their regional and political differences to help flesh out the structure of the nation's federal government. The painter John Trumbull, in an end-of-session letter to Senate president John Adams, captured the success of the First Federal Congress. "In no nation, by no legislature was ever so much done in so short a period for the establishment of Government, Order, . . . & general tranquility."[15]

I

Money and Politics

Electing US Senators

"COMPLETELY DYSFUNCTIONAL!" THAT WAS THE assessment of thirty-year Senate veteran Christopher Dodd in 2010 about the system for electing US senators.[1] For more than two centuries, Senate observers have pronounced similar verdicts against an election process that has occasioned anger, frustration, corrupt practices, and searing despair of ever getting it right. By the time of Senator Dodd's remarks, the election of senators had mostly fallen to the ferocious talents of squads of professional technicians, hired by the candidates and ready to savage every candidate's opponent. Dramatic thirty-second television attack ads enhanced the nastiness of their techniques. The costs were enormous, often tens of millions of dollars for a single Senate seat. In 2010, according to the Federal Election Commission, the Nevada election campaign of Senator Harry Reid ran up expenses equivalent to sixty-nine dollars for each vote he received, while his unsuccessful opponent spent ninety-seven dollars.[2] The methods of electing senators, which had been turned upside down, had profound effects on the character and thrust of the Senate.

To the making of the Senate went many considerations, none more important than the way senators were to be elected. The delegates at the federal convention in Philadelphia were supremely aware of that requirement when they designed the Senate. In shaping the House of Representatives, they had no choice but to follow the model of state legislatures and have the representatives elected by the people. That worried many of them, and they felt obliged to create the Senate as a check on the House to curb what Edmund Randolph called "the turbulence and follies of democracy" that they expected from the representatives.[3] Experienced legislators in their own right, they calculated that if they correctly drew the qualifications for senators and the method for choosing them, they would produce the restraint on the House that they thought necessary.[4]

In their debates, the Philadelphia delegates considered many options. They thought of denying senators a salary to make sure that only men of wealth could serve. To that same end, they considered requiring senators to own substantial property. They considered allowing the president to appoint the senators, and they pondered having the House of Representatives elect them from candidates nominated by a state's legislature. They agreed that senators be at least thirty years old, five years older than the minimum for members of the House. They had difficulty deciding how long a senator's term should run. Some wanted seven years; others wanted four; a few argued for nine years. Some even suggested that senators serve for life, on "good behavior," like federal judges. In the end, they concluded that the state legislatures should elect senators for terms of six years each, three times as long as for House members. Moreover, they decided that only one-third of the senators come up for election each two years, further to insulate the Senate from popular enthusiasms or turmoil.[5]

The intent of the Philadelphia delegates was obvious: they wanted the Senate composed of men little tempted to react hurriedly to any passing craze. How better to ensure that than to have them elected by already elected state legislators? The longer and staggered terms for senators further guaranteed that the Senate would make its judgments with appropriate deliberation. The delegates wanted as senators men of judgment and integrity, and they designed the election processes to that purpose. After all, who better would know the worthies of each state, in those days of spotty communications, than its own state legislators?[6]

The men who wrote the Constitution miscalculated the evolution of American politics, however, when they assumed that those future generations would shun partisan politics. They also assumed, in the case of electing senators, that state legislatures would continue to attract members who would choose those best qualified for the Senate. The delegates did not anticipate the partisan squabbling that broke out all over the country even before the Constitution was fully ratified, nor the bitter struggles over electing the members of the First Congress.

From the outset, the choice of senators proved a quarrelsome matter. In Virginia, Patrick Henry led the opposition to approving the Constitution, and later, in command of the state legislature, he blocked the election of James Madison to the Senate, choosing instead two of his own political supporters. Then, Henry tried to prevent Madison's election to the House of Representatives despite the reality that Madison was the single-most appropriate man to serve in the new Congress.[7] He had played the major role in drafting the Constitution and later a key role in the ratification battles, not only in Virginia, but also in the crucial state of New York. The fierce politicking in those first federal elections was only the beginning of the rough-and-tumble nature of American party politics. The decades that followed brought enormous changes in the nation's political methods and practices, but none more important than those for electing senators.

Organized political parties had taken form well before the conclusion of George Washington's first term as president, even as he sought to stay above such factionalism. Alexander Hamilton's Federalist Party asserted its great influence in the first decade of the Republic, and Thomas Jefferson's Democratic-Republicans dominated the next quarter century. Both sides knew the importance of holding a majority in the Senate as well as the House. The Senate and its political majority affected every aspect of the government's concern. The way to build that majority in the Senate was to gain party majorities in the state legislatures. From the first, those wanting a seat in the Senate did what they could to woo the members of their respective state's legislature. At times, that meant ballot after ballot before they reached agreement. Occasions where agreement could not be reached produced a vacancy in the Senate. In some states, the members voted their choices without outside guidance beyond the pleas of the hopefuls and their supporters. In others, the members met in caucus beforehand and picked a candidate. In still others, a party leader of domineering prominence simply overawed the legislators.[8] In 1821, for example, a group of Democratic legislators under the leadership of Martin Van Buren met in New York's capital to organize what became the nation's first political machine. Known thereafter as the "Albany Regency," its members elected Van Buren to the Senate and consequently launched his extraordinary national career.

The election of Andrew Jackson as president in 1828 polarized the nation's political classes and soon produced two political parties: the Jacksonian Democrats and the rival Whigs. As chief executive, Jackson instituted a full-scale "rotation-in-office" policy—to ensure that appointed officials did not come to view their jobs as lifetime sinecures.[9] To the Whigs, this seemed an unfair device for removing competent officials as political "enemies" and replacing them with less-than-competent "friends." "The people expect reform," Jackson told Martin Van Buren, then his agent for those removals. "They shall not be disappointed."[10]

In Senate debate on January 25, 1832, Whig leader Henry Clay took the floor to denounce this Jackson–Van Buren initiative as a "pernicious system of party politics."[11] New York's William Marcy, a new senator and a product of Van Buren's Albany Regency, responded by claiming that successful politicians were entitled to the "fruits" of their elections. "They see nothing wrong in the rule," Marcy answered Clay, "that to the victor belong the spoils of the enemy."[12] With that flashing phrase, the "spoils system" had been named. By Jackson's transformation of previous practice, the "spoils system" was put in use. That would change the meaning of senators' elections.

State legislatures experimented with a variety of methods for choosing senators, all of them sharply political. Illinois was typical. The joint debates between Abraham Lincoln and Stephen Douglas in their 1858 campaign are justly famed as the most significant in the history of Senate electioneering and among the most important in the history of the nation. The candidates met seven times over eight weeks at various sites in the state and extensively argued their views on slavery and the nature of the federal government. At the time, Senator Douglas had attracted great attention in the country and was presumed the Democrats' likely presidential candidate for 1860. Lincoln had already become one of the more conspicuous members of the newly created Republican Party. The debates wounded Douglas's prospects for the presidency and lifted Lincoln to such national renown that he was elected president in 1860, even though he lost the 1858 Senate election to Douglas.[13]

But there was much more to this election campaign than those joint debates. Both men, nominated by their respective parties' state conventions, vigorously canvassed the state through that summer and into the fall, making speech after speech urging the election of their partisans to the state legislature. Senator Douglas, by his own reckoning, made no fewer than fifty-nine set speeches at a length of two to three hours each, as well as more than seventy shorter speeches. The Lincoln-supported legislative candidates received more popular votes than did Douglas's, but Douglas won the legislature's vote, fifty-four to forty-six.[14] In their debates, each showed the other great courtesy, both making use of the word *friend* throughout. Although election opponents, they were indeed friends.

Yet the prize of public office placed enormous strains on even the closest of bipartisan relationships.

The Senate's constitutional authority to advise and consent to presidential appointments allowed senators, eventually, to gain near-absolute control over the selection of individuals to hold federal offices within their home states. This availability of patronage helped incumbents make the case to retain their seats, but it also gave challengers a way to embarrass incumbents. In his 1858 campaign, Abraham Lincoln taunted Stephen Douglas as a political spoilsman, reporting that his "anxious" party regulars were looking to the senator for a rich harvest of political spoils. "They have seen in his round, jolly, fruitful face," Lincoln said, "post-offices, land-offices, marshal-ships and cabinet appointments, chargeships, and foreign missions, bursting and sprouting out in wonderful exuberance, ready to be laid hold of by their greedy hands."[15]

Inherent in any system of elections lay the probability of corruption and fraud, and a year before the 1858 Lincoln-Douglas campaign the Senate received its first formal notice of just that. Sixty-nine members of the Penn-sylvania state legislature petitioned the Senate in 1857 to investigate the recent election to the Senate, "by corrupt and unlawful means," of Simon Cameron, a wealthy Pennsylvania businessman of sullied reputation.[16] A Democrat turned Republican, Cameron had used questionable tactics in bargaining with several dissident Democrats in the legislature for the votes he needed to win the Senate seat. Such dealings were not entirely new, recalling earlier rumors that some state legislators had accepted bribes in return for votes. Following a brief review, a Senate committee dismissed the charge of corruption as too vague. Its chairman, South Carolina's Andrew Butler, a states' rights man, argued that the Pennsylvania legislature, not the Senate, should investigate any corruption involved.

This was a disquieting episode in Cameron's Senate career. He quit the Senate in 1861 to serve briefly and disreputably as President Lincoln's sec-retary of war. He returned to the Senate in 1867, having by then built a political machine so powerful that, as its boss, he had the state legislature subservient to his will.[17] Simon Cameron was among the early party bosses elected to the Senate. His organization proved so effective that it became self-perpetuating. When he retired in 1877, he turned over the organization and his Senate seat to his son, J. D. Cameron. He in turn was followed by party bosses such as Matthew Quay and Boies Penrose, who maintained their control into the 1920s.

Under the spoils system, state after state fell under the grasp of party bosses who arranged their own election to the Senate. Among them were Rhode Island's Henry Anthony, New York's Roscoe Conkling, Wisconsin's

Matthew Carpenter, Indiana's Oliver Morton, and Michigan's Zachariah Chandler. In their home states, these party chiefs had thousands of dependent ward-heelers and political hirelings who held federal jobs and, in return, regularly paid party assessments. These bosses changed the Senate in fundamental ways. As working politicians, not legislators, they focused nearly exclusively on elections and political boodle. They rarely spoke in Senate debate on any topic. Simon Cameron, for example, made only one substantive Senate speech—on a tariff bill—during his fourteen-year tenure. He was better known for his chilling definition of an honest politician: "An honest politician is one," opined the Pennsylvania solon, "who, when he is bought, will stay bought."[18]

Over these years, in an offshoot of the spoils system, the state legislatures sent to the Senate a new type of member: men of great personal wealth, some of them party bosses, more of them industrialists and corporate chiefs. Writing in the 1880s, James Bryce, a British historian and politician, reported that the Senate had on its roster an unusual number of rich members. "Some," he wrote, "are senators because they are rich; a few are rich because they are senators."[19] That brought the charge that these members had transformed the Senate into a "Millionaires' Club." In those states with boss-controlled legislatures, the senator chosen was the boss himself or the candidate picked by the boss. Businessmen of great wealth found the Senate an appropriate reward for personal success. Nevada's James Fair, the richest of them all, amassed some $30 million ($600 million in modern value) from his gold and silver mines.[20] Isaac Stephenson, an immensely wealthy lumberman, gave $200,000 to Wisconsin's Republican Party and in 1907 the state legislature acknowledged his generosity with a Senate seat.[21] Other industrialists and corporate chiefs, conspicuously rich, included luminary oilmen like Ohio's Henry Payne, lumber barons like Michigan's James McMillan and Wisconsin's Philetus Sawyer, and railroad captains like West Virginia's Stephen Elkins. Representing more than their states, these men spoke for entire industries such as coal and steel and cotton. Among them were skilled corporate lawyers acting openly as counsels for their firms. By the start of the twentieth century, the Senate's ranks included more than two dozen multimillionaires.[22]

Meanwhile, widespread corruption flourished within the state legislatures, as price tags began to be attached to US Senate seats. In 1865, for example, Iowa's James Harlan, at the time secretary of the interior, accepted $10,000 from a railroad official to ensure his future election to the Senate.[23] *Harper's New Monthly Magazine* reported the going price in the Rhode

Island legislature for a vote for US senator was five dollars a head, a price apparently expected in other states. In some cases, the bribes amounted to many times that figure. Montana's William Clark, a copper-mining baron, and his equally rich rival spent huge sums in their fight for a Senate seat, as much as $100,000 in a single bribe. They paid off the home mortgages of legislators or simply handed them bags of cash.[24] In the 1870s, New York's Senator Roscoe Conkling boasted that he had $200,000 on hand in case of any difficulties with his state's legislators.[25]

In 1872, the Senate had ugly charges pending against both Kansas senators: Samuel Pomeroy, elected in 1867, and Alexander Caldwell, elected in 1871. The Senate's investigating committee heard a parade of witnesses. Both senators had brazenly bribed the state's legislators in their respective elections, with Pomeroy actually caught in the act. Caldwell paid one rival $15,000 to withdraw as a candidate from the race and purchased individual votes on a sliding scale ranging from $1,000 to $5,000 (or $100,000 in today's value). He claimed at one point that he was willing to pay as much as $250,000 total to buy the Senate seat, but in actuality he got the job done cut-rate, for merely $60,000 ($1.2 million in 2012 dollars). Pomeroy's Senate term ran out before the Senate could expel him.[26] Caldwell resigned. They put the stench of scandal on the Senate, and Pomeroy became a special target of Mark Twain's savage satire *The Gilded Age*.[27]

In the decades after the Civil War, the state party convention became a routine vehicle for nominating candidates to the Senate. These conventions allowed party managers to organize their people to maximum strength. They and their henchmen were able to tell the legislators just whom they were to choose for US senator. This was not as neat as that sounds, for the legislatures had within them party rivals and dissidents, and they created great confusion at times, tying up the legislature with their partisan intrigues. From 1891 through 1905, there were forty-five separate deadlocks in state legislatures unable to decide on a senator. That meant that in every such instance the state involved had to do without at least one of its senators in Washington. There were other tokens of political chaos. In 1896, for example, the legislature in Mississippi had to deal with thirty-six different candidates for senator—each nominated by its members out of courtesy or political calculation. In 1903, the North Carolina legislature had to pick from eighty-five candidates.[28] Even the weakest in the group believed they had a chance of winning this grand senatorial lottery.

Of course, not all state legislatures acted corruptly or in confusion during these years. On the contrary, some sent men of high principle to

Washington. In 1877, for example, the Massachusetts legislature elected to the Senate—without his knowledge or permission—George Frisbie Hoar, a man of distinguished family and high personal repute.[29] For that same Senate, the Mississippi legislature chose Lucius Quintus Cincinnatus Lamar, a former Confederate colonel and diplomat who advocated national reconciliation.[30] Two years later, the North Carolina legislature elected Zebulon Vance, another Confederate colonel, and South Carolina's legislators picked Wade Hampton, a Confederate lieutenant general. Like Lamar, these senators came from the Southern gentry, men of parts, and, among other causes, they struggled to block racists at home from disenfranchising their black constituents.[31]

Meanwhile, another device—the party primary—came into use, partly as a way to cleanse the election process and partly to approach the idea of popular election of senators. The primary had tentative beginnings as early as 1845 in Pennsylvania and eventually offered a way to lessen the ability of party bosses to dictate to the state conventions. By the 1880s, as James Bryce noted in *The American Commonwealth*, outside forces such as the primaries and party caucuses had largely superseded the state legislatures in the selection of senators.[32] The legislatures were reduced merely to ratifying those decisions. Some states adopted what they called "preferential" primaries, with party voters indicating just whom they wanted elected senator. Additionally, the state of Oregon required candidates for its legislature to pledge to vote for "the people's choice" for US senator—the candidate winning the preferential primary. In 1908, this resulted in the extraordinary phenomenon of the then-Republican-majority legislature actually electing the Democrats' candidate as senator.[33]

By then, some states had adopted the direct primary to nominate senators and bypass the rule of party bosses. This had major consequences especially in the South and the West. These primaries were enlarging the electorate, and out of the West came such political progressives as Wisconsin's Robert ("Fighting Bob") La Follette and Nebraska's George Norris. They and their like challenged the archconservative leaders of the Senate. Norris's Nebraska had adopted the "Oregon Plan," and in his year, 1912, the Democratic-controlled state legislature had to elect Norris, a Republican, because he had won the "people's choice" primary.[34] Out of the South came a strikingly different breed, populist demagogues such as South Carolina's Benjamin ("Pitchfork Ben") Tillman and Ellison ("Cotton Ed") Smith.[35] They won office with ugly racist rhetoric. Smith, for example, regularly campaigned by promising to keep the price of cotton up and the Negro down. They were forerunners for generations of Southern senators openly hostile to African Americans.

After federal troops were removed from the states of the former Confederacy in 1877, a long and bitter struggle began in the South, one that smacked of class warfare. Members of the planter class, mostly conservatives, the region's aristocratic elite, found themselves challenged and then gradually replaced in power by populist demagogues aghast at the advances African Americans had made during Reconstruction. As this new crowd gained political office in the 1890s and thereafter, they rewrote the state constitutions to withhold the vote from black citizens. They adopted "Jim Crow" laws to require racial segregation in public facilities throughout the South, and they readily tolerated lynchings of blacks. With their volatile constituencies of subsistence farmers and poorly educated laborers, they also elected their own to the US Senate.[36]

South Carolina's Tillman led the way, and there were many like him who followed to Washington. The likes of Wade Hampton and Zebulon Vance disappeared from the Senate roster, and a new kind of senator took their place. One of these was Arkansas' Jeff Davis, a lynch-law rabble-rouser popular with the hillbillies as the "Wild Ass of the Ozarks."[37] Others saw their chances, too. They aligned with what became the "Solid South," a regional bastion of the Democratic Party until the last decades of the twentieth century.

That Solid South played the crucial role in electing the first Democratic presidents in the new century: Woodrow Wilson in 1912 and Franklin Roosevelt in 1932. Each of them relied on the South's Democratic senators to provide the margins for passage of their party legislation. As such, neither dared risk alienating Southerners by offering any kind of legislative succor to African Americans.

With the Senate's damaged reputation as the "South's unending revenge upon the North for Gettysburg,"[38] it sustained a further blow in a series of articles published in 1906 by William Randolph Hearst's *Cosmopolitan Magazine*, entitled "The Treason of the Senate."[39] Written by a popular novelist, David Graham Phillips, they excoriated twenty-one of the Senate's wealthiest members, most of them Republicans, as thieves, perjurers, and bribe-givers. In sensational prose, Phillips described Rhode Island's Nelson Aldrich, the Senate's acknowledged leader, as the chief "traitor" among the "scurvy lot" in control of the Senate at the time. Phillips's extravagant language prompted President Theodore Roosevelt to classify such yellow journalists as "muckrakers," a name that stuck. Hearst, the son of former California Senator

George Hearst, and Phillips had a serious purpose, despite the flamboyant assaults. Their goal was the popular election of US senators. "The senators are not elected by the people," Phillips wrote in the first of his nine articles; "they are elected by 'the Interests.'"[40] His lamentations over Senate "corruption" were part of the growing public pressure on the Senate to change its election processes.

A few state legislatures petitioned Congress to propose a constitutional amendment for the direct election of senators. The corruption and confusion fomented by the existing system invited such pleas. As early as 1893, the House of Representatives approved by the required two-thirds majority just such an amendment. When that joint resolution reached the Senate, however, it died from neglect.[41] Three times more—in 1900, 1904, and 1908—the House approved the appropriate resolution, but to no avail.[42] Senators had little interest in changing the system under which they had won their seats. They argued, without apparent need for elaboration, that popular election of senators would turn the Senate into a small version of the House of Representatives—an argument employed with no little force even into the twenty-first century against "reforms" designed to increase the Senate's "efficiency." Some in the early twentieth century contended, as if it were not already happening, that direct election would encourage political demagogues to run, thereby lowering the Senate's stature.[43]

The 1910 elections brought the reformers new hope. Of the thirty senators newly elected to that Congress, fourteen had won through party primaries, which amounted to popular choice. More than half the states now had some version of the primary. The time had come, and the Senate finally joined the House in sending forward for state ratification what became the Constitution's Seventeenth Amendment, specifying direct election of senators—nearly ninety years after it first came before the Senate in 1826.

As this long-delayed reform finally materialized, senators had thrust on them a pair of painfully awkward disputed election contests: one in Mississippi suggesting the ugly price of popular elections and the other in Illinois illustrating the continuing need for election reform. The Mississippi contest involved Senator LeRoy Percy, a Delta planter-aristocrat seeking reelection. Chosen originally by the state legislature, Percy had as his principal rival in the party primary the state's former governor, James K. Vardaman, a flamboyant demagogue known widely as "the White Chief" for his racist harangues. "Every time you educate a nigger," he mouthed regularly as his battle cry, "you spoil a good field hand."[44] In this often sordid campaign, with charges of bribery and worse, the senator's son, William Alexander

Percy, feared for his father's life. The son later described the ill-dressed, surly crowds his father normally faced: "They were the sort of people that lynch Negroes, that mistake hoodlumism for wit, and cunning for intelligence, that attend revivals and fight and fornicate in the bushes afterwards. They were undiluted Anglo-Saxons."[45] He carried a pistol to protect his father. Vardaman won. This campaign failed to demonstrate the benefits of popular election.

The Illinois case involved William Lorimer, a wealthy Chicago businessman. The Republican had been elected to the Senate in 1909 following a months-long deadlock in the Illinois legislature, amid charges of bribe-taking by its members. Extensive hearings, beginning in 1910, broadcast details of the scandal even as the Senate was moving to consider the consti-tutional amendment to change the election process. At one point, senators debated the ugliness of Lorimer's election for a month and a half, with the majority Republicans tending to support him and the Democrats in oppo-sition. This launched a new round of awkward Senate hearings.[46] While this controversy was embarrassing the Senate, the House of Representatives again approved the constitutional amendment, with a proviso for controls at the state level. The Senate then adopted the amendment, but with federal controls. The two sides met in conference time after time, sixteen meetings in all, locked in stalemate, even as the Lorimer scandal cried for a decision. Finally the House conferees gave way, accepting the senators' version. Two months later, on July 13, 1912, the Senate invalidated Lorimer's 1909 election, giving him the painful distinction of being the last senator to be deprived of his seat for corrupting a state legislature.[47]

The first Senate elections under the new system came in 1914, and they produced some odd results. That year, two of the Senate's most distinguished members, New York's Elihu Root and Ohio's Theodore Burton, declined to run for reelection. Nearly six years earlier, in 1909, amid the clamor against party bosses, each had been elected to replace his state's party boss in the Senate by the boss's own political machine, as sops to the reformers. Neither man had any campaign savvy, and both lacked a political machine to smooth their way.

In 1910, anticipating the costs of conducting a statewide campaign for reelection when his term expired in 1914, California Senator Frank Flint decided not to run again. He calculated that his out-of-pocket costs to win the statewide party primary would amount to more than the total of his $7,500 annual Senate salary for the next six years. "It is purely a business problem for me," he explained.[48] Yet others, such as Pennsylvania's Boies

Penrose, one of the last of the powerful Northern party bosses, already three times elected senator by his state political machine, easily won reelection in the 1914 popular vote. "Look at me!" he exulted. "You and your 'reformer' friends thought direct elections would turn men like me out of the Senate! Give me the People, every time!"[49]

Gone before the Senate approved the Seventeenth Amendment were the Senate's "Big Five"—Rhode Island's Nelson Aldrich, Iowa's William Allison, Wisconsin's John Spooner, Connecticut's Orville Platt, and Maine's Eugene Hale. For the better part of the two decades the men had dominated the Senate with their conservative agenda. Allison and Platt had died, Spooner had resigned, and Aldrich and Hale, aged and now harried by young progressives, had declined to run for reelection in 1910. They were replaced by lesser men, part of the transformation away from the Senate they had helped to shape. This change was more than a change in degree. It was a change in kind, dramatically reflecting the way senators were now elected.

Journalists who covered the Senate during this period reported that the Senate and its members had fallen into serious decline. The *Washington Post*'s George Rothwell Brown saw that direct elections had fundamentally changed its character and thrust. The once conservative Senate, a check on the House of Representatives and the president, was becoming "a popular body, whose members were constantly under the necessity of bowing to the public clamor in order to retain their seats."[50] Under the new system, Brown wrote, senators had lost their dignified status as ambassadors from their states to become instead mere hustlers for partisan votes. "When the Senate became responsive to the popular will," he wrote, "it showed a striking tendency to be even more susceptible than the House itself to the constantly fluctuating opinion of the people and the passions and prejudice of the hour."[51] Charles Willis Thompson of the *New York Times* agreed. "Popular election of senators did not raise the character of the Senate," he wrote; "it lowered it. The Senate is now crowded with footless, ineffective men of narrow minds and small capacities."[52] The *Baltimore Sun*'s Frederick Essary acknowledged that party primaries and popular elections may have produced what he called "a somewhat lower grade" of senators, but he assumed that the new system at least prevented electing multimillionaires like Senator Lorimer just because of their great wealth.[53]

Senators were naturally reluctant to denigrate themselves or the Senate, but several of them admitted that they had "serious doubts" that popular elections had improved the body. Arkansas' Joseph Robinson, the chamber's then Democratic leader, said in 1927 that the new scheme had brought "no permanent improvement" to the Senate.[54] Massachusetts's David Walsh, acknowledging that the Senate of the 1920s had "defects" and "imperfections," claimed that at least it was no longer controlled by "political bosses and financial groups as formerly."[55]

George Haynes, then writing his two-volume history of the Senate, saw with dismay the Senate's loss of public esteem. "There can be no question," he wrote, "that in the years since the ratification of the Seventeenth Amendment the prestige of the Senate has suffered serious decline."[56] He blamed that partially on what he called "the vulgarization" of candidates' campaign tactics, especially in the new critical party primaries: "Present-day primary campaigning is largely a cheap bidding for notoriety."[57] Candidates were using "circus stunts" to try to draw attention to themselves and other degrading tricks, lowering the dignity of the office they sought. They were now using nicknames—"Al," "Bill," "Bob," "Ed," and so on—in place of their formal given names, with the idea that this would appeal to voters. "Men of higher type," Professor Haynes wrote, "find such cheap appeals most repugnant."[58]

In the first years after ratification of the Seventeenth Amendment, more than a dozen contested elections came before the Senate as candidates quarreled over their opponents' procedures and practices. Most explosive were three elections in which wealthy candidates spent extravagantly. The most spectacular took place in Michigan, pitting automaker Henry Ford against the equally wealthy industrialist Truman Newberry. Ford, running as a Democrat, had an initial advantage from his personal renown. Republican candidate Newberry and his friends spent hundreds of thousands of dollars to try to compensate, far beyond the $3,750 then allowable under federal and Michigan law. (Newberry was later indicted and convicted for this, although the Supreme Court subsequently overturned the verdict.) He barely won the 1918 election, and the Senate, with a Republican majority, allowed him to serve even though it did vote to condemn his excessive spending. He ended these difficulties by finally resigning from the Senate in 1922. The Ford-Newberry contest challenged the optimistic belief that, under the new system, no one now could buy a Senate seat. In the old system, men of wealth used cash to gain the approval of the state's legislature, but presumably now no one could purchase a majority within an entire state.[59]

In time, with changed views of members of Congress and rulings by the Supreme Court, lavish spending became critical to success in Senate election campaigns. In 1926, the senatorial elections in both Illinois and Pennsylvania held existing laws up to mockery. William B. McKinley, then senator from Illinois and a wealthy businessman in private life, found himself opposed in the Republican primary that year by another wealthy businessman, Frank L. Smith. In this ugly fight, marked by blatant fraud and corruption, Smith spent some $450,000; McKinley spent even more. Smith won the primary and then the election, but the Senate settled this "royal battle of the millionaires" by refusing to admit Smith, concluding that the blatant fraud and corruption of his campaign was "harmful to the dignity and honor of the Senate."[60]

The Pennsylvania election also centered on the Republican primary, which pitted the incumbent senator, George Wharton Pepper, against the governor, Gifford Pinchot, and William Vare, a member of the House of Representatives grown rich as party boss of the Philadelphia political machine. Pinchot spent moderate amounts on his campaign, but Vare unloaded millions and won the primary and the general election. He came under savage criticism for fraudulently voting persons who had died and others who were mere "phantoms." In his required submission of Vare's election certificate, Governor Pinchot reported that Vare's election had been "partly bought and partly stolen."[61] Vare considered his election as the ultimate honor of a long political career, but the Senate, after investigating, refused to seat him.[62]

Under the new system of direct popular elections, anyone who had the price of the filing fee could run for the Senate. That change invited clusters of hopefuls to take a chance at this new lottery, with not all of the aspirants of the caliber anticipated by the Constitution's framers in 1787. These grab-bag primaries at times made the process seem silly. In 1930, in Illinois, for example, there were twenty-three Senate candidates. With such crowds of contenders, runoff primaries were required, adding to the confusion.[63]

Shortly after the start of the new system, both major political parties—the Democrats in 1918, the Republicans in 1919—created senatorial campaign committees designed to help their respective Senate candidates. These bodies offered a variety of help such as speechwriting, political advice, and even some campaign cash. Later, as Senate elections evolved, these committees provided sophisticated services that included radio and television studios, skilled polling, and opposition-candidate research.

The conduct of election campaigns in the South evolved in the decades after the Civil War and Reconstruction with an overwhelming white commitment to keep African Americans in subservient status. Ever since the disenfranchising of blacks and Jim Crow segregation, Senate candidates had followed the lead of South Carolina's "Pitchfork Ben" Tillman and his commitment to "White Supremacy." Tillman made no apologies for the ways they prevented blacks from voting. "We shot them," he said in Senate debate. "We are not ashamed of it."[64]

Southern white leaders devised a variety of ways to deny the vote to African Americans, including grandfather clauses, poll taxes, and literacy tests. The redrafting of Southern-state constitutions removed most blacks who had earlier been eligible to vote. In Louisiana, for example, the year before the state constitution's 1898 revision, 130,344 blacks were registered to vote. Afterward the number shrank to 5,320.[65]

The state of Mississippi devised its own special way to keep blacks from voting. It required all those registering to vote to show that they understood the US Constitution, with white officials conducting the pass-fail test.[66] Georgia's Senator Hoke Smith admired the Mississippi plan and urged his state legislators to adopt it for their use. He explained how it worked. When a Negro tried to register, he said, do what they do in Mississippi: "Ask him what is the meaning of ex post facto law or some other question couched in language as you know he cannot answer. And when a poor, ignorant white man . . . comes, ask him some simple question."[67] White Southerners were amused at this ugly scheme. Mississippi-born Turner Catledge, later executive editor of the *New York Times*, built his early journalistic career by telling "nigger" stories, one of which was a rollicking old-boy yarn about this Mississippi plan: A Negro college professor came to register. The officials asked him to explain habeas corpus. He did. They asked him to explain a bill of attainder. He did. Finally they asked him about ex post facto laws. By then the professor knew their purpose. "Ex-post-facto laws," the professor replied, "means that in Mississippi a nigger can't vote!"[68] With that punch line came Catledge's laughter.

Not all Southern senators in these years were cut from Tillman's demagogic cloth, however. More took their representational roles seriously and acted responsibly. But Tillman did have imitators who matched his racist extravagances. Among them were South Carolina's Coleman Blease and Alabama's J. Thomas ("Cotton Tom") Heflin. "God Almighty," Heflin, the rabble-rouser, cried, "intended the Negro to be the servant of the white man."[69] While serving in the US House, Heflin shot and seriously wounded a black man who had confronted him on a Washington streetcar. Although indicted, Heflin got the charges dismissed. In subsequent home-state campaigns, he cited that shooting as one of his career's greatest accomplishments.[70]

Perhaps the worst of these racist senators was Mississippi's Theodore Bilbo, whom his own state legislature pronounced "unfit to sit with honest, upright men."[71] In one Senate election, he called an opponent "a cross between a hyena and a mongrel . . . begotten in a nigger graveyard at midnight."[72] He preached racial hatred and proposed deporting all African Americans to Africa. "I call on every red-blooded white man," he brayed, "to use any means to keep the niggers from voting."[73] If any tried, he said, pour gasoline on them. He won his last Senate election in 1946 that way, but the Senate balked at allowing him to take his seat again. He died in 1947, some said appropriately, from cancer of the mouth.[74]

Over these early years of direct popular voting for senators, those members seeking reelection, and the candidates opposing them, mimicked members of the House, long practiced in the arts of winning favor with voters. They advertised themselves as best they could in newspapers, magazines, and direct mail. After 1928, radio ads became commonplace, and so did the extensive speechmaking and handshaking later termed "retail politics." Much of these candidates' campaign rhetoric attacked or criticized their opponents, often unfairly, and sometimes dishonestly. There was an inherent nastiness in much of what they said and did. Occasionally, out of these partisan squabbles came unusual tactics or verbiage.

In 1926, for example, Alabama had an open Senate seat. In a shrewd, calculating maneuver, the two presumed leading Democrats arranged a series of debates between themselves as though they were the only serious candidates for the job. They excluded three other candidates, one of whom was a young lawyer named Hugo Black. Black countered their strategy with clever tactics of his own. He hired a mule-drawn dray to parade back and forth at their debate site carrying this bold notice: *Bankhead Says Kilby Won't Do. Kilby Says Bankhead Won't Do. Both Are Right. Vote for Hugo Black.* The voters elected Black.[75]

In 1930, Nebraska's George W. Norris, a progressive Republican hated by his party's old-guard reactionaries, sought reelection only to discover that his state party's bosses had devised a bizarre plot to defeat him. They had found a small-town grocery clerk whose name was identical to that of Senator Norris and persuaded the man to enter the Republican primary against the senator. That would have had the effect of canceling the votes for both of them, thus giving the nomination to the old-guard candidate. This double-dealing stratagem touched off a political firestorm that, among other responses, brought a Senate investigating subcommittee to Nebraska to take testimony. The grocery clerk was quickly disqualified; the senator won the primary and general election; and the grocery clerk and his old-guard sponsor were brought to trial, convicted of perjury, and sent to jail.[76]

In North Carolina's 1932 Democratic primary, challenger Robert ("Buncombe Bob") Reynolds contrived an ingenious bit of political skullduggery to help him defeat Senator Cameron Morrison. Reynolds learned that the hotel where Morrison stayed when in Washington listed caviar on its menu. "Friends," Reynolds announced in his campaign speeches, "it pains me to tell you the Cam Morrison eats fish eggs. This here jar ain't a jar of squirrel shot. It's fish eggs, and Red Russian fish eggs at that, and they cost two dollars." Reynolds assured the voters that he himself ate "good North Carolina hen eggs."[77]

Senatorial campaigns, of course, normally brought the candidates' varied responses to the political climate and anxieties of the time. They reacted differently in times of prosperity and times of recession. By 1950, with growing tension between the United States and the Soviet Union, the House of Representatives' Un-American Activities Committee (HUAC) had long been investigating suspected Communists, and Wisconsin's Senator Joseph McCarthy had that year launched his career of making reckless charges. That fall, with the Korean War under way, he campaigned around the country, attacking a dozen Democratic senators up for reelection by questioning their loyalty. Admirers credited McCarthy with causing the defeat of as many as seven of them, including Maryland's Millard Tydings, the senator who had chaired the investigating subcommittee that pronounced McCarthy's spectacular but unsupported charges as "a fraud and a hoax."[78]

The question of Communism also played a role in other 1950 Senate campaigns, including those in California and Florida. In California, Richard Nixon, a two-term Republican member of the House, battled Helen Gahagan Douglas, a three-term member of the House, for a vacant Senate seat. Nixon, a member of HUAC, accused his opponent of communist sympathies. "Why has she followed the Communist line so many times?"[79] Nixon asked. This was the campaign that gave Nixon the nickname "Tricky Dick," and the distaste of many Democrats. Nixon "was much too wise to have called me a Communist," Douglas complained. "He had deliberately designed [his campaign] to create the impression that I was a Communist, or at least communistic."[80]

In a somewhat similar campaign earlier that year, Representative George Smathers attacked Florida's Claude Pepper, a two-term senator who had acted as sponsor for Smathers in his initial political sallies. In the Democratic primary, Smathers labeled Senator Pepper as a "nigger-lover" and a political "Red." He repeatedly called him "Red Pepper" and accused him of advocating treason. Smathers won the primary and the general election. "I never knew what hit me," Pepper later complained. "In the vilification contest I was like a hummingbird fallen into a nest of screech owls."[81]

The Pepper-Smathers campaign produced one of the most extraordinary political speeches ever devised, a speech Smathers repeatedly denied ever making.[82] He delivered the speech, according to *Time* magazine, to naïve back-country voters. "Ladies and gentlemen," he began, "are you aware that Claude Pepper is known all over Washington as a shameless *extrovert*? Not only that, but this man is reliably reported to practice *nepotism* with his sister-in-law, he has a brother who is a known *homo sapiens*, and he has a sister who was once a *thespian* in wicked New York. Worst of all, it is an established fact that Mr. Pepper, before his marriage, habitually practiced *celibacy*."[83] In denying authorship of this belly-whopping bit of political fun, reputedly fabricated by an idle journalist, Smathers in effect claimed credit instead for the ugly campaign he actually did run against Pepper and his betrayal of the senator who had earlier befriended him. Had he declined comment, he could have been celebrated as a political wit of most excellent fancy.

These attack campaigns, like some others, contradicted the more traditional way many senators then sought reelection. They paid no attention to their opponents, assuming that even mentioning a challenger's name gave him a status he would not otherwise have. An incumbent senator normally had name recognition far beyond that of his opponent, and that translated into votes. This was the attitude of Missouri's Harry S. Truman, twice elected to the Senate. "The people want to see the man they are voting for," Truman explained, "and they want to know where he stands. My approach to the thing was always to explain the principles on which I was running. Don't attack your opponent. Whenever you do, it only gives him free advertising and another chance to attack you."

A similar philosophy governs the decision whether to debate. Sitting senators typically face a risky decision. In 1938, Ohio's Senator Robert Bulkley, a Democratic moderate, made the mistake of agreeing to debate his Republican challenger, Robert A. Taft, son of former president William Howard Taft. Bulkley, up for his third term, believed he could easily handle this young, shy, and diffident opponent. He was caught off guard, however, by Taft's aggressive attack on him as a Franklin Roosevelt rubber-stamp and by Taft's grasp of the political issues of the day. Their six debates were broadcast on statewide radio and attracted national attention. Those encounters not only helped Taft win the election, but they also gave him national standing when he reached the Senate the following January.[84]

In 1948, in Illinois, Paul Douglas, an economics professor nominated by the Democrats, challenged Republican Senator Wayland Brooks to a series of debates. After Brooks declined, Douglas devised his own form of debates with the senator. At his campaign appearances, afternoons and evenings, Douglas debated an empty chair designated for the senator. Not only did he recite his own campaign pledges and arguments, but from time to time he went over to the empty chair and made what he pretended were the senator's responses. Douglas won the election.[85]

Two years later, Everett Dirksen, a veteran member of the House, then out of office, challenged Senator Scott Lucas for the other Illinois seat in the Senate. Like Douglas, he proposed debates, and Lucas, like Brooks, declined. He suggested instead that Dirksen debate his own "revolving record" in the House of Representatives and all his political "flip-flops" there.[86] Dirksen copied Douglas's tactic of debating an empty chair. On the chair he placed a placard: "Reserved for Scott Lucas." Lucas, then the Senate's majority leader, had to remain in Washington with the Senate in late session. Dirksen won.[87]

In 1952, John F. Kennedy of Massachusetts, then a third-term member of the House, challenged Henry Cabot Lodge Jr. to a series of debates in their fight for Lodge's Senate seat. Working to elect Dwight Eisenhower as president, Lodge neglected his own reelection and soon fell behind. He therefore accepted Kennedy's challenge. In their first debate, Lodge condemned Kennedy's Democrats for national political failures, only to have Kennedy sharply retort: "If we are to be held responsible for everything that went wrong, we must be credited for everything that went right."[88] Lodge had not expected such rough handling from the younger man, and he made excuse after excuse to avoid any further debates. Kennedy won.

Every Senate candidate has had to work out a campaign plan, based on his or her credentials, party affiliation, and political realities of the time. In West Virginia in 1958, there happened to be two Senate seats up for election, both held by Republicans. The four candidates had strikingly different ways in their campaigns, but all typical of the period. The Republican senators were Chapman Revercomb, sixty-three, a strikingly handsome old-guard conservative with a talent for remembering constituents' names, and John Hoblitzell, forty-five, an active businessman recently appointed to the Senate to fill a vacancy. They were opposed by Democrats Jennings Randolph, fifty-six, an original New Dealer with cloying political mannerisms, and Robert C. Byrd, forty, seemingly the least likely candidate, then in his third term in the House of Representatives. All four scrambled to meet voters and gain their support. All four were secretive about their campaign funds and contributors, but the Republicans had at least twice the funds of either Democrat. Both Republicans suffered a major disadvantage, however, in that West Virginia was especially hard hit by a nagging economic recession then confronting the nation. They employed the usual election-year campaign tools such as posters scattered across the state, bumper stickers, and advertisements in newspapers, on radio, and even on television.

Senator Revercomb, Byrd's opponent, campaigned in the grand manner with a deep resonant voice. Reflecting his years in the Senate, he seemed somewhat pompous. Like the others, he worked the shops and factories, not always at ease with those he did not know. More than the others, he actually looked like a stereotypical senator, and he played that role with finesse. Hoblitzell, cheerful and engaging, all but raced through factories and offices as though in a desperate rush to shake hands with more voters than possible, "Hello," he greeted everyone, over and over, "I'm Senator Hoblitzell. Anything you can do November 4 will be appreciated."[89] He did not always tell voters that he was running for election to the Senate, a token of his lack of easy political know-how and brief seasoning time in Congress. Even so, with his quick smile, he seemed the most personally attractive of the four.

Randolph, heavyset and amiable, tried hard to seem pleasing while always anxious to avoid controversy. He relied heavily on endorsements from such touring party stalwarts as former president Harry Truman and Lyndon Johnson, then the Senate's majority leader. Representative Byrd campaigned harder than any of the others: factory gates at six in the morning, door-to-door after that, then a town's shops and offices all day and into the night wherever he might find voters. "I'm Bob Byrd," he said to each of them, offering his hand, sometimes spelling his name B-Y-R-D, "and I'm running for the US Senate."[90] He had a tough, hard-hitting political spiel, and with country folk in the hills, much like a preacher, he talked the Old Time religion. Afterward, he brought out his fiddle and entertained the crowd with such tunes as "Turkey in the Straw" and "Old Joe Clark." He was good, but he did not play the fiddle in the state's urban areas. Neither Revercomb nor Hoblitzell used the word *Republican* in their campaign materials, aware of the state's large Democratic majority. Byrd had struggled out of deep poverty, the adopted son of a coal miner, and he saw this as his great chance. He said then that if he could win this race, he would hold the seat reelection after reelection. He and Randolph won, both by a margin of well over 100,000 votes. (Byrd lived up to his promise, winning his next eight contests and serving until his death in 2010.)

Those West Virginia candidates, in their varied ways, marked the mid-century styles of Senate campaigners. Essentially, they were trying to meet and greet as many voters as they could and to leave with them a favorable impression. Criticizing opponents was not unknown, but Senate candidates tended to talk about themselves and what they could do for the state and its people. They had help, of course, mainly from friends and family, but they also had professionals for such functions as arranging rallies, raising campaign funds, and conducting public opinion polls. When he first ran for the Senate, John F. Kennedy largely relied on his immediate family, especially his mother and brother Robert. Also working for Kennedy was Larry O'Brien, a lawyer who emerged in the following few years as one of the country's most skillful campaign strategists. He put together a handbook, known later as *O'Brien's Manual*, a classic of its kind, to instruct the Kennedy team on how to solicit volunteers, to telephone registered Democrats, and to organize election-day drivers, among other functions. These were shrewd and effective tactics for their time.

In the years to come, however, the election of senators, like other elections, underwent revolutionary change. One principal cause was the advent of television, which Senate candidates, like other candidates, discovered could prove a telling campaign tool—not only to praise themselves, but more important, to savage their opponents, even with gross distortions and lies. Another cause for change was the "invention" of a new breed of independent election professionals, called political "consultants," ready to inflict those cruelties on any candidate's rivals. Tough-minded and highly skilled, they were available for a price, and they made themselves mandatory for hire by every serious candidate. They in turn, with television as their essential weapon, required every aspiring candidate for the Senate to have available huge amounts of cash, at first hundreds of thousands of dollars, then millions, and ultimately tens of millions. It was as though Congress and the states had added, by constitutional amendment, an extra requirement for membership in the Senate: plenty of cash.

2

The Collapse of Campaign Finance Reform

THE MANNER OF ELECTING US senators has disturbed the republic from its very beginnings. Ratification of the Constitution's Seventeenth Amendment in 1913 caused many to believe that chronic problems of electoral corruption and insufficient transparency about campaign contributions and expenditures would simply fade away. Yet, the twentieth and twenty-first centuries produced numerous acts of Congress and Supreme Court decisions designed to curb escalating problems associated with the financing and conduct of federal elections. Well into the second millennium, close observers of the US Senate realized that the process by which its members are elected is perhaps not at all subject to rational management. The Supreme Court's 2010 decision in *Citizens United v. Federal Election Commission* promised to open the floodgates to massive contributions from business and labor organizations—a flood of cash that makes early-twentieth-century funding limits appear hopelessly naïve.

For decades, the 1925 Federal Corrupt Practices Act had nominally governed the behavior of candidates seeking election to the Senate. In reality, that statute's gaping loopholes had made it easy to evade. In the years after World War II, the cost of running for the Senate increased dramatically, far in excess of senators' salaries or personal resources, and far in excess of the then-legal spending limit of $25,000. Elections came to cost hundreds of thousands of dollars and then escalated into millions. A loophole in the 1925 law conveniently allowed candidates to ignore campaign spending on their behalf conducted without their "knowledge or consent."[1] A candidate simply had to remain technically ignorant about contributions from friends and admirers.

Running in 1968 for his fourth Senate term, Illinois's Everett Dirksen, then the Senate's minority leader, knew precisely how to fund his campaign without breaching the law. As usual Dirksen had his half-dozen campaign committees, among them Bankers for Dirksen, Farmers for Dirksen, Lawyers for Dirksen, and Businessmen for Dirksen, each raising funds for his reelection. "I don't want to know who are on the committees or what you are doing," Dirksen told them, by his own account. "That's up to you . . . and don't tell me about it."[2] His supporters gave a fund-raising dinner for him at $100 a plate, and collected some $250,000. Dirksen attended the dinner and made a campaign speech, but he had nothing else to do with it. "I haven't received a penny," Dirksen boasted to reporters. "We have no ghosts in the closet, no skeletons to hide!"[3]

Some of Dirksen's Senate colleagues had other ways, outside the requirements of law, to raise and spend large sums on their elections. In this endeavor they acted in secret, dealt in cash, and kept no records. In the 1950s, senators and party candidates for the Senate had special access to such funds, with none as active as Texas' Lyndon Johnson, the majority leader, and his assistant, Robert G. (Bobby) Baker. They raised large amounts of cash from a variety of interest groups, with special generosity from the oil interests. On one occasion, an oil-lobby operative met with Senator Johnson in an ornate room just off the Senate chamber, to deliver a sealed envelope. Johnson slipped the envelope containing $25,000 in cash into his inside coat pocket. Unfamiliar with protocol in such matters, the operative asked Johnson for a receipt. "For what?" Johnson barked. "For the money," the man replied. Johnson countered, "What money?"[4]

As secretary-treasurer of the Democratic Senatorial Campaign Committee, Bobby Baker took charge of these secret funds, under Senator Johnson's overall supervision. "I was the official bagman for my party," Baker wrote in his memoirs. "It was my job to solicit, collect, and distribute funds among deserving senatorial candidates."[5] Senators gave credit to Johnson, of course, and Baker parceled out the available cash to where it would do Democrats the most good. This was a matter of delicacy, Baker found, for to him no senator ever seemed satisfied with the amounts received. Moreover, Baker knew that a $15,000 cash gift to a party candidate in a populous state, such as New York or California, amounted only to what he called "a drop in the bucket" for his campaign, while that same sum given to a candidate running in a less populated state, such as Montana or North Dakota, could decide the election.[6]

Over these years, campaigning senators and their challengers came to use television, casually at first, treating the medium as a useful gimmick. By

1970, however, more than half the Senate's candidates incorporated television in their campaign planning, even without truly understanding its full
potential. In 1968, there were two campaigns, one for a Senate seat and the
other for the presidency, that dramatically employed television as a political
weapon rather than a clever device. One was engineered by Joseph Napolitan, an innovative Democratic consultant, in Alaska's Senate election; the
other was the work of Roger Ailes, a Republican television producer hired
by Richard Nixon for his presidential campaign.

That year, Alaska's Senator Ernest Gruening, the eighty-one-year-old
"father" of Alaskan statehood, faced a Democratic primary challenge by a
thirty-eight-year-old real estate agent named Maurice ("Mike") Gravel. In
running the campaign for Gravel, a long shot at best, Napolitan wasted little
of Gravel's limited funds on such traditional campaign items as billboards or
bumper stickers. Instead, he husbanded his resources for the final days
before the primary. Meanwhile, he prepared a thirty-minute film embel-
lishing Gravel's credentials, as well as a series of television and radio spots.
Just before the primary, Napolitan launched what amounted to a political
blitz, playing the film dozens of times over Alaska's television stations and
saturating the air waves with television and radio spots. That changed everything, and Gruening panicked. "He hired a post-hole digger, dug some
holes, and put up some more billboards," Napolitan said. "It was a classic
example of the old against the new."[7]

In his use of television that year, Roger Ailes devised a series of one-hour
TV "shows," intended not so much to reveal who Nixon was, but to *conceal*
who he was. Nixon had fared badly on television in 1960, running against
John F. Kennedy for the presidency, and Ailes had to remedy his candidate's
discomfort with the medium. With his special skills in such details as
lighting, Ailes stage-managed the shows to make Nixon seem warm, self-
assured, and presidential. Ailes chose carefully those who would question
Nixon. For each show, he packed the TV studio with an audience of Republican loyalists who applauded whatever Nixon said. At the session's conclusion, the audience, as instructed, gave Nixon a standing ovation. It was
one triumph after another.

To record his campaign, Nixon gave journalist Joe McGinniss extraordinary access to his camp's operations and decision-making. Later, in his *The
Selling of the President, 1968*, McGinniss revealed with remarkable candor the
political machinations of Ailes and the others on Nixon's team. The book,
filled with detailed inside information, proved more than a report on Nixon's
election as president; it also offered a handbook for political professionals on

how to function in the new world of election campaign management. Thanks to McGinniss, Ailes had shown them how to use television as a political weapon, much as Joe Napolitan had in Alaska, each with widely different techniques.[8]

Meanwhile, fundamental changes became evident in the manner of electing one of the Senate's most powerful factions—its Southern bloc. In January 1961, although Democrats still held all twenty-two of the Old South's Senate seats, Georgia's Richard Russell had already publicly affirmed that the region was no longer solid. "The Old South, in a way, is dying,"[9] he said. Cracks in the Southern phalanx appeared in 1957 and again in 1960 as Congress adopted civil rights bills, largely of a token nature, but symbolically significant all the same. Tennessee's senators Estes Kefauver and Albert Gore Sr. were part of the changing South, and so was Texas's Lyndon Johnson, who, as Senate majority leader, had driven those civil rights bills through the Senate.[10]

There were other Southern senators long uncomfortable with the region's commitment to racism. A decade earlier, in 1948, Alabama's John Sparkman, up for reelection, took the Senate floor to denounce President Harry Truman for advocating a Fair Employment Practices Commission. Afterward, off the floor, Sparkman appeared badly shaken. "I love that man," he said of Truman.[11] He had made the speech only to protect himself politically in Alabama. His Alabama colleague, Lister Hill, had similar misgivings about routinely supporting the filibusters. "I had to do that to get elected," Senator Hill confessed years later after he had left the Senate. "We all did."[12] Arkansas' William Fulbright, like Lister Hill, had served in the Senate with distinction for thirty years, and he obliquely acknowledged that he, too, had to give way. "Everyone running for office has to compromise some of their views to get elected," Fulbright said. "It's a question of how far you go."[13]

In the Senate elections of 1958, the Democrats ousted more than a dozen conservative Republicans, giving the Senate a markedly liberal tilt, a political balance that would hold through the 1960s.[14] That change brought, among other measures, the enactment of three major civil rights bills, including the Voting Rights Act of 1965, which would radically change the South and those the South sent to the Senate.

With federal protectors at hand, hundreds of thousands of African Americans all over the South registered to vote—and voted. This revolutionized the South's electorate, a change not missed by that region's politicians. By 1978, the *New York Times* concluded that white racists could no longer be elected in the South.[15] That year, two of the South's most ardently racist senators were up for reelection: Mississippi's James Eastland and South Carolina's Strom Thurmond. Both had long fought against civil rights measures. On one, Senator Thurmond had made the longest floor speech in Senate history; Senator Eastland boasted that, as chairman of the Senate's Judiciary Committee, he had personally blocked scores of such bills.[16] The two men reacted differently to the new election registrations. Thurmond began hiring blacks for his Senate staff, he proposed blacks for federal offices, and, with much show, he enrolled his young daughter in an integrated public school. (He did not reveal that he quietly provided financial support to another daughter whom he had fathered with an African American maid.[17]) Thurmond failed to win a majority of black voters in 1978, but he attracted enough to be reelected. He won again in 1984 and 1990 and 1996, and only then did he finally agree—as he approached his one hundredth birthday—to retire from the Senate, a quarter century after the critical election of 1978.

James Eastland had a different fate. Not willing to follow Thurmond's efforts to accommodate changing times, Eastland realized belatedly that he had reelection problems. He tried to find help, consulting Aaron Henry, head of Mississippi's NAACP. What were his chances with the state's blacks, he asked. "Poor at best," Henry said. "You have a master-servant philosophy with regard to blacks."[18] Eastland left in tears, and a few days later he announced that he would not seek reelection. How badly Eastland had by then positioned himself became evident in the eight contenders who sought to fill his Senate seat, all of them wooing black voters. The winner was Thad Cochran, a Republican House member. "I campaigned in the black churches," Cochran explained, "gave the soul handshake."[19] White candidates' electoral relations with African Americans in Mississippi had traveled an unimaginable distance from the days of quizzing the state's black citizens on ex post facto laws.

By then, Republicans from the South had become regulars in the Senate, and those who elected them no longer abominated the word *Republican*— once evocative of Yankee carpetbaggers and post–Civil War occupation forces. John Tower of Texas, in 1961, and South Carolina's Thurmond, switching to the GOP in 1964, had led the way. When Cochran entered the Senate in 1979, he joined four other Southern Republicans. Within two years, they had nine. Clearly, Senate delegations had come to reflect a two-party South. In this new order of things, conservative Democrats were transforming themselves into Republicans, while blacks were becoming a significant Democratic voting bloc in that region. Yet, regardless of shifting party demographics, senators were united in their uses of incumbency for electoral advantage.

Senators both in the South and throughout the nation built widespread networks of state support to enhance their opportunities for reelection. They had the franking privilege, which allowed them to blanket their states with self-serving mail. They had the ability, through the legislative process, to channel federal funds and projects to their states—the pork-barrel bonanzas and earmarks about which they could boast come election time. With the help of their Senate staffs, they could respond effectively to all sorts of constituent requests, thereby assuring themselves of the electorally bankable gratitude of those constituents, their families, and their friends. Senators' staffs could also help through their knowledge of issues immediately important to their constituencies, and were available to take annual leave to assist in their boss's reelection campaign.[20]

Of course, not all constituents were always grateful. Senate Democratic leader Alben Barkley, a sparkling storyteller in his later years, loved to tell about a skeptical Kentucky farmer whom he had often helped, but who had since become reluctant to vote for Barkley's reelection. In self-mockery, Barkley's account had him list for the farmer all the ways he had helped him over the years—early discharge from the army, farm loans, building an access road to his farm, flood relief, appointment of his wife as postmistress. "Surely," Barkley pleaded, "you remember all these things I have done for you." "I remember," the farmer replied, "but what in hell have you done for me lately?"[21] Fellow senators especially liked that one.

Senate elections, like other American electoral contests, spawned questionable schemes and corrupt acts. States such as New York, New Jersey, Pennsylvania, Illinois, and Texas were long notorious for electioneering outrages, but these were not uncommon elsewhere. The people responsible used all the common practices, including hiring "repeaters," voting graveyard names, and buying blocs of votes from party bosses.

By the late 1950s, the story of how Texas Representative Lyndon Johnson had won his first Senate primary election in 1948 had achieved legendary status. Johnson had previously run for the Senate in a special 1941 election against Wilbert Lee O'Daniel, the state's governor. In those years, winning the Democratic primary in states of the Solid South, where there was little more than token Republican opposition, meant election. Both sides played rough, each justifiably accusing the other of stealing votes. On election night, with the vote tallies seemingly final, Johnson relaxed. But the governor's henchmen labored on and produced the "late" votes that ultimately elected O'Daniel.[22]

Lyndon Johnson had learned his lesson. In the 1948 primary, he ran against former Texas governor Coke Stevenson. In another ugly campaign, even by Texas standards, Johnson innovatively used a helicopter to campaign around the state. For almost a full week after the polls closed, both camps played politics Texas style, each side reporting held-back blocs of votes, "late" corrections and recounts, and fraudulent ballots by the thousands. In the end, it came down to Ballot Box 13 in Alice, Texas. That box held the two hundred obviously forged votes for Johnson that gave him the seat by an eighty-seven-vote margin. He came that close to losing his political career. Years later, the election judge in Alice confessed to the crime. "Johnson did not win that election," Luis Salas said. "It was stolen for him."[23] Owing to his bare victory, Johnson, to his chagrin, found himself nicknamed "Landslide Lyndon."

The worst election scandal ever came in 1972, not from a senator's election, but from the reelection of President Richard Nixon. The criminal offenses of Nixon and his associates were investigated by a Senate committee chaired by North Carolina's Sam Ervin. This vast conspiracy, known collectively as the Watergate scandal, sent to jail Nixon's campaign manager, his attorney general, and his principal White House lieutenants, among others, and compelled Nixon to resign the presidency. Most of the conspirators' operations were financed by often illegal solicitation of massive campaign funds, and that revelation forced a major rewriting of election laws.

Campaign money and its varied uses had long harried American elections. A scandal in 1867 forced Congress, for the first time, to forbid government employees from soliciting navy yard workers to contribute part of their pay for political party purposes.[24] In 1883, the Pendleton Act created a federal civil service and extended this ban to all federal employees.[25] In 1907, under the sponsorship of South Carolina Senator Benjamin Tillman, Congress enacted a toothless statute in hopes of curbing massive election spending of corporations and banks.[26] There were further attempts to tighten campaign spending—and to require disclosure by donors, culminating in the Federal Corrupt Practices Act of 1925, with its optimistic aim of limiting Senate campaign expenditures to $25,000.[27] The 1939 Act to Prevent Pernicious Political Activities, sponsored by New Mexico Senator Carl Hatch, limited party overall spending and individual candidate contributions.[28] In 1947, the Republican-controlled Congress forbade labor unions from making direct contributions to federal candidates.[29] A quarter century later, Congress repealed the ineffective 1925 law and put in its place an equally unsatisfactory statute—the Federal Election Campaign Act of 1971.[30]

That statute required candidates to disclose in detail who gave them contributions and how they spent those funds.

Quarreling over campaign funds and election law had long been a regular feature of Senate debate and a matter of grave concern to both political parties. The two parties had differing constituencies and, consequently, differing sources of financial support. In this, Republicans had an obvious advantage from their ties to business interests that were better off than the labor unions that formed a key sector of the Democrats' base. The Democrats generally tried to limit campaign money, while Republicans fought such restrictions.

President Nixon's Watergate scandal moved Congress to expand the 1971 law. The Federal Election Campaign Act Amendments of 1974 placed what at that time seemed like strict ceilings on campaign donations to congressional and presidential contests. This statute shaped modern campaign finance law.[31] In each election cycle, individuals could give as much as $2,000 for the primary and general elections of each candidate, and each political action committee (PAC) could give as much as $10,000. The law also allowed congressional campaign committees to give substantial campaign funds to their party's candidate, based on the number of eligible voters in their states or districts.[32] These limits, under scrutiny by talented lawyers, proved flexible. The PAC system, for example, under a clever new tactic of "bundling," emerged as a major loophole, providing candidates with large amounts of campaign cash.[33] The law also established the Federal Election Commission as an independent regulatory agency to publicize campaign finance information and enforce the relevant statutes. With its members appointed by the president and confirmed by the Senate, this commission became a political punching bag in the decades ahead, and some of its six seats remained vacant for extended periods.[34]

The 1974 law, with its ambiguities, came under immediate legal challenge, with New York Senator James Buckley and his allies bringing the principal suit. On January 30, 1976, in *Buckley v. Valeo*, the Supreme Court found important portions of the law to be unconstitutional, some for violating freedom of speech.[35] The court decided that Congress could not put limits on some types of campaign practices, including what any candidate spent on his or her own race. This was new law and opened an election loophole for persons of great wealth, inviting at least some of them to seek federal office.

One aspect of this statute initially pleased Republicans. It conferred legal authority for corporations and other business interests to create PACs and make campaign contributions where they would help most, thereby repealing the Tillman Act's 1907 prohibition of such contributions. As he was signing the 1974 amendments into law, President Gerald Ford observed, "We as Republicans insisted that business PACs be authorized, so we'd have some equity."[36] He assumed, as did other Republicans, that corporate PACs would largely support conservative Republicans. That did not go as planned.

From the start, the directors of all PACs tended to take a pragmatic, rather than an ideological, approach in making donations to candidates. Essentially, they wanted access to the power brokers in Congress, and they were willing to pay for it. They gave their money primarily to sitting members of Congress, not challengers, and they concentrated heavily on those chairmen and ranking members of committees most important to them. That gave them a natural bias toward those in the majority. This meant, for example, that the managers of corporate PACs in years of Democratic majorities in the Senate or House gave heavily to Democratic members of Congress. That offended important Republicans.

In 1976, the first campaign year of the new law's operation, Democratic senators, then in the majority, received more than twice as much PAC money as Republicans did.[37] These were trivial amounts compared to the tens of millions PACs would be offering in the years ahead, but they clearly forecast the exponential growth of PAC donations. That angered Republicans.

On reflection, President Ford suggested that there should be "some limit" on PACs, a reversal of his party's customary stance. Nevada's Paul Laxalt, like other Republican senators, denounced the directors of these corporate PACs as false "friends" unappreciative for Republican support on business questions. "When you have pushed water for them as long as we have," Laxalt said, "that's a little hard to swallow." As the new election practices evolved, Laxalt and other Senate Republicans would try to abolish all political PACs.

For PAC directors and their varied sponsors, federal legislation could easily jeopardize their interests. Their operations, serious cash-on-the-barrelhead politics with no nonsense, were not always understood by senators and others. Their cash contributions to members amounted to premiums on critical insurance policies against legislative disaster. They spoke in terms of seeking access so they could tell their stories. "We don't want the door shut in our face," explained a PAC director. "We don't want the deal decided before we get there." Others cited the "golden rule" of politics: "He who gets the gold rules."[38] In reality, they wanted more than access to members. They wanted results.

Corporate chiefs and their PAC managers rarely spoke candidly where they might be overheard on such matters, but in one instance the *Washington Post* disclosed "confidential" memoranda from General Electric's personnel on that company's spectacular success with its well-placed campaign contributions. Over a period of eight years in the 1980s, the company's PAC gave a little more than $2 million to members of the Senate Finance and House Ways and Means committees, the panels with jurisdiction over federal taxes. Those contributions, the memo reported, helped save GE more than $300 million in taxes. "Political contributions," another memo concluded, "are critical to the company's performance."[39] In 2011, the *New York Times* reported that General Electric, the nation's largest corporation, would, that year, thanks to having a tax department commonly referred to as "the world's best tax law firm," pay no federal income taxes on its American profits of $5.1 billion.[40]

By 1986, a dozen years after its tentative start, the new election system had come into full bloom. There were more than four thousand PACs, with more than one-third of them sponsored by corporations, and they were contributing millions of dollars to Senate candidates.[41] The entire election system had been transformed, not only by the immense sums committed to these campaigns, but also by the emergence of a new corps of freelance experts known as political consultants. Those in the group employed a wide array of clever, sophisticated, and often punishing campaign tactics and techniques. That year, major-party candidates in the thirty-four states holding Senate elections spent a total of $212 million, much of that figure on television advertising. Of that total, the energized PACs provided a little more than 20 percent. This was big business, largely managed by technicians of specialized talents.[42]

Political consultants, highly skilled craftsmen in election matters, were professionals for hire by the candidates who could afford them. They knew opinion-polling and manipulation; they understood print and electronic media, direct-mail campaigns, and how to schedule candidates' appearances for greatest visibility. And once they discovered television's capacity for image shaping, they all but reinvented political advertising. Most worked for candidates of one political party or the other. They acted much more like Renaissance condottieri, each with his train of cutthroat hirelings, than knightly troubadours who sang for their supper. They had become the new political bosses, stage-managing one election campaign after another, making success possible even for the weakest of candidates. As early as the 1970 elections, only five of that year's sixty-seven major-party candidates for the Senate neglected to hire some kind of political consultant. Today, only a foolhardy Senate candidate would forgo a political consultant's services. These technicians had reshaped the nation's election methods and principles, thereby reshaping the US Senate as an institution whose members have become excessively attuned to the fund-raising consequences of their every word and deed.

At first, as senators began to use television ads as a campaign tool under professional guidance, they tried to present themselves as appealing individuals, normally avoiding much mention of their opponents. That was old style—the way Harry Truman advised party candidates. The professionals' techniques became more sophisticated, and soon Senate elections reflected a new testiness, abandoning what was left of the assumed rules of the past in favor of attacking each other with the political equivalents of eye-gouging and knee-to-the-groin tactics.

In 1980, a private group, the National Conservative Political Action Committee (NCPAC), showed dramatically the effectiveness of television attack ads. NCPAC had its hit list of six liberal Democratic senators up for reelection, and the group's chairman, John ("Terry") Dolan, made no pretense at either fairness or honesty. "We're not people who crave respectability," he said. "A group like ours could lie through its teeth and the candidate it helps stays clean." Under the existing "stupid" election laws, he said, "We could elect Mickey Mouse."[43] Dolan's committee spent more than $1 million on its television attack ads against the targeted senators, who included South Dakota's George McGovern, the Democrats' 1972 presidential candidate; Idaho's Frank Church, chairman of the Senate Committee on Foreign Relations; and Indiana's Birch Bayh. Some of the Republican challengers took alarm at Dolan's tactics, fearing backlash. Dan Quayle, a member of the House running against Senator Bayh, tried to order Dolan and his associates out of Indiana. Four of the six senators whom NCPAC attacked lost their elections. "They weren't the only factor," Senator McGovern said of his defeat, but "they were crucial."[44]

These tough new campaign managers—hired guns, political mercenaries, if not paid character assassins—had a natural instinct for the political jugular. "Nobody hired a consultant for moral judgments," said one prominent consultant.[45] They had more at stake than electing client candidates: a winning record gave bragging rights and exposure to future high-paying clients. This prompted them to push beyond the ordinary limits of political tolerance to the distortions, misrepresentations, and nastiness that marred so many Senate elections. With intense research, they tried to discover the "nugget" in an opponent's past that could be exploited to savage him or her as off base on crime, national defense, Social Security, or women's rights, among other hot-button issues. Both sides worked this way, and their TV ads could poison the political atmosphere. Relentless in attack, swift in parry and riposte, these political duelists tutored the viewing public to a deeper cynicism about politics, politicians, and the US Senate.[46]

The major changes in the election processes grew out of the development of better political tools and worse strategies. "In just a few years the technology has changed dramatically," explained Mandy Grunwald, a Democratic consultant. "With more portable video cameras, better editing equipment and express mail, you can respond far more quickly—often in less than twenty-four hours. The result is that campaigns have really become video debates."[47] The newly devised tracking polls allowed campaign managers to fine-tune their candidates' responses, not only to changes in public opinion, but also to counter immediately opponents' ads and tactics. In earlier years, explained Robert Squier, another leading Democratic consultant, the candidates took polls, laid out their strategies, and then preceded in the final weeks to culminate their efforts. "Now," he said, "that whole process can take place in three days and be repeated over and over during the campaign." The short-term tracking polls permit consultants to measure public sentiments as often as every few hours, and then to act on that knowledge. There was danger in the new technology as well as opportunity. "The "techniques have gotten so refined, the weapons so powerful," said pollster Paul Maslin, "that if you don't use them, you will lose them, because the other side will use them on you."[48]

The new technology brought an increasing reliance on negative campaigning, with every Senate candidate no longer just proposing himself as hero, but assaulting his opponent as scoundrel. The candidates at times sounded like town scolds, screeching "liar" and "sleaze" at each other. Many thought themselves above such tactics only to have their campaign managers warn of certain defeat if they did not engage in the fight. One political consultant stated that this made election campaigns "just like mud-wrestling in a pigsty."[49]

Just a few months after the Supreme Court's 1976 rulings on election campaign financing, Pennsylvania's John Heinz, heir to the family pickle fortune and a member of the House, startled the political world by spending $2.5 million of family money, then a huge amount, to win election to the Senate. That year, more than a dozen other candidates for the Senate also gave substantial amounts, $50,000 or more, to their own campaigns, but none came close to Heinz's millions. He was the first legally to spend so much on a Senate campaign, and he was a forerunner of a new kind of Senate candidate: immensely wealthy and not unlike the millionaire "vanity" candidates of the late nineteenth century. This was a new option for the well-to-do to help themselves far beyond the supposedly legal limits of the previous decades.

In 1982, among the Senate candidates were rich businessmen who spent unusually large amounts of their own money on their campaigns: Minnesota's Mark Dayton, department store heir, $7.1 million;[50] New Jersey's Frank Lautenberg, data processing executive, $5.5 million;[51] and Ohio's Howard Metzenbaum, parking-lot franchise owner, $3.7 million.[52] In the 1983–84 election cycle, among other wealthy candidates, John D. ("Jay") Rockefeller IV, then governor of West Virginia and great-grandson both of the oil magnate and the late-nineteenth-century Senate titan Nelson Aldrich, spent a then-astonishing $12 million of his own money to win a Senate seat.[53]

Over the following years, it became almost commonplace for candidates of great wealth to continue to seek Senate seats. In the 1991–92 cycle, for example, there were at least fourteen multimillionaires running for the Senate. In the next cycle, no fewer than twenty-seven Senate candidates spent at least $100,000 of their own money on their campaigns. Edward M. Kennedy of Massachusetts, then more than thirty years a senator, was so seriously challenged by his Republican opponent, Mitt Romney, another multimillionaire, that he felt compelled to spend $1.3 million of his own money.[54] That was unusual for a Kennedy.

In 1994, California Representative Michael Huffington smashed all previous personal spending records for a Senate seat with a contribution of $28 million to his losing bid to unseat Senator Dianne Feinstein. Former Goldman Sachs executive Jon Corzine soon vastly exceeded Huffington's sum in awarding himself a record-shattering $62 million in his successful 2000 bid to represent New Jersey—for a job that then paid $150,000 per year.[55] Compared to that, former Hewlett-Packard chief executive Carly Fiorina's 2010 contribution of $5.5 million to her $21 million campaign chest, in a fruitless effort to oust California's other senator, Barbara Boxer, seemed like teenage allowance money.[56] In 2012, Connecticut Republican Linda McMahon boosted the record to a greater altitude by spending nearly $100 million of her own money for two unsuccessful Senate races within three years.[57]

The elections of 2000 produced other extraordinary Senate contests and other multimillionaire candidates. Among them, again, was Minnesota's

Mark Dayton. After his 1982 loss, he tried again, this time spending $12 million, and he won. In Washington State, Maria Cantwell, a multimillionaire in her own right, challenged Republican Senator Slade Gordon. She spent $11.5 million, most of it her own money, and upset the senator, who had only half that amount.[58]

Perhaps the most unusual Senate campaign that year came in Missouri, at first a seemingly ordinary battle of name-calling and expensive commitments to television attack ads. Three weeks before the election, however, Democratic candidate Mel Carnahan, the state's governor, was killed in an airplane crash. That seemed to give the election to his opponent, incumbent Republican senator John Ashcroft. In this difficulty, the Democrats decided to try to elect the dead man, a tactic without precedent, with the understanding that if he got the most votes, his widow, Jean Carnahan, would take his seat in the Senate. Carnahan was indeed elected, and the new governor then appointed his widow to the Senate.[59]

Another headline-producing 2000 campaign took place in New York. Democratic members of that state's congressional delegation encouraged First Lady Hillary Rodham Clinton to run for a soon-to-be-vacant Senate seat, even though she had never lived in New York State. After some hesitation, she agreed—and she won. That had never happened before. No wife of a president had ever before run for an important public office. She had a serious handicap, even more damaging than the cry of "carpetbagger"; she and President Bill Clinton prompted a malignant hatred from many critics over their political record and continuing ambitions. But she had formidable advantages as well, not least of which was total name recognition. She was known by all as an impressive woman in her own right. Despite the howling of their entrenched critics, she and her husband also enjoyed widespread popularity, especially in New York City.

To oppose Clinton, the Republicans nominated a little-known member of the House of Representatives, Enrico ("Rick") Lazio. A listless, ever-cheerful candidate with an ingratiating smile all but frozen on his face, Lazio proved unequal to the early projections that this campaign might prove great political theater. Their less-than-dramatic race had one additional extraordinary feature: between them they spent more campaign money than any previous or current campaign, actually $1 million more than that year's New Jersey's total with Jon Corzine's wild spending. Lazio spent $40.6 million and Clinton spent $30 million, a total of $70.6 million between them.[60] By contrast, the 2010 Boxer-Fiorina slugfest amounted to less than $50 million.[61]

Into the twenty-first century, Senate elections had largely become competitive contests in mudslinging and name-calling, with scant public attention to the substantive matters inherent in the jobs these candidates were seeking. All major-party candidates were fully armed in every Senate race with the professionals they needed to defend themselves and to attack their adversaries, both in the primaries and the general elections. "These are hired guns," said David Broder of the *Washington Post*, "They have no responsibility."[62]

"They know exactly what it takes to convince us in thirty seconds that one candidate is courageous and lovable, another one grasping and despicable," reported Alan Ehrenhalt of *Congressional Quarterly*. "The consultants have become so good that they are in the process of canceling each other out."[63] That did not diminish the ferocity of their work. They went on, election cycle after election cycle, abusing their clients' opponents and collecting their fees. Journalist Mark Shields offered an antidote to their excesses: "Put yourself through a car wash to get rid of the accumulated slime and grime."[64]

Ever since passage of the 1974 election law, designed to reduce campaign spending to rational levels, there had come more and more ways to raise ever more campaign cash. This had a large impact on senators. In 1988, the combined spending for all Senate candidates was $119.4 million. Just four years later, it had nearly doubled to $214 million, and then continued to skyrocket to $728 million in the 2009–10 cycle. These were immense sums, especially considering the relatively few campaigns for only one-third of the Senate seats each election year.[65]

The invention of "soft money," defined as contributions made to parties for their general operation rather than to benefit specific candidates and not subject to regulation under federal election law, played a major part in these dramatic spending increases. In 1988, a presidential year, the total soft money in federal elections amounted to $28 million, a modest amount compared to the astonishing outlays to come. Four years later, in 1992, the total more than tripled to $92 million, then in 1996 it tripled again to $270 million, and by 2000 to $570 million. In these presidential years, much of these funds went to the rival presidential camps, but candidates for the Senate shared richly in this largesse, too. In 2000, for example, candidates in the thirty-three Senate contests that year received the benefit of almost one-fifth of that year's soft money, more than $63 million for the Democrats, more than $44 million for the Republicans.

The vast expenditure of unregulated soft money in 2000 finally moved Congress to act, but only after turning aside a furious attempt to block any change. Under the leadership of Senator John McCain, an Arizona Republican, with major help from Senator Russell Feingold, a Wisconsin Democrat, Congress in 2002 enacted a statute intended to abolish soft money in federal election campaigns, and to restrict funding sources for pre-election broadcast advertising ("electioneering communications"). Critics instantly challenged this measure as unconstitutional, and the Federal Election Commission, through its enforcement decisions, quickly pockmarked it with loopholes.[66] The McCain-Feingold legislation, formally known as the Bipartisan Campaign Reform Act of 2002 (BCRA), banned national parties, federal candidates, and officeholders from raising soft money in federal elections, and it prohibited corporations and labor unions from using their general treasuries to fund independent campaign advertisements explicitly advocating the election or defeat of an individual candidate.[67] Contrary to predictions that this statute's soft-money ban would interfere with political parties' fund-raising activities, this did not happen.[68]

The Supreme Court, in its 2003 *McConnell v. Federal Election Commission* decision,[69] explicitly endorsed the McCain-Feingold soft money ban, noting that large contributions to political parties were improperly used to gain privileged access to elected officials. This came as a momentary setback for Senator Mitch McConnell, who in the years ahead, as his party's Senate floor leader, would expand his reputation as the leading Republican critic of campaign finance restrictions. As a later report in the *New York Times* explained, "Conservatives opposed to campaign finance restrictions acknowledge that they are driven partly by raw political motives and the belief that fewer limitations on wealthy individuals and companies would mean more money for Republicans."[70]

In 2007, partially in response to the free-wheeling spending ways of convicted lobbyist Jack Abramoff, Congress passed the Honest Leadership and Open Government Act (HLOGA) to add further disclosure requirements to lobbyists' campaign contributions.[71]

On grounds that campaign contributions are a form of free speech that deserve protection under the Constitution, the Supreme Court, on January 21, 2010, in its five-to-four *Citizens United v. Federal Election Commission* ruling, found to be unconstitutional the McCain-Feingold Act's prohibitions on any broadcast, cable, or satellite "electioneering communications" mentioning a candidate's name within a specified period before elections. This decision freed the treasuries of corporations and labor unions from further limits on campaign expenditures for such communications.[72] This decision continues the 1970s ban on corporations and unions making direct contributions to federal election candidates, although affiliated PACs may continue to contribute to candidates, parties, and other PACs.[73]

Justice Anthony Kennedy, in his opinion for the majority, wrote, "If the First Amendment has any force, it prohibits Congress from fining or jailing citizens, or associations of citizens, for simply engaging in free speech."[74] Justice John Paul Stevens, writing for the four dissenting justices, observed that the ruling "threatens to undermine the integrity of elected institutions across the Nation."[75]

Citizens United inspired an emboldened Republican Party to challenge the McCain-Feingold ban on soft money by arguing that the free-speech concept underlying the decision should be extended beyond unions and corporations to include national political parties. But in June 2010, the high court turned aside that effort in reaffirming the earlier decision.[76]

In an effort to undo the broadly unpopular *Citizens United* decision, the Democratic-controlled House, on June 24, 2010, passed legislation requiring greater disclosure by corporations of their campaign expenditures. Several weeks later, however, Senate Republicans killed the measure.[77] This collective action, at least for some time, finally erased the ban against corporate funding for federal election campaigns that the Tillman Act had initiated more than a century earlier.

The November 2010 congressional elections, the first to come under the *Citizens United* decision, witnessed an ever-greater outpouring of campaign funds. In the bitter, but unsuccessful effort of Nevada Tea Party candidate Sharron Angle to defeat Senate Majority Leader Harry Reid, the Angle campaign imported money by the bucketful, spending $31 million to attract 321,000 votes, against Reid's $25 million, to gain 362,000 votes.[78] This environment produced Super PACs to benefit presidential candidates. Under this new structure, independent of control by the candidates themselves, a few fabulously wealthy donors can contribute millions of dollars in unrestricted campaign donations, outside the restrictions that apply to the candidates themselves, for negative advertisements, while the candidates, relying on separate fund-raising sources, can maintain positive themes. A Democratic strategist observed, "The Supreme Court is saying that campaign spending is a matter of free speech, but it has set up a situation where the more money you have the more speech you can buy."[79] Despite the significant loosening impact of early-twenty-first-century legislation and court decisions, financial disclosure requirements and a majority of contribution limitations remained in place, offering a barrier—permeable though it may be—against corruption of the lawmaking process through the exchange of money for votes. Whether any such barriers will long survive, however, is one of the most serious questions confronting the institutional integrity of the modern Senate.

Prior to the 1970s, senators could enjoy acting as legislative "statesmen" for the initial four years of their terms, before taking on the onerous fund-raising duties of "candidate" for the final two. Today, senators who wish to keep their options open for another term must labor for six full years under the preoccupying urgency of amassing the many millions of dollars that such a campaign will be certain to require. More than at any previous time, these money-driven elections are discouraging otherwise promising potential candidates and are distracting members from optimal participation in the Senate's day-to-day legislative responsibilities.

3

Dancing with Presidents

A Wary Embrace

JOHN F. KENNEDY ONCE OBSERVED, "It is much easier in many ways for me, and for other presidents, I think, who felt the same way, when Congress is not in town."[1] From the start, senators have approached the nation's chief executive with caution. In the same line of work, but acting from differing positions under the US Constitution, they have recognized one another to be rivals in governing, as well as likely antagonists. New senators learn this quickly.

An early meeting between President George Washington and the Senate showed how difficult matters could become. On August 22, 1789, with the nation's temporary capital then in New York City, Washington traveled from his residence at 3 Cherry Street, near the East River, to visit the Senate on the upper floor of Congress's meeting place, Federal Hall, located at the corner of Wall and Broad streets. The president sought to flesh out his constitutional responsibility, "by and with the Advice and Consent of the Senate, to make Treaties." In this first exercise of that power, he sought the Senate's advice and consent to a plan to appoint a three-man commission to negotiate with the Creek Nation and other southern Indian tribes over land issues. He brought along Secretary of War Henry Knox to answer any questions the senators might have. But the senators had a different idea of how to proceed. They wanted to examine the accompanying documents over the coming weekend. This was not Washington's plan. Essentially, he wanted their consent on the spot, with or without their advice. The president departed in a huff, but returned two days later when the Senate finally granted its consent. Some of the senators reciprocated Washington's feelings of irritation. Pennsylvania Senator William Maclay, an irascible fellow, wrote in his journal, "I cannot be mistaken. The President wishes to tread on the necks of the Senate."[2]

This was not what anybody had expected. Under the Constitution, the president and the Senate were to work together constructively on important matters such as treaties and nominations, but the document lacked specific guidance on how they might do this. Washington and the senators, tentative in almost everything connected with the newly established federal government, moved with great caution.

In their deliberations two years earlier in Philadelphia, the constitutional convention's delegates seemed to suggest that they wanted the Senate, among its other duties, to serve as an executive council for the president.[3] The president and the senators understood this. Washington had presided over that convention, and half of the Senate's twenty-two members in 1789 had earlier served as its delegates.[4] Indeed, one of them, Pierce Butler of South Carolina, told his Senate colleagues that, in this meeting with Washington, they were acting as a "council" for the president.[5] But with considerable anxiety, they struggled on how to proceed. Vice President John Adams proposed that they provide the new president with a "throne" when he came to the Senate. Instead, Washington simply sat in Adams's chair at the rostrum.[6]

The senators then—and later—admired Washington to the point of reverence. He was the preeminent hero of the Revolution, unanimously elected as the nation's first president. Even before Washington had taken the presidential oath, senators had voted to bestow on him a royal title: "His Majesty, the President of the United States of America, and the Protector of the Rights of the Same."[7] Although the House of Representatives summarily rejected that grandiose title, it suggested how awed this first gathering of their colleagues in the upper chamber was by this first president. That died quickly as the Constitution's inherent obligations and provisions nudged the Senate in the direction of antagonism and rivalry, even with a president of Washington's stature. These first senators, many of them practiced parliamentarians, had an instinctive sense of their as-yet dimly defined institutional prerogatives.

Of course, from the very beginning, there was more to the Senate's relationship with the president than giving him advice, consent, and a fancy title. Besides their constitutional authority over treaties and federal appointments, senators had full legislative powers, equal to those granted the House of Representatives. Today, the US Senate is nearly alone among the bicameral legislatures of the Western world in its authority to exercise such coequal powers.[8] The constitutional checks and balances central to the federal government also placed sturdy barriers between the Senate and the president. Each could frustrate the other. Inherent institutional conflict came bundled with their respective roles as executive and legislators.

Even before this face-to-face meeting, the squire of Mount Vernon had had his troubles with the Senate. A little more than two weeks earlier, he had sent his first list of nominations for federal office to members of the upper chamber for their approval, but he did that without first discussing with them his selections. After the Senate quickly approved all but one of those nominees, it appointed a committee of three to confer with the president on the "proper" way for him to communicate such matters. The three deferentially asked Washington if he would be willing to appear before the Senate in person to present his nominations, as he was preparing to do for treaties. He responded politely, but firmly, that he preferred to transact such business in writing.[9]

The Senate's rejection of Washington's nominee to the post of naval officer for the port of Savannah, Georgia, annoyed the chief executive. Without prior announcement, he responded with a personal visit to inquire what the problem might be. Georgia Senator James Gunn, who had personal differences with the rejected nominee, explained his opposition while also making clear that he and his colleagues felt no obligation to share with the president their reasons, which they had discussed in secret session. Washington later sent the Senate a curt note suggesting that in the future whenever they had doubts about any one of his nominations, they simply ask him why he made it.[10] The contretemps over the rejected nomination and the slightly delayed treaty advice caused Washington to resolve never again to visit the Senate to discuss these matters. From that time onward, he and his successors would communicate only by written message.[11]

President Washington's inherent caution predisposed him to stand aloof from Congress and not to meddle with legislation under consideration in either chamber. The Constitution directed him to report to Congress "from time to time" on the state of the union and then to "recommend to their consideration such measures as he shall judge necessary and expedient."[12] In the understanding of much later presidents, this would seem an open invitation for them to initiate legislation, indeed full-scale legislative programs, but Washington treated this directive narrowly, as he did the option granted the president to approve or disapprove legislation the Congress recommended for his signature. Washington naturally showed great deference to Congress and its judgments. All through the Revolutionary War, he had served under the Continental Congress, whose members had picked him to command the American forces. That deference to Congress led members to believe that the president would consent to whatever legislation they adopted, unless he believed that the measure violated the Constitution. That was Washington's reason for vetoing his first bill (he vetoed only two),[13] and that became the grounds upon which presidents who immediately followed Washington judged legislation. As a result, those presidents rarely vetoed any bills. John Adams, Thomas Jefferson, and John Quincy Adams vetoed none. James Madison vetoed seven and James Monroe only one.[14] They had Washington's example to guide them. Indeed, in his 1796 Farewell Address, he advised all those who would succeed him as president not to interfere in the lawmaking process.[15] That was the business of Congress.

President Washington's distaste for meddling in Congress's deliberations did not stop others from playing an activist role, however, and no one proved more active than his treasury secretary, Alexander Hamilton. A fierce partisan, Hamilton had shaped an extensive legislative program of his own, including a national bank, which he pressed Congress to enact. He organized his own party apparatus within the Senate and House to sponsor the bills he wanted passed. He recruited senators and representatives as his agents, and he met them in private to plot strategy and line up the needed votes. Those in opposition to his measures had no organization, and they did little more than denounce their pliable colleagues as Hamilton's "Gladiators" and "tools."[16] Hamilton's politicking eventually brought him to a dueling ground in Weehawken, New Jersey, where he lost his life at the hands of the incumbent vice president, Aaron Burr. But his brilliant legislative concepts and clever tactics made him the first person outside Congress to hold real influence over its members. Hamilton's methods, though viewed darkly at the time, would become commonplace in modern times when presidents and others had no reason to assume a standoffish posture with Congress. Whatever Hamilton's successes, President Washington remained adamant in not encroaching on the deliberations of Congress.

When Thomas Jefferson became president in 1801, he observed the outward appearance of not interfering with Congress but, much like Hamilton, in private he worked closely with his political allies in the Senate and House to achieve his legislative goals. But he made one open change. With President Washington and his immediate successor, John Adams, the

State of the Union address was a highly formalized ritual, much to Adams's pleasure, with the president presenting his annual message in person. Later in the day, the vice president, attended by the Speaker of the House and members of both houses, visited the president's Philadelphia residence to make an address in reply. Jefferson, however, abandoned the practice as too reminiscent of British aristocracy and royal pretensions, or as one Antifederalist newspaper put it, "ridiculous pomp."[17] Instead, he dispatched his annual messages to the two houses with an aide and expected no response, as there was no protocol for replying in person to messages in writing. Jefferson let members know what he wanted in legislation through what then-senator John Quincy Adams called an "extra-official hint," taking pains to keep these matters secret.[18] In one instance, he asked a member to copy a bill he had sent to him and then to destroy the original, which was, culpably, in Jefferson's hand.[19]

A charming host, Jefferson regularly invited senators and representatives to dinner at the executive mansion in the new capital city of Washington. There, over choice wines and generous tables, Jefferson spoke freely and engagingly about his ideas for legislation. In this manner, he influenced both houses of Congress to the point that his opponents described his Capitol Hill loyalists as members of "the President's Party." Vermont Senator Stephen Bradley complained testily that, with his dinner invitations, President Jefferson "silenced" opposition in Congress and made senators even "more servile" to him than before.[20] For his part, Jefferson justified his "backstairs" approaches to senators and representatives by arguing that without such guidance, they would remain "in the dark" about his administration's intentions and desires.[21]

The presidents who followed Jefferson over the next twenty years wielded no such influence over Congress. Indeed, they actually lost ground to senators, as the latter exercised growing influence in determining who would receive federal appointments. James Madison, a diffident politician and a scholar at heart, proved utterly inadequate in the growing crisis with Great Britain, and offered no leadership to Congress. Kentucky's Henry Clay, the dynamic young Speaker of the House, led the War Hawks in both the House and Senate to force Madison into the War of 1812 against Britain. Clay called Madison "wholly unfit" to lead the nation or Congress.[22] John C. Calhoun of South Carolina described Madison as "a man of amiable manners and great talents" who could not control even the members of his own cabinet.[23]

Madison's successor, James Monroe, proved similarly inept in dealing with Congress. John Quincy Adams reported that Monroe had "not the slightest influence on Congress."[24] He sought no conflicts with the Senate or House. In 1818, during the Seminole War in Florida, Monroe's administration had created a military tribunal to try two British subjects for inciting Creek Indians against the United States. When the tribunal changed a sentence from death to corporal punishment, General Andrew Jackson disagreed and summarily had the subject shot. Facing a congressional outcry, President Monroe readily turned over confidential documents to allow Congress to investigate.[25]

In the 1824 presidential election, four candidates received votes in the Electoral College, but none got a majority. That put the choice to the House of Representatives, where Henry Clay, still Speaker, used his talents to elect Adams in preference to Andrew Jackson, who had received far more popular votes. Adams thereupon appointed Clay his secretary of state, the very job from which Madison, Monroe, and Adams himself had ascended to the presidency. Jackson and his fiery supporters regarded this as a profoundly "corrupt bargain" between Adams and Clay. Both suffered extraordinary abuse for all this throughout Adams's presidency. The bitter feelings Clay and Jackson had for one another fueled Jackson's rise to the presidency and Clay's evolution as leader of the Jacksonian opposition within the Senate.

Meanwhile, during the opening years of the nineteenth century, senators had begun to take their role as lawmakers more seriously. To that time, the House, much like the British House of Commons, had largely dominated congressional action. Most of the important debates took place in the House chamber, and major legislation tended to be introduced there. But the year 1820 signaled a change. With the coming of the great parliamentary struggle over the Missouri Compromise, the senators conducted the principal debate and came up with what they assumed was a solution to the deepening crisis between the North and the South over human slavery. Men of substance were coming into the Senate: Missouri's Thomas Hart Benton in 1821, South Carolina's Robert Hayne in 1823, and Massachusetts' Daniel Webster in 1827. They would make the chamber ring with their oratory, foreshadowing the times of greatness to come.

By this time, too, senators had begun to press their claims over presidential appointees to federal jobs. Senators argued that they should determine who received these positions within their home states. By law, the president had authority to remove those he appointed and replace them with others. Back in the First Congress, because the Constitution provided for Senate confirmation of executive appointees but remained silent on their dismissal, the House of Representatives had passed legislation requiring

Senate approval for the removal of those it had previously confirmed. On a tie vote, the Senate rejected that plan, thereby allowing the president to manage his cabinet and blocking the evolution of a parliamentary form of government with ministers responsible to the legislature.[26] This key decision made it possible for appointees to stay in their posts from one administration to the next. As early as Jefferson's presidency, these federal jobs had, in effect, become political sinecures, and senators had little opportunity to provide for their friends and political allies. Jefferson himself tried to place his adherents in federal positions, only to be hindered by this practice. "How are vacancies to be obtained?" he asked. "Those by death are few; by resignation, none."[27] Jefferson's words were soon shortened into the dictum "Few die and none resign."

In 1820, Congress passed the Four Years Act to limit these federal appointees to the length of a single presidential term unless they were reappointed.[28] But the law had little immediate effect because Monroe and his successor, John Quincy Adams, continued the old practice of allowing those in office to stay put. Change did not come until the 1829 arrival of Andrew Jackson, who burst onto the national stage with vastly different concepts of the presidency.

Victor of the Battle of New Orleans in 1815, Jackson took the presidential oath as an immensely popular folk hero. He remained angry and resentful that he had been cheated out of the job four years earlier. He blamed the Electoral College, John Quincy Adams, and Henry Clay for their "corrupt bargain" to deny him the office. Jackson brought to the presidency concepts contradictory to those of the six presidents before him. "The President," he said, "is *the* direct representative of the American people."[29] This was new doctrine, stunning members of the House and Senate. Daniel Webster and others protested that the president, indirectly elected, was not *the* representative of the people and responsible to the people as such. He was responsible to Congress, the people's representatives, and the laws Congress enacted.[30] From the start, Jackson's contrary views made conflict with Congress inevitable. In the political-parliamentary struggles to come, the Senate became the central arena for opposition to Jackson and his policies. This reality lifted the Senate into what became its Golden Age.

When he took office, Jackson enjoyed a sympathetic majority in the House of Representatives. In the Senate, however, his opponents won new recruits to battle his novel ideas about the president's enhanced role in government. "Old Hickory" had within him a moralistic fervor, which persuaded him that in all things he was right, and that anyone opposing him was corrupt, stupid, or both. This attitude set him especially apart from Henry Clay, a pragmatic politician recently returned to a far different Senate than the one he had known during a two-month appointment twenty years earlier. Unlike Jackson, Clay believed that two men could disagree and both be right, and that was the secret to the Kentucky senator's special talent for finding compromises.

Once in the presidency, Jackson promptly broke with the past by withdrawing all the nominations John Quincy Adams had made on which the Senate had not yet acted. Previously, new presidents simply re-nominated these carryovers. Jackson changed this practice by naming his own partisans to these, and other, posts. To him, this was democratic reform, partly on the theory of rotation-in-office, to give others an opportunity, and partly to have in place party loyalists who supported his administration.[31] By the time the new Congress met for business in December 1829, Jackson had sent the Senate 121 fresh nominations. Although many senators resented these tactics, they found themselves intimidated by Jackson's extraordinary popularity. Otherwise, Senator Webster stated, they would have rejected at least half of them.[32] The Senate debate over these nominations proved bitter and angry. It was marked by caustic and awkward arguments, which produced the spoils system across the country that in the next half-century became so corrupt that it badly fouled American politics. Some senators seized control of this system to build their own state parties and to make public appointments for their own private gain.

As part of his break with past practices, Jackson also changed the grounds for vetoing acts of Congress. His first veto, in 1830, killed an act of Congress authorizing construction of the sixty-mile Maysville Turnpike, located entirely with the Commonwealth of Kentucky. Under his interpretation of the Constitution, the federal government had no business funding projects that benefitted just one state. Further, Jackson believed his enemy Henry Clay was promoting that piece of home-state pork "rather for political effect than for public ends."[33] More directly, the president had pledged himself against public spending. "I stand committed before the country," he said, "to pay off the national debt"—a goal he actually reached.[34] Although many senators resented Jackson's action, he went on to veto other bills he stood in opposition to. In all, he killed twelve bills—more than the number vetoed by all the previous presidents combined.[35]

By basing his vetoes on policy, not their constitutionality, Jackson greatly enhanced the president's potential power, although only gradually did later presidents take up this parliamentary tool for their own use. In time, presidents found to their satisfaction that the mere threat of a veto could affect how members of Congress dealt with pending matters.

The 1832 presidential election campaign and the rising controversy over the Bank of the United States, a federally chartered institution that Jackson reviled as "the Monster," sparked Jackson's most ferocious fight with the Senate. To him, the bank was an antidemocratic creation of the moneyed aristocracy. In the fall of 1833, after Jackson's second inauguration, he acted to kill the bank outright by ordering the removal of all federal deposits. The move ultimately destroyed the bank and outraged Clay and other senators. His action set off a fierce debate about his authority to take such action without congressional approval.[36]

With a sympathetic majority in the House that made Jackson's impeachment impossible, Clay maneuvered to have the Senate formally repudiate the president for his actions against the bank. The Senate voted twenty-six to twenty to censure Jackson for violating the Constitution and federal law. The Senate's censure was an act without precedent and, although subsequently contemplated, never repeated.[37]

Senator Benton tried repeatedly to force the Senate to remove that blot from its journal. On January 16, 1837, less than seven weeks before Jackson's retirement from the presidency, Benton tried again, this time with a willing majority at his back. Near midnight, the Senate voted to "expunge" the rebuff to Jackson. In triumph, Benton presided as the Senate's secretary opened the 1834 Senate journal to the censure resolution, drew straight black lines around its text, and inscribed Benton's words renouncing the Senate's earlier action. With his Senate antagonists utterly foiled, Jackson watched in glory weeks later as his protégé, Vice President Martin Van Buren, once rejected by the Senate for an ambassadorial post, was sworn in as president of the United States.

Jackson's claim that he was the people's choice, responsible to them, changed the perception of the presidency. Using the veto as an effective parliamentary weapon to frustrate a hostile Congress, and acting arbitrarily on his own, as he had with the Bank of the United States, Jackson expanded the president's power and prestige beyond anything seen before. He saw no reason to defer to Congress—especially the Senate—and his defiance of the Senate changed the very nature of the presidency, of the Senate, and of the relationship between them.

But many senators' spirited opposition to what they perceived as Jackson's abuse of power also brought the Senate new prestige and power. They came through those struggles with Jackson with an enlarged view of their own role in the government, lifting the Senate to a new level of political prominence and ushering in the chamber's time of greatness. Before Jackson's presidency, the Senate, primarily, had immensely impressive style—but not real power—that was evident in the solemn, dignified way senators conducted their deliberations. When the young French aristocrat Alexis de Tocqueville visited the Senate's gallery in 1832, he was impressed; everywhere he looked on the Senate floor he thought he saw "statesmen of note, whose language would at all times do honor to the most remarkable parliamentary debates of Europe."[38] After Jackson's presidency, the Senate emerged with far more than style; it had substance, the power of decision, as its members conducted the great debates regarding the merits and meaning of the Constitution and the government founded on its principles. On many of the Senate's debates hung the fate of the nation, and many more senators were engaged in these extraordinary parliamentary battles than the three now remembered as the "Great Triumvirate," Webster, Clay and Calhoun.

The presidents who followed Jackson did not have his grandiose flair, his heroic posture, or his bristling self-righteousness. They were men of lesser stamp, and they did not challenge the Senate as Jackson had. His immediate successor, Martin Van Buren, was nicknamed the "Little Magician" for his political cunning, and was a notorious spoilsman well known to all senators. Tactful and courteous, a conciliator by instinct, he was utterly unlike the volatile Jackson. Van Buren, a senator through most of the politically charged 1820s, won the presidency in 1836 against a field of three incumbent senators and a former senator, General William Henry Harrison, all of whom attracted votes in the Electoral College. The Senates he faced from 1837 to 1841 had nominally supportive Democratic majorities, but the slavery question had already wrenched American politicians asunder, especially Democrats. Van Buren tried to placate both sides. In his inaugural address, he pledged to protect slavery in the slave states. For that waffling, he was labeled a "Northern man with Southern principles."[39] Although he escaped partisan quarreling over federal patronage by leaving most of Jackson's appointees in place, his years in the presidency were marked by a tenuous stalemate with the Senate.

A half century after Jackson retired from the presidency, the British statesman James Bryce, in an essay entitled "Why Great Men Are Not Chosen Presidents," described Van Buren and his successors until the time of Grover Cleveland in the 1880s as lacking in greatness. Lord Bryce made only two notable exceptions for those achieving presidential greatness: Abraham Lincoln and Ulysses Grant. "No President except Abraham

Lincoln," Bryce wrote, "has displayed rare or striking qualities in the chair. Who now knows or cares to know anything about the personality of James K. Polk or Franklin Pierce?"[40] Bryce offered several answers to his central question, including the reality that eminent men make more enemies than men of obscurity. The period he chronicled, however, was a time when the Senate functioned as the dominant branch of the federal government. Bryce called the presidents after Jackson and before Lincoln "intellectual pigmies" compared to the nation's "real leaders of that generation—Clay, Calhoun, and Webster."[41] The slight political talents of these presidents made them less than formidable rivals to the Senate's most preeminent members.

In 1840, when General Harrison defeated Van Buren for the presidency, he knew his place, and he said as much in his inaugural address. In his opinion, the president had no role in what he called "the legislative power" beyond making recommendations, and he would leave to Congress "the delicate duty" of legislating.[42] Taken aback by the Whig Party's nomination of Harrison for the presidency instead of himself, Senator Clay decided he would do whatever was necessary to take charge of the Harrison presidency. With Whig majorities in both the Senate and the House, Clay sought to reassert congressional supremacy in the governmental balance that Jackson had knocked asunder. Clay behaved so arrogantly and insolently that Harrison, the Whig president, broke with him, despite Clay's role as the recognized leader of the party and also of the Senate. Yet, Harrison did do what Clay wanted: he summoned a special session of Congress for May 31, 1841, when Clay planned to push to enactment the legislative program he already had in hand.[43] Shortly thereafter, Harrison became ill, and he died just a month after taking the oath of office. To the dismay of many, that made Vice President John Tyler the president.

No president had ever died in office, and some senators questioned whether Tyler should receive the title of president. Ohio's Senator William Allen, a Democrat, proposed that he be addressed as "The Vice President, on whom, by the death of the late President, the powers and duties of the office of President have devolved."[44] Although that motion did not pass, it suggested the skepticism that Tyler confronted in the Senate, and he was soon swept up in torrents of ridicule and abuse. Clay readily pushed through Congress his first legislative priority: repeal of the Democrats' sub-treasury system, designed to sever ties between the federal government and the nation's banking business, and Tyler signed that act. Clay had great trouble, however, with the re-charter of a new Bank of the United States, and when the measure finally reached Tyler, he vetoed it. With that veto, Tyler lost whatever chance he had with the Senate, because that bill was the corner-stone of Clay's and the Whig-controlled Senate's legislative agenda. Although Clay lacked the votes to override the veto, he and other senators punished Tyler by rejecting his most important nominations. And although Clay resigned from the Senate at the end of March 1842 to prepare another run for the presidency, the battering of President Tyler went on unabated. In all, the Senate rejected four of his nominations to the cabinet and four to the Supreme Court.[45] Despite these embarrassments and all his other difficulties serving as a president without a party, Tyler tried to win re-nomination in 1844, this time as a Democrat. His bid failed, however, as that party picked James K. Polk, a relative unknown.

Polk, a Jacksonian Democrat nicknamed "Young Hickory" after his mentor, held Jackson's views of the presidency as the people's representative and defender, but he lacked the political wherewithal to overawe Congress. "The people elect the President," he said, but that claim won him no special deference on Capitol Hill.[46] His party had a marginal majority in the Senate, but hardly a working majority. That several senators were actively maneu-vering to succeed Polk as president further undercut efforts to enforce party discipline. Although he consulted freely with many senators, and did not instinctively confront them as Jackson had, he complained privately about Democratic senators jostling among themselves for the party's presidential nomination. To him, the worst of the lot was John C. Calhoun, whom he called "the most mischievous man in the Senate," who was "perfectly des-perate" to gain the presidency.[47]

Polk had no interest in a second term. Fatigued and ailing, he died three months after retiring from office. Out of this partisan party scrambling, Michigan's Senator Lewis Cass gained the Democratic presidential nomi-nation. The Whigs turned aside bids from party members Daniel Webster and Henry Clay, awarding their nomination instead to another hero from the Mexican War, "Old Rough and Ready" Zachary Taylor. His political talents were admittedly meager. Polk called him "a well-meaning old man . . . uneducated, exceedingly ignorant of public affairs."[48] In his inaugural address, Taylor endorsed Clay's view of the limited role for the president, and pledged to leave to "the wisdom of Congress" what legislation to enact.[49] But sixteen months into his term, Taylor became suddenly ill, and on July 9, 1850, he died.

Vice President Millard Fillmore, a New Yorker, succeeded him. And, unlike Taylor, Fillmore favored the "omnibus bill," which Clay, now returned to the Senate, had introduced to reduce North-South tensions over the looming issues of slavery expansion and states' rights. In a dramatically changed strategy, Clay's supporters pushed through the Senate the individual titles within Clay's omnibus bill as separate measures, and President Fillmore signed them all.[50] This, the great compromise of 1850, staved off the fracturing of the nation—for a few years. In terms of historical reputation, the Senate of 1849–50 contained a galaxy of superstars. Ten of its sixty-two members, in terms of political skills and leadership stature, excelled any of that era's presidents. They included Thomas Hart Benton (D-Missouri), John C. Calhoun (D-South Carolina), Lewis Cass (D-Michigan), Salmon Chase (Free Soil-Ohio), Henry Clay (Whig-Kentucky), Jefferson Davis (D-Mississippi), Stephen Douglas (D-Illinois), Sam Houston (D-Texas), William Seward (Whig-New York), and Daniel Webster (Whig-Massachusetts).

In the tormented decade of the 1850s, the bitter quarreling over slavery continued to tear apart the fabric of American life, and the politicians of the day focused their efforts on dealing with this ongoing and frustrating national crisis. Not surprisingly, the three presidents of that era—Fillmore, Franklin Pierce, and James Buchanan—were much like those who had served in the 1840s, each a compromise choice, not a man of substance in his own right. Fillmore, the last of the Whig presidents, saw his party wither away into extinction, replaced shortly thereafter by the Republican Party. The Democrats chose Pierce, a New Hampshire lawyer of limited ambition, on the forty-ninth ballot of their 1852 convention after each of the four active and more prominent candidates failed to attract the two-thirds majority then required to carry the convention. An accidental candidate who became an accidental president, Pierce tried, without success, to bring harmony to his badly divided party. In 1856, Pennsylvania's James Buchanan won the Democratic nomination, but only on the seventeenth ballot. As president, Buchanan sought to leave legislation on substantive matters to Congress, but as president he proved hapless in an agony of indecision, first presiding over the smash-up of his party, and then, after the election of Abraham Lincoln, over the smash-up of the nation itself.[51]

By the close of this decade, the stalwarts of the Senate's Golden Age—Clay, Webster, Calhoun, and Benton—had long passed from the scene. Replacing them was a new generation of diverse talents. From these senators came the wildly emotional rhetoric that made the Senate chamber a cockpit of malignant recriminations, which no president could hope to control. Some among them struggled desperately to accommodate the estranged factions to save the nation and spare its people from a civil war. But in the weeks immediately after Lincoln's election, Southern states began seceding from the federal union, with South Carolina leading the way on December 20, 1860. By the end of January 1861, six other states had followed. To them, Lincoln was an obscure country politician with only two years of service in the House of Representatives a dozen years before, but they also saw in him the hopelessness of their slavery cause. Senators from these states, one after another, took the occasion to make farewell speeches to the Senate, bidding their colleagues good-bye, often in moving terms. The actions of these senators, unprecedented in history, marked their extraordinary response not to a president, but to a president-elect.

No president ever confronted such political catastrophe as Lincoln faced when he took the oath of office on March 4, 1861. Most of the Southern states had formally withdrawn from the Union; civil war seemed imminent, and Lincoln himself was in serious danger of assassination. Moreover, he had little past experience to qualify him to undertake the job ahead. In his inaugural address, he made an eloquent plea for restraint, which did little then to enhance his stature in this crisis. Massachusetts Senator Charles Sumner dismissed him as a "petty politician," and Ohio's Senator Ben Wade called him "poor white trash."[52] For his cabinet, Lincoln plucked three Republicans from the Senate—William Seward of New York for secretary of state, Salmon Chase of Ohio for secretary of the treasury, and Simon Cameron of Pennsylvania for secretary of war. All three had been Lincoln's rivals at the Republican Party convention in 1860. Seward assumed that he could act as premier and run Lincoln's administration. When he proposed foreign military adventures as the way to reunite the country, Lincoln gently but firmly rebuked him.[53]

Long an adherent of Henry Clay's politics of accommodation and compromise, Lincoln approached Congress with modesty. "Many of you," he said, "have more experience than I in the conduct of public affairs."[54] In the matter of legislation, the president supported Clay's views, too. "As a rule," he said, "I think it better that Congress should originate, as well as perfect its measures, without external bias."[55] In July 1862, however, Lincoln did send Congress the draft of a bill to compensate any state that abolished slavery within its borders. That touched off a firestorm of criticism, with his opponents denouncing this "usurpation" of power. In fact, the Senate exploded in an immediate debate over whether Lincoln had the authority to submit a draft of legislation he wanted.[56] Lincoln did not make that mistake twice.

In reality, Lincoln had little interest in legislation. He signed bills that he disapproved of, including the Second Confiscation Act and West Virginia statehood legislation.[57] He proposed few laws in his annual addresses to

Congress, and he used his veto sparingly. Of course, he had a far greater problem at hand: putting down an extraordinary rebellion, and this he did without deferring to Congress. When fighting broke out in South Carolina, he acted swiftly. Congress was not in session, and he did not call legislators into special session until July. Meanwhile, he suspended the writ of habeas corpus, a constitutionally questionable action that allowed him to direct the arrest of thousands of suspected Confederate sympathizers. He summoned the militia by the tens of thousands to fight this civil war. Never had the government been in such peril, and Lincoln acted decisively to put down the rebellion. On a few matters, like the suspension of habeas corpus, Lincoln later asked for Congress's approval, but for the most part he simply claimed authority to act under the war powers inherent in his office as president. These powers, he argued, went far beyond the powers allotted to Congress. "I conceive that I may in an emergency do things on military grounds," he said in one confrontation, "which cannot constitutionally be done by Congress."[58]

In January 1863, without authority from Congress, Lincoln issued the Emancipation Proclamation, a document that on military grounds freed all slaves then held in any territory occupied by the Confederates. Using this same executive power, Lincoln also appointed military governors over conquered Southern territory without the approval of the Senate. Lincoln's claim to such authority did not sit well with senators, and they objected at times with caustic oratory. They hounded Lincoln with demands: to fire Secretary Seward and reorganize the cabinet, to dismiss generals they believed inept, and to revise military strategy. Lincoln parried their varied thrusts as best he could, not always without offending them. He had his own ways of turning them back, usually with a stream of pithy stories.

One of Lincoln's most persistent antagonists was Ohio's Senator Wade, chairman of the Joint Committee on the Conduct of the War, which Congress created to investigate the Union's disasters at the 1861 battles of Bull Run and Ball's Bluff. Wade and other Republican Radicals never seemed satisfied with the prairie-lawyer president and they kept up their bitter criticism all through the war.[59]

Long before the end of the Civil War, Lincoln and the Republicans in Congress had begun to plan for how to deal with the rebel states once the war was won. In December 1863, at the beginning of a new Congress, Lincoln proposed a conciliatory plan to reestablish state governments in the Confederate states.[60] But Senator Wade and other Republican Radicals had no such intentions. They wanted to impose harsh terms on the "traitor" rebels, including trials for treason. Above all, however, they insisted that Congress have exclusive control over Reconstruction, to the exclusion of the president. "It belongs to us," said Wade.[61]

In 1864, an election year, not a single US senator favored a second term for Lincoln. In part, this reflected his often bitter quarrels with the Senate, but also the assumption by Republican senators—conservatives as well as radicals—that Lincoln had no chance for reelection. In the end, Lincoln easily won re-nomination at the June convention at Baltimore with his party renamed, for election purposes, the Union Party. Lincoln knew well the attitude of the Senate's Republicans. "They have never been friendly to me," he said.[62]

Despite Lincoln's strained relations with most senators, he was, without difficulty, reelected for a second term. He owed his political rescue to a dramatic upturn in the Union's prospects, primarily as a result of General William Tecumseh Sherman's devastating march through Georgia. But that did not lessen the opposition of Wade and other Republican Radicals to Lincoln's Reconstruction policies. They especially wanted "an eye for an eye and a tooth for a tooth," in Senator Wade's words. They ridiculed Lincoln's Reconstruction policies as "absurd."[63]

When Lincoln was assassinated in April 1865, these men had become his implacable opponents, and they did not stop to grieve. On the contrary, they saw his murder as a heavenly inspired "godsend," which put them in charge at last. "By the gods," exclaimed Wade, "there will be no trouble now in running the government!"[64] After Andrew Johnson became president, Michigan Republican Senator Zachariah Chandler, believing the Radicals would have Johnson's full cooperation, called him "a better man" than Lincoln.[65]

Senators Wade and Chandler and others in their camp let their resentment blind them to both Lincoln's greatness and to how he had changed the presidency itself. Out of sheer contempt, Wade saw Lincoln as a political weakling subservient to his secretary of state, William Seward, and presiding over a corrupt administration.[66] Because of their antagonisms to Lincoln's policies of conciliation, Wade and Chandler especially had no sense that Lincoln had immensely strengthened the executive office, or that his unseemly murder would lift him as political martyr to rank as the greatest American of the century, and the nation's greatest president. In fact, his tactical maneuvers and obfuscations, the very frustrations that Wade and Chandler read as evidence of Lincoln's ineptness and inadequacies, let Lincoln hold together the often antagonistic elements in the North, which in turn helped win the Civil War and save the nation. The struggles between Andrew Jackson and the Senate had brought the Senate its Golden Age; the struggles between Abraham Lincoln and the Senate heralded a similar cycle of parliamentary significance, a political phenomenon one of their presidential successors would label "Congressional Government."[67]

Only hours after Lincoln's death, Wade called an emergency meeting of his Joint Committee on the Conduct of the War, at which he and others voiced their disgust, in profane terms, at Lincoln's policy of conciliation. They decided to ask President Andrew Johnson for an immediate audience. They met with him the next day, Easter Sunday, and Senator Wade greeted him joyously. "Johnson," he said, "we have faith in you."[68] In the discussion that followed, Johnson delighted the Senate Radicals. "Treason is a crime," he told them, "and crime must be punished."[69] The next day, Wade again met with Johnson, this time to discuss among other matters the need for treason hangings. Johnson appeared surprised that Wade wanted so few, just what Wade called "a baker's dozen," starting with Jefferson Davis.[70]

Wade, Sumner, Chandler, and other Senate Radicals believed they now had one of their own as president. In less than a month, however, Johnson began to slip from their grasp. In early May, he began making Reconstruction decisions, instead of leaving them to Congress, by recognizing a restored government for Virginia. In late May, Johnson issued a general amnesty proclamation, pardoning most Confederates. By mid-summer, the president had abandoned the Radicals' cause and the savage retaliations they wished to inflict on the Confederate "traitors." By the time Congress convened in December 1865, following a nine-month adjournment, President Johnson had adopted most of Lincoln's approach on how to deal with the South and to restore national union. In just a few weeks, Johnson and the Congress were at war with one another. But Johnson, stubborn and tactless, soon showed himself to be his own worst enemy.

In late August 1866, with Congress again in adjournment and mid-term election campaigns under way, Johnson traveled to Chicago, stopping at city after city along the way to drum up support for his policies toward the Southern states. This "Swing around the Circle," as it was called, proved disastrous for the president. Not long into his travels, he was nastily jeered by hecklers in one crowd, and he made the mistake of responding in kind. From then on, he found hecklers in every audience, and his intemperate retorts to their taunts made him appear utterly undignified. The fall elections gave the Republicans overwhelming majorities in both the Senate and

House. By the time Congress reassembled in December, its members were talking impeachment.

In the new session of Congress, Republican radicals adopted the Tenure of Office Act to forbid the president from removing any senior federal official without the Senate's approval. This became their vehicle to try to oust Johnson as president. Although he vetoed this bill, Congress overrode his veto. And better to monitor Johnson, they kept Congress in continuous session, not allowing the usual extended break between sessions. Senator Wade and others made claims that Congress, and Congress alone, had the power to direct the government and set government policy.

Things came to a head in the summer of 1867, when President Johnson had a falling-out with Secretary of War Edwin Stanton and dismissed him. The Senate ordered Stanton's reinstatement, but in February 1868 Johnson again dismissed Stanton, defying the law. The House of Representatives promptly impeached Johnson, with all but one of the eleven articles based on Stanton's removal.

Johnson's trial before the Senate, an extravaganza of wild partisanship, marked a low point for the office of president and for the Senate itself. Even before the opening words, more than half of the senators—twenty-eight of the fifty-four—had pronounced the president guilty.[71] Immense pressures were brought on other wavering Republican senators through furious back-stage lobbying and even bribery. Representative Benjamin Butler of Massachusetts, one of the House impeachment trial managers, blurted out just such an offer. "Tell the damn scoundrel," he said of one senator, "that if he wants money, there is a bushel to be had!"[72] All twelve Senate Democrats supported Johnson. That meant that the Senate's decision hung on the moderate Republicans, a few of whom, like Maine's William Pitt Fessenden, were appalled at this judicial burlesque.[73] Others had grounds to fear for their safety, some with detectives spying on them.[74]

To the very end, the vote was in doubt, but when the Senate did vote, there were thirty-five for conviction and nineteen opposed, a one-vote margin shy of the two-thirds needed to pronounce Johnson guilty. Seven Republicans, including Fessenden, had voted "not guilty," and by their votes the Senate itself managed to escape from committing a parliamentary blunder that would have blackened its reputation for decades. None of the seven ever won reelection to the Senate.[75] One of them, Edmund Ross of Kansas, was singled out for special praise decades later by a young senator, John F. Kennedy of Massachusetts. In his book *Profiles in Courage*, Kennedy drew Ross as the hero of this dark episode in the Senate's history.[76] Ross's vote, Senator Kennedy argued, made the difference. But three other senators who stayed hidden—Edwin Morgan of New York, William Sprague of Rhode Island, and Waitman Willey of West Virginia—had also pledged privately to vote with Johnson if their support was needed.[77]

Not only had President Johnson escaped conviction by the barest margin, but he also received considerable sympathy because of the ugliness with which attacks were carried out against him. His own bungling and boorish remarks, however, earned him the contempt of senators who were not part of the scheme to convict him. Although enough senators ultimately shrank from inflicting on him that final indignity, Andrew Johnson left the presidency a much-weakened office. And, for a generation to come, the presidents who succeeded him had to deal with the intrigues of factions of senators hungry for party patronage and power. But perhaps as an unintended result, the more ambitious of these senators also tended to frustrate each other's aspirations for the presidency. In election year after election year, they saw their national party conventions pick lesser politicians for that great office, weakened as they had helped make it.

The first of these was Ulysses S. Grant, the general who crushed the Confederacy and thereby won the Civil War. "Let us have peace," he said on his nomination for president, and that was enough for him to win the election of 1868. But he was not an ideal choice, and his presidency started badly. Grant clumsily announced his cabinet choices without consulting party leaders, and that gravely offended the Senate's ranking Republicans. These senators formed what was called the "Senatorial Clique," a group of self-serving political bosses with such overall command of their party that they all but ruled the nation.[78] Among them were such party stalwarts as Simon Cameron of Pennsylvania, Zachariah Chandler of Michigan, and Roscoe Conkling of New York, each with his own train of retainers and hangers-on. At first they rebuffed Grant, but soon the president, naively ignorant of basic politics and government, fell prey to the blandishments of Conkling's flatteries. Thereafter, he relied on these men for advice and guidance. With Grant as a shield, they brought the party spoils system to spectacular new prominence. This, of course, outraged those in the party who were anxious for reform. Henry Adams, grandson of John Quincy Adams, found Grant so inept and primitive that he claimed he "upset" Darwin's theory of evolutionary progress, a Stone Age throwback who "should have lived in a cave and worn skins."[79]

Grant made several serious blunders in the men he nominated. The merchant prince he first proposed for secretary of the treasury was legally disqualified.[80] His first two nominees for chief justice—US Attorney General George Henry Williams and former US attorney general Caleb Cushing— had such tainted records that he had to withdraw their names.[81] For him, however, a larger problem came from the Senate, where members by now had perfected a system by which they actually could tell the president whom they wanted named to federal posts in their states and region. This was the fruit of the partisan patronage system developed over the previous half century. If the president nominated anyone without the approval of the respective state's US senator from the president's party, that senator had the option of appealing to his colleagues for what they called "the courtesy of the Senate," a demand that other senators stand by him and reject the nominee. As early as 1859, senators had begun to use "personally obnoxious" as the signal phrase to invoke the veto of senatorial courtesy.[82]

With this parliamentary tool, senior senators built up their home-state political organizations, the wherewithal of wealth as well as political power. For example, a prize political plum was the New York Custom House, whose chief was named by the New York's senior senator, Roscoe Conkling. He picked a political lieutenant, Chester A. Arthur, who in turn appointed more than a thousand party regulars to the agency, each of whom was required to donate a percentage of his salary to the party organization.[83] Other senators had similar arrangements in their states, and the corruption went far beyond the agencies involved to the senators themselves.

In these matters, senators were not inclined to take instruction from any president. George Hoar of Massachusetts, who entered the Senate in 1877, later wrote that the senators' control over party patronage, however untenable under the Constitution or injurious to the public interests, gave those senators such power that they could dismiss the claims of any president. "The most eminent senators," he wrote, naming nine of them, including Conkling, "would have received as a personal affront a private message from the White House expressing a desire that they should adopt any course in the discharge of their legislative duties that they did not approve. If they visited the White House, it was to give, not to receive advice."[84]

Grant ended up presiding over the most thoroughly corrupt administration of the nineteenth century. Scandals seemed everywhere. The Whiskey Ring defrauded the Treasury of millions of dollars in tax revenue. A similar scheme brought the looting of more millions from the US Post Office. One of the worst was the Credit Mobilier scandal, in which prominent members of the Senate and the House accepted stocks for a transcontinental railroad construction project at cut rates that amounted to bribery. Two Speakers of the House were implicated, and Grant's vice president, Schuyler Colfax, avoided impeachment only on a technicality. William Belknap, Grant's secretary of war, was caught accepting graft but escaped conviction in his Senate impeachment trial by resigning. Grant's bumbling performance as president did nothing to curb these outrages. On the contrary, he was by then the admiring friend of the Senate's principal power brokers, the ringleaders of the political pilfering. They, in turn, so admired Grant that they not only assured him of a second term but tried to get him a third term as well.[85]

Ohio governor Rutherford B. Hayes succeeded Grant. A dark-horse candidate, he had become the compromise choice when the Republicans' national convention deadlocked on better-known party members. Hayes pledged to seek civil service reform, the first major-party candidate to do so, at least in part to counter the deluge of party scandals during Grant's administration.[86] To prove he was serious, Hayes also pledged, if elected, to serve only one term. His election proved controversial and questionable, settled finally by a special commission created to count the disputed votes of Florida, Louisiana, South Carolina, and Oregon.[87] That panel, composed of five senators, five representatives, and five Supreme Court justices, reached a compromise that gave Hayes the presidency in return for his promise to remove the federal troops from still-occupied Southern states. But that deal managed to offend senators of both parties. The Democrats felt Hayes had thereby cheated their candidate, New York governor Samuel Tilden, out of the presidency. Recalling John Tyler's route to the presidency, which earned him the sobriquet "His Accidency," they bitterly nicknamed Hayes "His Fraudulency." Stalwart Republican senators despised Hayes for agreeing to remove the federal troops, the props that upheld the Republican carpetbagger regimes in those Southern states. President Hayes further outraged these Republican senators when they learned of his plans to curb their control over presidential appointments.[88]

Like Grant before him, Hayes started by proposing a cabinet of his own choosing, headed by an anti-Conkling New York attorney, William Evarts, as secretary of state.[89] Hayes had not only refused to consult the party's leaders on this, but he ignored the recommendations of Senator Conkling and other members of the Senatorial Clique. He intended, obviously, to break these senators' ability to dictate presidential appointments and to restore the appointing power to the presidency, where the Constitution had placed it. This was a stunning break with the attitude of President Grant, who had acted subserviently toward Conkling and the Senate's other party spoilsmen. By now, Conkling presumed himself to be the real leader of the Senate, and he retaliated against Hayes by maneuvering to block Hayes's nominees for the Cabinet.[90] Conkling and his Senate allies had to give way, however, under widespread protest against their tactics. This marked the beginning of four years of struggle between Hayes and key Senate Republicans over party patronage.

The battle raged back and forth with neither side predominant. When a Treasury-sponsored investigation demonstrated extensive corruption in the New York Custom House, part of Conkling's patronage, President Hayes acted to oust its chief, Conkling's man, Chester A. Arthur, along with Arthur's principal lieutenant. Hayes also ordered a stop to assessing federal employees a percentage of their salaries for party purposes, but the party patronage brokers overcame this by requiring the workers to "volunteer" these regular payments.[91]

Rutherford Hayes was a political moderate of modest talents, and he lacked the political means and will to push civil service reform legislation through Congress. He did, however, make a beginning in challenging the Senate's patronage spoilsmen. They, in turn, countered by trying to put in place a president more agreeable to their plundering ways when Hayes's term concluded.

For the 1880 Republican national convention in Chicago, Senator Conkling and his allies recruited slightly more than three hundred delegates committed to nominating former President Grant for a third term. They were the largest voting bloc at the convention, but not large enough to win. Opposing them were delegates favoring Senator James G. Blaine of Maine, former senator John Sherman of Ohio, and three other lesser candidates. Representative James Garfield of Ohio, then a senator-elect, was the head of Sherman's delegates, and he led the movement within the convention to stop Grant. The convention deadlocked among these candidates until the thirty-fourth ballot, when a few delegates voted for Garfield. Then, on the thirty-sixth ballot and to Garfield's embarrassment, the delegates chose him. Garfield's sudden success came in part from the votes of an anti-Conkling faction of the New York delegation headed by William Robertson, a judge whose gubernatorial nomination Conkling had earlier blocked.[92] This extraordinary turnabout at the convention was prelude to an astonishing confrontation between Conkling and Garfield after Garfield's election as president, in which Robertson played the inadvertent role of causing Senator Conkling's political ruin.[93] Beyond this catastrophe for Conkling, the events set in motion by this convention led in time to Garfield's assassination, adoption of civil service reform, and a significant lessening of the Senate's once-awesome political power in government.

In constructing his administration, Garfield picked as his secretary of state Maine's Senator James G. Blaine, a formidable politician with a take-charge attitude. This greatly alarmed Conkling, who for many years had been a bitter personal enemy of Blaine. Years earlier, in 1866, when they were both members of the House, they had engaged in an open quarrel during which Blaine excoriated Conkling in House debate with personal ridicule. He savaged Conkling, an astonishingly vain man, for his "haughty distain, his grandiloquent swell, his majestic over-powering turkey-gobbler strut," and compared him as "mud to marble, dunghill to diamond, a singed cat to a Bengal tiger, [and] a whining puppy to a roaring lion."[94] Conkling never forgave him, and now Blaine was advising Garfield, a veteran politician given to vacillation, on how to deal with Conkling and the Senate.

In a tense interview with Garfield, Conkling made his claims for party patronage so arrogantly that the president considered ordering him out of his presence. Even so, Garfield did yield to the senator nine federal offices for his party henchmen, but reminded Conkling that he also intended to reward the anti-Conkling New York Republicans who had helped him at the convention and in the election. Later, with Blaine's support and without consulting Conkling further, President Garfield nominated Judge Robertson, Conkling's principal New York antagonist, as head of the New York Custom House. This was a political thunderbolt. To Conkling, it meant war.

Conkling went before a closed-door caucus of the Senate's Republicans and asked that they stand by him and reject this nomination under the now traditional "personally obnoxious" doctrine.[95] In his patronage battle with President Hayes, Conkling had argued that the practice of allowing senators to pick federal officials for their states was based on the "beneficent principle" that they were "best fitted" to make those choices.[96] He passed over the reality that he and other senators had used this "courtesy" as the means to build their own home-state political machines by filling those federal offices with party loyalists. Now Conkling tried to argue that Garfield's action was not only an insult to him personally, but to the entire Senate.

In response to Conkling's ferocious attack, President Garfield withdrew his earlier nominations of Conkling's cronies and issued a dire warning to Republican senators. This, Garfield stated, was a fight to decide whether he, as president, was "the head of the government or the registering clerk of the Senate."[97] The president also stated bluntly that the senators' own careers were in jeopardy. "Senators who dare to oppose the Executive will henceforth require letters of introduction to the White House."[98] There was no vacillation in that threat, but Conkling retaliated with dramatic action. He resigned from the Senate and took with him his New York Senate colleague Thomas Platt. Their plan was to have the New York State legislature reelect them to show their political clout, but that did not happen. A few weeks later, on July 2, President Garfield was shot by Charles Guiteau, a rejected office-seeker. The assassin described himself as a Republican stalwart, like Conkling, and asserted that he shot Garfield to make Vice President Chester A. Arthur, Conkling's man, president.[99]

Garfield, gravely wounded, lingered over the summer and then died on September 19, 1881. Chester Alan Arthur's sudden succession to the presidency shocked everyone. Those familiar with his career as a sycophant of Conkling, the worst of the party spoilsmen, feared the worst. As president, however, he changed and was Conkling's man no longer. A genial and courteous politician, and always impeccably dressed, Arthur looked like a president, and now he tried to act like one, whatever his past shortcomings. He conducted himself with a dignity not expected, and he turned away from the most glaring aspects of the political spoils system. For starters, he declined to remove Conkling's enemy, Judge Robertson, from the New York Custom House, a signal that he was no longer catering to Conkling or other party bosses in the Senate. Moreover, when the new Congress met in December 1881, President Arthur endorsed the idea of civil service reform, startling for a longtime party spoilsman.[100]

With the downfall of Senator Conkling, the once-powerful Senatorial Clique lost influence. At the same time, senators of a new kind now were coming into prominence and power. Iowa's William Allison and Rhode Island's Nelson Aldrich cared more about such financial interests as coal, railroads, steel, and sugar than they did about political spoils. But that turnaround did not mean members of Congress had abandoned pork-barrel politics. In 1882, by overwhelming numbers, Congress approved the largest river-and-harbors bill ever, laden with pork projects. President Arthur won praise for vetoing the bill, even though Congress quickly overrode his veto.[101]

In the lame-duck congressional session beginning in December 1882, at President Arthur's urging, Congress adopted civil service reform with a bill proposed by Ohio's Democratic Senator George Pendleton. Only five senators voted against the measure, and the House acted so quickly that the debate lasted just a half hour. Arthur, the reformed spoilsmen, signed the bill on January 16, 1883.[102] The Pendleton Civil Service Reform Act of 1883 covered relatively few of the government's one hundred thousand employees, but it was real reform.

As president, Arthur had done much to reduce senators' influence, especially that of the party spoilsmen. But when he sought another term, the party convention instead chose James G. Blaine of Maine, the "Plumed Knight" of Republican politics and a formidable party power, despite a tainted reputation. The Democrats picked Grover Cleveland, the new governor of New York, who pledged to support more reform. The campaign proved ugly, with both Cleveland and Blaine charged with moral lapses, but Cleveland prevailed by a narrow margin.

President Cleveland had no legislative experience and no sympathy for the give-and-take of congressional compromise. Instead, he had courage, blunt and bold, and a singular lack of tact. He began his presidency holding to the traditional concept of the office, that he had no function in legislative proceedings. In his inaugural address, he made no mention of Congress. "I did not come here to legislate," he said later.[103] He spent much of his time reorganizing the executive departments.

It came as no surprise that Cleveland had immediate problems with senators—first the Republicans, then his fellow Democrats. By the time the first Congress of his administration convened in December 1885, he had suspended more than six hundred federal officials, most of them Republicans, and had submitted nominations for their replacements, most of them Democrats. Senate Republicans tried mightily to block him, the first Democrat in the White House since the Civil War. He responded tartly, "I shall not submit to improper dictation."[104] In a March 1886 message to Congress on the subject of presidential appointment and removal authority, he asserted, "I am not responsible to the Senate, and I am unwilling to submit my actions and official conduct to them for judgment."[105] Cleveland thus faced them down.

Then he offended the Democrats. He let them know that he intended to include under civil service many thousands more "not within the letter" of the 1883 law.[106] That pleased reformers, but to Democratic senators that meant leaving many Republicans in federal offices that they wanted for their friends and associates.

Once in office, Cleveland changed his mind about his role in the legislative process. He inherited a huge surplus of revenues, some $140 million, largely from the 1883 Republican tariff and its high protective duties. "I know nothing about the tariff," he confessed, and it was the tariff he planned to attack.[107] By the summer of 1887, he knew what he wanted: to slash the tariffs on such "necessities" of life as coffee, sugar, and clothing, the rates that most hurt working people. To dramatize his plan, Cleveland devoted the entire text of his annual message to Congress to the tariff. That message, presented December 4, 1887, shocked political Washington. "It is a condition which confronts us—not a theory," he said, and he resolved to meet it.[108]

In July 1888, the House, with a Democratic majority, approved a bill that supported Cleveland's goal, 162 to 149, with only four Democrats voting no. But Cleveland had no chance in the Republican-controlled Senate; his bold initiative had come to naught. What was significant was not that he failed, but that he had tried, against the odds and tradition, to play a significant role, as president, on adopting a major legislative measure.

Meanwhile, new elections were at hand, and Cleveland found himself opposed by Indiana's Benjamin Harrison, a former senator and the compromise choice of a deadlocked Republican convention. On the marquee issue of tariffs, Harrison was an ultra-protectionist, and the convention obligingly adopted a strong protectionist platform for his campaign. Nationally, Cleveland received 96,000 more popular votes than Harrison, but Harrison had more in the Electoral College.

A man of great piety, President Harrison saw himself as the choice of God. "Providence made me President," he boasted. "Providence," snapped Pennsylvania's Matthew ("Matt") Quay, "hadn't a damn thing to do with it."[109] Quay, a rough-and-tumble political brawler and now a senator from Pennsylvania and chairman of the Republican National Committee, made the difference for Harrison in one of the most corrupt elections in the country's history. Party bosses spent huge amounts to import thousands of "floaters" where they were most needed. Quay and New York's Thomas Platt had even "sold" Harrison's cabinet slots to help win the election. "I could not name my own Cabinet," Harrison complained.[110]

As president, Harrison proved to be a mere figurehead with a chillingly cold manner that offended almost everyone. Aloof and ungracious, he was frequently described as "a human iceberg."[111] Shunning Cleveland's lead, he reverted to the old style of a nonlegislating presidency. At the close of his administration, a prominent Washington journalist, Theron Crawford, reported that the president had scarcely any effect on legislation. "No one has apparently less influence upon Congressional legislation," he wrote, "than the President of the United States. His message is treated always as a perfunctory document, and while it is regularly and respectfully referred to the proper committees for consideration, it is very rare that any suggestion by the Executive has any practical result."[112] Cleveland had been an exception in 1884 and, elected again in 1892, he had another chance.

In the 1892 election, President Harrison had difficulties with Senator Quay and Quay's Republican allies, while Cleveland had his own problems dealing with Maryland's Arthur Gorman, now the leader of the Senate's Democrats. Senator Gorman had managed Cleveland's first presidential campaign in 1884, but Gorman was a protectionist and thus was shocked at Cleveland's 1887 tariff-slashing proposals. He declined to help Cleveland in the 1888 election, and in 1892 he ran against Cleveland for the Democratic nomination. But Cleveland won that nomination and then the election. And more important in that year's elections, for the first time since before the Civil War, the Democrats won majorities in both the Senate and the House of Representatives. That suggested an opportunity for President Cleveland to renew his initiative on tariff reforms.

When the regular session of Congress opened in December 1893, Cleveland asked for those reforms. But the Senate's Democrats were still split and angry over some of his strong-arm tactics, and the Republicans would not help reform the tariff schedules they had written into law. The House acted first and passed the bill, 204 to 140, which then went to the Senate. To defeat the House bill, Senator Gorman organized an informal bloc of eight Democratic senators from states that wanted tariff protections. Combined with protectionist Republicans, they had a clear majority of the Senate on tariff schedule after tariff schedule. In the five months the bill was before the Senate, with a mix of filibusters and power politics, they added 634 amendments to the House bill. To Cleveland, the bill had not simply been amended; it had been mutilated. So Cleveland wrote an ill-considered letter venting his outrage at the Senate and its amendments. Senators, Cleveland charged, were guilty of "party perfidy and party dishonor."[113] This caused a sensation, and Gorman took the Senate floor to respond in a speech that denounced the president for duplicity and cowardice. Moreover, he accused Cleveland of violating the very spirit of the Constitution by trying to encroach on the power of Congress to legislate American law. Gorman thus unleashed one of the most caustic attacks ever by a senator against a president of his own party.[114] His Senate colleagues approved Gorman's defense with wild applause. Gorman and his Senate Democrats gave Cleveland an ultimatum: they would accept no changes in their bill in conference with the House. They would not change a comma. President Cleveland found himself in an awkward dilemma. He would not sign the bill and he would not veto it either. He let the bill become law without his signature.

This was the end of President Cleveland's efforts to sponsor legislation. From this struggle, Cleveland became a party pariah. In his last two years as president, Democratic senators rarely visited the White House, and even he was appalled at his status with the Senate. "Think of it!" he exclaimed at one point. "Not a man in the Senate with whom I can be on terms of absolute confidence!"[115] His alienation from the senators became, in time, part of the Senate's institutional lore, long after the bitterness was forgotten. Decades later, old Senate hands still told an apocryphal story that late one night at the White House, Cleveland's wife shook him awake and whispered in his ear that there were burglars in the house. "No, no, my dear," the president supposedly replied, still half asleep. "In the Senate maybe, but not in the House!"[116]

In pragmatic terms, Cleveland's efforts had small results. In institutional terms, however, he had on his own, and in his imperfect way, set precedents that later chief executives could heed and copy. His bold intrusion into the legislative process offended senators of both political parties, and they openly voiced complaint. But what annoyed senators won admiration elsewhere from others anxious to have the president play a more meaningful role in national politics and lawmaking. Among those closely observing Cleveland's performance were two young men: Theodore Roosevelt, a Republican, and Woodrow Wilson, a Democrat. Roosevelt had known Cleveland ever since Roosevelt's years in the New York legislature when Cleveland was the state's governor. He admired Cleveland's bold, blunt ways, and so did Wilson. Already a published author, Wilson also wrote for the periodical press. He especially admired Cleveland's action in another struggle he had had with the Senate, this one on repealing the Sherman Silver Purchase Act of 1890. "Until he came on the stage," Wilson wrote, "both parties had dallied and coquetted with the advocates of silver."[117] Cleveland solved that dilemma, Wilson wrote, and in so doing reversed the flow of power from one end of Washington's Pennsylvania Avenue to the other, from the Capitol to the White House: "Power had somehow gone the length of the avenue and seemed lodged in one man."[118] Roosevelt and Wilson, both ambitious, would remember Cleveland's initiatives when each of them, in turn, reached the White House.

In 1896, William McKinley, former Republican governor of Ohio, won the presidency, and he brought to the office a far different attitude than that of Grover Cleveland. In his inaugural address, McKinley summoned Congress into special session but he offered no plan. He let the country know that he would accept "whatever action Congress may take."[119] He had thus lapsed back to the practices of early presidents, not mimicking Cleveland's legislative initiatives. McKinley had served more than thirteen years in the House of Representatives, and he had lived and thus understood the accommodations and courtesies common to congressional life. McKinley's soft words and gentle manners, and his obvious desire to please, helped him build with senators a cordial relationship that Cleveland had never known.

During this time, a crisis was building in Cuba, the Spanish colony ninety miles off the coast of Florida. The situation in Cuba had bothered American politicians for many years and, even as McKinley became president, a war spirit had taken hold in the United States, inflamed by jingoistic news accounts of outrages by the Spanish overlords. Vermont's Redfield Proctor led an anguished Senate debate detailing those horrors, but McKinley shrank from plunging the nation into war. "We are not prepared for war," McKinley argued. "I pray God we may keep the peace."[120] But on the night of February 15, 1898, a huge explosion sank the battleship USS *Maine* in Havana Harbor, resulting in the loss of 260 American lives. Congress immediately declared war on Spain.

One of the warmongers was Theodore Roosevelt, then assistant secretary of the navy. He wanted action, and he worked to bring it about. "McKinley," he said, "has no more backbone than a chocolate éclair!"[121] He quit his government post and worked frantically to recruit his own regiment, a bizarre mix of Western cowboys, Ivy League graduates, and sons of the socially prominent, among others. As lieutenant colonel and second in command, Roosevelt took wildly aggressive actions to get his regiment, nicknamed the Rough Riders, to Cuba as quickly as possible. Once there, he pushed to engage the enemy and emerged a national hero, his exploits heralded in American newspapers.

The war lasted four months, and American forces triumphed everywhere, seizing Spain's far-flung empire: Cuba, Puerto Rico, Guam, and the more than seven thousand islands that made up the Philippines. President McKinley wanted to keep them as prizes of war, but he needed the Senate to approve a treaty with Spain to do so. A vibrant debate in the Senate resulted, with most Democrats in opposition.[122] This seemed prelude to another instance of the Senate's inability to consent to the ratification of any treaty. For three decades, ever since the start of the Grant administration, intense partisanship had prevented the Senate from mustering the two-thirds vote required to approve any treaty. McKinley's secretary of state, John Hay, knew the Senate's record. So did McKinley. "There will always be thirty-four percent of the Senate on the blackguard side of every question that comes before them," Hay complained.[123]

To overcome this dilemma, President McKinley took extraordinary action, an action never before tried. McKinley named a five-member peace commission, including three members of the Senate's Foreign Relations Committee: two Republicans, including the chairman, Minnesota's Cushman Davis, and a Democrat, Delaware's George Gray. Although this was a shrewd maneuver, it was viewed as violating the Constitution's stipulation that no member of Congress hold any other federal office. That matter prompted another spirited Senate debate. The Senate's Judiciary Committee held hearings, but nothing came from them, and the senators went off to Paris, unchallenged, to help negotiate the treaty.

Meanwhile, Rhode Island's Nelson Aldrich, the Senate's ruthless dominating member, took over the chore of rounding up the needed two-thirds vote. Senator Gray, of course, was a special target, for as a ranking Democrat his support would influence other Democrats. He was not difficult; he was fifty-eight years old and was at the end of his Senate career, having recently failed to win reelection. By previous arrangement, once in Paris, Gray cabled McKinley that he could not endorse the treaty. McKinley cabled back: "Sign the treaty." Nothing else. To Gray, this meant that the president had approved the deal that Aldrich had offered, so Gray signed the treaty,[124] which then went to the Senate.

As part of his efforts to round up the necessary votes, Aldrich asked Foreign Relations Committee Chairman Davis for his help, but was roughly refused. "Get out of here," Davis said, "You can't show your stinkpot to me!"[125] Davis was fully aware of Aldrich's ugly tactics, including the offering of bribes and choice offices in return for votes. Aldrich openly worked the Senate floor, moving from desk to desk, making his offers.[126] On the morning set for the vote on the treaty, February 6, 1899, Aldrich still needed four more votes. Working desperately, Aldrich managed to get three of them, and then just five minutes before the appointed hour, he obtained the final vote he needed. During the roll call, still another senator signed on, so the tally ended up fifty-seven to twenty-seven, with ten Democrats, including Gray, making the two-thirds majority with one vote to spare.[127] Gray's Senate term ended on March 4, 1899, and a few weeks later, to show his gratitude, McKinley appointed him to a lifetime post as a federal circuit judge.

Although the strategy had violated the Constitution, and the tactics were ugly, McKinley and Aldrich had created a new way to improve chances for ratifying controversial treaties. Meanwhile, with the Spanish-American War won, Colonel Roosevelt returned to New York as one of the war's heroes, just in time to run for governor of New York. The state's Republican boss,

Tom ("The Easy Boss") Platt, now again serving as a New York senator, acquiesced in Roosevelt's campaign, but once in office Roosevelt proved highly unsatisfactory to the conservative Platt. By happenstance, in November 1899, Garret Hobart, McKinley's vice president, died, and Senator Platt saw that opening as a possible way to rid himself of Governor Roosevelt. Platt proposed to McKinley that Roosevelt fill the vacancy on the 1900 party ticket.[128] But Roosevelt flatly refused to go willingly into the ambiguous and innocuous office of vice president. Platt got Pennsylvania's political boss, Senator Matt Quay, to support his plan, but Ohio's Mark Hanna fought hard against it. Hanna pleaded with President McKinley to name someone else as his vice president. "Don't you realize," he argued, "that there's only one life between that madman and the presidency?"[129] McKinley declined to intervene, however, and the Republican convention picked Roosevelt to be McKinley's running mate. They were easily elected.

Hanna's word proved to be prophetic. In September 1901, President McKinley paid a courtesy visit to Buffalo, New York, and a Pan-American Exposition. There, at a public reception, he was shot twice by anarchist Leon Czolgosz. At first it seemed that he might recover, but after eight days he died. Senator Hanna was appalled, and not just for the loss of his friend. "Now, look!" he exclaimed. "That damned cowboy is President of the United States!"[130]

4

Struggling for Primacy
From TR to FDR

PRESIDENT THEODORE ROOSEVELT SEETHED WITH frustration over his relations with the Senate and House of Representatives, despite his party's substantial majorities in both houses. In a 1903 letter to his son Kermit, he vented, "I am having a terrific time trying to get various things through Congress and I pass my days in a state of exasperation, first, with the fools who do not want to do any of the things that ought to be done, and, second, with the equally obnoxious fools who insist upon so much that they cannot get anything."[1]

One of the "fools" Roosevelt had in mind was Senator Matthew Quay, the Pennsylvania political boss who personified Senate dominance of weak presidents. It was Quay who had helped engineer the election of Republican President Benjamin Harrison in 1888 and who boasted that Harrison would "never know how close a number of men were compelled to approach the gates of the penitentiary to make him president."[2]

Roosevelt and Quay stood at the pivot point in the balance of power between the Senate and White House. In the half century that lay ahead, all of the elements of the modern presidency would appear. Two world wars and a catastrophic economic depression necessarily placed a premium on the centralized leadership inherent in the presidency. As Congress fought to retain and bolster its constitutional prerogatives, a succession of presidents inexorably redefined the balance of governing powers, extending them in ways unimaginable to any senator serving at the century's beginning. Suddenly made president under appalling circumstances, Theodore Roosevelt found himself in a job seriously constrained by the Constitution and tradition. An assassin had raised President McKinley to the rank of martyred statesman, and Roosevelt did his best to defer to the memory of the man he now succeeded. That prompted his pledge to continue McKinley's policies and also to retain his cabinet.[3] He had other reasons as well to act with caution. At forty-two, he was the youngest president ever. He had served, however, in the administrations of Presidents Harrison, Cleveland, and McKinley, and during that time subtle changes had come to the presidency, and fundamental changes to the leadership of both houses of Congress. With boldness and parliamentary skill, Thomas B. Reed of Maine had lifted the House's Speakership to extraordinary power, a serious competitor to the president and the Senate's leaders. More important to President Roosevelt were the five men who had risen to dominate the Senate. The so-called Big Five included Rhode Island's Nelson Aldrich, Iowa's William Allison, Connecticut's Orville Platt, Maine's Eugene Hale, and Wisconsin's John Spooner. These five had so entrenched themselves in the Senate's influential committees and offices during the 1890s that they commanded the chamber's actions on most substantive questions.[4] Their obvious powers placed inhibitions on Roosevelt and any legislative initiatives he might make. With steely determination, the president set out to challenge these power brokers and their awesome authority over the federal establishment. He eventually bent them to his will. Functioning in these first years of the twentieth century, he would transform the White House into what he called the "Bully Pulpit," and thereby play a major role in ushering into reality what became the modern presidency.[5]

In his first months, Roosevelt actively sought to build a cooperative relationship with the Big Five and other senators. To Senator Mark Hanna, who had tried so hard to block Roosevelt's nomination as vice president, lest he succeed to the presidency, Roosevelt made a special plea, and Hanna generously promised to help him in any way he could. Hanna began by cautioning him to beware of making hasty decisions. Roosevelt followed that advice. His closest personal friend, Henry Cabot Lodge, already a senator for the past eight years, advised him that "a friendly Senate" could be the key to a successful administration, and Roosevelt began inviting senators to the White House.[6]

The new president had only weeks to prepare his first annual message to Congress. He invited each of the Big Five to consult with him directly on what he should say. In that message, Roosevelt took a moderate stance, proposing a department of commerce and new immigration restrictions, but avoiding mention of tariff reform, just as the Senate's Big Five had advised him. But he had strong reservations about the group's members. To him they were not just conservatives, but "reactionaries" with deep commitments to the corporate and business worlds that he did not share.[7] In the summer of 1902, in further token of his goodwill, he invited them to his home in Oyster Bay, New York, for what was called a "secret" conference on party policy. The next month, he attended another such conference at Senator Aldrich's mansion in Rhode Island.

Meanwhile, in administrative matters, Roosevelt had begun to act on his own. In February 1902, for example, he directed his attorney general, Philander Knox, to bring suit under the 1890 Sherman Antitrust Act to break up the Northern Securities Company, a giant holding company created by J. P. Morgan, the wealthiest of American financiers, and his associates. That stunned Senator Aldrich and his Senate colleagues, for they never imagined anyone trying to enforce the restraints of what they presumed was a moribund law. This was the beginning of Roosevelt's trust-busting career as well as his growing commitment to progressive politics.[8]

In still another concern of major consequence, Roosevelt took extraordinary and highly questionable action to ensure American control of what became the Panama Canal. The French government had tried and failed to build such a canal. In January 1903, Roosevelt sent the Senate a treaty under which the United States would pay the government of Colombia $10 million for the right to construct the canal through its territory.[9] The Senate approved the treaty, but the Colombians then decided to raise the price to $25 million. At that point, a rebellion broke out in that part of Colombia called Panama. With unseemly haste, Roosevelt promptly recognized the Panamanian rebels' provisional government and sent warships and marines to guarantee there would be no response from the Colombian government. In due course, Roosevelt submitted to the Senate a new canal treaty, this time with Panama, to build the canal. The president was proud of this escapade. He acknowledged later that he could have followed "traditional conservative methods" and submitted "dignified state papers" to Congress, but he chose not to. "I took the Canal Zone," he bragged, "and let Congress debate, and while the debate goes on, the canal does also."[10]

These events marked President Roosevelt as an inventive activist, pushing his authority to new borders. Such maneuvers did not, however, endear him to the conservative "stand-pat" Republican leaders of the Senate. To their chagrin, he was developing ideas about the president's administrative and legislative powers quite different from those they and their contemporaries held. He later explained, "I declined to adopt the view that what was imperatively necessary for the nation could not be done by the President unless he could find some specific authorization to do it. My belief was that it was not only his right but his duty to do anything that the needs of the nation demanded unless such action was forbidden by the Constitution or by the laws." This was new doctrine, justifying his bold administrative initiatives. "Under this interpretation of executive power," he went on, "I did and caused to be done many things not previously done by the President and the heads of departments. I did not usurp power, but I did greatly broaden the use of executive power. In other words, I acted for the public welfare. . . ."[11]

At the same time, Roosevelt was reinterpreting the president's legislative obligations. He knew the current assumption. "In theory," he wrote, "the Executive has nothing to do with legislation." In practice, however, Roosevelt found the chief executive offered "the only means" for the people to get the legislation they ought to have. "Therefore," he concluded, "a good Executive under the present conditions of American political life must take a very active interest in getting the right kind of legislation."[12]

In line with that thinking, Roosevelt had begun to force his personal legislative agenda on Congress. This included creation of a federal bureau to investigate corporate trusts. "With both Hanna and Aldrich," Roosevelt wrote, "I had to have a regular stand-up fight before I could get them to accept any trust legislation."[13] He was in his own way copying President Cleveland's legislative initiatives. "I am having a terrific time trying to get various things through Congress," he wrote to one of his sons in early 1903, "and I pass my days in a state of exasperation."[14] He was losing whatever awe he might have held for the Senate. Years before, he had confided to Senator Lodge that he would welcome the chance to serve as a senator. In dealing with senators, he found himself privately calling them unflattering names. "He has not got as much respect for the Senate," one of his friends reported, "as a dog has for a marriage license."[15]

In his November 1904 bid for reelection, he overwhelmed his hapless Democratic opponent, Alton Parker of New York, in a landslide triumph. That gave Roosevelt the presidency in his own right. In his campaign, he had spoken of offering "a square deal for every man," and the phrase *Square Deal* caught the public's fancy. This he tied into his hostile views about corporate monopolies, corrupt political bosses, irresponsible labor leaders, and radical anarchists. Here, for the first time, was the framework of a probable legislative program proposed by a presidential candidate of a major party. His stunning victory over Judge Parker at the same time had the semblance of a mandate to press Congress for that program.

The Senate's leaders took alarm at this demonstration of Roosevelt's immense popularity. "What will he do next?" Senator Platt asked Senator Aldrich. They were apprehensive that the president, with the public clamor he had stirred, would launch legislative attacks on trusts and the tariff schedules, too. "We are going to have lots of trouble," Platt predicted.[16]

In his December 1904 annual message to Congress, Roosevelt again ignored the tariff, but he proposed a variety of legislative measures on such matters as employers' liability, child labor, and the working hours of railroad workers. He startled and angered Senator Aldrich and his colleagues by also asking to arm the Interstate Commerce Commission (ICC) with the authority to set railroad rates. This was new, unmentioned in the party platform, and Roosevelt called this "the most important" measure needed to regulate corporations.[17] The House of Representatives did pass a version of the measure, but the senators balked.

When the new congressional session convened in December 1905, the president again submitted his railroad-rate proposal. To blunt the opposition, he proposed a change in his original recommendation, to provide that whatever rates the ICC set would be "subject to review by the courts."[18] As before, the House approved a version of the bill, but one less than satisfactory to Roosevelt. The real struggle came in the Senate through a bitter four-month debate. As a senior member, but not chairman, of the Senate's Commerce Committee, Senator Aldrich led the opposition. On the committee, Jonathan Dolliver of Iowa, a progressive Republican, favored the bill and under normal procedures he should have been designated its manager on the Senate floor. To frustrate Dolliver and embarrass Roosevelt, Aldrich devised a shrewd scheme. He contrived to name "Pitchfork Ben" Tillman, the ranking Democrat on the committee, as the bill's formal sponsor.[19] Designating a minority-party Democrat as the floor manager of a major bill before a Republican-majority Senate violated Senate precedent. There was more to Aldrich's maneuver than that, though: Tillman and Roosevelt were personal enemies.

Four years earlier, in February 1902, Tillman and his South Carolina colleague John McLaurin had engaged in a fistfight on the Senate floor. The Senate censured both combatants. President Roosevelt reacted, too, withdrawing Tillman's invitation to a White House state dinner, a public humiliation that enraged the senator.[20] He heaped abuse on the president, and the two of them had not spoken to each other since then. Aldrich's tactic complicated the Senate's consideration of the bill, but it did not work. By then, Roosevelt had long since learned to deal with senators as best he could, and he resolved his difficulty with Tillman: "I must work with the material that the states send me."[21]

The Senate debate ran on into the spring, and both Aldrich and Roosevelt worried about the outcome. Aldrich came to fear the public's reaction if he killed the measure. On his part, Roosevelt worried that Aldrich would do just that. Roosevelt approached Senator Allison and asked him to offer a face-saving amendment prepared for him. Allison agreed, and Aldrich accepted. That broke the deadlock. President Roosevelt did not get exactly what he wanted from the Senate, but he did achieve the essential: the ICC armed with regulatory authority to fix railroad rates and halt the industry's abuses of the public.[22]

This was not the only regulatory limitation that Roosevelt managed to push through the Senate and the House. In his 1906 novel *The Jungle*, Upton Sinclair created a national sensation with harrowing details of meat-slaughtering in the nation's stockyards. That gave impetus to another wave of reform, with Roosevelt pressing Congress for action. That produced not only a new law for federal meat inspections, but also measures on pure foods and drugs. Roosevelt relished his successes. "We have carried out with signal success the policies we have undertaken," he boasted.[23]

Looking back later at his struggles with Aldrich and the others, Roosevelt conceded the difficulties they made for him. "We succeeded in working together, although with increasing friction, for some years, I pushing forward and they hanging back. Gradually, however, I was forced to abandon the effort to persuade them to come my way, and then I achieved results only by appealing over the heads of the Senate and House leaders to the people, who were the master of us all."[24] He spoke persuasively to senators, one by one, "in such an emphatic, confidential, heart-to-heart sort of way," in a contemporary's description, that the senator found himself all but forced to agree. Senators were nonetheless reluctant, and that frustrated Roosevelt. He fought with many of them and took pleasure in ridiculing them to his friends. He said Aldrich was "a man to be shunned"; his close ally, Senator Hale, a man of "no conscience"; and Senator Joseph Foraker of Ohio a paid "agent" of the corporations.[25] And these were fellow Republicans! He labeled Senator William Peffer of Kansas, a sometimes Republican, "a well-meaning, pin-headed, anarchistic crank, of hirsute and slab-sided aspect."[26]

Roosevelt had a flair for colorful language, and he learned to use the Washington press correspondents to broadcast his views around the nation.

Impetuous and aggressive, he excoriated the financial barons as "malefactors of great wealth," and sought to persuade Congress to enact an inheritance tax to minimize the vast fortunes that they were building and passing on to their children.[27] His rhetorical flourishes gave zest to his speeches and newspaper interviews, making them all the more dramatic when compared with the stodginess of the Senate's Republican leaders. Roosevelt's flamboyance and his demands for legislation were changing the views of members of Congress, as well as those of the country at large, toward the presidency.

At Princeton, where he was now president of the college, Woodrow Wilson had watched Roosevelt's performance with special attention. He and Roosevelt had become casual friends, socially and professionally, and Wilson had already stirred speculation that he, too, might seek the presidency.[28] Roosevelt's Square Deal initiatives could be criticized as more show than substance, but there could be no argument that Roosevelt had enormously enhanced the stature of the executive office. Wilson saw this as well as anyone. Roosevelt had gone far beyond President Cleveland's precedents, so far that Wilson, the academic scholar, had changed his own assumptions about the president's role in the government. In his book *Congressional Government*, written before Grover Cleveland became president in 1885, Wilson deplored the fallen state of the presidency. He then saw the office as seriously reduced in prestige and authority by the dominance of Congress, especially by the usurpations and dictations of the Senate. "The President may tire the Senate by dogged persistence," he wrote then, in the mid-1880s, "but he can never deal with it upon a ground of real equality."[29] Nearly a quarter century later, toward the end of Roosevelt's presidency, Wilson had reversed his judgment entirely. "The President is at liberty, both in law and conscience, to be as big a man as he can," Wilson stated in one of a series of lectures published in 1908. "His capacity will set the limit."[30] The presidencies of Cleveland and Roosevelt had obviously changed his mind, and this revised view would dominate his behavior when he became president in 1913.

Meanwhile, however, Theodore Roosevelt found that he had to give up the presidency that he had held with such relish. On the night of his election triumph in 1904, he had abruptly pledged not to seek another term as president, a promise he came to regret as a personal blunder. He was reduced in his last two years as president to picking his Republican successor and ensuring his nomination. That was how William Howard Taft became president in 1909, somewhat against his will. He did not want to be president; he would have preferred to sit on the Supreme Court, but Roosevelt engineered his nomination as president, and there he was. He had little use for politicians, less for political "shenanigans." A kindly and modest man, judicial in temperament, he would prove an inept president with his tenure marred by a further damaging rupture within his Republican Party. He functioned historically as an interlude between two domineering presidents. The divisive split within the Republican Party, which Taft helped to create, actually made possible the election of Wilson and the return of the Democrats to national power.[31]

Like Roosevelt, Woodrow Wilson had a way with words, and he campaigned in 1912 for a program he called the "New Freedom."[32] He won in all but eight states, producing an overwhelming majority in the Electoral College, although in this three-way race he attracted only 42 percent of the popular vote. When he reached Washington, he had a mandate for his own legislative program.

Long a student of the federal government, Wilson had a scholar's book-knowledge of politics, not an understanding from hands-on experience. He wrote his first book, *Congressional Government*, at age twenty-seven. His goal was to abandon political theory in favor of showing how America's governmental institutions actually worked—"to present their weaknesses and strengths without disguise."[33] Of all the members of Congress serving during the time he wrote that book, he mentioned only one, Senator George Hoar of Massachusetts, and then only in passing.[34] As a result, he more nearly described the Congress of the 1850s than that of 1885, the year his book was published. Had he examined Congress firsthand, he might have sensed the extraordinary transformation already under way in both the Senate and the House.

In each chamber, the evolving precedents and parliamentary practices had so developed that both were poised to accept the strong party leadership that Woodrow Wilson had earlier complained they so badly lacked.[35] On becoming president in 1913, Wilson's lack of knowledge of the practical side of politics—and the Senate's party hierarchy that ushered in twenty years of party discipline—nearly led him to disaster. He had only recently become a committed political progressive, and, as president-elect, he had planned to push through Congress a legislative program of progressive reforms, relying both on Democrats and progressive Republicans. To achieve this, Wilson gave instructions to party leaders to exclude from committee chairmanships and party patronage the Democrats' senior conservatives, men he called "reactionary" and "stand-pat." Such individuals had opposed Wilson's candidacy at the Democratic nominating convention in Baltimore. Therefore, he wanted to reward only party progressives, but he had no idea of the price he would have to pay.

Wilson picked Albert Burleson, an eight-term congressman from Texas, as his postmaster general. In that post, Burleson had 56,000 postmaster jobs to distribute to deserving Democrats. Wilson told Burleson that he wanted all those jobs to go to "forward-looking" party progressives, none to the reactionaries. "When I heard that," Burleson said later, "it paralyzed me." He tried to persuade the new president that he risked political disaster by cutting off any Democrats from party patronage. They had been out of power, in the minority for eighteen years. "These little offices don't amount to anything," he told Wilson. "They are inconsequential. It doesn't amount to a damn who is postmaster of Paducah, Kentucky, but these little offices mean a great deal to the senators and representatives in Congress."[36] The offended Democratic members would retaliate, Burleson warned, by opposing every measure Wilson wanted enacted. They would wreck his administration. Stubborn and reluctant, Wilson refused to give way. Burleson was upset to find Wilson "absolutely ignorant" about this phase of politics. Only after several sessions did he finally yield to Burleson's argument.[37]

In the 1912 election that brought Wilson to the White House, the Democrats won overwhelming control of the House of Representatives, with a two-to-one margin over the Republicans, but only a bare majority in the Senate. That made the Senate the obvious battleground for Wilson's planned progressive legislation, complicated by the reality that under the Senate's seniority rules several archconservative senators were slated to chair major committees. Among these was North Carolina's Furnifold Simmons, ranking Democrat on the Senate's Finance Committee, the committee with jurisdiction over Wilson's most important campaign pledge: reform of the tariff schedules. Looking ahead to his plans for a special session in April 1913 to deal with tariff reform, Wilson asked that Simmons, who had opposed his nomination, be denied the chairmanship.

To plead his case, Simmons went to Josephus Daniels, a fellow North Carolinian whom Wilson had just named secretary of the navy. He asked Daniels, a party progressive, to tell the president that he had always been "a strong party man," never failing to stand by the party. As a party matter, he would totally support whatever legislation Wilson proposed. Secretary Daniels relayed Simmons's pledges to Wilson and told him that he could safely rely on those pledges. Reluctantly, as he did with Postmaster General Burleson's plea, Wilson again backed down, the political ideologue giving way to pragmatism. The Senate's Democratic caucus did confirm Simmons as chairman of the Finance Committee, and Wilson was rewarded.

Long before he became president, Wilson had come to regard the Senate as institutionally hostile to presidents, with veteran senators reflecting what Wilson called an attitude of "unmistakable condescension" toward whomever was president. "A member of long standing in the Senate," Wilson said in 1907, "feels that he is the professional, the President an amateur."[38] He lectured his classes at Princeton, however, that every member of Congress represented only his own state or congressional district, not the nation. "Only one man—the Chief Executive—is responsible to all the people," he said to them. "He must assume leadership and determine what is best for all."[39]

As president-elect, Wilson summoned key members of Congress to consult with him on his coming legislative program. Then as president, Wilson asked permission to address in person a special session of Congress that he had called. This surprised members of Congress. Not since the presidency of John Adams had a chief executive personally addressed Congress. Members of both houses, Democrats and Republicans, took alarm at this incursion by the president into their deliberations. Mississippi's Senator John Sharp Williams made a Jeffersonian protest that Wilson's move was but "a cheap and tawdry imitation" of royal pomposities, a speech from the throne.[40] On April 8, the day after the special session convened, Wilson did address the two houses in the hall of the House, and he scored a triumph. At first the atmosphere was tense, the great audience nervous, but Wilson, a skilled orator, soon put those there at ease. "The President of the United States," he began, "is a person, not a mere department of the government hailing Congress from some isolated island of jealous power."[41] He spoke for only ten minutes, but he had broken new ground in dealing with Congress. He outlined broadly what he wanted in tariff legislation, thanked the members for their "courtesy," and let them know that he would be back.

The very next day, April 9, Wilson returned to the Capitol, to meet with the Democratic members of the Senate's Finance Committee to discuss tariff reform. They met in the President's Room, just off the Senate's floor. Rarely used by any president, the room would serve Wilson as a convenient place from which to regularly lobby senators on what he wanted them to do.

Thus Wilson made an auspicious beginning as president, and in this Congress, the Sixty-third (1913–15), he would achieve remarkable successes. In later Congresses, he would face adamant opposition, primarily from the Senate, opposition that deeply embittered him. Finally, in his last great quarrel with the Senate, he broke down physically in trying to crack Senate opposition to the Versailles Treaty. He then came to hate the Senate with a hatred beyond that of any other president, and out of this hatred he would unleash against the Senate astonishing vitriolic abuse. In this, his first Congress, however, he devised even more techniques of presidential persuasion that made him, as president, the principal sponsor of the major legislative acts.

Just a month after Wilson's address to Congress, the House passed the tariff reform bill he requested, and the struggle began in the Senate. True to his pledge, Finance Committee chairman Simmons acted as the bill's chief sponsor. He had extraordinary help from the president, who put pressures on senators as no chief executive had done before. This was not an easy vote for all Democratic senators, for many of them, like their Republican colleagues, had home-state industries demanding protective tariffs. They found themselves under intense assault from a horde of lobbyists skilled in their craft. Wilson took dramatic action against these "insidious" lobbyists, as he called them, denouncing them for their onslaught and their spending money "without limit" against the public's best interests.[42] The Senate's Republicans resented Wilson's statement as questioning their integrity and demanded an investigation that would include the president's active efforts to influence the Senate's vote on the bill. Senator after senator testified under oath on his respective contacts in this party fight. Ironically, to the chagrin of the Republicans, the overall effect of this inquiry was to line up the Democratic senators more solidly for the bill. Michigan's Republican Senator Charles Townsend conceded that Wilson's attack on the lobbyists "may have saved the bill from mutilation or defeat."[43]

That was only the beginning for Wilson. He hosted many senators at the White House, where he set forth his arguments, largely couched in terms of party loyalty. Repeatedly, he went to the President's Room at the Capitol to summon senators to listen to him. He was there June 12 and he sent for twenty-one senators. Only seven could be found; most of the others were off at a baseball game. He returned on June 23 to meet with twenty-three additional members. At his request, a special telephone line was installed from there, just steps away from the Senate floor, to the White House so that he could reach senators quickly.[44]

With Wilson's obvious approval, Senate Democrats caucused secretly on his proposed tariff bill. They debated it for more than two weeks, and then voted to make this "a party matter," binding themselves to vote for the bill as a party "duty."[45] Chairman Simmons then brought the completed bill to the Senate floor.

The debate ran on through the hot summer months. In early August, the *New York Times* noted that Wilson's bold initiatives were part of his attempt to bring "effective leadership" to his party in Congress, "an important and intensely interesting experiment."[46] Wilson had long since abandoned his original ideas about counting on any Republican progressives for support. This was to be a party measure, and the Senate finally passed it on September 9 by a vote of forty-four to thirty-seven.[47] The president's success brought him immense personal prestige as a master politician. In institutional terms, he had lifted the presidency to an eminence in the legislative process far beyond anything achieved by Cleveland or Theodore Roosevelt.

Wilson wrote to Furnifold Simmons to express his admiration for what the senator had done. When he signed the bill into law, he used two gold pens, one of which he presented to the senator. He thanked both Secretary Daniels and Postmaster General Burleson for their advice on how to deal with the Senate. "What you told me about the old standpatters is true," Wilson said to Burleson. "They at least will stand by the party and the administration. I can rely on them better than I can on some of my own crowd."[48]

Meanwhile, in August 1914, war broke out in Europe. The conflict profoundly affected the United States and President Wilson, bringing him unprecedented opportunities for international statesmanship, lifting him to world stature far beyond any previous American president. That war and its aftermath also brought Wilson great difficulties with the Senate, painful and crippling, prompting him to unleash on the Senate and its members unprecedented verbal assaults.

The war created an immediate problem for the United States in a serious shortage of merchant ships. Wilson made proposals, but they proved complicated and controversial. Within the Senate, there was especially stiff resistance to Wilson's proposed ship-purchase bill, a resistance that took the form of a filibuster. Senators Henry Cabot Lodge of Massachusetts and Jacob Gallinger of New Hampshire, both Republicans, led the attack. In late January 1915, the Democratic leaders tried, unsuccessfully, to break the filibuster by holding the Senate in continuous session for thirty-seven hours. Later they tried again, this time holding the Senate for fifty-five hours, to no avail.[49] This was Wilson's first real taste of the Senate's ultimate weapon and he was angered. He denounced the filibuster as "contemptible."[50] In a public speech, he said Republicans used this filibuster to defy the public's best interests. He compared himself with President Andrew Jackson, a comparison openly revealing Wilson's assumption of his own moralistic superiority to his opponents. "You know Jackson used to think that everybody who disagreed with him was an enemy of the country," Wilson said. "I have never got quite that far in my thought, but I have ventured to think that they did not know what they were talking about."[51] The filibuster killed Wilson's bill. He reacted to this outrage, as he saw it, by drafting a formal statement accusing the filibustering senators of "disloyalty," questioning their patriotism, but he chose not to publish it.

The war in Europe soon preoccupied Wilson, greatly complicating his dealings with the Senate. By early 1915, the Germans had introduced a shocking new form of warfare: submarine attacks on ships at sea. In May, a German submarine sank the *Lusitania* with great loss of life, including many Americans. Wilson tried to serve as peace broker, catching criticism from the warring nations and members of Congress. In May 1916, he proposed creation of what he called a "feasible association of nations," to work out controversies between rival countries without resorting to war.[52] The idea was not then new, but this was the genesis of his commitment to the future League of Nations.

Wilson ran for reelection in 1916 on the slogan "He kept us out of war," and he barely won a second term. The war seemed largely stalemated in Europe with immense loss of lives, and Wilson again tried to broker a peace—"peace without victory," he called his proposal—and, as before, he came under withering criticism.[53] The Germans had continued their submarine attacks, and in January 1917, they announced unrestricted submarine attacks on all ships carrying supplies to the Allies. For the United States, Wilson said, this meant war.[54]

By late February, the Senate's Republicans had taken alarm. This Sixty-fourth Congress would end automatically on March 3, 1917, and the next Congress, under normal procedure, would not meet until December of that year. Congressional leaders feared leaving the government in Wilson's sole control for those nine months. In a party caucus, Republican senators made plans to stall needed legislation past the March 3 deadline so that Wilson would have to call Congress into special session. That way, they could monitor his actions.

By then, a controversy had arisen surrounding a proposal to arm American merchant ships against the German submarines. Wilson knew he had legal authority to do this on his own, but he requested an invitation to appear before Congress to seek its "special warrant." On February 26, 1917, he addressed a joint session to seek approval of a bill he had drafted himself to give him anew the power he already had. Even before he spoke, senators had begun a filibuster. There were eleven members actively engaged, five Democrats and six Republicans, led by Wisconsin's Robert La Follette and

Nebraska's George Norris. They stymied any action in the Senate to the end. Before that end, seventy-five other senators—more than three-quarters of the Senate—signed a manifesto denouncing their intransigence.[55] Wilson was furious. He issued a public reprimand of them in striking savagery: "A little group of willful men, representing no opinion but their own, had rendered the great Government of the United States helpless and contemptible."[56] In response, the shaken Senate promptly adopted a new rule, its provisions incorporated in Rule 22, to provide a means to stop filibusters.[57] On March 12, Wilson acted on his own to arm the merchant ships.

The president did call Congress into special session starting April 2, 1917, a session that ran until early October. On that first day, as he had many times before, Wilson addressed the Congress again, this time to ask the members for a declaration of war. This was a momentous occasion, as flag-waving members repeatedly cheered his remarks with explosions of applause.[58] Two days later, the Senate gave its approval with only six senators dissenting; the House followed with its approval the next day.

President Wilson turned control of the fighting over to the military, picking General John Pershing as the US commander in Europe. In speech after speech, often dramatically eloquent, Wilson voiced an idealistic array of war aims not always pleasing to Great Britain and France. He proclaimed this a war to save democracy and in January 1918 he announced his Fourteen Points, his own terms for the peace settlements.[59] In sum, he laid down what amounted to a charter for a new world order based on decency and territorial integrity, monitored by an international body named the League of Nations. These speeches lifted Wilson to an unprecedented popular eminence, but they did not delight Henry Cabot Lodge and other senators.

In late October 1918, with the war in Europe all but concluded, Wilson made a dramatic plea to the nation. This proved to be the first in a series of blunders that brought about his political ruin. He asked that voters continue to elect Democratic majorities in both the Senate and the House. As so often in the past, he couched this plea in personal terms: the election of a Republican Congress would repudiate "my leadership."[60] This shocked almost everyone. The Republicans called Wilson's words "an insult" to their patriotism. Senator Lodge and other Republican congressional leaders issued a protest: "This is not the President's personal war."[61] In the elections, despite Wilson's appeal, the voters elected Republican majorities for both houses, with forty-nine Republicans and forty-seven Democrats in the Senate. In the upcoming Congress, Senator Lodge would take over as chairman of the Senate's Foreign Relations Committee, the committee with jurisdiction over the peace treaty.

In the 1918 election cycle, President Wilson not only sought to defeat Republicans, he went out of his way to punish Democratic members of Congress who had opposed his measures. In a notable instance in August, he attacked Senator James Vardaman of Mississippi in his primary fight with Byron ("Pat") Harrison, then a member of the House. "Senator Vardaman has been conspicuous among Democrats in the Senate," Wilson wrote in a letter widely published just before the primary, "in his opposition to the administration."[62] Harrison won the primary and with it Vardaman's seat in the Senate. Wilson's retaliation against party defectors did not go unnoticed in the Senate or elsewhere.

Just three weeks and two days after the November 11 armistice that ended World War I, Wilson sailed for Europe as head of the American delegation to negotiate the peace treaty. This was the first time that an American president had taken on such a role, and even his partisans questioned the wisdom of placing oneself across the table in confrontation with the prime ministers of Great Britain, France, and Italy.[63] More important, Wilson declined to name any senator, Democrat or Republican, to this delegation. He knew that President McKinley had done so in the negotiations with Spain, and with success, but Wilson, like Democrats in McKinley's day, argued that this would breach the constitutional prohibition against members of Congress holding any other federal office.[64] Significantly, for this peace delegation, the men Wilson picked were his subordinates. That made Wilson himself *the* delegation; the others merely went along as advisers. He would make the decisions. In time, this proved a major misstep, for he coupled it with his own high resolve that whatever those decisions might be, the Senate would have to agree to them without change. This would give Senator Lodge, now nursing a malignant hatred for Wilson, the wherewithal to attack the president's treaty obliquely and, with the help of other senators, ultimately to prevent its approval.

Wilson's extraordinary welcome in Europe, where he was hailed as the savior of mankind, gave no hint of the troubles he would find at home. That welcome also did not temper the tough bargaining he faced in Paris at the hands of the other delegations. Wilson returned to the United States in late February 1919, to be available for the final week of the Sixty-fifth Congress. By then, in Paris, Wilson had in place his proposal for a League of Nations. With the congressional session concluded, he started back to Paris the next day to complete the treaty. Before he left, in the last hours of that Congress, Senator Lodge read to the Senate a formal resolution declaring senators' opposition to the League of Nations "in the form now proposed to the Peace

Conference." Thirty-seven senators and senators-elect, all Republicans, had signed this "Round-Robin" letter, far more than the one-third plus one of the Senate needed to reject any treaty.[65]

When Wilson returned to Washington in July 1919, he returned in triumph, the Versailles Treaty in hand. On the day after he arrived, July 10, Wilson went before the Senate and presented the treaty. Weeks before, in late May, Senator Lodge had begun his campaign to reject the League of Nations. In consultation with Idaho Senator William Borah, he then acknowledged how "hopeless" any effort would be to defeat the League "by a straight vote in the Senate."[66] He decided to hold extensive hearings and then work to quash the League with amendments or "reservations" to the treaty. He calculated that in this he would have the support of most of the Senate's Republicans. That was his plan before Wilson returned, and Lodge knew Wilson well enough to assume that the president would not tolerate the Senate tampering with his masterwork.

Some Democratic senators cautioned Wilson that the Senate would not approve the treaty without reservations. They suggested that he meet with Lodge and other Republican senators to that end. Wilson refused. He insisted that the Senate accept the treaty as is. All the same, he started inviting Republican senators, not less than fifteen of them by Lodge's count, to the White House to plead for their support. Frustrated at their lack of information about the treaty, members of the Foreign Relations Committee asked Chairman Lodge to ask the president to meet with them. When Lodge did that, Wilson agreed and invited them to lunch. This was new and extraordinary. In a pre-lunch meeting on August 19 that lasted more than three hours, Wilson responded to the committee's questions. He held fast to his insistence that any reservations to the treaty would unravel its support from other nations. He knew soon enough that he had not made converts.[67]

Faced with this resistance, Wilson resolved to make a direct appeal to the nation and try to force the Senate's compliance. He set out on September 3 by train to tour the country, concentrating especially on states with Republican senators. He was less than successful. He spoke to large audiences in many states, but under great strain, he collapsed in Pueblo, Colorado. His physician ordered cancellation of further speeches and a swift return to the safety of the White House. Several days after returning to Washington, Wilson suffered a massive stroke, from which he never fully recovered.[68]

Thus wounded, Wilson carried on his fight for his treaty with a gallantry admired by his supporters, but he was frequently irritable, reviling the Senate and its members. Cut off by his wife from contact with anyone other than his secretary, Joseph Tumulty, Wilson did send out messages from his White House sick-room to bolster his stand. On November 18, for example, he sent word to the Senate that Lodge's proposed reservations, if adopted, would nullify the treaty.[69] The Senate was already voting on them, and Wilson regarded them as personal insults. The next day, November 19, the Senate rejected the treaty as amended with reservations, thirty-nine to fifty-five.[70] On January 8, 1920, Wilson sent a letter to a Democratic dinner asserting that he did not accept that Senate action as "the decision" of the nation. "We must take it without changes," he wrote.[71] The struggle resumed in the Senate. On March 20, that body tried one more time, but again, by a forty-nine to thirty-five vote, failed to reach the necessary two-thirds majority.[72]

With his treaty rejected, Wilson's bitterness against the Senate crystallized. He coined one favorite insult. "The senators of the United States have no use for their heads," he said repeatedly, "except to serve as a knot to keep their bodies from unraveling."[73] His anger distorted his judgment, for as president, largely through his earlier successes with the Senate, he had in the eight years of his administration lifted the presidency far beyond the power and prestige achieved by any of his predecessors. In his first term, he had overawed the Senate into adopting a dramatic legislative program. In his second, he had reached the rank of acknowledged world statesman, a stature future presidents would also enjoy. Remarkably, with the sheer power of his public denunciation of the Senate's "little group of willful men" and their filibuster of 1917, he had intimidated that body into adopting, for the first time, a way to halt filibusters in the years to come. In institutional terms, he had changed the checks-and-balances equation between the president and the Senate. The upper house could still frustrate and defeat the president, of course, as senators did with Wilson's treaty, but they were no longer competing with the president on a level playing field. Wilson had given the presidency special advantage, and even the Senate's most arrogant members would come to treat the president, as president, with something like awe. Ironically, Wilson's own stubbornness had brought his defeat on that treaty, when with a more accommodating attitude he could have had success.

With obvious contempt, Wilson disparaged Senator Warren Harding's 1920 presidential election victory and what he called his "bungalow mind" (that is, it had no upper story)—an epithet he also applied to others among Harding's Senate colleagues.[74] Even the Republican senators who had arranged Harding's nomination regarded him as a political mediocrity. Harding himself knew his own shortcomings. "Come down to brass tacks,"

he asked his campaign manager, Harry Daugherty, before the party convention. "Am I big enough for the race?" "Don't make me laugh!" Daugherty replied. "The day of giants in the presidential chair is passed."[75]

In political terms, Warren Harding had one great asset: he looked like a
president. He was elected by the greatest popular majority to that time, and
with that majority he did try to act like a president, notably presenting
himself before Congress to ask for enactment of his legislative program. Like
Wilson, he had particular difficulties with the Senate, despite his own service
there and the personal friends he had made among senators of both parties.
He had successes just the same, and in one notable instance, rejecting
Wilson's tactics, he scored a personal triumph with the Senate in the very
field of Wilson's greatest defeat—diplomacy.

Harding summoned the newly elected Sixty-seventh Congress into
special session, and before the members assembled on April 11, 1921, he
invited the leaders of the Republican majority in the Senate and House to
the White House for consultations. He made plain he wanted no quarrel
with the Congress such as marred Wilson's last years in office, and he offered
what he called a "program of cooperation." On April 12, in the style of
Wilson, Harding addressed Congress with a speech proposing an extensive
legislative program that included reduced federal spending, lower taxes,
tighter immigration restrictions, and a new budget system to end the
government's fiscal chaos.[76] This last was not a new idea, but Congress
adopted it on Harding's initiative as a badly needed reform.

Delivering on a campaign pledge, Harding asked for legislation to protect
black Americans from racist mob action: "Congress ought to wipe out the
stain of barbaric lynching."[77] He did not suggest how, but left that to
Congress. In due course, the House passed such a bill to make lynching a
federal crime. Southern and border state senators predictably filibustered the
bills. They argued that this was a states'-rights question, not federal, even
though they knew, as did everyone else, that no white Southern jury would
ever convict any lynch-mob participant. For the previous decade, and for
years to come, such mobs lynched victims on the average of one every week.
This was the beginning of a struggle in Congress for black rights, a struggle
that lasted half a century, protracted all that time by Senate filibusters.

Harding's dealings with the Senate were seriously handicapped by a crippling split within the Republican Party that pitted Old Guard conservatives
against insurgent progressives. Combined, they gave the Republicans a clear
party majority in the Senate. That meant claiming the committee chairmanships and other offices, but they did not provide a working party majority

for Harding's legislative proposals. Republicans also lacked an effective party leader. As senior Republican and chairman of the party's Senate caucus, Senator Lodge had the designation of "majority leader," but, as journalist Mark Sullivan reported, "He doesn't seem to know how."[78] Another journalist dismissed Lodge as merely an "irascible old man with worn nerves" and questioned how long he could last.[79]

Even so, Harding persisted in personal appeals to Congress. Like Woodrow Wilson, he appeared in person before a joint session to give his annual address in 1921 and 1922, and for a special session he called in November 1922 to discuss promotion of the American merchant marine. To back up his demand for a subsidy for merchant shipping, he let Republican members know that he would cut off party patronage to those who failed to support him.

In the aftermath of World War I's horrors, Senator William Borah, a ranking member of the Foreign Relations Committee, had proposed an international conference to consider major arms reduction. President Harding seized that idea as his own. In June 1921, just three months into his presidency, he invited Great Britain, France, Japan, and other naval powers to send delegates to Washington to negotiate treaties to halt an arms race already under way. He addressed their opening session that November, but unlike Woodrow Wilson, he named his secretary of state, Charles Evans Hughes, to head the American delegation. Even more important, again unlike Wilson, he named two pivotal senators as delegates: Republican floor leader Henry Cabot Lodge, and Oscar Underwood of Alabama, leader of the Senate's Democrats. As fellow senators, Harding and Underwood had become close personal friends. Harding wanted senators directly involved in drafting these treaties, however questionable constitutionally, as a way to commit those senators as champions of those treaties later in the ratification debate.[80]

In due course, the delegates produced three major treaties carrying out naval cutbacks. Then Harding put his strategy into play. The struggle in the Senate centered on the controversial Four-Power Treaty, an accord by the United States, Great Britain, France, and Japan. Lodge, the senator most responsible for defeating Wilson's treaty, won over most of the Senate's Republicans for Harding's treaty. The Democrats were more difficult. They had not forgotten or forgiven the role of Lodge and his Republicans in rejecting the Versailles Treaty. In personally presenting these treaties to the Senate, Harding had told the senators that as a former senator himself he perfectly understood the Senate's "proper jealousy" in the treaty-making process and that was why, at his direction, Senators Lodge and Underwood had "shared" in drafting these treaties. With that flattering endorsement, the Senate voted sixty-seven to twenty-seven for the Four-Power Treaty.[81] The president's strategy worked. Underwood produced twelve Democratic votes for the treaty, the votes needed to provide the necessary two-thirds margin that gave Harding this extraordinary achievement and the most important of his presidency. This renewed a critical precedent. A quarter century later, under the guidance of President Harry Truman, this precedent set the stage for deeply involving senators from both political parties in a new national commitment to a bipartisan foreign policy.

Harding's unexpected death in August 1923 thrust into the presidency Vice President Calvin Coolidge, a pinch-faced introvert, peevish and often rude, utterly unlike the genial and gregarious Harding. As vice president, Coolidge had presided over Senate debates for two years. He found the debates interesting and entertaining. "At first I intended to become a student of the Senate rules," he wrote in his autobiography, "but I soon found out that the Senate had but one fixed rule, subject to exceptions, of course, which was to the effect that the Senate would do anything it wanted to do whenever it wanted to do it. When I had learned that, I did not waste much time on the other rules, because they were so seldom applied."[82]

Hardly a convivial fellow, Coolidge stayed largely apart from senators, and senators left him alone. What he enjoyed most were the many dinners he and his wife, a gracious woman, attended. As ranking guests, they arrived last and left first, "so that we were usually home by ten o'clock."[83] Coolidge's pleasure in accepting both this flattering deference and free food did not suggest a dynamic party chieftain with ambitious political goals.

Coolidge kept Harding's cabinet, and he pledged to carry out Harding's legislative program. He brought no pressure on Congress to pass these measures, and Congress ignored them all, except for a minor reorganization in the diplomatic service. In 1924, Coolidge easily won the presidency in his own right and did not again bother to go before Congress for any purpose. Each December thereafter, he sent the Senate and House a perfunctory message, asking for little more than a new cut in federal taxes, made feasible by the annual budget surpluses produced by the nation's booming prosperity. Despite his pinching ways, that prosperity made Coolidge a popular president.

By 1927, Coolidge was so popular that he seemed certain of reelection, and he startled everyone with his unexpected and cryptic announcement that he did not "choose" to run in 1928. In the Republican Party struggle thereafter, Commerce Secretary Herbert Hoover emerged as the successor to Harding and Coolidge. Coolidge mocked him as "The Wonder Boy." "That man has offered me unsolicited advice for six years," Coolidge declared about Hoover, "all of it bad."[84] Part of Hoover's advice to Coolidge had cautioned him to try to deter the wild and reckless speculation on margin in the stock market.

Hoover's active opponents for the nomination all came from the Senate. Eight years earlier, in 1920, one of their own, Warren Harding, had been nominated by a cabal of Republican senators, and that again seemed a good idea to Republican senators of 1928. Several of these senators tried to organize a "Stop Hoover" scheme before the convention, but they failed. These senators, professional politicians all of them, had little use for Hoover, the nonpolitician, and their annoyance at his success made them less than cooperative when Hoover won the presidency.

As the incoming president, Hoover knew that for the past decade and more many federal operations had been neglected, with Coolidge especially "reluctant to undertake much that either was new or cost money."[85] Hoover had an extensive list of needed reforms on such matters as water resources, conservation, and child welfare. For starters, he called a special session of Congress beginning April 15, 1929, primarily to relieve the plight of the nation's farmers. He did win from Congress a new federal agency to help farmers market their produce, but his plan for a limited revision of the tariff for similar purpose went awry with protectionist senators and representatives exploiting his modest requests into the Smoot-Hawley Act with the highest tariffs ever.[86] Meanwhile, in mid-October came the stunning collapse of the stock market, triggering a catastrophic depression that devastated the national economy for the next decade.

During similar crises in earlier years, the federal government played but a minor role. These complex problems were left largely to the business community to solve. Federal officials and the US Treasury stood aside, for the government then had no apparent way to deal with such matters. In the 1929 emergency, however, President Hoover took actions then, and in the three years following, that went far beyond anything tried by any prior president.[87] He speeded up federal construction projects, encouraged state and local governments to do so as well, and wrung pledges of new capital investments from railroads, utilities, and other private enterprises. This was a new concept of government. Presidents Roosevelt and Wilson had greatly expanded presidential decision-making, and this was a further elaboration of their initiatives. Hoover clearly recognized his responsibilities in this crisis.

Others did so as well, and they would hold him responsible as no president had ever been held responsible before.

On paper, Hoover had a clear Republican majority in the Senate, but the Republican progressives normally voted with the Democrats, creating a much different majority. Moreover, the Senate's Republican leadership was antagonistic, too. They were Kansas's Charles Curtis, a longtime senator, now vice president and the Senate's presiding officer; Indiana's James Watson, the Senate's majority leader; and New Hampshire's George Moses, the Senate's president pro tempore. All three were Old Guard arch-conservatives, ill-disposed to Hoover's brand of progressivism. They did not like Hoover, and the feeling was mutual. Curtis and Watson had challenged Hoover for the party's nomination, and they resented Hoover's new eminence. Majority leader Watson proved especially difficult for Hoover, because he took pleasure in Hoover's defeats and embarrassments. Hoover judged Watson's legislative talents as merely "spasmodic."[88] Hoover tried to get along with him, even arranging a private telephone to his home so they could consult at any time, but he held in contempt the advice Watson gave him.

Meanwhile, President Hoover had begun his own strenuous efforts to curb the Depression, constantly consulting those in business, labor, politics, and industry who might help. With Congress back in session, and with millions suddenly unemployed, Hoover laid out a program of public works that included new highways, federal buildings, and improvements to rivers and harbors. Even as he took these actions, he had hesitations, for he believed that the new "ascendancy" of the president over Congress had gone too far. "Far from merely advising Congress," Hoover later wrote of the president's role, "he is expected to blast reforms out of it."[89] Whatever his resentments at his Senate critics, he felt he had to respect the "independence" of Congress. "I had little taste for forcing Congressional action or engaging in battles of criticism."[90] That did not stop him from asking for help from senators, and he did so constantly.

Like many others, Hoover badly miscalculated the depth and ruinous effects of the economic depression, and his proposals proved utterly inadequate. The Republican majority in the House was sympathetic to his efforts, but senators regularly attacked his proposals and him, with Democrats especially vindictive. In the 1930 congressional elections, they named this ongoing national calamity after him: "The Hoover Depression."

The Congress elected in November 1930 for the term beginning in March 1931 convened, as the Constitution then provided, on the first Monday in

December, thirteen months later. By then, the Democrats had a bare majority in the House and almost a majority in the Senate. Privately, Hoover proposed to the Senate's Republican leaders that they allow the Democrats to organize the Senate, arguing that would make matters easier for him.[91] Republican leader Watson bluntly refused. Hoover believed that giving the Democrats majority responsibility would end the "sabotage" and "demagoguery" against him and his proposals. He damned Watson and the other Republican senators for wanting to hold their titles, chairmanships, and "the nicer offices in the Capitol." He had no real understanding that majority control also meant power.[92]

By then, the Senate's Democrats were demanding direct federal cash assistance for the jobless. Hoover shrank from that. He favored charitable help as long as he could, and then he proposed that state and local governments provide such aid and work with the Red Cross. Senators came up with hopelessly inadequate proposals. Alabama's Hugo Black proposed a thirty-hour workweek so people could share the available jobs.[93] Idaho's William Borah and others proposed the Treasury issuing "fiat money" to the jobless.[94] The Democrats accused Hoover of indifference to those suffering, and he accused them of "playing politics at the expense of human misery."[95] The orchestrated attacks in time reduced Hoover, a renowned humanitarian, to a public caricature of a do-nothing, cold-blooded miscreant. In reality, Hoover worked long hours every day, to the point of exhaustion, but partisanship was intense. The Senate's Democrats, out of power since 1919, knew they had a splendid chance to take over again in 1933. Hoover confronted what he called an "economic hurricane," and his responses never proved adequate to stem its devastation.[96]

At their 1932 party convention, Republicans nominated Hoover for a second term, despite the public battering and abuse he had for so long endured. With considerable irony, New York's governor, Franklin Roosevelt, the Democrats' nominee, easily won with a campaign denouncing Hoover for what Roosevelt called his reckless spending and unbalanced federal budgets.[97] In his coming years as president, balancing the budget was not a prime concern for Franklin Roosevelt. That was obvious almost immediately.

On inauguration day, Saturday, March 4, 1933, Roosevelt dramatically took charge of the government with an eloquent, self-confident speech that boldly announced: "The only thing we have to fear is fear itself." He summoned the new Congress into special session for the following Thursday, March 9, and ordered a bank "holiday," closing the nation's collapsing banking system until further notice. "We must act, and act quickly," he declared.[98] In effect, he thus announced himself to be the vital center of the government, ready to give orders. In the confusion of the time, with many Americans badly frightened, Roosevelt's radiant smile and rich, resonant voice gave added confidence to his ebullient optimism.

In the 1932 elections, the Democrats won sweeping majorities in both the Senate and the House. With Roosevelt pointing the way, they seemed willing to do whatever he asked. On that first day of the new session, Roosevelt submitted the text of an emergency banking bill to congressional leaders and asked that they arrange for its immediate consideration. With no copies available, the House shouted the bill through after a debate of only forty minutes. The Senate acted with similar dispatch. Not bothering with committee hearings or any other review, the senators voted the bill through in less than four hours after its arrival from the House. President Roosevelt signed the measure into law that evening, with the presumption that the nation's banking system had been saved. In the Senate's terms, this was a dizzying pace, with the senators acting, in Senator Henry Ashurst's phrase, like so many "whirling dervishes."[99]

This was just the start. In the next few weeks, Roosevelt submitted fourteen other bills for action, and the Senate and the House approved them all, with many Republicans joining the Democrats in assent. They were a jumble of measures, inconsistent and even contradictory, not a systematic plan, in what the historian Richard Hofstadter called "a chaos of experimentation."[100] Never before had a president so successfully scored so many goals so early in the game. For the Senate, long the slow-moving half of Congress, this was astonishing. These measures began Roosevelt's "New Deal," enacted in what would be called the "Hundred Days," an unprecedented surge of sudden legislation.[101] Roosevelt himself defended the hit-and-miss thrust of these new programs. "It is common sense to take a method and try it," he argued in starting. "If it fails, admit it frankly, and try another, but above all, try something."[102] At his goading, Congress was doing something, and that brought hope to the nation.

Franklin Roosevelt began his presidency with warm regard for the Senate and its members. He invited no fewer than six senators to serve in his first cabinet, and three of them accepted, including Tennessee's Cordell Hull as secretary of state. From the beginning, the president worked closely with his party's leaders in Congress. In the Senate, that meant primarily Arkansas' Joseph Robinson, for ten years the Democrats' floor manager and now the Senate's majority leader. Equally committed to Roosevelt were Mississippi's

Pat Harrison, a seasoned legislator, now chairman of the Senate's influential Finance Committee, and South Carolina's James Byrnes, a shrewd backroom operator. These three Southern senators, despite their skepticism about Roosevelt's progressive and even radical ideas, formed the nucleus of his legislative team in the Senate. They restrained their conservative bent out of party loyalty, much as had the party conservatives in the Senate early in Wilson's time. They had not tasted majority power in the Senate for a painfully long time. Backing them was Kentucky's Alben Barkley, a lesser talent but an orator of ability.

Most surprising of all in this cadre of skilled Roosevelt-aligned legislators in the Senate was the new vice president, John Nance Garner, the Texan nicknamed "Cactus Jack." As Speaker of the House and a candidate for the 1932 Democratic presidential nomination, he had played the crucial role at the party convention in swinging that nomination to Roosevelt. As a party activist, Garner not only regularly advised Roosevelt on Senate strategy and tactics, but he also worked to line up senators to vote for Roosevelt's bills. This was extraordinary. Traditionally, vice presidents had long been relegated to the innocuous role of presiding over the Senate's sessions. Garner had special influence with senators from Southern states, many of whom he knew well from their years in the House.[103]

Roosevelt met frequently with the principal Democratic leaders of the Senate and the House on legislative and other political matters, and this small group was nicknamed the "Big Four." The Senate's contingent was Vice President Garner, recognizing his unprecedented legislative stature, and Majority Leader Robinson; the House's leaders were the Speaker and his lieutenant, the House majority leader. Senator Robinson had unique stature of his own, the first majority leader of the Senate with command of the party regulars in caucus, committed to the legislative program of his party's president. From Robinson's tenure dates the Senate's "modern" majority leader, able to represent the president's wishes to his party's senators and vice versa.[104] This could be a matter of great delicacy from time to time, and his successors in this post copied his performance with variations of their own. Robinson had one great ambition that deeply spurred his commitment to Roosevelt: he wanted to serve on the Supreme Court.

Roosevelt's hold on the Senate's Democratic leadership went far beyond that of Woodrow Wilson's, and he initiated several ways to assert his control of legislative action. For example, he had members of his cabinet work closely with party members in the Senate and House. In those first weeks, he instructed Postmaster General James Farley, his patronage broker, to inform party members in Congress that he would make no political appoint-ments until they had enacted the bills he wanted.[105] He himself met often with members of both houses, and he used the telephone to lobby members as no president before had done. With them he was cordiality itself, calling them by their first names, sharing confidences, coaxing, pleading, and flat-tering with a beguiling charm that worked wonders.[106]

In another innovation, he assigned two young administrative assistants, Thomas ("Tommy the Cork") Cochran and Benjamin Cohen, as personal agents to lobby members of Congress for his bills. They had other chores as well, including drafting legislation, but their work lobbying members began tentatively what became an extraordinary method for later presidents to promote their causes on Capitol Hill. Not acknowledged openly until late in the Eisenhower administration, and then only gingerly, this strategy evolved over time into presidents maintaining a formal lobbying staff of their own in the White House. Cochran and Cohen did more than merely talk to senators. They signaled those waffling on an issue and in need of a call from the president or, perhaps, from a party boss back home. They pro-vided draft bills for members to introduce, and, often with the help of the Democratic National Committee, they offered ghostwritten speeches for members to deliver.[107]

Gone now was any pretense that the president and his men did little more than recommend subjects for Congress to consider. Under Roosevelt, presidential initiation of legislation became so customary that on one occasion a member of Congress, upon introducing a bill on his own, boasted that no official of the executive branch had even been consulted on its drafting. Roosevelt's bills were "administration" bills, routinely introduced in the Senate or House "by request."[108] This was fundamental institutional change so great that, later, in 1947, when President Harry Truman asked Congress for an anti-inflation bill, Republicans assumed he really did not want the bill enacted because he had failed to submit a text. "He ought to submit a bill," protested Michigan's Senator Homer Ferguson.[109]

By an alchemy of his own, Franklin Roosevelt transformed the funda-mental relationship between White House and Congress, in which he dom-inated both the House and the Senate. Democratic Party leaders in both chambers had become his political lieutenants, committed to enact the "must" bills he proposed. Part of this change came from the party loyalty of Democratic senators, but they were as well captured by the sheer force of Roosevelt's ebullient personality. He was the first president to exploit the possibilities of radio, from time to time making what he called "Fireside

Chats" to the nation, building anew his already formidable personal popularity.

With Roosevelt's great popularity, the Democrats in the 1934 off-year elections accomplished the remarkable feat of gaining additional seats in both the Senate and the House, an accomplishment no other administration had previously achieved. Two years later, Roosevelt himself won overwhelming reelection and with him a Congress in which the Republicans were reduced to a hapless minority. There were only sixteen Republicans left in the ninety-six-member Senate.[110]

For all his successes with Congress, Roosevelt met devastating opposition from another quarter. In case after case, the Supreme Court struck down as unconstitutional major elements of his New Deal. By early 1937, the justices had undone six of the most important among them and pending before the court were legal challenges to several others, including Social Security. With his new election mandate, Roosevelt decided to cripple the court's capacity to nullify any more of his measures. He consulted no one in Congress in advance. Then, on February 5, he stunned the leaders of Congress and everyone else by unveiling a surprise plan. He proposed a complicated "reform" of the court under which he as president could name as many as six additional justices. Many recognized this as an attempt to "pack" the Supreme Court with justices favorable to the New Deal. The proposal touched off a struggle that rocked political Washington for the coming six months. Roosevelt assumed that with his massive majorities in the Senate and the House he could carry this scheme to fruition, but this proved an error that all but ended his formidable hold on Congress in legislative matters.[111]

Roosevelt mounted a full-scale campaign directed at the Senate. "We must bring the Court in step with the New Deal," he said. The Senate's Democratic leaders loyally, if reluctantly, supported this effort, but many party colleagues, in Postmaster General James Farley's judgment, were "lying low to see how the wind would blow from home."[112] By party agreement, the Senate's handful of Republicans opted out of this fierce conflict lest their open opposition give Roosevelt grounds to recast this as a partisan party fight. They would vote "no" when the time came. Meanwhile, they would silently watch the maneuvers of the opposition Democrats.[113]

Over these months, the background realities that prompted this political brawl changed dramatically. The court started validating Roosevelt's measures, including his new labor law and Social Security. Then one of the most conservative justices, Willis Van Devanter, resigned, giving Roosevelt the vacancy he wanted. Still, Roosevelt insisted on his plan. But the sudden death of majority leader Robinson brought the administration's campaign to a halt. Many senators attended his funeral in Little Rock, and on the special train returning them to Washington, Vice President Garner sounded them out on the court bill. He took his findings to Roosevelt in the White House. The bill was dead—Roosevelt's first great defeat on legislation.

He responded recklessly by deciding to punish those Democratic senators up for reelection in 1938 who had soiled his record. This was a repeat of Woodrow Wilson's party purging in 1918, only far more brazen; both presidents, after six years in office, displayed a politically dangerous self-confidence. Like Wilson, Roosevelt sought to deny senators party renomination. He had eight on his list for punishment, but some of them, like Nevada's Patrick McCarran and Colorado's Alva Adams, were beyond his reach. He concentrated on Georgia's Walter George, Maryland's Millard Tydings, and South Carolina's Ellison ("Cotton Ed") Smith. He was most dramatic with Senator George, denouncing him to his face on a public platform in Georgia. "I accept the challenge," George told him. Party chairman James Farley was aghast at Roosevelt's attempted vengeance, knowing that violated "a cardinal political creed" to stay out of local matters such as primaries.[114] Senator George used Roosevelt's attack to play the martyr, and so did Smith. Tydings campaigned actively that he was not Roosevelt's "rubber stamp," or his "ventriloquist's dummy."[115] All the senators on Roosevelt's hit list won their primaries and reelection, and that meant trouble for the president. Back in Washington, "Cotton Ed" Smith and Walter George discussed their escape from Roosevelt's attempted purge. "Roosevelt is his own worst enemy," Smith suggested. "Not as long as I am alive," George replied.[116]

Roosevelt's heavy-handedness sent a chill through the Senate. Senators could retaliate, and those offended did. Farley pleaded with Roosevelt to end this feuding with senators by restoring their party patronage. Roosevelt refused. This, of course, made matters worse. By January 1939, Roosevelt had lost his legislative options. In those 1938 elections, Republicans had gained seven new seats in the Senate, beginning a steady erosion of Roosevelt's once massive majority. In the next three national elections, while Roosevelt was president, the Republicans gained more Senate seats each election year. And, by then, they had informally developed a working understanding with the South's disgruntled Democratic senators to create the so-called "Conservative Coalition." This formidable group, allied with Western Republicans, would largely control much of the Senate's decision-making for the coming twenty years.[117]

After these failed party purges ended the New Deal, Roosevelt turned to international matters. He had years more to serve as president, and now the dangers in Europe and the Far East brought him harrowing new concerns. He acted to deal with them, ignoring most legislation beyond what was needed to carry on these new responsibilities. Ironically, despite all his New Deal laws, the country still languished in deep economic depression.

The threat of war and then war itself lifted Franklin Roosevelt to world prominence just as it had Woodrow Wilson a generation earlier. FDR struggled to help the embattled British. He acted on his own to "lend" them fifty naval destroyers. After the Japanese attack on Pearl Harbor, he acted for the United States in setting the two-war strategy, choosing commanders, and meeting from time to time with Winston Churchill and the leaders of other allied nations to work out war policies and later peace aims. These pursuits, fraught with dangers, gave Roosevelt a stature that made senators seem like political pygmies. In this vast struggle, they could hardly challenge him. In 1940, with Europe falling under German attack, Roosevelt so manipulated political matters at home that he had himself "drafted" for the presidency again, thus breaking the two-term tradition for presidential tenure. Four years later, in the midst of all-out war, he was reelected once more. There were senators who wanted his job, but they had no chance.

Roosevelt's final summit meeting with Churchill and the Soviet Union's Joseph Stalin took place at Yalta in early 1945, where the three tried to reach accommodations for the world after the war. On the way back from Yalta, Roosevelt expressed to diplomat Charles Bohlen his frustrations over the major role the Senate would play in that postwar world. Roosevelt described senators as "a bunch of incompetent obstructionists" and said "the only way to do anything in the American government was to bypass the Senate."[118] A few weeks later, he was dead.

Whatever Roosevelt's animosity toward the Senate, he had long since achieved an unprecedented dominance over Congress. When he died, he left the government and the presidency far different than when he began. He had redefined the government in strikingly new ways, centralizing all sorts of national activities under often-competing bureaucracies. He redefined the presidency, too. He set a new pattern of laying down a legislative program for Congress, and then actively lobbying for that program. Roosevelt had gone far beyond the traditional responsibilities of the nation's chief executive, and became for a while Congress's chief legislator. Later presidents would copy his innovations, with embellishments of their own, most with far less success. The country came to regard the president as the one to propose legislation, with Congress responsible for responding to his proposals. Within a few years of Roosevelt's death, journalists began evaluating each session of Congress on how adequately members of Congress responded to the president's initiatives. Some benighted souls actually came to believe that the Senate and House work for the president.

5

Losing Ground to the Imperial Presidency

IN ITS MODERN-ERA RELATIONS WITH the White House, the Senate, with brief exceptions, has moved to a decidedly weaker position. In their dealings with foreign nations, presidents have chosen to bypass the Senate treaty ratification process through the use of executive agreements. When executive agencies experience difficulty in obtaining statutory approval for a regulatory action, they seek to act unilaterally. From Korea to Libya, when a chief executive has believed the time has come to take the nation to war, especially if he doubts the depth of congressional support, he has defined "hostilities" to suit his purposes and given the Pentagon its marching orders.[1] As the Cold War accelerated under threat of nuclear devastation, and then ended after four decades to give way to the global war on terrorism and its randomly executed atrocities, the framers' delicate constitutional balance has been knocked asunder in the name of national security.

For the better part of the 1930s, the activities of dictators in Europe and Asia had preoccupied members of Congress. On the home front, these same senators and representatives had grown increasingly resentful of a dictatorship lodged within the executive branch—Franklin Roosevelt's aggressive assumptions of legislative power. Many still remembered his September 1942 demand for legislative action on a farm price-support bill: "In the event that Congress should fail to act, and act adequately, I shall accept the responsibility, and I will act."[2] This challenge underscored House Speaker Sam Rayburn's warning that the ability of a democratic form of government to survive under wartime pressures was directly related to Congress's ability to balance demands for adequate discussion with demands for prompt action.[3]

In 1941 and 1942, the American Political Science Association studied the increasingly evident imbalance between Congress and the presidency and concluded that Congress must "modernize its machinery and methods to fit modern conditions if it is to keep pace with a greatly enlarged and active executive branch."[4] In early 1945, with World War II still raging and Roosevelt beginning his fourth term in office, the frustrated Senate and House of Representatives created a joint committee to conduct an extensive review of congressional operations.

Within a year, they would adopt an overall plan, the Legislative Reorganization Act of 1946. This landmark statute would become the single most influential institutional reform measure in the Senate's history—restructuring its committees, raising members' salaries, and permitting members and committees to hire professional staff equal in competence and compensation to their counterparts in the executive branch.[5] With these new tools, Congress would enter the modern era in its relations with the presidency. For good measure, as soon as congressional Republicans regained majority control of Congress two years later, having long suffered under Roosevelt's dominance, they would push through a constitutional amendment to limit future presidents to two four-year terms.

Just fifteen weeks into the 1945 session, Vice President (and former senator) Harry Truman found himself, upon Roosevelt's death, president of the United States. The nation was at war in Europe and Asia, and he was almost totally uninformed about Allied strategy and military operations when he took the oath of office on the evening of April 12, 1945.

The next day, he traveled to Capitol Hill to have lunch with a dozen key senators in a private room just off the Senate floor. This was Truman's idea, one that shattered previous tradition. An unassuming fellow, Truman did not stand on protocol. He wanted their help. The Speaker of the House, Sam Rayburn of Texas, was there, and so, too, was Joseph Martin of Massachusetts, the House Republican leader. Truman told them that from then on, things were going to be different; he offered them "full cooperation" in all matters.[6] Arthur Vandenberg of Michigan, ranking Republican on the Senate's Foreign Relations Committee, was especially pleased, as he recorded the occasion in his diary: "It means the days of executive contempt for Congress are ended; that we are returning to a government in which Congress will take its rightful place."[7]

Truman, however, seemed a sorry substitute for Franklin Roosevelt. He had none of FDR's debonair nonchalance, his persuasive eloquence, or grand manner. He had none of Roosevelt's arrogance either, or his political guile. And he had a far different idea of how to treat senators. As a senator for a decade, beginning in 1935, Truman devoted himself to his work, earning the respect of his colleagues, some of whom he found "the finest men I have ever known."[8] He knew, of course, in his phrase, that others among his colleagues were "liars, trimmers and pussy-footers," and that, typically, those most anxious for personal publicity were the ones who did the least real work.[9] Truman's skill as chairman of a special Senate committee overseeing the defense effort had landed him the 1944 Democratic nomination for vice president.

In Truman's first presidential decision, he directed that there be no postponement of the international conference scheduled for less than two weeks later at San Francisco to create the United Nations. Senator Vandenberg, chosen by Roosevelt, was the Republican senator in the American delegation. Roosevelt and Truman did not want to repeat Woodrow Wilson's 1918 mistake. Less than a month after Roosevelt's death, Germany surrendered in total collapse and the war effort now concentrated on vanquishing Japan. The postwar era was at hand, and Truman and Congress scrambled to deal with the pell-mell confusion at home and abroad. In mid-summer, Truman gave the order to drop an atomic bomb on Japan and, after the military dropped a second bomb, Japan quickly capitulated.

On September 6, just four days after Japan's formal surrender, Truman sent Congress one of the longest messages ever, outlining a vast domestic program to return the nation to peacetime pursuits. This was the beginning of his "Fair Deal," an extension of Franklin Roosevelt's "New Deal," and it marked Truman's claim to full presidential authority. He included an array of new proposals, including a civil rights bill, and informed Congress that he shortly intended to ask also for a national health program and an expansion of Social Security. He was acting as chief legislator, but he did not have the command of Congress that Roosevelt had in 1933.

In this Seventy-ninth Congress (1945–47), Democrats still held majorities in both houses, but that did not mean that Truman could count on either body for support. Senior Southern senators, like Georgia's Walter George and Tennessee's Kenneth McKellar, held powerful committee chairmanships, and they worked closely with Ohio's Robert Taft and others in his Republican leadership team. Their informal alliance had the votes to block Truman's initiatives. This was a time of intense and widespread economic and political turmoil, as the nation acted to transition the wartime economy to peaceful purposes. Among other difficulties, President Truman found himself confronting industrial strikes that threatened national safety.

In the 1946 congressional campaigns, the Republicans adopted a telling party cry: "Had enough?" For the first time since Hoover's administration, they won substantial majorities in both the Senate and House. That meant special trouble for President Truman, for they intended to undo many of Franklin Roosevelt's domestic programs. On January 6, 1947, for the first time since becoming president, Truman appeared before a joint session of Congress to deliver his State of the Union address. Among other proposals, he asked Congress for a new law to lessen labor-management tensions, but one that was not "punitive" to organized labor.[10] In the months that followed, Truman and this Republican Congress fought on many matters. Twice he vetoed Republican bills to cut taxes, but the principal struggle came on labor law. Senator Taft himself sponsored the Republican version, rejecting Truman's. Taft's bill outlawed closed shops and secondary boycotts and applied "tough" restrictions on labor unions and labor leaders. Congress overrode Truman's veto.

The 1947 session of Congress, and the 1948 session, too, in part foreshadowed the coming presidential elections. Truman asked and asked, and the Republican Congress denied and denied. In February 1948, he sent Congress a special message urging a broad civil rights program, a proposal Senate Democratic leader Alben Barkley ignored but which deeply offended senators from the South. The Republicans passed a third tax-cut bill, and this time they passed it over Truman's veto. By the summer of 1948, reflecting the president's dismal legislative record, party bosses, labor leaders, and other prominent Democrats tried to organize a "Dump Truman" strategy for their party's national convention. That effort collapsed, and Truman emerged as the party candidate.

Appearing before the convention, long after midnight, to accept its nomination, he startled everyone with a fiery speech denouncing Republicans and what he called the "Do-Nothing Republican Congress." In a clever maneuver, he summoned Congress back into session on July 26, "Turnip Day" in Missouri, and challenged the Republicans to pass some real laws. With that speech, Truman launched his campaign. "I'll give 'em hell," he said.[11]

To the Turnip Day session, Truman presented an extensive list of legislative proposals, more than Congress normally handled in a full year, no less in a few days. The Republicans treated Truman's antics as mere desperation. "We're not going to give that fellow anything," Senator Taft announced.[12] An adjournment was called after two weeks, and Truman had what he wanted: a further excuse to damn the Republicans for their "Good-for-Nothing Congress." With that theme, he set out on a nationwide "whistle-stop" tour by train, making as many as sixteen speeches a day. A feisty battler, he played the role of underdog, and, ignored by professional pollsters, party regulars, and journalists, he scored with voters. To almost everyone's surprise, Truman not only won the election, achieving the most stunning upset in presidential politics, but he carried Democratic majorities in both the Senate and the House. Thereafter, Harry Truman held the presidency in his own right.

In his inaugural address on January 20, 1949, and his State of the Union address two weeks earlier, President Truman laid out for Congress an extensive legislative agenda that included repeal of the Taft-Hartley labor law, federal aid to education, and a new program of low-cost housing.[13] He pledged a "fair deal" for everyone, but from this Congress he won only mixed results. Despite a majority of fifty-four Democratic senators, Truman suffered constant frustration with the Senate, partially because of the conservative coalition of Midwestern Republicans and Southern Democrats, but also with the moderates and liberals of both parties. He grew to resent the Senate's new Democratic leaders, Illinois' Scott Lucas, as majority leader, and Pennsylvania's Francis Myers, as majority whip. They lacked "the guts of a gnat," he complained privately.[14] Hesitant to press all of Truman's requests because of the stiff resistance in the Senate, they did what they could, and they paid dearly for aligning with Truman as much as they did. In the 1950 elections, both Lucas and Myers were defeated for reelection.

In June 1950, communist North Korea attacked South Korea, a country President Truman immediately resolved to protect. The war that resulted, described as merely a "police action," dominated the remainder of Truman's presidency and strained anew his relations with the Senate. Truman considered asking Congress for an endorsement of his action. Secretary of State Dean Acheson had such a resolution drafted, but Truman rejected that course in favor of his claim that he had constitutional authority as commander-in-chief so to act. Robert Taft and other Republican senators questioned the constitutionality of Truman's action and argued for a congressional resolution authorizing what he had done.[15] Acheson had on hand a memo citing eighty-seven instances of previous presidents acting on their own in troublesome times.[16] But Truman's major military commitment, which ultimately cost thirty-seven thousand American lives, was not another instance like those on Acheson's list. As the casualties mounted, so did the partisanship.

By June 1951, Taft joined in the cry that Korea was Truman's war, a "useless and expensive" mistake.[17] This was only part of the misery that the

Senate heaped on President Truman. In April 1951, Truman dismissed General Douglas MacArthur from command in Korea for his obvious insubordination, and that touched off a near frenzy of outrage by congressional Republicans, with some senators calling for the president's impeachment. Truman received little outward support from the senators at the time, but weeks later he was largely exonerated by a Senate investigation conducted by Georgia's Senator Richard Russell.[18]

Other Senate investigations examined a variety of scandals within the Truman administration. One, chaired by North Carolina's Clyde Hoey, embarrassed the president with revelations that some of his White House aides were engaged in helping questionable lobbyists obtain government contracts.[19] An inquiry chaired by Arkansas' William Fulbright uncovered similar corrupt activities within the Reconstruction Finance Corporation.[20] On his desk in the Oval Office, Truman kept a small placard with the words *The Buck Stops Here*. He did not duck responsibility, but he snapped back testily at his critics, many of whom had not thought him up to the job he inherited. His popularity fell disastrously.

Despite his lost public approval, Truman understood that he had responsibility to tell members of Congress what legislation they should enact for the good of the nation and then demand that they do so. In this, he basically assumed the role of "Chief Legislator." By way of acknowledging the president's ascendancy in legislative matters, a Washington weekly publication, *Congressional Quarterly* (*CQ*), founded in 1945, began scoring what its editors called the president's "batting average" with Congress on his legislative requests. The staff of *CQ* credited Truman with making 167 such requests to that Congress and then counted seventy-eight that Congress had approved. (This new way of appraising the president and Congress continues today.)

On the large questions of national government and foreign policy, Truman had left a rich inheritance for his successors in the White House. He had, of course in all this, drawn on precedents and initiatives from presidents before him, but he added more of his own, immensely strengthening and expanding the office he held. On his watch and under his guidance had evolved the modern presidency, with the form and thrust his successors, with modifications, would copy, in peace- and wartime.

In 1952, as in 1920, a war-weary nation rejected the wartime leadership of its Democratic presidents in favor of lower-key Republican successors. Dwight Eisenhower began his presidency in 1953 with a vast treasury of goodwill and only a limited legislative agenda. Yet, at the outset, insensitive to the Senate's distinctive political culture, he unintentionally irritated his own party's Senate majority leader, Robert Taft. Without consulting Taft, he named as his treasury secretary Taft's longtime home-state opponent, George Humphrey. Taft swallowed that offense, but worse came when Eisenhower chose as his secretary of labor, plumbers' union president Martin Durkin, a Democrat and an avowed opponent of the Taft-Hartley labor law. "Incredible!" Taft exclaimed.[21]

A chastened Eisenhower assured Taft he would seek his advice on future major appointments requiring Senate confirmation. But still greater trouble came with Eisenhower's appointment of Charles Bohlen, a brilliant career diplomat, as ambassador to Moscow. Eisenhower had cleared this nomination with Taft, but his party's conservative "Taft wing" in the Senate exploded in fury. Wisconsin Senator Joseph R. McCarthy questioned Bohlen's loyalty and blamed him for the "treason" of the 1945 Yalta conference agreement President Roosevelt had negotiated with Soviet Premier Joseph Stalin. The assault on Bohlen became so intense that Eisenhower asked Taft and Democratic Senator John Sparkman from Alabama to examine the "raw" files at the FBI for whatever "derogatory" information they might contain on Bohlen. The two senators cleared Bohlen.[22]

Alarmed at McCarthy's instinct to attack, Republican leader Taft tried in his reorganization of the Senate to curb the Wisconsin senator's continuing spree of demagogic accusations by blocking him from becoming chair of the Senate Internal Security Subcommittee—formerly Senator Patrick McCarran's vehicle for Communist-hunting. Eisenhower refused to utter McCarthy's name in public. Taft had him assigned to chair the Senate Committee on Government Operations, and McCarthy then appointed himself to chair that panel's Permanent Subcommittee on Investigations. Despite Taft's misplaced optimism that "We've got McCarthy where he can't do any harm," the determined senator went on to use that panel in his self-styled campaign to root out Communists in government, a government now controlled by Republicans.[23]

Frustration among Senate conservatives of both parties flared anew over the nation's growing postwar involvement in the United Nations and other international organizations. Nurturing isolationist sentiments that had been set aside for the duration of World War II, these conservatives feared that the UN Charter and Universal Declaration of Human Rights might be at odds with the protections of the US Constitution and laws—a possible threat to American sovereignty. This inspired Robert Taft's Ohio colleague, John Bricker, to propose a constitutional amendment to limit the president's powers to negotiate treaties and executive agreements with foreign powers by providing that the United States could not be a party to any treaty whose provisions conflicted with its own Constitution. Although endorsed by the Republican Party in its 1952 platform, this projected constitutional change triggered a tumultuous struggle between Senate conservatives and Eisenhower. The president saw in the broadening of the amendment's text to include "all executive and other agreements with any foreign power" a major legislative branch incursion into presidential prerogatives to conclude executive agreements in lieu of treaties. This especially included the conservatives' particular bête noire—the 1945 Yalta agreement.[24]

With most Senate Republicans in favor of the proposed amendment, Eisenhower turned to Senate Democratic leader Lyndon Johnson for support. After extended debate, the Senate in 1954 rejected the amendment, sixty to thirty-one, just one vote shy of the number needed to send it to the states for ratification. Three years later, the Supreme Court more or less settled the issue by ruling that the Constitution superseded any international agreements ratified with Senate approval.[25] Eisenhower confided to his press secretary, "If it's true that when you die the things that bothered you most are engraved on your skull, I am sure that I'll have there the mud and dirt of France during the invasion and the name of Senator Bricker."[26]

In 1955, the Senate returned to Democratic control by a paper-thin majority. Eisenhower's relations with the new majority leader, Lyndon Johnson, proved more open and amiable than they had been with the dour California Republican, William Knowland, who had succeeded to that post with Robert Taft's death in mid-1953. But, as Eisenhower headed into the final two years of his second term, the skies darkened with an economic recession, White House influence-peddling scandals, and concerns about Soviet breakthroughs in outer-space exploration. In this troubled climate, Senate Democrats scored huge victories in the 1958 midterm congressional elections, picking up thirteen Republican seats and two more when Alaska joined the Union—making it the largest transfer of seats from one party to another in the Senate's history. When the dust settled, there were sixty-four Democrats against only thirty-four Republicans.[27] This electoral fortune animated Democratic hopes of regaining the presidency in the 1960 elections.

Seeking an issue on which they could conspicuously oppose the Eisenhower administration, Senate Democrats lit on the pending nomination of Admiral Lewis Strauss to the plain-vanilla cabinet post of commerce secretary. The outspoken, suffer-no-fools Strauss had previously earned influential enemies on Capitol Hill during his tenure as chair of the Atomic Energy

Commission. The president named Strauss under his recess appointment authority with agreement from Senate leaders that they would act favorably early in the 1959 session. But that deal was struck *before* the 1958 Democratic electoral blowout.

Among Strauss's Senate enemies was New Mexico's Clinton Anderson, chair of the Joint Committee on Atomic Energy. Strauss had once publicly criticized the short-fused Anderson for having a "limited understanding" of Cold War atomic energy issues. During his 1959 confirmation hearings, Strauss—ignoring the perennial advice to nominees to let the senators do as much of the talking as possible—displayed a condescending attitude toward his interrogators. His insistence on remaining at the witness table to cross-examine hostile witnesses, as well as senators, delighted Anderson. With the support of his 1948 Senate classmate Lyndon Johnson, Anderson decided to make Strauss the first cabinet nominee to be rejected in thirty-four years. At thirty-five minutes past midnight, on June 19, 1959, in a packed Senate chamber, Johnson and Anderson delivered the votes to defeat Strauss, forty-six in favor, forty-nine opposed. No senator present on that occasion ever forgot its drama. A furious Eisenhower, recalling the Senate's 1868 impeachment trial of President Andrew Johnson, branded the occasion "the second most shameful day in Senate history."[28] The Strauss rejection heralded a period of legislative stalemate for the final eighteen months of the Eisenhower administration.

As he left office in January 1961, Eisenhower told Republican Senate and House leaders that the "Party must have a voice while it's out of power . . . based on the collective judgment of the congressional leaders."[29] This suggestion sparked creation of the Republican Congressional Joint Leadership Conference.[30] The most notable feature of that ponderous-sounding body was its weekly press conference with the party's Senate and House leaders. These sessions became an instant hit among journalists. The *New York Times'* Tom Wicker dubbed it "The Ev and Charlie Show," for the Senate's Everett Dirksen and House leader Charles Halleck.[31] This forum reached a national audience and influenced policies of the new John F. Kennedy administration. On one occasion, it pressured President Kennedy to cancel a planned trade of tractors for the release of political prisoners in Fidel Castro's Cuba and, on another, motivated the unanimous adoption of a Senate resolution against seating Communist China in the United Nations.[32]

On January 20, 1961, John F. Kennedy became only the second person ever to move directly from the Senate to the White House. Following the precedent of Dwight Eisenhower in developing a legislative liaison office,

Kennedy appointed as his congressional liaison chief Lawrence O'Brien, the key strategist of his election campaign. Concerned that his former Senate colleagues would take advantage of that relationship to advance their pet programs, Kennedy devised an effective response: "Have you discussed this with Larry O'Brien?"[33] That quickly spread the word that O'Brien was the man to contact at the White House. This gave President Kennedy his own White House lobbying staff with which to deal with congressional matters, and strengthened his influence over legislation. In this, he owed a great deal to the precedents set by Bryce Harlow, who, in the final years of the Eisenhower administration, had the low-profile title of deputy assistant to the president for congressional affairs.[34] The Larry O'Brien files preserved at the Kennedy and Lyndon Johnson presidential libraries contain vast detail about the personal habits, idiosyncrasies, and favors accorded to members of Congress. Never before had the White House known so much about so many senators—information that had a high political market value.

Powerful Senate committee chairmen disdained working with former majority leader and now vice president Lyndon Johnson. They resented the strong-arm tactics of his Senate days, but they also stood at a distance from President Kennedy, who as a member of the Senate had had a cool relationship with many of his colleagues. Senate "workhorse" Warren Magnuson, chair of the influential Commerce Committee, complained that Senator Kennedy had been away from the Senate "more than any other member I can recall," that he had treated the Senate merely as "a stepping stone to the White House."[35] For his part, Kennedy proved to be uncomfortable in his relations with Senate power brokers. Consequently, his initiatives, including those to advance legislation for Medicare, education, natural resources, agriculture, and housing, languished in the Senate, stymied by the coalition of conservative Southern Democrats, who held key committee chairmanships, and their Republican allies. He also had difficulty advancing economic proposals to curb inflation and a recession. Aware that he lacked support in Congress to pass legislation establishing a Peace Corps, he created that agency by executive order and only later secured enabling legislation. Many of Kennedy's thwarted initiatives in areas such as civil rights, tax reduction, trade expansion, health, and education passed only after his death in 1963, under the Great Society banner of Lyndon Johnson's administration. One Senate insider attributed the indifference of Senate committee chairs to Kennedy's youth and impatience to get his programs enacted. "The Old Bulls up here could not see what it was he wanted to do. They were not used to that kind of pace. He was younger than most of them, and so they just wanted to take their time to make sure whatever he was doing, it was the right thing to do."[36]

Kennedy became embroiled in several Cold War–inspired foreign policy crises. They included the 1961 construction of the Berlin Wall, which isolated West Berlin in East Germany and closed an escape route for East Germans seeking to flee to the West. Of at least equivalent magnitude was the abortive effort in 1961 to land an invasion force at the Bay of Pigs in Cuba—a plan already in place at the time Kennedy entered the White House—and the resulting Cuban Missile Crisis, which brought the United States and the Soviet Union to the brink of nuclear holocaust in 1962. His administration brought to a successful conclusion years'-long negotiations with the Soviet Union that produced the first arms-control agreement of the Cold War era—the 1963 Nuclear Test Ban Treaty, banning tests in the atmosphere, under water, and outer space, but not underground. The Senate approved this landmark agreement eighty to nineteen, following close bipartisan cooperation between its leaders, Mike Mansfield and Everett Dirksen. The Kennedy administration also escalated US involvement in Vietnam from several hundred "advisors" when he took office to fifteen thousand at the time of his assassination in November 1963.

In the wake of President Kennedy's murder, Lyndon Johnson entered the presidency with enormous goodwill. The subsequent 1964 elections produced a Senate with sixty-eight Democrats, the largest majority in thirty years, plus support from moderate and progressive Republicans. Large numbers of Democrats helped weaken the conservative coalition that had blocked civil rights and health care legislation. Johnson had a better grasp on the politics and culture of the Senate than any other president, before or since. "There is but one way for a President to deal with Congress," he asserted, "and that is continuously, incessantly, and without interruption."[37] His ability to work effectively with committee chairmen, who were then the gatekeepers of legislative accomplishment, proved fundamental to the success of his Great Society legislative agenda.

In his years as the Senate's majority leader, Johnson had used rough-and-tumble tactics on his colleagues. As president, he fretted over successor Mansfield's always considerate dealings with everyone. "Why do I have to have a saint for majority leader?" Johnson complained. "Why can't I have a politician?"[38] On the other side of the aisle, he had an extraordinary relationship with Republican leader Everett Dirksen. They battled directly over many of Johnson's legislative proposals, but on larger matters Dirksen stood boldly for Johnson despite growing criticism from his own ranks. With

Congress in session, Dirksen normally met privately with Johnson at the White House two or three times a week, and they constantly talked by telephone. They confided in each other and helped out when they could. During the difficult days of the Vietnam War, rumors circulated that Johnson even had Dirksen help him pick bombing targets in North Vietnam.

Despite heavy criticism from his fellow Republicans, Dirksen hardly wavered in his support of Johnson on the war. By 1966, many senators—Democrat and Republican alike—openly opposed continuing the conflict, among them Senator J. W. Fulbright, chairman of the Senate's Foreign Relations Committee. Some Republicans wanted to label this "Johnson's War," much as Republican senators had labeled Korea as "Truman's War." Dirksen checked them with his continuing backing of Johnson. Less actively, Majority Leader Mansfield, a former Marine, quietly opposed the war; he carried up-to-date casualty lists in his breast pocket.

Even more than Kennedy, Johnson made extensive use of the White House lobbying operation, retaining Larry O'Brien in that post. On occasion, however, he took charge himself. In one such instance, the Senate Finance Committee one morning suddenly voted to repeal a host of excise taxes, at great potential loss in federal revenues. Johnson acted instantly, telephoning the chairman and others during the committee's luncheon recess while ordering his assistants into action. By the time the committee reconvened, he had lined up the votes to cancel the morning's vote, to the amusement of Republican Leader Dirksen, who had engineered the original vote. Dirksen taunted Connecticut's Abraham Ribicoff, a Democrat, for switching sides. "Well," Ribicoff replied, "what do you do when the President gets you on the phone and eats your consummate ass out? He told me what a low-life bastard I was: 'You better get right with God before it is too late!'"[39]

In 1964, as US involvement in Vietnam began to escalate, President Johnson bamboozled the Senate and House into approving the Gulf of Tonkin Resolution, a limited measure. Later, he tried to argue that the resolution was the equivalent of a declaration of war. In the years of the Cold War with the Soviet Union, a time of great international tension, the Washington community adopted what became a hackneyed slogan: "Don't tie the President's hands." There was an assumption that, with his vast sources of information, President Johnson knew best.[40]

In June 1963, President Kennedy had proposed an omnibus civil rights bill to cool rising racial discord. For more than forty years, Southern senators had derailed sporadic attempts to enact such laws, but they were no longer the solid bloc they had been. They had defectors, but they still had eighteen committed members, enough to filibuster such a measure indefinitely. With Majority Leader Mansfield opposed to trying to break filibusters by keeping those who chose to use them on their feet around the clock, it was necessary for the measure's sponsors to muster the two-thirds vote needed to invoke cloture. Cloture could not be attained without Republican votes, and only Everett Dirksen could round up enough of them. Dirksen worked steadily on changes he wanted in Kennedy's original measure. He had what amounted to a veto on the bill, which gave him power to dictate terms. Not until late March 1964 did the Senate take up the bill. By then, the House had passed its own version.

This was an extraordinary piece of legislation, and the Senate treated it accordingly. The debate ran on through April, but not until June 10, when Dirksen finally had the votes for cloture, did the Senate vote: seventy-one to twenty-nine. The rest was anticlimactic.[41] Some Democrats resented Mansfield's deferring to Dirksen in moving this vital legislation, but not President Johnson or his White House assistants. "Without Dirksen on these votes like civil rights," said Larry O'Brien, "we're gone!"[42]

When Congress enacted the 1964 civil rights bill, most members assumed that the issue had been adequately dealt with. African Americans and their allies, angered that so much had been cut away from the original measure, renewed their protests. In Selma, Alabama, these demonstrations took an ugly turn. President Johnson went before Congress and dramatically asked for new legislation, primarily to guarantee everyone the right to vote.[43] That made Senate Republican leader Dirksen again the center of the contest, for he again had to muster enough Republicans to invoke cloture on that bill. Again, Dirksen played a major role in drafting the legislation, and he and Mansfield jointly introduced the bill on March 18, 1965. The hostile Southern senators had been shaken by their loss on the civil rights bill of the previous year, and they again resorted to a filibuster. "You can't get cloture in the Senate," said Larry O'Brien, "without Dirksen working like hell for it."[44] Not until mid-May did he have enough. "All I know is that mathematics is the greatest of the sciences," Dirksen said. "There you add and subtract. I try to count and count hard." On his motion, backed by Senator Mansfield, the Senate voted seventy to thirty for cloture, and the bill became law.[45]

The next year, 1966, with civil rights protests still rampant, President Johnson tried to quiet national turmoil on racial equality. He proposed another bill, this one to provide federal guarantees on the right of everyone to buy or rent a place to live. This time, Dirksen balked. When Johnson's faction managed to bring this "open housing" measure before the Senate, Dirksen denounced it: "This is a package of mischief."[46] Twice Mansfield tried to invoke cloture against the Southerners' filibuster, and twice he failed. With Dirksen in opposition, he had no chance. This was the "Dirksen Veto." He could not push through the Senate his own pet measures, but he could decide the legislative fate of any measure subjected to a filibuster.

In early January 1968, President Johnson again asked for an open housing law, and again Senator Dirksen applied his veto. When, in late February, Senator Mansfield moved to invoke cloture, Dirksen rose in his place to oppose his motion. Three times in the 1960s the Senate had invoked cloture, and in each instance Dirksen had been the instrument of success. Now he equated cloture with "gagging" the Senate: he hoped "that the Senate will not gag itself."[47] Mansfield's motion failed, but this struggle was not over.

Dirksen worried about the consequences of this opposition for his Republican Party in the 1968 presidential election year. Some younger Republican senators, including his son-in-law, Howard Baker of Tennessee, wanted action on the bill. With their help, Dirksen fashioned a variant of Johnson's bill, "the Dirksen substitute," and put that before the Senate. "I do not apologize for my conduct," Dirksen said, and now he asked his colleagues to vote for cloture—to "gag" the Senate—on his version. Despite an initial rejection, many of his party members rallied to help capture the necessary two-thirds vote, sixty-five to thirty-two, on cloture. His influence in the Senate was diminishing. His Republican senators were increasingly annoyed at him, principally for his cozy dealings with President Johnson.[48]

In mid-June 1968, Chief Justice Earl Warren notified President Johnson that he wished to retire. On receiving Warren's letter, Johnson telephoned Dirksen and asked him to come to the White House. There, they discussed this unexpected development and whom Johnson might choose to replace Warren. Only late in the conversation did Johnson propose Abe Fortas, his longtime friend and a sitting Supreme Court associate justice. Dirksen said Fortas would be the easiest for the Senate to approve, and Johnson nominated him a few weeks later.

By then, a freshman Republican senator, Michigan's Robert Griffin, had organized his own campaign to block Senate confirmation of anyone Johnson might name. Johnson had announced in late March that he would not seek another term as president, and Griffin reasonably argued that the next chief justice should be picked by whomever won the presidential election in November, quite possibly a Republican.

Dirksen dismissed Griffin's maneuvers, but even before the hearings began Griffin had enlisted more than half of the Senate's Republicans to his cause, a matter of sudden alarm for Dirksen. From the start, Griffin planned to filibuster the Fortas nomination and, in this, he knew that he could count on help from most of the Southern Democrats. That was what happened. When Mansfield moved to invoke cloture, he barely had the support of half the Senate, certainly not the two-thirds vote needed at that time. By then, Dirksen had been badly outmaneuvered. He made a lame excuse and then voted against Fortas, too.[49] A dispirited President Johnson withdrew the nomination.

Richard Nixon ran for president in 1968 with the promise that he had a "secret plan" to end the war in Vietnam. After his election victory, he pledged to help "Vietnamize" the conflict to allow the United States an honorable departure. Instead, Nixon expanded the war into neighboring Cambodia and Laos. With that, Senate Majority Leader Mansfield dropped his instinctive deference to the president's acquired prerogatives in establishing the nation's foreign policy. In 1970, his voice rising in anger, he asserted, "For many years, we have seen our role in matters of war and peace largely as one of acquiescence in the acts of the executive branch. If we have had doubts, we have swallowed them. . . . We have gone along. We have rocked few boats." Mansfield demanded that the Senate move "to curb the further expansion of the war."[50]

Two years later, as continuing reverses dictated withdrawal of American forces, the Nixon administration adopted a new priority: opening relations with China. Soon after the president's historic visit there, Senate leaders Mansfield and Hugh Scott followed in his steps. Both senators had academic training and long-standing interests in the Far East and believed this initiative should have come much earlier. Mansfield noted the irony of opening doors to China at the same time the United States was waging war in Vietnam, which, "to put the best face on it, was sanctioned by what has now become a discredited policy towards China. The President's visit to China had the symbolic effect of marking the end of that policy. If the old China policy is no longer valid, is not the present involvement in the Vietnam war which derived from that policy also invalid?"[51]

In response to Nixon's capricious war-making in Southeast Asia, Congress adopted the 1973 War Powers Resolution—over his veto—to try to limit the president's authority on such occasions. Later presidents continued to take the country into military actions, largely ignoring these supposed limits, but none seriously challenged that law constitutionally. In the first Iraq War, and then the second, Congress did vote a kind of permission to the president, but by then the Senate and the House had lost their old authority in such matters. These wars—Korea, Vietnam, and Iraq—cost many thousands of American lives and vast amounts of treasure; the Senate and House docilely followed wherever the presidents led.[52] (In 2011, President Barack Obama challenged the 1973 resolution's definition of "hostilities" and proceeded to ignore its letter and spirit in dispatching air power to Libya against the regime of Muammar el Qaddafi. The Senate and House rushed to pass resolutions supporting the president's action.[53])

As in war-making, President Nixon went too far in financial matters. In 1972, with congressional spending seemingly out of control, he asked permission to break any previous law to keep the appropriations that year under $250 billion. The House approved, though its leaders protested, but the move was ultimately blocked by the Senate.[54] Nixon then gravely offended members of both houses by announcing that hereafter he would treat all appropriations bills as offering the president options on what he could spend. He "impounded" those appropriations he chose not to spend, and he impounded many billions. Appropriations bills when enacted became the law of the land, and Congress reacted by drafting an entirely new system, one restoring to Congress much of its power over government spending. That law, the Congressional Budget and Impoundment Control Act of 1974, also approved over Nixon's veto, made the House and Senate responsible to draft the annual budget and involved the president only later.[55]

The Nixon administration chilled relations between the White House and Capitol Hill. One long-serving Senate staffer noted, "As tough as Johnson was as a leader, nevertheless he did not have the disrespect for the Congress that Nixon and his people seemed to have."[56] The major agent for this deterioration—aside from Nixon—was the president's domestic affairs assistant, John Ehrlichman. On one typical occasion, he went to the Hill to convince the Senate and House Republican leaders to support legislation that those leaders concluded had no chance of passing. To their astonishment, the tone-deaf Ehrlichman issued the following threat: "OK, you can tell everybody that's going to vote against us that we're going into their state, or their district, and campaign against them." One participant recalled that House Republican Leader Gerald Ford "looked at Ehrlichman like this guy's got to be bonkers. Does he think for one minute that the President of the United States is going to go into some Republican state and campaign and campaign against some Republican that's running? That's crazy!"[57]

As the scandals linked to Nixon's 1972 presidential reelection campaign became public and began to multiply, the president turned to Senate Republican leader Hugh Scott for help. In early 1973, Majority Leader Mansfield sponsored a formal investigation by a select Senate committee of the Watergate break-in and other election-year abuses. This was a matter of great party concern, and Hugh Scott did what he could to undercut the process, an ongoing chore for the next year and a half. In private, Nixon assured Scott that he had nothing to do with this gathering crisis. "Stupid I'm not," he told Scott. "We have nothing to hide. . . . No one in the White House was involved."[58] Scott accepted his word and publicly proclaimed Nixon's innocence. To his dismay, as with other Republicans, the committee hearings brought astonishing revelations against Nixon and his people, including that Nixon himself had actively tried to cover up his administration's scandals. Then, in the hours of Nixon's greatest peril, Scott played a central role in two momentous incidents that led to Nixon's removal as president.

The first came in mid-October 1973, with the so-called Saturday Night Massacre. Cornered by the Senate committee, a federal judge, and the special prosecutor, Nixon ordered his new attorney general, Elliott Richardson, to fire the special prosecutor and abolish his office. This touched off a firestorm of wild controversy. Nixon had consulted no one in the congressional leadership, and Scott, already betrayed, reacted in ferocious anger. He summoned legislative liaison Bryce Harlow, one of Nixon's closest advisers, to meet with Senate Republicans. With their backing, Scott directed Harlow to relay their ultimatum to Nixon: The president must appoint a new special prosecutor with guarantees of his independence. If Nixon refused, they would call for his resignation. Nixon had no option but to comply. Meanwhile, the Speaker of the House, Oklahoma's Carl Albert, had ordered the House Judiciary Committee to begin impeachment proceedings.[59]

The second major event came in August 1974, after the House committee had voted three articles of impeachment against Nixon, and White House tapes, revealed by order of the Supreme Court, confirmed his guilt in the cover-up. With political Washington in utter turmoil, Scott, as the Senate's Republican leader; the House's Republican leader, Arizona's John Rhodes; along with Senator Barry Goldwater, the most esteemed of Republicans, met privately with Nixon at the White House. Rhodes told him that impeachment by the House was certain. Scott and Goldwater told him they had canvassed the Senate and that he could not escape conviction. They doubted whether he could get more than a dozen Senate votes in his favor. Nixon asked them to name the twelve. They could name only five. But that night, in a speech to the nation, Nixon announced that he would resign the next day, and he did.[60] The collective impact of Nixon's management of the war in Vietnam and his Watergate-related scandals greatly weakened the authority of presidential leadership, as Congress moved to strengthen its constitutional prerogatives with legislation such as the War Powers Resolution and the Congressional Budget and Impoundment Control Act of 1974.

With the October 1973 resignation of scandal-ensnared Vice President Spiro Agnew, President Nixon had selected as his replacement House Republican Leader Gerald Ford, considered the most likely to be quickly confirmed by the House and Senate under the Constitution's Twenty-fifth Amendment. On the day Ford took his oath as vice president, December 6, 1973, a correspondent for a national newsmagazine visited him in his House leadership office. The journalist recalled,

> We were alone and we chatted about his new job, vice president, and the one of president he was likely to inherit. "What this country needs most," I said, "is a president with simple republican manners." "You don't think I will change, do you?" he answered. "There are many who will try" to make that happen, I said. He asked me to listen to him practice his inaugural speech planned for later that day. He started firmly, voice resolute. He loved the House of Representatives, where we had worked for a quarter century and tears formed in his eyes as he spoke about leaving that place. This was a painful moment for him and soon he was weeping. His words were badly muddled and he stopped. Then he began again. He spoke anew to his commitment to the rule of law. Now, he could only speak two or three words at a time, his voice cracking. It was so touching, so touching. I joined him in his tears.[61]

As the new vice president anticipated on that extraordinary day, within nine months Nixon's resignation placed Gerald Ford in the White House. Proclaiming "Our long national nightmare is over," Ford entered office with wide support in both houses of Congress, and throughout the nation. In an address to Congress, he pledged "communication, conciliation, compromise, and cooperation."[62] On August 20, he nominated former New York Governor Nelson Aldrich Rockefeller, grandson of Senate baron Nelson

Aldrich, to succeed him as vice president and Senate president. Ford promised to make Rockefeller a full partner on domestic policy decisions. Later, when Ford was asked what he believed his top achievement of his first hundred days in office to be, he answered, "Nominating Nelson Rockefeller."[63] (But two years later, preparing for the 1976 presidential election, he allowed party conservatives to force the liberal-minded Rockefeller to withdraw as his running mate. Of that turn of events, Ford subsequently observed, "It was the biggest political mistake of my life. And it was one of the few cowardly things I did in my life."[64] As Rockefeller's replacement, Ford chose Kansas Senator Bob Dole.

James Cannon, an adviser to Rockefeller and Ford—and later chief of staff to Senate Majority Leader Howard Baker—described the new president as having "an abundance of character and three other qualities that every modern President needs most: an understanding of how the Federal government works, common sense, and the guts to say 'Yes' or 'No.'"[65] But he also identified a missing characteristic of national leadership: "Presidents are remembered more often for their words than their actions, and Ford was never eloquent. His thoughts and words were plain, direct, everyday; there was no poetry in his native speech or his being."[66]

Ford's initial popular support evaporated overnight with his September 8, 1974, pardon of Richard Nixon. Facing 12 percent inflation, rising unemployment, severe energy shortages, and a mild recession, Ford spent valuable time and political capital trying to explain his decision. And he blundered in his conclusion that inflation was the country's most significant challenge. The former University of Michigan football star developed a public relations offensive to "Whip Inflation Now," complete with "WIN" buttons, which he displayed in a nationwide televised address. That offensive bled into triviality and undermined the serious image he sought to cultivate. Ford shifted to the more fundamental problem of rising unemployment.

These issues, along with the collective outrage over Nixon and Watergate, dominated the 1974 midterm congressional elections. House Democrats enjoyed a major sweep, adding forty-nine members, while the number of Senate Democrats rose to sixty-one. An energized cadre of "Watergate Babies" in the House and their counterparts in the Senate moved quickly to reassert the powers and prerogatives of Congress. As Republican Senator Mark Hatfield lamented about President Ford, "A man of Congress who had wanted to restore a sense of cooperation and conciliation between the executive and legislative branches . . . confronted a hostile legislature that turned his presidency into a clash of vetoes and veto overrides."[67] James

Cannon summarized the lasting impact of that election and the Nixon scandals that shaped it. "The election of 1974 swept aside the House and Senate traditions that respected experience and ensured accountability. Instead, Congress became a loose congregation of independent operators serving parochial interests, local constituencies, and the highest goal—the next election."[68]

Senator Robert Byrd noted the change in attitude on Capitol Hill following Nixon's resignation. "The Watergate crisis brought home to members of Congress the realization of how unbalanced and unchecked presidential powers had become. For years, presidential actions had circumvented Congress, kept Congress in the dark about major foreign policy initiatives, and frustrated congressional intentions in a wide range of areas from the use of American troops abroad to the spending of federal funds at home."[69]

Through this shift, Ford concurred with Nixon's belief that the United States should continue its military and civilian operations in Vietnam to thwart the advance of Communism in that region. But by the time he took office, Congress and the general public had tired of that costly and fruitless struggle. In an address to Congress, Ford urged the nation to stand with the Vietnamese, and to direct large amounts of additional funding for military and humanitarian aid. This concerned members of the Senate Foreign Relations Committee so much that they traveled to the White House for an intense consultation. New York Republican Senator Jacob Javits delivered the committee's verdict to the president. "I will give you large sums for evacuation, but not one nickel for military aid."[70]

Ford realized he had no choice but to hasten US withdrawal. But an incident involving the capture by Cambodian forces of an American merchant ship, the SS *Mayaguez*, in international waters, allowed him to reassert US determination to display its military resolve. Ultimately, American forces boarded and seized the ship and rescued its captured forty-member crew. The cost of this adventure proved high, however, with the loss of fifteen US Marines and twenty-three air force security troops. Democrats in Congress commissioned an investigation by the General Accounting Office. The verdict: the use of military force had been unnecessary. Ford gamely concluded that the episode "restored American morale, got us back up out of the depths of the defeat in Vietnam, and renewed respect around the world for America."[71]

Gerald Ford's experience for most of his twenty-five years in Congress was as a minority party member seeking to thwart majority initiatives. This gave him a lot of experience in fighting losing battles. Now, as president, he was obligated to abandon that perspective. He wrote, "When I was in Congress myself, I thought it fulfilled its constitutional obligations in a very responsible way, but after I became President, my perspective changed."[72] What he observed from the other end of Pennsylvania Avenue was a parochial, single-issue body unwilling to accept his legislative leadership. Congressional Democrats focused on the nation's high levels of unemployment and lags in worker productivity, while Ford initially emphasized the need to combat the inflationary spiral. When Congress passed social-welfare legislation, as well as measures that he saw as working against his goal of a balanced federal budget, Ford rejected them, vetoing sixty-one bills during his two years in office. Congress went on to pass twelve of those acts over his veto, the largest number of overrides since the presidency of Harry Truman. These vetoes put Ford on record as opposing issues widely popular with voters, and they contributed to his 1976 election defeat by a Georgia peanut farmer named Jimmy Carter. Naturally disappointed, Ford concluded, "Considering the mess I inherited, I was convinced that I had done a good job and should have won on the merits."[73]

Ford biographer James Cannon concluded, "Ford's moment in history arrived when the highest powers in Congress were looking for an honest man. They knew exactly where he was; he was one of them. His choice was the act of a Congress that no longer exists, performed by old-time leaders who could swiftly put aside partisan differences to make a momentous decision in the highest traditions of representative government."[74]

Despite the best efforts of Senate insiders Birch Bayh, Lloyd Bentsen, Robert Byrd, Frank Church, Fred Harris, and Henry Jackson to gain the 1976 Democratic presidential nomination, it went to former Georgia governor Jimmy Carter, a little-known public figure who campaigned against the Washington establishment.

Initially, Carter displayed little active interest in developing close working relations with congressional leaders. Senator Edward Kennedy concluded, "I think he simply had convinced himself he was going to do it his way. He was an outsider, and he was going to run things from an outsider's point of view. That was true of his dealings with the Senate, and one of the principal reasons that he never won that body's cooperation."[75] Carter later acknowledged that when he arrived in Washington, he did not know many members of Congress and "had not spent much time studying about them."[76] House Speaker Thomas O'Neill considered Carter "the smartest public official I've ever known . . . but when it came to the politics of Washington, DC, he never really understood how the system worked."[77]

For his part, Carter complained that congressional leaders seemed to have an insatiable desire to be consulted and that they seemed to take offense when bypassed. To that, Senate Majority Leader Robert Byrd responded that congressional leaders were trying to convey to the president a message "about appreciating the institution of Congress and how it works; about working with Congress rather than fighting against it."[78] Byrd and others particularly objected to Carter's decision to swamp Congress all at once with a variety of ambitious and controversial legislative proposals—some of it in areas of his personal interest but without broad constituencies—in areas including energy independence, tax and budget reform, arms control, federal water projects, airline deregulation, national health insurance, human rights, and control of the Panama Canal. Carter later acknowledged, "It would have been advisable to have introduced our legislation in more careful phases—not in such a rush. We would not have accomplished any more, and perhaps less, but my relations with Congress would have been smoother and the image of undue haste and confusion could have been avoided."[79]

Longtime Hill observers questioned this view. In one Senate aide's opinion, "Volume isn't always necessarily the answer. . . . [I]f the programs are good, and if the country is responsive to those programs, this body will enact them. But if it isn't, it doesn't matter whether you send two programs or two thousand, it won't make any difference."[80]

Carter's major initial blunder, from a congressional perspective, was his campaign pledge to cut funding for nineteen water projects located in seventeen states. Senator Byrd privately acknowledged that the public works bill contained obsolete and unnecessary projects, but "many of these water projects were vitally important to members' home states and had gained the support of senators and representatives from both parties, of all ideological persuasions." Byrd continued, "Instead of marshaling his forces against the worst excesses of the pork barrel, and building support on a case-by-case basis, Carter leveled his fire against the whole package, thereby alienating more members than he attracted."[81] Carter responded by targeting more proposed projects. Washington journalist Martin Schram observed, "Although Carter's actions may have been valid on the environmental and budgetary merits, his zealotry on water projects stirred up so much political ill will on Capitol Hill that his presidency never recovered."[82]

Symbolic of this new distance between the chief executive and congressional power brokers was Carter's decision to sell the presidential yacht *Sequoia*. Presidents back to the days of Herbert Hoover had used the vessel for intimate gatherings with members and their spouses. A simple sail down the Potomac to Mount Vernon at sunset could pay big dividends in cordial relations. Carter intended a new, and ultimately unrealistic, order of business in which members of Congress appeared to be junior partners—to be summoned as needed.[83]

At a White House session with Democratic congressional leaders early in the Carter administration, Byrd lectured the president. "It would be wise," he told him, "to consult senators who are in important committee positions and allow them to make their contributions." He might have added in reference to a public relations problem that was setting an indelible mark against the administration: "It would also be wise to return these members' telephone calls and keep their scheduled appointments." Carter soon began to pay heed, and that inspired greater cooperation from Byrd and others.[84]

In August 1977, President Carter had proposed a pair of treaties, long in negotiation, to turn over the Panama Canal to Panama. As a treaty, this was a matter for the Senate alone and it proved far more difficult than ordinary legislation. Not only did these treaties invite jingoistic demagoguery from opponents—a campaign already under way—they required two-thirds votes by the Senate. Five months later, Byrd called up the treaties for Senate action. By January 1978, the Senate Foreign Relations Committee had conducted formal hearings and many senators, including Byrd and Republican Leader Howard Baker, had traveled to Panama for on-the-spot inspection of the canal and consultations with local officials. Despite these preliminaries, the opposition was strong and strident, and the Senate's power players were actively engaged in a scramble to woo their colleagues' votes. Professional polls indicated that four out of five Americans opposed the treaties. There was a desperate struggle ahead.[85]

Nevada Republican Senator Paul Laxalt took charge of the Senate's opposition. Senate Republicans, moderates versus conservatives, were sharply divided. They understood that this controversy would affect the party's next national convention, a matter of special concern to Senator Baker, among others. Laxalt and his lieutenants sent "truth squads" of senators around the country to drum up opposition, and, with the help of professionals, they stimulated a blizzard of protest mail to senators' offices.

The debate ran on until mid-March. By then, Byrd and Baker openly supported the treaties, but California's Alan Cranston, the Democrats' Senate whip, in his count, was still five votes short of the sixty-seven required, assuming that all senators showed up. Only a few senators, all under intense pressures, remained uncommitted. Byrd scheduled the vote anyway, gambling on last-minute negotiations with those still in doubt. He and Baker, with Carter's reluctant support, worked to persuade the necessary additional senators. As insurance, the super-cautious Byrd had had one "safety" vote in hand, a pledge by his West Virginia colleague, Jennings Randolph, but only if his vote alone was needed to agree to the treaties.[86] With approval assured, Byrd turned to solve the obvious hazard for all those voting for the treaties. With just the exact number needed to approve, every senator voting "aye" risked election-year attack that his or her vote was the one that "gave away" the Panama Canal. To spare all of them, Nevada's Howard Cannon, a Democrat strongly opposed to the treaties, agreed to vote for them under these extraordinary circumstances. That made the recorded vote sixty-eight to thirty-two, and that gave a campaign reprieve for the sixty-seven. No one cast the decisive vote.[87] Despite this clever parliamentary tactic, the treaty vote ultimately ended the Senate careers of several supporters, including Foreign Relations Committee chair Frank Church.[88]

President Carter was less fortunate, however, in efforts to gain ratification of a treaty that would have sharply reduced strategic nuclear weapons in the United States and the Soviet Union. Although Senate conservatives stoutly opposed the so-called SALT-II Pact, Senator Byrd—harboring his own reservations—wished to give the president an "up or down" Senate vote. Byrd traveled as Carter's emissary to meet with European leaders, including Russian President Leonid Brezhnev.[89] Ultimately, the 1979 Soviet invasion of Afghanistan shelved consideration. Carter considered this failed opportunity to harness the nuclear arms race as "the most profound disappointment of my Presidency."[90]

Despite his rocky relations with Congress, Carter was able to point to significant legislative accomplishments, including comprehensive civil service reform; creation of the federal departments of Energy and Education; deregulation of transportation, energy, and communications programs; and placement of inspectors-general in all government agencies.

His administration failed, however, to resolve a crisis growing out of a revolution in Iran. In November 1979, Islamic militants seized the American embassy in Tehran and held fifty-two Americans. An attempt to rescue the hostages in April 1980 failed and resulted in the deaths of eight American servicemen. In a defiant gesture, the Iranian revolutionaries held on to their captives until the inauguration of Ronald Reagan, who—with the help of double-digit inflation and an energy crisis—had defeated Carter in the November 1980 election.

A former movie actor and California governor, Ronald Reagan won election with smooth media performances and his searing question to the American people: "Are you better off today than you were four years ago?" At a time of rampant inflation and national humiliation over the Iranian hostage episode, the answer was obvious to many voters. Although Reagan had been favored to win, few expected that his party would also take control of the Senate for the first time in twenty-six years. His coattails made a difference in at least three Senate races, allowing the Republicans, with only forty-one seats in the previous Congress, to take twelve seats from the Democrats—the largest pickup since 1958. The 1980 election, along with those of 1976 and 1978, brought a major turnover among senators, introducing fifty-five new members throughout that period, many of them Republican and conservative. It also closed out an era of bipartisanship and progressive legislative accomplishment that had dated back to the early 1960s.[91]

The Senate's new majority leader, Howard Baker, recalled his January 1981 choice. "I had to decide whether I would try to set a separate agenda for the Senate, with our brand-new Republican majority, or try to see how our new president, with a Republican Senate, could work together as a team to enact our programs. I chose the latter course and I believe history has proved me right. Would I have done the same with a president of the opposition party? Lyndon Johnson did with President Eisenhower and history proved him right as well."[92] Reagan respected Baker and worked easily with him. In 1987, he continued the relationship by choosing Baker, then a former senator who had abandoned his own presidential ambitions, as his White House chief of staff.[93]

The sixty-nine-year-old Reagan took up his duties with vigor, promising a new "morning in America." "America is back" became the theme as he brushed aside the lingering pessimism of the Carter years. Reagan's genial personality, his evident desire to get along with Congress and its leaders, his willingness to stake out an apparently unshakable position, but then compromise while declaring victory, and the tide of public sympathy that followed his good-natured recovery from an assassination attempt made him, at the outset, an effective force on Capitol Hill.

Unlike Carter, Reagan had the advantage of a well-supported congressional liaison office. During his first hundred days in office, Reagan managed to meet personally with 467 of the Senate and House's combined 535 members. This led some of his staff—on subsequent legislative matters—to fret that "if the president doesn't call them personally or see them, the White House doesn't care."[94]

Reagan followed a "chairman of the board" leadership style, delegating authority to his senior staff and showing little interest in the evolving details of his policies and programs. When congressional leaders met with him at the White House, they brought back tales of his detached manner. One recalled that the president "usually made a few remarks, reading the cue cards with perfection. As amiable as Reagan was, he rarely made any truly personal comments to any of us."[95] The president's fondness for afternoon naps and frequent trips to his California ranch—where he would spend the equivalent of nearly one year out of his eight years in office—quickly eroded any image of a fully engaged chief executive.[96]

With vital assistance from Senate Majority Leader Baker, Reagan's administration, in its early months, secured legislation granting a major reduction in income tax rates along with a significant boost in military spending. Reagan's failure to push for comparable reductions in other spending accounts created huge budget deficits. His biographer, Lou Cannon, explained that the president's "faith that the tax cuts would spur economic activity to such an extent that the government would receive added revenues from lower rates proved unfounded. As a result, the national debt nearly tripled during the Reagan presidency, the trade debt quadrupled, and the United States became a debtor nation."[97]

Robert Byrd soon became a principal Senate voice against the Reagan administration. "From a position of guiding the president's program through the Senate, I found myself and my minority party in opposition to many of the new president's foreign policy initiatives."[98] Byrd objected to the president's decision to sell high-altitude AWACS radar planes to Saudi Arabia on grounds that the transaction would destabilize the Middle East. Byrd also opposed injecting American peacekeeping forces into a Lebanese civil war, a decision that ultimately cost the lives of 241 US Marines in October 1983 and forced US withdrawal from the conflict the following year.[99]

To address this increasingly troubling situation—annual budget deficits during the Reagan years would increase from $79 billion to $173 billion—Senator Bob Dole, who became majority leader with Baker's retirement in 1985, and Budget Committee chair Pete Domenici put together a deficit reduction package in May 1985 in the expectation that it would save $135 billion over three years. That plan included the politically dangerous withholding of Social Security cost-of-living benefits for one year. Dole counted carefully and determined that he had exactly fifty senators willing to pass the bill, with the anticipated tie to be broken by Vice President George H. W. Bush.

Suddenly, one of Dole's troops, Republican Senator Pete Wilson of California, was rushed to Bethesda Naval Hospital for an emergency appendectomy. Dole arranged, against medical advice, to have Wilson brought back to the Senate chamber by ambulance for a 2 A.M. vote. Wilson, in his hospital garb and wheelchair, dramatically arrived to vigorous bipartisan applause. With the vice president's help, the bill passed the Senate, fifty to forty-nine.[100] Recalling that event years later, Dole added, bitterly,

> But unfortunately, the story didn't end there. One thing you learn as leader is that biting a bullet carries the risk that it may explode in your face, which is exactly what happened when [chief of staff] Don Regan at the White House, [House Speaker] Tip O'Neill, and House Republicans made a separate deal [to spare Social Security] that, in my opinion, avoided the hard choices. In the next election, [we] Republicans lost our Senate majority, and more than a few pundits believed the vote on the deficit package was a contributing factor.[101]

Those Republicans shared Dole's sense that President Reagan had betrayed them.[102] The honeymoon with the Senate had come to an end.

Texas Senator Phil Gramm proposed a plan that would allow Republicans who did not wish to be recorded as voting to increase the debt limit to create a mechanism for blocking future budgetary expansion. Designed to cut the budget deficit, which was then at an all-time high of $2 trillion, the Gramm plan provided for automatic spending cuts, or "sequestrations," if Congress failed to hit an exact deficit target. The implementation of what became known through its Senate sponsors as the Gramm-Rudman-Hollings Balanced Budget and Emergency Deficit Control Act of 1985 proved to be complex and soon triggered legal action and quickly made its way to the Supreme Court, which in 1986 declared the process for determining the spending cuts to be unconstitutional.[103] Congress reworked the statute in 1987, but it ultimately failed to prevent sizeable budget deficits.

The other major domestic legislative accomplishment of the Reagan years, owing to the heavy lifting of a bipartisan congressional coalition, was the Tax Reform Act of 1986. This landmark measure greatly simplified the tax code by reducing the number of exemptions and tax brackets, while expanding the sources of tax revenue.[104] It also included the largest corporate tax increase in history, along with an increase in payroll taxes to keep Social Security solvent.[105]

Reagan's final two years in office, with the Senate back under Democratic control, produced few legislative accomplishments. After November 1986, his administration became preoccupied with the Iran-Contra scandal, in which enterprising high-level Reagan aides, with the president's at least passive acknowledgment, had sought to provide arms to Iran, contrary to an embargo, to secure release of American hostages held in Lebanon. Profits from that transaction would go to support the Nicaraguan Contras in their efforts to overthrow that nation's Communist government, despite a congressional prohibition against such aid. Attorney General Edwin Meese, facing criticism for his management of the resulting investigation and for ethical lapses, resigned in 1988. Senator Byrd identified Meese as "the crown jewel of the sleaze factor in Reagan administration history."[106] President Reagan also ran into trouble in the Senate with his late-term Supreme Court nominations. Earlier, he had easily obtained its approval for Sandra Day O'Connor, the first woman justice, and Antonin Scalia. He had greater difficulty in 1986 in elevating associate justice William Rehnquist to chief justice, with thirty-three senators voting in opposition. In 1987, with less than two years remaining in his increasingly scandal-plagued administration, and with the Senate returned to a Democratic majority, Reagan's luck soured with the nomination of federal appeals judge Robert Bork. Uncommonly combative for a high court nominee, Bork responded to his critics with a cockiness that guaranteed an acrimonious and ultimately futile confirmation battle. After a replacement nominee also failed the Senate's scrutiny, Reagan appointed and the Senate confirmed US appeals court judge Anthony Kennedy, who took his seat early in 1988.

Despite his troubles on Capitol Hill, Reagan experienced late-term success in his relations with the Soviet Union through his willingness to negotiate arms reductions with leader Mikhail Gorbachev. The two men conducted five summit meetings and produced the Intermediate Nuclear Forces (INF) treaty. The president's reputation as an unyielding anti-Communist nullified instinctive opposition among his party's conservative senators and resulted in the Senate's overwhelming approval of that pact—greatly improving US-Soviet relations and therewith easing tensions that underlay the Cold War.

After serving eight years as Ronald Reagan's vice president, George Herbert Walker Bush earned the right to be considered the logical successor to the presidency. His decisive 1988 electoral victory over Democrat Michael Dukakis made him the first vice president to move directly to the presidency by election since Martin Van Buren succeeded Andrew Jackson in 1837.

Some critics described Bush's victory as simply a third term for Ronald Reagan.

Bush, a successful oilman, began his career in Texas politics with a failed bid in 1964 to unseat liberal Democratic Senator Ralph Yarborough. In 1968, he won a seat in the House of Representatives, where he waited two years for another chance to join the Senate—hoping to emulate his father, Prescott Bush, who had represented Connecticut in the Senate while the son was in his thirties. But he lost his 1970 race as well, to conservative Democrat Lloyd Bentsen. Presidents Nixon and Ford subsequently appointed Bush to a series of high-profile administrative posts. In 1980, Bush failed to win the Republican presidential nomination, but the successful candidate, Ronald Reagan, selected him as his vice-presidential running mate.

In his 1988 presidential victory, Bush lacked the coattails to add to his party's forty-five Senate seats. In his inaugural address, he called for a return to bipartisan cooperation. Noting the increasing divisiveness of Congress, owing in part to the fracturing experience of the Vietnam conflict, he urged an end of "the hard looks," the unhelpful challenging of each other's motives, the climate "in which our great parties have too often been far apart and untrusting of each other." Sitting nearby were Senate Republican Leader Bob Dole, whom he had defeated for their party's presidential nomination, and Democratic majority leader George Mitchell, a no-nonsense former federal prosecutor and judge. The new president looked in their direction. "I am putting out my hand to you. . . . This is the age of the offered hand."[107]

Working with the Senate and House, the Bush administration forged bipartisan agreements for its initial budget to tame the Reagan administration's soaring deficits and for a plan to help the troubled savings and loan industry. Yet this positive spirit quickly faded into the political realities of a strongly Democratic Congress pitted against a resolute Republican administration.

The Senate dealt the Bush administration a stunning blow after less than two months in office. By a vote of forty-seven to fifty-three, it rejected the president's nomination of former Texas senator John Tower to be secretary of defense.[108] This was the first failure to confirm a cabinet officer since the Lewis Strauss debacle thirty years earlier, and the first ever for a member of a president's initial cabinet. Senator Robert Byrd explained that his party's opposition grew out of "Tower's employment as a consultant to defense contractors after his service as an arms control negotiator; evidence bearing on a perceived pattern of excessive drinking in the not far-distant past; and allegations and rumors of womanizing."[109] After this, Republicans responded to the Democratic majority by blocking its efforts to override Bush's vetoes—of his forty-four vetoes, Congress overrode only one—and obstructing Senate action on legislation opposed by the administration.[110]

Despite being a Washington insider, President Bush displayed no interest in personally pressuring members to support his programs. Rather—and contrary to presidents from Johnson to Reagan—he preferred to have his staff make the sales calls.[111] Part of his difficulty on Capitol Hill could be traced to his "take no prisoners" chief of staff, from 1989 to 1991, former New Hampshire governor John Sununu. Holding a PhD in mechanical engineering from MIT, Sununu seemed to take a dim view of the average member of Congress. That attitude sparked a long-remembered incident during a 1990 off-campus "summit" meeting that White House officials held with senators and representatives to discuss crucial budget issues.

Sununu sat reading a newspaper with his feet propped up on a desk while lecturing his audience. Appropriations Committee chairman Robert Byrd reacted angrily. "Let me give you a piece of advice. You are the king's men. Right now the king is riding very high. But six months from now, when our boys are still sitting in the sands of Saudi Arabia, when the economy is in a nosedive and unemployment is skyrocketing, you boys will be back here begging for our help. Don't ever forget that." Byrd concluded that "President Bush would be ashamed to know that his staff had behaved so rudely," but later commented that the closed meeting then "proceeded in an atmosphere of greater respect and civility."[112] Sununu, whose personal spending of government funds for questionable purposes later brought him extensive media attention, resigned the following year. Eventually, the more diplomatic James Baker took the reins.

President Bush sent the Senate two Supreme Court appointments for approval. His September 1990 nomination of New Hampshire judge David Souter, whom Sununu and New Hampshire Senator Warren Rudman actively supported, passed easily, despite lobbying by groups representing women and blacks. Completely different in judicial philosophy was federal judge Clarence Thomas, an African American whom Bush appointed in July 1991 to succeed the court's first black member, Thurgood Marshall. Thomas's opposition to a woman's right to an abortion mobilized the National Organization of Women, which feared he might vote to overturn the court's 1973 *Roe v. Wade* decision. No one on a fifteen-member American Bar Association review board rated him as "well qualified"; thirteen put him down as "qualified," and two as "unqualified."[113] After extended hearings, the evenly divided Senate Judiciary Committee sent his nomination to the Senate without a recommendation.[114] As the Senate was preparing to vote, new charges emerged that Thomas had, a decade earlier, sexually harassed his personal assistant, Anita Hill, in the federal Office of Civil Rights. The Judiciary Committee reopened his hearings in an atmosphere characterized as a "media circus." Thomas charged the committee with perpetrating "a high-tech lynching for uppity blacks who in any way deign to think for themselves."[115] The Senate subsequently confirmed Thomas by a vote of fifty-two to forty-eight.

The Bush presidency and Congress produced notable legislation in 1990 to revise the Clean Air Act and to establish the landmark Americans with Disabilities Act. During his administration, the Berlin Wall was torn down and the Soviet Union collapsed. His notable foreign policy actions included sending twenty-four thousand US troops to Panama in 1989 to oust and capture former president Manuel Noriega, who had blocked the installation of a democratically elected successor. The secrecy, speed, success, and public approval of that operation eliminated the opportunity for Senate Democratic opposition.

A year later, when Iraq's Saddam Hussein invaded neighboring oil-rich Kuwait, Bush responded with diplomatic and military action, assembling under UN auspices a coalition of thirty-four nations, with American forces playing the dominant role. In the run-up to that conflict, he reiterated the opinion of his immediate predecessors that the 1973 War Powers Resolution was unconstitutional. But, as he later noted, his sense of obligation to consult fully with the Senate resulted in numerous personal meetings and phone calls."[116] In a 1999 address to the Senate, he observed, "If I had to pick one vote, I'd say the Senate vote of January 1991 authorizing me to use 'any means necessary' in order to liberate Kuwait was the key Senate vote during my presidency." He continued, "To be honest, for weeks, we debated whether to try and push such a resolution in the Senate. I'm glad we did bring it here and pleased that it passed. But the 52-to-47 margin was the slimmest Senate margin ever to vote for war, and naturally I regret that we couldn't convince more in the majority to help us send a clear and united signal to Saddam, and the world, about our resolve to lead."[117] Shortly before the Senate adopted that resolution, Hawaii Senator Daniel Inouye, a respected Senate elder, reflected Democratic misgivings in advising Bush, "If things go wrong, you could well be impeached."[118]

The allied forces liberated Kuwait and advanced into Iraq. In the Senate and elsewhere, Bush received intense criticism for failing to "complete the job" when he decided not to attempt to continue the drive and capture

Baghdad. Later events would demonstrate the wisdom of his restraint. Bush's conduct of the Persian Gulf War boosted his public approval to an astounding 91 percent. But an intractable recession, growing deficits, and a failure to keep his "Read my lips: no new taxes" pledge to the 1988 Republican National Convention—along with widespread "Reagan-Bush fatigue"—reduced his popularity on the eve of his 1992 election, which he lost to Democrat Bill Clinton with 38 percent of the vote to Clinton's 43 percent.

Bill Clinton's electoral margin could hardly be interpreted as a compelling mandate for a specific agenda. His greatest political assets on entering office were that he was not George H. W. Bush and that he seemed to hold the credentials of a centrist Democrat. But struggling to sort out his legislative priorities, he failed to get his administration off to a focused start. His proposal to improve treatment of gays and lesbians in the military muddied his relations on Capitol Hill, diverting lawmakers' attention from larger issues. He stumbled in naming members to his cabinet. Minor ethical lapses doomed his first two attorney-general nominees and caused the Senate to drastically tighten reporting requirements for all senior administration appointees—thereby adding serious delays to its already sluggish approval process. But Clinton avoided possible Senate controversy in his choice of two nominees to fill the Supreme Court vacancies that opened during his tenure. He chose easily confirmable federal judges Ruth Bader Ginsburg (1993) and Stephen Breyer (1994), a onetime Senate Judiciary Committee chief counsel.

The 1992 elections made Bob Dole, the Senate's minority leader since 1987, the most prominent Republican holding national office. As such, even before Clinton took on his new office, Dole announced his intent to oppose the president-elect and his legislation in new and dramatic ways. Clinton, he observed, had won the presidency in a three-candidate election by only a minority of the popular vote, and he, Dole, would now represent those who had not voted for him and serve as the president's "chaperone."[119] In carrying out that threat, Dole adopted the filibuster as his party's weapon of choice. This was new. Never before had a party leader adopted the filibuster as an instrument of overall party policy. Filibusters had always been the tool of party minorities, decade after decade, but not this way. Dole's filibusters came on measure after measure. On some he won outright; on others he forced substantive change.

This greatly frustrated Majority Leader George Mitchell and his Democrats. President Clinton's health-care plan came under fire, too. Mitchell assumed that Dole and his Republicans would not dare to filibuster so popular an idea, but filibuster they did, even as Dole pledged cooperation at the start. Secretly negotiated under the guidance of First Lady Hillary Clinton, her many advisers unknown, the bill came under savage television attack from an effective lobby campaign by the medical trade. It fell of its own weight, more than 1,300 pages of largely unreadable legislative minutiae and administrative gobbledygook.

In this Congress, Dole demonstrated impressive skills as party leader. He set a course that would lead him to the Republican nomination in the 1996 presidential election against Clinton. When he resigned from the Senate in June to prepare for that upcoming contest, he was succeeded by Mississippi Senator Trent Lott, a wily and experienced legislative tactician in his own right. Trent Lott considered Bill Clinton "the oddest president I have known." Despite a public comment that they "weren't friends," the president called the Republican leader dozens of times monthly, occasionally in the morning's small hours. "I seemed to offer some sort of rare Zen role for Clinton—the careful listener on the other end of the line who politely acknowledged the high-level ramblings of the commander in chief, and just as promptly forgot them."[120]

When Tom Daschle succeeded George Mitchell as Democratic leader in 1995, as the Democrats moved into the minority for the rest of Clinton's time in office, he, too, received many late-night calls. Daschle began to think that Clinton got "the bulk of his work done between midnight and sunrise."[121] As Senate Democratic leader, Daschle had to try to maintain effective relations with Clinton through two difficult periods. The first related to Clinton's strongly asserted belief that the Constitution gave presidents the authority to selectively veto individual line items in appropriations bills as he received them for his signature. The second involved a Senate impeachment trial.

As governor of Arkansas, Clinton had exercised line-item vetoes, which were common in other states as well. The line-item veto on the national scene had gained special attention in 1986 when President Reagan asked Congress to "give me the authority to veto waste and I'll take the responsibility. I'll make the cuts. I'll take the heat." In January 1996, Senator Bob Dole introduced the Line-Item Veto Act and the Republican-controlled Congress sent it to Clinton for his signature within three months. Immediately, a group of six senators challenged the statute's constitutionality. Although a federal district judge found it unconstitutional, the Supreme Court dismissed the case on grounds that the senators as plaintiffs were not personally and specifically injured by the law's provisions. President Clinton used the veto against provisions of the Balanced Budget Act of 1997 and the Taxpayer Relief Act of that same year.

The law was challenged a second time by parties having obvious standing, with friends of the court briefs filed by senators, including Robert Byrd. In dogged opposition, Byrd had in 1993 delivered a series of fourteen Senate floor speeches, each of which he recited from memory, decrying this abdication of legislative constitutional prerogative.[122] On June 25, 1998, the Supreme Court, in *Clinton v. City of New York*, affirmed a lower court's finding and declared the act unconstitutional on grounds that the Constitution's Presentment Clause does not allow the president to unilaterally amend or repeal portions of statutes passed by both houses of Congress.[123]

In 1995, with the House of Representatives newly under Republican control, Speaker Newt Gingrich, with the cooperation of Senate Republicans, launched a barrage of investigations of President Clinton and his government. In the midst of those investigations, most of which came to not much, Clinton was caught in a shocking sexual scandal with a young White House intern, and then he lied about it under oath. That prompted House Republicans to seek impeachment. The mathematics of the process was simple: an ordinary majority of the House of Representatives was needed to impeach, two-thirds of the Senate to convict. The Republicans had a House majority and the Senate had fifty-five Republicans. If all Republican senators voted "guilty" on an article of impeachment, they still would need a dozen Democrats to join them in order to remove Clinton.

The House Republicans badly botched the proceedings. They seemed to start well, with the Judiciary Committee chairman, Illinois' Henry Hyde, pledging balanced and responsible hearings. Then he and Republicans let loose, in ugly partisanship, their anger and fury at Clinton. To make their case, they released a special prosecutor's massive report that contained graphic and lurid details of Clinton's sexual exploits. The party whip, Tom DeLay, a pest exterminator in private life with a pest exterminator's attitude toward political opponents, turned the proceedings into a Republican Party issue, strongly pressuring House Republicans to vote for impeachment. That was a classic blunder. It had the effect of discouraging Democrats from joining this Republican assault on "their" president. With no chance for the Senate to convict Clinton, the Senate held only an abbreviated trial, with acquittal preordained.[124]

Clinton concluded his presidency in 2001 on a high note. Thanks to positive economic news, with budget surpluses from 1998 to 2001, and the lowest unemployment rate in nearly thirty years, his end-of-term public approval rating had soared to 66 percent, higher than any of his post–World War II predecessors going back to Harry Truman.[125]

Thus ended the twentieth-century duel between Senates and presidents— leaving the Senate in a far weaker position than when the century had begun. The terrorist attacks of September 11, 2001, with their awful losses, led the nation into a series of costly and essentially unwinnable wars in the Middle East. Following the model of their predecessors, Presidents George W. Bush and Barack Obama denied any responsibility to seek congressional approval to launch military action under the War Powers Resolution of 1973, and turned a blind eye to the US Constitution's explicit grant of authority to Congress, in Article I, section 8, "to declare war." President Obama argued over the definition of "hostilities," stating that his 2011 military intervention in Libya was not a "war."[126]

Political leaders in the White House and on Capitol Hill decided in the face of an uncertain economy not to finance these wars through tax increases and had difficulty—until passage of the Budget Control Act of 2011—in targeting spending reductions. In fact, the George W. Bush administration and Congress, as in earlier times, put in place significant tax cuts, particularly for the wealthy. Once in place, those cuts proved politically impossible for subsequent administrations to rescind. The huge revenue losses from the tax cuts and the astronomical costs of waging open-ended wars created record deficits that severely challenged Congress's ability to keep the nation's financial house in order. These issues defined the 2012 presidential and senatorial election campaigns and seemed certain to challenge legislative-executive relations to a degree unimaginable on that August 1789 day when George Washington angrily withdrew from the Senate chamber.

6

Living with the House of Representatives

SENATE MAJORITY LEADER HARRY REID was fed up. The Republican minority showed no intention of yielding in its opposition to a lengthening list of nominees for federal judgeships. He knew their tactic well, because his own Democrats had refined it during their recent four years in the minority. On May 10, 2007, turning from his center-aisle Senate chamber desk, he gestured to the back of the room, to the swinging doors that open to the long stone corridor leading south through a small Senate-side rotunda, into the grand rotunda, through Statuary Hall and, finally, to the chamber of the House of Representatives. Concluding a bitter statement on Republican interference with judicial nominees, Reid said, "There are times, I can tell my colleagues without any reservation, when I wish I were the Speaker of the House. The Speaker of the House doesn't have to worry about the minority. They [in the House majority simply] run over everybody. That is the way it is set up."[1]

Four years later, during a battle between a Democratic-controlled Senate and a House under Republican management, Senate Appropriations Committee chairman Daniel Inouye issued a statement on the "facts of life" in relations between the two bodies. "It is my sincere hope that the parties will remain reasonable as we seek to fund the federal government for the remainder of the fiscal year. Neither house of Congress is in a position to dictate terms to the other, so I remain hopeful that we will come to a sensible accommodation."[2] This perhaps sounded like Civics 101, but it needed to be said.

The lack of reasonableness among the parties would not have surprised the delegates to the 1787 Philadelphia constitutional convention. They

149

deliberately designed the Senate and the House to be rivals and antagonists, each to act as a restraint on the other on the road to "a sensible accommodation." On balance, the convention delegates seemed to fear the House more than the Senate, as the members of the House would be elected directly by the people. Presumably, that would make them susceptible to popular enthusiasms and transient passions, and lead them to act in haste. They also believed that the US House, like the British House of Commons, would tend to dominate the national government. As James Madison explained, the House of Representatives, backed by the people, would not permit the Senate to usurp power. The real challenge for the delegates was how to curb the House.[3]

"The people immediately should have as little to do as may be about the government," said Roger Sherman, a convention delegate from Connecticut, warning against a popularly elected House.[4] Out of these fears and alarms came a special role for the Senate: that chamber would bridle the expected recklessness of the House. "The use of the Senate," Madison said, "is to consist of its proceeding with more coolness, with more system, and with more wisdom, than the popular branch."[5] He expected the Senate to stand as "a necessary fence" against the "fickleness and passion" of majority rule.[6]

Creation of the Senate alarmed others, including Thomas Jefferson, who like John Adams, had been abroad during the Philadelphia convention. According to one legend, Jefferson asked George Washington, who had presided over that convention, why the delegates proposed a senate. "Why did you just pour your coffee in your saucer?" Washington replied. "To cool it," Jefferson answered. "Even so," Washington supposedly said, "we pour legislation into the senatorial saucer to cool it."[7]

Shaping the two houses of Congress as adversaries predictably set the members of each at odds with members of the other, and for more than two centuries they have struggled over matters great and small. Sometimes they have seemed to be bickering over trivialities. On other occasions, they have engaged in quarrels of great moment, deciding the nation's history. Underlying this heat lay a never-ending contest between them for power and prestige.

The Philadelphia convention provided not only that the Senate and the House have different powers and legislative jurisdictions, but that those serving in either chamber be subject to different qualifications and have different constituencies and terms of office. While each state in the Union would have just two senators, the size of a state's House delegation would reflect the extent of its specific population. With far fewer members, the Senate presumably would act with more prudence than the House. The convention delegates understood that larger groups were more likely than smaller ones to resort impulsively to hasty and ill-considered actions. Madison famously wrote, "Had every Athenian citizen been a Socrates, every Athenian assembly would still have been a mob."[8] If the members of the House were to be elected by popular vote, the delegates decided that senators would be chosen by each state's legislature.[9] That would make senators the elect of the elect, doubtlessly men of probity and sound judgment. The six-year term for senators and their elections on a staggered basis, with one-third of the seats subject to renewal every two years, gave senators the political security of greater continuity in office, unlike House members, whose two-year term made them so immediately responsive to popular excitements. Senators had to be at least thirty years old, five years more mature than the minimum age set for representatives.[10]

To further restrain the two bodies, the framers gave the Senate and House powers, some separate and distinct, that set them at odds. The Senate was charged with giving advice and consent to the president on treaties with foreign governments and on his appointments to federal office.[11] This gave the Senate preeminence in Congress over foreign affairs and, in time, over federal patronage. The House was assigned original jurisdiction over "all bills raising revenue," the power that Madison and other delegates assumed would give the House command of the national government much as similar power had done in Great Britain.[12] The House alone had power to impeach federal officials. The Senate alone had the authority to conduct trials to decide whether to remove said impeached officials.[13]

The very specifics of their construction as legislative bodies put them in natural competition with each other. Each regularly encroached on the privileges and authorities of the other, and each, jealous of its own prerogatives, has often bitterly rebuffed the aggressions of the other. They have long engaged in this high rivalry, each protesting from time to time the other's pretensions. Yet out of sheer necessity, the two chambers are forced to get along. Thus their formal relationships have normally seemed correct and even, at times, cordial, but beneath this veneer of formal courtesy has raged an institutional combat often marked with ridicule and mutual contempt.[14]

In his years as vice president, from 1797 to 1801, Thomas Jefferson compiled a *Manual of Parliamentary Practice* to mollify the antagonisms between senators and representatives that he, as the Senate's presiding officer, had witnessed firsthand.[15] In time, both the Senate and the House came to use Jefferson's manual to guide their own proceedings. Under his strictures, the members of both houses were forbidden to criticize the other chamber, or its members, or even to refer to them in debate. This, he wrote, would avoid "misunderstanding" between the houses. He proposed that the Speaker of the House immediately silence any member of that chamber who condemned the Senate or any senator.[16] Over the years, relying on Jefferson's manual, Speakers of the House regularly forced their colleagues to cease their floor remarks on grounds that they had broken this rule. Eventually, House members found ways to bypass Jefferson's decree so that they could continue to vent their chronic and structural hostility. They devised euphemistic phrases, such as designating the Senate as "the other body," as though referring to some remote and indistinct place.

House members enjoyed ridiculing the Senate, an instinctive response to the evident presumptions of senators about their superiority. In 1911, Wisconsin Representative Victor Berger grew so frustrated with corruption associated with state legislative election of senators that he introduced a constitutional amendment to provide for a unicameral Congress composed solely of the House of Representatives.[17] Years later, Representative Samuel Hobbs of Alabama routinely opened sessions of the House Judiciary Committee with this proposal: "Mr. Chairman, I move to abolish the Senate!"[18]

One of the most trenchant House critics of the Senate was Speaker Thomas B. Reed. In the 1890s, he regularly mocked the Senate as "a nice quiet sort of place where good representatives go when they die."[19] He once wrote a sham "history" of the 1940 presidential election, then fifty years in the future. By then, he imagined, the nation would have tired of the lackluster presidents chosen the old way and would have amended the Constitution to have the Senate, "the wisest body of men," pick "the wisest man" among them as the next president. To the astonishment of the country, in Reed's telling, when this procedure was tried for the first time, every senator received exactly one vote! Not until that moment, Reed scoffed, did the American people realize that "the Senate of the United States was one level mass of wisdom and virtue, perfect in all its parts, and radiant from North to South with that light of intelligence, which never shone on sea or shore."[20]

Finally, in 1987, two centuries after the signing of the Constitution, the House modified its rule so as to allow members to call the Senate by its actual name. But that change did not go so far as to permit members to criticize the Senate or its members. "This amendment," explained Martin Frost of Texas, its sponsor, "will allow members the freedom to make necessary reference to the Senate, but will not allow name-calling."[21]

The struggle for dominance between the Senate and House began the moment they convened for the first time in April 1789. The Senate devised a plan for sending messages and legislation between the two chambers. Under this plan, its clerk would handle that chore for all documents heading for the House. But the Senate then specified that the House should designate two of its members to carry papers to the Senate. The House collectively laughed and sent its own clerk. By all accounts, early sessions of the Senate were dull affairs, conducted behind closed doors for the first few years and with only a handful of members present. House proceedings were never dull, with dozens of members present and competing for attention. In the earliest decades, it was not uncommon for a six-year Senate term to be filled, successively, by as many as three or four individuals, as members resigned to run for the House, or for a state office closer to the real-world concerns of their constituencies.

In the First Congress, Senator William Maclay of Pennsylvania had hostile reactions whenever he visited the House. "The House," Maclay wrote in his journal of 1789, "have certainly greatly debased their dignity, use base invective, indecorous language; three or four up at a time, manifesting signs of passion, the most disorderly wanderings in their speeches, telling stories, [and] private anecdotes."[22] That first House had sixty-five members, compared to the Senate's twenty-six. As the nation grew, so did the size of the House, and so, too, did the discord of its debates.

The House-Senate balance began to shift in the 1820 as issues related to the westward expansion of slavery moved to the forefront. As Northern states picked up proportionally more representatives with each decennial census, Southern states—equal in number, but not population, to the Northern states—came to understand that the Senate alone would be their preferred vehicle for equal influence on Capitol Hill. Thus, by the early 1830s, the Senate entered its Golden Age, a time of great orations and telling debate on the very nature and thrust of the Constitution and the federal union. In their debate on the 1820 Missouri Compromise, senators had won high praise for the caliber of their arguments. Where the House had earlier dominated the Congress's response to national questions, the Senate now moved to take over that role.

In 1827, with grave misgivings, Daniel Webster left the House to represent Massachusetts in the Senate.[23] The next year, the election of Andrew Jackson as president turned the political world upside down. Partially at Webster's invitation in 1831, former House Speaker Henry Clay returned to the Senate he had left twenty years before. Like Webster, he hesitated initially. "My habits are formed for the House," the Kentuckian said, "and I doubt if I should feel so much at home elsewhere."[24] The third member of this fierce triumvirate arrived in 1832. No longer comfortable as vice president, South Carolina's John C. Calhoun quit that office for the greater freedom of expression available to him from the Senate's floor than from its presiding officer's rostrum. The three men transformed the place—rivals united against President Jackson. They quickly became champions of their regions: Webster of the North, Calhoun of the South, and Clay of the West.[25] Opposing them in the Senate was Missouri's mighty Thomas Hart Benton, a formidable parliamentarian and Jackson's special ally.

Andrew Jackson had his own ideas about the role of the president and that of the federal government, ideas that clashed with those of previous chief executives. He intended to take control of the legislative process and to pay off the national debt. Although he had support in the House of Representatives, the Senate would mount tough resistance to his new brand of partisan democracy. In the first Congress to meet after Jackson's inauguration, the Senate caught the nation's attention and admiration with an extraordinary series of debates. Ostensibly on public-land policy, the debates between Webster and South Carolina Senator Robert Hayne expanded into a historic argument about the meaning of the Constitution. Many senators took part, starting in January 1830, each expounding his views on states' rights and whether the Constitution had created a single nation or a compact among mutually dependent but ultimately sovereign states. This debate greatly enhanced the Senate's prestige, at least partly at the House's expense.[26]

Two years later, in January 1832, the young French aristocrat Alexis de Tocqueville, spent a fortnight in Washington at the end of a nine-month study-tour of the United States. He visited the Senate and the House several times. Later, in his book *Democracy in America*, Tocqueville described his impressions of both. Echoing Senator Maclay's 1789 observation, he savagely criticized the House for the "vulgar demeanor" of its members, "mostly village lawyers, men in trade, or even persons of the lower class of society." He lavished praise on the Senate and its members, "the celebrated men of America," men more congenial to this young nobleman. "The Senate," he wrote flatteringly, "is composed of eloquent advocates, distinguished generals, wise magistrates, and statesmen of note, whose arguments would do honor to the most remarkable parliamentary debates of Europe." Tocqueville attributed this "strange contrast" between members of the House and the Senate to the election of House members by "the folly of the people" and senators "by the wisdom of state legislatures." An acute observer, Tocqueville was not much of a prophet in writing that unless the Constitution was amended to provide for indirect election of representatives, like senators, the American republic would risk "perishing miserably among the shoals of democracy."[27]

Senator Thomas Hart Benton emerged as Tocqueville's chief congressional critic. A former House member, he interpreted the Frenchman's book as an aristocratic attack on President Jackson and his brand of democracy. Drawing on his experience in both bodies, Benton wrote that senators and representatives were much the same, not haughty patricians in one house and peasants in the other. "The Senate," he asserted, "is in great part composed of the pick of the House."[28] Among the forty-eight senators Tocqueville interviewed, nearly half, including Webster and Clay, were former House members—not an unusual composition. From the Senate's earliest days, House members had sought to join its ranks, although the increasing tide had become more evident after the 1820s. Throughout the Senate's history, between one-third and one-half of its members at any one time had previously served in the House.

The House that Tocqueville so harshly censured had 215 members, and that body, like every House before it, had, in Tocqueville's phrase, a "startling" difference from the Senate: the confused roar and seeming chaos of its debates.[29] The hurly-burly of House debates, a byproduct of congested and acoustically deficient chambers, had long marred the House's reputation and long would continue to do so. With far fewer members, the Senate had the luxury of conducting its debates with dignity and decorum, a difference readily noticed by observers both foreign and domestic. Visiting the House in the 1880s, James Bryce, the British author and diplomat, was struck by the "noise and turmoil" of the House's debates, a din so loud as to drown out the words of the orator of the moment.[30] The House would continue to expand its membership until space considerations finally forced the modern cap of 435, set early in the twentieth century.

By the late nineteenth century, of course, the House's debates were not as incoherent as they seemed to casual visitors. Forced by its sheer numbers, the House had long since taken steps to limit its debates. The first of these restrictions came in 1811, when under Henry Clay's guidance the House revised its moribund "Previous Question" rule to allow a majority of its members to cut off all further debate and force an immediate vote on the pending question.[31] In 1841, again under Clay's guidance, even though he had by then moved back to the Senate, the House adopted its "one-hour rule" and applied it to all House speeches.[32] This hardly proved an effective deterrent with so many members entitled to an hour on every bill and every amendment.

In the years after the Civil War, the House's Speakers and their lieutenants gradually strengthened their controls over the body's operations. Speakers had long appointed members to the various standing committees, but Maine's James G. Blaine, first elected Speaker in 1869, used that authority for political advantage as he packed key committees with his supporters.[33] Kentucky's John Carlisle, Speaker in the 1880s, immensely strengthened the Speakership by taking control over who would speak. "For what purpose does the gentleman rise?" Carlisle intoned to any member seeking recognition. The member had to explain and Carlisle then decided whether to allow him to speak.[34] In these years, the House's leaders gradually strengthened the chamber's Rules Committee, not only to decide which measures would come before the House but also under what terms they would emerge.[35]

By the 1890s, these practices placed the House in what amounted to a legislative straightjacket, with minority party members all but relegated to irrelevance. Speaker Thomas B. Reed's merciless use of those new weapons gained him the sobriquet "Czar Reed." He explained his view of the two-party system. "The best system is to have one party govern and the other party watch; and on general principles, I think it would be better for us to govern and for the Democrats to watch."[36] His successor, Illinois' Joseph Cannon, studied Reed's methods and improved on them. A bitter House revolt against Cannon in 1910 modified some of these strictures and curbed the Speaker's powers, but those changes still left the House as a leadership-controlled legislative machine. Speaker Reed himself had stated as much during his reign: "The House of Representatives is no longer a deliberative body."[37]

If these changes made the House a more effective legislative machine, able to move with promptness and purpose, they left the House's members confronting what seemed a bewildering maze of parliamentary practices and precedents. Asher Hinds, for many years the official House parliamentarian, vividly pointed to the declining importance of the body's individual members. In 1907, he published five massive volumes of House legislative precedents. In careful detail, he listed a total of 7,346 separate and distinct technicalities of House procedure, almost all of which restricted the behavior of that chamber's members. "The pages of these volumes," Hinds wrote, "show a constant subordination of the individual to the necessities of the whole House as the voice of the national will."[38]

The Senate had taken a far different course. In their separate and starkly contrasting evolutions as legislative bodies, the House and the Senate became inversions of each other: the House a legislative factory with factory methods, the Senate often a courtesy-ridden debating society with each member entitled to speak for as long as he or she could remain standing. Senators came to revere the filibuster and what they called their "freedom of debate," while representatives prided themselves on their legislative efficiency and dispatch. For much of the nineteenth century, however, the House had its own form of filibuster under which members of the minority could cripple the majority. With the House going first, and the Senate soon to follow, both chambers adopted what they called the "Disappearing Quorum."

For any legislative activity to take place, each body had to have a quorum, a majority of duly elected members, present. Under this tactic, those opposing a particular action would respond to their names on a quorum call. On the roll call vote that followed, however, they would remain silent, thereby causing the quorum to disappear. On occasion, in the throes of this tactic, both chambers went through a long series of quorum calls and roll call votes with no voting quorum, until the majority finally gave up. In 1890, the newly ascendant Speaker Reed put an end to this form of filibuster by a simple tactic of his own: he counted as "present" those members of the minority still in their seats who had refused to vote. That provided the quorum. His action set off a near riot on the House floor—but the House's filibuster was no more.[39] A master parliamentarian, Reed made himself the House's most powerful Speaker ever. Six feet two inches tall and over 250 pounds, he devised his own sardonic way of informing the minority party leaders of his plans for the House. "Gentlemen," he would say in language unthinkable on the Senate side, "we have decided to perpetrate the following outrage."[40]

There were obvious shortcomings in the legislative methods of both the Senate and the House. These shortcomings had become plain with Speaker Reed's near dictatorship and senators' skillful use of the filibuster. In 1906, a congressional correspondent, O. O. Stealey of the *Louisville Courier-Journal*, shrewdly contrasted the legislative sins of both chambers. "The majority in the House is undoubtedly unfair and unjust at times to the minority," he wrote, "and . . . in the Senate the minority is often unquestionably unjust and unfair to the majority."[41] Ironically, to casual visitors in their galleries, the two houses in session seemed the very reverse of their actual realities: the Senate orderly and restrained, the House obviously undisciplined. As late as the 1930s, before introduction of a voice-amplification system, the House in operation still acted with all the familiar turmoil and confusion that had upset visiting observers from the beginning. "Debate in the House is indescribable," a congressional reporter wrote in 1931. "It is a shambles of low humor, impossibly absurd assertions made as statements of fact, violent partisanship, clamor, confusion, and burlesque. Members wander about the hall, laughing and talking."[42]

This was a time when senators took exceeding care to appear dignified and sober, dressed in formal wear for their Senate chamber appearances. They did at times have moments of high tensions, angry recriminations, and even awkward disarray, but often these tensions were concealed through debates that offered a high degree of mutual respect and courtesy. Long before the twentieth century, the Senate's processes tended to exalt every senator, even as those of the House tended to denigrate every representative.

From the beginning, members of the Senate and the House found natural grounds to quarrel over their legislative rights and prerogatives. As early as 1792, they came into conflict over government spending. President George Washington wanted to submit a treaty with Algiers as an orderly way to pay ransom to the Barbary pirates for Americans they had captured. He had Secretary of State Thomas Jefferson sound out members of both houses on how best to provide the money for the bribes. Jefferson learned that although senators were willing enough to approve such a treaty, they did not want the House involved in the transaction. They feared that members of the House would use this as a precedent to encroach thereafter on the Senate's special authority over treaties. In the end, President Washington did submit the treaty to the Senate, and the House went along with voting for the tribute money.[43]

Several years later, a more significant treaty propelled the House and Senate into angry confrontation. The Jay Treaty of 1794 sought to settle US-British disputes left over from the Revolutionary War that threatened to reignite hostilities. Adherents to the two recently formed political parties were bitterly divided; the Jeffersonian Republicans attacked the measure's provisions as near-treason. They failed in the Senate to block the treaty, and in the House and Senate to deny the appropriations necessary to carry it into operation. House members nonetheless gave spirited notice to the Senate that as long as the House had a role in passing appropriations and other legislation, senators would not have exclusive control over treaties.[44]

This threat flowed from the Senate-House quarrel, dating from 1789, over the Constitution's language granting the House the initiative on bills "raising revenue." House members came to insist that the Constitution gave them original jurisdiction over all money bills—taxes, tariffs, and appropriations.[45] Senators argued for a much narrower definition. In 1833, Henry Clay creatively contended that a revenue bill he sponsored could properly originate in the Senate because it reduced revenues rather than raised them. His colleague Daniel Webster disagreed. "If it was a money bill," Webster said, "it belonged to the House of Representatives to originate it."[46] Nonetheless, senators continued to originate such revenue-raising bills, with some finding their way into public law, much to the aggravation of their House counterparts.[47]

In the years before the Civil War, the Senate largely refrained from challenging the House on appropriations bills, most of which also carried provisions for raising revenue as well as spending it. Only once, in 1857, did the Senate actually originate a spending bill, but this caused no trouble: the House simply ignored it. In the aftermath of the Civil War, with the immense increase in the federal government's spending activities, the House and the Senate restructured their money committees. Until then, the House Ways and Means Committee and the Senate Finance Committee had primary jurisdiction over taxes, tariffs, and appropriations. In 1865, the House created a separate appropriations committee, and the Senate echoed that innovation two years later.[48] This new arrangement seemed to clear the way for the Senate to initiate appropriations bills, but the House then and thereafter stoutly resisted any change in the old ways of dealing with money matters. Senators protested from time to time, but they continued to acquiesce to the House's claim of jurisdiction. Even so, by then senators had gained two concessions from the representatives. The meetings of House-Senate conference committees would take place in the Senate's committee rooms, and a senator would always preside. Conference committees played a crucial role in the legislative process in settling the differences between House and Senate versions of the same measures. The place of meeting had little actual significance, outside of deference to the senators, but the chairmanship surely did matter. Whoever presided over these sessions not only set the agenda for their discussions, but also proposed the ways to compromise their differences.

In time, however, senators came to rely on their acknowledged authority to amend House bills as their way to initiate desired provisions. Even before the Civil War, particularly under the influence of the large revenue needs of the 1846–48 war with Mexico, the Senate had been making substantial increases by amendment to House-passed appropriations.[49] In 1872, devising a dramatic new tactic that senators would use ever after, the Senate tacked onto a minor and unrelated House bill an extensive revision of the tariff laws, an adroit maneuver that deeply offended House leaders. Technically speaking, the senators were not originating anything. In these years, senators also developed other techniques to impose their will on the House. One was to strike everything after the enacting clause of a House bill and then substitute an entirely different measure.[50] Another, despite Senate rules against it, was to offer proposals for freestanding legislation as amendments to high-priority House appropriations bills.[51] To curb this practice, the House in 1875 adopted a rule forbidding House-Senate conference committees to accept such Senate amendments unless they were germane to the subject at hand and also reduced actual spending.[52]

By this time, the handling of appropriations bills had become a familiar routine. The House committee and the House normally cut funds requested by the administration. The Senate committee and the Senate then responded by restoring the funds cut and adding more appropriations. Finally, a House-Senate conference committee would work out a compromise. The Senate had become a "court of last resort." Acting always after the House had acted, senators assumed an appellate stance, reviewing critically what the House had done and then considering pleas to reverse those decisions. These came not only from executive branch officials, but also from frustrated House members whose own colleagues had denied valued home-state projects.[53]

In these years, senators acted aggressively on all kinds of money bills, often to the House's dismay. In 1883, there arose widespread demand for tariff revision. When the House failed to act, senators again used the tactic of adding major tariff provisions to a trivial bill that the House had already agreed to.[54] In 1897, working on a new set of House tariff revisions, the Senate added 872 amendments, savaging the House-passed bill.[55] In 1901, the House approved a bill repealing some stamp taxes; the Senate struck out everything after the enacting clause and substituted language to reduce taxes on beer and tobacco.[56]

Within a decade after creating their respective appropriations committees, the Senate and House complicated their mutual relations by transferring control over funding decisions for politically lucrative rivers and harbors projects, and for new post offices and post roads, from those spending panels to legislative committees.[57] This handicapped both of the appropriations committees on overall budget decisions and inadvertently weakened the House in its struggles over these measures with the Senate.

It also led to what the House's conservative members regarded as spending extravagances. This situation persisted until 1921 when, in a reform of committee jurisdictions, the House and Senate restored full appropriations jurisdiction to their appropriations committees.[58]

Throughout their two-plus centuries of guarded relations, the Senate and House have had their most direct contact through conference committees— especially those to resolve differing versions of appropriations bills. Early in the First Congress, both chambers agreed to settle disagreements on legislation by appointing members from each body to negotiate a mutually acceptable final version. If they failed to find common ground, the measure failed. These conference committees, whose members are called "managers," played an obviously important role in the legislative process. Over the years, the managers devised tactics and stratagems of their own, and they became so important in time that collectively they amounted to a "third house" of Congress. Conference committees formed a natural battlefield for the rival houses, with senators and representatives occasionally engaged in furious political combat.[59]

By the nature of their assignment, the managers for the Senate and the House were expected to defend their chamber's version of the legislation and to make their decisions on adjustments within the terms of the two measures at hand. Within a year, however, managers violated that assumption. In June 1790, the two houses had passed bills to create the US diplomatic service. Both versions had set $30,000 for the expenses of American ministers abroad. On the recommendation of Secretary of State Thomas Jefferson, however, the conferees increased the amount to $40,000. In reporting back the conference agreement to the House, the conferees drew criticism for exceeding their authority, but both the House and the Senate ultimately approved the adjusted bill. The conferees apparently acted almost casually in approving the increase, but here they set a precedent of great significance.[60]

In that 1790 conference committee, the senators had a designated chairman and so did the representatives. In function, however, the senators' chairman, New York's Rufus King, appears to have actually chaired the conference meetings and to have spoken on behalf of the other members. This was a natural role for the senator, as natural as senators' presumed superior rank over mere representatives, and it would become the pattern for conference committee operations. Not only did a senator routinely chair the committee sessions, but, as was customary, those committees customarily met in the senators' quarters, thereby subjecting the House's conferees to what they came to resent as a second humiliation. In spirit, this was not unlike the difficulties between senators and representatives over revenue measures. Decade after decade, until well into the twentieth century, senators insisted on their prerogatives in conference committees, embittering the representatives caught in their pretensions.[61]

Senior members of the House, meeting senators in conference committees, had confidence that normally they could out-argue and outmaneuver the senators. "Senate snobs to the contrary," explained Missouri's Representative Richard Bolling, a party strategist in the 1970s, "House members have generally shown themselves more knowledgeable than senators about particular bills in conference." That was a view shared by most representatives. Gerald Ford, a veteran of many years in the House, had no doubts about this. "We thought the members of the Other Body were not the best legislators," he said, reminiscing about his House days, "We were."[62]

House members were limited to service on only one major committee. That tended to make them especially knowledgeable in fields of their specialization, a reality that senators grudgingly respected. And, they had another advantage. Traditionally, the House conducted far more intensive committee hearings on legislation than the Senate did. This was notably true on appropriations and tax measures, areas of the House's traditional authority.[63]

Senators developed their own methods of operations for the often difficult chores involved in these confrontations with the House, but they suffered from a significant handicap. There were, of course, far fewer senators than members of the House. That meant that senators each had to assume a larger share of the legislative workload than their House colleagues did. Senators routinely served on many more committees and subcommittees than representatives. Prior to reforms in the 1970s, some senators served on more than thirty. That logically had the effect of making them less than attentive to the majority of these panels' work.

All the same, the Senate had its own powerful weapons, which included a roster of senators skilled in legislative maneuvering and substantive expertise. When they spoke, they commanded attention. Moreover, the Senate's members had two distinct advantages in comparison with members of the House: one structural, the chairmanships of House-Senate conference committees; the other extra-legal—the option to threaten a filibuster.

Over the years, senators have commonly complained that their conferees too often failed adequately to defend the Senate's position on disputed bills. In 1948, for example, Arkansas Senator J. William Fulbright sardonically congratulated Senate conferees for blatantly disregarding the majority votes of the rank-and-file members of the Senate. "It is quite clear," he said in a Senate speech, "that regardless of what the common members of the body may wish, the conferees make the decision."[64] In 1981, when Oregon's Mark Hatfield became chairman of the Senate Appropriations Committee, he tried to mobilize his committee colleagues to confront House conferees, because, in his words, the Senate generally gets "taken to the cleaners."[65] In cases when senators failed to prevail in House-Senate conferences, they have been known to apologize to the Senate. "If we stayed there until the cows came home," explained Rhode Island's John Pastore to the Senate about his fellow conferees' failing to face down the House members, "the answer would have been the same. The House was adamant, but the Senate did try."[66] In 1970, Senate Majority Leader Mike Mansfield complained that senators did not make a real effort in these confrontations. "All I'm asking," Mansfield pleaded, "is that senators stand on their feet and not give in too often or too easily, as they do on occasion with the House."[67]

Not all legislation passes through conference committees. In the modern Congress, only about one of every ten bills undergoes this scrutiny. And, in the bitterly partisan early twenty-first century, complex bills have been pulled back to avoid the additional opportunities a conference provides for derailing "must-pass" legislation. This results in one chamber having no option but to pass a less-troublesome version enacted by the other house. But, until the twenty-first century, almost every measure of importance had to survive conference-committee examination, and these conference committees from the start operated with extraordinary powers. Their sessions were customarily informal and until the 1970s conducted behind closed doors. In the mid-nineteenth century, the House and Senate adopted a joint rule providing that conference committee reports on legislation could not be amended. That meant that each house had to vote the measure up or down as it emerged from the conference committee—an immense power for the conferees.

Just as differences between the House and Senate eroded efforts to operate conference committees, so, too, have those differences made it difficult to maintain a system of joint rules, which members considered essential in the early years of congressional operations.

The general purpose of the joint rules, as indicated in the earliest journals of the two houses, was "for the enrollment, attestation, publication, and preservation of the acts of Congress, and to regulate the mode of presenting addresses, and other acts to the President of the United States." The greatest single burst of activity occurred on August 6, 1789, with the adoption of

seven rules added to four earlier regulations governing conference committees and the presentation of messages. Both chambers agreed to a few
additional rules during the early and mid-nineteenth century, but only once,
in 1822, did they bring consistency to the entire set through a general
revision. Implicit in the survival of the joint rules were two potentially crippling procedural questions: Could one house repeal a joint rule without the
other's consent? And was it necessary for the House, all of whose members'
terms expired every two years, to readopt these joint rules at the start of each
Congress? During any given session of a Congress, a controversial joint rule
could spark the destruction of the entire system. In 1876, Joint Rule 22 did
just that.

Adopted in February 1865, Joint Rule 22 established new procedures for
counting presidential electoral votes and was employed without controversy
in 1865, 1869, and 1873. The disputed presidential election of 1876, however,
imposed an unsustainably heavy burden for Joint Rule 22. Under the provisions of this rule, either house was allowed to invalidate any state's electoral
votes. In recent contests, the Republican Party had controlled both houses,
but in 1876, party control was divided with a Democratic majority in the
House. Early that year, anticipating difficulties, the Republican Senate had
voted to repeal Joint Rule 22 on the grounds that each chamber had a constitutional right to establish its own procedures. By ignoring the Senate's
action, the House created a deadlock in the vote-counting process. Under
threat of grave constitutional crisis, both bodies devised for this occasion a
special electoral commission to decide on the validity of the disputed ballots.
In 1887, Congress removed the matter from the control of joint rules by
enacting a statute that required concurrent action by both houses to reject
electoral votes. Three years earlier, as part of a general revision of its rules,
the Senate had proposed an updated code of joint rules. The House failed to
act on this code and other related proposals that followed over the next few
years. By 1889, as Congress celebrated completion of its one hundredth year,
it acknowledged the distinctiveness of its two houses by abandoning further
efforts to revive the joint rules. Despite this lapse in an official system of
joint rules, many of the procedures they instituted have endured, embedded
in statute or common practice.

Joint committees are obvious appendages to a bicameral legislature. They
have existed both as temporary, goal-oriented panels, and permanent bodies
designed to maintain competence in complex subject areas. The Senate and
House established the first temporary joint committees in the spring of
1789, one to prepare their joint rules and the second to manage acts of

Congress being sent to the president for signature. Early in the nineteenth century, the two houses created joint panels, with equal representation from both chambers, but chaired by a senator, to oversee the Library of Congress (1802) and congressional printing operations (1846). During the Civil War and Reconstruction eras, Congress increased the number of its joint committees to investigate matters related to the conduct and aftermath of that conflict, but for the remainder of the century, with separate parties controlling the two houses for much of that time, there was little incentive for continuing the joint cooperation that such committees were created to foster.

In the immediate post–World War II era, congressional reformers once again landed on the idea of joint committees, attracted by the inherent efficiency in centralizing expertise in one bicameral panel. They believed this would avoid the need to have witnesses spend long, repetitive hours on both sides of Capitol Hill. It would also promote the deepening of staff expertise in highly complex topical areas.[68] Among those that flourished in the postwar era were the Joint Economic Committee (1946–), the Joint Committee on Atomic Energy (1946–77), and the Joint Committee on Defense Production (1950–77). Until 1953, just as with conference committees, senators traditionally chaired joint committees. That changed when House members of the Joint Committee on Atomic Energy insisted that one of their own serve as chairman. In the years that followed, the individuals involved gradually worked out an arrangement to rotate between the House and Senate the chairmanships of such committees every Congress. By the 1960s, however, the concept of joint committees had again lost its appeal as each house found more reasons to guard its hard-won prerogatives in a climate where antagonisms between the House and Senate regularly exceed those between each chamber's political parties. In 1995, Republican Speaker Newt Gingrich enjoyed amusing his audiences with this jibe: "We should never forget that House Democrats are our adversaries; the Senate is our enemy."[69]

Rarely did the Senate or House grant joint committees authority to report legislation—a power held closely by the standing committees of each house. At its demise in 1977, the Joint Committee on Atomic Energy became the last panel to have such reporting authority. Until the 2011 creation of the short-lived Joint Special Committee on Deficit Reduction, Congress had continued to rely on joint panels for periodic special events, such as the quadrennial Joint Committee on Presidential Inaugural Arrangements. But for high-profile investigations, such as the 1970s Watergate affair and the 1980s Iran-Contra scandal, where the investigative efficiencies of a single joint committee would have seemed warranted, the two chambers have chosen to work sequentially or in parallel.[70] The Iran-Contra committees met jointly but as separate panels, each with its own chairperson.

As of the second decade of the twenty-first century, there were four joint committees: the Joint Committee on Printing, the Joint Committee on the Library of Congress, and the Joint Committee on Internal Revenue Taxation—all of whose congressional members also served on their chambers' directly corresponding standing committees—and the more broadly constituted Joint Economic Committee.[71]

Members of these joint committees, taking a historical view, have had reason to reflect on a shift that surely would have surprised James Madison and his fellow Constitution drafters. The fundamental changes in the manner of electing senators have tended to reverse the institutional roles of the House and the Senate. By the end of the nineteenth century, most of those seeking election to the Senate publicly campaigned for the job, not unlike those campaigning for House seats. The state legislatures had long before lost the substance of their constitutionally assigned role to choose senators, at first owing to creation of political parties and state party conventions, and later to the newly developed party primaries, in which state legislators committed to endorse those who won the popular vote. By 1913, when the states ratified the Constitution's Seventeenth Amendment, mandating direct popular election of US senators, most senators—many of them former House members—were already experienced campaigners, fully familiar with election tactics and maneuvers.

These changes had significant impact on the Senate and its members' attitudes. One of those who witnessed these changes as they were adopted, George Rothwell Brown, a savvy congressional correspondent, saw the new election processes stripping each senator of the once-dignified rank of ambassador from his state and making him instead a mere "hustler for votes." This, Brown reported, had dramatic consequences for the Senate's relationship with the House. "When the Senate had been made up of ambassadors of states, and not the representatives of the people, it was conservative, and performed the function of being a check upon the House, but when the Senate became responsive to the popular will it showed a striking tendency to be even more susceptible than the House itself to the constantly fluctuating opinion of the people and the passions and prejudice of the hour."[72]

Although members of the House liked to denigrate the Senate and mock senators' pretensions, it was natural for some of them to consider running for the Senate as it was for senators to consider running for the presidency. Some of the House's ablest members preferred to remain in the House, but for many, despite their complaints, the Senate held an almost mystical allure. To them, in reality, the Senate seemed grand, and every election year a small band of them, some with great trepidation, risked their political careers to try for the Senate. The odds against them were formidable, and a majority of those who tried normally failed. That reality scared away some representatives from making the attempt, but every election year a new group volunteered.

There was much about a senator's job to tempt a House member. The six-year term came from the Constitution, but there were many other advantages to a career in the Senate, not least of which were broader public recognition, the gravity assumed for senators' opinions, and the fawning attention of administration officials, lobbyists, and hostesses, both in Washington and at home. Almost every senator had ready access to generous campaign contributions, and, until the 1980s, substantial speaking fees as well. Most important of all, a senator held real power in the government, unlike the obscurity that was the fate of most members of the House. There was much more, including party patronage, the ability to steer large projects to one's state, and, of course, the freedom to voice her or his views from the Senate floor to one's heart's content, a far cry from the stringent limits imposed on just about every member of the House.

Former House members, elected to the Senate, universally comment on one major difference: Senate leadership. In the House, the Speaker leads from the rostrum (his or her party governs, the other party watches); in the Senate, the leaders of both parties carefully watch one another as they govern from the floor.

7

The Center to Which Everyone Comes

FOR DECADES, THE SENATE CARRIED on without a strong, formal leadership structure. No one seemed to notice or care. This vacuum was not particularly surprising in a legislative body whose members arrived viewing themselves as ambassadors of semi-sovereign states, equal in the councils of the Senate irrespective of their states' population size or natural resources. The most any nascent leader could hope for was to be politely regarded as first among equals. Yet as former Senate leader Howard Baker explained, "Someone must speak for the party. Someone must speak for the Senate. Someone must create an indelible position out of one hundred contending voices. Someone must make sure that the Senate functions."[1] At its origins in the late eighteenth century, the Senate had so few members that there seemed to be no need for complicated procedures or official leaders to guide its operations. The delegates at the Philadelphia Convention made no provision in the Constitution for Senate leadership, nor did the authors of *The Federalist*, who aimed to explain in detail how that document would operate, concern themselves with this question. To give the vice president something to do when he was not checking on the health of the president, they made him president of the Senate. His leadership role would be to convene and adjourn the Senate, appoint officers and aides, settle procedural disputes, and announce the decision of the Senate at the conclusion of votes. In his absence, the Senate would appoint one of its members president pro tempore to perform those same functions.

At first, those in the new government dismissed partisan politics as mere "factionalism," but within a few years, senators—and House members, too—began to divide into what amounted to political parties: the Federalists supporting strong government and the Anti-Federalists favoring limited government.[2] Party feelings had grown so intense by 1797 that, according to Thomas Jefferson's account, some quarreling senators refused to speak to each other outside the Senate chamber and would "cross the street to avoid meeting."[3] The unexpected development of organized partisanship suddenly made it mandatory to have strategists available to outwit the opposition and push a contested legislative agenda through to enactment.

A significant example of such leadership, applied from outside the Senate, appears in the activities of the first secretary of the treasury, Alexander Hamilton, who unhesitatingly presented Congress with a series of controversial proposals to establish the government's credit and financial resources. He then worked shrewdly to line up the votes in both bodies to enact them into law. These maneuvers soon pitted him against Thomas Jefferson, then Washington's secretary of state, and brought down on Hamilton savage complaints of his "corrupt squadron" at the Treasury and his kept "gladiators" in the Senate.[4] Hamilton had formidable allies in the Senate, including both of New York's senators: Phillip Schuyler, his father-in-law, and Rufus King. Hamilton saw himself as the president's prime minister with a legislative program to enact.

The earliest sustained impetus to the development of internal leadership hit the Senate with great force during the presidency of Andrew Jackson, from 1829 to 1837. Jackson seized the reins of presidential power more forcefully than had any of his six predecessors. Such a polarizing figure, fiercely intent on subordinating the Senate to his purposes, summoned into existence an identifiable class of visible and eloquent Senate leaders. Daniel Webster of Massachusetts and Henry Clay of Kentucky expressed bitter reservations at Jackson's new democracy and the dramatic changes he brought to the presidency in his arbitrary way. Clay shaped the Whig Party, which emerged in opposition to Jackson's Democrats. The president vetoed bills merely because he did not like them. He opposed federally financed public works projects, and he made plain his hostility to the "Money Monster," the federally incorporated US Bank, which was dear to the young country's money interests as well as to Clay and Webster.

Senator Thomas Hart Benton of Missouri, a politician of startling vanity, took upon himself the role of Jackson's chief defender and apologist. Leading the opposition in the Senate, as though by right, was Senator Clay, a political and personal enemy of Jackson. Clay and Benton, both talented parliamentarians, knew how to work behind the scenes to secure votes. They used those skills to the fullest. They assumed leadership in the Senate by the sheer force of their personalities. These were not timid men.

By the early 1840s, leaders had arisen in the Senate as champions for the contending arguments: the Senate's Great Triumvirate was composed of Webster for the North, Calhoun for the South, and Clay for the West. Benton had his own role as leader of the Jackson Democrats. All four constantly debated each other, all with eloquence. John C. Calhoun was the theorist, calculating how Negro slavery was morally good and necessary. Daniel Webster was all talk, from time to time unburdening himself of a statesman's oration, paying little attention to the mechanics of leadership and the nitty-gritty of lining up votes. Henry Clay and Thomas Benton worked those details, one for the Whigs, the other for the Democrats, and in their struggles they found their colleagues not always cooperative.[5]

In earlier years, the House of Representatives largely initiated and debated Congress's significant legislation. But, now, as legislation focused more intensely on issues dividing the nation's sections and now, as the Senate, unlike the House, provided equal representation to the thirteen states of the North and the thirteen states of the South, that burden had shifted to the Senate.[6] That made Clay and Benton the principal power brokers for the entire Congress. Until 1841, Clay had the handicap of needing to get along with Jacksonian Democrat Martin Van Buren in the White House. That changed with the 1841 inauguration of the first Whig president, William Henry Harrison, and with him, a Whig majority in the Senate. Clay resolved to make the best of his new reality. From his desk in the Senate, he would act as a kind of prime minister for President Harrison. He treated the chief executive brusquely, all but giving him orders. This moved Harrison to protest, "Mr. Clay, you forget that I am the President."[7]

Clay began by calling his Whig senators into caucus. He had them vote to urge President Harrison to call a special session of Congress. Harrison summoned the session for late May 1841, but by then Harrison had died unexpectedly, and Vice President John Tyler, a sometime Democrat and doubtful Whig, had replaced him. Tyler made a few suggestions to the new Congress, but Clay dismissed them to offer his own legislative program. Among his major proposals were creation of a new national bank and a new way to distribute the proceeds of public land sales.[8] A master of Senate politicking, Clay had a Whig majority at his back and assumed he could proceed at will. Benton soon taught him otherwise.

Working behind the scenes, Benton rallied his Democrats to undertake what amounted to the Senate's first organized filibuster in order to block

Clay's measures.[9] Under Benton's leadership, his minority party colleagues not only spoke at length against Clay's purposes, but offered crippling amendment after crippling amendment to harass the Whig leader. After each day's combat in the Senate, Benton and his stalwarts met privately to concoct another batch of dilatory amendments.[10] Clay succeeded in passing legislation to create a new national bank only to have Tyler veto it. Humiliated, Clay publicly denounced the president so violently that he could no longer function as the party's unofficial floor leader in the Senate. A few months later, in March 1842, he quit the Senate, intending never to return.[11] Benton stayed on to take up with Webster and Calhoun the ever-increasing quarrels over the nature of the government, the extension of slavery into the territories, and states' rights.[12]

The admission of Texas as a state in 1845, acquisition of the vast territories in the Southwest and West, and spoils of the 1846–48 war with Mexico greatly increased the stakes for which Washington politicians were gambling. At risk was the life of the nation. Senators, including the leaders, spoke openly of potential secession and the ensuing breakup of the federal Union. The hysteria of much of their quarreling made reconciliation difficult.

When Henry Clay returned to the Senate in December 1849, he resolved to seek a "comprehensive scheme" to reconcile the warring factions. In January 1850, he announced eight separate measures granting concessions to both the Southern firebrands and their Northern antagonists in what he hoped would produce a reasonable settlement of all controversial questions.[13] The most controversial were admitting California as a free state and adopting a more effective fugitive slave law. The debate ran on for three months, and it was an extraordinary one. Clay was past seventy years old and seriously ailing, but he stayed on the Senate floor to manage the legislation as best he could.[14]

For all his eloquence and parliamentary skills, Henry Clay was unable to pass his plan, now an "omnibus" bill—a vehicle carrying lots of passengers. Stephen Douglas, the Democratic senator from Illinois, took over the leadership. He shrewdly commented, "By combining the measures into one Bill the Committee had united the opponents of each measure instead of securing the friends of each."[15] He pressed the Senate to enact the parts of the omnibus bill, separately, and the Senate passed them all. It was he, with skilled leadership, who passed Clay's "Compromise of 1850."[16] With a generosity not common in the Senate then or later, Douglas gave full credit to Clay, for it was Clay's ideas that won out and spared the country for another decade from the catastrophe of civil war.

The senators who had led the Senate for so long now were leaving the scene forever. As the old leaders fell away, a new generation appeared, but they lacked the stature of their predecessors. These senators were also caught in the whirlpool of debate over slavery. The times were out of joint, and no group of senators had the wherewithal to set them right. It would take a generation and more before the Senate again would find that rare breed of member capable of providing leadership on matters of high state.

In the absence of dynamic individual leaders, senators began to use their respective party caucuses as an instrument of leadership. While senators had naturally met in party caucus from the Senate's first years, they now took up in caucus some of the organizational problems of running the Senate. The most pressing of these was the determination of committee rosters.[17] Until the mid-1840s, Senate rules provided that the Senate would vote on filling each seat of each committee at the start of each new congressional session. But balloting for committee assignments proved tedious and time consuming. That prompted them on several occasions to give the choice to the vice president, the Senate's presiding officer, or his substitute as president pro tempore, but that move, too, proved unsatisfactory when the vice president held political views at odds with those of a majority of the Senate. Finally, in 1845, senators began to make their party's selections in caucus and had the caucus chairman present for Senate approval the slate they'd chosen. That led to the caucus chairman taking on other chores in the organization of the Senate in each session, giving him special status among his colleagues. Eventually, the senator chosen chairman of the majority party's caucus would be called the "leader" of the Senate, even though other senators of his party might hold more power and influence within the legislative body.[18]

"Time can be saved and much trouble obviated," said Senator Jesse Bright of Indiana in December 1851, as he presented the Democratic caucus slate for committee assignments and asked for immediate approval.[19] More than time and trouble were involved, however, for senators had learned long before then the importance of committee assignments. The committees formulated the legislation on which the Senate acted. They also made recommendations on approving presidential appointments. In the years before the Civil War, senators from the slave states tried to make sure that they had a majority on the Senate's Judiciary Committee. That gave them influence over who served on the Supreme Court and other federal courts. This was of the gravest consequence, and Senator Hannibal Hamlin of Maine explained why: "On the organization of committees every senator knows the form and direction of the business of the Senate is mainly dependent."[20] Republican

Senator Zachariah Chandler of Michigan was not so polite. The Democrats then held a Senate majority. "You can elect your committees as you see fit," he told them, "but, gentlemen, beware! For the day is not far distant when the measure you mete to us today shall be meted to you again!"[21] Just four angry years later, Chandler's prediction came true with the secession of the Southern states and the resignations of their senators. By then, Hamlin had become vice president and Chandler a senator of great power among his colleagues. They would mete unto the South such punishments as would never be forgotten.

With the departure of Southern senators, the Republicans found themselves in total control of the Senate, with commanding majorities throughout the Civil War and for a dozen years afterward. In the Civil War years, several Republicans reached considerable stature within the Senate. William Pitt Fessenden of Maine, a moderate, held great power as chairman of the Finance Committee—which then also managed most appropriations legislation, especially in the final few deal-making weeks of each congressional session when panicked expediency could vanquish principled opposition. Charles Sumner believed his chairmanship of the Foreign Relations Committee gave him rank above all other senators. Among Northern abolitionists, Benjamin Wade of Ohio was his sometime rival. Chandler, by one account, "carried the Republican organization in his breeches' pockets."[22] None gave way to any other, however, and others also had claims to the Senate's attention. Solomon Foot of Vermont, president pro tempore during the Civil War Congresses, also chaired his party's caucus. In both capacities, he had so many chores to perform in the Senate chamber that his colleague William Stewart of Nevada called him the body's "Master of Ceremonies."[23] That did not, by any means, make Foot the Senate's policy leader. Rhode Island's Henry Anthony, his successor in both offices, never achieved that status either.[24]

By the time of the Civil War, the Republicans had begun to use their party caucus as an instrument of party discipline, but, without accepted and designated leaders, gaining agreement on what to do often proved difficult. Senator Anthony assumed the caucus chairmanship in 1862 and held it until he died twenty-two years later. At one point during his tenure, in 1869, Republicans filled sixty-two of the Senate's seventy-four seats. The Republicans were using the party caucus to bind party members to vote on the Senate floor in a way that was faithful to what party members had decided in their respective caucuses. The "binding caucus" came to full flower during Senator Anthony's tenure as caucus chairman.[25]

In 1873, George Alfred Townsend, a prominent Washington journalist, described the Republican caucus as "an irresponsible and unrecognized master of the Senate," and he described the penalties for any senator who bolted. Those senators invited to attend the caucus, by special private notice, met in secret under strict party discipline. "Whoever goes into the caucus must abide by its verdict or be dishonored," Townsend wrote. "He must obey the party behest, conscience or no conscience." A senator who disobeyed, Townsend observed, "forfeits his right to meet in the private sessions of his party again, and one might as well be in limbo now-a-days as in no party." That prospect threatened the party pariah with losing all his party benefits, including reelection.[26]

The caucus sessions, held in private, became a magnet for criticism, both internal and external. Senator Lyman Trumbull of Illinois, for example, denounced the party's binding caucus for muffling party dissent and forcing some senators to vote against their own better judgment. Senator Justin Morrill of Vermont saw no reason to apply party rule. "I think the Senate are quite competent to express their own judgment without any whip," he said. "We have never had what is called a whip in the American Senate."[27] Despite these protests, the Senate's Republicans continued their party caucus with its binding power for another half century, ending it then only in response to public outcries so damaging that they then renamed the party *caucus* as the party *conference*.[28]

Seeing themselves as ambassadors of their states, senators were instigated by that high charge to the very independence that made them less than enthusiastic about following anyone's lead, including that of any president. Yet they experienced new counterpressures, which forced a change. One was the escalation of the Senate's legislative and political workload in the years after the Civil War. Another was the growth of the nation and its economy and the resulting increase in new states. In 1889, the nation had forty-four states and the Senate eighty-eight members—exactly four times as many senators as had sat in the first session a century earlier. The sheer number of senators made change mandatory. Many came to realize that the larger the body, the greater the need for careful organization. The adoption and growth of the committee system had reflected that expansion a half century earlier. So, too, had the evolving development of the party caucus system. Increasingly, senators recognized that poor organization produced ineffective legislation. As early as 1874, the Republicans tried to correct this problem within their own caucus by appointing a few of their colleagues to suggest what bills they should consider. In 1878, this evolved into the party's Steering

Committee, which comprised senators picked to offer some party superintendence of their legislative agenda.[29]

Numerous commentators pointed to the then-leaderless state of the Senate and the haphazard methods of legislating that resulted. The *New York Times* reported in 1878 that the Senate had no "distinctly recognized leaders," despite the growing legislative workload. "Business," the newspaper stated, "is left to the initiative of individuals or of the numerous unconnected committees."[30] A decade later, in 1888, James Bryce in his study *The American Commonwealth* confirmed anew that the Senate had no "recognized leaders." He found "no chieftains" heading the majority or the opposition parties that any other senator would likely follow. The party caucus, he stated, was "the regular American substitute for recognized leadership," and had the advantage of seeming to treat every senator of that party equally, at least in theory. Senators were jealous of their supposed equality, but that worked against their recognizing any senators as leader. "No senator can be said to have any authority," Bryce wrote, "beyond that of exceptional talent and experience."[31]

Bryce noted another ill effect of the system. He reported that the Senate's majority caucus had so taken over the decision-making process that Senate debate had become meaningless, speeches offering "mere rhetorical thunder" for the audience in the galleries and constituents back home. Even earlier, one journalist reported that senators paid no attention to those speeches or much else. As soon as the chaplain finished the opening prayer, he wrote, "The senators at once fall to work at their task of paying no attention to what is transpiring in the hall. Some are engaged in conversation, some in writing, some in reading newspapers."[32] They even neglected on occasion to vote when their names were called. That utter indifference to floor proceedings, Bryce stated, resulted from the reality that the majority party's majority had already decided the matter in caucus.[33]

In 1885, Woodrow Wilson, then a young scholar at Johns Hopkins University, produced a remarkable study of the Senate and House of Representatives. His wove into his *Congressional Government* animated phrases that would make him famous as he criticized the inadequacies of Congress. He was especially harsh on the lack of party leadership, a "defect" he found unacceptable. He acknowledged that some senators were mentally and morally "stauncher" than others and one or another occasionally became "conspicuous" in the Senate's deliberations. "The public now and again picks out here and there a senator who seems to act and to speak with true instinct of statesmanship and who unmistakably merits the confidence of colleagues and of people," Wilson wrote. "But such a man, however eminent, is never more than *a* senator. No one is *the* senator. No one may speak for his party as well as for himself; no one exercises the special trust of acknowledged leadership. The Senate is merely a body of individual critics."[34]

Even as Wilson wrote this study, senators were in place to change the institution and its ways. They set out to establish for themselves a leadership oligarchy in command of the Senate. William Allison of Iowa entered the body in 1873, Orville Platt of Connecticut in 1879, and Nelson Aldrich of Rhode Island and Eugene Hale of Maine in 1881. These Republicans were already taking charge of the Senate's most important committees, and in a few years they would, in effect, seize control of the Senate.[35]

Meanwhile, Senate Democrats had a caucus chairman, Maryland's Arthur Gorman, who displayed effective party leadership. Elected in 1880, Gorman brought to the Senate the professional skills that had made him both the political boss of Maryland and a multimillionaire. His colleagues picked him as caucus chairman in 1889, and he soon proved far more forceful than those who preceded him. He made his special mark in 1891 when he organized his minority Democrats to defeat, by filibuster, a Republican bill that would have brought federal control to elections in the former states of the Confederacy—a measure hugely unpopular in the South.[36] For almost two months, he arranged for a relay of Democratic senators to keep the filibuster going. In 1892, he competed with former president Grover Cleveland for their party's presidential nomination. With Cleveland back in the White House and Gorman the de facto Senate majority leader, they engaged in a brutal quarrel over tariff schedules that smashed the Democratic Party asunder.[37] In the 1894 election, they lost their short-lived majority in the Senate, and they did not regain it for almost twenty years.

In the Fifty-second Congress, 1891–93, with Republicans in the majority, Allison chaired the Appropriations Committee and served with Aldrich on the Finance Committee. That committee's chairman, Vermont's Justin Morrill, then eighty-one years old, no longer could function effectively, and Aldrich, helped by Allison, had largely taken over as ad hoc chairman. That gave them substantive control of the Senate's two most powerful committees. Senator Hale, chairman of the Census Committee, also served on Allison's Appropriations Committee, and Senator Platt chaired the then-important Territories Committee. Combined, they held formidable power within the Senate, and they were soon called the "Big Four."[38] In the 1896 elections, the Republicans gained an increased majority in the Senate and, critically, a sympathetic new president in Ohio's William McKinley. Allison, as senior Republican, claimed the vacant post as chair of the Republican caucus. That move had the effect of giving the Big Four a monopoly of the party's political machinery within the Senate.[39] As they moved into their positions of authority, Aldrich and Allison and their immediate allies came to realize, as had none before them, that holding these posts offered the opportunity to control the Senate's operations. The party committees, created by the party caucus, were equally important to their ascendancy. Through the Committee on Committees, they packed the important panels with their adherents. Through the Steering Committee, they managed the Senate's schedule. As an ally reported to Allison, "We should use the machinery for our own benefit and not let other men have it."[40] Allison himself acted in these matters with grave concern. "It is of the utmost importance," he wrote a member of the leadership cabal, "that we should make no mistake in reorganizing the committees of the Senate."[41] By 1897, they dominated the Senate as no other group of senators had ever done before.

Also in the 1896 elections, Wisconsin's John Spooner, after an absence of six years, won reelection to the Senate. A punishing debater, he added an extra dimension to the Republican leadership faction. He had a way of humiliating Democrats in floor debates, and he was trusted and admired by the "Big Four." They quickly added him to their leadership clique.[42]

These men operated in tandem, each with a special role. Spooner was their orator, the best in the Senate. Chief, of course, was Rhode Island's Aldrich, now in full command of the Finance Committee. A multimillionaire in his own right, he had powerful allies in business and politics throughout the nation. His daughter had married John D. Rockefeller Jr. Aldrich was the manager, the "school-master of the Senate," one colleague called him. Diffident in manner, Aldrich rarely spoke on the Senate floor and then only laconically. He regarded the public with contempt. Haughty and arrogant in appearance, but privately charming, Aldrich had an extraordinary flair for leadership, coupled with a mastery of legislative trivia and parliamentary tactics that amounted to brilliance. He had the manner of command.[43]

Indifferent to public praise or blame, Aldrich carried himself with dignity and self-assurance, but his engaging manners masked an iron will to have his way on matters of state. "With his skill in legislation and intimate knowledge of the rules," wrote New York's Senator Chauncey Depew, "he was the leader whenever he chose to lead."[44] He and his lieutenants did not always succeed. They tried to prevent the war with Spain, and they blamed

President McKinley for giving way to the journalistic jingoism of the time. Losses were few, however, and around him grew legends that he had "but to whisper" his desires and the Senate responded. Mostly, Aldrich operated behind closed doors; but he worked the Senate floor, too, lobbying senators on pending measures. He played the serious business of politics with ruthless tactics. He kept in touch with political managers and business leaders throughout the country and he used them, when needed, to pressure Senate colleagues on specific votes. Central to his power was the ability to decide who would receive campaign funds and how much they would get.

William B. Allison, a shrewd parliamentarian, was the group's legislative tactician. Cautious and tactful, a man of modest means, Allison worked to reconcile whatever differences arose among the group. Connecticut's Orville Platt, a lawyer of renown, acted as the chief legislator, creatively drafting the desired bills just the way his colleagues decided. Senator Eugene Hale acted as the leadership's press spokesman. The others avoided public statements, refusing on-the-record press interviews. The five normally consulted in private, conducting in those sessions what knowledgeable contemporary observers called the Senate's real debates on pending public matters.

They had, of course, the support of the party regulars in the Senate, and that support reached unusual levels. For example, Senator Thomas Platt, New York's political boss (not to be confused with Connecticut's Orville Platt) put in writing to Allison his full commitment to whatever they decided. "What you say goes," he wrote. "Kindly keep me posted as to what you do, so that I may not go astray."[45] It was that sort of followership that gave the Big Five their control.

For all his outward show of affability, Aldrich on occasion acted with extraordinary ruthlessness, much as he did on McKinley's peace treaty with Spain. McKinley had used questionable tactics in appointing three senators to the peace commission, but that was not enough. The commission's Democrat, Delaware's George Gray, reflected the views of his party colleagues by balking at the pact's proposed annexation of the Philippines. For Aldrich, this became a desperate struggle to line up votes. With the Senate in customary closed session for treaty debate, he worked the floor, moving from one senator to another, offering blandishments. On the morning set for the vote, February 6, 1899, Aldrich was still four votes short. With McKinley's help, they had secured Senator Gray. His Senate career would be over on March 3, and he had no hope of reelection, so deadlocked was his state's legislature. For his support, they promised him a federal judgeship, which he readily accepted. Aldrich did not quit, pleading even with senators who had openly opposed the treaty. To South Dakota's Richard Pettigrew, leader of the Senate's opposition, it was obvious what Aldrich was doing: blatant bribery. And he was succeeding, picking up the last supporter needed just five minutes before the vote, and then a spare for safety during the roll call. The vote was fifty-seven to twenty-seven, with ten Democrats ensuring the two-thirds margin required.

In the 1890s, the Senate's ranking Republicans met most Thursday nights for dinner and poker at the lavish residence of James McMillan, a wealthy Detroit industrialist first elected to the Senate in 1889. These started out as casual get-togethers with Senator McMillan always the genial host, but after Allison and Aldrich became regulars, they took on a special significance. Assured of total privacy, members talked freely on politics and Senate business. As a jest, they called themselves the School of Philosophy Club, but their seminars dealt with practical politics and legislation, not philosophy. The convivial sessions built lasting friendships among the attendees, and gave the party leaders even more control of the Senate's operations and decision-making.[46]

The 1901 assassination of William McKinley elevated Theodore Roosevelt to the White House. At first, Roosevelt tended to defer to the Senate leaders, all of them much older than he. But in 1904, he won the presidency in his own right with a smashing victory and pledges for a "Square Deal" legislative program stoutly opposed by Nelson Aldrich and his conservative Senate partners. Increasingly, Roosevelt assumed a headstrong style of governing. While the Senate debated the Panama Canal, Roosevelt took direct action on his own to build it. When he proposed railroad-rate reform, Aldrich maneuvered deliberately in an ultimately futile bid to defeat the measure.

In another blunder, Aldrich openly opposed Roosevelt's proposal to pass pure food and drug legislation. Despite his inherent reluctance to address the Senate, Aldrich took the floor to argue that Roosevelt's proposal risked the freedom of Americans by trying to have the federal government decide what people could eat. His campaign collapsed with the shocking revelations of stockyard filth depicted in Upton Sinclair's novel *The Jungle*. The Senate passed the bill sixty-three to four.[47]

Aldrich still held command in the Senate, but these losses to Roosevelt suggested an erosion of his control. By then, he and the Senate itself had come under attack from many quarters. The most savage thrusts came from writers who would eventually be labeled "muckrakers." Their platforms were such popular national magazines as *Nation* and *Independent*.

The most spectacular blasts came in 1906 in a series of nine articles titled "The Treason of the Senate" in the monthly magazine *Cosmopolitan*.[48] Their author, David Graham Phillips, joined other muckrakers in finding no redeeming virtues in any of the party leaders. These journalistic assaults did nothing for the morale of the senators. A few months after the conclusion of the *Cosmopolitan* series, Senator Spooner, disheartened by the abuse, resigned.[49]

By then, there were other factors starting to undo the authority of Senator Aldrich and his leadership lieutenants. One was their advancing age and its attendant hazards. Connecticut's Senator Platt, then seventy-seven, died in April 1905, and Allison, seventy-nine, died in 1908. Although caucus chairman Eugene Hale by 1906 had come to be addressed out of courtesy as "Leader of the Senate," Aldrich remained in charge. Three years later, approaching seventy, he finally became the caucus's official leader.[50]

Another change under way seriously challenged Aldrich's command of the Senate. Party primaries were picking progressive candidates, including talented Republicans, for state legislatures to send to the Senate. Wisconsin's Robert La Follette arrived in January 1906. Soon there were others: Indiana's Albert Beveridge, Iowa's Jonathan Dolliver, and Minnesota's Moses Clapp. At first, Aldrich did not recognize the political convulsion at hand, but these new party primaries were undercutting the formal party organizations and eroding the party cohesion previously created. The Republican progressives were openly antagonistic to the Old Guard and standpatters. La Follette and his fellows intended revolution. They protested the secrecy of party caucuses and party rule and, more important, challenged the party's longtime commitment to the worlds of business and finance. They selected for their first major fight the tariff bill presented to the Senate in 1909 by Senator Aldrich.[51]

Aldrich followed his usual practice. He called his committee's Republicans into closed session, and in two days they made some six hundred increases in the three-hundred-page House bill. Aldrich provided no written report, and when he asked the Senate to approve this bill, he made no explanation of its provisions other than to estimate its expected revenues. La Follette and other progressives were ready. They attacked Aldrich's bill, questioning schedule after schedule in such detail that Aldrich actually fled the Senate chamber. "The Senate boss was thrown into confusion," La Follette later boasted. "He had been accustomed to issue orders—not furnish reasons."[52] They embarrassed Aldrich, but they could not woo the votes to make any substantive changes. Even so, they took satisfaction in confronting the Senate's leader in such telling terms and gaining recognition for the progressive movement.

The significance of this party revolt was not lost on Nelson Aldrich. He and Senator Hale, each a thirty-year Senate veteran, decided not to seek reelection in 1910. Two years later, La Follette and other progressives challenged Taft for the presidential nomination. They split the Republican Party so badly that a Democrat, Woodrow Wilson, won the White House. The 1912 elections also gave the Democrats majority control of the Senate for the first time in eighteen years. These changes brought important alterations in the style and thrust of the Senate's leadership.

Recent congressional scholars have assumed that the first senator to combine the chairmanship of his party caucus with effective majority leadership in the Senate was John Kern of Indiana, a mere freshman Democrat with little legislative experience of any kind. Offering scant evidence, they credited him with muscling through the Senate in 1913 the legislation demanded by just-elected President Wilson. It was true that Wilson had great success with the Senate that year and that Kern had the nominal title of majority leader, but the heavy lifting on legislation was done then, as for years before, by the committee chairmen with jurisdiction over the measures. Kern had been a senator less than a year when the elections of 1912 gave the Democrats a working majority in the Senate for the first time since 1895. Not a single Democrat in the new Senate had ever served in the majority, and party progressives and conservatives alike eagerly looked forward to the political control and spoils the Senate's majority normally enjoyed.

Wilson had won his party's nomination and then the presidency with campaign pledges for dramatic progressive reforms, but he quickly ran into a steel wall of resistance by conservatives and also moderates who, as the collegial culture of the Senate would have it, argued against an ugly fight that would ruin chances of enacting his legislative program. Consequently, Wilson abandoned his plan to rely on the progressives in favor of working with party regulars. That shift in strategy made possible his extraordinary successes. The regulars got the federal patronage they wanted, and they delivered the leadership and the votes to enact Wilson's reforms. At the party caucus, the progressives mustered the votes to elect Senator Kern chairman of the caucus, with the nominal title of Senate majority leader.[53]

With his legislation passed, Wilson was both pleased and surprised. "My head is with the progressives in the Democratic Party, but my heart, because of the way they stood by me, is with the so-called Old Guard in the Senate."[54] In all of this, Senator Kern did what he could to help. That meant tending the Senate floor, scheduling what bills he could, and pleading with senators to show up for important votes. Without much seniority or experience, however, he had little influence in the deal-making and bargaining needed to shape and pass the Wilson program.

Kern's colleagues quickly recognized his inability to carry out even the limited responsibilities of the position. After just a few weeks, Democrats caucused to address that matter. They elected a party "whip," an office never before created in the Senate and one technically in basic conflict with every senator's sense of being an independent operator. For the new position they picked another freshman senator, J. Hamilton Lewis of Illinois. They designated Lewis as Kern's "assistant" and assigned him to do what Kern was supposed to do. "Mr. Lewis's chief duty will be to see that Democrats are present or paired at every roll call," the *New York Times* reported. "The appointment of an assistant to Senator Kern, though brought about in a way to avoid wounding the majority leader's pride, is in fact partly explained by general dissatisfaction with Mr. Kern's leadership."[55] Two years later, in 1915, the Senate's Republicans copied this Democratic initiative and elected a party whip of their own. Nearly two decades would pass, however, before the post of majority leader became a meaningful leadership office.[56]

In the years after the collapse of the Aldrich oligarchy, the Senate's Republicans functioned without strong leaders. In 1911, they chose as chairman of the party caucus and nominal floor leader their most senior member, eighty-two-year-old Shelby Cullom of Illinois, a twenty-eight-year Senate veteran. "Who has succeeded Aldrich as leader of the Senate?" Cullom himself asked that summer. Then he answered his own question: "No one."[57] He explained that even though the Republicans still had a majority in the Senate, this was not a working majority: the party progressives frequently voted with the Democrats. "Under these circumstances," Cullom wrote, "real leadership is out of the question."[58] That year, the party progressives and the Old Guard quarreled so bitterly over committee assignments, chairmanships, and other party posts that they were unable to elect a Senate president pro tempore.[59] That party split dictated the choice of Cullom as caucus chairman; at his age, they did not expect him to actually lead the Senate or the party. Indeed, with the continuing ideological conflicts within the party, the Senate's Republicans removed the caucus chairmanship from controversy by robotically awarding it to whomever happened to have the most seniority.

Shelby Cullom retired from the Senate in 1913, when he was eighty-four years old. The caucus chairmanship went automatically to the next most senior Republican senator, New Hampshire's seventy-six-year-old Jacob

Gallinger. He held the nominal title of Republican leader for almost six years, during a period of Democratic majorities, until his death in 1918. The position then fell to Henry Cabot Lodge of Massachusetts, at that time the Senate's senior Republican. This was just a few weeks before the 1918 congressional elections, which returned the Senate's Republicans to majority status. Lodge, again by seniority, became chairman of the Senate's Foreign Relations Committee.[60]

Lodge gloried in his new title. "As leader of the Senate Republicans," he wrote to Theodore Roosevelt, his longtime friend, "I am seeing people all the time. . . . I am the center to which everyone comes."[61] First elected to the Senate in 1893, Lodge was sixty-eight years old. That November, the armistice between Germany and the Allied forces had ended World War I. The peace treaty negotiated by President Wilson with the other allied leaders came before the Senate and to Lodge's committee for what proved a momentous political struggle. Senator Lodge by then had a malignant hatred for Wilson, and he took the lead in the Senate to defeat Wilson's treaty. He did so not as the Senate's nominal majority leader, but as the chairman of the committee with jurisdiction over the treaty.[62]

In the new Senate, Lodge's Republicans held a bare majority; defection of a single senator would cost them that status. On the treaty, as on other matters, they were starkly divided. Some were in favor of it; others, such as Idaho's William Borah, among the "Irreconcilables," opposed the treaty totally. Between these two factions were those who wanted some reservations added to the treaty, and they included Senator Lodge. Lodge saw his job as holding together enough Republicans to deny Wilson the two-thirds vote he needed to ratify the treaty, unless modified, and its proposed League of Nations. Lodge used his committee chairmanship to that end. Following Lodge's guidance, the committee added to the treaty so-called reservations designed to anger Wilson. The Senate failed to approve the treaty that way when it was brought to a vote in November 1919. Wilson defiantly resubmitted his version of the treaty and the struggle began anew in January 1920.

When William Borah discovered that Lodge was secretly negotiating with Senate Democrats on the treaty, he called an emergency meeting of his fellow Irreconcilables. They, in turn, summoned Lodge from a meeting with the Democrats. When the annoyed Lodge arrived, Borah confronted him directly: "We think we ought to know what is going on in that meeting you are attending." Lodge became even angrier at this questioning of his party loyalty. If they distrusted him, he said, they could elect a new leader. "I won't give you a chance to resign," Borah snapped.[63] He would take the Senate floor Monday morning and explain why they needed a new leader. Lodge was badly rattled and started visibly trembling. Struggling to regain his composure, he asked one of the senators to escort him back to the earlier meeting. There, he told the Democrats that he had to cancel their negotiations. The next day, Borah sent Lodge a letter threatening to bolt the party if Lodge tried any more compromises with the Democrats. That defection would cost the Republicans their majority and Lodge his committee chairmanship. The Senate finally voted on the treaty with Lodge's reservations on March 19, 1920, and failed to achieve the two-thirds margin. This was counted as Lodge's great victory over President Wilson, but the senator had offered something less than stalwart leadership.

In the summer of 1920, Lodge presided over the Republican convention in Chicago that nominated Ohio senator Warren Harding for president. That prompted *New York Times* correspondent Charles Willis Thompson to savage them for their unsavory political scheming. He sarcastically contrasted Lodge's "Big Dozen" in the Senate's leadership with Senator Aldrich's "Big Five" two decades earlier. Aldrich and his colleagues were "statesmen," he wrote, dealing with legislation and public policy, not mere "politicians" trying to control who lived in the White House.[64] Lodge still held the title of leader of the Senate, but he offered a sorry performance in the Senate of 1921 and 1922.[65]

Now in his seventies, Lodge had great difficulties temperamentally and personally in the role of leader. He had the manners and speech of the Boston Brahmin he was, offering snorts and sneers at opponents and underlings. He had little taste for conferences or the nitty-gritty of legislative action. For all his aristocratic airs, he was a political boss in Massachusetts, with an intense craving for party patronage that did not endear him to his Senate colleagues. There were reports that President Harding himself made overtures to Senator Borah to act as his spokesman in the Senate, in place of Lodge. That assumed Lodge now was too old and infirm without enough drive to do the job. Borah, a fierce individualist uninterested in the compromises associated with leadership, declined.[66] Within the Senate, party regulars tried unsuccessfully to reorganize the Steering Committee in such a way as to provide some structured party leadership. As a Washington journalist saw it, "There was absolutely no leadership in the Senate whatever."[67]

These changes brought about the disintegration of the old system. The disappearance of party cohesion immensely complicated the job of the Senate's leaders then and for decades to come. Senator Lodge hardly tried.

As his party's nominal Senate leader, he repeatedly voted against his party's positions even on important measures like the tariff. He barely won reelection in 1922, and by 1924 he had become such a political pariah that he was booed at the party's national convention. He failed to recover from major surgery that fall and died at age seventy-four in December 1924.[68]

After a single term, Senator Kern lost reelection in 1916, and the chairmanship of the Democratic caucus reverted to Thomas Martin. By then, war was at hand, and Martin's chief responsibility was to provide Senate approval of adequate funds for the American military. Even so, he played a critical role in one of the Senate's most dramatic reforms. It fell to him, as designated majority leader, to respond to the national uproar over the successful filibuster that denied President Wilson formal authority to arm merchant ships against marauding German submarines. Wilson's fiery denunciation of that "little group of willful men"—La Follette and his Senate allies—who carried out that filibuster created near hysteria in the country. When Wilson demanded that the Senate change its rules to limit future filibusters, overawed senators reacted quickly. Under Martin's leadership, a bipartisan committee promptly proposed a cloture plan that would allow a supermajority of two-thirds to halt extended debate. Martin offered the necessary resolution, and after a brief debate, the Senate approved seventy-six to three. At their leisure, senators could deplore their instant surrender to this extraordinary outside intimidation on a matter over which senators had quarreled for so long. The procedural reform quieted the public outcry, but, embodied in Senate Rule 22, it proved as difficult to execute as some of its nominal sponsors might have expected.[69]

Following Martin's death in November 1919, Senate Democrats chose Alabama's Oscar Underwood as head of their party caucus. By then, the Republicans had a majority in the Senate, and they would hold that majority for more than a dozen years. Underwood had a special relationship with President Harding. They had become close friends as senators even though they were of opposing political parties. When Chief Justice Edward White died in May 1921, Harding tried without success to convince Underwood to become White's successor. His friendship with President Harding did not sit well with some of his Senate colleagues, and that along with his plans to run for president prompted him to resign as the Senate's minority leader, a post that he seemed not to value. When he wrote his memoirs, he neglected to mention his leadership of the Senate's Democrats.[70] To replace him, at the opening of the next session of Congress, December 3, 1923, the Democrats picked Joseph T. Robinson of Arkansas, a rough-and-ready political partisan who, in time, became the real majority leader of the Senate.

Under the Republicans' seniority rule, the senator in line to inherit Lodge's nominal party leadership was eighty-one-year-old Francis Warren of Wyoming, but he and Senator Reed Smoot, next in line, were not interested. Finally, by seniority, the office went to Charles Curtis of Kansas, an Old Guard conservative.

As Senate leader, Curtis had even greater difficulties with the Senate's activist progressives than Senator Lodge did. They continued to resist party discipline, and in 1924 two of the Senate's most talented members, Robert La Follette and Burton K. Wheeler, had run for president and vice president, respectively, as a bipartisan progressive slate. That raised resentments among the party regulars. The Republican caucus, with Curtis as chairman, punished La Follette by voting to expel him from the party along with three other progressives. Curtis found himself at odds with President Coolidge, a taciturn New Englander not sympathetic to Midwest farmers. Curtis offered the Senate little leadership. Not interested in sponsoring legislation, he led the Senate during the administration of a president similarly uninterested in legislative initiatives. According to one cynical assessment, Curtis's "big job" each day was to close the Senate's session with the cry: "Mr. President, I move we adjourn."[71]

In 1928, Senators Curtis and Indiana's James ("Sunny Jim") Watson, along with several other senators, ran for the Republican presidential nomination against Commerce Secretary Herbert Hoover. They launched a "Stop Hoover" campaign in last-minute desperation, but Hoover won despite their attempts. As good party men, they had long considered Hoover, an engineer turned humanitarian, not their kind of partisan Republican. Hoover regarded them as little more than political hacks. When Hoover took the oath as president in March 1929, he discovered to his distress that he had Watson to contend with as the newly designated Republican leader of the Senate.[72]

Watson, a flamboyant orator in the bloviating style of Warren Harding, reluctantly accepted Hoover as the party's leader and boasted later that he, as the Senate's majority leader, had put Hoover's "entire program" through the Senate.[73] That was no small accomplishment, for despite much malicious belittling to the contrary, Hoover proved an activist president fighting the disastrous economic depression that engulfed his administration. Hoover and Watson were far apart, a shy, reserved president and a boisterous, extroverted senator. When they spoke with one another, a frequent occurrence, they often talked at cross purposes. "I don't talk to the President," Watson said. "I talk at the President."

Hoover sensed Watson's hostility and complained that Watson was "supposed to be the Republican leader of the Senate," but preferred "to play his own politics against me."[74] They had breakfast at the White House at least once a week when Congress was in session. "On those occasions," Watson remembered, "he was always very courteous and affable and willing to listen to my advice on legislative matters in the Senate."[75] So that they might talk freely at any time, Hoover had a private telephone line installed from the White House to Watson's home. These were recognitions of the Senate leader's status institutionally, but Hoover's problem was that he did not like politicians and he made no exception with Watson. Watson, the politician, wanted to talk politics. That bored Hoover. "I never could induce him to pay the slightest attention to anything I said about the organization of the party or the management of the campaign," Watson complained.[76] Hoover shrank from Watson's constant harping on party politics. "Oh, he's here again," Hoover once groaned, spotting Watson, "telling me what to do!"

Hoover had troubles with both wings of the Republicans in the Senate. The Old Guard thought him too progressive, and the progressives thought him too conservative. He did, however, have a remarkable, somewhat concealed alliance with Senator Joseph Robinson, leader of the minority Democrats. Hoover regularly consulted with Robinson about appointments and legislation.[77] By then, Robinson had achieved considerable party stature. In 1928, party managers had picked him to run as their candidate for vice president, offering the Arkansan to balance the ticket headed by Governor Alfred Smith of New York. In that campaign, Senator Curtis, Senator Robinson's counterpart, was the Republicans' candidate for vice president, an obvious acknowledgment of the growing prestige of the Senate's designated floor leaders.[78]

When Franklin Roosevelt won the presidency in 1932 and swept Democrats into commanding majorities in Congress, Senator Robinson had already become a formidable floor leader and parliamentarian. By then, he had had ten years' experience perfecting his leadership techniques. A massive man physically, with a booming baritone voice and explosively hot temper, he cowed at least some of his colleagues with his bullying tactics. In debate, Robinson put on an extraordinary show, pounding his desk, flailing his arms, and roaring insults as he worked himself into a nearly incoherent frenzy. On several occasions he came close to fistfights on the Senate floor, and more than once outside the Senate he punched antagonists in the face.

In 1932, he and Louisiana Senator Huey Long engaged in an ugly shouting match in the Senate chamber that climaxed with Long resigning his committee assignments and threatening to campaign against Robinson's reelection in neighboring Arkansas.[79]

In 1933, as the Senate's new majority leader, Robinson tried to reinstate the binding caucus, in which support for a measure by two-thirds of the caucus would generally bind all party members to support it on the Senate floor. He intended to act as the president's man in the Senate and to enact whatever legislation President Franklin Roosevelt proposed. Like others before him, he had responsibility to set the Senate's schedule. But he also brought to the job a new dimension and a new commitment that made him the first of the modern leaders of the Senate. Politically, and in parliamentary terms, he had the wherewithal to induce the Senate to follow where he led. In the special session of Congress immediately following Roosevelt's inauguration, known later as the Hundred Days, Congress enacted a series of major bills—fifteen out of the fifteen requested—with astonishing speed. Robinson boasted that he shoved every Roosevelt bill through the Senate "in record-breaking time."[80]

The crisis atmosphere of these initial days of Roosevelt's presidency gave special urgency to members of Congress to respond to the president's dramatic requests. Roosevelt quickly learned that he could work closely and cooperatively with Robinson and other party leaders in the Senate. As did Woodrow Wilson in the early months of his administration, Franklin Roosevelt relied more on party regulars, conservative though they were, than on party progressives. The regulars, most with considerable seniority, were prepared as party loyalists to back Roosevelt, even on measures they did not like. Roosevelt's political blunders would, in time, weaken that steadfastness, but Robinson's willingness to accept the president's direction so unquestioningly changed the thrust and purpose of the Senate's majority leadership. This enhanced the leader's role as a meaningful player in the great game of Washington politics, but it also made the Senate's leader a mere lieutenant of the president.

Robinson drove his colleagues the way he drove himself, and in his case that became medically dangerous. He was frequently frustrated by the negligence of fellow senators. "Some of these men," he said, "need to be taken by the scruff of the neck and the seat of the trousers and shaken into sense."[81] Robinson was a political conservative, far more conservative than Roosevelt's legislation, but for him passing these measures was a matter of party duty, not ideological first principles.

Despite his ferocity in action on the Senate floor, Joe T. Robinson was a convivial fellow off the floor, playing golf and attending baseball games with Senate colleagues who were friends. Among these was Oregon's Charles McNary, who succeeded to the Senate's Republican leadership after Senator Watson's electoral defeat in 1932. McNary had seen Senator Robinson's unusual cooperation with President Hoover. He offered similar cooperation with President Roosevelt. "We wish the new administration an abundance of success," he said in 1933. McNary went far beyond good wishes; he voted for most of Roosevelt's New Deal legislation.[82]

Robinson and McNary worked together to set the Senate's schedule. They normally met daily at noon in Robinson's Capitol hideaway for strategy sessions. Responding to McNary's accommodations, President Roosevelt treated him as a personal and confidential friend, consulting him on matters of state and rewarding him with federal projects in Oregon. On signing one rivers and harbors bill, Roosevelt said, "I've got to give Charlie his dam!"[83] This was authorization for the mammoth Bonneville Dam.

In the 1936 elections, President Roosevelt scored a personal triumph of extraordinary extent. His sweeping victory lifted the Senate's Democratic membership to seventy-five, an unprecedented margin for any party in the Senate. Roosevelt had seemingly gained total command of the Senate and the House, where the Democrats held a similar margin. Senator McNary, leader of only seventeen Republicans, could hardly mount any opposition; they were so few that they had not bothered to choose a party whip. Yet, ironically, it was in this Congress, the Seventy-fifth, that Roosevelt lost his hold over his Senate and House party members.

FDR had become increasingly frustrated and annoyed at the Supreme Court for negating his New Deal legislation in decision after decision. Now, with huge party margins in both houses, Roosevelt tried to strong-arm through Congress a radical plan to pack the Supreme Court with a half-dozen extra justices handpicked by him. Senator Robinson accepted Roosevelt's proposal as marching orders and set out to push the legislation through the Senate. After an initial canvass of senators, he reported that as many as fifty-five senators could be persuaded. Party resistance ran stronger in the House, and so the managers chose to have the Senate act first.

For Republican leader McNary, Roosevelt's scheme posed a complicated problem because his party regulars were all but hysterical in their opposition. He saw that if Republicans screamed wildly against the proposal, Roosevelt could use their opposition to treat this as a Democrat-versus-Republican war and thus woo back his own party members. McNary proposed a shrewd strategy: a conspiracy of Republican silence. They would withhold partisan criticism and let the Democratic bolters carry the fight. "Let them do the talking," McNary said. "We'll do the voting."[84]

Prior to the introduction of the court-packing legislation, Robinson had had little trouble leading the Senate. From the start, he had important help from Southern senators and from Vice President John Nance Garner, a veteran member of Congress and one unusually active legislatively for a presiding officer. The court-packing bill changed that, however, badly splitting the Democrats. Robinson went to Roosevelt to plead for a compromise: "This bill's raising hell in the Senate."[85] Roosevelt refused. Robinson appealed to his colleagues to little avail. Then, unexpectedly, Justice Willis Van Devanter announced his retirement. That would give Roosevelt his way with the court, and Robinson's Senate colleagues flocked to congratulate their leader, for they knew of Roosevelt's pledge to name him to the first Supreme Court vacancy.[86] Roosevelt stalled and evaded. Robinson struggled on as best he could, to the point of exhaustion. He had heart trouble, and the pains came, but he did not quit. On the morning of July 14, 1937, a maid found him dead on the bedroom floor of his Capitol Hill apartment, a copy of the *Congressional Record* at his side.[87]

That was the end of the struggle over the Supreme Court, although the controversy dragged on a little longer. As the Senate's political leader, Robinson had repeatedly mastered the Senate, but he did so in subservience to a master of his own, the president. He had elevated the dual role of Senate majority leader and majority party caucus chairman to a level not previously achieved, but he did so in such a way that left in doubt whether he truly was the Senate's leader or just the president's obedient lieutenant.[88]

Even before Senator Robinson's funeral, a behind-the-scenes contest began over who would succeed him as majority leader. Senate Democrats were divided between Mississippi's Pat Harrison and Kentucky's Alben Barkley, the party whip. Roosevelt intruded with an open letter to Barkley—"My dear Alben"—treating him as the "acting" leader of the Senate.[89] Harrison read Roosevelt's motives correctly: he was signaling that he wanted Barkley. In a private talk with Harrison, Roosevelt assured the senator that he really was neutral in this fight. Despite this, he worked through his aides to gain votes for Barkley. That made the difference: Barkley won the job with thirty-eight votes, just one more than Harrison.[90] If Roosevelt's decision to intervene suggested the increased importance of the Senate's majority leader, Barkley's willing submissiveness to the president disclosed what the Senate's majority leadership was becoming in the 1930s, a dependency that would continue into the 1950s.

FDR's duplicity in the leadership race eroded his support among many Democratic senators. In early 1939, there were no fewer than twenty Democratic senators, bristling with bitterness at Roosevelt, ready to vote against anything he requested. There would be no more New Deal legislation. Instead, these disgruntled senators were the making of a conservative coalition with the Republicans.

In the aftermath of the court fight, changes of some institutional significance came to the Senate's leadership. Roosevelt, like earlier presidents, frequently consulted leading members of Congress, but he did that haphazardly. The new House majority leader, Sam Rayburn of Texas, suggested that Roosevelt meet every week with his party's chiefs in Congress. "We could tell him what we're planning," Rayburn said, "and he could tell us his plans. It would eliminate a lot of confusion."[91] Roosevelt adopted the idea, and that became a regular practice also for his successors. Each week when Congress was in session, Vice President Garner, Speaker of the House William Bankhead, Barkley, and Rayburn met with Roosevelt at the White House, often in the president's bedroom. They were called the "Big Four," but they played a different role than the "Big Four" of Senator Aldrich's day.

In 1944, responding to Roosevelt's insulting language in vetoing a major tax bill, Barkley took the Senate floor, denounced the president for his unseemly attack, and dramatically resigned as majority leader. In doing so, he defined his role as Senate party leader in an extraordinary manner. In one way, he saw himself as a crucial figure in the government's major operations. At the same time, as the president's man in the Senate, he described himself as little more than a political sycophant taking orders from FDR.

As Barkley spoke, word spread quickly and senators soon crowded the Senate floor. They listened in hushed silence as he answered point by point the president's offensive veto and asked his colleagues to override that veto. For years, he said, he had "carried the flag" for Roosevelt, but now he had to resign as majority leader. "I felt," he said, "I ought not to remain as the Administration's floor leader."[92] When he finished, his colleagues gave him a standing ovation.

Like Senator Robinson, Barkley believed that as the Senate's majority leader he had to represent President Roosevelt and support his measures, even though he was chosen by, and ultimately answerable to, his Senate colleagues. He had been criticized for being merely a White House "errand boy." Subsequent Senate majority leaders would take differing views of their role and responsibilities. For Barkley, his resignation as leader amounted, in effect, to a resignation from Franklin Roosevelt's staff. The Senate's Democrats promptly reelected him as their leader. Despite those heroics, Senator Barkley soon lapsed into his familiar role as the president's man in the Senate.[93]

Senator McNary died in February 1944 and was succeeded as Senate Republican leader by a lesser figure, Maine's Wallace White, a kindly, affable Senate veteran. White grew up under strong Senate influences. His grandfather, William Frye, who had represented Maine in the Senate for three decades at the turn of the twentieth century, had been an influential chairman of the powerful Senate Commerce Committee. The grandson, however, had no pretensions to leadership. He deferred to a talented group of conservative Republican activists led by Ohio's Robert A. Taft, son of President Taft.

Robert Taft strove to create a tough partisan leadership style distinctly unlike McNary's convivial cooperation with the FDR administration. "The role of the opposition is to oppose," Taft said repeatedly, and he intended to provide that opposition. Taft could have claimed the formal party leadership for himself, but he had no taste for the tedious chores imposed on the senator designated as party leader. These included remaining on or near the Senate floor, monitoring the seemingly endless speechmaking, and finding accommodations for all the problems, great and small, of other senators.[94] Taft would be the real leader of the Senate's Republicans without the title. Senator White knew his role. When reporters questioned him on Senate matters, he had a stock answer: "Taft is the man you want to see."[95]

In April 1945, with the war in Europe almost won, the sudden death of President Roosevelt catapulted into the Oval Office Vice President Truman, in many ways uninformed on military matters. The former Missouri senator immediately signaled the Senate's leaders that he would seek a more cooperative working relationship with them, an assurance that most legislators greeted warmly.[96] The political tilt of the Senate's majority was changing. Ever since Roosevelt's triumph in 1936, each biennial election had eroded the Democrats' Senate majority. Then, in the 1946 elections, in the aftermath of wartime restrictions and shortages, the Republicans gained majority control of both the Senate and the House.

For Taft and his party lieutenants this meant new responsibilities and new opportunities as they returned to power after fourteen years in the minority. In the reorganization of the Senate, Wallace White remained as designated floor leader. Senator Eugene Millikin of Colorado, Taft's most influential ally, became chairman of the powerful Finance Committee and doubled as chairman of the Senate Republican caucus. In Arthur Vandenberg, a senator from Michigan, Taft had a potent rival; both men had deeply rooted presidential ambitions. These politically astute senators quickly came to an amicable agreement: Vandenberg took charge of foreign policy, Taft of domestic matters.[97] Vandenberg became chairman of the Foreign Relations Committee and president pro tempore of the Senate, a post of special importance with the vacancy in the vice presidency. Taft remained the party's real leader, as chairman of the Republicans' newly created party policy committee. He took on as well, to the surprise of many, the chairmanship of the Senate Committee on Labor.[98]

Robert Taft came to dominate the councils of the Senate's Republicans by the sheer force of his intellect. He had none of the easy affability of a professional politician. Candid to the point of cruelty, often indifferent to the sensibilities of others, Taft was so intent on his public responsibilities that he sometimes inadvertently snubbed close personal friends.[99] Without grace notes in his manners, he lacked the ingratiating ways and pleasantries of the successful office-seeker, but his candor, however partisan, won admiration even from adversaries. "I held him in the highest respect," said President Truman.[100]

Among other changes, Taft had determined to rework the labor legislation that was part of President Roosevelt's New Deal. President Truman vetoed the restrictive bill he sponsored, the Taft-Hartley Labor-Management Relations Act of 1947, but Congress overrode that veto. Organized labor responded angrily to the statute's narrowed definition of acceptable work stoppages, its outlawing of exclusively unionized workplaces, and the ban on union donations to federal political campaigns. One of the most controversial measures of this Eightieth Congress, it provided President Truman with an issue that earned him enthusiastic and crucial support from American labor in his 1948 election campaign.

In his quarrels with this Congress, Truman vetoed no fewer than seventy-five bills, and in his 1948 whistle-stop campaign, he denounced it as a "Do-Nothing Congress" not worthy of reelection. For all Truman's campaign bluster, this Congress actually accomplished a great deal under the guidance of Taft and Vandenberg. In domestic matters, Congress enacted major housing and education legislation. In foreign concerns, it approved the Marshall Plan to rebuild Europe, aid to Greece and Turkey, aid to block Soviet aggression, and the unification of the armed services. The Republicans had a creative record in this Congress, but Truman won the presidency in his own right.

The 1948 election did more than give Harry Truman four more years in the White House. He had picked Senator Barkley, a popular figure at the party nominating convention, as his running mate, and their victory made it necessary for Senate Democrats to elect a new floor leader. The post went to Scott Lucas, a downstate Illinois lawyer reluctant to take the job.[101] Within the Senate, the majority leadership had become "a misery without splendor."[102] Senator Lucas agreed to accept the post only at the urging of party leaders. He soon found that he had serious additional burdens beyond the expected routine. With his startling election victory, President Truman assumed he had won a national mandate to press Congress for the commitments set forth in the Democratic Party platform. He expected Lucas to guide all of them through the Senate.[103]

Lucas had a majority in the Senate, fifty-four Democrats to forty-two Republicans, but this was a majority not likely to approve Truman's "Fair Deal" legislative program of civil rights, public housing, and national health care. The party's conservatives, notably those from the South, had drifted away into informal alliance with like-minded Senate Republicans. Even so, in the tradition then building, Senator Lucas felt obliged to push for President Truman's progressive legislation despite formidable opposition. He risked his health and his Senate seat trying to respond effectively to the president's goading. For his troubles, he lost his 1950 reelection race.[104] The demands of his leadership position were partly to blame.

On the Republican side, Wallace White, in his seventies, had declined to run for reelection in 1948. Some of his younger Republican colleagues, upset at their party's failures, tried unsuccessfully to install new leadership in the Senate, but Taft remained in command. The Republicans picked Nebraska's Kenneth Wherry, a bumptious and aggressive conservative, to replace Senator White. All were soon enmeshed in further controversies that prompted new partisanship and new rounds of political vitriol. Not least of these were Wisconsin Republican Senator Joseph R. McCarthy's charges of treason within the Truman administration. Taft encouraged McCarthy to "keep talking"; if one case did not work, try another. The outbreak of the Korean War in June 1950 gave new tension to their operations. Truman sent American troops to turn back the North Korean invasion of South Korea.

Taft and the other Senate Republicans at first endorsed Truman's decision. "The time had to come sooner or later," Taft said.[105] As casualties mounted, however, the opposition Republicans pulled back, and Senator Wherry labeled the conflict "Truman's War."[106] For all his chilly personality, Taft grew steadily in reputation among Republicans to the point that he came to be called "Mr. Republican."[107]

Senator Wherry seemed unaware of his own growing reputation as a bumbler loose on the Senate floor. His malapropisms became so startling that reporters covering the Senate collected them as "Wherryisms." In debate, he called Chinese leader Chiang Kai-shek "Shanghai Jack," and he made an hour's speech about a place he called "Indigo-China." He assured a fellow senator that he would have "opple ampertunity" to make a speech.[108] He was not as discombobulated as he sometimes sounded, for his real role in the Senate was to conduct the daily routine, not to lead. Others in the Senate's Republican hierarchy knew to rely on Taft. Notable among them was New Hampshire's Styles Bridges, a creature of the political shadows who had a shrewdness about him bordering on cunning, which was useful in difficult times.[109] Another was Eugene Millikin, who looked and voted like a prosperous banker, but who had a robust, ribald sense of humor that often set the Senate cloakroom in a roar. When Millikin first heard the extent of President Truman's planned economic mobilization for the Korean War, he pretended astonishment. "Well," he cried, "I'll paint my ass white and run with the wild antelope!"[110] As in the many years of Senator Aldrich's ascendancy in the Senate, the Republicans still divided party leadership among several members, a kind of collegial commission of Republican chieftains with one of special talent the most prominent. In this they differed dramatically from the Senate's Democrats, who lodged in the one senator responsibilities for floor leadership, and chairmanships of the caucus and the principal party committees.[111]

With the defeat of Senator Lucas, the Democrats had to pick a new floor leader, and Lucas's defeat had sapped any latent interest among fellow Democrats in taking his place. Stuck in Washington as the Senate's leader, even as his opponent campaigned all over his home state, Lucas had also been hurt by Democratic scandals, Truman's flagging popularity, and the war against North Korean communists. The war continued, and so did the administration's scandals. After much back-and-forth consultation, party regulars drafted Arizona's Ernest McFarland, a party moderate who harbored serious questions of his own about Truman's policies and proposed legislation. "I was not a candidate," he stated later. "There seemed general agreement that I should run for majority leader."[112] McFarland proved an ineffective leader, a mere figurehead in the job. He addressed the Senate as little as possible, and he saw no reason to promote legislation that President Truman urged on Congress. "I felt," McFarland said later, "that my principal job was that of a senator from Arizona."[113] With mounting casualties in Korea and an administration rife with scandals, Truman lost the popularity he once enjoyed, and McFarland paid for it. Up for reelection in 1952, McFarland found himself opposed by a handsome and provoking Republican businessman, Barry M. Goldwater. He attacked McFarland as "Truman's majority leader in the US Senate," and blamed him for the "no-win" policy in Korea and the Truman scandals, a telling combination that ended McFarland's career in the Senate.

In the 1950 elections, along with Scott Lucas, the Democrats' Senate whip, Francis Myers of Pennsylvania, had also been defeated for reelection. In January 1951, in addition to naming McFarland their leader, Senate Democrats selected a new whip, or assistant leader, responsible for counting heads and rounding up party members for key votes. A forty-two-year-old Texas Democrat elected to the Senate only two years earlier, Lyndon Baines Johnson, saw the trivial whip's job as one loaded with promise. With little difficulty, he persuaded party elders, most notably Georgia's Senator Richard Russell, to let him have it.[114] With Senator McFarland defeated in 1952, Johnson skillfully maneuvered to become the new Democratic floor leader. Thus began the most extraordinary Senate leadership tenure since the rule of Nelson Aldrich.

8

Leadership Empowered

The Modern Era

AS THE POLITICAL SEASON OF 1952 came to a close, with President-elect
Dwight Eisenhower preparing to take office, the Senate's Republicans and
Democrats turned to choosing new floor leaders. Both jobs were vacant: the
Democrats' because of the election defeat of Senator Ernest McFarland and
the Republicans' because temporary Republican leader Styles Bridges, with
his party back in the majority, preferred the less-demanding office of Senate
president pro tempore.[1] Presumably the choice would not be easy. The two
previous Democratic majority leaders, McFarland and Scott Lucas, had to
be drafted for the job. Both had lost their Senate reelection bids, at least
partly because they had taken that post. While necessary for promoting
orderly Senate floor proceedings, the party floor leader's role entailed more
drudgery than prestige, prompting both parties to shunt the job off to their
less captivating members. An astute Washington journalist, the *New Yorker*'s
Richard Rovere, described the process as picking senators to reward their
"enterprising mediocrity."[2]

In his 1938 history of the Senate, George Haynes dismissed as insignificant the job of party floor leader.[3] Even though President Franklin Roosevelt had intruded on the Senate Democratic caucus decision in 1937 to pick
Senator Barkley as majority leader, that move did not make Barkley the
most influential among the Senate's Democrats. Over these years, there had
been occasional token events suggesting some status to the men who served
as their party's floor leaders. In 1927, as a convenience to himself, Senator

Joseph Robinson claimed the front-row, center-aisle desk on the Democratic side of the chamber. Ten years later, Senator Charles McNary did the same on the Republican side. These, then, were merely housekeeping changes, but years later, as their positions became politically powerful, they placed the party leaders at the very center of the Senate's floor action. In these years, the titles of the two parties' floor leaders awarded them a degree of public prominence, and occasionally both national parties picked one or another of them as candidates for vice president to "balance" the party's presidential ticket. In 1928, both Senator Joseph Robinson, the Democratic leader, and Senator Charles Curtis, the Republican leader, were so nominated. In 1940, the Republicans chose Senator McNary as their vice-presidential nominee, and in 1948, the Democrats selected Senator Alben Barkley. Both Curtis and Barkley won this "promotion."

In another sphere of the Senate's operations, Vice President John Nance Garner, as the Senate's presiding officer, made a few seemingly minor changes in the Senate's parliamentary processes. Those adjustments would, however, take on great significance years later. As a longtime member of the House and its Speaker just before becoming vice president, Garner saw no reason to change the way he chose to recognize members to speak. Under the Senate's rules, the presiding officer is obligated to recognize the senator who first seeks recognition. Garner changed that procedure on May 25, 1933, a few weeks after becoming vice president, when he recognized Virginia's Carter Glass instead of Indiana Senator Arthur Robinson, who had addressed him first. Robinson instantly protested, accusing Garner of the unforgivable sin of substituting House rules for the Senate's. Garner asserted that his policy was to give preferential recognition to the senator serving as floor manager of the pending bill. Glass, chairman of the Appropriations Committee and a former treasury secretary, then had charge of a pending banking bill: in effect he was temporarily the Senate's "acting" floor leader. Garner meant this only as a courtesy to the bill's high-status manager, nothing more, but this was new doctrine. No senator challenged his ruling, thereby giving it the consequential status of a Senate precedent.[4]

Four years later, still vice president, Garner enlarged his policy on recognition. He would recognize the Senate's majority leader or the Senate's minority leader whenever either of them sought the floor. When he stated this to the Senate on August 13, 1937, claiming he saw the procedure as his "duty," his words touched off a somewhat confused debate, but no senator seriously challenged his decision, which seemed of no great importance.[5] But, through the 1940s and into the early 1950s, this Garner precedent would mature into the floor leader's "right" to orchestrate the Senate's operations with extraordinary control.

In January 1953, both parties believed they would have to draft from their ranks someone willing to take the onerous job of floor leader. To the surprise of many, two senators volunteered for these party posts. Robert Taft of Ohio and Lyndon Johnson of Texas each had differing motives for his decision.

Robert Taft, a longtime senator, lost his bid for the 1952 Republican presidential nomination to Dwight Eisenhower, a five-star general and legendary World War II commander who a year before had not belonged to any political party. Taft took his defeat graciously, pledging to help Eisenhower in the coming campaign, but Taft's loyalists in the Senate were bitter, deeply resentful that their candidate, a lifelong Republican and son of a Republican president, had lost the nomination to a professional soldier. They nursed that bitterness with an antagonism that made Eisenhower's first years in the White House especially difficult.[6]

Aware that these resentments stirred many of his fellow Republican senators, Taft seriously considered offering himself as the Senate's new majority leader as a way to ease matters for President Eisenhower, but he hesitated in recognition that his political views were sharply more conservative than the new president's. "I have a good bit of doubt," he said at the time, "largely because I don't know whether I can agree with the Eisenhower administration, and if I can't, perhaps I'd better have a more independent position."[7] Taft's words reflected the prevailing assumption that the Senate's floor leader of the president's party would support the president's program, and that he would serve as the president's political lieutenant in the Senate. That was not easy for Taft.

The Republicans had been out of the presidency for twenty years, and Taft, whatever his misgivings, resolved to try his best to make this new administration a political success. Publicly, he stated that he took the job as a matter of practical, orderly procedure. "You can't have a lot of fellows running down to the White House and then coming back to the Senate to speak for the President," Taft said then.[8] Privately, however, he had deeper purposes. He would speak to the president for the Senate according to appropriate Republican principles, and he would do what he could to pacify the party conservatives in the Senate on the president's behalf. He would serve as the president's political adviser, a kind of prime minister.

By accepting the majority leadership, Taft did more than position himself to counsel the new president and guide his administration. In institutional terms, he had lifted the leader's job to a new level of dignity and authority.

As the true leader of the majority Republicans, not merely their titular head, Taft commanded a respect among conservative Republicans that amounted to near reverence. By changing his own view of the majority leader's status, Taft also changed the Senate's view, suggesting that there was far more to the post than previously assumed. Taft, of course, did not intend to act merely as the scheduler of the Senate's daily agenda, but the job he took proved daunting.[9]

How successful Taft might have proved as the Senate's formal leader was not to be tested. The party regulars forgave his blunt ways, but that style could have hurt him with other senators. In mid-spring 1953, Taft became ill with cancer. He tried to attend to his duties in the Senate, hobbling about on crutches, but his illness became more widespread. On June 10, at a party caucus, he told his colleagues that he had to step aside temporarily, and in the meantime he "appointed" California's William Knowland as "acting" floor leader in his absence.[10] This was an extraordinary decision, made possible by Taft's great prestige and done to keep the leadership in the control of a Taft-wing conservative. There was no protest among fellow Republican senators, but this selection from outside the party's leadership cadre had serious consequences. Taft died seven weeks later, and Knowland, already in place, automatically succeeded to the leadership, bypassing party whip, or assistant floor leader, Leverett Saltonstall of Massachusetts. Lacking Taft's national stature and Saltonstall's political tact, Knowland would prove to be ill-suited to the challenges ahead.

Robert Taft had undertaken the majority leadership out of party loyalty. Lyndon Johnson, his Democratic counterpart, had far different motives. A forty-four-year-old freshman senator, Johnson saw for himself the party's floor leadership as a pathway to power and prestige. Intensely ambitious and compulsively energetic, Johnson from the start intended to make his mark on the Senate. Johnson knew firsthand where power rested in the Senate— in the chairmanships of the most important committees, the due reward to those senators of great seniority. In 1949, Johnson's first year as a senator, Tennessee's Kenneth McKellar, a senator since 1917, chaired the Appropriations Committee, and Georgia's Walter George, a senator since 1922, chaired the Finance Committee. Johnson, far too impatient to wait his turn as the senior members had, sought a different route to power and party influence. By odd chance, he found a shortcut in the 1950 elections, when both the party's Senate leaders, Scott Lucas and Francis Myers, the party whip, failed to win reelection. Johnson promptly consulted Georgia's Richard Russell, leader of the Senate's Southern Democrats, and with Russell's tacit approval,

Johnson actively campaigned for the job of party whip, surprising some senators whom he called to ask for their votes in caucus. He had no competition and, after just two years a senator, he became part of the Senate's formal leadership.

In the 1952 elections, opportunity came again to Johnson with Senator McFarland's reelection defeat. Again Johnson appealed to Senator Russell and again he won his endorsement. Johnson knew the hazards of the leader's job; he had witnessed the defeats of Lucas and McFarland, and he himself would face the voters of Texas in 1954. He had ideas, however, on how to enhance the leader's position, and he gave a demonstration of his parliamentary prowess almost immediately.

At the Senate Democratic caucus in January 1953, Johnson announced a cooperative policy toward President Eisenhower and the Republicans. This came as a dramatic contradiction to the confrontational opposition the Republican Taft had long shown Democratic presidents Roosevelt and Truman. "I have never agreed with the statement that it is the business of the opposition to oppose," Johnson said, paraphrasing Taft. "I do not believe that the American people sent us here to obstruct." Johnson's words had a statesmanlike ring to them not customary in the Senate's partisan battling. In the years that followed, Johnson regularly supported Eisenhower on many matters, sometimes teasing him that he, the Democratic leader, supported Eisenhower more than did the Republicans in the Senate.[11]

For his own colleagues in the Senate, Johnson had a startling reform. Traditionally, each new crop of senators in their first years had little choice on any of the spoils of office, including their committee assignments. These went to party seniors, and the newcomers got what was left. Johnson saw this allocation of committee assignments as a waste of party talent and also a possible means for him to endear himself to rank-and-file Democrats. He intended for them to share in the elite committee memberships. First, of course, he consulted Senator Russell, who tried to dissuade him. "You are dealing with the most sensitive thing in the Senate—seniority," Russell told him.[12] But Johnson launched into a frenetic campaign to persuade the most senior Democrats to allow the freshmen a more equitable portion of the choice assignments. With sheer persistence and a few humorous stories, Johnson secured the concessions he wanted.[13]

With the argument won, Johnson arranged for the newer Democrats to get assigned to committees they actually wanted. His plan not only helped fellow freshman Democrats but built a reserve of good feelings among all the party members in the Senate. This was a matter of concern to Johnson, for the Democrats had deep ideological splits that he wanted to bridge. In time, with the success of his plan on assigning committees, it became known as the "Johnson Rule," and the Senate's Republicans copied it, in part.[14]

As the party's designated leader, Johnson chaired the Democratic caucus, the Democratic Steering Committee, and the Democratic Policy Committee. He had little use for calling sessions of the caucus, lest these meetings produce nasty quarreling and infighting. But he turned the steering and policy committees to his own leadership purposes—the first to control committee assignments, the second to set a legislative agenda for the party. On both panels he sprinkled Democratic liberals, but he supplied each one with an adequate number of dependable party stalwarts. By transforming those moribund committees into effective tools of leadership, Johnson strengthened his hold on the Democratic senators. More than ever, he could help or hurt his fellow party members, and they knew it. "Lyndon has the power," said Senator John F. Kennedy, "because he hands out the loaves and fishes."[15]

As the Senate's leader, Johnson gradually assumed personal responsibility for just about all major bills, abandoning the tradition of entrusting that sensitive chore to the chairman of the committee that had reported the bill. This naturally lessened the role and authority of the committee chairmen, but many of them had a lackadaisical attitude toward their bills, as compared to Johnson's intense interest. They were content to make the presentation speech opening the Senate's debate on the bill, and then stand by while Johnson lined up the votes needed. With Bobby Baker's head count and his own, Johnson decided when to take up any given bill for consideration, then what amendments might be needed to ensure passage, and finally when to press for a vote. In his off-the-floor office, he conducted the often intricate negotiations on each bill and its needed amendments, but he did not hesitate, when the Senate was in session, to roam the Senate floor and openly apply his high-pressure methods on senator after senator.[16]

With Robert Taft gone, William Knowland emerged as a lackluster substitute. A ponderous politician, grimly given to scowling and grumbling, he proved inept, humorless, and bull-headed with few political skills and no parliamentary finesse. His bristling manners offended his own Republican colleagues; in the cloakroom they called the forty-five-year-old leader "a young fogy."[17] His awkwardness in legislative matters made him a ready foil for Lyndon Johnson, enhancing the Democratic leader's reputation as a clever legislative tactician. Repeatedly, Knowland called up bills for a Senate vote only to have Johnson tease him in whispered taunts across the center aisle: "Bill, you know you don't have the votes, don't you?"[18] Johnson had the

Senate carefully counted; Knowland did not bother with such details. On one dramatic occasion, Knowland blithely announced that he was holding the Senate in night session, but he had failed to consult Johnson. "That is no way to run the Senate," Johnson told him.[19] Johnson promptly moved to adjourn, and as usual he had the votes, again humiliating Knowland.

As the Senate's minority leader in 1953 and 1954, Johnson scored some substantive victories over Knowland and his Republican conservatives. On the touchy matter of Senator Joseph McCarthy's continuing personal denunciations of many Americans, Johnson remained aloof, seemingly indifferent. Working quietly, he finally fashioned a special Senate committee to consider censuring McCarthy and appointed to it three stalwart Democrats, all conservatives. Then, with the matter in hand, Johnson advised all Democrats to stay out of the Senate debate to prevent McCarthy's apologists from claiming Democratic partisanship.[20] When the vote came, the margin was overwhelming. Every Democrat who cast a vote supported censure, a show of party unity engineered by Johnson. Only twenty-two of the Republicans, the discredited remnants of the more conservative Taft wing of the party, supported McCarthy at the end. Johnson arranged for that vote to be held after the 1954 November elections to lower partisan pressures. In those elections, the Democrats narrowly won control in both houses of Congress. That made Johnson the Senate's majority leader.

Johnson had shown his mastery of the Senate's business. Obsessed with legislative matters, the Texan prowled the Senate floor and cloakrooms, seeking information and working his parliamentary magic, staying late at night, indifferent to such personal welfare considerations as diet and rest. He tried to speak to every Democratic senator, every day. He wanted to know where they were and where they would be, in case of the need to act. He relied much on Bobby Baker, the staff insider whom he named to the key post of Senate Democratic secretary.[21] Baker mingled constantly with senators, swapping confidences and favors. He claimed he could produce an accurate head count of the Senate on any pending question within an hour.[22] On his own, Johnson closely studied every senator, his background, his family, his hobbies, his drinking habits, his womanizing (among some), his allies back home, the economic interests and parochial biases of his state, his personal strengths and weaknesses, anything that could help Johnson win his vote in the hour of need. "He seemed to sense each man's individual price and the commodity he preferred as coin," Baker explained, "whether it might be money, flattery, vote trade-offs, public works projects, or other of the tools of power."[23]

Johnson had cordial relations with President Eisenhower, for he and House Speaker Sam Rayburn, Johnson's fellow Texan, offered the president their cooperation on many matters, especially foreign concerns. Both men personally liked Eisenhower. From time to time, the president invited them to the White House for evening drinks and pleasant talk about matters of state. "Mr. Eisenhower," Johnson said, "is the only President we've got."[24] Johnson's cooperative attitude brought complaints from some Democrats, and his supportive bent stood in striking contrast to Senator Knowland's bristling independence. Unlike previous Senate floor leaders, Knowland felt no obligation to his party's president, regularly finding fault with Eisenhower's policies and programs. In those instances, he left his front-row-center leader's desk and spoke from the rear of the Senate chamber, explaining, "I do not speak for the administration."[25]

Eisenhower met every Tuesday morning with the Republican congressional leaders. Knowland made these sessions an ordeal for the president, constantly proposing what Eisenhower called "cockeyed notions."[26] "It is a pity," Eisenhower wrote a friend, "that his wisdom, his judgment, his tact, and his sense of humor lag so far behind his ambition."[27] In 1958, Knowland left the leadership and the Senate to run for the governorship of California, an office he assumed would give him a better chance to win the 1960 presidential nomination. He lost that election, and a few years later he committed suicide.[28]

Meanwhile, Johnson's growing command of the Senate brought him great national prominence and recognition as his party's highest-ranked elected official. By then, he had built a cadre of senators on whom he could rely. They ranged from senators of formidable talent such as Richard Russell of Georgia and John Stennis of Mississippi to men of lesser stamp such as Delaware's Allen Frear and Florida's George Smathers. To some he was deferential, to others autocratic. Once, when he miscalculated on a close Senate vote, he shouted across the crowded Senate chamber to Senator Frear: "Change your vote!" Frear hesitated. "Change your vote!" Johnson ordered again. Frear did.[29]

Johnson liked to argue that as party leader, he had no means other than persuasion to influence fellow senators. "About all the leader can do is recommend," he said. "There is no patronage, no power to discipline, no power to fire senators."[30] In this, he ignored what he did have at his disposal for distribution to helpful senators: choice offices in the Senate Office Building, private hideaways in the Capitol, congressional delegation trips overseas, campaign money often in substantial amounts, committee assignments, and, as important as any, the willingness to call up for Senate action any senator's pet bill or resolution.[31]

Above all, however, was Johnson's spectacular power of persuasion, often so overwhelming that this talent of his was named the "Treatment." When a senator proved reluctant to do Johnson's bidding, Johnson subjected him to his persuasive wiles. Shameless in flattery, he appealed for the senator's help, to his patriotism and party loyalty, to his sense of history and his place within it. He pleaded and begged. One moment obsequious, the next boastful, he told jokes, mimicked colleagues, whispered gossip and personal confidences, relentless in pursuit of the senator's help. If begging failed, he would threaten, suggesting party favors he could prevent. "Let us reason together," he argued over and over, with a variety of entreaties, some of them vulgar: "The ox is in the ditch," "Your leader needs you," and "My ass is on the line."[32] All this while, in difficult cases, Johnson worked his targeted senator with his hands and arms, hugging, patting, squeezing, caressing, and then poking the senator in the chest with a bony finger to emphasize his argument.

These appeals made senators intensely uncomfortable, and he had a wide array of options for the reluctant senator. Perhaps the senator could withhold his vote until the end of the roll call and then vote Johnson's way only if his vote made the difference. If not that, perhaps the senator would agree to take a "live pair" with an absent senator, thereby negating his own vote but still on record the way he wanted. If worse came to worse, maybe the senator could arrange to be elsewhere and simply duck the vote.

Constantly consulting the Senate's parliamentarian, Johnson made himself a master of the Senate's rules and procedures.[33] Some of them he expanded in unprecedented ways. The Senate had long used unanimous consent agreements as a way to untangle the clutter of debate and set a time certain for the Senate to vote on a pending measure. Johnson seized on this procedure to package several measures and the amendments to them, along with complex side agreements, in order to satisfy significant numbers of complaining senators, any one of whom could defeat this deal-making simply by objecting. These intricate negotiations took time, and Johnson often found that time by using extended quorum calls that put the Senate, in effect, into suspended animation, sometimes for hours at a time. In institutional terms, this had the effect of denigrating Senate debate, but Johnson wanted results, and this worked to give him the outcome he desired. "What do you want," he asked in one such typical bargaining session, "houses or a housing issue?"[34]

Some Democrats complained that he compromised too readily, that he did not achieve in these bills all that he could. He had a stock response: "I got the best bill I could with the votes that I had."[35] In one such instance, suggesting his indifference to the substance of a measure, Senator Fulbright came to him, asking help on a treaty, and started to explain its provisions. "I don't give a damn about that," Johnson said to him. "Just tell me how many votes you need."[36]

As a regular instrument of his Senate leadership, Johnson relied on his "right" to recognition whenever he chose to speak. This was an outgrowth of Vice President Garner's practice of extending priority recognition to the majority leader as a courtesy. Johnson called this "the power of recognition," and he exploited this power tactically and with great skill. With it, he orchestrated the Senate's proceedings however he wished under the terms he dictated. When he had conditions just right, with his head count favorable and his members at hand, he could act. In one such instance, on a quiet day in 1955, with a minimum-wage bill on the schedule, Johnson noticed the careless absence of the opposition's designated sentry for this bill, Florida's Spessard Holland. Johnson asked for recognition, moved a brief quorum call, brought the bill before the Senate, and passed it by voice vote. Senator Holland belatedly rushed into the Senate chamber, protesting furiously. "Well, Spessard," Johnson said to him, "I had a little quorum call. If you fellows aren't on the job around here, I've got legislation to pass."[37]

With extraordinary talent and his driving ambition, Johnson came to dominate the Senate and its decisions as no senator before him, not even Henry Clay or Nelson Aldrich. Seemingly in perpetual high gear, he lifted the majority leadership to new power and prestige. Partly he was able to do this because of the lackluster leadership of Senator Knowland. Principally, however, he rose to this stature because he had a Republican in the White House and that Republican had only a casual interest in most legislative matters. As the leader of the Senate's Democrats, Johnson had no party obligations to President Eisenhower. He treated the president with tolerance. Between the two men there existed a kind of parity that Johnson could never enjoy with a chief executive of his own party in the White House.

With his elevated status in political Washington, Johnson began to take on airs that troubled some of his colleagues. Never a modest man, he bristled at anything smacking of criticism. He ordered press photographers never to take his photograph from his "bad side," the right profile, or when he was wearing eyeglasses.[38] As though to complement his stature as the Senate's leader, Johnson claimed for his use a large committee room just off the Senate floor and made it his leadership office.[39] The great room was a show-place, its ceiling richly decorated with elaborate frescoes. Johnson had it embellished with trappings of his own, including a private restroom (the ultimate status symbol in a building with a dearth of such facilities) and fully stocked bar, discreetly concealed, with a bartender available when needed. Here Johnson entertained those he wished to impress. In mockery, Senate media correspondents nicknamed Johnson's gorgeous new headquarters the Taj Mahal.[40]

These imperial pretensions did not last. In the 1958 congressional elections, the Democrats made spectacular gains in both the House and the Senate. Until then, as majority leader, Johnson had to work with just a bare majority in the Senate, a margin so narrow that it gave credence to Johnson's attempts to keep his Democrats united. Now, in the 1959–60 Senate, Johnson suddenly had an overwhelming majority of sixty-five Democrats to only thirty-five Republicans, a net gain of fifteen Democrats, most of them liberals. They proved less than responsive to Johnson's domineering ways. Also, Senate Republicans gained a new leader in Everett Dirksen of Illinois, a skilled legislator deeply committed to President Eisenhower. Then, too, Eisenhower himself had taken alarm at these Democratic gains and resolved to fight this presumed threat with heavy use of his presidential veto.

The party's liberals had long resented Johnson's dominance and strong-arm tactics. In early 1959, one of the freshman senators, Wisconsin's William Proxmire, went public with these complaints in a series of speeches denouncing what he called Johnson's "one-man rule." "The typical Democratic senator," Proxmire said, "has literally nothing to do with determining the legislative program and policies of the party." He chided Johnson for not allowing regular meetings of the party caucus and for setting party policy on his own on an "off-the-cuff" basis. Proxmire received little public support from colleagues, and one senator, Oregon's Richard Neuberger, berated Proxmire as an ingrate. "You are biting the hands that feed you," Neuberger told him. "Everything you've got in the Senate was given to you by Lyndon Johnson." That was exactly Proxmire's point. Johnson decided everything from committee assignments to what legislation the Senate would consider. "There has never been a time," Proxmire said, "when power has been so sharply concentrated as it is today in the Senate."[41]

Johnson, of course, deeply resented his critics, but he took solace in the results of his management of the Senate, and he tried in 1960 to parlay his accomplishments as his party's Senate leader into the Democratic presidential nomination. At the party's national convention in Los Angeles, however, the nomination went to John F. Kennedy, almost ten years Johnson's junior and a back-row senator who was not part of Johnson's Senate leadership. When Kennedy offered him the vice-presidential nomination, Johnson had to make what many of his allies thought an impossible choice.

In previous years, Johnson had repeatedly declared, often in vivid and vulgar terms, that he would not accept a nomination as vice president, and he did so in such strident language that even his colleagues expressed surprise when he accepted Kennedy's offer. Kennedy's nomination substantially changed Johnson's political prospects. If Kennedy won, he would presumably be re-nominated in 1964, and that meant that Johnson would have no chance at the presidential nomination for another eight years. If Kennedy lost, Johnson would remain the Democratic leader of the Senate, operating as he had with Eisenhower with a new Republican president. Kennedy's success threatened to turn Senator Johnson into a mere presidential lieutenant, or in Johnson's terms a political pygmy. Nonetheless, he opted for the vice presidency. Perhaps he could do something with that office. He had transformed the bland majority leadership into the Senate's power center, and he had the energy and arrogance not to be shunted aside at this point in his career.[42]

After the election, Johnson as vice president–elect undertook a somewhat bizarre scheme to make his new job even more powerful than the one he was leaving. Traditionally, the vice president had little authority over anything, but that did not trouble Lyndon Johnson. With his ingenuity, he saw possibilities in the vice presidency. With his formidable talents, he hoped to carry the power he had won as majority leader into his new job as the Senate's presiding officer, to transfer control of the Senate from the Senate floor to the vice president's chair. "Power is where power goes," he preached.[43] Johnson expected to retain his power as though it belonged to him personally, rather than being innately rooted in the job he had held.

He began immediately to make the needed arrangements, starting with the choice of his successor as the Senate's majority leader. He wanted Mike Mansfield of Montana to take the job, but Mansfield balked. Mansfield finally relented after President-elect Kennedy said to him: "I need you."[44] Mansfield had served as the party whip for Senate Democrats for four years, and his promotion to floor leader seemed natural and in keeping with a growing Senate practice. In another negotiation, Johnson arranged for Minnesota's Hubert Humphrey to replace Mansfield as party whip.

With the new leadership settled, Johnson conferred with Mansfield, whose acquiescence he needed for his planned operations as vice president.

For his headquarters, he wanted to keep the Taj Mahal, the fancy suite he had created for himself as party leader. That was no problem. Mansfield, an unusually modest man, did not want it. Then Johnson asked Mansfield to keep Bobby Baker, his longtime special agent, in his Senate job. Finally, he asked Mansfield to allow him, as vice president, to preside over the sessions of the Senate's Democratic caucus. This was an extraordinary request. Since the 1890s, the senator the Democrats picked as their caucus chairman also served as their designated party floor leader. But Mansfield saw no institutional hazards in Johnson's request, and Mansfield himself, as Johnson knew, had little use for the badges and spoils of public office. He agreed to make such a motion at the next party caucus. Johnson was delighted at Mansfield's responses. "It's going to be just like it was," he told Bobby Baker.[45]

At the party caucus on January 3, 1961, Mansfield was unanimously elected party leader, and he made the motion to have Johnson, as vice president, preside over sessions of the caucus in the coming Congress. That shocked many of the senators, including some of Johnson's best friends, among them New Mexico's Clinton Anderson and Virginia's Willis Robertson. Anderson told his colleagues that this could not be done, that such an arrangement would violate the Constitution's separation of powers. Senator Albert Gore Sr. supported Anderson: "The distinguished Vice President is no longer a Democratic senator."[46] Johnson sat there, embarrassed, his face ashen. Senators were treating his plan as a power grab. Mansfield was upset at this uproar, and he threatened to quit as party leader if his motion was rejected. The caucus, by secret ballot, voted forty-six to seventeen to approve the motion, but Johnson knew what that really meant. He stalked out of the room. "Those bastards sandbagged me," he muttered.[47] From that moment, Johnson fell into a sulk, refusing to have any role at all in the Senate's deliberations. Although he returned to an occasional caucus meeting, he left leadership to Mike Mansfield.[48]

Johnson and Mansfield were polar opposites, an astonishingly vain and domineering extrovert versus a self-effacing introvert. Mansfield made no deals and he deferred to the committee chairmen, assuming they would act responsibly. When a committee chairman brought a bill to the Senate floor, Mansfield turned over his front-row leader's desk to the man, the better for him to manage the debate and voting. Mansfield then took a seat in the back of the chamber or, inconspicuously, with the Senate's clerks.[49]

With Mike Mansfield, there would be no rough tactics. He had no system of rewards and punishments for his colleagues, and he never tried to browbeat any of them into voting the way he wanted. "I've always urged the

Democrats to vote as their consciences dictated," he stated, "but if they had any doubts, to give the administration the benefit of that doubt."[50] Unlike Johnson, Mansfield had a Democratic administration to support.

Mansfield abandoned Johnson's tactic of holding late-night sessions, partly because of the unseemliness of senators answering quorum calls after midnight in pajama tops, but principally because of the risk to the health of the older senators. Instead, he wanted to improve senators' quality of life, not subject them to physical punishment. "I've tried to hold the Senate to a reasonable hour," he said, "so senators could get home to their families for dinner."[51] He did battle filibusters from time to time, and he did so with success but without endangering any of his colleagues. In time, he created a new technique to tolerate filibusters in daylight hours without paralyzing other Senate operations.

"My job is to represent the Senate to the President," Mansfield said, "and the President to the Senate. I'm the Senate's agent primarily. . . . I'm not the leader really," he said. "My Democratic colleagues are the leaders. They don't do what I tell them. I do what they tell me. When they call, I jump." He saw himself as a kind of den mother. "My job is just keeping the party together, smoothing over the differences, keeping tempers, and trying to achieve the possible despite the differences inherent in the party."[52]

Mansfield's view of his leadership role reflected his personality and also the clearly expressed attitude of other Democratic senators, who had grown tired of Johnson's bullying tactics. Johnson had wielded a fiercely burning torch of leadership authority; Mansfield was content to be guardian of one hundred flickering senatorial candles.

Mansfield's seeming abdication offered a leadership invitation to Minnesota Senator Hubert Humphrey, newly elected as his party's Senate whip. Humphrey plunged joyfully into the early Senate struggles over President Kennedy's legislative program. An instinctive enthusiast with uncommon vitality, he was agog over this opportunity, and he gave new importance to the secondary office he held. When Mansfield had been whip, the job meant little. "As whip," Mansfield confessed, "I was really a figurehead."[53] Majority Leader Johnson had done everything. Humphrey had no such difficulty, and much of the Kennedy administration program flowed from ideas first proposed by Senator Humphrey. "I am in the thick of things," he boasted to a friend.[54] That did not mean, however, that he received much credit. In one notorious instance in 1961, he and Mansfield, with major help from White House operatives and lobbyists, worked strenuously to save a housing bill from defeat. Later they met with the press. "John Sparkman deserves the full credit," Mansfield said, citing the Alabama senator who was chairman of the sponsoring committee. "He did the job."[55] Senator Humphrey gagged, and Sparkman himself was startled, for he had played only a minor role in this struggle. Mansfield wanted credit to go to the appropriate chairman, not himself.

By 1963, Mansfield, in his guileless way, had begun building a remarkable partnership with Senate Republican leader Everett Dirksen. By no means did this partnership work on much domestic legislation, but in a few critical areas of foreign policy and civil rights, Mansfield found in Dirksen the ally who made Senate action possible. During Dirksen's ten years as leader of the Senate's Republicans, he never had much more than a third of the Senate backing him. Even so, by the odd happenstances of the struggles in which he engaged, he managed to become the Senate's most influential member. Not only did he have control of some of the Senate's most important decisions, but by his flamboyance and eloquence he even achieved the notoriety of folk hero.

Elected to the Senate in 1950, Dirksen had special reason to resent Eisenhower's convention victory over Senator Taft in 1952. Had Taft won the party's presidential nomination, Dirksen had hopes that Taft would pick him for vice president. In Eisenhower's first years as president, Dirksen joined with other Taft-loyalist senators in various displays of their displeasure at Eisenhower's success. During the Senate's 1954 proceedings to censure Joseph McCarthy, Eisenhower's abusive antagonist, Dirksen served as McCarthy's chief defender. Later, with Taft gone and McCarthy rebuked and his own reelection in 1956 in doubt, Dirksen underwent dramatic change. Gradually, he became the most ardent supporter in the Senate of the immensely popular Eisenhower, a switch that the president rewarded with high praise and flattering approval. After the 1956 elections, with Senator Knowland now likely to depart the Senate, Senator Bridges and other party leaders arranged to elect Dirksen as the Senate's Republican whip. That put Dirksen in place to succeed Knowland when he left. Then, as Knowland absented himself to campaign in California for the governorship, Dirksen slipped into the role of the Republicans' "acting" floor leader. The party's progressives made a belated and listless effort to run one of their own against Dirksen for the party leadership, but Dirksen readily won the job in 1959. He had already shown Eisenhower and his colleagues that he had far different ideas than Knowland on how to behave in that post.[56]

Eisenhower found Dirksen far more congenial than the often pompous Knowland, and he came to rely more and more on the colorful leader.

In personal terms, this was heady stuff for Dirksen. A veteran of sixteen years in the House, Dirksen had formidable skills in parliamentary maneuver. He had watched Knowland's often bizarre antics with dismay. He had watched Lyndon Johnson's performance, too, and he knew the difference. As the Republicans' designated leader in the Senate, he would shun Knowland's gaucheries as best he could, and he would employ Johnson's techniques using his own variations. For starters, he wanted to try to unify the Senate's Republicans, long bitterly divided between the Old Guard conservatives and the progressives. With the approval of New Hampshire Senator Styles Bridges, at the party caucus that elected him leader, Dirksen quietly made sure that the party chose California's Thomas Kuchel as party whip. Kuchel, an engaging politician with a rollicking sense of humor, was the progressives' candidate for that post, and Dirksen's token gesture in this was not missed.[57] Then Dirksen adopted Johnson's tactic of ensuring all of his party members at least one choice Senate committee, a plan that did Dirksen no harm in the appreciation of freshmen senators. This sort of "reform" hardly pleased the party's seniors, but Dirksen, to show the way, gave up his best committees, Appropriations and Labor, to new senators. "The leader takes what's left," Dirksen stated. "Every man got a first-class committee."[58]

In another area, Dirksen revived the Senate Republicans' policy committee, which Knowland had allowed to lapse, and arranged for its members to meet each week for lunch to discuss party policy and strategy. In time, he enlarged this gathering to include all of the Senate's Republicans. At the conclusion of these lunches, Dirksen showed up at the Senate's press gallery to report what the party members had considered and decided. Perched on a table, sipping coffee from a paper cup and cadging cigarettes from reporters, Dirksen put on a remarkable show, fielding questions and offering confidences that on occasion helped to gather as many as sixty journalists for a recap. He tried to act responsively, understanding the political value of publicity, and he had a sophisticated knowledge of the reporters' needs: a catchy phrase that might make a headline for the wire services, somber analysis of the crisis of the moment for serious newspapers, and graphic details of behind-the-scenes carryings-on for the newsweeklies. From these sessions, Dirksen gained a considerable national audience.

Some senators, tutored in Johnson's coercive methods, also complained that Mike Mansfield did not crack the party whip. In early November 1963, at a night session, Connecticut Democrat Thomas Dodd, a Johnson intimate, took the Senate floor to attack Mansfield's leadership.[59] Republican leader Dirksen asked for recognition and then unleashed on Dodd a savage verbal assault, accusing him of "cerebral incoherence."[60] Dirksen would not tolerate the abuse. Dodd apologized to Mansfield the next day. The year before, in a similar incident, Oregon's Wayne Morse, an unusually vain politician, renounced Mansfield as party leader and in effect called him a liar.[61] Instantly, Dirksen was on his feet and called Morse to order for his "indecorous language" under the Senate's rarely invoked Rule 19.[62] That silenced Morse and forced him to take his seat, a stinging rebuke to the senator.

By this time, each floor leader had become, in institutional terms, the principal power of his party in the Senate. Whoever held the post still had many of the nagging routine chores that smacked of a janitor's duties, but there was now far more to these jobs than hanging around the Senate all day and, when the day's work was done, turning off the lights. Senator Taft had given special stature to the majority leadership, and then Lyndon Johnson had demonstrated how powerful that post could become. Operating from a totally different stance, Mansfield caught criticism for his self-effacing style, but he shared with Johnson a deep commitment to get legislative results, and get them he did. Under his leadership, however unobtrusive, the Senate passed an extraordinary volume of meaningful legislation. Those measures included the landmark civil rights bills, none of which Johnson could have risked in his own Senate years, and an array of domestic legislation, including Medicare, that reshaped the nation and its people. For his part, too, Senator Dirksen, for all his bombast and political shenanigans, made the minority leadership meaningful as never before.[63]

Mansfield had shown, as Dirksen had, that there was more than one way to lead the Senate effectively. Mansfield welcomed criticism. "I have been criticized," he said at one point. "The criticism is justified." He willingly took the blame for what he called "my principal failures"—any legislation that the Senate failed to pass. "I have no successes," he said, "because what we've done, the Senate has done." "When it comes to parliamentary tricks," Mansfield said, "I have none, and if I had any, I wouldn't use them. I make no deals of any kind."[64] Mansfield distributed authority and credit among his Senate colleagues, and they liked that.

The enhanced prestige of the party floor leaders had the effect of making their assistants, the party whips, more important than ever, primarily because whoever held that post had the best chance of succeeding to the leadership. Created a half century earlier as a secondary position to the designated floor leader, himself then a secondary figure in the Senate's hierarchy, the whip had little to do of significance for the next several decades. Senator Humphrey, as whip, had played a major role in floor operations under Mansfield's leadership, especially with the Civil Rights Act of 1964, and when he was elected vice president later that year, the post attracted no fewer than six senior Democrats to consider campaigning for it. Louisiana's Russell Long won on the second caucus ballot. He found the job less than exhilarating. "The majority leader makes the decisions," he complained.[65] His disinterest became obvious, and that enticed Senator Edward Kennedy of Massachusetts to challenge him in January 1969. Kennedy won, but he also soon proved less than enthusiastic about the required work. That prompted West Virginia's Robert Byrd, an ally of Senator Long, to challenge Kennedy in January 1971. On his own initiative, Byrd had taken on Kennedy's neglected chores as party whip, and that won him the title to match the work.[66]

Meanwhile, in 1969, the post of the Senate's Republican whip became vacant, and that touched off another intraparty fight. Senator Dirksen wanted the job to go to Nebraska's Roman Hruska, his closest ally in the Senate, but Pennsylvania's Hugh Scott, a longtime Eisenhower Republican, won out over Hruska, twenty-three to twenty.

When Dirksen died later that year, Scott, as party whip, had an initial advantage in the struggle to succeed him. Several senators, including Hruska, considered challenging Scott, but in the end the party conservatives backed Tennessee's Howard Baker Jr., a political moderate, but more conservative than Scott. Scott won the caucus vote, twenty-four to nineteen. He brought to the Senate a far different kind of party leadership than Dirksen had provided, a style that pleased at least some of his colleagues but offended President Richard Nixon.

As the Senate's minority leader, Scott had his own set of priorities, and President Nixon did not come first. His priorities lay with his Pennsylvania constituents and his Senate colleagues. Scott did not see himself as the president's man in the Senate beyond informing his Republican colleagues about Nixon's wishes on legislation and other matters. Certainly, he would not act as the White House enforcer of the president's demands. That opened a breach between Scott and the White House. Nixon lieutenants H. R. Haldeman and John Ehrlichman, ignorant of Washington ways, began their White House service with unusual contempt for members of Congress—a "herd of mediocrities," in Ehrlichman's phrase.[67] They held the leaders of Congress in total disdain, including Senator Scott, whom they regarded as a political hack, and Michigan's Gerald Ford, the House Republican leader. They expected Scott and Ford to take orders from the White House. "We existed, they seemed to believe," Ford later wrote, "only to take their instructions."[68]

At the close of 1976, Senators Mansfield and Scott both retired from the Senate. That touched off a scramble within the two parties to choose their successors, now a matter of full competition. The party whips, West Virginia's Robert Byrd and Michigan's Robert Griffin, had an early advantage, because each had functioned as his party's assistant floor leader. Under Mansfield's benign management, Byrd had assumed much of the routine of the Senate's daily operations, demonstrating a mastery of the Senate's rules as well as a talent for devising complex unanimous consent agreements to speed legislation to fruition. He had also proved instrumental in proposing several reforms in sloppy Senate practices to make the place more dignified and orderly. Robert Griffin was President Gerald Ford's closest friend in the Senate, with special skills of his own as a legislative tactician.

Gerald Ford's 1976 presidential election defeat hurt Griffin's chances. Not only did he lose his obvious White House clout, but with Democrat Jimmy Carter now president, Senate Republicans needed their leader to be a charismatic spokesman. Griffin hardly fit that billing, but until the last moment he seemed the only candidate. Tennessee's Howard Baker had been privately lining up votes for himself, however, but he did not decide to run until the party caucus had begun. He won by the barest margin, nineteen to eighteen. Baker had gained widespread acclaim for his prominent role in the Senate's Watergate investigating committee. As Republican leader, he brought to the job a much different outlook than Senator Byrd.

Byrd, a consummate parliamentarian, well versed in tactical and strategic maneuvers, knew ways, with patience, to turn even a hostile Senate into favoring seemingly hopeless causes. He had a deep commitment to the Senate, but less so to any president. Byrd had long since worked out his own creed about presidents. Standing before the party caucus that had elected him leader, Byrd pledged that his first responsibility was to the Senate. "I trust that God will give me the courage and the wisdom always to act for the highest good of the Senate," he said then. Not the president, not the country, not the party, but the Senate.[69] In his years as senator, Byrd had aligned himself with a small group of conservative senior members, whose devotion to the Senate evoked a sense of religious commitment. They felt that their service in the Senate and to the Senate was a higher calling than vouchsafed to other men. Presidents came and went. The Senate endured.

"I don't want a confrontation," was how Byrd explained his relations with President Jimmy Carter. "I'm the President's friend, but I'm not the President's man. I'm the Senate's man. That doesn't mean I won't cooperate with the President. I will. I want him to succeed. I don't see myself as the President's man. I was here before he came, and I will be here after he goes."[70]

Robert Byrd and Howard Baker took care not to take each other by surprise. "We're not going to come up on the blind side of each other," Baker had said in the midst of one struggle.[71] They led opposing parties, but this was more than mere courtesy. Each was a close student of the Senate's ways, and they both understood the need for cooperation and compromise. After Byrd moved into the leadership ranks in the late 1960s, he abandoned some of his more conservative views. "One had to stand on the middle ground to get the votes together to pass things," he explained.[72]

Senators with their varied demands, Byrd said, made him at times "a traffic cop, babysitter, welfare worker, minister, lawyer, punching bag, target, lightning rod—all this and more."[73] He regularly tried to hold the Senate to a full five-day workweek, but senators constantly objected to votes on Mondays and Fridays, when they wanted to be elsewhere. A talented master himself of the filibuster, he complained also that this once rarely used tactic was now used "promiscuously" on even trivial matters. It was an increasing problem for Senate leaders.

Senator Baker, a sophisticated lawyer in private practice, had an engaging way as a politician of lapsing into a shorthand Tennessee cornpone drawl. "Ain't got no dog in that fight," he said repeatedly about not meddling in other senators' controversies. "No education in the second kick of a mule," he said from time to time as he cautioned colleagues not to repeat a mistake.[74] His relaxed, self-effacing manner won him admiration from his Senate colleagues of both parties as well as the national press corps. As a new senator, Baker studied closely the Senate's ongoing operations and methods, fascinated by the play of power politics. All this made him an unusually skilled legislator long before he won the party's leadership.

In those 1980 elections, to the surprise of many, the nation's voters elected so many new Republicans to the Senate that they had a clear majority for the first time since 1954. That made Baker the Senate's majority leader. California's Ronald Reagan, the Republican nominee, won the presidency. "I am the president's point-man here," Baker said. "I'm going to stay loyal to him."[75] He met privately with Reagan shortly after his inauguration to give him those assurances. "Look, Mr. President," he said, "there are some things on which you and I may disagree, and if we do and if I must take a separate position, I will try to let you know in advance. You should know that on every issue where it's a close call, I'm going to resolve the issue in your favor."[76]

With the Senate in session, Baker kept close to the Senate floor, on the alert for whatever came up. "The cloakroom becomes my office," he explained. "The floor is my domain."[77] He had quickly shown himself an effective leader of the Senate, largely responsible for President Reagan's legislative successes. With his mild manners and easy ways, he won remarkable support from his colleagues, for there was stern resolve behind his smiles.

Whatever his commitments to Reagan, Baker saw that the fundamental responsibility of the Senate's leader was "to make the place work."[78] That was not easy. His Senate Republicans, particularly after the 1980 election, had deep ideological splits. Baker saw his job as bringing them together if he could. "That's the only way you can get things done," he said. "The education of a Senate leader ends in the third grade," he said. "When you learn how to count, you've completed the educational requirement."[79] To juggle those numbers to create a Senate majority, however, was immensely complex. He had many ways to persuade legislators. "Look," he would say, "I've got to have this vote. What can I do to make it easier for you?" "If you'll not offer your amendment on this particular resolution, I'll find another vehicle for you."[80]

Baker had in his ranks some especially difficult senators, among them North Carolina's deeply conservative Jesse Helms and Alaska's irascible Ted Stevens. Connecticut's Lowell Weicker, not a modest fellow, had his own agenda. "I used to call him in every now and then," Baker disclosed years later, "and say, 'Now, Lowell, you can only be a moral giant once this week.'"[81] In dealing with these contrary senators, Baker relied on his extraordinary patience and private persuasion.

Baker found solace in the assumption that he failed in his 1980 try for the presidency primarily because he was handicapped by his leadership job. He knew that Nixon, Carter, and Reagan, the three most recently elected presidents, had run for the office unencumbered by holding any other public office. He decided to copy their example. He chose not to run for reelection in 1984. "I make no bones about it," he said. "I want to be President."[82]

Senator Bob Dole disagreed with Baker that Senate leadership was a handicap. Setting out to replace him as Republican leader, the Kansan had stiff competition. Four other senators also announced for the position, the most ever. At the party caucus in mid-November 1984, Republican senators had to vote four times, each time by secret ballot—with the contestant polling the fewest votes dropping out of the next round—before Dole emerged as the new majority leader.

Dole had a skeptical view of President Reagan's seemingly simple-minded approaches to complex problems, and that made him less inclined than

Baker to follow the president's lead. Four years earlier, in 1981, as the new chairman of the Senate's Finance Committee, Dole had gone along with Reagan's requests for massive tax cuts, but only with deep misgivings. Those tax cuts helped produce a serious recession and then huge budget deficits. Reagan and his advisers supported the theory of "supply-side economics," believing that by slashing taxes they could spur economic growth and thus bring the Treasury more revenues. That had not happened, and Dole, in his sardonic way, used gallows-humor good-news, bad-news taunts to show his annoyance. "The good news is that a bus full of supply-siders went off a cliff," Dole said repeatedly. "The bad news is there were three empty seats."[83]

In 1982, to counter the huge budget deficits then afflicting the nation, Dole pushed through Congress a bill to retrieve about one-third of these lost revenues. With flair and great skill, he had maneuvered the measure through the Finance Committee, the Senate, and the House, then persuaded President Reagan that what he proposed was tax "reform," not tax increases. As Senate leader, he made plain that he intended to pursue his own agenda, without coaching from President Reagan or his lieutenants.

In his role as majority leader, Dole took drastic action in trying to cut the massive deficits in Reagan's budget proposals and to help ensure reelection for those of his Senate Republicans then campaigning. "We have to make tough decisions," he said of Reagan's budget, and not just "nickel and dime" the huge deficits. Reagan had made major changes difficult. "You can't touch defense, and you can't touch Social Security," Dole said, quoting Reagan, "and you can't raise revenues." With help from Republican senators, Dole produced an alternative "leadership" budget that not only cut Reagan's defense requests, but also proposed a freeze on Social Security cost-of-living adjustments and some increased taxes.[84]

With the 1986 elections in the offing, he devised a clever new tactic not only to frustrate the Senate's Democrats, but to monopolize sponsorship of popular amendments to the budget for his fellow Republicans. He did this by claiming his "right" to immediate recognition from the presiding officer. This went far beyond Vice President Garner's policy of recognizing the majority leader as a mere courtesy. Day after day, Dole offered amendment after amendment, and amendments to the amendments. Then he would farm each to those Republican senators most helped by sponsoring the amendment at hand.

The most notorious came on those Social Security cost-of-living adjustments, always a popular election-year target for Democrats. For the Democrats, New York's Daniel Patrick Moynihan had ready an amendment to cancel Dole's proposed freeze on benefits. Dole cut him off. Claiming his priority right to recognition, Dole offered on his own a copycat version of Moynihan's amendment and then transferred its sponsorship to two Republicans, New York's Alfonse D'Amato and Florida's Paula Hawkins, both up for reelection in states with large constituencies of Social Security beneficiaries. Dole himself opposed the amendment he offered, and subsequently voted against it. In this, Dole had turned the amendment process upside down, and Democrats were outraged. Traditionally, any senator could offer any amendments to almost any measures without restriction.

Dole's tactic, brand-new in Senate proceedings, was an obvious abuse of the Senate's normal proceedings, and the Democrats' leader, Robert Byrd, angrily denounced this "hard-ball" innovation. "The minority is gagged," he protested. "The minority is shut out from offering amendments."[85] Under Dole's management, and as a consequence of the polarizing election of 1980, the Senate was becoming a more partisan place. Under his control, Democrats could offer amendments only with his permission, and they had to show him each amendment in advance. On August 5, 1986, apparently by accident, the Democrats slipped one past him without permission, and he voiced his annoyance at this "surprise." Byrd exploded in anger. "I have had enough of this business of having the majority leader stand here and act as a traffic cop on this floor," he shouted. "He determines who will call up an amendment, when they will call it up, and what will be in the amendment."[86] Dole did not apologize for his tactic. "I did not become majority leader to lose," he said.[87]

For all his scrambling and hardball tactics, Dole failed in his purpose in the 1986 elections. Republicans lost a net of eight seats, thereby giving the Senate's Democrats a majority of fifty-five to forty-five in the new Congress. That again reduced Senator Dole to the minority. He would complain later that as majority leader he had not had the "tools of persuasion" that Lyndon Johnson used when he was majority leader. "In this age of weakened party loyalties," Dole argued, "any Majority Leader is part ringmaster and part traffic cop. He is an architect, building a legislative house brick by brick, commitment by commitment. Most of all he is a juggler, keeping half a dozen balls in the air while looking down the road to see where vectors of policy and politics converge."[88] Whatever his complaints, he stayed on as Republican leader in the next Congress, and Senator Byrd again became the Senate's majority leader. Byrd continued in that post for two more years, before taking on the more politically rewarding assignment as chair of the Appropriations Committee in 1989. Dole returned to the majority leader's role in 1995, but having come to recognize its drag on presidential aspirations, he resigned in 1996 to lock up his party's presidential nomination. He went on to lose the general election to the incumbent Bill Clinton.

Party leaders' increasing abuses of the Senate's traditional ways of proceeding had a meaning beyond the episodes themselves. They were part of a less-than-gracious change coming within the Senate that was making the place more strident and partisan. There were still friendships across the Senate's center aisle, but the continuing loss of comity within the Senate was causing alarm. In the years immediately ahead, Senate party leaders, including Byrd and Dole, would use more high-handed methods, with the traditional senatorial courtesies not always forgotten, but certainly badly neglected.

To replace Senator Byrd, Senate Democrats on November 29, 1988, elected Maine's George Mitchell. The *New York Times* observed about that contest what might be said of any modern-era Senate leadership election: "The process is at once as quaint as electing a class president, as solemn as selecting a new Pope, and as laden with intrigue as a shake-up in the Kremlin."[89]

Mitchell owed his rapid ascent to leadership to the fatherly patronage of two powerful senators: Edmund Muskie and Robert Byrd. He had joined Muskie's Washington staff in the early 1960s, out of Bowdoin College and Georgetown University Law School. Several years later, he returned to Maine to practice law. After two unsuccessful campaigns for statewide office, and with Muskie's crucial endorsement, the Senate confirmed his late 1970s appointment to be US attorney for Maine, and subsequently to a federal district judgeship. In 1980, Mitchell returned to the legislative branch as an appointed US senator, filling the seat Muskie vacated to become US secretary of state. Two years later, against oddsmakers' predictions, he decisively won the seat in his own right.

Majority Leader Robert Byrd—Muskie's 1958 Senate classmate—took an immediate liking to his friend's former protégé. Admiring Mitchell's tough-minded competence and low-key manner, Byrd saw to it that he received choice committee assignments. That confidence eventually netted Mitchell the chair of the Democratic Senatorial Campaign Committee for the 1986 election cycle. The resulting crop of eleven new Democratic senators, who returned that party to majority status in 1987 for the first time in six years, earned Mitchell appointment to the honorific post of deputy president pro tempore, previously held only by Senator and former vice president Hubert Humphrey.[90] Mitchell's participation in the 1987 congressional investigation of the Reagan administration's missteps in the Iran-Contra affair enhanced his image for quiet and tough-minded competence. Drawing on a physical presence and judicial manner that prompted one senator to observe that "people don't lie to George Mitchell,"[91] the Maine senator earned headlines for his skillful questioning of Lieutenant Colonel Oliver North—"Recognize that it is possible for an American to disagree with you on aid to the Contras and still love God, and still love his country, just as much as you do."[92]

As majority leader, Mitchell blocked several of President George H. W. Bush's efforts to redeem a campaign pledge to cut the capital gains tax. In 1992, the Senate replaced what Mitchell branded "a tax cut for the rich" with a middle-class tax cut.[93] This provoked Bush to veto the legislation in the middle of his own reelection campaign, thus helping to elect Bill Clinton. Although Mitchell was subsequently unable to push Clinton's health-care plan through Congress, he could claim credit for enactment of other landmark legislation, including the Americans with Disabilities Act, the Clean Air Act Reauthorization, and the North American Free Trade Agreement.

A talented negotiator and as competitive on the Senate floor as he was on the tennis court, Mitchell helped unite his fellow Democrats during increasingly fractious times. Republican Trent Lott, who arrived in the Senate in 1989 at the start of Mitchell's leadership tenure, later observed, "He came across as moderate and thoughtful, yet he was a very vicious liberal partisan. . . . The schedule was terrible and there was no certainty. Some days we wouldn't know whether there would be further votes until after nine o'clock in the evening." The future Republican majority leader blamed this on Mitchell, "a driven bachelor who didn't seem to understand that other senators had families."[94]

Mitchell carried on the tradition of working closely with his Republican counterpart, Bob Dole, explaining that he told Dole "that I would never, ever surprise him, in a procedural or other way, that I would notify him in advance of what I would do, that I had no desire or interest in embarrassing him in any way, that the job was difficult enough in the best of circumstances."[95]

In 1994, Mitchell announced his retirement, suggesting that he was ready for a less strenuous way to spend his days. Addressing the departing leader's effectiveness, veteran congressional correspondent Adam Clymer concluded, "The very characteristics that deny Mr. Mitchell attention—the control of his temper, the willingness to yield center stage and the sometimes tedious command and explication of detail—were essential to success."[96]

His successor, Tom Daschle, added, "In the heat of the fiercest debate, George was able to maintain a moderate, reasonable, well-balanced tone, even as he doggedly pursued a different agenda."[97]

Daschle won the leadership election by a single vote over the more combative but equally liberal-leaning Christopher Dodd. Daschle faced a rising conservative tide, with Republicans preparing to return to the majority after eight years, eager for combat with President Clinton, who was burdened by a 54 percent public disapproval rating.[98] Tough times lay ahead for the Senate's Democrats. One of them, Louisiana's John Breaux, when asked why he did not enter the leadership race, laughed and sheepishly explained, "I was afraid that if I ran, I might have won."[99]

Like George Mitchell before him, Tom Daschle had been a senator for only eight years, had previously learned about Senate operations from the "in the weeds" perspective of a onetime staff aide, had the reputation among influential senior members of being a "rising star," and had a prestigious berth on the Senate Finance Committee. Noted for "a deft intellect and feverish ambition," Daschle was also described as "soft-spoken and gentle."[100] He approached his leadership responsibilities with guarded optimism, but was well aware of the challenges that moved columnist Mary McGrory to compare leading the Senate to leading the Metropolitan Opera—a task of "juggling enormous and fragile egos."[101] In the manner of Lyndon Johnson, Daschle realized that the effective leader must patiently study each member to decipher what it is that motivates that senator, and what makes him or her willing to consider casting a vote against personal or constituency interests.[102]

Trent Lott reflected on the years between 1996 and 2002 when he and Daschle served as their respective parties' floor leaders. "I found him to be a formidable opponent, and a committed Democratic partisan—a Prairie Populist. But there is a side of him you can trust."[103] Daschle returned the compliment, noting, "To Trent's credit, he was sometimes able to resist forces within his own party who wanted to close off all lines of communication between us many times."[104] Both leaders took pride in their unfettered communication. Daschle later urged future Senate leaders to "install a hot-line where you just pick the phone and it goes directly to the other leader. Trent and I were on it a lot."[105]

Daschle found his own leadership skills under assault in the 107th Congress, between 2001 and 2003. He later described that chaotic period as "like no other time"[106] in the life of the nation. It began with the Supreme Court's five-to-four decision to award the presidency to George W. Bush, and with the unprecedented Senate party division of fifty Democrats and fifty Republicans. That split allowed the Democrats, with Vice President Al Gore providing the tie-breaking vote, to organize the Senate from January 3 through January 19, 2001, with Daschle leading this temporary majority. When Dick Cheney replaced Gore as vice president on January 20, Daschle reverted to minority leader, only to be restored to majority status in June, as Vermont's independent-minded Senator James Jeffords, under Daschle's vigorous lobbying, abandoned the Republican Party to caucus with Senate Democrats. Then came the terrorist attacks of September 2001 on New York City's World Trade Center, and, within viewing distance of the US Capitol, the Pentagon. Weeks later, in an atmosphere of acute crisis, an envelope packed with a lethal dose of anthrax spores, addressed to Daschle, arrived in his Senate office building mailroom. For the next three months, half the Senate's members and their staffs were displaced from the quarantined Hart Senate Office Building.

The 108th Congress (2003–05) brought the Senate's acquiescence to the Bush administration's later-discredited case for going to war with Iraq in retaliation for the September 11 attacks. As Daschle entered his 2004 reelection campaign, his prospects for victory seemed assured, despite close margins in the preliminary polls. Then, in a decision without precedent that reflected the searing partisanship of that period, William Frist, his Republican counterpart as floor leader, traveled to South Dakota to campaign for Daschle's opponent. Frist's intervention may or may not have made the difference, but on November 2, Daschle became the first floor leader to lose his Senate seat since the 1952 defeat of Ernest McFarland. Years later, Daschle counseled the Senate's Republican and Democratic leaders to try to get along better—perhaps, he suggested, by seeking an invitation to the presidential retreat in the Maryland hills, sixty miles outside Washington. "Nothing breaks down communication barriers more effectively than bowling in the Camp David lanes."[107]

As Daschle entered the Senate's leadership ranks in 1994 by a one-vote margin, so, too, did Trent Lott in his bid to become the Republican's assistant minority leader, a job that he believed would position him to become party leader.[108] Political observers interpreted his narrow victory over that post's less confrontational ten-year incumbent, Alan Simpson, as a sign that the party's conservative elements were restive under the more accommodating leadership of Bob Dole and influenced by the tide that had just swept in hardliner Newt Gingrich to be the next Speaker of the House of Representatives. Lott disdained the existing Senate whip's operation, in sharp contrast to what he had known in the House, as basically staff-driven. "There's a world of difference between a staff member politely inquiring how a senator might vote and another senator bringing to bear peer and partisan pressure."[109]

Two years later, when Dole resigned to pursue his bid for the presidency, Lott's Republican colleagues, by a vote of forty-four to eight, elected him leader over his state's other senator, Thad Cochran. Lott moved quickly to put some distance between himself and Gingrich. "We will work very hard to have a good relationship with the House. But we in no way will try to make the Senate like the House."[110] As the only Senate leader ever to have served previously in a House leadership post—as minority whip from 1981 to 1989—Lott brought special insight to Senate-House relations. From his House perspective, he considered the Senate that he entered in 1989 as a cold and inefficient place—"devoid of courtesy and festering with hate."[111]

The passage of seven years and the shift of control to his party disposed him to rethink those conclusions. As minority whip in both chambers, he had necessarily focused on parochial party matters. As Senate majority leader, he recognized his responsibility to lead and speak for the entire Senate, and to try to make its proceedings, "sometimes arcane and very difficult to follow," better understood by the American people.[112]

Following the instinct that motivated Vice President Thomas Jefferson in the 1790s to explore his Senate leadership role by compiling a manual of helpful precedents to guide his successors, Majority Leader Lott set out to compile a historical manual of his own. He conceived a series of historical lectures on the essence of Senate leadership. The audience for those lectures, gathered in the historic old Senate chamber, included current and former senators, along with innumerable C-SPAN television viewers. The roster of speakers included five former majority leaders and four recent vice presidents.[113] Mike Mansfield inaugurated the series in 1998 with a version of a speech that he had intended to deliver on November 22, 1963, asserting his consultative philosophy of leadership against his senatorial critics. That day's assassination of President John F. Kennedy delayed for thirty-five years Mansfield's delivery of this remarkable assessment.

Lott's tenure as Republican leader coincided with that of his across-the-aisle counterpart Tom Daschle. The two leaders made a point of consulting every morning the Senate was in session, focusing where possible on matters that they considered ripe for agreement. These ties moved Daschle initially to respond empathetically in December 2002 to a crisis that would drive

Lott from his party's leadership just as it was about to return to majority control.

On the occasion of South Carolina Senator Strom Thurmond's one hundredth birthday party, Lott jocularly observed that the United States would have been better off to have followed Mississippi in voting for Thurmond as the Dixiecrat Party's candidate for president in 1948: "We wouldn't have had all these problems over the years either." The Mississippi senator's off-the-cuff remark, which he later described as "innocent and thoughtless," provoked a firestorm of outrage for its racist overtones.[114] Privately, Lott explained to Daschle, "I screwed up. I didn't intend for it to come out the way it did."[115] Although Lott had little choice but to step down in 2002, that act ultimately did not end his Senate leadership career. Four years later, he staged a comeback to his earlier job as Senate Republican whip, winning by a one-vote margin over Tennessee Senator Lamar Alexander. Lott replaced Mitch McConnell, who moved up to replace William Frist, who had succeeded Lott in 2003.

William Frist can be considered the "accidental majority leader." Unlike other modern-era Senate leaders, he had shown no indication of harboring a secret desire to become the chamber's "first among equals." Although he lacked the parliamentary skills that traditionally came with newly elected floor leaders, Frist—as a senator brought up from the rank-and-file—offered a clean break from the recent past. Fellow Senate Republicans, turning aside rumors that pressures from the George W. Bush White House had forced their selection, noted they were rewarding his success for having energetically directed the 2004 Republican Senatorial Campaign Committee. That committee had raised sufficient cash to propel eight new party members into the Senate, for a net gain of two seats—and majority control. Frist's Tennessee colleague Lamar Alexander, once a Senate leadership staffer, explained, "He may not be steeped in the political experience of a Bob Dole or a Howard Baker, but he's a terrific student. And he starts out with a tremendous amount of good will for being willing to do this, because we all know he'd rather be working on his health care issues."[116]

From the start of his Senate career in 1995, this heart and lung transplant surgeon had stood apart, his unique status reflected in the "Dr. Frist" incised on his chamber desk's brass name plate and in the gold-leaf lettering on the door of his Capitol leadership suite. The product of a bitter election cycle that favored candidates who appeared not to be traditional politicians, this self-anointed "citizen legislator" had pledged to serve only two Senate terms, ensuring that his tenure as leader, from the perspective of 2003, would not extend beyond four years. Frist's party colleagues could reasonably believe his term of office would open a transition back to normal leadership patterns. They respected his stunning 1994 defeat of Democratic incumbent James Sasser, who had entered that contest a plausible successor to outgoing majority leader George Mitchell, and they appreciated his reputed "ability to plunge into a subject with a surgeon's focus, a hunger to win and a powerful ambition."[117]

Political columnist David Brooks viewed Frist in his early Senate years as a Howard Baker Republican, "conservative but pragmatic, energetic, but not confrontational." But, as the tireless Frist settled into his majority leader's role, Brooks observed a subtle change, not uncommon among senior senators, evolving from "the beloved community leader who made such a mark on Nashville" into a "stiff, ideological politician."[118]

Frist's leadership tenure, accompanied by the intense scrutiny accorded to those harboring presidential ambitions, brought challenges involving the ultimately successful confirmation of two conservative Supreme Court nominees. Frustrated with the Democrats' delaying tactics, the majority Republicans considered pursuing a so-called nuclear option strategy designed to obtain a parliamentary ruling permitting the Senate to end filibusters on judicial nominees by a simple-majority decision. Democrats, perceiving this as the entering move to eliminate filibusters altogether, promised a nuclear meltdown in response. A bipartisan "gang" of fourteen senators came forward with an accommodation that ultimately made it unnecessary for Frist to pull the nuclear trigger.

In March 2005, Frist suffered a permanent political black eye with his long-distance intervention in the controversial decision by a Florida husband to end hospital life support for his brain-damaged wife, Terri Schiavo. Speaking as a heart surgeon, after reviewing family-produced videotapes, the majority leader challenged her physicians' diagnosis that she had fallen into a "persistent vegetative state."[119] Responding to critics, Frist offered an explanation that spoke to the incompatibility of his roles as physician and Senate leader. "It is the surgical personality. You act, you just don't sit and talk about things."[120] Frist later disavowed plans to run for the presidency, and at the close of his Senate term, in January 2007, he returned to private life.[121]

Frist's relations with Harry Reid, his Democratic counterpart beginning in 2005, proved consistently frosty. Two years earlier, the plain-spoken Reid—as assistant floor leader—observed of Leader Frist, "He was selected by the [George W. Bush] White House and that has put a pall over what he'd done." Reid noted later that this was "the first time in Senate history

"Webster Replying to Senator Hayne," by George P. A. Healy (1843–50). This grand history painting, prominently displayed in Boston's Faneuil Hall, depicts Massachusetts Senator Daniel Webster in the final hours of a January 1830 debate with South Carolina Senator Robert Y. Hayne. Orators of great skill and intellect, they attracted a capacity audience to the Senate chamber during a weeklong series of verbal confrontations over the nature of the federal union. *Boston Art Commission*

SOUTHERN CHIVALRY — ARGUMENT versus CLUB'S.

John L. Magee's cartoon depicts South Carolina Representative Preston Brooks as a faceless bully in his May 22, 1856, Senate chamber attack on Massachusetts Senator Charles Sumner, who is armed only with a quill pen and his moral superiority. In a bitter speech several days earlier, Sumner had mocked the absent Senator Andrew Butler, Brooks's South Carolina kinsman. *New York Public Library*

On February 12, 1874, the occasion of the late President Abraham Lincoln's sixty-fifth birth anniversary, forty-one of the Senate's seventy-four members gathered with Senate officials for a unique outdoor photo session on the US Capitol's East Front steps. *US Senate Historical Office*

In Joseph Keppler's 1889 *Puck* cartoon, "The Bosses of the Senate," well-fed "monopolists," representing interests ranging from steel, copper, and oil to paper bags and envelopes, oversee a chamber of compliant senators. The public gallery stands empty, its door bolted against visitors. This widely circulated image fostered concern over the influence of industry over government and contributed to passage of the 1890 Sherman Antitrust Act. *Library of Congress*

The group of no-nonsense Senate Republican leaders known as the "Senate Four" gathered in the summer of 1903 at the Rhode Island estate of Senator Nelson Aldrich. From left, they are Connecticut's Orville H. Platt, Wisconsin's John C. Spooner, Iowa's William B. Allison, and Rhode Island's Aldrich.

MARCH

COSMOPOLITAN

TEN CENT

The Treason of the Senate

by

David Graham Phillips

Publisher William Randolph Hearst acquired *Cosmopolitan* in 1905 as a vehicle for his campaigns against corruption in state legislative elections of US senators. He hired novelist David Graham Phillips to prepare a series of sensational articles, including one from March 1906 focusing on New York's Senator Chauncey Depew. *US Senate Historical Office*

"The closing days of the Senate present their customary arguments in favor of a revision of the Senate rules," a cartoon by John T. McCutcheon, ran in the *Chicago Tribune* on May 26, 1928. Twentieth-century political cartoonists significantly shaped public attitudes about the Senate at work—or at filibuster. McCutcheon reached a national audience with his satirical and on-target drawings. *Library of Congress*

Freshmen senators gathered at a Georgetown athletic field for a photo opportunity in 1953. Mike Mansfield (D-Montana) umpires behind catcher John F. Kennedy (D-Massachusetts) as Henry M. Jackson (D-Washington) tries his best. *US Senate Historical Office*

The Johnson Treatment, December 17, 1963. As Senate majority leader, Lyndon Johnson perfected his one-on-one style of persuading reluctant colleagues. As president, he drew on that talent to convince Senate Armed Services Committee chairman Richard B. Russell (D-Georgia) to serve on the Warren Commission investigating the assassination of President John F. Kennedy. *Lyndon Baines Johnson Library*

Senator Margaret Chase Smith (R-Maine) arrives at the Republican National Convention in San Francisco, July 26, 1964. The first woman elected to both houses of Congress, Senator Smith became the first of her gender to have a major party convention place her name in nomination for president of the United States. *Associated Press*

Republican leader Everett Dirksen holds a 1960s Senate press conference. Known as the "Wizard of Ooze," the mellifluous Illinois senator enraptured audiences, from the Senate chamber in Washington, DC, to the Tournament of Roses parade in Pasadena, California. His bestselling album, *Gallant Men*, earned him a 1968 Grammy Award. *US Senate Historical Office*

In response to intensifying congressional criticism over his conduct of the war in Vietnam, President Richard Nixon meets in 1971 with a bipartisan group of congressional leaders, including, from left, House Republican leader Gerald Ford, House Speaker Carl Albert, Senate Republican whip Robert Griffin, Senate Majority whip Robert C. Byrd, and Senate Republican leader Hugh Scott. *US Senate Historical Office*

The Russell Senate Office Building's marble-clad caucus room accommodates a capacity audience as the Senate Watergate Committee, formally the Senate Select Committee on Presidential Campaign Activities, began nationally televised hearings in May 1973. As a result of the panel's findings, Richard Nixon became the first president to resign from office. *US Senate Historical Office*

Chairman Frank Church (D-Idaho) of the Senate Intelligence Committee displays a CIA poison dart gun—"the nondiscernible microbioinnoculator," as co-chairman John Tower (R-Texas) looks at the weapon during the panel's probe of the Central Intelligence Agency. The committee met on September 17, 1975, in the caucus room of the Richard Russell Senate Office Building. *Associated Press*

On June 2, 1986, the first day of regularly televised Senate floor proceedings, Senator John Glenn (D-Ohio) uses a makeup brush to satirize how live coverage could transform his media-conscious colleagues. *C-SPAN*

Displaying frenetic campaign energy, supporters of veteran Senator Joseph Lieberman (D-Connecticut) rally in Hartford two days before the 2006 election. Lieberman, who had left the Democratic Party to run as an Independent Democrat, won that race. *Associated Press*

that the president had chosen a Senate party leader."[122] The two leaders emerged from starkly different upbringings: Frist, the beneficiary of privilege, wealth, and an Ivy League education—a politician by avocation; Reid, the soft-spoken son of a hard-rock miner and laundress, educated in modest rural schools, a graduate of state universities and an evening law school program, which he financed by working days as a US Capitol policeman—a politician by sheer determination.

After serving in various Nevada state offices, Reid won a newly created Nevada US House seat in 1982. Four years later, he entered the Senate. By 1995, his journey up the Senate leadership ladder began in earnest with his appointment as co-chair of the Senate Democratic Policy Committee, alongside Tom Daschle. With his party recently returned to the minority, Reid worked closely with colleagues seeking to shape the Clinton administration's legislative goals. In 1999, he moved up a rung to become Democratic whip. There, his aggressive defense of his party's legislative interests and his command of Senate procedure earned him the deep respect among Democrats that made him an effective whip. In 2004, Reid's colleagues unanimously elected him as floor leader to replace Daschle.

Typically, this selection complicated Reid's relations with his constituents. No longer was he simply their senator; overnight he had become the public face of all Senate Democrats. As a national polling director observed, "His whole profile changed; his numbers changed. This is exactly what happened with Tom Daschle."[123] Through 2009 and 2010, Reid reinforced that profile as he tenaciously advanced comprehensive health-care legislation, working against a unified Republican caucus to secure a filibuster-proof sixty-vote victory margin. As President Barack Obama told a journalist, "Harry has the toughest job in Washington. He's done as good a job as anybody could have done. He just grinds it out."[124]

Reid's leadership accomplishments nearly defeated his nationally riveting 2010 reelection bid. He was saved from the plight of previous Senate party leaders Lucas, McFarland, and Daschle only by massive infusions of campaign cash, a smoothly orchestrated advance voter-registration drive, visits by President Obama, and, most crucially, an inept opponent.

For much of his tenure as party whip and then as floor leader, Reid had Senator Mitch McConnell as his Republican counterpart. The Kentucky senator once lauded Reid as being "as strong as new rope when he needs to be."[125] Despite the imperatives of leading their parties through some of the most contentious struggles in all of the Senate's history, both men worked to preserve open communications with one another in the style of Lyndon

Johnson with Everett Dirksen; of Howard Baker, Bob Dole, and Trent Lott with Robert Byrd, George Mitchell, and Tom Daschle. Remembering the break from that tradition in Frist's 2004 journey to South Dakota to help defeat Daschle's reelection bid, Reid pointedly traveled during a busy legislative period in October 2007 to the University of Louisville to speak on the topic of bipartisanship at the congressional studies center named after Mitch McConnell.

Kentucky voters first elected Addison Mitchell McConnell Jr. to the Senate in 1984. As a child, with the prodding of a determined mother, McConnell overcame the effects of polio and in the process nurtured a steely determination that admirers and adversaries were quick to respect. A well-read student of American political history and author of a college senior thesis on Henry Clay, McConnell had long desired a US Senate seat. Prior to starting law school, he took a Senate internship with Kentucky's legendary John Sherman Cooper and had a ringside seat for high-level legislative maneuvering as Cooper worked for passage of the 1964 Civil Rights Act. Following law school, McConnell returned as a legislative assistant to Senator Marlow Cook and served as Cook's coordinator for two of Richard Nixon's ultimately unsuccessful Supreme Court nominations. Later, from 1978 until winning his first Senate race, he served as judge-executive for the Kentucky county that includes Louisville.

As a senator, McConnell followed what had become the traditional stepping-stones to floor leadership, chairing second-level legislative committees and his party's senatorial campaign committee. As assistant floor leader from 2003 through 2006, he again looked to Henry Clay, whose desk he occupied in the Senate chamber, seeing the whip's role as one of shaping legislation through a series of timely and well-placed compromises.[126] Following the 2006 elections, which returned the Senate to Democratic control, McConnell's Republican colleagues unanimously elected him to succeed William Frist as their floor leader. This honor was perhaps as questionable as the honor Democrats accorded Tom Daschle in 1994—on their way back to minority status.

McConnell previously had gained Senate and national attention through his efforts to derail campaign finance reform legislation. His colleagues appreciated him as a master of arcane parliamentary procedures, a well-prepared and tireless legislative tactician, drawn more to cloakroom negotiations than committee-room legislative drafting; a leader dry of humor, and relentless and calculating in his pursuit of a conservative legislative agenda. His colleague Robert Bennett of Utah, who had first come to know the Senate's culture as the son of a long-serving member, believed McConnell possessed "the best political mind" in that body."[127] During the brief period following the 2008 elections that found Senate Democrats with a sixty-vote, filibuster-proof majority, McConnell iron-handedly enforced unity among his colleagues. In the struggle against legislation that ultimately became the Patient Protection and Affordable Care Act of 2010, he cautioned moderate Republican senators not to be tempted by Democratic appeals for their backing. Just one or two defections, he argued, would allow Democrats to shift public opinion in their favor with claims that the measure had bipartisan support. "It's either bipartisan or it isn't," and his ranks held when solidarity really mattered.[128] As floor leader in the early Obama years, McConnell managed his party caucus to block energy legislation and jobs bills, and, until the final hours of the 112th Congress, to prevent repeal of Bush-era tax cuts for the nation's richest families.

Former majority leader Howard Baker captured the frustration faced by Mitch McConnell and generations of other elected Senate leaders. That frustration "is trying to make ninety-nine independent souls act in concert under rules that encourage polite anarchy and embolden people who find majority rule a dubious proposition at best."[129] In a ceremonial lecture to the Senate in its historic former chamber, the respected former Tennessee senator offered a "Baker's Dozen" of rules for Senate leaders to follow. In addition to counseling patience, civility, truthfulness, and respect for senators' family lives, Baker advised his successors to "Consult as often as possible with as many senators as possible, on as many issues as possible," to "Listen more than you speak," and to "Count carefully and often. . . . Fifty-one today may be forty-nine tomorrow." Leaders from Joseph Robinson to Alben Barkley and Lyndon Johnson would have appreciated his primary recommendation. "Understand [the Senate's] limits. The leader of the Senate relies on two prerogatives, neither of which is constitutionally or statutorily guaranteed. They are the right of prior recognition under the precedent of the Senate and the conceded right to schedule the Senate's business. These, together with the reliability of his commitment and whatever power of personal persuasion one brings to the job, are all the tools a Senate leader has."[130]

9

The Senate Investigates

"WHAT DID THE PRESIDENT KNOW, and when did he know it?" That simple question, uttered in 1973 by Senator Howard Baker, vice chair of the Senate Select Committee on Presidential Campaign Activities, evokes an image of that chamber's investigations at its most effective. It represented a turning point in the Senate's inquiry of corrupt actions directly ordered by President Richard M. Nixon, and it set in motion decisions leading to his resignation in disgrace. In the methods and procedures employed to reach its successful conclusion, the Senate Watergate Committee drew on the cumulative experience of nearly two dozen far-reaching Senate investigations conducted since the eve of the Civil War.[1]

The framers of the US Constitution awarded Congress three vital powers for maintaining its equilibrium in relations with the government's executive and judicial branches: the power of the purse, the power to declare war, and the power to conduct investigations. In the decades since World War II, each of those powers has come under serious challenge by presidents pursuing the contrived doctrine of "executive supremacy." The war power has been a dead letter since the beginning of the Korean War in 1950. President Richard Nixon set out in the early 1970s to destroy the other two with his policies of "impounding" congressional appropriations and claiming immunity from congressional inquiries about his administration's conduct. In a move toward restoring the intended equilibrium, the Supreme Court struck down Nixon's theory of withholding lawfully appropriated congressional funding, and the US Senate, through its Watergate investigation, helped destroy the notion of unreviewable executive privilege.[2]

In its early decades, the Senate proved reluctant to conduct investigations of any kind, largely leaving such matters to the House. From 1789 to 1814, the House of Representatives undertook twenty-seven separate investigations, while the Senate embarked on only three, and these on relatively trivial matters.[3] In 1800, with Congress nearing the end of its decadelong residence in Philadelphia, senators took offense at what they regarded as malicious falsehoods published about them in the *Aurora*, a local anti–John Adams administration newspaper. A Senate Committee on Privileges brought charges against the editor, William Duane, whom it found to be guilty through his false statements of exciting against senators "the hatred of the good people of the United States."[4] Under a Senate order to appear in its chamber to hear the charges on which a majority of the body, without a trial, had found him guilty, Duane complied on March 24, 1800. Allowed two days to confer with his attorney, Duane decided to go into hiding for the several weeks remaining before the Senate's adjournment. The Senate, unable to locate the fleet-footed Duane and preoccupied with preparations to move to the new capital in the District of Columbia, adopted a face-saving resolution requesting the president of the United States to seek Duane's arrest.[5] The matter was then quickly forgotten.

Not until 1818 did the Senate take up a major inquiry, this on the arbitrary actions taken by General Andrew Jackson in conducting what amounted to open warfare against the Seminole Indians in Spanish Florida and, in the course of that campaign, executing two British subjects. The Senate granted its committee full subpoena powers, a significant first, and the committee in due course voted a censure of Jackson.[6] Owing to Jackson's popularity, however, the full Senate decided not to pursue the matter.

Other such investigations of consequence conducted by the upper house were its 1828 inquiry into the management of the Internal Revenue Bureau and an 1830 review of US Post Office operations.[7] The House, however, continued to dominate this aspect of congressional affairs, so much so that one prominent senator, Thomas Hart Benton, contrived in 1834 to have the House undertake an investigation he wanted to pursue.

For all the reluctance of senators to involve themselves in investigations, now and again they simply had no choice. In 1846, for example, a Washington newspaper, the *Daily Times*, published a series of articles charging that several senators, Democrats and Whigs, had engaged in corrupt talks with the British minister over the then hotly disputed Oregon Territory. The Senate responded by appointing a five-member select committee to investigate. The committee held hearings and concluded, in one senator's phrase, that the charges were "utterly and entirely false." The Senate voted to bar the newspaper's representatives from the Senate press gallery.[8] In institutional terms, this investigation set precedents confirming that the Senate not only had the power to investigate questions of libel but also to punish those responsible.

This was not much of an advance in the Senate authority, however, and senators remained reluctant to engage on such matters. They seemed to assume that under the Constitution they were the jury, not the prosecutors, for official misconduct trials. Impeachment trials were rare; only four were conducted between 1789 and the Civil War.[9] This senatorial queasiness was present even in 1856 when one of its own, Charles Sumner of Massachusetts, was physically assaulted on the Senate floor and beaten unconscious by a House member, Preston Brooks of South Carolina. This was a parliamentary outrage without precedent, made even more offensive in that Brooks attacked Sumner for words Sumner had spoken in Senate debate, therewith violating Sumner's constitutional rights. The Senate immediately appointed a five-member select committee, none of them friendly to Sumner, to study the matter. But shrinking from recommending any action, they concluded that the Senate lacked the constitutional authority to discipline a House member. The House set up its own committee and ultimately voted, short of the necessary two-thirds majority, to expel Brooks. In the face of this condemnation, Brooks resigned his seat.[10]

Three years later, on October 16, 1859, amid the tensions rising between North and South, the revolutionary abolitionist John Brown and his putative army of twenty-one seized the federal armory at Harpers Ferry, Virginia. Their goal was to trigger a slave rebellion in the Southern states. Brown and his men were quickly defeated, and those captured were put on trial. On the opening day of the Thirty-sixth Congress, December 5, 1859, seven weeks after the incident and three days after Brown's execution, Virginia Senator James Mason demanded a full-scale review of this event, which had horrified much of the South. For more than a week, senators debated the proposal. Mason wanted to uncover who had supported Brown, financially or otherwise, but he couched his resolution in terms of considering whether this offense required any new legislation to preserve the peace. On December 14, the Senate voted unanimously for a select committee of five to conduct the inquiry. This was the Senate's most ambitious inquiry to date, the real beginning of the Senate as a fact-finding body. There were senators still doubtful about the legislative body's authority in such matters, and the investigation itself proved less than successful, openly defied by several important witnesses. From that time on, however, the Senate was prepared to act in such matters, and, in this particular instance, the House of Representatives deferred to the Senate.[11]

With Mason chairing the committee and Jefferson Davis of Mississippi as one of its members, scores of witnesses were summoned. Senators Mason and Davis were trying to discover the extent of Brown's conspiracy, but witnesses who refused to testify sorely tested the senators' patience. The committee had the Senate order the arrest of several of them. John Brown's son avoided arrest by going into hiding. Thaddeus Hyatt, a wealthy New York businessman, was caught and brought to Washington, where the committee's conduct provoked an important Senate debate.

Hyatt refused to testify under the compulsion of the committee's subpoena. He argued—and certain influential senators agreed—that the Senate had no legal or constitutional right to compel him to do so. Chairman Mason asked the Senate to send Hyatt to jail for his contempt and to keep him there until he relented. On March 12, 1860, the Senate voted, forty-four to ten, in favor of Senator Mason's resolution. That sent Hyatt to the common jail in the District of Columbia, where he remained until the committee completed its work three months later. More important, that vote established the Senate's powers to investigate, a precedent that would be of immense importance in the decades to come. Hyatt was not the first person whom the Senate punished with imprisonment, but he was the first affected by such a broadly based investigation not of the Senate's immediate concern.

Hyatt treated his three months in jail as a joke. He had his cell elaborately decorated and invited prominent friends to visit. He had his bank checks printed with his new address: "Washington Jail." In its report, the committee did little more than recite the facts of what had happened and came to this conclusion: "The committee, after much consideration, are not prepared to suggest any legislation."[12] The idea of proposing corrective legislation was the primary justification for conducting this investigation, and Senate committees from then on would use the claim of recommending legislation as an all-purpose excuse to inquire into just about all phases of American life.

With the outbreak of the Civil War in 1861, senators threw off previous restraints and proceeded as if their lawmaking responsibilities naturally included the power to investigate. When Congress met in early December, Senator Zachariah Chandler of Michigan, a party boss and fiery Republican radical, proposed that the Senate investigate in full the Union's recent defeats at Bull Run and Ball's Bluff. He did not argue the possible need for corrective legislation. On the contrary, he stated that the Senate owed it to the nation to investigate these disasters and fix the blame on those responsible.[13] This was a senator urging his colleagues to assume the role of prosecutor. After debate, the Senate decided to broaden Chandler's proposal to cover all aspects of the war. To do this, a joint investigating committee with the House was created. This committee, the Joint Committee on the Conduct of the War, was made up of three senators and four representatives, with Ohio Senator Benjamin Wade as chair. Wade was as radical a Republican as Chandler, and in this Senate the Republicans had little Democratic opposition, since almost all the Southern senators had defected to the Confederacy. That meant there was little to inhibit the committee members or to persuade them to use caution.[14]

The committee did investigate the defeats at Bull Run and Ball's Bluff, condemning those officers they found derelict, and continued in such inquires until the end of the war in 1865. Committee members traveled widely to the scenes of the battles, and everywhere they pressed to discover and criticize mistakes or blunders by those in command. Not one member of the committee had any military experience, but each one felt fully competent to tell President Lincoln and his generals how to run the war.[15]

From the start, Senators Wade and Chandler regarded anyone who opposed them as "traitors and fools," and they did not exempt Lincoln from their often nasty attacks. They regularly urged Lincoln to cashier the generals in charge. Lincoln considered the committee members a meddlesome group of congressional busybodies constantly harassing him with their demands and recommendations. The committee always met in secret, and its high-handed methods smacked of star-chamber proceedings. It summoned subordinate officers and demanded that they find fault with their superiors. In their committee meetings, the members saw themselves engaged with plots and counterplots, all sorts of schemes and intrigues, and treasonous conspiracies fomented by wicked connivers. Periodically they published fat volumes of hearing transcripts, obviously contrived to help Republican candidates in their current election campaigns.[16]

The committee's work was not valueless, though. In the early phases of the war, President Lincoln used its brusque criticisms to try to goad the timid General George McClellan into action, and the committee's published hearings provided contemporaries and later historians with important on-the-spot testimony about the details of many battles. But the committee members' arrogant methods offended even their own

Republican colleagues and did not enhance the public's confidence in congressional investigations.

By the 1880s, senators had set aside earlier misgivings and began to assume an ever greater role in conducting investigations, acting as though no phase of American life was exempt from their examination. Even as the Senate was assuming a greater investigative role, the Supreme Court handed down a decision that chilled congressional investigations for the next half century. That 1881 decision, *Kilbourn v. Thompson*, rebuked an 1876 House investigation, which had examined the financial dealings of a Washington real-estate pool.[17] The head of the pool, Hallet Kilbourn, refused to respond fully under the claim that the House had no authority to investigate the "private business" of those engaged in that business. On orders from the House, its sergeant at arms, John Thompson, arrested Kilbourn and brought him before the bar of the House. He still refused to testify, and the House convicted him of contempt and ordered him jailed. After six weeks, Kilbourn won his release with a writ of habeas corpus and promptly sued the Speaker of the House, members of the investigating committee, and the sergeant at arms for false arrest and imprisonment. That suit reached the Supreme Court and prompted a far-reaching decision questioning the authority of the House and the Senate to conduct investigations and to punish recalcitrant witnesses.

In the Kilbourn decision, the court ruled that congressional investigations were limited by the Constitution and therefore subject to review by the federal courts. The court decided in this case that the Speaker and members of the House were constitutionally immune from the civil suit, but not the sergeant at arms. In broader terms, the court ruled that the House and the Senate lacked "general power" to investigate the private affairs of citizens unless that investigation could fill their need for information to write "valid" legislation. In the court's judgment, this was not so in Kilbourn's case. Privately, as revealed in the correspondence of Justice Samuel Miller, who wrote the decision, he and his colleagues were aghast at the excesses of congressional investigations, with a majority of them inclined to deny the House and the Senate any power to punish witnesses for contempt.[18] In the Kilbourn decision, the justices left unresolved just what authority the House and the Senate did hold to investigate. For decades, the 1881 decision was treated as an effective limit on the scope of congressional investigations.[19]

All the same, in the following decades, the Senate conducted investigation after investigation, scrutinizing the conduct of the executive departments, root and branch. They repeatedly examined the Treasury's tax and customs collections, the administration of Indian Affairs and the land office, and the operations of the civil service, among other concerns. Armed with the power of subpoena, senators searched out blundering and misconduct in succeeding administrations, and if these investigations were less than an ideal method for appraising officials' performance and deportment, their exposure of political and economic abuses proved an important part of managing the government. They did bring changes and corrections. In one especially notable instance, the Senate created a five-member select committee to investigate the alarming rate wars then under way among the nation's railroads. The committee toured the country, taking testimony, and then produced the Interstate Commerce Act of 1887 with a federal commission to regulate monopolistic practices within that industry.[20]

The 1912 presidential election campaign triggered several major congressional investigations, and those inquiries developed and refined investigative practices in both House and Senate. The Republican-controlled Senate conducted what became a sensational investigation under the chairmanship of Minnesota Republican Moses Clapp.[21] This inquiry pitted Republican regulars against that party's progressives, with the Senate's Democrats chortling over the startling revelations of what they called Republican "sins" and "crimes." What set the Republicans into this spiteful political brawl was the 1912 campaign of Theodore Roosevelt to regain the presidency from President Taft. The Clapp inquiry ran through the summer and into the fall, ending just before the election. It brought disclosures of huge cash contributions to the party from business interests and charges of widespread dishonesty. The investigation succeeded in undermining the Republican candidacies of Taft, as the party's designated nominee, and of Roosevelt and his Bull Moose supporters. Elected instead was Democrat Woodrow Wilson. This malign competition between the Republican regulars and progressives would plague the party for years to come and make possible spectacular Senate investigations in the 1920s.

In his 1912 campaign, Wilson had castigated the vested interests that long had intimidated Congress, and only a few weeks after his inauguration, he found their lobbyists threatening to defeat his major initiative to reform the nation's tariff system. Following House passage of a bill, the Underwood Tariff Act, which significantly lowered rates for the first time since the Civil War and established a tax on high-income individuals, the spotlight turned to the Senate, where the Democrats held a narrow majority. As swarms of lobbyists seeking to maintain higher rates and fight the new tax provisions descended on the Senate, an angry Wilson issued a statement denouncing their "insidious" efforts to mislead the Senate and the public for their private profit.[22] That created a sensation. Republican senators especially resented, as they saw it, Wilson's questioning of their integrity, and one of them, Albert Cummins of Iowa, proposed forming a select committee to investigate the charge.[23] The Democrats did not object. Senator Robert La Follette suggested that all senators testify on what properties they held that might be affected by lowering the tariff schedule. What Wilson began as a tactical maneuver to help pass the tariff bill quickly became a sweeping investigation of the Washington lobbyists, the first ever, and also the first public disclosure of senators' financial assets. Senator after senator came before the committee to list their holdings. North Dakota's Asle Gronna acknowledged a nine-thousand-acre farm; Rhode Island's Henry Lippitt, extensive holdings in textiles; North Carolina's Lee Overman, shares in cotton mills. The committee produced four volumes of testimony, and those hearings proved crucial in stiffening the resolve of the Senate to pass Wilson's bill.[24]

If Wilson successfully used one congressional investigation for his own purposes at the start of his presidency, he found himself and his administration harassed by a rush of congressional investigations at its close. Despite his plea to the public during the 1918 midterm election cycle to elect another Democratic Congress, Republicans won majorities in the House and the Senate. The legislators had felt Wilson's contempt for them, and now they wanted to punish him. In the next two years, 1919 and 1920, they undertook no fewer than fifty-one investigations of his administration, almost all of them conducted by House Republicans.

The Senate's Republicans were equally aware of the "wild extravagance" of the Wilson administration during the just-ended world war, but they, too, were cautious. They feared that such investigations might backfire on the investigators and they had more important concerns in mind. For one, they wanted to regain the presidency in 1920, so they chose not to risk the party's image unnecessarily. For another, they were already plotting to defeat President Wilson on a far more important measure: the Versailles Treaty.

Warren Harding's 1921 inauguration as president changed the political ground rules. As stories of questionable dealings began to emerge, a coalition of progressive Republicans and Democrats pushed ahead with various investigations. Other senators realized that their colleagues who supported these inquiries would not be silenced. Better, the party leaders decided, to let the senatorial sleuths have their way. On the resolution to investigate irregularities in leasing US naval oil reserves at Teapot Dome, in Wyoming, the Senate vote was unanimous, fifty-eight to none. On the resolution to investigate allegations of wrongdoing by Attorney General Harry Daugherty and his Justice Department, the Senate voted sixty-six to one.[25]

From the start, Senator Robert La Follette and conservationists in and out of Congress suspected the worst of Albert Fall, whom President Harding named secretary of the interior in March 1921. They knew Fall well. For the nine years immediately before joining Harding's new cabinet, Fall had served in the Senate, and his record there persuaded them that he was not a fit guardian of the nation's public lands and resources. A self-styled cattle baron, Fall lived on a sprawling ranch outside Tularosa, New Mexico. As one of his state's first senators, he had demonstrated his belief in the private exploitation of the country's natural resources. In the Senate chamber, Fall's desk was placed next to Harding's, and the two had become such warm friends that Harding, as president-elect, even considered appointing him secretary of state. If Fall had made admiring friends in the Senate, like Warren Harding, he had also made enemies among those senators he had crossed over the years. Senators who considered themselves conservationists expressed deep unhappiness at Fall's new job. Besides his long opposition to their causes, in the past he had engaged in sharp practices both in election politics and as a Western rancher. He would bear watching.[26]

They did not have long to wait. In his first weeks in office, Secretary Fall persuaded Edwin Denby, the new secretary of the navy, to transfer from his department to the Interior Department the untapped oil-rich fields reserved for the navy: Teapot Dome in Wyoming and Elk Hills in California. President Harding agreed to the transfer on May 31, 1921. Then secretly, without seeking outside bids, Fall in April 1922 leased the Teapot Dome reserve to Harry Sinclair's oil company. Conservationists regarded this as a clearly illegal act, and Robert La Follette proposed a full-scale Senate investigation.[27]

That inquiry, one of the most celebrated in Senate history, had extraordinary consequences far beyond its revelations of one of the worst scandals ever uncovered in a president's administration. In ordinary criminal terms, the Senate investigators discovered that Secretary Fall had bargained away immensely valuable government properties in return for pretended "loans" to himself of more than $400,000 from the venturesome freebooters in on the conspiracy. Those disclosures led to Fall's indictment, trial, and conviction in federal court for bribery. He thus became the first cabinet officer ever sent to prison.[28] More than this, the public exposure of Fall's crimes triggered a series of fifteen further Senate investigations of corruption within the Harding administration. These inquiries produced sensation after sensation, and if the committee sessions at times proved overly dramatic, the corruption they so often revealed was true enough. That, in time, brought the Senate an enhanced reputation for its investigative capacities. If malfeasance was suspected, those who were apprehensive looked to the Senate.

In the 1930s, the Senate's investigations took on a far different purpose than exposing the misdeeds in the executive branch of government. They were used then, in part, to help the administration legislatively and politically. With the election of Franklin Roosevelt in 1932, the Senate's Democrats, now in the majority, had a president they wanted to support. With their investigations, and the techniques devised to maximize their impact, they set the stage for enacting the laws Roosevelt proposed. These vastly expanded the government's authority and its powers to regulate the nation's economic life. Telford Taylor, a student of the process, called the investigations "the arsenal" of the New Deal's social revolution.[29] They created broad public support for Roosevelt's many proposals.

This cooperation with the White House actually began in 1932 under President Hoover. He asked the Republicans on the Senate's banking committee to undertake an investigation of the country's stock exchanges. Up for reelection in the midst of the worst economic depression in the nation's history, Hoover hoped that the investigation would fix blame for the economic devastation on the reckless speculations of Wall Street's stockbrokers. Initially this investigation proved ineffective, suggesting a whitewash of stock-market practices. Witnesses were evasive and uncooperative. The committee chairman, Peter Norbeck of South Dakota, fired the chief counsel. In the regular postelection, lame-duck session of the Senate, still under a Republican majority, the committee hired a new chief counsel, Ferdinand Pecora, who quickly put together a professional staff. He started formal hearings in February 1933, just days before Roosevelt became president and the Democrats became the Senate's majority party.[30]

Pecora stayed on the job, and from his first witness, the president of a major national bank, he produced spectacular revelations of the high-handed methods of the country's "money-changers," the shocking corruption within the banking system and the stock exchanges. Pecora summoned before the committee the country's most prominent financiers. With massive documentation, he exposed their insider dealings and exploitations of the financial system. In a time of cruel poverty for many millions, Pecora showed that some of these men, including J. P. Morgan, paid no income taxes in some years despite their immense incomes. Pecora also showed himself a master propagandist, playing for headlines with a skill that would be mimicked by later Senate investigators. He timed his revelations on a schedule to make a daily round of headlines in the country's afternoon newspapers, then another round later in the day for the next morning's papers. He, rather than the senators, ran the hearings, and his exposure of the greed and exorbitant profits of these people, their price fixings, and riggings of stocks provided the factual underpinning for much of Roosevelt's early reform legislation, starting with the Banking Act of 1933. These hearings continued until June 1934 and built up pressure behind passage of other measures Roosevelt championed, including the Securities Exchange Act of 1934 and the Public Utilities Holding Company Act of 1935. In all, Ferdinand Pecora produced twenty-two volumes of testimony.

Not all of these measures were easily enacted. At great cost, the public utility companies staged a renegade campaign to block abolition of their holding companies, a campaign marked by ugly tactics. After a struggle, the Senate barely passed an administration-sponsored bill in May 1935, but, under heavy lobbying pressure, the House balked. At the urging of the White House, Senator Hugo Black of Alabama proposed a Senate investigation of that lobbying. As the committee chairman, Black proved fraud and corruption behind the blizzard of telegrams inundating the Capitol in opposition to the bill. He had a tip from a Pennsylvania House member that almost all the hundreds of telegrams he was receiving came from persons whose surnames began with the first letter of the alphabet. On investigation, Black discovered that agents of the utility companies were taking these names from telephone books in a fraudulent effort to suggest widespread opposition to the legislation. A militant prosecutor, Black used ruthless methods of his own, which raised serious questions about their propriety. He had two committee aides seize the chief of the utility lobby, Philip Gadsen, in a downtown hotel and bring him immediately before the committee members waiting to question him at the Capitol. As Gadsen testified, a committee staffer rifled his office and personal files. Committee agents seized another witness in his bed at one A.M. and brought him immediately to Washington to testify. Black was widely criticized for his brazen tactics, and he defended them with the claim that those sought by the committee for questioning were evading them and destroying evidence. In a national radio broadcast, he berated the "highly paid mouthpieces of greed and grab" who were the targets of his investigation.[31] Like Pecora, Black skillfully timed his hearings for maximum newspaper play. Reporters who covered his hearings admiringly called them "Chairman Black's Three-Ring Circus."[32]

Black had proved his mettle as an investigator on another provocative inquiry, this one started in May 1933 to scrutinize the US Post Office's mail contracts with airline and shipping companies.[33] As chairman of the special committee, Black cleverly beguiled the executives to admit the large salaries they drew from the hidden subsidies awarded by such contracts. This investigation's real significance, however, went much further than exposing the ability of skilled lobbyists to gain lucrative government contracts. In the course of the inquiry, a prominent Washington attorney, William MacCracken, refused to turn over to the committee subpoenaed papers belonging to his clients, to protect his attorney-client relationships. On Black's motion in February 1934, the Senate voted to have the Senate's sergeant at arms arrest MacCracken and bring him before the Senate. The Senate put MacCracken on trial, found him guilty, and then, for his contempt, sentenced him to ten days in jail. The case, of course, created a sensation. MacCracken appealed through the judicial system, and in February 1935 the Supreme Court unanimously ruled in favor of the Senate.[34] MacCracken served ten days in jail.

In jailing MacCracken, the senators copied the methods the Senate had used back in 1860 when they dealt with another intractable witness, Thaddeus Hyatt. MacCracken, however, had appealed his conviction all the way to the Supreme Court, and the Supreme Court's decision gave the Senate new authority in its investigative powers, powers that could be invoked in the legislative body's hours of need, even against the president of the United States.[35]

One major investigation unexpectedly caused serious difficulties for the Roosevelt administration. This was a three-year investigation of the munitions industry, chaired by Senator Gerald Nye of North Dakota.[36] Nye was a Republican and a zealous isolationist. The Democrats had allowed him the chairmanship because he had introduced the resolution authorizing the inquiry, but they later came to regret this gesture. Beginning in early 1934, Nye took advantage of a cooperative press corps to turn the hearings into a provocative investigation of what he called "merchants of death." The North Dakotan exploited the hearings to enhance the status of isolationists at a time when Roosevelt was becoming increasingly troubled by the militancy of dictatorial regimes in Europe and Japan. With their rough questioning of witnesses, Senator Nye and his chief counsel, Stephen Raushenbush, prompted protests from France and Great Britain, among other foreign governments. The committee helped produce the neutrality acts of 1935, 1936, and 1937, legislation that Roosevelt deplored. This complicated the administration's diplomatic maneuvering in the war crises looming in Europe and Asia.[37]

In 1936, in rapport with Roosevelt's pro-labor sympathies, Wisconsin's Senator Robert La Follette Jr. followed in his late father's progressive footsteps and undertook a ticklish investigation of working conditions in the United States. Concentrating on the rights of workers, the inquiry covered sharecroppers in the South, factory workers in the North, and the appalling conditions under which they labored. A tough, even chilling, investigator, La Follette used the often dramatic hearings to reveal the shocking methods used to intimidate these workers. He called as witnesses the thugs many companies hired as strikebreakers and the spies they hired to infiltrate the ranks of their employees. The hearings brought widespread public revulsion at these brutal tactics and did much to further President Roosevelt's efforts to protect workers' rights with federal legislation. La Follette continued these investigative hearings well into 1940, two years after Congress had passed the Fair Labor Standards Act, the last of the major New Deal laws. In all, La Follette produced almost one hundred volumes of testimony and formal reports.[38]

These Senate investigations, like the ones before them, often had a partisan bias, recognized by those who were their targets. In 1936, a presidential election year, the Senate's Democrats undertook a critical inquiry into the Republican Party's financial structure, an investigation that outraged the Republicans' presidential candidate, Kansas Governor Alfred Landon. He protested publicly and bitterly that, ever since 1932, the Senate's Democrats had been using investigations to harm President Roosevelt's opponents. They were designed not "to get the crooks," he said, but "to get the critics."[39]

With the outbreak of a new world war and then the United States' major role in it, official Washington underwent painful political convulsions amid much confusion as senators and members of the House tried to rationalize their past records with new realities. There were anguished cries and angry demands to assign blame for war-related crises and to determine what the country must do to meet this unprecedented challenge. Out of this government bedlam emerged one committee that from its start made both sense and effective policy. This was the Senate's Special Committee to Investigate the National Defense Program, the idea of Harry S. Truman of Missouri, who had just won election to a second Senate term.

A student of history, Senator Truman was aware of the dangers ahead from unscrupulous men taking greedy advantage of the massive military buildup already under way. He sought to prevent graft on arms contracts, as well as waste, negligence, and noncompliance. He also knew of the dangers of a congressional committee meddling with military strategy and tactics, as had been the case during the Civil War with the Committee on the Conduct of the War. The Senate approved Truman's resolution setting up the select committee on March 1, 1941, nine months before the Japanese attack on Pearl Harbor. Truman, as chairman, resolved to conduct its work in a completely nonpartisan way and to avoid the mistakes of past committees in wartime.[40]

The Truman committee worked largely in private, without pretensions. Through their dedication, the senator and his committee members first won praise and admiration, then prestige, and finally power and influence over the defense program. "The committee wants to see results," Truman said. Results they did achieve. Just weeks after the Japanese attack, the committee issued a biting report on the blunders and "ineptness" of the officials at the Office of Production Management, a report that goaded President Roosevelt to replace that agency promptly with one to take effective charge of war production.[41] The committee helped settle an angry quarrel within the administration over who should use limited oil resources: those pressing for production of synthetic rubber or those wanting high-octane airplane fuel. The committee repeatedly caught companies delivering defective military equipment with falsified tests and forged inspection reports, some dishonestly certified by military and naval officers. They even caught a few members of Congress making improper claims, and one of them went to jail.[42]

Truman and his colleagues saved many billions of dollars for the government. They formed what amounted to a domestic high-command that effectively coordinated competing aspects of the war effort. They rooted out graft and corruption and thereby built public confidence in official Washington. In its three-and-a-half years under Chairman Truman, the committee filed thirty-two unanimous reports, all nonpartisan, and twenty-four volumes of testimony. But on August 4, 1944, Truman resigned as chairman. Roosevelt had chosen him as his next vice president.

The Truman committee's work, distinguished as it was, constituted only a small part of a massive proliferation of investigations by the Senate and the House of Representatives during the war. The war itself disrupted much of American life, creating widespread dislocations and shortages. The government suddenly became engaged in an extraordinary variety of new activities, many of which invited congressional investigations. There were more than one hundred formal inquiries during the war, investigating wage disputes and manpower policies, gasoline shortages and rationing inequities, and scores of other problems. Senators and representatives, anxious to become involved, regularly proposed committees to investigate whatever seemed appropriate at the moment. And, permanent standing committees, to forestall intrusions on their turf by rival panels, launched investigations of their own. Organized groups had become skilled in bringing pressure on Congress for what they wanted, and now they used letter-writing campaigns and other effective tactics to seek relief from their varied wartime grievances. These were grounds for investigations. There was considerable confusion and duplication in all this activity, and that had to hurt the war effort. In the midst of the war, on April 17, 1943, with the outcome in doubt, General George Marshall, the army's chief of staff, complained in a confidential memorandum that "unnecessary" and over-lapping congressional investigations—almost thirty ongoing then—were tying up his people and wasting their time.[43]

General Marshall did not question the right of the Senate and the House of Representatives to conduct investigations, just the "tremendous loss of time" caused by their duplications. These examinations, whatever their faults, had a beneficial effect; they kept those running the government's war effort fully aware that their conduct was subject to the scrutiny of Congress. The magnitude and intensity of the war effort had prompted this burst of inquiries, but by now both the Senate and the House had grown accustomed to using them for their legislative purposes. In the decades to come, they would find additional methods and techniques, for good and ill, to conduct their investigations. The advent of television, rising to immense popularity in the years immediately after the war, transformed congressional probes, especially in the Senate, to a new level of public attention.

10

The Watchdogs

WELL BEFORE ALLIED FORCES BROUGHT World War II to a triumphant close, thoughtful members of Congress had become alarmed at the immense new powers of the president and the daunting disarray of Congress. They had yielded Franklin Roosevelt unprecedented authority, first to fight the Great Depression, and then unparalleled further powers to fight the most widely spread war in human history. Meanwhile, the members of Congress made do with the tools they had. By war's end, they knew that they had to make drastic changes to outfit themselves for a vastly changed postwar world. In early 1945, with the wars still raging in Europe and the Far East, the House and Senate voted to create a Joint Committee on the Organization of Congress. The idea was to reassess the role of Congress for the legislative-political struggles to come. In this, they regarded the congressional investigation as an especially useful instrument.

After months of hearings and study, the joint committee proposed new approaches for congressional operations, and both houses quickly approved many of the reforms. The reforms slashed the number of standing committees and authorized the remaining panels to hire professional personnel. Members obtained additional staff for their personal offices, along with a pay raise. And, for the first time, lobbyists were required to register with Congress.[1]

Having learned powerful lessons from the experience of the Truman Committee and other wartime inquiries, the Senate and House placed a new emphasis on investigations. They passed legislation directing each of their reorganized committees to oversee federal agencies and programs as never

245

before, and gave each standing committee full subpoena powers. During the year and a half they spent considering this reorganization, the two houses of Congress authorized more than fifty separate new investigations.

Towering among them was a 1945–46 investigation into the Japanese attack on Pearl Harbor, a matter that spawned intense partisan bickering, a not uncommon ingredient in many congressional investigations. Senate Republicans seemed determined to blame President Franklin Roosevelt rather than the Japanese for the disaster, but Senate Democrats seemed equally intent on placing the blame on almost anyone else. Majority Leader Alben Barkley proposed a joint committee investigation and had himself named chairman. After extensive hearings, the committee fixed the blame for the negligence at Pearl Harbor on the commanding officers there, even as Republicans continued to protest that it was Roosevelt's fault.[2]

In these postwar years, both the Senate and the House undertook scores of investigations and explored all sorts of subjects, not always to the credit of those conducting the investigations. With every committee charged to oversee the federal agencies and programs under its jurisdiction, this was an expected result, but none of those who had urged this course in reorganizing Congress could have imagined either the explosive controversies that would soon take place or the bitter partisanship. As part of the reorganization, the Senate created a special permanent investigating subcommittee for its Committee on Government Operations, essentially giving that subcommittee oversight over the entire government. Meanwhile, in 1945, the year before the reorganization, the House had promoted its almost moribund Committee on Un-American Activities (HUAC) to the status of a standing committee. Begun in 1938 on a temporary basis, that committee had engendered much criticism for the attacks by its chairman, Martin Dies Jr., of Texas, on many targets, among them Roosevelt's administration and various minority and other groups, including Communists.[3] But the entrance of the United States into World War II and the resulting alliance with the Soviet Union all but silenced Dies and his committee, and Dies did not seek reelection in 1944. As revived in 1945, however, the committee embarked on a wild career of investigative abuses that, in the judgment of legal scholars, threatened the fabric of American law and civil rights. In these extravagances this House committee led the way, but the Senate's own investigations would quickly follow.

Chairman Dies had devised a distinctly new kind of investigation, quite different from those that had been held before. His purpose was to punish those whose ideals and politics the committee members disliked simply by exposing them publicly at committee hearings and pronouncing them un-American. The idea was to humiliate the witnesses rather than to gain information, and the witnesses summoned were often stigmatized as disloyal to the nation. It was exposure for exposure's sake, with no pretense of a legislative intent. Since the committee's hearings were not judicial proceedings, courtroom safeguards were not applicable to protect witnesses from vilification. Indeed, because the federal courts declined to intervene, a witness before a congressional committee had no right or avenue to question his or her treatment.

The notoriety of this House committee did not obscure the reality that the government had cause for concern. President Truman repeatedly criticized the panel for its excesses, but he also established a loyalty-security system within the government. The Senate also took up the cause. In 1950, Nevada's Patrick McCarran, chairman of the Senate Judiciary Committee, set up a special subcommittee on internal security, essentially to investigate Communist infiltration. As that panel's chair, he emulated the unsavory tactics of the House investigators and was joined in this by other senators, including Indiana's William Jenner, Mississippi's James Eastland, and Wisconsin's Joseph McCarthy. McCarthy's exploits would soon attract enormous attention and make him the most infamous investigator in the Senate's history. So ugly were his methods that his name morphed into a word of reproach, *McCarthyism*, and became a way to define repugnant smear politicking.[4]

Although Joseph McCarthy's career as investigator began casually, almost inadvertently, it gave him more than four years of national notoriety unmatched by any other senator. In his first years in the Senate, before he "discovered" the threat of Communism, he had served inconspicuously in a few investigations. In one of these, an inquiry into the high cost of housing, he had defined correctly the committee's proper course: "We should conduct an investigation, not an inquisition."[5] In his years of prominence, however, as he harangued the Senate with rash accusations, some compared him with Torquemada, the inquisitor-general of fifteenth-century Spain.

As an obscure senator first elected in 1946, McCarthy began to worry about his reelection well before 1952. Anxious to ingratiate himself with party leaders, journalists, and anyone else who might help him, he told two congressional reporters in December 1949 that he needed something to call attention to himself, something to use in his reelection campaign. He was thinking of going after the navy. He handed them a navy document stamped "Secret." "You might make a story out of this," he said.[6] He talked to others, of course, and the head of Georgetown University's School of Foreign Service, the Reverend Edmund Walsh, suggested that he look into Soviet imperialism and Communist subversion.[7]

In February 1950, McCarthy took that theme for a series of Republican Party speeches he prepared and made around the country during the Lincoln's Birthday recess of Congress. But because he was not previously versed in these matters, he had to scramble to put these speeches together by borrowing what material he could find, including some newspaper clippings from a friendly journalist. In the first of these speeches, to a woman's club in Wheeling, West Virginia, McCarthy made the astonishing claim that he held in his hand a list of 205 Communist Party members who were operating as a spy ring in the State Department—and, worse, that they were known to Secretary of State Dean Acheson. Although he quickly backed away from that number, stating that these individuals were "bad security risks" and that the card-carrying Communists actually numbered only fifty-seven, he repeated his charge that the State Department was riddled with Communists. But in a bizarre, six-hour speech to the Senate on February 20, 1950, McCarthy offered still different numbers and a ragtag collection of individual "cases," some of which involved persons who had never worked at the State Department, which made it obvious that he had had no list in the first place.[8] With these wild speeches, however, he had so dramatized his sensational accusations that the Senate ordered them investigated.

Senator Millard Tydings of Maryland chaired the special subcommittee. The conservative Democrat now had a chance to chastise this impudent newcomer whose charges were so wild that even Senator Robert Taft had at first dismissed them as "perfectly reckless," although later even Taft encouraged McCarthy to "Keep talking!"[9] So McCarthy continued with his charges and added more. When asked for proof, however, he claimed that the State Department had all the evidence under seal. When President Truman subsequently ordered those files opened, McCarthy asserted they had been riffled.[10]

Having a delightful romp, basking in his new visibility, McCarthy failed to stop even after Federal Bureau of Investigation director J. Edgar Hoover checked the files and declared them intact. And McCarthy seemed genuinely confused that persons he had accused of disloyalty were angry at him when he greeted them later. McCarthy had learned the rhythms of the press, not only the daily deadlines of reporters, but the restraints of the "objectivity" they imposed on themselves in their reports. As United Press correspondent George Reedy observed, "We had to take what McCarthy said at face value. Joe couldn't find a Communist in Red Square—he didn't know Karl Marx from Groucho—but he was a United States Senator."[11] Whatever extravagances he uttered, however dubious, reporters and editors treated them as valid news simply because he was a US senator. He exploited this presumed professional virtue of conscientious reporters into what one of them called "a recording device for Joe."[12] With this technique, McCarthy built large popular support for himself around the country. But after weeks of hearings, the Tydings subcommittee reported that McCarthy had perpetrated a "fraud and a hoax" on the Senate.[13]

While McCarthy and other senators were copying and perfecting the techniques of Martin Dies and his committee associates to achieve "exposure for exposure's sake,"[14] members of Congress somewhat inadvertently discovered still another way for congressional investigations to grab political publicity. This occurred in early 1951 when Tennessee's Estes Kefauver, a freshman Democratic senator, casually allowed a local television station to broadcast live a hearing he was conducting in New Orleans as part of an organized crime investigation. Indifferent to the station's request and preoccupied with managing his panel's proceedings, Kefauver was at first unmindful that the hearing was being broadcast. The public's reaction, however, was spectacular. Tens of thousands of viewers watched with fascination as the prim senator and his chief counsel, Rudolph Halley, questioned defiant professional gamblers about their wide-open operations in New Orleans. The televised hearings prompted a public outcry and an immediate crackdown by local authorities.[15]

Kefauver had actually started his investigation in May 1950 with hearings in Miami, and he and his entourage traveled from one city to another, issuing subpoenas to a bizarre assortment of underworld figures and corrupt law enforcement officials. The senator and his committee were exploring the seamy side of American life, and Kefauver's Senate colleagues and others were less than pleased with the goings-on. By the time this road show reached New Orleans in late January 1951, it had become a very touchy subject for senior Democrats, because they feared that any such investigation could disclose compromising arrangements between their party's big-city political bosses and unsavory local elements.[16]

At this time, with relatively few TV sets in American households, television was still a novelty and those in charge of television programming had not yet latched onto public affairs as suitable television material. In 1948, television stations had used brief segments of HUAC hearings on their evening news shows, but not until Senator Kefauver's hearings in New Orleans did the stations start covering hearings as they took place. Although Kefauver himself was skeptical, he acquiesced in allowing television at his hearings in Detroit, St. Louis, and Los Angeles. But, under mounting criticism, he tried to bar television cameras when his committee reached San Francisco. He was too late—the local people had already made their arrangements. A few witnesses had objected to testifying on camera, and Kefauver had respected their wishes, but clearly television had become a compelling new tool for congressional investigators.[17]

Through his television fame, Kefauver had suddenly achieved the status of "folk hero," a champion battling the forces of evil wherever he could find them. There was talk that he should run for president. The Tennessee senator gave the viewing public an unexpected glimpse into the criminal underworld. The Kefauver Committee summoned to testify a rogue's gallery of racketeers and gangsters, the henchmen of such notorious criminals as Al Capone, Meyer Lansky, "Bugsy" Siegel, and "Lucky" Luciano. Many had colorful nicknames: Murray "The Camel" Humphrey, Sam "Golf Bag" Hunt, Anthony "Tough Tony" Capezio, and Jacob "Greasy Thumb" Guzik among them. Some talked. Some balked. Some just said, "I don't remember." Some claimed the protection of the Fifth Amendment against self-incrimination. Preliminary hearings were closed, but the open hearings attracted huge television audiences. Almost accidentally, Senator Kefauver stumbled onto a publicity jackpot, a real-life melodrama starring a motley collection of genuine felons and outlaws. In their wake, his committee members left a trail of arrest warrants, contempt citations, and newly convened grand juries offering criminal indictments. Kefauver had a cast of hundreds playing to an audience of millions, and this was before he took his traveling troupe to New York City for the most dramatic hearings of all.

Frank Costello, reportedly the "prime minister" of the criminal underworld, a political fixer grown wealthy as the power broker for lawless gangs all over the country, emerged as the star witness. Costello's lawyer objected to his client televising his face, however, and therefore while Costello testified the cameraman focused only on his hands. Those hands, nervous, twisting and turning, crumpling a handkerchief, grasping a water glass, caught strikingly Costello's evasiveness and the tension of his ordeal, creating a sensational and memorable episode in the early history of television.[18] This was the climax of Kefauver's year of investigating crime and criminals, later described as "the outstanding theatrical production of the 1950–51 season."[19]

The Senate's senior members looked aghast at Kefauver's investigative methods: the careful staging of the hearings, the promise of new sensations to come, and the recklessness with which these investigations summoned whomever they wanted to appear and perform. As chair, Kefauver logged fifty-two thousand miles of travel across the country to preside over these hearings. His committee called almost eight hundred witnesses to testify, and cited forty-five of them for contempt.[20] Those summoned were mostly hoodlums and corrupt officials, and few chose to protest the unfairness of their treatment. *New York Times* correspondent William S. White described the punitive spirit of Kefauver's hearings as "parodies of grand jury proceedings" in which the investigators "held up men to public scorn and contempt for having had past brushes with the law."[21] Although that alone was troubling, so was the failure of Kefauver and his colleagues to produce or propose any corrective legislation. By the time the hearings had concluded, however, an estimated 30 million Americans had seen through television at least one of these "performances," and Kefauver himself had emerged as a hero.

If Kefauver showed his Senate colleagues, and everyone else, the possibilities of television, his investigative forays reflected badly on some of his fellow Democrats, and eventually on himself. They revealed unwholesome alliances between some of the party's bosses and criminal elements. Through his hearings, five sheriffs, among others, were indicted. In late 1950, party leaders pleaded with Kefauver to stay out of Chicago, where Scott Lucas, the Senate's majority leader, was running a close race for reelection. Kefauver ignored the plea. He held a new round of hearings in Chicago just days before the November election. Although they were closed to the public, a Chicago newspaper managed to obtain and print the testimony of the Democrats' candidate for sheriff, Dan ("Tubbs") Gilbert, reputedly the world's richest cop. That testimony was devastating to the Democrats and was blamed for the defeat of Senator Lucas.[22] President Truman and other Democratic regulars never forgave Kefauver. Truman held Kefauver in contempt, and privately he called him "Senator Cow-fever."[23] In the 1952 campaign year, Kefauver won most of the presidential preference primaries, and he arrived at the party's Chicago national convention with the largest committed bloc of delegates. But President Truman and other party leaders deliberately blocked his nomination.[24]

The Kefauver investigations, along with McCarthy's, were not the only Senate investigations that were troubling to President Truman and his White House staff. Another of these was an inquiry, begun in August 1949, into what were called "influence peddlers" or "five-percenters," an odd assortment of political hangers-on who, for a price, would help businessmen gain lucrative contracts with the government. While some of these brokers operated in grand style with fancy and expensive downtown offices, others were sleazy, fly-by-night hustlers, and all of them preyed on frustrated businessmen in a time of great shortages of many critical commodities. Through their insider contacts with high officials, these brokers arranged ways to bypass the tedious, often baffling contracting processes to gain the desired deals for their clients.[25]

The chairman of the Senate committee that investigated these practices was Clyde Hoey of North Carolina, the last of the old-time frock-coated senators, but the real work was done by the committee's chief counsel, William P. Rogers, and his chief investigator, Francis ("Frip") Flanagan. As a result of the investigation, Harry Vaughan, President Truman's military aide, turned up as one of the principal targets for these "influence peddlers." Vaughan was a longtime friend of the president, and he had willingly responded to the brokers' requests for help. From the White House, he wrote notes for them to agency heads and made requested telephone calls. He saw nothing improper in this, even as he became identified as the White House "fixer."[26] And he saw nothing improper with accepting gifts from the grateful: the most notorious of these gifts were freezers, which an anxious client gave to Vaughan and others he suggested, including Mrs. Truman.[27] Vaughan's ethical laxity was not unique in the Truman administration, and gave the Republicans grounds for their partisan cry about "The Mess in Washington," which became a campaign slogan.

Another troubling investigation was a 1951 inquiry by a Senate banking subcommittee into the operations of the Reconstruction Finance Corporation (RFC). After a quiet initial study, the subcommittee chairman, Senator J. W. Fulbright, reported that those managing the RFC were yielding improperly to political pressure in granting loans. Truman denounced the report as "asinine" and called Fulbright, who was a Rhodes scholar, "an over-educated S.O.B." and "Senator Halfbright."[28] Fulbright responded by holding public hearings in which several prominent Democrats were quickly implicated in the RFC's misconduct, among them the Democratic national chairman, William Boyle, and some of Truman's White House aides. The testimony also disclosed that Donald Dawson, Truman's special assistant, was "the man to see" for those wanting favorable action on RFC loans. The favoritism was obvious, and it did not help that during the investigation it was revealed that a White House stenographer had received an expensive mink coat as a gift from a lawyer-lobbyist with clients before the RFC.[29]

Things got worse for Truman. On April 11, 1951, he dismissed General Douglas MacArthur as commander of US and UN forces in the Far East, then in the midst of the Korean War. That action triggered a firestorm of criticism against the president. In their fury, Senator Taft and other Republican conservatives called for Truman's impeachment, but lost in this seeming political hysteria were Truman's grounds for acting: MacArthur's blatant insubordination. Joseph Martin of Massachusetts, the House minority leader, on his own decided to invite MacArthur to address Congress, and MacArthur did so with a dramatic and emotional speech that drew national attention. New York City gave the general a parade that attracted more than 7 million cheering spectators.

There were demands, of course, for a congressional examination of Truman's cashiering the five-star general. Georgia's Senator Richard Russell, chairman of the Senate's Armed Services Committee, maneuvered quickly and shrewdly to take charge, thereby preempting any action by the Republicans or any other congressional committee. He called his committee members into session, and they authorized an investigation. When members of the Senate's Foreign Relations Committee indicated they also wished to look into the matter, Russell invited them to join in his inquiry, making it clear that he would act as the chairman.[30] In his years in the Senate, Russell had earned a reputation as a judicious and knowledgeable colleague, a man to turn to in a crisis, and he used that reputation to control the proceedings at hand. He and his colleagues had watched the carnival atmosphere of Kefauver's televised hearings, and Russell intended to prevent any such extravagances in these hearings. "I do not propose to act as ring-master of a political circus," he said.[31] Accordingly, he announced that the hearings would be closed, barring both television and the print press. The committee would release "sanitized" versions of each day's testimony, cleansed of anything that might compromise national security (and the drama of each witness's testimony and cross-examination). Chairman Russell made it plain that he wanted a dispassionate, nonpartisan inquiry, and only then did the Republicans realize that Russell's terms would have a chilling effect on the frenzied emotionalism that Truman's action had inspired.

Russell started the hearings in the Senate's Caucus Room on May 3, 1951, with General MacArthur as the first witness. He treated MacArthur with near reverence, describing him as one of the "great captains" of history.[32] For three days, MacArthur explained his ideas, and the transcripts showed clearly not only how deeply he had opposed what he called Truman's "no-win" policy in Korea, but also how openly insubordinate he had been to the nation's commander-in-chief.[33] The other witnesses who followed MacArthur—George Marshall, secretary of defense; Dean Acheson, secretary of state; General Omar Bradley, the chairman of the Joint Chiefs of Staff; and several other military and naval commanders—all agreed with Truman's decision to remove MacArthur. General Bradley's testimony was particularly devastating. MacArthur's plan, he said, would have put the United States at war with Communist China. "This strategy," he said, "would involve us in the wrong war, at the wrong place, at the wrong time and with the wrong enemy."[34]

The hearings ran on for almost two months, longer than Russell wanted, but they had the effect he sought: he had muzzled most of the pro-MacArthur partisanship. In fact, the hearings had evaporated the explosive controversy of mid-April to such an extent that Russell and his Democratic colleagues saw no reason even to file a report. Some Republican senators mildly protested, of course, but even they were aware that the hearings had simply petered out into insignificance. It was an extraordinary achievement by Senator Russell. General MacArthur had seen this controversy as his chance to seek the Republican nomination for president in 1952, but Chairman Russell's hearings had trivialized those prospects, too.

Meanwhile, with his successful influence in the 1950 elections, Senator Joseph McCarthy assumed a new level of swagger and arrogance, equating himself as the American patriot fighting a desperate fight, against fearful odds, to expose Communist subversion and homegrown traitors. He was highly skilled in this. Journalist Richard Rovere called him "the most gifted demagogue ever bred on these shores" with a sure, swift "access to the dark places of the American mind."[35] To his party's conservatives, he had by then become a valued asset, and with their support he became ever more reckless. In June 1951, in an extraordinary Senate speech, McCarthy charged that General George Marshall, one of the nation's most revered leaders, was disloyal, engaged in "a conspiracy so immense and an infamy so black as to dwarf any previous such venture in the history of man."[36] Although in other places he prudently spoke in more general terms, McCarthy made defamatory speeches like this in the Senate, where his words were constitutionally immune from legal challenge or retaliation.

If his extraordinary partisanship pleased some of his Senate colleagues, he appalled others. Senator Fulbright called him "a ruthless boor . . . disgusting and irresponsible."[37] Connecticut's William Benton formally asked the Senate to expel McCarthy for his deceit, perjury, and "despicable" behavior. An investigation was ordered, and that touched off months of new charges from McCarthy. By the time the subcommittee finally filed its report in early January 1953, McCarthy himself had been triumphantly reelected, and the Republicans had won the White House and majority control of both houses of Congress.[38] That meant that McCarthy, under the rules of seniority, would become chairman of the Senate's Committee on Government Operations and its permanent subcommittee on investigations.

McCarthy began a new career as investigator extraordinaire. In the previous three years as a member of the minority, McCarthy had made headlines by denouncing, insulting, and vilifying those whom he attacked. He faked documents that he claimed proved his charges. He redelivered in the Senate his original West Virginia speech in grotesquely bowdlerized form. Most of his speech attacking General Marshall, tens of thousands of words long and written by others, he did not bother to deliver in the Senate. He simply stuck it in the *Congressional Record* as though it had been read.[39] In these years, his weapon was talk, often reckless and overbearing. Now, with his chairmanships, he could act, not just talk, and the special subcommittee was an irresistible invitation to launch investigations. He announced that he intended to pursue his campaign to expose Communism in government.[40] That meant he would be trying to find Communist subversives in President Eisenhower's Republican administration.

McCarthy started by renewing his assault on the State Department. He hired new staff, and with them he looked throughout the government for likely prospects. By their reckoning, McCarthy and his staff conducted 445 "preliminary inquiries" and 157 "investigations," of which seventeen resulted in public hearings.[41] Of course, by the very nature of his scattergun approach, McCarthy sent a chill throughout the executive branch. One of his aides, Roy Cohn, boasted later that McCarthy "terrorized" the Eisenhower administration.[42]

After looking into such agencies as the Government Printing Office and the Voice of America, McCarthy turned his attention to the US Army, an investigation without precedent in its nastiness and the triviality of the matters in dispute. President Eisenhower, against his will, was dragged into these controversies. "I refuse to get in the gutter with that guy," he had said privately, but that diffidence did not let him escape McCarthy's wrath.[43] The senator had earlier called the Democrats "the party of treason."[44] Now he charged Eisenhower with "treason." Conservative Republicans who had supported Senator Taft were proud of McCarthy. "Joe," said Indiana's Senator William Jenner, "you're the kid who came to the party and peed in the lemonade."[45] McCarthy found conspiracies everywhere he looked. In

New Jersey, he located a New York dentist, Irving Peress, who had been drafted and commissioned an army captain and later automatically promoted to major. Peress had complied with the army's required loyalty certification, but he had refused to answer questions about membership in subversive organizations. Out of this, McCarthy built a national crisis: "Who promoted Peress?"[46] He summoned the local commander, Brigadier General Ralph Zwicker, and demanded information on Peress that Zwicker was under orders not to disclose. McCarthy, in a rage, told the general he was "not fit" to wear the uniform.[47] Army Secretary Robert Stevens then ordered Zwicker not to appear again before McCarthy, so McCarthy went after Stevens with bullying tactics that quickly had Stevens all but groveling, giving way to all McCarthy's demands.[48] That brought in the secretary of defense, Charles Wilson, and President Eisenhower, and then the Republican leaders of the Senate and House of Representatives. From this seemingly innocuous trifle, McCarthy accused the army of a basic policy of promoting Communists. The resulting tumult seemed political lunacy, and the Senate had no option but to undertake a formal investigation of McCarthy's investigations.

The Army-McCarthy hearings attracted extraordinary national attention and were played out on television to an audience numbered in the tens of millions. McCarthy gave up his subcommittee chairmanship temporarily to another Republican senator, South Dakota's Karl Mundt, but, throughout, McCarthy dominated the proceedings from the sidelines. "Point of order, Mr. Chairman," he shouted constantly, "point of order!"[49] He harassed witnesses, subcommittee members, and the attorneys with objections, often irrelevant, and accusations that they were helping the Communists. Over and over McCarthy showed himself to be reckless, humorless, and dictatorial. With his dark, glowering demeanor and abusive rhetoric, he looked and sounded brutal and menacing, much like a theatrical villain. Even his allies saw that he was now a political liability. The hearings, begun on April 22, 1954, ran on for two months of turmoil and political confusion. In a rash moment, on June 9, McCarthy attacked a young lawyer not involved in the investigation, and the army's special counsel, Joseph Welch, took him to task with withering scorn. "Have you no sense of decency, sir, at long last?" he asked McCarthy. "Have you no sense of decency?"[50] That brought wild applause from the audience present, and McCarthy looked bewildered. "What did I do?" he asked.[51]

What he did was make himself vulnerable to political retribution. Two days later, on June 11, Senator Ralph Flanders of Vermont, a Republican moderate, formally proposed removing McCarthy from his chairmanships, a motion the Senate Republican leader, William Knowland of California, angrily rebuked as "contrary to established procedure in the Senate."[52] Flanders then changed his resolution to call for the Senate to formally censure McCarthy. The Senate created a select committee of three Republicans and three Democrats to conduct the inquiry. Named chairman was Arthur Watkins of Utah, a respected Republican senior senator who was fully aware of what he called McCarthy's "genius for disruption." He and his committee members devised rules and procedures to keep McCarthy in check. Their hearings were open and brief, confined largely to the tedious reading of past testimony, and there was no television. When McCarthy tried to disrupt the hearings, Watkins gaveled him into silence. On September 27, the select committee unanimously recommended the censure of McCarthy.[53] But with the 1954 congressional elections at hand, the Senate leaders put off further action until late November.

In those elections the Republicans lost majority control of the Senate to the Democrats, a loss in part blamed on McCarthy's extravagances. If that somewhat eased the pressures, voting against McCarthy—the self-proclaimed patriot exposing Communist subversion—was still a ticklish matter for many senators. McCarthy violently attacked the committee, accusing its members of using Communist methods to help the Communist conspiracy. To prevent McCarthy from blaming the Democrats for his troubles, Senate Democratic leader Lyndon Johnson repeatedly stated that this was not a party matter, but was instead a question for every senator to resolve for himself.[54] Illinois' Everett Dirksen tried to save McCarthy from censure by pleading with him to sign an apology of sorts to the Senate, but McCarthy was defiant. "No," he told Dirksen. "I don't crawl."[55]

The censure debate was often bitter and biting, even bordering at times on hysteria. At Johnson's urging, the Democrats mostly stayed quiet, leaving the quarreling to the divided Republicans. In the end, the vote was sixty-seven to twenty-two to censure McCarthy, with all of the Democrats voting to reprove the Wisconsin senator.[56] The Republicans voting "no" were the Taft Republicans, including the party's designated leaders in the Senate. In the months after this official rebuke, McCarthy continued making wild charges, but now he was being ignored. The press corps no longer hung on his denunciations, and even the timid wire services paid him no attention. He took to drinking heavily, and his health soon failed. He died in May 1957 at age forty-eight, ostensibly of hepatitis, but the gossip around the Senate was that he drank himself to death.[57]

McCarthy was not alone in abusing the Senate's investigative powers. There were others just as notorious as he, among them Nevada's Senator Patrick McCarran, chairman of the Senate's Judiciary Committee. With the help of his chief counsel, Jay Sourwine, an investigator of unusually nasty disposition, McCarran used deliberately vindictive tactics to bait and harass witnesses they suspected of disloyal leanings.[58] Senator William Jenner, who had served on this committee, publicly proposed that any American ever tainted with Communism be deprived of his rights and employment: "Let them earn their living as dishwashers or ditch diggers!"[59] Mississippi's James Eastland, a senior committee member who would become chairman in 1956, held notorious one-man hearings in New Orleans in which he pilloried longtime critics of his "white-supremacy" racism as Communist sympathizers. When one witness demanded to know the "ground rules" of this investigation, Eastland testily replied: "I will decide those as we go along and announce them when I desire."[60]

Despite these abrasive tactics, the federal courts stood aloof. In a 1953 ruling, a federal court of appeals stated bluntly: "In general a witness before a Congressional committee must abide by the committee's procedures and has no right to vary them or to impose conditions upon his willingness to testify."[61] Thus, by the nature of the process, witnesses before any committee could find themselves under attack. Under hostile questioning, witnesses at times seemed more like victims than deponents. Much quoted privately in these years was the shorthand version of advice, attributed to General Carl Spaatz, air force chief of staff, to a first-time congressional witness: "Be polite. Don't tell any lies, but, for God's sake, don't go blabbing the truth!"[62]

Abe Fortas, a Washington lawyer who later became a Supreme Court justice, graphically described what he and his clients faced before investigating committees: "There are no standards of judgment, no rules, no traditions of procedure or judicial demeanor, no statutes of limitations, no appeals, no boundaries of relevance, and no finality. In short, anything goes and everything frequently does—and often on television."[63] These abuses prompted widespread protests in and out of Congress, and the Eighty-third Congress (1953–55), in response to these demands for "fair play," considered a flood of proposals for new rules to protect witnesses from the investigators. More than twenty senators sponsored resolutions for "codes of fair practice" by Senate committees. Editorial writers also took up the cry, and Edward R. Murrow, the CBS television journalist, devoted an entire program to excoriating McCarthy for the "comfort" he was giving to the nation's enemies at home and abroad.[64] In the aftermath of McCarthy's formal censure, both the Senate and House took several actions intended to protect witnesses at congressional hearings. Members of the Senate's Committee on Rules and Administration suggested a dozen guidelines for Senate panels on the treatment of witnesses. Senator John McClellan, then chairman of the Permanent Subcommittee on Investigations, revised the committee's rules of procedure to safeguard the rights of witnesses and to prohibit the one-man hearings that McCarthy had so often exploited. Although these hardly amounted to a "bill of rights" for those subpoenaed, future witnesses had assurances of some due process, including the right to counsel of their choice.

Neither the abuses by investigators nor the reforms intended to curb their high-handed methods stifled the Senate's use of investigations then, or later. Senator J. W. Fulbright, a talented investigator in his own right, defended the Senate's use of investigations as "perhaps the most necessary of all the powers" of any legislative body.[65] In Fulbright's view, investigations properly conducted provided the Senate's members with "eyes and ears" to understand the options that lay before them. No senator had fought Senator McCarthy harder than Fulbright. He had confronted McCarthy head on during the 1950 hearings on Columbia University law professor Philip Jessup, and he was shaken by McCarthy's bizarre accusations that the distinguished scholar was a security risk for his affiliation with Communist-front organizations. "So that's Joe McCarthy!" Fulbright muttered over and over, as he left the hearing room."[66] From then on, Fulbright opposed McCarthy at every turn.

In fact, the Senate conducted many useful investigations. For example, at the outbreak of the Korean War, Lyndon Johnson, as a freshman senator, saw the need and the opportunity to create a special subcommittee of the Senate Armed Services Committee to monitor the military buildup then under way. After considerable backroom negotiations, Johnson won approval for a defense preparedness subcommittee and got himself appointed as chairman. Johnson modeled his subcommittee's investigation on those of Senator Harry Truman during World War II: nonpartisan, deliberately shunning publicity. He disarmed any White House criticism by directly consulting President Truman. Johnson insisted that every investigative report—there were forty-four in all—be approved unanimously by the subcommittee, and he muffled any Republican dissent by openly criticizing faults and failures of Truman's Democratic administration.[67] His subcommittee investigated a wide array of military matters, ranging from defense production to the excessive number of generals and admirals stationed at the

Pentagon. When the subcommittee criticized the chairman of the Munitions Board for his inept performance, President Truman promptly fired him. Under Johnson's deft management, the subcommittee became the acknowledged "watchdog" of the war effort, and that enhanced Johnson's stature in both the Senate and the nation.[68]

Through the 1950s and '60s, the Senate conducted many investigations, some fact-finding for possible legislation and others overseeing the administration. These had become a routine procedure for the Senate and took up much of its time and attention. The subjects were as varied as life in the United States. Some were quickly completed, while others ran on for years. Most caught the attention of only those immediately concerned, but some attracted national audiences and rattled the country's political system. A few even became significant for the opportunities they offered senators seeking political promotion, including their respective party's presidential nomination.

One of these was the Senate investigation of racketeering and corruption in labor unions, an investigation begun in January 1957 and culminating almost three years later in the adoption of a tough new labor reform law.[69] Arkansas Senator John McClellan, by then a veteran of Senate investigations, chaired the panel. Committee member John F. Kennedy's preoccupation with presidential politics created a special problem for McClellan. He had to castigate the criminals controlling some unions without alienating those unions that were traditional allies of Kennedy's Democratic Party. In hearings around the country the committee concentrated largely on the Teamsters Union, the leaders of which typically supported Republican political contenders. The senators investigated other unions as well, including those for textiles, laundry, and auto workers. In 270 days of public hearings, the committee issued more than eight thousand subpoenas and questioned some 1,500 witnesses, more than three hundred of whom refused to testify, claiming the protection of the Fifth Amendment.[70]

The committee's hearings were often dramatic and tense, and they drew huge television audiences with the exposure of extensive criminal activities, an unsavory mix of extortion and intimidation, goon squads, and hoodlums. Many union officials were caught looting their unions' pension funds, as well as taking bribes and payoffs for sweetheart contracts with cooperating companies. Some unions were infiltrated by gangsters and known felons. Successive presidents of the Teamsters Union, Dave Beck and James Hoffa, were summoned as witnesses; later both were indicted and sent to jail. The many scandals these hearings revealed called loudly for remedial legislation. In January 1959, Senator Kennedy introduced a moderate reform bill designed to prevent financial misconduct by union officials. The measure was important to Kennedy's presidential campaign as a way to show his legislative prowess, but it was constructed so as to escape damnation by legitimate union leaders for "union busting."

After formal hearings on the Kennedy bill, the real struggle came first on the Senate floor, then in the House of Representatives, and finally in the Senate-House conference that resolved the differences between the two chambers' bills. The final version was far harsher on organized labor than Kennedy had planned, and Kennedy's supporters blamed Lyndon Johnson, the Senate's majority leader, who also had presidential ambitions. Johnson stood aside in the Senate fight, letting conservatives pass their amendments, but in the House showdown Johnson was suspected of secretly persuading many in the Texas delegation to vote against the Kennedy version. After many concessions in the conference, Kennedy barely managed to produce a bill he could support. "I think it's the best bill we can get—and get a bill," he said. "Compromises are never a happy experience."[71] Even so, in the investigation of labor-union corruption and the reform legislation that resulted, Senator Kennedy demonstrated the political and parliamentary skills that helped him win his party's nomination and subsequently the presidency in 1960.

In October 1957, the Soviet Union startled the world by launching a man-made earth satellite, *Sputnik*, an achievement that raised grave fears about Soviet intentions. President Eisenhower dismissed the Soviet success, but Democrats in the Senate reacted quickly. Missouri's Stuart Symington, a former secretary of the air force, called for a full-scale investigation of the nation's space program, a move expected to raise his profile and help his presidential candidacy. But Senator Johnson promptly acted to block Symington and to take charge of the investigation himself. He consulted President Eisenhower, the administration's senior cabinet members, and the Senate's other Democratic and Republican leaders. Then Johnson proposed that he revive his preparedness investigating subcommittee to find the proper response to the Soviet threat. He was now the Senate's majority leader, after all, so he was able to take over. Johnson set rules to prevent partisan politicking. In the months that followed, he and his subcommittee filed seventeen reports, all unanimously approved, that reordered the American space program. Among his subcommittee's recommendations was the creation of the National Aeronautics and Space Administration (NASA), the agency that a decade later celebrated the American triumph of placing men on the moon. Johnson conducted the hearings with skill and imagination to dramatize the new peril of Soviet aggression. He was widely praised for the "minor masterpiece" of this investigation.[72] In the process, Johnson gave credence to his own claims for his party's presidential nomination.

In 1962, another extensive Senate investigation resulted in tough reform legislation, in this case almost inadvertently. Late in 1959, Senator Kefauver, with his presidential ambitions spent, began what became a two-and-a-half-year investigation of the drug industry's high prices and monopolistic practices in hopes of enacting remedial legislation. Kefauver's subcommittee explored many aspects of the trade, among them sharp marketing practices, often misleading advertising, the inadequacy of the Food and Drug Administration's oversight, price fixing, violations of antitrust laws, and the huge markups over cost that produced wildly excessive profits. With his bumbling manner, Kefauver had previously seemed to be a naïve hillbilly seeking publicity, but by now he was a skilled investigator who laid bare the reasons for those high prices for prescription drugs. The drug companies fought back fiercely, and they had on the Kefauver Committee open apologists for their prices and tactics, including Everett Dirksen of Illinois, now the Senate Republican floor leader, and Roman Hruska of Nebraska. In June 1962, when the time finally came to mark up a bill, Dirksen and Hruska took charge, offering a series of amendments that defeated Kefauver's purposes.[73] Kefauver could not support the bill that emerged from committee.

But before that bill went to the Senate floor, a stunning revelation abruptly reversed its momentum. Scientists had discovered that the drug thalidomide, used widely as a sedative and treatment for morning sickness among pregnant women, had caused terrible deformities in thousands of babies born in Europe and Canada. A drug company had distributed millions of samples of thalidomide to American doctors for testing on their patients. But a medical officer at the Food and Drug Administration, Dr. Frances Oldham Kelsey, had managed to block the drug's general use in the United States.[74] Those who had gutted Kefauver's bill were at once embarrassed, and they quickly agreed to restore much of his proposed language. "I have been pretty well excoriated in the press," Dirksen said. "I do not whimper."[75] Both the Senate and the House approved the strengthened bill unanimously, and President Kennedy awarded Dr. Kelsey the President's Award for Distinguished Federal Civilian Service for her heroism.

By the 1970s, the Senate had long held clear preeminence in conducting congressional investigations. Over the decades, senators simply assumed responsibility for undertaking formal inquiries into complex questions, including enemy atrocities during the Korean War, military procurement irregularities, civil disorders, and home mortgage fraud, and they had by then achieved formidable investigative powers. The Senate armed its investigators with the power to subpoena witnesses and documents, and to put those witnesses under oath, subject to criminal prosecution for perjury or the refusal to testify. The Senate could cite rebellious witnesses for contempt, a felony. Routinely the Senate sent such citations to the Department of Justice for prosecution under an 1857 law, but senators had the power themselves, under the MacCracken precedent of 1935, to put such persons on trial before the Senate and, upon conviction, to send them to jail.[76] There were but minor restraints on the Senate's investigative powers and almost no limitations at all on what or whom senators could investigate.

In 1970, as part of an act to control organized crime, Congress authorized its investigative committees to grant immunity to witnesses likely to claim the protection of the Fifth Amendment. So-called use immunity protected the witnesses only against self-incrimination from their testimony, but offered no immunity from prosecution with evidence otherwise obtained. While a nuisance to federal prosecutors, use immunity gave Senate and House investigators the ability to explore matters where significant witnesses would otherwise have refused to testify. This new authority shortly proved critical to the Senate's most extraordinary investigation ever, its formal inquiry into the criminal activities of President Nixon's White House and his reelection campaign of 1972, an accumulation of illegal and sordid offenses known collectively as Watergate.

Accustomed to deferring to the Senate on such matters, the House's leaders stood aside while the Senate's investigators acted to expose the Watergate scandals. No one seriously questioned the Senate's jurisdiction, even though from early on there was compelling evidence of high crimes and misdemeanors by the president, or those under his command, and therefore grounds for the House to consider articles of impeachment. The Senate's investigating committee uncovered startling revelations of massive corruption within the Nixon administration. The House's leaders acted only after the senators located the damning evidence against the scofflaw president and, in so doing, precipitated a national political crisis. The Senate's investigation, a classic of its kind, stemmed from a seemingly trivial incident, the botched break-in of the Democratic Party's national headquarters in Washington, but its consequences were enormous. They included the forced resignation of Vice President Spiro Agnew and then of President Nixon, the jailing of more than a dozen of his closest associates, and the adoption of significant new legislation reforming the national budget process, the president's war powers, and the management of election campaigns.[77]

In the early hours of June 17, 1972, Washington, DC, police arrested five intruders inside Democratic headquarters in the Watergate Office Building. National Chairman Lawrence O'Brien quickly learned that those arrested had been hired by President Nixon's reelection campaign, and O'Brien brought suit against them in an attempt to exploit what he took to be a major scandal. He had little success at first, as the press treated the incident as a somewhat bizarre political caper, and the White House dismissed the break-in as a "third-rate burglary."[78] But the matter did not end there. Over the months that followed, congressional doubts about this strange caper festered to the point that the Senate launched a full-scale investigation that uncovered a gaudy array of political crimes. In the end, that botched "third-rate burglary" brought down the Nixon presidency.

A few newspapers, notably the *Washington Post*, took an early interest in the break-in and published stories that increasingly indicated that there was far more to it than originally assumed. That summer and fall, Massachusetts Senator Edward Kennedy, chair of a Judiciary subcommittee, had his staff undertake a preliminary inquiry, primarily to secure documents in anticipation of a full-scale investigation. The Senate's majority leader, Mike Mansfield, also became more interested in the matter and let it be known that he would press for just such an investigation after the new Senate convened in January 1973. After Nixon's reelection, Mansfield sent formal notices to the chiefs of relevant government agencies warning them against allowing destruction of any materials relative to the coming Senate investigation.

In February 1973, the Senate voted unanimously for the investigation Mansfield wanted, and Mansfield, in a move to block a high-profile role for Senator Kennedy, chose North Carolina's Sam Ervin, a highly respected senator, to chair the committee.[79] By then, the Watergate burglars had been put on trial in federal court, where they all pleaded guilty and were awaiting sentencing from Judge John Sirica.

The Senate's Republican leaders picked Tennessee's Howard Baker as their ranking member on the investigating committee, and Chairman Ervin promptly named him vice chairman, an unusual gesture reflecting Ervin's desire to keep the proceedings as nonpartisan as possible. Baker, a talented politician with national ambitions, was not a likely apologist for Nixon.

In mid-March, one of the burglars, James McCord, who was facing twenty years in jail, volunteered to tell the Ervin committee all he knew.

Higher-ups were involved, he said; and he fingered John Mitchell, Nixon's onetime attorney general, and John Dean, the White House counsel, among others.[80] Word that McCord was talking spread rapidly, and soon some of the White House officials, among them John Dean, also began to testify before a federal grand jury about what they knew. The Ervin committee staff, headed by Chief Counsel Samuel Dash, began negotiating for these men to appear as committee witnesses. For cooperation, Dash could offer them use immunity and the hope of leniency in their sentencing.

Nixon announced at the outset that, as a matter of executive privilege inherent in the presidency, he would not permit any White House official to testify before the Senate committee. He professed to be defending the presidency, not himself, but Senator Ervin, a constitutional scholar, dismissed Nixon's claim. "Executive privilege," he said, "is executive poppycock."[81] The senator knew in detail the MacCracken case of 1935, the one on which the Supreme Court ruled that the Senate had power to arrest, convict, and jail an uncooperative witness.[82] Ervin let it be known that he was prepared to have the Senate order the arrest of any White House official who defied a committee subpoena. He had his committee members vote to require every White House witness to testify publicly and under oath. The vote was unanimous. Nixon thereupon backed down and tried to negotiate easy terms for his aides.

Not until mid-May was the committee ready to start taking testimony, and then James McCord, the burglar, testified sensationally that the burglars were paid to plead guilty. He also testified that he himself was offered a presidential pardon if he kept silent. In April came the revelation that Nixon had created within the White House a special lawless unit called the "Plumbers," two of whose agents had burglarized the office of the psychiatrist Daniel Ellsberg, then on trial for disclosing the Pentagon Papers. Growing panicky, Nixon fired John Dean as White House counsel and forced the resignations of his principal White House aides, H. R. Haldeman and John Ehrlichman, and the attorney general, Richard Kleindienst.

Meanwhile, a federal grand jury seemed about to indict others involved in the conspiracy. On May 8, the new attorney general, Elliot Richardson, named Archibald Cox from Harvard Law School as special Watergate prosecutor. Cox promptly demanded that the senators postpone their investigation until he had completed his. The senators refused.

To save himself, John Dean became what proved to be the committee's principal witness. For five days in late June, under a grant of immunity, he gave riveting details of White House intrigue and criminality, directly accusing Nixon of far more than the Watergate burglary. Dean told the committee that Nixon's strategy was to feign cooperation with the committee, but to hide as much as possible.[83]

Dean's testimony shocked political Washington and the country at large. Senator Baker put the matter succinctly: "What did the president know, and when did he know it?"[84] Significantly, Dean's charges also stirred action in the House of Representatives, and the House's new majority leader, Thomas P. O'Neill, started to plan for impeachment.

By mid-July, Ervin's committee made a startling new discovery. Alexander Butterfield, a onetime Nixon aide, revealed under questioning that President Nixon had secretly wired the principal rooms in the White House, Executive Office Building, and Camp David to record all conversations, twenty-four hours a day.[85] This revelation suddenly suggested a surefire way to prove exactly what the president and his men had been doing regarding the charges of a cover-up. The committee subpoenaed tapes of conversations they knew had taken place. So did Archibald Cox, the special prosecutor. But Nixon refused to honor either, so both Cox and the committee sued him in federal court for those tapes.[86]

The Ervin committee summoned the president's men to testify, including John Mitchell, H. R. Haldeman, and John Ehrlichman, who presented themselves in various guises. Haldeman offered himself as a courteous, cooperative witness, but he lied to the committee and went to jail for his perjury. Ehrlichman, scowling and snarling, acted like a culprit and went to jail, too. So did Mitchell, Nixon's former attorney general. Over the weeks of testimony, astonishing disclosures of political nastiness and dirty tricks emerged, as well as complicated schemes by Nixon's White House to conceal what the president and his men had done and were doing.

Carried live on national television, the committee's hearings fascinated millions of Americans and made those who appeared regularly on camera well known throughout the land. With his gentle wit and kindly manner, Chairman Ervin became immensely popular, a folk hero to those who saw him bringing to justice the Watergate conspirators. Out of a natural modesty, Ervin posed as a simple country lawyer, but he was, in fact, a skilled questioner, a former judge, and a highly talented Harvard Law School graduate with a profound commitment to the Constitution. Despite Senator Baker's efforts to spare Nixon and his fellow Republicans the full brunt of these scandals, he also emerged with an enhanced reputation.

Overall, the committee hearings and their extensive disclosures had a devastating impact on Nixon, so much so that in early September Robert

Dole, a loyalist Nixon senator, tried to have the committee ordered "to turn off the TV lights" and conduct its hearings in secret. Dole charged that the television hearings were squeezing "the last drop of anguish and printer's ink out of Watergate."[87] His efforts failed.

In fall 1973, the investigation turned melodramatic with the sudden news that Spiro Agnew, the vice president, faced criminal indictment. Constitutionally he was the heir apparent to Nixon's presidency, and that raised grave questions about impeaching Nixon. As governor of Maryland, Agnew had joined a conspiracy to extort cash payoffs from businessmen seeking state contracts. The federal prosecutors estimated that he pocketed more than $100,000 in bribes. In public, Agnew angrily protested his innocence, but in private he quietly negotiated a plea bargain. Nixon's difficulties let Agnew gain highly favorable terms. In return for resigning as vice president and acknowledging his evasion of income taxes, Agnew was let off with a fine and probation. He escaped jail, but resigned in disgrace on October 10, 1973.[88]

Two days later, President Nixon, under provisions of the Twenty-Fifth Amendment to the Constitution, nominated Gerald Ford, the House Republican leader, to replace Agnew as vice president. Nixon sought to present this as a joyous occasion, with much advance hoopla and suspense over whom he would choose, but he was in more trouble than ever. The Senate committee had subpoenaed five of Nixon's White House tapes; the special prosecutor had subpoenaed nine tapes; and Nixon was struggling in federal court to block the motion. On October 19, a Friday, nine days after Agnew resigned, Nixon began a series of maneuvers that precipitated a new political crisis the following night.

He started by summoning Senators Ervin and Baker to the White House. He told them that he wanted their committee to have the tapes they had subpoenaed, but not the nonrelevant matters on those tapes. He proposed submitting the tapes to Mississippi's John Stennis, a senator of great personal integrity, and to have him provide the committee with those segments pertinent to their investigation. Both senators told Nixon that they could not agree to that arrangement.[89]

Nixon subsequently directed Attorney General Richardson to fire prosecutor Cox, but Richardson refused and resigned as attorney general, as did Deputy Attorney General William Ruckelshaus. Nixon then ordered Solicitor General Robert Bork to fire Cox, and Bork complied. Thereupon the White House announced that Nixon had "abolished" the Special Prosecutor's Office, and Alexander Haig, Nixon's chief of staff, ordered FBI agents to seize the offices of Cox, Richardson, and Ruckelshaus. All this smacked of a palace coup, one carried out on live television before a startled and bewildered national audience.

These stunning events, promptly labeled the "Saturday Night Massacre," touched off a firestorm of protest. Congressional offices were flooded with telegrams and letters, and their telephone switchboards were jammed with calls. Especially angered were the Senate's Republicans, none of whom Nixon had consulted. Their leader, Pennsylvania's Hugh Scott, summoned Bryce Harlow, one of Nixon's chief advisers, to a closed meeting with Republican senators. There he gave him an ultimatum for Nixon: he must reestablish the Special Prosecutor's Office promptly and with sure guarantees of the prosecutor's independence. If Nixon refused, the Republican senators would turn on him.[90]

Nixon had badly miscalculated. The country was outraged, and he was now in defiance of the court's order to yield the tapes and liable to be cited for contempt. That could force his resignation. On the first business day of the new week, more than eighty members of the House filed resolutions for Nixon's impeachment. House Speaker Carl Albert announced that the House Judiciary Committee would now undertake a full-scale impeachment inquiry.[91] That committee processed Ford's nomination as vice president as quickly as it could, and he took the oath for that office on December 6, 1973. Congratulated by a friend on coming through the committee examinations without a blemish, Ford had a cryptic answer: "They didn't ask the right questions."[92]

The House Judiciary Committee declined to undertake any original investigations of the many accusations against Nixon contained in the scores of impeachment resolutions. They held the committee's meetings in private and relied primarily on the data compiled by Senator Ervin's committee and the special prosecutors. By the end of July 1974, the committee members took up proposed articles of impeachment and subsequently approved three.

Three days before the first vote, the Supreme Court ruled unanimously that Nixon had to turn over the sixty-four tapes now subpoenaed by the special prosecutor.

The tapes showed that just six days after the Watergate burglary Nixon had clearly ordered a cover-up. "Play it tough," he had told Haldeman, his chief of staff. He ordered Haldeman to tell the director of the CIA, Richard Helms, to tell the head of the FBI, L. Patrick Gray, to "lay off" its Watergate investigation.[93] That was obstruction of justice, a grave criminal offense. As word spread of these incriminating statements, any remaining support for

Nixon collapsed. Even so, Nixon tried to hang on, arguing that he might still save himself with a speech to the nation. In the end, he had to resign, and he did so on August 9, 1974.[94]

The success of the Senate Watergate investigation and widespread anger at the executive branch's disastrous course in Vietnam ushered in a brief period of congressional reassertion of legislative branch constitutional prerogatives, particularly with regard to the management of American foreign policy.

On December 22, 1974, investigative journalist Seymour Hersh published in the *New York Times* alarming accounts of Central Intelligence Agency activities intended to destabilize foreign governments.[95] His research also produced new information that the CIA was conducting illegal intelligence operations against large numbers of American citizens. Soon after the Senate convened for the Ninety-fourth Congress in January 1975, it adopted the model of the previous Congress's Watergate Committee to establish an eleven-member Select Committee to Study Governmental Operations with Respect to Intelligence Activities.[96] Chaired by Idaho's Frank Church, with John Tower of Texas as vice chair, the temporary committee's goal was to reassert legislative oversight of the nation's intelligence agencies. Reflecting the enormity of such an enterprise, the Senate authorized the hiring of 135 staffers, including fifty-three investigators. Over a period of nine months, the committee conducted 250 closed sessions and twenty-one days of public hearings, interviewing more than eight hundred people.

At the committee's initial public session in the ornate Senate Caucus Room, Chairman Church dramatically displayed a CIA poison dart gun—known technically as the "Nondiscernible Microbioinnoculator"—to support findings that the agency had violated a presidential order by keeping a supply of shellfish toxin sufficient to kill thousands.[97] That weapon ended the career of CIA chief William Colby, whose cooperative attitude with the committee enraged members of the intelligence community. He later acknowledged that "the impact of the toxin spectacular [media circus], and especially the fact that I had delivered the dart gun when Congress demanded it, blew the roof off."[98]

Unlike the Watergate Committee, however, the so-called Church Committee—dealing with classified national security information—lacked bipartisan support for full disclosure. Among those in opposition were the administration of President Gerald Ford, vice chairman Tower, and Republican military affairs stalwart Barry Goldwater. As journalist Daniel Schorr explained, the resistance to cooperation grew out of "ingrained convictions that an intelligence secret was forever and its disclosure close to treason."[99] The December 1975 assassination of a CIA station chief in Greece reinforced this intransigent attitude. Neither Tower nor Goldwater signed off on the committee's fourteen-part final report issued in the spring of 1976, in the midst of a presidential election campaign.[100] The committee recommended enhanced oversight of the national intelligence activities, and its report inspired creation of the permanent Senate Select Committee on Intelligence, as well as a presidential executive order banning US support for the assassination of foreign leaders, and passage of the 1978 Foreign Intelligence Surveillance Act.[101] President Ford later described the investigation as "sensational and irresponsible," and others agreed with his assertion that its damage to the nation's intelligence-gathering efforts would be long lasting. On the other side of this politically divisive issue were journalists who concluded that the final report stood as a landmark public document in the history of American intelligence.[102]

The theme of illicit CIA involvement in the affairs of sovereign nations burst back into the headlines in 1987 with the revelation of that agency's efforts to undermine the Cuban-backed Sandinista government of Nicaragua with aid to a rebel group known as the Contras. Five years earlier, Congress had attached to appropriations legislation Representative Edward Boland's rider explicitly prohibiting such aid if used for military support of efforts to overthrow Nicaragua's regime. President Ronald Reagan interpreted this ban to apply only to US intelligence agencies, such as the CIA and units within the Defense Department, leaving him free to funnel resources to the Contras through his administration's National Security Council. Congress subsequently tightened the Boland Amendment to ban all funds for military support. This led the White House to seek financial support from foreign sources in a scheme managed by National Security Council director Robert McFarlane; his successor, Vice Admiral John Poindexter; and his deputy, Lieutenant Colonel Oliver North.

Despite Reagan's pledge not to do business with terrorist states and not to trade arms for hostages, he agreed in late 1985, without consulting Congress, to Poindexter and North's clandestine plan to sell missiles to Iran—despite an arms embargo—for its war against Iraq. In return, the United States would win the release of several American hostages held in Lebanon. Less than half of those funds actually reached the US Treasury. Lt. Col. North later explained that he, with Poindexter's permission, had been diverting a portion of them to aid the Contras. When a Lebanese newspaper exposed this deal in November 1986, President Reagan at first denied it, only to recant several months later.[103]

In that year's midterm congressional elections, Senate Democratic picked up a net gain of eight seats, and thereby returned to the majority for the first time in six years. Later that month, Poindexter resigned and Reagan fired North. Public anger and disillusionment caused Reagan's public approval polls to plummet from 67 percent to 46 percent.[104]

When the Democrats organized the Senate in January 1987, they collaborated with the House to create an eleven-member Senate Select Committee on Secret Military Assistance to Iran and the Nicaraguan Opposition and a fifteen-member House counterpart.[105] The two committees operated jointly but had their own chairmen and separate staffs. The Senate retained noted legal strategist Arthur Liman as its committee's chief counsel. Throughout the committees' proceedings, Liman proved to be a relentless questioner. Yet he and the committee became targets of widespread public anger throughout this politically galvanizing inquiry either for pushing too forcefully or not vigorously enough.[106]

After three months of investigation and 250 hours of testimony from twenty-eight witnesses, including sharp questioning of McFarlane, Poindexter, and North, among others, the joint committee uncovered the major elements of this scheme, but without being able to identify the exact role of President Reagan. The careful employment by White House staff of the doctrine of "plausible deniability," along with paper-shredding machines, decimated the documentary trail and ultimately blunted serious talk of impeachment proceedings against the president. The committees made a strategic error in not calling Reagan to testify and in granting limited immunity to encourage testimony of key witnesses. Although North and Poindexter were later convicted, their congressional immunity proved decisive in their pleas to have their convictions overturned on appeal. This unforeseen consequence of providing "use immunity"—allowing convicted felons to go free—would cause future congressional investigators to have second thoughts about using all available tools to assess the guilt of the key players. Ultimately, this investigation failed to answer the question that the Watergate committee had so decisively resolved: "What did the president know, and when did he know it?" In the final report of the congressional investigation, the two chairmen—Hawaii Senator Daniel Inouye and Indiana Representative Lee Hamilton—were left to conclude simply that "fundamental processes of government were disregarded and the rule of law was subverted."[107]

The next significant Senate investigation had its roots in a 1978 purchase by Arkansas attorney general—and soon to be governor—Bill Clinton; his wife, Hillary; and their business partners, Jim and Susan McDougal of 230 acres of mountain property on the south bank of the White River in the Ozark Mountains of Arkansas. The partners had borrowed $203,000 to finance this purchase for developing vacation home sites, and they created the Whitewater Development Corporation to manage the sales. The deal soon soured because of skyrocketing mortgage interest rates that kept prospective buyers away and because the tract was on the much less desirable side of the river—remote from amenities and inaccessible during periods of flooding.[108] The Clintons and McDougals maintained their financial and personal relationships through the 1980s. Jim McDougal helped Governor Clinton with fund-raising events to help pay off the latter's campaign debt, but also weakened the relationship by agitating for interest payments from them on the Whitewater loan. Ultimately, the McDougals lost their investment.

The Whitewater issue surfaced more than a decade later during Clinton's 1992 presidential campaign when Jim McDougal, suffering declining physical and mental health, and by then deeply alienated from the Clintons, contacted the *New York Times*.[109] He later wrote, echoing Clinton's own campaign language, "The Whitewater case unfolded because I wanted Bill Clinton to feel my pain."[110]

Six months after Clinton's 1993 inauguration, Vincent Foster, a White House staff attorney who had been handling the complex matter for the Clintons, was found dead in a park along the Potomac River. Speculation flared among their imaginative political opponents that the Clintons had had him murdered to cover up possible illegal Whitewater-connected dealings, including the transfer of funds from two bankrupt Arkansas financial organizations. In 1993, a House committee examined the matter and agreed with previous findings that his death was by suicide. The Senate Banking Committee jumped onto that bandwagon a year later and reached the same conclusion.

Bowing to intensifying Republican demands to fully investigate a related series of seemingly unsavory disclosures, President Clinton in January 1994 directed the US attorney general to appoint an independent special prosecutor—a decision that later caused him to remark, "I was so naive."[111] That prosecutor, Robert Fiske, subsequently received several other cases, unrelated to Whitewater, but touching on the Clintons. On August 5, 1994, a judicial panel replaced Fiske with former federal appeals court judge Kenneth Starr.

The 1995 return of the Senate to Republican control resulted in the creation on May 17 of a separate committee under the jurisdiction of its Banking Committee to continue the inquiry. The Special Committee to Investigate Whitewater Development Corporation and Related Matters, chaired by New York's Alfonse D'Amato, with Maryland's Paul Sarbanes as the ranking Democrat, hired as its lead counsels Michael Chertoff and Richard Ben-Veniste, the latter a former official in the Watergate special prosecutor's office. Over its fourteen-month existence—the longest congressional inquiry into the actions of any incumbent president—the Senate Whitewater Committee took more than ten thousand pages of testimony from nearly 250 individuals, and reviewed more than 1 million pages of documentary evidence.[112] On June 18, 1996, the panel's Republican majority issued an eight-hundred-page report sharply critical of First Lady Hillary Clinton. The Democratic minority found no evidence of wrongdoing by either of the Clintons.[113] Senator Christopher Dodd (D-Connecticut) attacked the inquiry as a taxpayer-funded effort by the committee's Republican majority to help their party in the upcoming 1996 election campaigns— "the most partisan and polarized hearing in the history of the Senate."[114]

The failure of committee Democrats and Republicans to forge a unified report underscored how thoroughly the political climate had deteriorated in the twenty-three years since the Watergate Committee's 1973 final report. Committee chairman D'Amato was then serving as co-chair of Bob Dole's presidential campaign and Christopher Dodd presided over the Democratic National Committee.[115] Unlike Watergate and Iran-Contra, this investigation failed to sustain long-term media attention. As one observer noted, there simply was no "smoking gun."[116]

Special prosecutor Kenneth Starr continued his separate investigation, which came to focus on issues unrelated to Whitewater, but directly related to President Clinton's intimate behavior as governor and president. Pursuit of these issues ultimately led to Clinton's impeachment by the Republican-controlled House of Representatives, on charges of perjury and obstruction of justice for his efforts to conceal extramarital affairs, and his subsequent acquittal by the Senate on February 12, 1999.

The Senate Whitewater investigations proved to be the antithesis of the Watergate inquiries a generation earlier. Where Watergate set new standards for bipartisan cooperation, Whitewater demonstrated the futility of deeply partisan proceedings. In hindsight, it marked the end of the era of major twentieth-century congressional investigations. Although the Pecora Committee, the Truman Committee, the Ervin Committee, and the Church

Committee, among others, operated in inherently partisan climates, partisanship did not fracture the ultimate integrity of their inquiries. It is no wonder that Congress subsequently shunned its long investigative traditions in deciding instead to hand over high-profile investigations to outside panels, whose assiduously crafted final reports were quickly forgotten, of possible value only to future students of governmental dysfunction.[117] Notable examples of this shift away from Congress's constitutional responsibility to investigate include the 2002–4 National Commission on Terrorist Attacks Upon the United States (the 9/11 Commission), a panel short on time, funding, and executive branch cooperation that ultimately left many questions unanswered; and the 2009–10 Financial Crisis Inquiry Commission.[118]

In 2005, Senate Democrats, in the minority, called for a national commission to investigate governmental inaction in response to that year's Hurricane Katrina, which devastated the nation's Gulf Coast. Republicans in the Senate and House decided to refer that responsibility to their standing committees on governmental affairs. The administration of George W. Bush, which came under ferocious attack for its inept handling of the emergency, ultimately refused to provide the panels with vital information, citing separation of powers and executive privilege considerations. Nonetheless, the final reports of both committees, and related congressional inquiries, rendered a clear indictment of the administration's performance, but they offered little substantive guidance for protecting against such disasters in the future.[119]

In times of early-twenty-first-century investigative need, senators are quick to look back to the landmark Senate investigations of the twentieth century. The Truman Committee is fondly recalled as a model for scrutinizing the rampant corruption, fraud, and mismanagement revealed during the nation's extended military operations in Iraq and Afghanistan. To explore the financial meltdown of 2008, senators suggested a committee along the lines of the Pecora Committee on the Stock Market Crash. But times have changed. Aside from crippling partisanship, a major barrier to creating such a panel composed entirely of senators is the enormous commitment of time and talent necessary to master the complex issues involved. Senators of the current era are simply too busy and too distracted to actively participate in investigations that could extend for years. Consequently, the latter-day Pecora Committee became the Financial Crisis Inquiry Commission. That panel included no incumbent member of the Senate or House. Therefore, it—and similarly constituted outside commissions—lacked advocates whose investment in the issues under study would motivate them to follow up as sponsors of legislative remedies, with the persistence and congressional tenure to ensure that recommendations remained before Congress for action rather than on a library shelf. If the Senate and House pursue this pattern into the twenty-first century, they will be abdicating the fundamental constitutional right—under the doctrine of separation of powers—of the Senate and House to hold the executive branch accountable. That would be an incalculable loss for Congress and for the nation.

11

Debate, Deliberation, and Dispute

FOR GENERATIONS, SENATORS HAVE TAKEN special pride in the Senate's reputation as a great deliberative body, an institution exulting in its freedom of debate. Its members, they believe, have the capacity, by means of persuasive speeches, to lead the nation. In every Senate since 1789, there have been members perfectly confident in their eloquence and oratorical skills. Indeed, the Senate's roster has rarely if ever been shy of men and women deeply convinced of their own brilliance and prepared to show this to their colleagues and the world. Yet over those same generations, Senate debate in the grand manner of ancient tradition has steadily fallen into disuse and the Senate's day-to-day debates have come to be largely ignored—not only by the outer world, but by the senators themselves. For more than a century, the standard ingredient in any recipe to restore public confidence in Congress has been improving the quality of Senate floor debate in order to inspire and inform the public.[1]

Those who drafted the US Constitution in 1787 intended the Senate to act as a deliberative body, to advise the president prudently on domestic and foreign matters, and to restrain the expected rashness of the larger and popularly elected House of Representatives. From the start, senators sought to achieve that high purpose through their debates. And by the end of the 1820s, the Senate had begun to establish a reputation as a forum of eloquence and wisdom. For the next few decades, the nation listened when senators debated. By then, the Senate had become what Daniel Webster called "a body to which the country looks with confidence for wise, moderate, patriotic, and healing counsels."[2] Over the third of a century that preceded the Civil War, the Senate regularly debated the meaning of the Constitution and the nature and thrust of the government it created. These were the glory years of Senate debate.

Whatever the intentions of those who wrote the Constitution, the Senate failed to achieve legislative preeminence before 1820. The important debates and the significant legislative initiatives consistently took place in the House of Representatives. Men of ambition sought election to the House, not the Senate, and it was as House members that Daniel Webster, Henry Clay, and John C. Calhoun, among others, first achieved national stature. The House's debates, often boisterous and chaotic, were the debates that counted in shaping the nation's laws.[3]

From 1789 to 1795, the Senate met in secret, behind closed doors. This not only concealed what senators were saying but also gave them little incentive to take pains with their speeches. On occasion, they had so little to say that they fell silent, but stayed in closed session anyway. "We used to stay in the Senate chamber till about two o'clock," Senator William Maclay of Pennsylvania confided in his private journal, "whether we did anything or not, by way of keeping up the appearance of business."[4] Not surprisingly, their debates were largely ignored.

From the spring of 1789 to the summer of 1790, they spoke to one another in a grand setting—a handsomely restored chamber in New York City's Federal Hall on Wall Street. Situated on the second floor above the House chamber, the Senate occupied a richly carpeted space forty feet long and thirty feet wide. The chamber's most striking features were its high arched ceiling, tall windows curtained in crimson damask, fireplace mantels in handsomely polished marble, and a presiding officer's chair elevated three feet from the floor and placed under a crimson canopy. The ceiling was adorned in the center with a sun and thirteen stars.[5]

In December 1790, under an agreement that would place the seat of the federal government in the District of Columbia by 1800, the government took up residence for ten years in Philadelphia. Congress occupied Philadelphia's recently constructed county courthouse, located on Chestnut Street adjacent to the state house—today's Independence Hall. Named Congress Hall, this building offered the Senate accommodations considerably more elegant than those available to the House one floor below. In addition to the double row of members' desks and red leather–upholstered chairs, the room's furnishings included a specially woven large carpet brightly designed with an eagle clutching an olive branch and thirteen arrows.[6]

It was in that chamber, in 1795, that the Senate first opened its doors—and oratory—to the public, although the doors remained shut when the members discussed "executive" business such as treaties and presidential appointments. The availability of an audience, seated in a just-completed spectators' gallery, encouraged the chamber's would-be orators to do their best. Philadelphia's *Aurora* sent a reporter to cover the proceedings, but soon opted to take that trouble only for debates of high political interest. The locked doors had attracted that era's highly partisan press much more than the substance of the chamber's debates.

The early Senates included men of distinction who felt the honor of election to a legislative body partially modeled on the British House of Lords.[7] It was this sense of honor that persuaded senators from the beginning to conduct their debates in a solemn and dignified manner befitting themselves and the Senate. They won praise for this attitude from the start, especially when their debates were compared to the brawling, rambunctious shouting matches in the four-times-larger House of Representatives. Senators' sense of decorum prompted them to speak in grave and subdued tones. They dressed accordingly in high style: knee breeches, buckles, and ruffled shirts, almost as though their fashionable clothes were more important than what they said.[8]

For many, however, Senate membership proved a somewhat empty honor. DeWitt Clinton resigned in 1803 to become mayor of New York City, a job that paid $8,000 a year, a princely sum, especially compared to the Senate's six dollars per day.[9] Clinton's colleague Theodorus Bailey quit the Senate a few weeks later for a post closer to home, becoming New York City's postmaster. Resignations were frequent under the stimulus of more attractive alternatives to the long journeys and difficult living conditions associated with Washington, DC.

In 1804, the New York legislature picked Samuel Mitchill, a member of the House, to replace one of those resigned senators, and he wrote unhappily to his wife that she would henceforth read little about him in the newspapers. "Senators are less exposed to public view than representatives," he informed her.[10] The public paid scant attention to Senate debates.

But by the early 1820s, the membership of the House of Representatives had nearly tripled to 181, whereas the Senate consisted of not more than forty-eight. The Senate's less crowded chamber and consequently more permissive procedures increasingly served as an incubator for aspiring orators. The debate that finally ushered in a remarkable new era of Senate oratory came in January 1830 on a resolution by Connecticut's Samuel Foot to restrict the sale of public lands. Missouri's Thomas Hart Benton, a ferocious debater and defender of westward expansion, boldly challenged Senator Foot's resolution as a blatant attack by the North on the West, and he called on the South for help. The next day, South Carolina's Robert Hayne denounced Foot's proposal as a new effort to consolidate the federal government and thereby threaten the sovereignty and independence of the several states. Hayne was a disciple of Vice President John C. Calhoun, the Senate's presiding officer. As Hayne argued Calhoun's doctrine of states' rights, Calhoun ostentatiously sent him helpful notes from the rostrum.[11]

Webster, new to the Senate, could not let Hayne's speech pass unanswered. He responded in kind. Hayne came back with a further speech so brilliant that Webster's supporters feared it could not be effectively answered. Webster thought otherwise. His four-hour reply swept like a wildfire through the chamber and across the nation. Some of Webster's listeners wept openly. The United States under the Constitution, he argued, is not a casual confederation of separate states, each free to interpret that charter for itself and to nullify whatever federal laws it disliked. No, he cried, this is a nation, a union of states: "Now and forever, one and inseparable!"[12] Webster did more than answer Hayne; he gave new meaning to the Constitution as the bond that united the states into an indivisible nation. As he did this, he also gave new meaning and stature to the Senate—and to its oratory.

"Sir," Webster said to Hayne, "the gentleman seems to forget where and what we are. This is the Senate, a senate of equals, of men of individual honor and personal character, and of absolute independence. We know no masters, we acknowledge no dictators. This is a hall for mutual consultation and discussion, not an arena for the exhibition of champions."[13] Despite that protest, Webster had made himself the champion of the North.

Elected to the Senate three years earlier, Webster had been reluctant to become a senator. Henry Clay, back in private life in 1830, also preferred the House to the "solemn stillness," he called it, of the Senate, where he briefly had served twenty years earlier.[14] But Clay returned in 1831, partly at Webster's invitation. John Calhoun, aware of the Senate's rising importance, resigned the vice presidency at the end of 1832 to accept election to the chamber over which he had been presiding for the past seven years. Only then were all three in the Senate together, and together they changed the Senate forever.

At times they were allies and political partners, joining in fierce fights with their common enemy, President Andrew Jackson. At times they were rivals, for all three wanted the presidency, and all three repeatedly tried for it. Each, however, was recognized as the champion of his region: Webster of the North, Calhoun of the South, and Clay of the West. They engaged in many debates. Their quarrels, even if couched in the stylish courtesies of Senate oratory, were often bitter and personally offensive. Clay hated Jackson and Calhoun. Benton hated Calhoun. Calhoun hated Clay and Jackson, and John Quincy Adams hated Webster. And—to complete the circle of animosity—Jackson hated Calhoun and Clay.[15] At times, only the dignified and artificial politeness required in Senate speech-making allowed them to converse with one another at all.

In his prime, Daniel Webster struck listeners with awe. His voice was a rich baritone, and when he spoke his eyes glistened like burning anthracite. One admirer said that God Almighty had never made a man who looked half as wise as Webster. Another said his every word seemed to weigh twelve pounds. He was master of gorgeous prose, and he delivered his speeches in profound and measured tones. Describing Alexander Hamilton's contributions as the nation's first treasury secretary, he said this: "He smote the rock of national resources, and abundant streams of revenue gushed forth. He touched the dead corpse of public credit, and it sprang upon its feet."[16] Reserved socially and at times personally unpleasant, Daniel Webster was respected and admired, but not popular.

John Calhoun, austere and cold in public, was a kind and engaging man in his private dealings. When he rose to speak in the Senate, he spoke forthrightly, without adornment, cold, stiff, and grim, but at times with eloquence. Calhoun seriously claimed that his political career from its beginning was totally consistent, despite obvious evidence to the contrary, and that he never had even slight interest in becoming president. The South Carolina legislator, aware of the profits reaped by his state's plantation owners, bent his powerful intellect to a justification of human slavery: "a good, a great good!"—"Slavery is indispensable to republican government," he argued.[17] For slave owners, and the South, John Caldwell Calhoun was a hero.

By far the most colorful of the three, Henry Clay was elegant in debate. Haughty and imperious at times, gracious and chivalric at others, he commanded a fiery eloquence that won him national popularity. As an orator, he could be witty and clever, dignified and high-toned, bold and impetuous—whatever posture seemed appropriate—and he was especially genial and winning. He had a readiness in debate that Webster greatly admired as "a precious thing in the hour of need."[18] Above all, Clay had a special gift for bringing even antagonistic senators into agreements by compromise. A passionate advocate himself, he was willing to take high political risks to achieve his legislative purposes. "What is a public man worth," he asked, "who will not sacrifice himself if necessary for the good of his country?"[19]

The time from Webster's initial Senate oath-taking in May 1827, to the death of Clay, the last of the three, in June 1852, amounted to little more than a quarter century. Over those twenty-five years, however, the three men served together in the Senate for less than ten years. All quit the Senate at various times—Webster twice—only to return later. For two years, from March 1843 to March 1845, all three were absent. The reality was that they found the Senate in their time less glorious than its later reputation. Part of that flowed from the nature of Senate debate.

Clay himself could be savage. So could many others. In 1832, Clay and Benton engaged in a shouting match so ugly that senators feared a fistfight on the Senate floor. They were gaveled into silence. Both apologized to the Senate, but not to each other. On another occasion, Clay in debate denounced Alabama's William King for making false and cowardly remarks to the Senate. King promptly sent Clay a challenge, and only extensive negotiation averted the demanded duel. Clay disparaged Jackson in language so offensive that the president, in a fury, likened Clay to a drunk in a whorehouse.[20] In a badly chosen moment, Calhoun once boasted that he had bested Clay in an earlier debate. "I had the mastery over him on that occasion," Calhoun bragged. Clay was on him instantly. "My master! Sir, I would not own him for the meanest of my slaves!"[21] Calhoun was crushed by the reply, and for years he refused to speak to Clay. In a remark that has been taken as illustrative of the peculiar nature of friendship in the Senate, Calhoun said of Clay, "I don't like Henry Clay. He is a bad man, an imposter, a creator of wicked schemes. I wouldn't speak to him. But by God, I love him."[22]

Under the Constitution, no senator could be held legally accountable outside the Senate for anything he said in the Senate, but in the years before the Civil War that did not protect senators from the hazards of dueling. Southern senators took special pride in the Irish "Code Duello" and their region's related manual, *The Code of Honor; or Rules for the Government of Principals and Seconds in Dueling*.[23] They larded their Senate speeches with the attention-getting boast that they were prepared to answer for their words in debate "here and elsewhere." Before he became president, Andrew Jackson had killed a man in a duel, and, in an ugly brawl with Thomas Hart Benton and Benton's brother, Jackson was shot in the shoulder. They reconciled later when they were both senators, and still later Benton became President Jackson's staunchest defender in the Senate.

Benton counted himself an authority on dueling; in one of his duels, he had killed a rival lawyer. In 1826, he presided over an extraordinary duel between Henry Clay, then secretary of state, and Senator John Randolph of Virginia, both experienced duelists. Clay challenged Randolph for the abuse the senator had poured on him in his Senate speeches. Both missed on the first shot. On the second, Clay's bullet pierced Randolph's coat. Randolph made the grand gesture, firing his shot harmlessly into the air. "You owe me a new coat, Mr. Clay," he said, advancing and offering his hand. "I'm glad the debt is no greater," Clay gallantly replied. Benton called this "about the highest toned duel" he had ever been privileged to witness.[24]

Benton was a boisterous braggart, given to excessively long speeches, filled with bombastic grandiloquence and self-righteousness. He was vain far beyond the Senate norm. "Benton and the people! Benton and Democracy are one and the same, sir!" he cried. "Synonymous terms, sir! Synonymous terms, sir!"[25] It was said of Benton that when he went West, he thought the East tilted up. He hated Calhoun for his advocacy of slavery, but when word was brought to him that Calhoun had died, Benton adjusted his attitude: "When God Almighty puts His hand upon a man, sir, I take mine off, sir!"[26]

Benton was a principal in one of the most astonishing episodes ever to take place on the Senate floor, a dispute stemming from abusive Senate debate. The Missourian had long quarreled with Mississippi's Henry S. Foote, a senator almost as vain as Benton and, like him, given to verbose speech-making. He was known as "Hangman" Foote for threatening in Senate debate to help hang New Hampshire Senator John P. Hale if he ever came to Mississippi. Hale replied that if Foote ever came to New Hampshire he would be pleasantly welcomed and entertained.[27] The bickering between the burly Benton and the diminutive Foote had been reduced to hurling personal insults, and when Foote again began a harangue against Benton, on April 17, 1850, Benton, in a rage, jumped to his feet and moved menacingly up the center aisle toward his antagonist. Foote shrank back, but then he drew a pistol. Benton hesitated for a moment, and then—in a great theatrical gesture—threw wide his arms, baring his chest. "I disdain to carry arms," he roared. "Stand out of the way and let the assassin fire!" The Senate, of course, was in an uproar, members shouting "Order! Order!"[28]

Senate debates were often violent and sometimes ugly. Those involved were aware that under Senate rules they could be called to answer for their words. For Northerners, dueling in time became a politically unacceptable way to settle quarrels, and they tried to avoid such encounters. When Webster was approached with what amounted to a challenge from Virginia's John Randolph, he declined. "I told him I did not choose to be called to account for anything I said," Webster replied.[29] In 1835, Mississippi's George Poindexter began a challenge to Vice President Martin Van Buren, a New Yorker and once a senator, who had allegedly called Poindexter a "bloated mass of corruption." Van Buren cautiously managed to evade the challenge, but he feared Senator Poindexter might attack him at any moment. For several days, Van Buren concealed on his person a pair of loaded pistols, and he wore them in the chair as the Senate's presiding officer.[30]

For Southern firebrands and Western senators, there were no inhibitions about dueling, even after Congress passed a law in 1839 forbidding the practice in the District of Columbia.[31] For these men, dueling pistols, some inlaid with gold, were part of their normal outfits. Northerners were viewed as mere tradesmen and cowards. That did not raise the tone of Senate debate. Increasingly, in both houses of Congress, debate reached such provocative levels that members routinely carried arms, with the pocket-size Derringer a particular favorite after the mid-nineteenth century.

Clay and Webster and Calhoun gave the Senate its fame—and its power—but there were others of almost equal talent. Among them were Benton, a formidable parliamentarian despite his unmatched egotism, and New York's Silas Wright. They had great subjects to debate, almost all involving the interpretation of the Constitution, and they, rather than members of the House of Representatives or those in the executive branch, debated them at length. When political crises arose, the Senate became the forum for their debate, and these debates gave the Senate a claim, on political questions, to the intellectual leadership of the nation.

Their debates, of course, did not pass legislation. Far more than eloquent speeches was needed to persuade senators how to vote on any pending question. More vital than oratory was the backroom vote-hustling and bargaining that had marked, from its origins, the Senate's decision-making. Henry Clay had that special talent, along with the tactical parliamentary skills, needed to create a working majority. Clay's mastery of vote-hustling prompted Senate opponents to call him a "dictator." They came to assume that when he moved to enact a bill, he had the needed votes already pledged. This was not always so, but they assumed that he had in mind a much more complicated strategy to pass the measure than merely depending on Senate speeches.

A dramatic example of a brilliant Senate debate failing, while clever tactical maneuvering succeeded, came in the parliamentary struggle that produced the Compromise of 1850. The nation was again in crisis, with North and South bitterly divided by the controversy over slavery. In this emergency, Henry Clay returned to the Senate after an absence of several years and tried to save the nation with a legislative solution. This was the last Senate in which Clay, Calhoun, and Webster would serve together, and a new generation of senators destined for prominence had already arrived, among them Stephen Douglas of Illinois, Jefferson Davis of Mississippi, William Seward of New York, and Salmon Chase of Ohio.

Clay introduced a series of resolutions, some to appease the North, some to appease the South, and a select committee bulked them together in an omnibus bill. In a two-day speech, Clay opened the debate, which subsequently ran on sporadically for more than seven months. He begged senators to listen to reason and to accept "some mode of accommodation" to restore harmony and peace to the nation. Calhoun, suffering from the disease that would kill him four weeks later and too weak to read his own speech, had another senator deliver it for him. He wanted no accommodations, and he blamed Northern "agitators" for the crisis. Webster was wary. Clay privately had implored him for help, but he and Webster knew that his Massachusetts constituents would never forgive him if he endorsed the proposed concessions to the South. Even so, Webster resolved to stand by Clay. On March 7, 1850, Webster rose in a crowded Senate and made one of the great speeches of his long career. "Mr. President, I wish to speak today, not as a Massachusetts man, nor as a Northern man, but as an American, and a member of the Senate of the United States . . . ," he began. "I speak today for the preservation of the Union. 'Hear me for my cause!'"[32] Other senators opposed Clay's compromise. Mississippi's Jefferson Davis resented the bill's limits on slavery, and slavery, he argued, was sanctioned by God. New York's William Seward, in the opposite camp, wanted no concessions at all to slavery, and in his speech he used these flashing words—"There is a higher law than the Constitution"—that would follow him for the rest of his career.[33] With so many opposed, often for contradictory reasons, Clay's compromise failed.

The omnibus bill, with concessions to both sides, pleased no one and had the effect of maximizing the opposition. Senator Douglas found a strategy to minimize the strength of the opponents: divide the omnibus bill into its component parts and offer each separately. Southern firebrands voted against those for the North, and the Northerners voted against those for the South, but the Senate approved them all. Douglas was pleased. "The North has not surrendered to the South," he said, "nor has the South made any humiliating concessions to the North."[34] The long debate, one of the most remarkable in the Senate's history, had failed to produce a majority for the omnibus bill, but by an astute shift of strategy, the bill's proponents enacted its substance into law. Legislative tactics and maneuver had proved more important than the Senate's oratory.

A few years later, the slavery question again arose sporadically in Congress. Debate ran wild and partisan in the Senate, the political storm creating a new crisis, and a need for new legislation. With great skill, Senator Douglas managed that legislation, the Kansas-Nebraska Act, to final approval, and he dismissed the Senate's extended debate as meaningless. "I had the authority and power of a dictator throughout the whole controversy," he bragged later. "The speeches were nothing. It was the marshaling and directing of men, guarding from attacks, and with ceaseless vigilance preventing surprise."[35]

In these years, the Senate was undergoing changes that in time transformed it into the most powerful upper chamber of any legislative body in the world. Long known for the dignity, even solemnity, of its proceedings, it had become a great deal more than a polite debating society, and its debates were not always admirable. With its growing power and influence, the Senate became a political cockpit of fierce combat and ferocious partisanship. Under the cloak of gracious manners, senators struck out at one another with almost savage contempt. One of the elegant grace notes of senatorial decorum then was for senators to ask the Senate's formal leave to introduce a bill or make a speech. Permission, however, was not automatic. In a dramatic instance, Senator Charles Sumner of Massachusetts was refused when he first asked leave to speak in 1852.[36]

The Southern senators knew what he planned: a violent harangue excoriating them over the horrors of slavery, and they did not intend to permit it. When Sumner first came to the Senate, Benton told him that he had come too late; the great men were gone, and "there was nothing left but snarling over slavery, and no chance whatever for a career."[37] Sumner thought otherwise. "A seat here is a lofty pulpit with a mighty sounding board," he said, "and the whole widespread people are the congregation."[38] He intended so to use the Senate. "I must speak," he protested when denied the floor. "By God," replied Virginia's James Mason, "you shan't." Sumner had to wait three months before he found his chance, and then he berated the Southerners in a speech of almost four hours.[39]

Sumner was not the only Northerner who detested Southerners. Ohio's Benjamin Wade was just as vehement, but none spoke such visceral hatred as Sumner. Sanctimonious in his self-righteousness, Sumner enraged his

Senate colleagues, North and South alike, for he did not confine his abuse to Southerners. For example, he accused Senator Douglas of a skunk-like vileness that offended ordinary decency with the "perpetual stench" of his ugly personality.[40] South Carolina's James Chestnut called him a slanderer guilty of vulgar malice, mendacity, and cowardice, who whined at the feet of aristocrats, craving pity.[41]

On May 19, 1856, Sumner took the Senate floor to deliver a speech he called "The Crime against Kansas," one of the most vitriolic ever uttered in the Senate. Among others, he berated South Carolina's Senator Andrew Butler as stupid and at times an incoherent advocate of the "shameful imbecility" of human slavery.[42] On May 22, at the close of the day's Senate session, South Carolina Representative Preston Brooks, a kinsman of Senator Butler, attacked Senator Sumner in the Senate chamber, striking him again and again with a cane until Sumner collapsed unconscious. Brooks was arrested, freed, tried, and fined a token amount. A motion of expulsion in the House of Representatives failed to gain the required two-thirds majority, but Brooks soon resigned. Sectional antagonism had reached such a level that Sumner was hailed as a martyr in the North, and Brooks as a triumphant hero in the South. Senate debate was leading the nation, seemingly, to political madness. To some, Sumner's speech and Brooks's assault were the first blows of the Civil War.[43]

Violence and the threats of violence were commonplace. Mississippi-born William Gwin, a senator from California, exchanged three rounds in a duel with a South Carolina representative before they discovered they had misunderstood each other. The times were tense and dangerous. For some time, senators had been attending the Senate with concealed weapons, but now, according to South Carolina's Senator James Hammond, some senators were armed with two revolvers and a Bowie knife. In 1859, Senator David Broderick, home in California, was killed in a duel by that state's former chief justice.[44]

When the break did come and Southern states voted to secede from the federal union, the senators from that region, one by one, undertook an extraordinary series of Senate speeches. Each in turn announced his state's decision, and then each renounced his own allegiance to the United States. These were farewell speeches, couched in dignified and sometime bitter words. There was a heroic tone to the speeches, a "My-regiment-leaves-at-dawn" gallantry, for these senators knew that civil war was at hand. They were prepared for it. "The union, sir, is dissolved," said Georgia's Robert Toombs in his speech. "We will trust to the blood of the brave and the God of battles for security and tranquility."[45] Some cited the slander and insults they had endured, among them Louisiana's Judah Benjamin, who concluded his speech with a plea: "Let this parting be in peace."[46] Some gushed defiance. Most of them graciously offered thanks to those remaining for courtesies of the past. Jefferson Davis concluded by calling his speech "a final adieu."[47] There was grandeur to it all, even in this time of great anxiety and tension. Many in the galleries wept openly.

The departure of the Southern firebrands did not mellow the Senate's debates. The tension and blunders of the war heightened senators' sensibilities, at times, into political frenzy. Many lapsed into a moralistic radicalism that persuaded the men that they alone were fit to run the government and the war. They made life difficult for President Lincoln and miserable for his successor, Andrew Johnson. Senator Willard Saulsbury of Delaware seemed deranged in a wild speech denouncing fellow senators and labeling Lincoln as an "imbecile."[48] When called to order and physically restrained, he pulled a pistol and threatened to kill the Senate's sergeant at arms. Longtime friends turned against one another. Maine's William Fessenden, a Republican moderate, privately recorded that if he were allowed to cut the throats of a half-dozen Republican senators, he would start with Charles Sumner as "by far the greatest fool of the lot."[49]

In the 1870s, Senate debate had fallen to such a sorry state that senators themselves ignored each other's orations. That, however, did not slow the steady flow of words. James Bryce, the British commentator, noted that any senator attentively listening to a colleague's set speech was presumed a freshman not yet conversant with the Senate's ways. On "show days," Bryce reported, "each senator brings down and fires off in the air a carefully prepared oration which may have little bearing on what has gone before."[50]

Two of the most prominent orators of this time were Sumner of Massachusetts and Roscoe Conkling of New York, both vainglorious politicians who took immense pride in their stylish orations. Sumner flooded the Senate chamber with his organlike voice; Conkling delivered his in loud stentorian tones. Those who heard the New Yorker, however, knew that he cared more about how he looked—he was fastidious to a fault, his hair parted just so—than what he said.[51] By contemporary account, just about every senator felt obliged to make one such full-blown speech per session, printed in the *Congressional Globe*, and from 1873 the *Congressional Record*, for free mailing to his constituents back home.

By the 1890s, this sort of speech-making had become so vacuously insignificant that one congressional correspondent described "mock" speeches having "nothing to do with the legislation to be enacted."[52] The real debates, he reported, took place in whatever committee room the Senate's bosses— Senators Aldrich and Allison—happened to meet with their chief lieutenants to decide the Senate's policy. They controlled the Senate's decisions. The senators making speeches in the Senate chamber were merely entertaining the tourists in the galleries.

Over these decades, however ineffectual Senate debate had become, senators built a reputation for long-windedness, a reputation sustained by their refusal to adopt restraints on their speech-making. As early as the 1830s, John Quincy Adams complained that every senator's great effort was "to show that he could make a tiresome, long speech."[53] Even earlier, Thomas Jefferson, for four years as vice president and the Senate's presiding officer, attributed the talkativeness of the place to the fact that so many senators were lawyers, "whose trade it is to question everything, yield nothing, and talk by the hour."[54] He tried to restrain irrelevant speeches with rules he proposed for the Senate, but without great success. A generation and more later, Henry Clay failed in a similar attempt, to his own disgust. Then and ever after, senators made obvious their sheer pleasure in voicing their views extensively on whatever occurred to them. "I love to hear the sound of my own voice," Illinois Senator William Mason admitted as he began a filibuster in 1903.[55] Senators boasted about their prowess in making long speeches. Alabama's John T. Morgan, a Confederate brigadier during the Civil War, won special renown for long-windedness. He claimed that he could talk for two or three days on any subject he understood. "If it were upon a subject matter which I knew nothing about," he said, "I could talk for two or three weeks."[56] It was said of him that he took ten days to prepare a speech, ten days to deliver it, and then ten days to celebrate.

Not surprisingly, Senate debate and its inadequacies brought ridicule from the outside world. H. L. Mencken, who enjoyed mocking senators, called them "perhaps the windiest and most tedious group of men in Christendom."[57] Finley Peter Dunne, speaking through his fictional Mr. Dooley, described Senate debate this way: "Well, Hinnissy, ye see, there ain't anny rules in th' Sinit. Ivrybody gets up whin he wants to, an' hollers about annything that comes into his head."[58]

The most biting criticism, however, came from senators themselves. West Virginia's Matthew Neely, many times elected, called Senate debate "the tedious, tasteless, dreary, weary period of loquacity, confusion and chaos."[59] Arizona's Barry Goldwater spoke harshly about the place after he retired:

"The Senate floor is often a babbling market place of pet projects and personal promotion instead of measured debate on major issues."[60]

Under Jefferson's rules, first published in 1801, no senator was to "speak impertinently, beside the question, superfluously, or tediously." For decades, presiding officers called senators to order under this rule when they failed to speak to the matter at hand.[61] Yet, presiding officers invoked the rule inconsistently. In the mid-1820s, Senator John Randolph of Virginia, ferociously vindictive, spoke at great length almost daily about whatever popped into his head in speeches so eccentric that they raised questions about his sanity.[62] The failure of John C. Calhoun, then vice president, to call Randolph to order became the death knell for Jefferson's rule of relevancy.

On February 29, 1872, John Sherman of Ohio called Charles Sumner to order under the old Jefferson rule. In the chair sat Schuyler Colfax, the vice president, and he bluntly denied Sherman's point of order. The Senate itself had let the rule lapse, but Colfax went far beyond that. "The chair decides," he said, "that under the practice of the Senate he cannot restrain a senator in remarks which are, in the opinion of the senator, pertinent to the issue before the Senate."[63] Under Colfax's ruling, every senator could define relevancy for himself. This freed senators to speak interminably and tediously about anything. Two generations later, Colfax's decision underlay Huey Long's decision to spice his debates with recipes for frying oysters and making potlikker.[64]

In the early years of the twentieth century, changes came to the Senate that greatly affected its debates, some in admirable ways and others not so admirably. The most important was the popular election of senators, a reform brought by adoption of the Seventeenth Amendment to the Constitution in 1913. Popular elections eventually changed the caliber of the men elected to the Senate and altered as well the substance and style of Senate oratory. This new breed of senators was less dependent on political parties and more dependent directly on voters' approval. These senators appealed with sense and nonsense to their constituents, often with volatile rhetorical extravagances that permeated their speeches on the stump and in the Senate. The notorious rabble-rouser Benjamin ("Pitchfork Ben") Tillman of South Carolina was the first of many Southern firebrands to arrive by popular choice, demagogues replacing the aristocrats and men of parts, and for decades to come their voices echoed in the Senate chamber with white-supremacist racial abuse of black Americans. The new electoral system also coincided with reform initiatives associated with the so-called Progressive Era. Senators, mainly from the Middle West and the Far West, including Robert La Follette of Wisconsin, George Norris of Nebraska, and Hiram Johnson of California, argued eloquently and at length in favor of such measures as pure foods and against the monopolies and trusts of the corporate world.

Another change had the effect of diminishing senators' attendance in the Senate chamber. This was the 1909 opening of the first Senate Office Building, large enough to give every senator a private office not far from the Capitol. Earlier, some senators had on their own rented office space in nearby buildings and, of course, each senator who chaired a Senate committee had for his use the committee's room in the Senate wing of the Capitol. Now, with private offices of their own, senators had less reason to stay in the Senate chamber, less reason to make up an audience for any colleague delivering a speech. In time, with their ever increasing workload and preoccupation with other matters, senators found that they had better ways to fill their time. In the decades that followed, two additional office buildings were added for senators, and it was in these offices and committee rooms that they spent most of their time.

By bizarre happenstance, senators learned to exploit the tediousness of Senate debate as a parliamentary weapon that gave them individually and collectively immense legislative and political power—more so than any other legislators anywhere. This was the filibuster. Originating tentatively out of the verbose speech-making of senators in the middle decades of the nineteenth century, the filibuster had, by the 1880s, developed into an effective tactic to defeat measures they opposed. The idea here was not to persuade colleagues of the merits or demerits of a pending matter, but to defeat it, or to threaten to defeat it, simply by talking it to death. The reluctance of senators to limit debate, even innocuous, functionless debate, resulted in much empty and irrelevant talk. For a century, senators resorted to full-scale filibusters only occasionally and on matters of great concern, at least to them.

Over the years, a pattern of indifference to actually taking up legislation once it had been scheduled for floor consideration understandably irritated some senators. Senator John Pastore of Rhode Island, a master of cut-and-thrust debate, said this indifference had deadened and dulled Senate debate. "You can see it from attendance on the Senate floor," he said. "The excitement is gone." In 1963, he proposed a new rule to require senators to speak on the pending subject for the first three hours of each day's session. He argued that senators discussing their self-serving press releases on irrelevant subjects ranging "from the price of eggs to conditions of the Great Lakes" stalled the Senate hours on end every day.[65]

Everett Dirksen of Illinois, the Senate's Republican leader, laughed at the idea. "Ha, ha, ha," he said, "and you might add Ho, ho, ho." Dirksen's rambling speeches were crowded with irrelevancies. "It is somewhat difficult to reply to such a speech," complained his Illinois colleague, Paul Douglas, "which covers everything and touches nothing." Dirksen was amused at such complaints. "I have a surprise for you," he told his Senate colleagues one day. "I shall depart from my usual custom and talk about the bill that is up for discussion today."[66] Senators adopted the "Pastore Rule" in 1964 but seldom enforced it in the following decades.[67]

Some senators came to believe that their speeches were not just speeches, but action itself. To them their words were deeds. In one such reported case, South Carolina's Ellison ("Cotton Ed") Smith made an astonishing claim. "When I started my last speech in the Senate, cotton was ten cents," he boasted. "When I finished four hours later, cotton was twelve cents. I will continue to serve you in this way."[68]

Much as senators bewailed the denigration of Senate debate, it all the same played a necessary role in the legislative process. On any matter of consequence, disagreement was likely, if not automatic, and no legislative leader dared to neglect or ignore the Senate's formal debate. That would risk the desired outcome. Much preliminary work in lining up votes had already been done, of course, in committee, in the back offices, and by the interested lobbying organizations, but no sponsor could afford to yield any debating points by default. On the contrary, all sides engaged in the struggle and tried to muster all the political strength they could, including having on hand their most articulate spokesmen to argue the cause on the Senate floor.

There was another compelling concern about Senate debate. Traditionally, the words spoken for and against a measure and the amendments offered formed a significant part of the measure's legislative history, the under-standing of its intents and purposes. Those in the executive branch who administered the resulting law automatically consulted the Senate's debates on the measure, as did those in the House of Representatives. So did judges and lawyers responsible for reviewing it judicially. Senators might grieve that in their speeches they spoke only plain-song prose, not gaudy rhapsodies, but the sum total of their prosaic remarks could amount to a special persua-sive eloquence of its own. Their speeches helped explain the legislators' intentions. That, however, was not necessarily the way this always worked.

Knowing that the courts and others relied at least in part on the Senate's debates, senators have been tempted to tamper with the evidence. They have loaded committee reports and Senate speeches with their own spin on a bill's meaning, seeking to influence the later interpretation of the measure.

Some laws passed by Congress have been vague and unclear, some even deliberately ambiguous. Federal judges have taken advantage of that, casually dismissing congressional debate and deciding for themselves a measure's meaning and intent. One federal judge put it this way: "Visiting legislative history is like going to a cocktail party and looking through the crowd for your friends."[69] The judges could pick and choose what they liked. This has offended senators and representatives, but they, too, have tried to take similar advantage. The Senate's handling of the Civil Rights Act of 1991 was a notorious example. Democrats and Republicans both crammed the *Congressional Record* with their contradictory arguments on what the bill's language meant and what Congress intended. Those tactics led one administrative official charged with interpreting this law to protest that "some legislative history is, frankly, garbage."[70]

Within the Supreme Court there has been the view that the mess of Senate and House debates was, frankly, just that—garbage. Justice Antonin Scalia asserted, in effect, that the law was the law, and the courts should read that law through its own language. He declared that researching a law's legislative history was not only a "waste" of time but a "false" method of discovering its intent. "We are governed by laws," he wrote, "not by the intentions of legislators." He wanted the federal courts to ignore debate in the Senate and the House, not only because the debaters so often disagreed, but because those speaking did not necessarily represent the majority. "The greatest defect of legislative history," he wrote, "is its illegitimacy."[71]

That the Senate normally handled its routine business in a routine way was hardly surprising, but in this, the Senate's stylized mannerism of speech gave even these routine matters a tone of elegance and dignity often far beyond the seriousness of the matter under consideration. Deferential courtesies by senators to each other, sometimes cloyingly spoken, gave the Senate's debates a solemnity much admired by foreign observers and other casual visitors to the Senate galleries. Here, certainly to them, was an assembly of statesmen and exemplars, men of propriety and excellence. There could be fun in this as well. Senator Tom Connally of Texas, capable of scalding sarcasm, could reduce a colleague to a laughingstock by addressing him as the *distinguished* senator.

In 1945, Kentucky's Alben Barkley, then the Senate's majority leader, gave this advice to that year's freshman class: "If you *think* one of your colleagues is stupid in debate, which you will if you are here long, refer to him as 'the able, learned and distinguished senator.' If you *know* he is stupid, which you probably will, refer to him as 'the *very* able, learned and distinguished senator.'"[72] Barkley was being playful, of course, but there was a serious side to his commentary.

Despite the required courtesies, the Senate chamber has occasionally witnessed nasty debates and put-downs, which have sparked dangerous anger. An incident in the 1850s inspired consideration about adopting a rule to curb such excesses, but the Senate finally did so only after an ugly episode during a debate in 1902. South Carolina's "Pitchfork Ben" Tillman accused his South Carolina colleague, John McLaurin, of selling his vote for federal patronage. McLaurin called Tillman a malicious liar. Tillman lunged at him, striking him above the left eye. McLaurin hit Tillman back with an upper-cut to the nose. They were separated by other senators, and the brawl caused consternation throughout political Washington. Senator George Hoar of Massachusetts seized the occasion to propose a rule he long had had in mind: "No senator in debate shall, directly or indirectly by any form of words impute to another senator or to other senators any conduct or motive unworthy or unbecoming a senator."[73] Once adopted, senators had the means of instantly quieting raucous or abusive debates. When called to order under this rule, Rule 19, the offending senator had to take his or her seat, and could not proceed further without the permission of the Senate. The language of the rule was deliberately vague. Under it, said Senator Barkley, a senator could be actually ruled out of order for reciting the Lord's Prayer. Only rarely has the rule been enforced, and then with resentment. Senators regarded its use as an insult. Once so threatened, Pennsylvania's Hugh Scott, in a hissed whisper clearly heard in the galleries, counter-threatened savage retaliation. The other senator backed down. In another instance, Senator Dirksen used the rule to force Tennessee Senator Albert Gore Sr. to take his seat. Gore had accused Dirksen of "pompous verbosity," a charge not without merit. The next day, Senator Gore regained the Senate floor, and to every-one's amusement ridiculed Dirksen with mock praise as "the inimitable and euphonious sockdolager from Illinois, one of the most ariose, mellifluous, dulcifulent orators" in the Senate.[74] Gore thus evaded the rule, which was not hard to do. In the 1920s, Kentucky Senator Richard Ernst showed the ease of this. He had engaged in a nasty floor quarrel with Michigan's James Couzens, and in conclusion he asked the Senate's presiding officer whether there was any way under the Senate's rules that he could call another senator "a willful, malicious, wicked liar." The senator in the chair told Senator Ernst that under the Senate's rules he could not do what he had just done.[75]

For all their deference toward each other, senators have traditionally taken the view that they themselves were little influenced by Senate debate. Virginia's Carter Glass, a twenty-six-year Senate veteran, put this bluntly: "I have never known a speech to change a vote."[76] In the earliest years of the republic, senators' speeches had more influence persuading other senators than in more recent times, but even then only in relatively few cases. "Speeches in the Senate in most cases have very little influence upon the vote," Senator William Plumer of New Hampshire stated in his journal in 1806. "A large majority of the Senate have made up their opinion."[77] He estimated, however, that in roughly 5 percent of Senate debates, the arguments did change votes. Otherwise, undecided senators tended to vote the way the administration desired, or made up their minds after conversations with their colleagues.

So many influences—including home-state concerns and the exertions of professional lobbyists—have played on a senator's judgment that even he or she would normally have trouble identifying what finally caused him or her to vote a certain way. Occasionally, senators have given credit to a colleague's speech. In his memoirs, Vermont's Ralph Flanders could cite only three such instances over his twelve-year service when he was so persuaded.[78]

In his time, Senator Everett Dirksen was a notable debater. When he first came to the Senate in 1951, his Senate speeches were so pompous that one journalist styled him "The Wizard of Ooze."[79] Later, as he found his bearings and gained power and influence, he evolved into an effective, amusing, and often eloquent orator, who could and did change votes. The civil rights bills of the 1960s were enacted largely through his persuasive powers in floor debate and in the backrooms. His flamboyance tempted writers to try to capture him in words. "Now he conjures moods of mirth, now of sorrow," one wrote in *Time* magazine. "He rolls his bright blue eyes heavenward. In funereal tones, he paraphrases the Bible ('Lord, they would stone me . . .') and church bells peal. 'Motherhood,' he whispers, and grown men weep. 'The Flag!' he bugles, and everybody salutes."[80]

Dirksen's speech in support of legislation to name the marigold the national flower—"It is as sprightly as the daffodil, as colorful as the rose, as resolute as the zinnia. . . ."—was widely regarded as a classic, if unsuccessful.[81] Dirksen knew well the limits of long-winded speeches. "No souls are saved," he said, "after the first twenty minutes."[82]

One of the Senate's curious traditions, routinely honored in the breach, assumed that senators deferred to their seniors and kept discreetly quiet for their first few years in that body. As a freshman senator in 1953, John F. Kennedy asked Georgia's Walter George, a senator with more than thirty years' tenure, this question: "What is the difference between members now and when you came to the Senate?" "When I arrived here," George replied, "it was the custom for freshmen to keep a respectful silence."[83]

That was the standard response, richly redolent with maudlin senatorial nostalgia, but it was not true. Freshman senators were quick to take the Senate floor in the 1920s, and this included Walter George. They were not hesitant in earlier times, either. In his memoirs, Illinois Senator Shelby Cullom reported that he made his first Senate speech on January 11, 1884, scarcely a month after he first became a senator. He admitted that he had often suggested silence to new senators. "I was not quite as modest," he wrote, "as I have since advised younger senators to be."[84]

In modern times, some among the Senate's seniors still deplore the newcomers' ignorance of the Senate's venerable traditions, but they no longer bother to advise them to stay silent and remain in the shadows. As demanded by their constituencies, with their access to twenty-four/seven news coverage, freshmen had become active everywhere: in committee, in the backrooms and corridors, and on the Senate floor in debate.[85]

The Constitution gives members of Congress broadly interpreted legal immunity for words spoken in debate. One of the classic abusers of that special privilege was Wisconsin's Joseph McCarthy. From early 1950 through March 1955, McCarthy repeatedly took the Senate floor to charge Americans, in and out of government, with disloyalty. His vilifications went on even after the Senate formally censured him for his scandalous behavior.[86] McCarthy had imitators within the Senate, among them Indiana's William Jenner, Kansas's Andrew Schoeppel, and Idaho's Herman Welker. With reckless charges, McCarthy won a national popularity that intimidated at least some of his Senate colleagues, but he did not go unchallenged. In June 1950, Maine's Senator Margaret Chase Smith took the Senate floor to scold her colleagues for tolerating McCarthy's demagoguery. She criticized them for allowing McCarthy, a fellow Republican, to use the Senate chamber as "a publicity platform" for his verbal assaults on so many Americans.[87] Senator Smith was widely praised for her speech, but the Senate did not act on her advice. Earlier, Arkansas Senator William Fulbright had openly opposed McCarthy and continued his opposition despite McCarthy's threats against him. In 1954, the year that the Senate finally censured McCarthy, Fulbright made an eloquent Senate speech deploring what he called "that swinish blight so common in our time, the blight of anti-intellectualism." This, he said, was "the last refuge of the mentally insecure and the intellectually bankrupt."[88] He was criticizing not only McCarthy, but also the Cold War climate that bred McCarthy and his admirers. Fulbright told senators that they could not, like so many witch doctors, cure the nation's troubles by beating drums and chanting cabalistic incantations. They would have to use common sense.

During his Senate career from 1945 to 1975, Fulbright was a victim of the decline in the Senate's attention to its own debates. A thoughtful scholar turned politician, Fulbright made occasional speeches expressing his views on national affairs, as he had on McCarthy and the country's growing anti-intellectualism. In the years immediately after the close of World War II, he and other senators could hold an attentive audience of senators when they made important Senate speeches. Michigan's Arthur Vandenberg, Fulbright's predecessor as chair of the Foreign Relations Committee, could hold seventy senators in their seats through a three-hour speech. Gradually, however, that audience disappeared. In his later years as a senator, Fulbright gave up trying to speak directly to his colleagues in these speeches. He still had an audience but an audience outside the Senate. To reach that target, he continued his Senate speeches, but he mumbled his way through them, often skipping words and sentences, even paragraphs. He sent full copies of these speeches to the Senate press galleries, however, and they were widely reported by the national press.

For all the Senate's admiration of great oratory, its members have not always admired its silver-tongued speakers. Part of this came from the arrogance of some of the declaimers themselves. Indiana's Albert Beveridge came to the Senate in 1899 heralded as a boy orator of wondrous skill. Vain far beyond the Senate's broad tolerance, Beveridge addressed the Senate early and often with word symphonies of his own that brought him more ridicule than praise. "T'was a speech ye cud waltz to," said Mr. Dooley in mock admiration of Beveridge's first effort.[89]

Oregon's Wayne Morse, a senator of perhaps even greater personal conceit, added to his boasting and arrogance a quarrelsome nature and a sanctimonious pedantry certain to give offense. "He massaged his ego twenty-four hours a day," said Arizona's Barry Goldwater.[90] Morse talked and talked and talked, normally to an all but empty Senate chamber, but to his own obvious delight. Over a single stretch of twelve years, by one estimate, he filled more than four thousand pages of the *Congressional Record*.[91]

Until motion pictures, then radio, and finally television dramatically homogenized the spoken American language, the Senate chamber rang with many regional, even parochial accents—the nasal twang of New England

Yankees, the mellifluous drawl of Southerners, the flat drone of prairie senators, and the special tonalities of Westerners. The Downeasters from Maine talked through their noses. Out of Massachusetts came Boston and Harvard accents. The New Yorkers had their own variants, too, and the Georgians pronounced words such as "first" as "foist," much like New York's Brooklynese. In his final years in the Senate, Lyndon Johnson used two accents, depending on circumstances. When cajoling Southerners on Southern matters, he talked "Southern." With others, he adopted the slouch and slang of the Western cowboy, tall in the saddle.

South Carolina's Burnet Rhett Maybank was a special case. In the late 1940s and early 1950s, he was a senator of consequence especially in matters of the Korean War, but he spoke a variation of Gullah, a dialect native to the Georgia-Carolina coastline, which was almost incomprehensible to reporters in the Senate's galleries. One of those reporters, Warren Duffee of the United Press, originally from Georgia, acted as translator for his fellow reporters. The Senate's floor had been a melodious treasury for the student of phonetics, but by the 1990s there were only a few regional accents in the Senate, those of South Carolina's Ernest Hollings and Massachusetts's Edward Kennedy. Most senators by then spoke "American," in the neutral intonations of television newscasters.

In June 1986, with grave misgivings, the Senate opened its daily sessions to gavel-to-gavel television coverage. The change had long been discussed, and there had even been a few false starts. Senators were wary that the cameras would change the Senate in unexpected and undesirable ways. Senators favoring the change argued that it offered "an electronic bridge to the American people," in the words of Senator Bob Dole.[92] "This marvelous extension of the Senate gallery will prove to have lasting value for our people," said Kentucky's Wendell Ford, a sponsor of the plan.[93] Those opposed feared that "every senator with an inflated ego" would exploit the system by grandstanding to the cameras with his or her own self-serving demagoguery. This would damage the Senate's image and destroy the Senate's special role as a deliberative body. "Gavel-to-gavel coverage of the Senate would be a consummate bore," predicted Connecticut's Abe Ribicoff.[94]

Other legislatures around the world had already made the change, however, without ill effect. Closer to home, the House of Representatives had opened its proceedings to television almost seven years earlier, and the effect had been to increase greatly the public's attention on the House. Not only did the House debates themselves now have a national audience, but television stations across the country regularly used snippets from those debates on their morning and evening news programs. By one estimate, the House was receiving ten times more television news coverage than the Senate, and this for senators became a matter of institutional jealousy. "Without television," Senator Robert Byrd argued, "we are going to become the invisible half of Congress."[95] Stories began to circulate of senators' experiences walking through their home-state airport with a House member in which passersby would recognize the representative and ignore the senator. This readily enlarged the ranks of those who supported televising of Senate proceedings.

The Senate weathered its new openness without difficulty. At first there was a noticeable increase in senators' verbosity, as more members made more speeches, but that did not last. For a few weeks, senators wore blue suits and blue shirts to improve their television appearance, and Ohio's John Glenn mockingly pretended on the Senate floor to gussy himself up with cosmetics to the laughter of his colleagues. By the end of July, the novelty was gone, and by a year later senators had accepted the televised proceedings as routine. Televising the debates had not changed the Senate markedly, nor ruined its reputation, despite the energetically expressed concerns of some senior members. Senator Robert Byrd submitted data to show that televised coverage had not altered the way the Senate conducted its business. "Our fears were unfounded," acknowledged Louisiana's Bennett Johnston.[96] Yet neither had the televised debates greatly enhanced the Senate's image, as some had hoped. If some viewers were "appalled," as one from California wrote in, at the "ignorance and arrogance" they saw in some senators, others were "impressed" with the "statesmanship" they witnessed in others.[97] By opening its debates to television, the Senate shared the national audience with the House of Representatives. The Senate in session had always been the Senate on public display, and senators simply adjusted to the new conditions.

In earlier times, American audiences relished the oratorical extravagances of senators and other politicians, listening attentively for hours at a time, but all that changed in the modern era with the quickening of American life. Senators still indulged themselves with long speeches, but they did not ignore the shrinking of the public's attention span. Stately orations gave way, especially in campaign speeches, to bumper-sticker brevity, preferably with a telling quip that could catch a newspaper headline or a mention on television news programs. "Like it or not," Senator Dole said, "the days when Webster, Calhoun and Clay filled the halls of Congress with great oratory have gone the way of spittoons and snuffboxes. Americans today prefer their eloquence in thirty-second sound bites."[98]

Aware of that audience, senators began to adopt the methods of show business and the lecture circuit in their Senate speechmaking. They used charts, posters, and maps to illustrate what they were arguing. These visual props offered a new simplification to their explanations, but they did not necessarily increase the substance of their speeches. One critic suggested that Senate debates had been made to resemble one of those motel seminars on how to make millions in real estate. In early 1992, a presidential election year, Senate Republicans placed in the Senate chamber, and thus on television, a large chart counting each day that the Senate's Democrats failed to act on President George H. W. Bush's economic program. The Democrats retaliated with an even larger chart counting the days of the "Bush Recession." In 1993, with a large chart in blue, yellow, and orange, Senator Dole used a huge pencil to point out the advantages of his budget plan. The chart was simple and effective, but Dole looked silly. By then, through their staffs, senators had a regular, organized system to produce these devices, and they became a staple of daily Senate debate.

From the start, television cameras revealed to the public at large an extraordinary aspect of the Senate's procedures: the seemingly endless quorum calls that at times could last up to five hours. The Senate seemed in a state of suspended animation, all but paralyzed institutionally. A normal "live" quorum call took relatively little time and summoned senators to the Senate chamber. In the distant past, when senators did not understand fully what they were doing, perhaps tangled in parliamentary confusion, a quorum call gave them time to figure out that dilemma. In the 1950s, Majority Leader Lyndon Johnson routinely used extended quorum calls to stay the Senate's action while he scrambled with his sometimes magical gifts of persuasion to line up offstage the votes needed to pass or defeat the pending proposal. This Johnson tactic became a regular practice for party leaders in the years after Johnson's departure, frequently interrupting Senate debate. In late October 1985, the year before Senate television began, Arkansas' Senator David Pryor reported that in the twenty-eight weeks that the Senate had so far met that year, the Senate had stalled proceedings a total of 247 hours and forty-eight minutes on extended quorum calls, almost one-quarter the time of that Senate session. "We seem to be in a never-ending series of quorum calls," Senator Pryor said, and asked his colleagues to correct this frustrating waste of time.[99] His colleagues did nothing.

Into the twenty-first century, these extended quorum calls were as make-believe as they were with Lyndon Johnson. Television viewers, often bewildered at this inaction, saw only the all-but-empty chamber, legislatively frozen, with unfortunate senators taking hourlong shifts sitting in the presiding officer's chair. The unblinking camera showed the same scene, hour after hour, as though the stock-still Senate might soon spring to life. Senators defended this bizarre procedure, unknown to the House of Representatives or other legislative bodies, as a necessary time-out while they worked in the backrooms to fashion the Senate's decisions. It was exactly the sort of parliamentary eccentricity that had persuaded some senators to doubt the wisdom of putting the Senate on gavel-to-gavel television in the first place.

Opening the Senate to television coverage did not increase the influence of the Senate's debates in its decision-making processes. On the contrary, after a quarter-century of television coverage, there was evidence that it might be having a contrary impact. Broadcasts of their speeches tended to make senators more provocative, more partisan, and more intractable than they had once been. In any case, the tested methods of the past—corralling the necessary votes—still remained the obvious way to win the Senate's approval on any pending question.

That meant give-and-take bargaining to find the accommodations and compromises needed. From the earliest years, such behind-the-scenes negotiations had always had more influence than debate on the Senate's judgments. Televising the Senate's debates seemed to hamper finding those accommodations and reaching the required compromises, a further limit on the effectiveness of the Senate's debates. Complicating the process was the growing use of offensive language by some freshmen ideologues, conservative and liberal, members with little sense of the Senate's traditions and little tolerance for others' views.

In the early summer of 1995, Adam Clymer, congressional correspondent for the *New York Times*, reported that the televised debates amounted to little more than "wildly exaggerated" arguments. "In fact," he wrote, "almost all debate here is for sound bites fed by the hope that network television will use an extreme comment. Most members speak as if they think that not one of their colleagues is listening seriously or could be persuaded by thoughtful arguments."[100]

Norman Ornstein, a respected congressional scholar, noted that few of the newer members in the Senate or the House of Representatives were interested in "the give-and-take of legislating," but only in their own "crusades." This, Ornstein stated, produced the frustration of "partisan bickering, ideological ranting and gridlock" that offended the public everywhere.[101] The mix of television coverage with morally righteous new members made more difficult the process of finding accommodations and compromises to solve the nation's problems. Senator William Cohen found that televising the debates had worked a subtle psychological effect on the Senate. He served eight years in the Senate before television and then a decade when debates were televised. Before the C-SPAN broadcasts, Cohen said, senators enjoyed a sense of camaraderie and a willingness to accommodate their conflicting views. Television had changed that. "When the lights are on, it is theater, and I think we have evolved into more performing than deliberating and working things out in an intimate atmosphere." There were "positive benefits," he acknowledged, to letting the country watch the Senate in action. "On the other hand," he said, "there is less willingness to drop one's rigid position, to find some kind of common ground."[102]

The testiness in debate discouraged senators, making some of them less interested in continuing their political careers. Election year after election year, senators declined to run for reelection even when it seemed assured. Senator Byrd blamed what he called the "sour inflammatory rhetoric" that too often marked Senate debate. "It is no wonder," he said in December 1995, "that good men and women, who have served honorably and long in this body, are saying they have had enough."[103]

Senate debate, on its own, naturally tended to a degree of anarchy, but the filibuster was the deliberate creation of legislative chaos. There was constant temptation among senators to resort to filibuster as a means to have their way. By the twenty-first century, senators so frequently used the filibuster, or threat of a filibuster, that this parliamentary device became commonplace, reducing Senate debate at times to near irrelevance. The filibuster had evolved to give Senate debate a meaning far beyond the meaning of the words spoken.

12

Dilatory Tactics

IN MARCH 1925, MINUTES AFTER being sworn into office at the rostrum of the Senate chamber, Vice President Charles Dawes launched an attack on a sacred Senate tradition—the filibuster. Unless the Senate reformed its rules of debate, he asserted, it would surely sacrifice its own "effectiveness, prestige, and dignity."[1] Senators who had been expecting this outsider—this legislative greenhorn—to deliver the standard "I'm not worthy to preside over your deliberations, but I shall earnestly tend to my homework" address at once registered their shock at his willful temerity. Here he was, charging that the Senate, in its use of extended debate, was trampling the rights of the American people. This shockingly unprecedented event inspired Columbia University professor Lindsay Rogers to compose a book-length lecture to the vice president. "The undemocratic, usurping Senate is the indispensable check and balance in the American system, and only complete freedom of debate permits it to play this role," he wrote. Contrary to Dawes, Rogers cautioned the Senate against further limiting this freedom. "Adopt closure in the Senate, and the character of the American Government will be profoundly changed."[2]

Like every legislative body, the Senate has devised its own peculiar rules, precedents, and practices. None of these was more striking than its special brand of filibuster. Tactics aimed at impeding the flow of controversial legislation were not new to this senate—they were in evidence as far back as the senate of ancient Rome. Yet the way they evolved in the American Senate over the decades produced a distinctly original and powerful parliamentary technique that became one of that chamber's most distinguishing features.

Designed as a conservative body to restrain impetuous, ill-considered actions by either the House of Representatives or the president, the Senate developed its ways of proceeding to ensure calm deliberation on matters of consequence. In time, this made the filibuster what it has become: the ultimate method not merely to slow consideration of such matters, but to halt them completely. If on occasion the Senate acted with reckless haste or unseemly political passion, its instinct institutionally has been to delay, to argue, and to deny. Although the filibuster has brought down upon the Senate the often harsh criticism of many, it has also given the Senate immense political influence in the country and throughout the world. It offers senators extraordinary powers, for good or ill, and every senator has learned that quickly.[3]

In defending the filibuster over the years, senators have argued that theirs was the deliberative body, theirs the assembly of dignity and power, and that under the Senate's rules and procedures a small band of senators, even a single senator could stand against the contemporary flood of any popular enthusiasm. In the fullness of the filibuster's effectiveness, one senator, independently, could paralyze the government when and if, in that senator's judgment, such drastic action was required. Richard Russell of Georgia, leader of the Senate's Southern bloc in the mid-twentieth century, called the filibuster a "bulwark against oppression," the very means to protect freedom of speech itself.[4] Less charitably, its many opponents have come to characterize the filibuster as a device to promote self-serving special interests at the cost of the nation's perceived best interests.

It took a half-century for the first intimations of the filibuster to appear in the Senate's deliberations—a by-product of the institutional instinct of senators to talk at great length—and then another half century for the filibuster to become a truly effective parliamentary weapon.[5] Not until well into the twentieth century did the Senate begin to take corrective action to curb its abuse, and debate about the need for continuing reform echoed well into the twenty-first century.

By the 1930s, a time of growing awareness of the inequities in American life, the filibuster had become the instrument of Southern senators for blocking antilynching bills and other civil rights legislation. In the years that followed, Southerners in the Senate used the tactic so frequently against such measures that the filibuster became identified in the public mind as the tool of white supremacists to keep black Americans subjugated in racial segregation.[6]

Not until the civil rights laws enacted in the 1960s did the filibuster emerge from that onus, and then senators came to use the filibuster in new ways that constantly threatened political gridlock. They used the filibuster so frequently and so casually that it became a matter of concern on every bill and nomination of consequence, a matter of almost constant alarm for those responsible for the running of the American government.[7]

In the Senate's earliest years, senators took pride that they conducted their debates with appropriate decorum, in stark contrast to the brawling so common in the House of Representatives. The Senate first convened in 1789 with only twenty-two senators, representing the eleven states that had then ratified the Constitution. The very smallness of the membership gave an intimacy to the Senate's proceedings impossible in the larger House, and that intimacy worked as a restraint on how senators behaved. In 1790, Pennsylvania Senator William Maclay noted with disdain that Southern senators were conspiring to defeat a pending bill with dragged-out speeches. "The design of the Virginians and a Carolina gentleman was to talk away the time," he wrote in his journal, "so that we could not get the bill passed."[8] Generally, senators declined to tolerate excessive speech-making and shouted down the offenders. In 1791, Maclay reported, "And every one that attempts to speak is Silenced with the Cry of 'the Question!'"[9] In these first decades, for a senator blatantly to try to use extended debate as a means to defeat a measure or to extort legislative or political spoils was not acceptable. Only much later did senators discover the possibilities in what came to be known as the filibuster.

In his *Manual of Parliamentary Practice*, Vice President Thomas Jefferson offered guidance on the need to control Senate debate. He wrote: "No one is to speak impertinently or beside the question, superfluously or tediously."[10] Although never incorporated into the Senate's rules, the provisions outlined in this manual became the Senate's guide in the years to follow. Jefferson's dictum on debate offered a more dignified way to proceed than shouting members down.

In these years, there was no need for the Senate to constrain debate beyond what Jefferson proposed. A decade earlier, in 1789, a committee of senators had set out to draft a set of rules to guide Senate proceedings. They borrowed heavily from the rules of the recently expired Congress, which had operated under the Articles of Confederation. Five of the original nineteen rules pertained to the potentially explosive topic of debate management, and two of those touched on debate limitation. Rule Four stated that no member would be permitted to speak "more than twice in any one debate on the same day" without Senate permission. Rule Nine introduced a term then common in parliamentary circles: the "Previous Question." Its brief text has spawned centuries of misunderstanding. "The Previous Question being moved and seconded, the question from the Chair shall be: 'Shall the main question be now put?' And if the nays prevail, the main question shall not then be put."[11] As used today, under such popular guides for conducting meetings as *Robert's Rules of Order*, a call for the Previous Question requires an immediate vote, not itself subject to debate, on the matter then before the body. If agreed to, it blocks further amendments, thereby eliminating further opportunities for debate. If not agreed to, debate may continue.

But in 1789, the Previous Question rule as understood in the Senate, the House of Representatives, and the British House of Commons, when invoked, did not halt debate and require an immediate vote. Rather, the motion was used to postpone the pending question and to take up another. In his manual, Jefferson described the Previous Question as then used as the proper way to set aside a "delicate" subject better left alone.[12] In the Senate, the Previous Question rule was not used as a mechanism for closing debate in order to vote on the matter at hand. Consequently, it was dropped when the Senate revised its rules for the first time in 1806.[13]

On February 28, 1811, the House of Representatives, with a full-scale filibuster under way, radically changed its own Previous Question rule by a pair of dramatic post-midnight votes. The House overruled the Speaker to make the Previous Question motion, henceforth, the means of cutting off all debate and forcing an immediate vote.[14] Later in the nineteenth century, when the filibuster became a serious problem in the Senate, its reformers repeatedly tried without success to persuade senators to adopt the House's strengthened form of the Previous Question.

Virginia's John Randolph often receives credit as the first senator to seriously employ the filibuster. Many times elected to the House of Representatives, where he earned a reputation as a vitriolic and sometimes malicious orator, Randolph served in the Senate for slightly more than fourteen months, starting in December 1825—but what extraordinary months they were. Day after day, he strode into the Senate chamber, often with a pair of hounds at his heels, and harangued his colleagues for hours on whatever struck his fancy. In ranting so wild at times as to raise questions of his sanity, Randolph obviously relished vilifying his many enemies, and none more so than President John Quincy Adams. Randolph's ridicule of Adams's secretary of state, Henry Clay, prompted Clay to call him out to the dueling grounds. They exchanged fire twice, without injury to either.[15] Booted and spurred, Randolph continued his flamboyant performances, unmatched in the Senate's history. His speeches, however, were not filibusters. He sought neither to block legislative business, nor to extort any kind of political concession. He had no other purpose than to lecture at length his captive fellow senators. Some of them had what Senator Martin Van Buren of New York called a "corrective": they walked out on him.[16]

Randolph's speeches gave great offense. As complaints grew, there were demands that Vice President John C. Calhoun call Randolph to order. Calhoun refused; he was prepared to call a senator to order for disorderly conduct, but he shrank from reprimanding a senator for words spoken. That, to him, would be an assumption of unwarranted, even despotic, power. On May 1, 1826, an article excoriating Calhoun for that decision appeared in a Washington newspaper. It was signed "Patrick Henry," but many, including Calhoun, believed the author was none other than President Adams himself. Using the pen name Onslow, after a long-serving member of the British House of Commons, Calhoun replied in a newspaper article of his own, and over the next several months the two writers kept up a verbal duel, eleven articles in all.[17]

The articles by "Patrick Henry" were particularly furious. He accused Calhoun of "shameless" tolerance of Randolph's "most flagrant indecencies" and his "rhapsodies" of vilification that went on "hour after hour, day after day, week after week, and almost month after month."[18] "Patrick Henry" made the valid points that Randolph did not confine his remarks to pending measures and that, under the guidance of vice presidents before Calhoun, the Senate had conducted its proceedings with a "decorum almost rising to solemnity."[19] The Senate's presiding officers had earlier called senators to order for breaching Jefferson's rule on impertinent and superfluous speeches.

In his own defense, Calhoun argued that only another senator could call a senator to order for his speech-making, not the vice president. Two years later, Calhoun claimed vindication of his position when the Senate, in revising its rules, voted to give the vice president formal authority to call a senator to order. But the Senate also added an escape clause, which permitted the overruling of any such action by a majority vote of senators present.[20]

If John Randolph was not in fact engaged in filibustering as such, his seemingly endless speech-making at least suggested how Senate debates might deteriorate once the filibuster became part of each senator's tool kit. Calhoun's reluctance to interfere had significance, too. In part, it reflected the silencing of the vice president as the Senate's presiding officer (contrary to the growing prerogatives of the House Speaker). It also underscored the Senate's ultimate decision to let each senator decide, in his own speech-making, what was pertinent or tedious.

Thomas Hart Benton of Missouri, whose service from 1821 to 1851 would make him the first thirty-year Senate veteran, dated the tentative beginnings of serious legislative obstruction in the Senate to 1829, at the start of Andrew Jackson's presidency. By his vetoes and his extravagant view of himself and his office, Jackson infuriated many senators. They denounced him repeatedly, opposed his often high-handed actions, and at one point formally censured him. His Senate opponents, however, lacked other weapons to frustrate his course. They had not yet devised the tactics of obstruction that later would be called the filibuster. In 1833, for example, Jackson demanded troops to collect the revenues South Carolina owed, but refused to pay, the federal government. John C. Calhoun, then one of that state's senators, and his supporters raged at Jackson's demand. They called him dictator and even talked of civil war, but they did little more than vent their wrath in their Senate speeches. When the revenue collection bill came to a vote, they dramatically stalked out of the Senate chamber, refusing to vote. That vote came on February 20, less than two weeks before the mandatory end of the Twenty-second Congress. They could have talked that bill to death, had they known how.[21]

Four years later, in 1837, that idea had matured. It was then that Senator Benton, Jackson's special defender, moved to expunge from the Senate's journal that body's 1834 censure of the president. Benton had the needed votes, but he understood that Henry Clay and his Senate allies intended to block his expunging resolution with their extended speeches—in reality, a filibuster. Benton therefore prepared for an all-night session. He stocked a nearby committee room with a sumptuous feast of hams, turkeys, and choice wines. His plan was to outlast the speech-making, to hold the Senate in session as long as it took to accomplish the vote, while sustaining his supporters throughout the ordeal to come. Clay and his talkers did try, but they soon gave up and let Benton's resolution pass.[22]

Four years later, in 1841, the political tides had turned, with Benton in the minority and Clay with a majority and a legislative program to enact. Benton readily adopted obfuscating tactics to block Clay's bills. For many years, members of the House of Representatives had been using such tactics to derail measures, and it was not surprising that senators, some as former House members, had begun to adopt their techniques. The previous summer, Benton had proposed killing a Whig bill simply by holding the Senate floor until adjournment date. Now, in 1841, he and his Democratic allies took a different tack. "The Democratic senators acted upon a system," he later confessed, "and with a thorough organization, and a perfect understanding." Each night, they met in caucus to draw up amendments with which to attack Clay's pending bill. The next day, they offered these one after the other, arguing for them "not by formal orations . . . but by sudden, short and pungent speeches."[23] On one bill alone they offered almost forty amendments, and they forced delaying roll call votes on thirty-seven of them.

Stiff opposition in the House, along with Benton's stalling tactics, frustrated Clay. House Democrats were using long speeches to block action on measures Clay supported. As that body's former Speaker, Clay arranged to undermine this effort with backstage maneuvers to convince the House to adopt a one-hour limit on its speeches. He succeeded on July 8, 1841, and four days later broadly hinted that he would push for the same limit in the Senate.[24]

That threat triggered a wild response. Benton and Calhoun were furious. They and others dared Clay to try to "stifle" debate and "gag" the Senate. Clay had routinely consulted his Whig colleagues beforehand, but they had not expected such an explosive reaction. Now they retreated; Clay had to switch course. On July 15, he abandoned the one-hour rule and proposed instead to adopt the House's redefined version of the Previous Question, the instant halting of debate by simple majority, to force a vote.[25] Partisanship had long been tense and bitter. This set off another political firestorm. Alabama's William King lashed out at Clay. Only weeks before, they had directed such seething language at each other that King challenged Clay to a duel—a duel cancelled only by the intervention of a magistrate who placed them both under peace bond.[26]

"Did he understand," King snapped at Clay, "that it was the intention of the senator to introduce that measure?"

"I will, sir!" Clay said. "I will!"

"I tell the senator, then," King said, "that he may make his arrangements at his boarding house for the winter."[27]

Thus, the summer of 1841 witnessed the coming of the filibuster, full-blown, to the Senate. King and his colleagues were prepared to stall the Senate as long as necessary—six months or more—to defeat Clay's proposed change in the rules. They would not tolerate that change, and they had available the practical parliamentary tricks and tactics to delay Clay's proposal indefinitely. Confronted thus, Clay had no choice. He backed down.

Despite the Democrats' spirited attacks, Clay's bills were not talked to death, nor were they defeated by all those amendments thrown at them by Benton and his partisans. Frustrated as he was by the difficulties of moving measures, Clay renewed his ambitions for the presidency and resigned from the Senate at the end of March 1842 to plan for his campaign.

Delaying tactics continued in the Senate year after year, and these harassments strained the Senate's traditional graciousness and courtesies. Senators, however, hesitated to use such methods actually to kill pending measures. That did not occur until 1846, when a Massachusetts senator, John Davis, deliberately blocked a final vote on a controversial appropriations bill for a reserve fund of $2 million for any territory that the United States might acquire from Mexico during their ongoing war. Once recognized, Davis talked until the hour already agreed upon for the end-of-session adjournment. President James Polk wrote in disgust, "Should the war now be protracted, the responsibility will fall more heavily upon the head of Senator Davis than of any other man, and he will deserve the execrations of the country."[28]

In the growing crisis over slavery and states' rights, Henry Clay returned to the Senate in 1849, hoping to negotiate peaceful accommodations among the warring partisans. Working conditions in the Senate had deteriorated during his seven-year absence. Senators were abandoning the old ways of courtesies and decorum. They now largely ignored Jefferson's suggested rule against long-winded and irrelevant speeches. They increasingly made such speeches as a matter of routine, encouraged by advances in communication that made it possible for their remarks to be reported in home-state newspapers more quickly and in greater detail. This greater accessibility to the public ear would, in time, play an important role in effective filibustering. They grew less tolerant of each other. When Henry Foote of Mississippi began what they knew would be a lengthy speech, his Senate colleagues started to howl and hiss to silence him. That did not stop Foote. "I know my rights," he shouted at them, "and will maintain them too, in spite of all the groans that may come from any quarter."[29] Senators no longer habitually requested formal permission to make a speech on a bill. They would speak whenever they pleased.

They were making changes that would become significant in the Senate's brand of filibuster. For example, senators had fallen into the practice of routinely debating motions to take up measures for consideration. This proved a critical innovation and, in the arsenal of later Senate filibustering, a formidable weapon, for it gave opponents two separate chances to attack, first on the procedural motion to take up the matter, then on the substantive matter itself.

By mid-century, the House of Representatives had developed an extraordinary parliamentary tactic to prevent legislative action—the Disappearing

Quorum. On a roll-call vote, the proponents would vote for the bill; the opponents would remain silent. In a narrowly divided House, with its usual share of absentees for illness or travel, that meant the required majority of the whole House had not voted and a quorum call was automatic to summon the absent members. For this tally, the previously silent opponents answered to their names and a quorum magically reappeared. The roll call vote was repeated and the opponents once again fell silent. The quorum disappeared. Again and again this time-consuming process played out: roll-call vote followed by quorum call, followed by another roll-call vote. On one long session, the House had 101 such calls of the roll and accomplished nothing. In January 1851, several senators imported this House stunt, refusing to vote. Two of them—David Yulee of Florida and Andrew Butler of South Carolina—were called to order for it. After a confused parliamentary wrangle, the chair ordered them to vote, as the Senate's rules required. They again refused, but the Senate failed to punish them. That was the beginning of the Disappearing Quorum in the Senate, a stratagem that filibusterers would employ with great effect for more than a half century.[30]

It was at this juncture that senators began to describe as "filibuster" the various and sometimes complicated delaying tactics they used to block legislative action. They made long and often irrelevant speeches to kill time. They offered all sorts of motions, one after the other, to tie up the Senate: motions to lay the proposal on the table, to postpone it indefinitely or to a time certain, and to adjourn. On each of these, the filibusterers demanded roll-call votes.

One notable instance occurred at the close of session in 1863, in which senators tried to kill a habeas corpus bill. Members were speaking "at length" and making all sorts of time-consuming motions. Senator Lyman Trumbull of Illinois called them "a fractious opposition."[31] What they were doing, said Senator Lazurus Powell of Kentucky, was "what is commonly called filibustering."[32] This marked the first recorded use of the word in Senate debate to describe the complex of dilatory tactics. A decade earlier, senators had used "filibuster" in a different meaning to denote the bands of lawless American adventurers then illegally trying to seize control of Latin American countries. The word itself was an English corruption of the Dutch *vrijbuiter* ("freebooter") and was originally used to describe seventeenth-century English buccaneers who plundered Spanish ships and settlements in the Caribbean.[33] The word, of course, had strong connotations of illicit behavior, stemming in part from its origins, but also from the unseemliness of the methods it described in legislative proceedings. Whatever the unsavory aspects of the word and the tactics, the filibuster then and later came to help shape the Senate into the most powerful legislative body in the world.

In the aftermath of the Civil War, political partisanship reached levels of new intensity. That was obvious in a remarkable 1879 filibuster by Republican senators—briefly reduced to minority status—against a proposal by Southern Democrats to prohibit using army regulars as "a police force" in Southern elections. The Republicans went to unprecedented extremes in their filibustering, reducing the Senate to hopeless confusion. In an all-night session, they used the trick of the Disappearing Quorum as never before: in just one night, they forced thirty roll-call votes and nine quorum calls. Ohio's Allen Thurman, the Senate's president pro tempore, lamented that this extravaganza was "a new idea" in the Senate.[34]

In 1881, it was the Democrats who launched a filibuster as bitter as any. The Senate was closely divided along party lines, and this was a fight over party patronage and committee assignments, subjects likely to excite the worst in working politicians. The filibuster created a political stalemate that deadlocked the Senate for weeks, preventing any action. Georgia's Joseph Brown, a Democrat, said he and his colleagues were prepared to maintain their filibuster, begun in early March, until June, or, if necessary, December. In the end, the assassination of President James Garfield caused the two parties to settle on a compromise, with Republicans keeping their prime committee assignments and the Democrats undisturbed in their ability to award patronage jobs.[35]

These filibusters attracted national attention. Clearly the tactic had become in the Senate an accepted vehicle for the minority in opposition to the majority's measures. Although frustrating to those trying to move legislation to enactment, filibusters did not arouse much public resentment. In his 1888 study, *The American Commonwealth*, British historian James Bryce noted that filibustering was used as an "extreme safeguard" against "abuse" by the majority.[36] He blamed its increased prevalence in part on the ever expanding size of the Senate, as new states entered the Union, making prompt dispatch of the Senate's business ever more difficult. He questioned whether the Senate, with pride in its traditions, would do anything about it, liking to "mark the contrast between its good manners and the turbulence of the more turbulent House."[37] With thirty-eight states in the Union, and seventy-six members in the Senate, there was a growing strain on those good manners.

In January 1890, the newly elected Speaker of the House, Thomas B. Reed of Maine, ruling from the chair, effectively put an end to the Disappearing

Quorum filibusters that had long been paralyzing that body. When the minority Democrats sought again to use the familiar tactic to block a Republican proposal, Reed confounded them by coolly counting as present those Democrats who had refused to respond on the roll-call vote. That meant that the measure had passed, a quorum being present, and the House could move on to the next matter. For all the anguished cries, Reed's ruling held, and in time that became the House's accepted way to ensure orderly proceedings. For its part, the Senate tolerated the Disappearing Quorum for another eighteen years, finally adopting the House's precedent in 1908. By then, senators had so many other ways to filibuster that loss of the Disappearing Quorum made little difference.

In December 1890, the Senate's majority Republicans took up a bill that the Democrats fought with steel-edged ferocity. The measure in dispute proposed federal supervision of congressional elections in the South. This, to the Democrats, especially those representing Southern states, was, in the guise of protecting civil rights, an unconstitutional use of force—a "Force Bill." Their speeches in opposition ran to great length and attracted widespread attention. The Republicans tried to break the filibuster by holding the Senate in all-night sessions. The Democrats supplemented the Disappearing Quorum tactic by going into hiding. In desperation, the Republicans at one point ordered the sergeant at arms to search out the missing senators, arrest them, and bring them bodily into the Senate chamber. Still the filibuster ran on as senators strenuously opposing limits on their prerogatives tossed aside schemes for ending debate by simple majority vote. The Democrats with their filibuster managed to defeat the "force" bill and thus demonstrated anew that on matters of great party concern the available dilatory tactics were indispensable. These methods were equally useful to the Democrats and the Republicans, whoever was in the minority.[38]

The year 1893 brought these matters again to a boil, primarily by means of a two-month filibuster that Western senators launched to block repeal of the Sherman Silver Purchase Act, a filibuster characterized by raw partisanship and searing invective. The filibusterers, encouraged by senators representing silver-mining states, used a variety of methods, including the Disappearing Quorum and lengthy speeches. The bill's principal sponsor, Daniel Voorhees of Indiana, countered with tough tactics of his own, holding the Senate in around-the-clock session to break the filibuster. Several senators, among them Massachusetts Senator George Hoar—a Senate rules specialist and grandson of a Constitutional framer—again proposed invoking cloture by majority vote, a proposal again ignored, despite the gravitas of its supporters.[39] The long struggle finally wore down the filibusterers, and they gave up.

In the public press and on the Senate floor, there was much talk of the "degradation" of the Senate by these filibusters. Henry Cabot Lodge of Massachusetts, a new senator, deplored filibustering for discrediting the Senate's public reputation. "There is another right more sacred in a legislative body than the right of debate, and that is the right to vote," he said. "To vote without debating may be hasty, may be ill considered, may be rash; but to debate and never vote is imbecility."[40] In time, Lodge would change his mind, when he learned the uses of delaying tactics, but his complaints and those of others had little effect on those initiating a filibuster.

There was another disquieting aspect to these filibusters: Senators were taking obvious pride in their sometimes extraordinary garrulousness, however tedious and repetitive their words. In the 1891 filibuster, West Virginia's Charles Faulkner held the Senate floor overnight, for eleven and a half hours, a feat that startled observers.[41] In the 1893 filibuster, Nebraska's William Allen held the floor overnight, too, this time for fourteen hours, a new record. In both cases, the senators were helped by frequent quorum calls and the support of cooperating colleagues. Their achievements would seem trivial when compared to those of filibustering senators in the twentieth century, but they strengthened the identification between an excessively long speech and a heroic act. In the 1893 filibuster, senators gleefully outdid themselves. Nevada's John Jones made one speech that took him seven days to deliver and filled one hundred closely printed pages of the *Congressional Record*.[42]

These one-man efforts suggested a new kind of filibuster: the threat by a senator to tie up the Senate indefinitely unless his colleagues conceded to him what he wanted. The Senate was most vulnerable to this tactic in the last days of a Congress when time was severely limited and much legislation was still pending. The first to try this was Pennsylvania's Matthew Quay, a political spoilsman, who, in the last days of the Fifty-fourth Congress in 1897, tied up the Senate with his own filibuster. Acting for the steel barons of his state, he demanded that the Senate increase the price the navy paid for armor plate. He settled in for a long siege, until action in the House eventually defeated his plan. Thus thwarted, Quay contented himself with stuffing into the *Congressional Record* the materials he had planned to read, 176 pages' worth.[43]

Of course, others soon imitated Quay. In 1901, Montana's Thomas Carter killed a rivers-and-harbors bill with a one-man filibuster, holding the Senate floor for thirteen hours. His colleagues had denied him an appropriation for his home state, and he was retaliating.[44] The most notorious case came in 1903, again in the last hours of that Congress. South Carolina's "Pitchfork Ben" Tillman threatened to defeat all pending legislation with a filibuster unless he got a $47,000 appropriation to compensate his state for expenses claimed from the War of 1812—which had ended nearly a century earlier. His Senate colleagues had no choice but to yield. After this, Tillman regularly threatened to filibuster at the close of each Congress's final session, his way to grab what he called "a generous appropriation for South Carolina, a nice dish of pork." He was brazen in this: "I am looking out all along the line to get 'my share of the stealing.'"[45]

Filibusters came on many subjects: shipbuilding subsidies, statehood for territories, appropriations bills, and Panama Canal tolls, among others. Some tied the Senate up for weeks, and these brought round-the-clock sessions. Often, the debates turned ugly. None was worse than a filibuster in 1908 conducted by progressives from the Midwest against an emergency currency bill, which they considered to be another scheme to benefit the wealthy. The measure was sponsored by Rhode Island's Nelson Aldrich, the de facto leader of the Senate, and his Old Guard Republican allies. The fight lasted only two days, but brought great partisan bitterness and parliamentary violence without previous parallel. Aldrich and his partisans, who included Vice President Charles Fairbanks, used high-handed and questionable tactics to set new precedents hampering filibustering and then, finally, to break the filibuster at hand.

Wisconsin's Robert La Follette began the filibuster shortly after noon on May 29, 1908. He held the floor through the night until 7 A.M. the next morning, for a record-breaking total of eighteen hours and forty-three minutes. In that time, he forced no fewer than thirty-two calls of the roll, compelling Aldrich to scramble to keep a quorum present to wear down the filibusters. La Follette sustained himself with glasses of milk and whipped raw eggs. During one roll call, he took a large swallow and instantly reacted to the vile taste. Later analysis revealed a potentially lethal dose of ptomaine in the glass—administered either by Mother Nature or a stealthy opponent.[46]

Aldrich and his allies repeatedly tried to take La Follette off his feet, calling him to order again and again, but the Senate shrank from silencing him. Aldrich threatened retaliation against any senator joining La Follette. With the connivance of Vice President Fairbanks, he and his partisans did force La Follette to lose the floor, if only temporarily. La Follette had allies, too, and they took up the fight where he left off. In the early afternoon of

May 30, during a planned shift of speakers, Aldrich directed Fairbanks promptly to order the vote on passage of the measure, even though another senator was shouting for recognition. In a blatant violation of the Senate's rules and traditions, Aldrich cunningly used it to break the filibuster.[47]

Out of this struggle came two important precedents, both engineered by Aldrich, to make filibustering more difficult. The first came on a point of order he raised, and the Senate confirmed, that a senator could not enter more than one quorum call until some intervening Senate business had taken place. The Senate confirmed that debate did not count as "business." Under this ruling, individual senators could no longer force a majority to remain on hand for endless quorum calls. The other precedent came after a roll call that turned out to be one senator shy of a quorum. Aldrich prompted Vice President Charles Fairbanks to rule that another senator then present had not answered to his name; therefore a quorum was present. In so ruling, Fairbanks had, in effect, counted a quorum, much as Speaker Reed had done eighteen years earlier. That 1908 ruling ended for the Senate the filibusterers' old trick of the Disappearing Quorum.[48]

A surprising further reform came nine years later, in March 1917, prompted by a totally unexpected source: President Woodrow Wilson. This was a time of national tension; a great war engulfed most of Europe, and Wilson had asked Congress for legislative authority to arm American merchant ships. In the final days of this Sixty-fourth Congress, several progressive senators led by La Follette blocked the measure with a dramatic filibuster. Wilson was outraged. A master of righteous indignation and flamboyant language, he denounced them in a tough public statement: "The Senate of the United States is the only legislative body in the world which cannot act when its majority is ready for action. A little group of willful men, representing no opinion but their own, have rendered the great Government of the United States helpless and contemptible."[49] The only remedy, Wilson said, was for the Senate to change its rules so that the majority could act.

The response to Wilson's attack was extraordinary. From all over the nation came condemnations of the filibusterers and of the Senate itself. The senators were called cowards, moral perverts, and traitors. Public fury intimidated most members. A new session of Congress, specially called by Wilson, was already under way, and senators of both parties hurriedly met in party caucuses to decide on quick action. The Senate's designated majority leader, Virginia Democrat Thomas Martin, proposed a cloture rule as the way to halt future filibusters. After a brief and perfunctory debate, the Senate approved the rule that same day, March 8, 1917, by an overwhelming vote, seventy-six to three.[50]

The Senate had acted with great haste to placate public opinion, but privately its members had no intention of abandoning the filibuster as a parliamentary tactic. The rule they adopted provided for only a modest restriction on debate, and few senators expected that it would have much effect on future obstruction activities. During the debate, New Hampshire's Henry Hollis proposed cloture by a simple majority vote, but he was quickly persuaded to withdraw that idea.[51] The reform language, attached to Rule 22, provided that on the petition of sixteen senators, the Senate would vote two days later to close debate. If two-thirds of the Senate then voted for the motion, cloture was invoked. That meant that thereafter each senator was limited to just one hour of further debate. This was hardly radical bypass surgery on the Senate's clogged legislative arteries. With the Senate's membership at ninety-six, that meant a potential of a dozen eight-hour days of further debate after cloture. Moreover, inasmuch as most filibusters came in the final days of a Congress, the restrictions were less than strict. The Senate's prompt action quieted the national clamor, but senators knew what they had done. Colorado's Charles Thomas put the matter bluntly: the Senate's new rule was "literally the offer of a stone in response to a demand for bread."[52]

Ostensibly, the Senate's majority could silence its filibusterers in due course, but the reality was something else. The new rule left in place the now-familiar ways of stalling and derailing legislation, including the endless talk. Filibusters continued from time to time, wrenching the Senate away from its members' preferred image of a deliberative body. The cloture rule did little to improve matters. In the first forty years under that rule's provisions, the Senate voted only twenty-two times on cloture, hardly once each Congress. On these votes, the Senate actually invoked cloture only four times, and of those four, only one came on a matter of great moment, the Senate's consideration of the Versailles Treaty in 1919.[53]

When the Republicans were in the minority, they filibustered the Democrats' bills. When the Democrats were in the minority, they filibustered the Republicans' bills. On some occasions, the filibusters came from regional blocs like that of the farmers; at other times, they came from ideological blocs like the isolationists. Throughout the 1920s, senators employed filibusters on a wide variety of legislative proposals. Some came in mid-session and lasted for weeks. Others emerged at session's end, when the inherently chaotic nature of legislative proceedings made them most effective. On those occasions, an individual senator with steely resolve could gain his colleagues' undivided attention. It was so with Arizona's Henry Ashurst, whose oratorical flourishes earned him the sobriquet "the silver-tongued sunbeam of the painted desert."[54] In one dramatic instance, he demanded an appropriation for a group of his constituents. "You are going to pass that Indian bill," he told the Senate, "or you will not have any legislation." He would block everything. Senators asked him to be patient. "No!" he shouted. "You sang me that kind of song two years ago—'wait, wait, wait'—and we waited forever. Now the iron hand: you will pass the Indian bill, or you will get nothing." The Indian bill was passed.[55]

These filibusters brought continuing criticism to the Senate. Some of the members proposed strengthening the cloture rule, but nothing was done. These were inconveniences, sometimes worse, to the senators, but they preferred to suffer them rather than to invoke further limits on themselves. How strongly they felt about this was revealed in 1925 when they came under a most extraordinary assault. On March 4, Vice President Charles Dawes delivered as his inaugural speech as the Senate's new presiding officer a scathing attack.

From the chair, for thirty minutes, Dawes denounced a variety of Senate practices, including its rules and seniority system. At length, he called for basic reform to abolish the filibuster with a new rule to cut off debate by majority vote—majority cloture. "Who would dare maintain," he asked, "that in the last analysis the right of the Senate itself to act should ever be subordinated to the right of one senator to make a speech?" The senators were shocked and offended. Mindful of the tradition that the vice president, as presiding officer, should be seen and heard only when he was announcing results of their votes, senators of both parties excoriated Dawes for his lecture and his impertinence. The speech also blighted his budding relationship with President Calvin Coolidge, whose own inaugural address, delivered minutes later, was overshadowed by Dawes's rant. Mississippi's Pat Harrison mocked Dawes, a man with no legislative experience, for having "all knowledge" about the Senate. Nebraska's George Norris said that the vice president's plan would destroy the Senate as "the only forum in our country where there is free and fair debate."[56] Senators were not prepared to let this vice president—or any other one, for that matter—tell them how to run the Senate.

Charles Dawes was not silenced by the counterattack. He toured the country that summer and fall in a campaign for what he called "my" new rule for the Senate. He threatened, without success, to try to defeat senators up for reelection if they balked at adopting it. Dawes spent the next four years presiding unhappily over the Senate, witnessing senators regularly using the filibuster to coerce the majority, in his words, "into legislative concessions dictated by selfish and sectional interest."[57] What bothered him most was the way those engaged in filibustering were treated. "The most determined obstructionists are fawned upon, cajoled, flattered—anything to get their acquiescence that the Senate may do its constitutional duty," Dawes wrote in his journal. "It is a shameful spectacle."[58] When his term expired in 1929, he quipped, "I should hate to think that the Senate was as tired of me at the beginning of my service as I am of the Senate at the end."[59]

To end the abuse of the filibuster in the final days of a Congress, Senator George Norris came up with a remarkable solution: a constitutional amendment to change the meeting dates of Congress so as to leave the day of final adjournment open-ended. Each new Congress would meet for the first time on January 3, just two months after Election Day; the president would take the oath of office on January 20 after his election. This would eliminate the notorious "lame-duck" sessions of Congress, Norris argued, and the old absolute deadline for adjournment on March 4. "No limitation of a session would exist," he said, "and no filibuster would even be attempted."[60] Norris first proposed this plan in 1923, and his Senate colleagues approved it by an overwhelming margin of sixty-three to six. The House, however, blocked it then and on four more occasions during the 1920s. In 1932, both the Senate and House approved the proposal. The necessary number of states quickly ratified the amendment, the Constitution's twentieth, and it took effect in January 1934.

Despite Norris's claim that this schedule would prevent the worst of filibusters, the results were far less than that. Senators' use and abuse of the filibuster continued largely unimpeded. Each Congress still had to end, and in those closing days senators used the filibuster, and the threat of filibuster, to intimidate and frustrate their colleagues. Mid-session filibusters continued as before, and in the evolving use of the filibuster there came new and troubling developments. A few senators discovered that filibustering was a tactic by which they could claim national attention. The first of these was Huey Pierce Long of Louisiana, a freshman senator who made himself a likely presidential candidate with his often bizarre filibusters. More significantly in these years, senators from the former slave states of the South found themselves relying on the filibuster as their way to block all civil rights legislation. In time, this gave the filibuster the appearance of a parliamentary weapon for racists.

From his first days in the Senate, Long, the flamboyant former governor of Louisiana, captured national attention with his self-promoting filibusters. In speech after speech, he heaped enough scorn on his colleagues to become a prime Washington tourist attraction. His demagogic "Share Our Wealth" scheme—capping incomes of the rich and providing financial support to the poor ("Every man a king, but no one wears a crown")—signaled his intention to run against President Franklin Roosevelt in the 1936 election, and was credited with prompting Roosevelt to propose the Social Security system. Long's Senate colleagues detested him. The majority leader, Joseph Robinson from neighboring Arkansas, called Long's speeches the ravings of a madman.[61]

Long was a braggart and vulgarian, provocative and offensive, given to feigning anger and indignation as he insulted and abused his fellow senators. In his most famous speech, a filibuster in June 1935, he held the Senate floor for fifteen hours and thirty-five minutes, regarded as an extraordinary physical feat. His speech ranged almost as widely and erratically as John Randolph's half-mad speeches of the 1820s. Long spoke of all sorts of irrelevant matters, Frederick the Great, Victor Hugo, and potbellied politicians. When he demanded that senators be required to stay in the chamber and listen to his ramblings, Vice President John Nance Garner ruled that such an order would violate the Constitution's specific prohibition against cruel and unusual punishment.[62]

For all his offensiveness to the Senate's norms, Long shared with other senators from the South an antagonistic attitude toward black Americans. "We just lynch an occasional nigger," he once said.[63] For years before he entered the Senate, white mobs had been lynching African Americans in a reign of terror promoted by such lawless groups as the Ku Klux Klan. These were crimes without penalty, for those in the lynch mobs knew that no local jury would dare to convict them.[64] In 1922, the House of Representatives finally passed a bill that made lynching a federal crime. As soon as the House bill reached the Senate, Southern members launched a filibuster to kill it. Led by Oscar Underwood of Alabama, then the Senate's Democratic minority leader, they relied primarily on dilatory tactics, mostly just stalling indefinitely the approval of the Senate's journal for the previous day. "Under the rules of the Senate," Underwood stated, "when fifteen or twenty or twenty-five men say you cannot pass a certain bill, it cannot be passed."[65]

That was the beginning of the calculated obstruction by filibustering Southern senators of all civil rights measures, a systematic campaign that would torment the Senate's deliberations for the next half-century and more.

Underwood insolently asserted, "We have no apologies."[66] And in that vein for decades to follow, Southern senators flaunted what they were doing, sure of enthusiastic support from voters back home. They argued that these bills were unconstitutional and by opposing them they were defending "the Southern way of life," by which they meant the subjugation of blacks to legally enforced racial segregation. In this long struggle, the Senate's filibuster became for them a positive good, the means of protecting their cherished principles, such as they were, from outside intrusion. To those sponsoring anti-lynching legislation, the filibuster became an obvious evil, ugly and crude, used to perpetuate the humiliation of millions of African Americans in a continued attempt to deny them their rights. Earlier, the filibuster was available to any senator without giving more offense than the obvious annoyance he caused his colleagues. The filibuster became a parliamentary tactic some senators relished as an affirmation of the Senate's special brand of free speech, but one that other senators abhorred as the Senate's fundamental institutional flaw as a legislative body.

Both sides avowed high moral principles, and the emotional content of their contradictory claims had the effect of warping the way they perceived the filibuster. Senators from the South came to believe with religious fervor that they could not under any circumstances vote to halt any filibuster against any question, that the filibuster was a tactic they must defend at all costs. By contrast, those favoring civil rights legislation came to question whether they could ever properly resort to a filibuster to defend or advance any of their causes. In times of trial, there were sometimes exceptions by both sides, but then only by a few and then usually with apologies for their breach of their normal ground rules.

The South's senators organized themselves early as a working bloc to fight these bills, and they picked senior and influential senators as their leaders. Following Oscar Underwood was Byron Patton "Pat" Harrison of Mississippi, chairman of the Senate's Finance Committee. "We would hold a meeting," one senator reported, "lay out our battle plan and give Pat leeway to arrange our speakers so that the fight would go on without a break."[67] Harrison was succeeded by Thomas Connally of Texas, chairman of the Senate's Foreign Relations Committee, a skillful parliamentarian notoriously rough in debate. He was persuaded that Northern senators proposed these bills only as a way to woo black voters in their home states. "We Southern members were made to look like fiends," Connally said, "even though all of us opposed lynching."[68] He was succeeded as Southern caucus leader by Richard Russell of Georgia, chairman of the Senate's Armed Services

Committee, an even more skillful parliamentarian. Like the others, he held that it was up to the states, not the federal government, to deal with lynching and civil rights. In his time, the Southern bloc was nicknamed "Dick Russell and his Dixieland Band," and he and they proved effective only into the 1960s. He was adamant to the end to protect any filibuster, not just those on measures that the Southerners opposed.[69]

A constant problem for those trying to outlast or undermine a vigorous filibuster was the need to muster a quorum of the Senate at any hour, day or night. Without a majority of the Senate's membership at hand, the Senate could not function legally, thereby aiding those mounting the filibuster by further delaying Senate business. It increased the pressure on senators who had other legislative matters they wished to advance to set aside the contentious legislation that had sparked the filibuster. During any filibuster, absenteeism was rampant. Senators had better ways of spending their time, particularly in the small hours of the early morning. Added to this difficulty, those conducting the filibuster were not inclined to cooperate. They did not merely absent themselves on quorum calls; they went into hiding.

Under its rules and the common practice of other Western legislatures, the Senate had power to force the attendance of the absentees. This was a ticklish matter, likely to offend those arrested, and therefore rarely used in recent decades. In earlier times, however, the practice was familiar, if not common. The senators present first directed the sergeant at arms to request the absent senators to return to the Senate chamber. If this failed to produce a quorum, they then could order the sergeant at arms to arrest the missing members and deliver them to the bar of the Senate to answer for their negligence, where they would then be subject to punishment.

In the 1920s, the Senate several times ordered the arrest of absent senators. In one such case, on a midnight quorum call in February 1927, Sergeant at Arms David Barry reported his inability to persuade many of the absentees to return. Some claimed they were sick. Delaware's Thomas Bayard explained he had a funeral to attend. Michigan's Woodbridge Ferris said he was too tired. New Hampshire's Henry Keyes said he would "think it over." The senators present voted to have Barry arrest the absentees, and it took him close to three hours to round up enough of them to make a quorum.[70] Two years later, in a series of end-of-session filibusters, the Senate again ordered its sergeant at arms to bring in those who had not answered the after-midnight quorum call. Vice President Charles Dawes, presiding off and on during the filibusters, wrote in his diary that he enjoyed listening to the sometimes profane excuses of the arrested senators as a welcome break from the "driveling and irrelevant talk" of those conducting the filibuster.[71]

There were hazards involved in these arrests. In November 1942, during a filibuster, the sergeant at arms brought Senator Kenneth McKellar of Tennessee into the Senate chamber. McKellar's rage was incandescent. A nastily cantankerous Senate veteran and chairman of the Senate's Appropriation Committee, he partially slaked his thirst for retaliation by having the sergeant at arms fired. He then turned to Senator Barkley, the majority leader who had made the motion to order his arrest. Barkley scrambled desperately to placate McKellar, even arranging to have his name removed from the official list of those arrested. McKellar refused to talk to Barkley for weeks, and any hopes Barkley might have had for a Supreme Court nomination died that day.[72]

Throughout the 1920s and 1930s, Southern senators had no great difficulty in blocking the anti-lynching bills. In those decades, they held power through the filibuster to issue and enforce ultimatums on legislation. "We are going to transact no more business," Senator Underwood said on such an occasion, "until we have an understanding about this bill."[73] They could obstruct all business indefinitely. Senate leaders shrank from trying to break these filibusters with round-the-clock sessions, and that made the filibustering relatively easy. During a six-day talkfest in 1938, for example, Louisiana's Allen Ellender actually addressed the Senate for little more than twenty-seven hours, less than five hours a day. This brought sharp criticism against the floor leaders for tolerating these "feather-duster" and "pink-tea" filibusters instead of confronting the offenders.[74]

By the early 1940s, mob lynchings had largely stopped, and the goals of the civil rights struggle in Congress shifted, first to enactment of anti–poll tax bills and then to fair employment practices (FEPC) legislation. The Southern senators filibustered and defeated anti–poll tax bills in 1942, 1944, 1946, and 1948. In 1946, and again in 1950, they filibustered and defeated FEPC bills. In these years, all efforts to invoke cloture on these and other filibusters failed, and that led in the mid-1940s to serious attempts to change the cloture rule, to make cloture easier to invoke, a new struggle that would bedevil the Senate's deliberations in one form or another for the next seventy years.

Rule 22's provisions for cloture, as originally adopted, provided for ending debate on "any pending measure" when approved by "a two-thirds vote of those voting." In 1948, Senate President Pro Tempore Arthur Vandenberg rendered a devastating decision. He announced that while the cloture rule did apply to a proposed anti–poll tax bill, it did not apply to the motion to proceed to take up that bill for debate. A filibuster against a motion to consider a measure could not be stopped by any number of senators under Rule 22. "In the final analysis," Vandenberg said, "the Senate has no effective cloture rule at all." The Senate's rules, he said, did not provide for absolute cloture. "They still leave the Senate, rightly or wrongly, at the mercy of unlimited debate ad infinitum."[75]

Early in the following Congress, on March 10, 1949, the new vice president (and former veteran Senate Democratic leader), Alben Barkley, reversed Vandenberg's ruling, stating that Rule 22 did indeed apply to motions to take up measures. The Senate promptly overruled him.[76] Weeks of back-and-forth maneuvering and negotiations produced a troublesome compromise. The old rule was revised so that it did apply to motions to take up proposals, but cloture could be invoked only by a two-thirds majority of all senators "duly chosen and sworn," instead of just two-thirds of those who showed up to vote.[77] That made cloture harder to impose. Of the Senate's then ninety-six members, at least sixty-four had to vote "aye" to invoke cloture, no matter how few senators were present.

That did not settle the matter. Year after year, at the beginning of each new Congress, senators found themselves once more engaged in yet another angry quarrel over their rules of debate and the filibuster. This was a contest of great importance, for the outcome determined in large measure the substance of what legislation the Senate would approve. And it deepened the sense of reformers that the filibuster was essentially a tool for evil deeds.

Senators from the South thought otherwise. As new members from that region arrived, it became a virtual ritual of initiation to announce support for the unrestrained filibuster. These arriving freshmen members were signaling their Southern colleagues that they were all right on the filibuster and on cloture. Frequently they chose their maiden speech in the Senate to make these pledges. Russell Long of Louisiana, Huey's son and a freshman in 1949, made just such a speech a few weeks after first taking his senatorial oath in defense of the Constitution. "Today," he announced, "I ask for the right of unlimited debate in the defense of my people, in defense of their customs, traditions and society." He referred, of course, to racial segregation. Long became one of the Senate's most skilled filibusterers, promising in one such struggle that "I'm going to be standing here fighting it until God calls me home."[78] Likewise, his classmate Lyndon Johnson, in his own maiden speech, offered the familiar pledges. As a Southerner, he said, he celebrated the Senate's "freedom of unlimited debate" and promised to defend the

South from "the tyranny of momentary majorities," those seeking cloture.[79] These orations required little intellectual effort, their phrasing had become so common.

The Southerners were not the only senators opposed to limiting debate. Conservative Republicans, allied with Southern Democrats in a working coalition since the late 1930s, normally opposed cloture simply because they were conservatives and deplored aggressive legislative initiatives. They had few African American constituents back home. More significant, however, were senators from the less populous states, Democrats and Republicans alike, who regarded the filibuster as their ultimate weapon to protect their constituents. They had only tiny delegations in the House, some with only one or two members. Overwhelmed by the then massive delegations from such states as New York, Pennsylvania, and Ohio, these isolated members had little chance under the House's stringent rules and party controls to make their mark on anything. In the hour of need, when the interests of one's state were at hazard, a senator could disrupt the Senate indefinitely, using the filibuster or other dilatory tactics. With no obvious restraints, the member could effectively practice legislative blackmail. "Yield to what I demand or suffer the parliamentary bedlam I might inflict!" This was a blunt but effective legislative weapon, and senators knew its value. These senators did not favor all filibusters by any means, but they did not want the filibuster weakened by allowing cloture to become a matter of routine. That lay behind their policy of resisting any motion for cloture.

Meanwhile, the squabbling over Rule 22 and the filibuster continued. Occasionally, there was a breakthrough, bewilderingly obscure to the outside world, but of grave meaning to senators. One such came in January 1957, at the opening of the Eighty-fifth Congress. Vice President Richard Nixon, from the chair, offered an opinion that sent chills through the ranks of the Southerners. At the beginning of each new Congress, he stated, the Senate could adopt whatever new rules the majority saw fit, and the new Senate was not bound by any previous rule of the Senate.[80] What made Nixon's words frightening to the South's senators was that he was thus announcing how he would rule if this question came before him. That year, the Senate brushed aside efforts to change the rules, but the Southerners understood their danger. If Nixon's opinion carried, that could mean cloture on filibusters by a simple majority, not two-thirds of those duly chosen and sworn. A ruling by the Senate's presiding officer, if sustained by a mere majority of senators, could end the South's ability to block measures they opposed.

When Lyndon Johnson became the Senate's majority leader in 1955, he well understood the anxiety of his fellow Southerners. When the next Congress convened in 1957, he maneuvered to bring them some relief by engineering Senate passage of a pending civil rights bill. He told the Southerners that he believed black Americans had become "pretty uppity." "We've got to give them a little something."[81] Otherwise, the South might completely lose the filibuster with all that implied. Then Johnson went after the sponsors of the legislation. He warned them that unless they drastically cut back its provisions, the Southerners would filibuster the bill to death, as they had done so often in the past. Johnson thus persuaded both sides to give way, and the Senate then passed a much weakened civil rights bill without confronting a real filibuster. In the closing hours of debate, South Carolina's Strom Thurmond, a career segregationist, launched his own one-man filibuster, holding the Senate floor for twenty-four hours and eighteen minutes, the longest unbroken speech in the Senate's history. Thurmond won himself headlines across the nation and he embarrassed his less vocal Southern colleagues, but he had no effect on the substance of the bill or its passage.[82]

Thurmond's exploit was a matter of showing off, and he was hardly the first to gain public notoriety through excessively long and noisome filibustering speeches. Some Southern senators whose real interests were in national legislation gave only token commitment to any filibuster, including those on racial matters, but there were other senators, not all from the South, who seized whatever opportunities there were to address the Senate at great length. One of the most notorious was Wayne Morse of Oregon, a quarrelsome politician with an insatiable craving for publicity. For years, Morse used to claim the Senate floor after the day's business was done and harangue the Senate's all-but-empty chamber for hours on end. In 1953, he spoke for twenty-two hours and twenty-six minutes in a filibustering speech, to that date the longest uninterrupted speech in the Senate's history. Morse was proud of his talents. "Give me six men true and blue bound to have dinner together in Washington on Christmas Day," he said one mid-September, threatening a filibuster, "and that is exactly what will happen."[83]

In 1959, responding to Nixon's proffered opinion two years earlier, Majority Leader Johnson negotiated backstage a deal to safeguard Rule 22 at the start of each new Congress. In return for permitting cloture by two-thirds of those "present and voting," the Senate's existing rules would continue automatically from one Congress to the next unless altered under the two-thirds rule, not the simple, "constitutional" majority Nixon proposed.[84]

That made cloture somewhat easier to invoke, but reform of the Senate's rules much harder.

Tampering with Rule 22 suggested the weakening of the Southern bloc's once formidable power. Additionally, Tennessee Senators Estes Kefauver and Albert Gore Sr., both with presidential ambitions, had openly defected on civil rights measures, and so had Lyndon Johnson. An on-again, off-again candidate for president, Johnson had now resolved to sponsor a civil rights bill of his own and push it through to Senate passage. He informed his colleagues in advance that he would act on February 15, 1960. The South's leader, Senator Russell, despaired. "[O]ur ranks were too thin and our resources too meager," he said."[85] The Southerners could filibuster, of course, but Russell assumed that now they had no hope of winning. They would have to make concessions. Johnson sensed that, too.

Johnson had made himself a master of the Senate's rules and practices, and now he took action that startled Senator Russell and everyone else. On the day he designated, February 15, an hour before noon, Johnson routinely called up for action a minor House-passed bill dealing with some real estate in a Missouri school district. Then, with that bill before the Senate, Johnson invited senators to use that measure as the vehicle for civil rights amendments. This stunning announcement was a brilliant maneuver, which badly crippled Southerners in the struggle to come. First, Johnson had neatly bypassed the sentinels Russell had posted to counter any Johnson move. That meant the bill was already before the Senate and that Russell and his band had lost the chance to filibuster the motion to take up the bill. More important, by his tactics Johnson had also bypassed the Senate's Judiciary Committee, the committee with jurisdiction over such legislation. The committee was chaired by the Senate's most ardent racist, James Eastland of Mississippi, who was certain to squelch in committee any civil rights measure.

Johnson let the filibuster run for two weeks. Then, on Monday, February 29, he announced his intention to break it by holding the Senate in continuous session, around the clock, "until a vote is reached."[86] This, too, had never been done to the extent Johnson intended. Senator Russell pledged that he and his partners would use "every legal means at our command" to block the bill. To that purpose, the Georgia senator organized his filibusterers into three platoons, each with six senators, and they served eight hours on duty, sixteen hours off, each team relieved in turn by another squad fully rested and refreshed. The filibusterers relied partially on talk, but principally on time-consuming quorum calls. Johnson held the Senate in continuous session for the full week, from Monday morning until Saturday evening, 125 hours and thirty-one minutes, with only one fifteen-minute break to tidy up the Senate chamber, the longest ever unbroken sitting of the Senate.[87]

The filibustering senators, following Russell's plan, demanded quorum calls night and day, and that meant Johnson had to produce a majority of senators every time. The dinner hour was a favorite, but even more punishing were the roll calls in the early hours of the morning—three o'clock, five o'clock—when senators were not readily available. Johnson ordered army cots and bedding placed in nearby offices and committee rooms so that senators might catch a little sleep between quorum calls. Disheveled and sprawled on these cots, senators offered a less-than-dignified image of a great deliberative body. The filibustering senators stayed away, refusing to answer to their names, and that made Johnson's burden more difficult. Johnson's strategy, as countered by Russell's, exhausted the bill's advocates and Johnson, not the filibustering senators. The debate and filibuster dragged on for several more weeks before the Senate passed a much-diluted bill worked out in backstage conferences.[88]

Majority Leader Johnson managed to win approval of that bill without invoking cloture on the filibuster. As of that time, the Senate had not invoked cloture on anything in more than thirty years, and never on a civil rights bill. The fight over the rules, especially those dealing with the filibuster, went on then and for many years to come. At times this debate took on aspects of convoluted logic seemingly ridiculous to those uninitiated in the parliamentary maze of the Senate's precedents and practices. Nixon's 1957 opinion, of course, was never put to the test, and it lapsed in 1961 when he left the vice presidency. Those seeking reform tried to devise new stratagems, immensely complicated, to bring their proposals to the Senate floor for a direct vote, and those opposed had their own intricate arguments to counter those efforts.

One of these centered on defining the very nature of the Senate itself, whether or not the Senate was "a continuing body," a legislative assembly whose institutional life had never been interrupted since its origin in 1789. The House of Representatives died with every final adjournment and came back to life with every new Congress, the members then electing anew their officers, re-creating their committees, and readopting their rules. The Senate was different. Unlike the House, only one-third of the Senate's seats were put to election every two years. The other senators routinely continued in office, as did the Senate's committees and rules. This supported the notion of the Senate as a continuing body.[89] If accepted, it would spike the reformers' arguments to change the Senate's rules by a simple majority at the start of each new Congress.[90]

In this often bitter quarreling, the Northern Democrats had so regularly denounced the filibuster and the way the Southerners used it that they were embarrassed to use the filibuster themselves when, for reasons of conscience or expediency, it might have served their legislative purposes. Similarly, the Southerners were so committed to defending the filibuster as a legitimate tactic that they could not bring themselves to vote for cloture under any circumstances. Both sides, however, did make exceptions, if awkwardly. In 1953, for example, Northern Democrats openly filibustered the tidelands oil bill, and again the next year they filibustered a natural gas bill. Senator Paul Douglas of Illinois, who took part in both, argued that they were not really using these filibusters to kill the bills: they were only trying to build opposition to them. He felt obliged to explain, "Our purpose was to dramatize our case, to alert the people, and to convince our colleagues, but it was not to forever prevent a vote."[91]

While important symbolically, the civil rights acts of 1957 and 1960 hardly dealt with the inequities long imposed on black Americans, and all through the 1960s the Senate confronted further efforts to redress the wrongs of segregation and racial bias. The Southerners still used the filibuster, as they had before, but the tactic no longer gave them a legislative veto. Despite their efforts, the Senate passed three landmark bills: the omnibus Civil Rights Act of 1964, the Voting Rights Act of 1965, and the Open Housing Act of 1968. On each, the Southerners filibustered, and on each they failed. Their failure and the substance of the measures enacted into law had a profound effect on the country and the Senate.

The first intimations that the Senate would make this break with the past came in 1962 on a bill proposed by President Kennedy. Kennedy's election as president in November 1960 carried Lyndon Johnson from the Senate floor as party leader to the Senate's chair as vice president. Montana's Mike Mansfield succeeded Johnson as the Senate's majority leader, and he brought to that post a totally different approach, based partially on his respect for his colleagues. In dealing with the Senate's operations, including filibusters, Mansfield—responding to intensifying complaints from Democratic colleagues—rejected Johnson's often abrasive, strong-arm tactics and his dissembling methods. Those who missed Johnson criticized Mansfield for his "weak" leadership, but under his guidance the Senate invoked cloture for the first time in a generation and went on to pass one bill after another, the most significant civil rights legislation in modern history.[92]

The first filibuster of this era to be cut short by cloture came on Kennedy's communications satellite bill. Leading that delaying action—in an ironic role reversal—were ten Senate liberals who saw the measure as an unacceptable government giveaway to private industry. The large financial stakes in this bill, they argued, were warrant enough. "While the rules exist," said Senator Paul Douglas, one of those filibustering, "I shall not strip their protection from those who are fighting for what they believe to be the defense of the American people."[93]

Even as the Senate's liberals were starting to abandon their inhibitions against filibustering, their conservative colleagues in both parties were changing, too. They supported the communications satellite bill and shrank from allowing a filibuster to defeat it, despite a chronic reluctance to vote for cloture. On August 14, 1962, no fewer than seventeen Republicans who regularly voted against cloture voted for cloture on this bill, and they included senators from such thinly populated states as Utah and Idaho.[94]

The Southern Democrats had a more painful problem. They wanted this law, but they split on the cloture vote. Some gave way and actually voted for cloture for the first time ever, while others simply stayed away. With the other switches, their disappearance allowed the Senate to invoke cloture, sixty-three to twenty-seven, three votes more than the two-thirds majority needed. This was the first time since 1927 that the Senate had voted for cloture. This was not a civil rights measure, but what had been done once could surely be done again.

This vote had serious implications for the Senate. Those who had long demanded reform of Rule 22 now faced the argument that cloture was indeed possible under the existing rules. Senators from some of the less populous states found themselves catching testy home-state criticism for what they had done. Most of the Southern senators had stuck with their leader, Senator Russell, and he was resolved to give no ground. "I will vote to gag the Senate," he said, "when the shrimps start to whistle 'Dixie.'"[95] He knew better than most, however, that his Southern ranks were broken and that Republican votes for cloture were more likely now than ever.

The great test for the filibuster came in 1964 on the omnibus civil rights bill that President Kennedy proposed the year before. This was legislation certain to disrupt the Senate's Democrats, pitting the Southerners against those from the North and West. Kennedy's awareness of that certain outcome had led him to delay in proposing the measure. Under the pressures from widespread public protests, he could not, however, wait past June 1963. Once he made the request, the old antagonisms arose again among the Senate's Democratic factions.[96]

The measure had just begun its legislative course when Kennedy was murdered in Dallas. That made Lyndon Johnson president, and as president he resolved to pass Kennedy's civil rights bill as a way to honor the slain president's memory. The bill was a great deal more than the "little something" that Johnson, as senator, had pushed through the Senate in 1957. Under the strategy adopted, the House of Representatives would act first. President Johnson, in his January 8, 1964, State of the Union address, strongly urged Congress to approve the bill, and on February 10 the House did pass it.[97]

The Senate debate began in early March, and the Southerners, again led by Senator Russell, filibustered from the start. Johnson tried to persuade Mansfield to break the filibuster by holding the Senate in around-the-clock session, but Mansfield refused. That was not his way, and he remembered the 1960 filibuster when Johnson had tried that tactic for almost a week, exhausting the bill's advocates, but not those filibustering. "This is not a circus or a sideshow," he explained. "We are not operating in a pit with spectators coming into the galleries late at night to see senators of the republic come out in bedroom slippers, without neckties, with their hair uncombed, and pajama tops sticking out of their necks. There will be no pajama sessions of the Senate."[98]

Mansfield did bring the Senate into session early each morning and held it in session well into each night, but his refusal to use harsh methods made filibustering easy for the Southerners. For three full weeks, they filibustered Mansfield's motion to take up the bill for consideration. Senator Russell then let that motion go to a vote, fearing that further stalling on that initial question might prompt a successful motion for cloture. Only then did the Senate technically start debating the bill itself. In this struggle, those favoring the bill created their own special organization to answer the arguments and speeches of the filibusterers. Mansfield named Hubert Humphrey of Minnesota, the Democratic whip, to take charge of the Democratic supporters. Senator Thomas Kuchel of California, the Republican whip, became his party's floor manager for this bill. They and their supporters met daily to exchange information and arrange their own schedule of speakers. Senators were assigned titles of the bill to defend whenever attacked. This was extraordinary. In the past, those filibustering had to keep talking. Now they were answered, often cogently. The speech-making was not just one-sided. Senator Mansfield relied on the prospect that eventually the Senate would settle this legislative contest by invoking cloture. He could not hope for enough Democratic votes; Senator Russell's faction was too large. He had to gain Republican votes for cloture, votes that most Republican senators normally shunned. "The key," Mansfield said, over and over, "is Dirksen."[99]

He was speaking of Everett Dirksen of Illinois, the Senate's Republican leader. Mansfield, modest to the point of self-abnegation, had no difficulty deferring to Dirksen. Neither did Senator Humphrey. President Johnson repeatedly urged Humphrey to flatter Dirksen, to offer him the role of statesman in this historic undertaking. "I began a public massage of his ego," Humphrey reported later, "and appealed to his vanity."[100] Much as Dirksen enjoyed the stroking, he knew that the task of rounding up Republican votes would not be easy. By the head counts of those supporting the bill, they needed twenty-five of the thirty-three Republicans then in the Senate to ensure cloture, and no one but Dirksen had any chance of persuading so many. Worse for the bill's advocates, Dirksen had special problems of his own about supporting this bill. In his 1962 reelection campaign, his state's African American leadership had opposed him, and that still rankled. Dirksen pronounced the bill unsatisfactory.

As the filibuster droned on week after week, Dirksen put aside his personal resentments and entered a complex series of backroom negotiations with senators sponsoring the legislation, staff experts, and officials of the Justice Department led by Attorney General Robert F. Kennedy. A gifted legislator able to compose law, unlike many of his colleagues, Dirksen began to propose changes in the pending bill. Resentful at Dirksen's sudden prominence in this operation, Robert Kennedy tried to block them, but Dirksen had his way. He had a telling argument: without these amendments he could not hope to deliver the votes of his Republicans for cloture. Dirksen offered amendment after amendment, some seventy in all, and he insisted on them as his price for supporting the bill. He so altered the bill that it was now called "the Dirksen package," something deeply satisfying to Dirksen the legislator.[101]

In the midst of these negotiations, Senator Russell tried to woo Dirksen into opposition, but the blandishments of the bill's sponsors were much preferable. On a deeper level, Dirksen had assessed his party's prospects. This was a presidential election year; the likely Republican candidate was Senator Barry Goldwater of Arizona, Dirksen's close friend, and Dirksen wanted to position his party and its candidate favorably in that context. Even with his own version of the bill in hand, Dirksen faced a tough assignment in his pledge to persuade Republicans to vote for cloture. Goldwater, for example, had never voted for cloture in his years in the Senate.

"I got on my knees to some senators," Dirksen said later, "and said 'Please give us a vote for cloture.'"[102] Many of his colleagues were reluctant. Some refused. He asked North Dakota's Milton Young. "Damn you," Young snapped, "don't you ever ask me again for cloture."[103] He had voted for cloture in 1962, at Dirksen's plea, and he had taken criticism for that from his people back home. Some senators bargained hard. "We went to the leaders," South Dakota's Karl Mundt confided, "and told them we had the controlling votes on cloture." Mundt insisted that the Senate vote on three amendments his allies wanted "before we would consider cloture." They got their Senate votes.[104]

In the debate, Dirksen, a theatrical politician, now supported the bill with his gaudy oratory. "Stronger than all the armies is an idea whose time had come," Dirksen exhorted his colleagues, quoting Victor Hugo. "This is an idea whose time has come. It will not be stayed. It will not be denied."[105]

The Senate's debate, unusual in its often intense parry-riposte duel of words, was important, but the significant parliamentary battle centered on lining up the needed votes for cloture. To Dirksen's dismay, Senator Goldwater refused to vote for cloture and for the bill itself. That undid Dirksen's party strategy for the fall elections. Meanwhile, Goldwater's Senate colleague from Arizona, eighty-six-year-old Carl Hayden, privately committed himself to vote for cloture if his vote made the deciding difference. A senator since 1927, Hayden concealed himself in the Democratic cloakroom during the vote until cloture was assured. During the vote, Senator Clair Engle of California, dying of a brain tumor that left him speechless, was rolled into the Senate chamber in a wheelchair and voted "aye" by pointing to his eye. This vote for cloture was seventy-one to twenty-nine. Twenty-seven Republicans had voted "aye."[106]

Dirksen and his fellow Republicans numbered less than one-third of the Senate's membership, but by the realities of the filibuster and the need for cloture, he had achieved a remarkable power far in excess of his party's Senate strength. Through his talent at persuading his colleagues to follow his lead, he was able to decide not only whether this bill would pass but the very substance of its contents. This was heady stuff for Dirksen, and he found the Senate's way of conducting its affairs much to his liking. He wanted no tampering with Rule 22, no weakening of this weapon of the minority. "I do not propose to forfeit any weapon or shield of the minority," he said. The filibuster gave him special command in the Senate, whichever side he was on, and he knew that. The civil rights bill he did so much to pass was the first ever adopted by the Senate through cloture, but all had not been accomplished.

Scarcely had the civil rights bill become law than new demonstrations in Alabama met ugly police brutality, which prompted headlines and outrage all over the country. The protesters were demanding the right to vote. President Johnson took alarm and ordered his attorney general to draft "the goddamndest, toughest voting rights act that you can devise."[107] In March 1965, to underscore his grave concern, Johnson went before a special joint session of Congress and demanded that this bill be enacted. He wanted immediate action.[108]

In the Senate, Majority Leader Mansfield, with Dirksen's approval, had the bill referred to the Judiciary Committee with instructions that it be reported back in less than three weeks. Senator Russell was ill and absent. Louisiana's Allen Ellender, a veteran filibusterer, took over in his place and pledged to speak against this bill "as long as God gives me breath."[109]

The debate began in mid-April, and the Southerners filibustered. Dirksen conceded that they were having the usual difficulty persuading senators to vote for cloture, despite some promised conversions. Senator Russell returned on May 24, the day before the scheduled vote. "If there is anything I could do, I'd do it," he said in resignation, "but I assume the die is cast."[110] The vote for cloture was seventy to thirty, and the next day the Senate approved the bill 77 to 19. Larry O'Brien, Johnson's chief liaison with Congress, gave the credit to Dirksen. "You can't get cloture in the Senate," O'Brien said, "without Dirksen working like hell for it!"[111]

However dramatic the passage of the 1964 and 1965 bills, their enactment did not remove the searing problem of racially oppressive laws. In January 1966, in his State of the Union address, President Johnson asked Congress for further civil rights legislation, this time an open housing law.[112] This faced strenuous opposition not only from Southern senators but also from conservative Republicans including Dirksen. Like others, he did not see how real estate, for rent or purchase, could be included in interstate commerce. Dirksen pronounced the measure unconstitutional, and his allies blocked it and subsequent versions until early 1968, when Dirksen agreed to support a new version that included his modifications. It was Dirksen who now moved for cloture. This again was a presidential election year, like 1964. "I was thinking of the party's future," Dirksen said. He himself was up for reelection.[113] Finally, on March 4, 1968, after repeated setbacks, Dirksen rallied enough Republicans to produce a vote of sixty-five to thirty-two, cloture by a two-thirds margin.[114]

This maneuver assured Senate passage of the Civil Rights Act of 1968, commonly known as the Fair Housing Act, and that completed enactment of all the long-pending major civil rights measures. Only dimly understood at the time, the three bills of 1964, 1965, and 1968 would dramatically change the nation politically, ending the Democrats' hold on what was once called the Solid South, and radically altering the way voters chose presidents and members of Congress.

In this new form, the filibuster would fundamentally change the US Senate. Within the Senate, the filibuster became an entirely different mechanism, freed at last from the onus of racial discrimination, but caught up in its revised use as an instrument of even more frequent legislative gridlock.

13

Reform and Reaction

IN FEBRUARY 1988, SENATE MAJORITY Leader Robert Byrd decided to get tough with Republicans planning to filibuster legislation that would place limits on federal campaign spending. Mindful of recently installed C-SPAN television cameras, he announced that he saw "no point in having a nice easygoing filibuster here . . . Let us have it out here on the floor . . . where the American people can see."[1] Republican Whip Alan Simpson responded, "We are ready to go all night. We will have our sturdy SWAT teams and people on vitamin pills and colostomy bags, and Lord knows what else."[2] As the session headed into evening hours, Simpson's fellow Republicans stayed away from the Senate chamber to avoid the quorum calls necessary to transact business, and the Senate presiding officer ordered the arrest of the absentees. A cleaning lady revealed to Capitol police that she had just seen Oregon Senator Robert Packwood slip into his private office. Officers apprehended Packwood and escorted him to the chamber. At 1:17 A.M., he insisted they carry him across the threshold and into the room, his body theatrically limp. Although his presence established the necessary quorum of fifty-one senators, Republicans subsequently managed to defeat the bill. One of their number, Warren Rudman of New Hampshire, wryly commented, "The events of the last 48 hours were a curious blend of 'Dallas,' 'Dynasty,' 'The Last Buccaneer,' and Friday night fights."[3]

The filibuster as we know it today, cleansed of its racial overtones, took shape in the early 1970s as the nation began a significant move toward political polarization. Composition of the Senate shifted as a consequence of this change. The elections of 1976, 1978, and 1980 brought fifty-five new members, with a large percentage of them, and those who would arrive in the following decades, embracing the filibuster as a tactical weapon to be used routinely in pursuing specific legislative agendas. Over the next four decades, this extreme partisan polarization contributed to an excessive use of the filibuster by large minorities, including, on occasions, the entire minority party. Beginning with its 2013 session, the Senate faced the urgent challenge of making long-needed changes, such as eliminating filibusters on routine procedural motions, while preserving its stature as a place for sober second thought, a place where the simple possibility of filibusters will continue to force senators to strive for consensus.[4]

The enactment of the 1968 Fair Housing bill, last of the major civil rights measures, had profound effects on the Senate; even that body's most savvy members did not immediately recognize its significance. The new law cleared the once-thick portfolio of civil rights legislation so long demanded. The years ahead presented agonizing problems for African Americans and other minorities, but the great struggle over federal legislation was over. There were no pending civil rights measures for Southern senators to filibuster. Within a few years, they came to realize that the filibuster was no longer their special weapon for protecting what they called the "Southern way of life." The recently enacted bills, especially the 1965 Voting Rights Act, were changing the South dramatically, and Southern senators who had so long stifled the hopes of their black constituents soon found themselves anxiously currying favor, trying to win their votes. This extraordinary transformation had effects as well on other senators, many of whom had vilified the filibuster as the tool of racism. With the taint of racial prejudice largely washed away, the filibuster became for them a handy instrument for their own purposes.

In time, with every senator now free to indulge without embarrassment, the filibuster came into such regular use that senators sponsoring any bill of substance found they had to muster enough votes to invoke cloture to halt the almost automatic filibuster. At the same time, the techniques of filibustering had become so foreshortened that the old-time filibusters of the past, some lasting months, ceased to exist. Indeed, in this new parliamentary world, the senators gradually evolved a variation of the filibuster called the "hold," a tactic under which any senator objecting to a bill or a nomination could prevent Senate action merely by informing his party's floor leader privately that he wished the matter delayed, sometimes indefinitely. This development alarmed many, including senators, for these dilatory excesses were pushing the Senate toward legislative anarchy.

For the first few years following its surge of civil rights legislation, the Senate operated under its earlier complicated methods, and under those methods the Senate dealt with an extraordinary presidential nomination: President Johnson's choice for a new chief justice of the United States. In June 1968, just a few weeks after passage of the open housing bill, Earl Warren privately informed President Johnson that he wished to retire as chief justice. Before Johnson had time to choose a successor, a freshman senator, Robert Griffin of Michigan, resolved to block whomever he chose.[5] Johnson had declined to run for reelection, and Senator Griffin wanted the new chief justice chosen by the incoming president, who as likely as not would be a fellow Republican. He decided to defeat Johnson's nominee, no matter who that was, with a filibuster.[6]

This was an appointment of enormous significance, and Johnson acted with his usual shrewdness. He invited Senate Republican leader Everett Dirksen to the White House to help him pick the candidate. With Dirksen's public endorsement, Johnson's nominee would have little trouble winning Senate confirmation. Dirksen also served as the ranking Republican on the Senate's Judiciary Committee, thereby becoming a key player for the opposition party on such matters.

At the White House, the two talked over the choices for ninety minutes. "You got any suggestions?" Johnson began. "You ought to have suggestions," Dirksen replied. Among those they considered were Cyrus Vance, then in Paris negotiating with the Vietnamese; Treasury Secretary Henry Fowler; and a senior federal judge in Illinois whom Dirksen suggested. Finally Johnson proposed his close friend, Abe Fortas, already on the high court as an associate justice. Dirksen approved. He would be easier to confirm than anyone from outside the court. Dirksen dismissed Senator Griffin's maneuvers. "There will be a little ruckus," Dirksen said. "He'll be confirmed, period."[7]

Even before Johnson announced his choice, Griffin had quickly lined up eighteen other Republican senators to sign a round-robin statement declaring that the new chief justice should be chosen by the president taking office in January 1969. They were prepared to block anyone else with what Griffin called "extended discussions" in the Senate. Griffin had calculated that with his committed Republican colleagues he already had the wherewithal to reject cloture on their filibuster. He was sure that almost all the Southern Democrats would join them automatically, in their traditional response, to oppose cloture, as would at least a few of the Democrats from the small states who routinely and steadfastly opposed the tactic. Only belatedly did Dirksen realize how poorly he had miscalculated. By late September, Griffin had taken most of the Republicans away from Dirksen, and Dirksen found himself scrambling to escape his earlier commitment. In the end, he joined Griffin in openly opposing Fortas. Griffin's filibustering strategy ultimately caused Fortas to abandon the fight.

The decline of the filibuster as a weapon against civil rights legislation accelerated following the 1971 death of Georgia's segregationist Senator Richard Russell. His obvious successor as leader of the Southern Caucus was John Stennis of Mississippi, a talented parliamentarian of great personal probity. Stennis immediately confronted problems beyond his control. For one, the caucus was itself disintegrating. Under varied new pressures, including the voting rights legislation, it had already lost six members, and would soon be losing more. The once-solid Democratic South was turning Republican. Even more important, Stennis, that champion of unrestricted debate, found himself forced to ask the Senate to invoke cloture on a filibuster he believed risked the safety of the nation.

By 1968, America's commitment to the war in Vietnam had become so unpopular that Lyndon Johnson backed off running for reelection, and Richard Nixon, in his quest for the Republican nomination, announced he had a "secret" plan to end the war.[8] Three years later, in 1971, with Nixon as president, the war still raged on, casualties continued to mount, and many senators wanted to stop the killing. The vehicle at hand was Nixon's request for a two-year extension of the military draft, due to lapse at the end of June. Senator Stennis, as chairman of the Senate's Armed Services Committee, sponsored the new legislation. After formal hearings, he presented the bill to the Senate in early May, and Senator Mike Gravel of Alaska, a liberal Democrat, promptly announced his intention to defeat the draft with a filibuster. "If thirty-four senators hang tough," he said, "we will have no draft. That is all I seek."[9] Stennis replied that such a sudden ending of the draft would devastate the military and the 525,000 US troops then in Vietnam.[10] Gravel had many allies. Senators William Proxmire and Harold Hughes were openly supportive from the start. They and other non-Southern Democrats were changing their views of the filibuster. "I for one do not consider the filibuster horrendous," said Senator Alan Cranston of California, who also supported Gravel. "I think the draft and Vietnam far worse. I look upon the filibuster as a means, not an end."[11] This was a new attitude from senators so long appalled at how their Southern colleagues had used the filibuster.

Debate on eliminating the draft, often intense, continued week after week, but not sustained by merely dilatory tactics and long-winded speeches.

The draft been extended four times since 1951 and the Korean War, in each instance by lopsided Senate approval. This time was different, and senator after senator had amendments to offer, some for withdrawing troops, others for ending the war altogether—so many that Gravel and his fellow filibusterers scarcely needed to speak at all. Stennis and his allies defended the legislation, and they had President Nixon backing them. At last, Stennis had to call a halt. With immense reluctance, he did something he had never done before: he offered a motion to invoke cloture on the ongoing filibuster. "As everyone knows," he told the Senate, "I do not have enthusiasm about a motion for cloture." He did so now, he said, only out of dire necessity. This bill had to pass. He tried to minimize what he was doing. This was after all, he said, "purely a question of procedure."[12]

Purely a question of procedure? So was the filibuster. So were all the precedents and practices the Senate had accumulated over the decades that guided and controlled how senators conducted their legislative business. For senators from the South, voting against cloture was more than political dogma; it was patriotic and heroic, defending the South's way of life. Stennis had never before voted for cloture; neither had a dozen of his colleagues before this year. Now he was asking them, in this changed Senate, to vote with him. Enough of them did and Stennis's motion carried, sixty-one to thirty. The group voting in the affirmative included such stalwarts of the Old South as Mississippi's James Eastland and South Carolina's Strom Thurmond. In the turnaround, most of those now in opposition were Democratic liberals. This was a dramatic break with the past, evocative of a Senate in transition.

Even before this shift by senators from the South, the filibuster was becoming much more commonplace than in earlier years. More and more senators were exploiting the filibuster for their own purposes. They obviously felt freer to use the filibuster, or the threat of filibuster, to attack any question they opposed. In the final months of the 1970 session, for example, senators were filibustering all sorts of pending matters, ranging from foreign aid and welfare reform to the supersonic transport plane and national defense appropriations. "We are having filibusters," complained Senator Mansfield, the majority leader, "and filibusters on filibusters, and filibusters within filibusters. Some people are against everything and will talk to defeat anything."[13] This parliamentary confusion deeply troubled Mansfield; he openly worried that the Senate was reducing itself to what he called "an innocuous House of Lords."[14]

The confusing and often conflicting filibusters so muddied the Senate's deliberations that Mansfield agreed to try a scheme to lessen their impact.

Every one of them, while in operation, normally halted all other Senate action. West Virginia's Robert Byrd, the Democratic whip and by now a skilled parliamentarian, suggested that in these circumstances the party leaders have authority to set aside the filibustered matter to take up other legislation and then, in due course, return later to the filibuster.[15] Mansfield adopted a two-track system to let the Senate complete some matters even while a filibuster otherwise stymied the chamber. This plan made filibustering even easier than under Mansfield's already relaxed management, and tended to increase the number of filibusters, but it certainly made them less painful and less frustrating. Filibusters no longer froze the Senate automatically in gridlock.[16]

Following the cloture vote on extending the draft, the Senate had only three senators who had never voted for cloture: Arkansas' John McClellan and Louisiana's Allen Ellender, two veteran filibusterers; and a new freshman Democrat, Alabama's James Allen. The filibuster against the draft had also altered the attitude of some of the Senate's longtime reformers. Since the early 1950s, they had been pressing to lower the margin to invoke cloture from the original two-thirds of those voting to three-fifths, the difference in a full Senate between sixty-seven votes in the old form and sixty. Senator Frank Church had led the fight in early 1971 to try to set the lower number, but now he said he was ready to eat his words. The filibuster, he argued, could prove "a most useful tool" in the years ahead.[17] Clearly, the filibuster as a parliamentary procedure was under review.

"Change is in the air," Senator Mansfield warned his colleagues, "and we cannot avoid it, much less ignore it." Unless the cloture rule was modified, he said, the "new voices" would succeed in setting a mere majority to invoke cloture. "I warn the Senate," he said. "The basic character of the Senate as a deliberative body . . . will be a thing of the past."[18] He asked his colleagues to accept the three-fifths compromise or risk adoption of simple majority rule and the loss of the Senate's power and prestige.

Senators blocked reform on cloture then and again in 1973 at the opening of the next Senate. In the Senate of 1969–70, the leaders had moved for cloture six times; in the Senate of 1971–72, twenty times, a startling increase; and two years later, the number had jumped to thirty-one. This brought a new attempt to amend the Senate's procedures when the Ninety-sixth Senate convened in January 1975.

These moves alarmed the Southerners. After ten days of back-and-forth squabbling, Louisiana's Russell Long offered a somewhat surprising compromise on behalf of those Southerners: cloture by three-fifths of all senators, not just those present, except on changing the Senate's rules when a vote of two-thirds of those present would still be required. Under Long's proposal, cloture would need sixty "aye" votes to invoke in the one-hundred-member Senate no matter how few senators actually voted.

Senator Mansfield and the others seeking change quickly agreed to Long's suggestion. The principal exception was Alabama's James Allen, who had already made himself a master of parliamentary obstruction. He showered the 1975 proceedings with an extraordinary array of dilatory maneuvers: quorum calls, motions to reconsider, challenges of rulings, and ingenious diversions to stall any final action. After five weeks of parliamentary scrambling, Robert Byrd took charge and moved for cloture. The vote was seventy-three to twenty-one, with seven Southern Democrats voting "aye." Senator Allen had put on a spectacular display of dilatory maneuvers, but he gave up once cloture was invoked. Then the Senate, on March 7, 1975, passed the pending resolution fifty-six to twenty-seven.[19]

By that margin, the Senate provided that thereafter it could halt filibusters with a mere sixty votes, a long-desired reform. There was much more couched in that vote, however, than just an easier way to stifle filibusters. With the Senate's new practice of frequently applying filibusters on pending matters, it then became necessary to gather sixty votes for cloture before an up-or-down final vote. That meant, in reality, that to approve any matter of importance the sponsors needed to muster a super-majority. An ordinary majority was not enough. This was a dramatic break with the Senate's past, one that would complicate the Senate's proceedings for decades to come.[20]

In 1975 alone, under the changed rule, the Senate again endured a flood of filibusters and threats of filibusters that prompted twenty-three cloture motions. James Allen continued in these struggles to hone his skills in dilatory tactics, By the year's end, he had found, remarkably, what amounted to a technical flaw in Rule 22 that allowed him or any other senator to continue filibustering indefinitely even after cloture had been invoked. He was experimenting in post-cloture filibustering, and in 1976 his experiments came to fruition.

Under the 1975 rule, once the Senate voted cloture, every senator had one hour each for debate, seemingly an absolute limit. The rule, did not apply, however, to time taken for Senate votes, quorum calls, or reading the texts of proposed amendments. In a moment of special insight, Senator Allen realized that those exemptions could be exploited into a new form of post-cloture filibustering. In June 1976, he put his new concept to the test. The Senate had voted cloture on an antitrust enforcement bill, and Allen started a post-cloture filibuster by calling up pending amendments to the bill. On each amendment, he demanded a roll call vote, each of which took at least fifteen minutes, and then, after that vote, another vote on reconsidering the previous vote.[21] At every stage, Allen demanded quorum calls, and each of them lasted until the needed number of senators showed up. None of this counted against his allotted one hour, and he was prepared to continue indefinitely day after day. "Cloture," he warned in wicked understatement, "may not be the easiest way to get a bill passed."[22]

Allen's scheme amounted to little more than taking an existing rule and treating it in an ingenious new way. Over the decades, the Senate had frequently voted on amendments to a bill on which cloture had been invoked. On the 1964 civil rights bill, for example, the Senate had 560 amendments pending after cloture, and senators spent a full week voting on ninety-nine of them before finally passing the bill. No one then thought of using those amendments as a way to continue the filibuster indefinitely to kill the bill. That was the flaw in the rule that Senator Allen had spotted. His shrewd insight attracted little attention outside the Senate, but within the Senate this was a matter of great moment.

Later that year, Allen undertook another post-cloture filibuster, this time against a bill authorizing fees for civil rights attorneys, and South Dakota's James Abourezk, paid close attention. He stated publicly that he and several of his colleagues had "learned their lessons very well from the senator from Alabama" and would themselves use Allen's techniques for their own purposes. He had taught them something worth remembering.

The Congress that convened in 1977 received a telling parliamentary challenge in the form of President Jimmy Carter's energy legislation. Carter submitted a flawed bill that lacked a natural constituency. Powerful special interests quickly moved to oppose it. An earlier vote showed that the Senate favored deregulating federal controls on natural gas, but not Carter's plan, and this dismayed Senator Abourezk and his new freshman ally, Ohio's irascible Howard Metzenbaum. By their calculations, the opposition's substitute, if adopted, would cost consumers many tens of billions of dollars over the next few years. They undertook to defeat it with a lethal filibuster, utilizing Senator Allen's post-cloture techniques. In preparation, Abourezk and Metzenbaum introduced 508 amendments, almost all of them technical changes and all of them presumably eligible for consideration after cloture had been invoked.

Robert Byrd, as newly installed Democratic majority leader, vowed that the Senate would act. To cut off Abourezk and Metzenbaum, he moved for cloture and, two days later, on September 26, 1977, the Senate voted to end debate, seventy-seven to seventeen. Abourezk and Metzenbaum then launched their plan of harassment, calling up amendments from their stash, insisting that the Senate clerk read them in full—some as long as twenty pages, and demanding quorum calls between roll call votes. Drawing from his kit-bag of time-tested tactics, Byrd tried to break their filibuster by holding the Senate in session overnight on September 27–28. Senior senators were catnapping on cots set up in offices ringing the Senate chamber. In this first all-night session in more than a dozen years, Abourezk and Metzenbaum forced no fewer than thirty-eight calls of the Senate's roll.[23] There was little sleep for anyone. Byrd tried to negotiate a compromise, but nothing dissuaded the two filibusterers as they pursued their campaign with assistance from other senators. Their thirteen-day battle enraged Byrd and moved him to conceive an ingenious plan to crush the frustrating offensive. What he did no one had ever done before, and his actions triggered a wild melee in the Senate chamber by outraged senators of both parties.

Byrd had concocted his stratagem several weeks earlier when the new vice president, Walter Mondale, had ineptly recognized another senator to speak ahead of Senate Republican Leader Howard Baker, who was on his feet seeking recognition. Byrd was furious. This was a violation of his and Baker's prerogatives as leaders. Byrd unleashed on Mondale a long-remembered tongue-lashing. "When several senators seek recognition," he lectured the vice president, "the leadership will be accorded that recognition."[24] Byrd had decided to claim a right to preemptive recognition as the club to beat down this filibuster.[25] Abourezk and Metzenbaum had perfected Senator Allen's post-cloture filibuster to a new level of legislative obstruction, a tangle seemingly beyond unraveling. With Mondale in the chair to make the rulings, armed with a point-of-order-confirmed agreement that the presiding officer, operating under cloture, must strike down "all amendments which are dilatory or which on their face are out of order," Byrd made his move on October 3.[26]

He had briefed Mondale on his scheme to avoid "endless roll calls that could otherwise consume weeks" and had handed him a typewritten sheet of responses he was to make.[27] Byrd would claim the floor and make motion after motion, allowing no interference from other senators as the vice president dutifully did his part. After some preliminaries as the Senate took up again the day's business, Byrd addressed the chair.

"I call up amendment number eight-nine-oh," he said.

"It is not in order," Mondale responded.[28]

Byrd called up another and another and another. To each, Mondale replied the same way. Stunned senators started shouting protests. Abourezk tried to appeal Mondale's rulings, but the vice president ignored him. To be heard, Byrd and Mondale had to raise their voices in their strange singsong duet. With their high-handed tactics, they blocked any appeal, a grave violation of Senate practice.[29] Maine's Edmund Muskie was trying to be heard. Maryland's Paul Sarbanes shouted, "Outrageous!"[30] The Senate's floor was bedlam, and still Byrd and Mondale carried on, killing amendment after amendment. The Senate's majority leader and the vice president, in this utterly unprecedented duet, took nine minutes to dismiss thirty-three of the Abourezk-Metzenbaum amendments as delaying and not in order. They did this to a wild chorus of senators yelling their disapproval.

A dozen senators shouted for recognition. Muskie bewailed Byrd's arbitrary changing of the Senate's rule—initiating "a new order of things."[31] When Byrd finally spoke, he was as angry, he confessed later, as he had ever been in his life. He excoriated his critics for their negligence of the dangers of the post-cloture filibusters, which he alone was trying to correct. He acknowledged that he had taken "extraordinary advantage" of his right, as leader, to priority recognition. "One has to fight fire with fire," he said, "when all else fails."[32]

More quietly, Byrd assured the senators he would never again use that tactic. Abourezk and Metzenbaum gave up their filibuster, complaining that they had received no help from President Carter, whose legislation they had tried to protect. Later, Byrd assessed this as "the roughest filibuster I have experienced during my thirty-one years in the Senate, and it produced the most bitter feelings."[33]

In institutional terms, this struggle had far-reaching effects on the Senate and its leaders. Senator Howard Baker now shared Byrd's alarm over the post-cloture filibuster and worked with his counterpart to find a solution. More important, Byrd's claim of his leadership prerogative to preferential recognition moved that to the status of an absolute right, far beyond the simple courtesy Vice President Garner had initiated so many years before. Byrd would use this right again, as would those who followed him as leaders of the Senate. Future majority leaders would use this prerogative not just to remove a few out-of-order amendments, but to control the Senate's entire amending process.

The day after the Senate passed its version of the energy bill in the fall of 1977, Byrd and Baker acted to seek a legitimate way to halt future post-cloture filibusters. They created separate ad hoc committees of Democratic and Republican senators to study the problem and propose appropriate changes to Rule 22. The floor leaders acted partly to cool the anger of their colleagues and partly to come to terms with the post-cloture filibuster. As things turned out, the ad hoc committees failed to meet or to draft recommendations. Filibusters ran on unheeded as before, although early in 1979, the Senate would vote seventy-eight to sixteen to limit post-cloture filibusters to no more than one hundred hours after cloture, no matter how many amendments were at hand.[34]

Some months before that, in the spring of 1978, Utah's Orrin Hatch and Indiana's Richard Lugar, both freshmen Republicans, undertook a sophisticated filibuster to defeat organized labor's prime legislative goal, a complex bill to revise the nation's labor laws. First, they relied on traditional tactics—much talk, quorum calls, and all the other dilatory maneuvers. They copied the Southerners' old strategy of creating three platoons, each of a half-dozen senators, to spell each other over the next several weeks. Next they adopted Senator Allen's post-cloture strategy, introducing more than 1,200 amendments with which to continue their filibuster indefinitely. Robert Byrd tried six times to invoke cloture and failed.

This victory by conservative Republicans was the most notable that they had so far achieved, and the editors of *Congressional Quarterly* concluded that Republican filibustering had changed the dynamics of the Senate's legislating. The Republicans, they said, "had retrieved for themselves a weapon of enormous legislative importance," so important that now, for practical purposes, the Senate could not approve any controversial measure without producing a sixty-vote super-majority. The younger Republicans took a provocative attitude toward their responsibilities. "We just don't filibuster for the hell of it," said Nevada's Paul Laxalt, the Republican who led the 1977–78 fight against the Panama Canal treaties. They had made the filibuster a matter of everyday life in the Senate. Even the mere threat of a filibuster had become a serious matter for those trying to pass legislation.[35]

Meanwhile, in an extraordinary development, there evolved in the Senate what amounted to a new short-circuit form of filibuster, one that spared its users even the bother of showing up on the Senate floor to block whatever they wanted blocked. This was the "hold." Originally intended as only a common courtesy to senators, the hold allowed any senator to inform his or her party's floor leader that he or she wished a nomination or other matter set aside for the time being. For decades, under its traditions of senatorial courtesy and mutual deference, the Senate had acceded to such requests. This casual and informal arrangement, however, did not last through the growing partisanship in the Senate in the 1970s. Senators from that time began to treat this common courtesy more like a right, and to use it as a weapon in their parliamentary struggles.[36]

At the beginning of the 1970s, the two party leaders had the option of honoring hold requests or ignoring them. By the end of the decade, however, the hold, like the filibuster, had become an instrument of senatorial power, and senators expected their holds to hold. For a while, the hold proved useful to the party leaders as a sign of a member's intention to filibuster. That offered party leaders a special insight on how to plan the Senate's schedule. Later, the hold became a virtual filibuster itself, blocking indefinitely the targeted bill or nomination. To break this hold, with its implicit message of the requestor's determination to block unanimous consent agreements, vital to the Senate smooth procedural operation, the Senate leader had to invoke cloture, just as with a regular filibuster. What made the hold tellingly effective was the anonymity of the senator or senators invoking that hold. The senator informed the party leader privately of his or her hold, thus escaping any counterattack or maneuver from those sponsoring the matter involved.

As the tactic came into more regular use, senators broadened the ways they used it. One of these was private retaliation for past offenses. The original hold, politically innocuous in that it sought delay only in order to obtain additional information, became known as "the Mae West hold," as in her familiar "Come up and see me some time." Far more complicated were those called "blanket holds," and "block holds," which stopped all action in entire fields of legislation. Some of these amounted to private conspiracies by groups of senators willing to reassert a hold that a colleague had been forced to withdraw, thus continuing the frustration. They went under such names as "rolling holds," "revolving holds," "ping-pong holds," "fuzzy holds," and "hand-to-hand holds." In time, senators began to use the hold as a device to force action in totally unrelated matters, such as blocking diplomatic nominations in order to force, for example, the secretary of agriculture to consult with the senator on a farm problem. This amounted to political blackmail, a form of extortion. Less flagrantly, senators invoked the hold in an attempt to force legislative concessions, much as they used a formal filibuster or threat of filibuster. Early in 2010, Kentucky's Jim Bunning, a practiced wielder of the hold, used it to delay extensions of unemployment and health insurance for millions of people, thereby becoming a reviled symbol of hold abuse. A year later, the Senate, under intense criticism, voted ninety-two to four to abolish the secret hold.[37]

By the mid-1980s, obstructionism had become commonplace in the Senate, dramatically changing the nature of what senators still liked to call the world's greatest deliberative body. Filibusters, the threat of filibusters, and the use of holds had made the Senate a far more partisan place than before. Party strategists looked to election years now as a chance to win enough seats to give their senators a sixty-vote, "filibuster-proof" majority. Not until 2009–10 would this happen—and then only briefly—but with significant legislative results.

In the 1980 elections, the Republicans defeated enough Democrats to gain a majority in the Senate for the first time since 1954. That did not slow the use of the filibuster in the coming Congress. Long out of power, the Republicans had their own legislative agenda, at least parts of which would automatically trigger filibuster after filibuster. These filibusters started in June 1981, when Jesse Helms offered a tough anti-school-busing amendment. This was only one of several similar controversies as South Carolina's Strom Thurmond and other party conservatives pushed their measures on the Senate's attention. In 1982, they caused Majority Leader Baker recurring legislative nightmares. The filibusters began to mount in the spring and ran on, one measure after another, for the rest of the year. So tangled was the Senate in filibusters that Baker had to call a lame-duck session after the November elections. "You're uniquely at the mercy of a few people who want to obstruct," he complained.[38]

The postelection period proved even more divisive. North Carolina's Helms had already deeply annoyed senators by his parliamentary antics. At one point, Arkansas' Dale Bumpers in debate mistakenly called Helms "the senator from South Carolina." He quickly corrected himself. Then he apologized to South Carolina.[39] New filibusters strained tempers. Senators forgot normal courtesies, shouting at each other in disparaging terms. They prevented the Senate from adjourning for the year until two days before Christmas. There was much talk, within the Senate and without, about the need to change the body's rules and ways. As the Senate's leader, Howard Baker had already taken preliminary action at least to consider doing just that.

Under a Senate resolution the previous spring, Baker had appointed two former senators, Kansas's James Pearson and Connecticut's Abraham Ribicoff, both highly respected, to undertake a year's study of the Senate's operations and then submit recommendations for improvements. They filed their report in April 1983, and the Senate's Rules Committee held brief hearings on their recommendations.[40] They proposed several changes in floor procedures: to eliminate holds and to allow each senator to propose only two amendments after cloture. By then, the Senate's daily sessions had reached such a sorry shape that the Senate's chaplain opened one day's meeting with a prayer asking God's help to save the Senate from becoming like Humpty Dumpty, "so frustrated and fragmented that no one will be able to put it together again."[41] Even so, even in these dire circumstances, the Rules Committee did nothing about the Pearson-Ribicoff recommendations, and neither did the Senate.

In early 1984, at the instigation of Indiana's Senator Dan Quayle, the Senate created a select committee, with Quayle as chairman, to study anew the Senate's procedure and practices.[42] By November, the committee members had a report ready for the opening of the next Congress in January. Again they went after the filibuster, this time suggesting a more difficult way to invoke cloture but making it easier to enforce once invoked. "Filibuster and cloture were meant for great issues," Quayle stated, "but they have been trivialized as recent history clearly demonstrates."[43] As with the Pearson-Ribicoff proposals, the Quayle committee's recommendations were discussed and then ignored.

Senate Republicans met in caucus on November 28, 1984, and picked Senator Robert Dole as their new leader. As majority leader–designate and in the spirit of the recent Quayle committee report, Dole invited all senators, Democrats and Republicans, to an unusual meeting a week later to consider ways to improve what he called the "quality of life" in the Senate. The session was informal and private; even staff assistants were excluded. Some seventy senators attended, and they discussed a variety of their frustrations, including filibusters and holds. By that time, senators were using holds literally to veto pending bills and nominations. To put a stop to this, the senators agreed to arrangements that would identify which members were secretly blocking action. In practice, however, this nonbinding attempt at reform had little effect, either then or for the coming quarter century.

In November 1985, Senator Thomas Eagleton of Missouri pronounced an extraordinary indictment on all senators for the sorry state of the Senate's deliberations. "The Senate is now in the state of incipient anarchy," he began. "The filibuster, once used, by and large, as an occasional exercise in civil rights matters, has now become a routine frolic in almost all matters. Whereas our rules were devised to guarantee full and free debate, they now guarantee unbridled chaos." Eagleton was fifty-six years old, at the height of his career, completing his third six-year term in the Senate, and he told his colleagues that he would not again seek reelection partly because of the

Senate's procedural frustrations and gridlock. "We, the great deliberators, are deliberating ourselves into national ridicule and embarrassment," he said.[44]

The question of changing the rules for limiting debate came up sooner than anyone expected. In February 1986, during the debate over whether to allow gavel-to-gavel television coverage of its proceedings, senators expressed alarm because of the filibuster. "Just how silly are we going to look?" protested Bennett Johnston of Louisiana. "We're not going to look good."[45] The viewing public would not tolerate the repetitive debates, the seemingly endless quorum calls. The Senate's procedures, he argued, were "a messy, untidy spectacle to watch, but . . . vital to the nation." Opening the Senate to television, he said, conceivably could add pressures for rules changes that would reduce its debate to mere five-minute speeches, as in the House of Representatives.[46]

For all the talk and worry about speeding up the Senate's procedures to meet the faster pace of television, the senators made only two minor changes in the rules. One was to reduce the post-cloture debate limit from one hundred to thirty hours. The other was to deny debate on approving each day the Senate's journal of the previous day, long a favorite target of some of the Senate's most talented filibusterers.[47] Despite these changes, filibusters went on in the Senate, only now on national television.

In the 1986 elections, the Democrats regained their majority over the Republicans by a fifty-four to forty-six margin, and the filibuster took on added meaning. As Republican minority leader, Robert Dole had to challenge Democratic proposals, and he relied on the filibuster whenever the need arose. For Dole, that was a powerful tool. Senator Byrd, restored as majority leader, but without the sixty party votes needed to invoke cloture, suffered the legislative frustrations that Dole had the talent and ability to inflict.

In the opening months of 1987, Dole and his Republican colleagues undertook four filibusters in a row against a variety of Democratic proposals on such measures as cutting off aid to rebels in Nicaragua and election campaign financing. By the time of the August recess, they had forced fifteen cloture votes, and they were threatening many other Democratic bills. Senator Byrd and his fellow Democrats protested this blatant obstructionism by the Republicans as "scorched earth" tactics.

Yet, these filibusters were hardly in the mold of the Senate's classic talk-fests. The flamboyance was gone. No senator took on the chore of talking for hours and hours until he or she could be relieved by another filibusterer. Byrd had the Senate meeting each morning at nine o'clock and adjourning late that afternoon. Using the double-track legislative system, he frequently set aside the bill under challenge to take up noncontroversial matters. Much of the time counted as part of the filibustering actually was spent on hourslong quorum calls while negotiations took place in back offices. Television viewers witnessed a Senate that seemed suspended. The World's Greatest Deliberative Body sustained a public-relations black eye.

The Senate's nominal majority no longer ruled. In those first fifteen filibusters of 1987, the majority Democrats succeeded only once in invoking cloture, and that was on a bill to give senators a salary increase. The minority Republicans had what Senator Richard Lugar called two "magic numbers": with thirty-four votes they could keep Congress from overriding any veto by President Reagan, and with forty-one votes they could block cloture on their filibusters. "We're not going to be content to be spectators," said Mississippi's Thad Cochran, an activist Republican senator.[48]

These guerrilla tactics and the extraordinary frequency of filibusters and threat of filibusters had forced a change that was not part of the rules. In the past, with a filibuster under way, the party leader hesitated to ask prematurely for cloture. He had to wait until senators had debated the matter for some time. Otherwise, senators were reluctant to vote for cloture. Now, however, the sponsors of any matter threatened with filibuster moved for cloture even as they asked the Senate to start the debate.[49] The Senate's heavy workload denied them the luxury of keeping to the more leisurely approach, but, more important, the successful filibuster no longer depended on the talent of the filibusterers to keep talking endlessly. The real fight was on mustering sixty votes for cloture. Senator Byrd, who revered the Senate, grieved at this trivializing of the Senate's procedures to what he called "the point of ridiculousness."[50]

In January 1989, at the start of the 101st Congress, Senator Byrd yielded his floor leadership post to Maine's George Mitchell. Over the past nine years, Byrd had undertaken a series of speeches on the history of the Senate, an extraordinary set of lectures published in two volumes by the Senate in 1988 and 1991.[51] Despite all the harassment and frustration he had suffered from filibusters, Byrd roundly defended the filibuster in those Senate speeches as "the main cornerstone of the Senate's uniqueness." He cited the abuses, painful at times, but argued that the filibuster, the right of unlimited debate, had made the Senate the most powerful legislative body in the world. "Without the right of unlimited debate, of course, there would be no filibusters, but there would also be no Senate, as we know it," he said. "The good outweighs the bad, and not all filibusters have been bad, even though they may have been exasperating. . . . Filibusters are a necessary evil, which must be tolerated lest the Senate lose its special strength and become a mere appendage of the House of Representatives."[52]

With those words, Senator Byrd neatly described why he and other senators shrank from drastically altering Rule 22 even to remedy the debilitating legislative chaos into which the Senate was plunging. To them, the alternative seemed worse, but now the job of keeping the Senate constructively engaged fell to Senator Mitchell. He would hold that post for six years, never free from the discord and disarray of his filibustering colleagues.

Following Democrat Bill Clinton's 1992 election to the presidency, Republican leader Robert Dole let him and the nation know that he could expect not much from the Senate. For starters, he denied that Clinton, elected with less than a popular majority, had any mandate whatsoever. Dole argued that this justified refusing Clinton the traditional honeymoon that Congress normally offered each new president. For this strident opposition, Dole would rely primarily on the filibuster, an extraordinary elevation of this dilatory tactic. Never before had the Senate's minority party as a matter of party policy chosen to depend on the filibuster.

Dole's strategy had brought him new national attention as the president's principal Republican opponent, and much speculation that he was emerging as Clinton's likely presidential opponent in 1996. In a legislative body whose normal pace ranged from slow to stop, Dole now commanded great power. Part of this stemmed from his parliamentary skills and political nerve, but principally it flowed from his willingness to use the filibuster to carry out his purposes. Senate filibusters in this form and to this purpose proliferated over the following decade, lifted on ao current of ever increasing partisanship. The filibuster had made the minority party, Democratic or Republican, a far more effective force than it might otherwise have been.

These developments fueled a dangerous confrontation in 2005, as the Senate's Republican majority leadership, frustrated at Democratic efforts to block President George W. Bush's conservative slate of appeals court nominees, dusted off the parliamentary tactic known to its advocates as the "constitutional option." They so labeled it because they believed it derived from an authority superior to any Senate rule. Democrats, in opposition, adopted the term *nuclear option*, because of the explosive consequences of its use. As both sides saw it, this parliamentary procedure would begin with a senator moving to amend the rules by lowering the cloture requirement from sixty to a simple majority. That would surely ignite a filibuster. Those supporting the motion would seek cloture. If more than a majority, but fewer than sixty senators voted for cloture, the presiding officer could announce that cloture had been adopted by a simple majority vote. This would trigger an appeal to the full Senate to reverse the chair's ruling. If a simple majority sustained the ruling, it would make majority cloture a binding precedent of the Senate. As two seasoned observers of Senate floor procedure observed, "A simple majority could set a new Senate precedent that would alter the operation of the Standing Rule while leaving its text untouched."[53]

Angry Democrats warned that if the Republicans executed this plan, the resulting explosion would annihilate the Senate "as we have known it." Republicans justified this extreme step to counter what they claimed was an unprecedented campaign to filibuster judicial nominations. In this, they overlooked their own party's 1968 extended debate against the nomination of Abe Fortas to be chief justice of the United States.

The decision to pull the "nuclear" trigger lay with Majority Leader William Frist, who had suddenly risen to that high office as a consensus candidate following Republican leader Trent Lott's abrupt resignation from the position. Senate traditionalists feared that Frist might be tempted to execute that plan. Ultimately, a bipartisan "Gang of Fourteen" senators emerged to defuse the issue. With the Senate divided among fifty-five Republicans and forty-five Democrats (including one Independent who caucused with the Democrats), the withholding of six Republican votes would prevent a simple majority vote to establish majority cloture. The seven Republicans agreed that they would withhold the votes necessary to invoke the nuclear, or constitutional, option, and the seven Democrats would deny their party's leadership the votes necessary to sustain filibusters of judicial nominees. The deal included a safety valve that permitted any of the fourteen senators to opt out of the agreement in what an individual might define as "extraordinary circumstances." Under that agreement, five of the ten filibustered nominees were allowed to be confirmed. Later, the fourteen agreed to support the Supreme Court nomination of Samuel Alito, forestalling a likely filibuster. Any chance that the Republicans might invoke the nuclear option during the following congressional session ended with the 2006 elections, which returned majority control to the Democrats.

Over the next six years, however, an increasingly steadfast Republican minority took up the filibuster tool as recently sharpened by the Democrats to produce legislative stalemate throughout the early years of Barack Obama's presidency. Even its most stalwart advocates acknowledged that the filibuster was being abused and overused. Senate partisanship seemed sharper than before, with the exception of the immediate pre– and post–Civil War eras. Filibusters came on all sorts of measures, not all of them, initially, confrontations between Republicans and Democrats. But by 2009, with the Democrats temporarily wielding their long-sought sixty-vote majority—their first since 1968—party polarization seemed complete.[54] Not one of the forty Senate Republicans, nor for that matter any House Republican, broke party ranks to vote for the national health care reform legislation of 2010.

This situation revived discussion of remedies including the nuclear, or constitutional, option; the "talking filibuster"; and the "declining filibuster." Assistant Democratic leader Dick Durbin advocated the "talking filibuster" to prevent a senator who initiated a filibuster and started the thirty-hour post-cloture clock running from leaving the floor and thereby stopping the Senate cold. "What is suggested," Durbin argued, "is that if you believe [in] it, if it is important enough to stop the business of the Senate, for goodness sakes, stand up and tell us why. Defend yourself. Stand up for your principles."[55] Under this plan, one senator would be obligated to speak for seven hours and then find another twenty-three colleagues, each of whom would speak for an hour to fill the thirty-hour post-cloture debate requirement. Under a "declining filibuster," once debate has begun, the number of votes needed for cloture would successively be lowered until only a simple majority would be sufficient for passage.[56]

At the beginning of the 112th Congress in January 2011, Senate leaders forged a compromise under pressure from a public and senators angry at the interparty stalemates that prevented passage of every one of that fiscal year's thirteen appropriations bill, blocked adoption of the annual budget resolution, and left hundreds of House-passed bills and presidential nominees in Senate limbo. In the previous two Congresses, an astounding 33 percent of all Senate roll call votes had required a sixty-vote cloture margin to take place—three times that of just fifteen years earlier.[57] Recently elected members also beat the drums of reform. Many of those senators had previously served as majority-party members of the House of Representatives and were attracted to the relative efficiency of simple majority rule. The reformers had carefully studied the changes of the mid-1970s and the 2005 "constitutional option" debate and sought to change the Senate rules, including the sixty-vote cloture rule, by a simple majority vote on the first day of a new Congress. Against the reformers stood the minority-party Republicans, well aware, as Democratic minorities had been before them, of the protections offered by their ability to block legislation with forty-one votes. Senate

Republican Conference Chair Lamar Alexander, emphasizing the consensus-forming value of requiring sixty votes to move controversial legislation, observed that what the Senate needed was not a change in rules, but a "change in behavior."[58] Later, he added, "[A] great many of us feel that the Senate is a shadow of its former self in terms of its ability to function as a truly deliberative body." He recalled his service in the early 1980s as legislative assistant to Majority Leader Howard Baker. In those days, members were allowed to offer as many amendments as they wished, knowing that time pressures would eventually make it possible to get just one or two adopted. In more contemporary times, he lamented, the majority party began to limit amendments. The minority responded with filibusters and holds and other delaying tactics that spawned gridlock.[59]

Striving to avoid the bitterness that grew from that paralysis, Democratic floor leader Harry Reid and his Republican counterpart, Mitch McConnell, pledged to limit the use of the filibuster and to eliminate filibuster-spawning confirmation requirements for nearly one-third of the federal agency nominees subject to Senate approval. With the goal of encouraging more substantive debate and more votes on more amendments, the two floor leaders pledged to end two major delaying tactics: the secret hold and the practice of senators having legislative floor clerks read aloud amendments, some of them lengthy, now publicly available on the Internet. Reid further agreed to abandon the majority-party tactic of blocking minority-party members' efforts to freely pose amendments. For his part, McConnell pledged to limit Republican filibustering of Democratic efforts to bring up generally noncontroversial measures for debate. The leaders also agreed not to create a "constitutional option" precedent of permitting rules' changes at the start of a two-year congressional term by simple majority vote. Their pact appeared to be the most significant effort to address the management of extended debate since the Senate in 1975 lowered the cloture requirement from a two-thirds majority to sixty votes.[60]

In a colloquy extraordinary for its expression of interparty good will, Reid said, "Our discussion today is in the spirit of bipartisan cooperation to express hope and anticipation that the 112th Congress will be different in many ways than the 111th. We look forward to greater comity on both sides of the aisle so that we can move legislation and nominees that have bipartisan support from the majority of senators in this body."[61]

McConnell warmly endorsed Reid's call, observing, "Neither party has all the solutions to the problems our Nation faces."[62] In the management of filibusters and cloture, this appeared to be one of the Senate's rare moments of institutional self-adjustment. It raised hopes for a more functional Senate in the years ahead, but also a Senate that would continue to guarantee all of its members the essential requirement for extended debate. By mid-2012, however, under the intense pressure of renewed bipartisan wrangling, Reid disavowed his statement of cooperation. Many Reid-watchers realistically dismissed his change of position as the consequence of legislative combat fatigue. Perhaps fresh air of the coming session, or the one beginning in 2015, or 2017, would indeed bring overdue reforms to this slow-paced institution.[63]

Shortly before his death in 2010, Senator Robert Byrd referred to the vital importance of preserving the opportunity for extended debate. He cautioned, "We must never, ever, tear down the only wall—the necessary fence—this nation has against the excesses of the Executive Branch and the resultant haste and tyranny of the majority."[64]

TO THE FUTURE

THE US SENATE FACES GRAVE challenges as it moves through the twenty-first century. The Senate's challenges are the nation's challenges. They include a sluggish economy with chronic unemployment and a damaged housing market; a disproportionate distribution of income that gives 20 percent of the nation's population control of 84 percent of its wealth;[1] a trillion-dollar-plus annual budget deficit; unsustainable and unpopular military interventions that Congress chose not to fund with increased taxes or reduced spending; and the ever-present possibility of terrorist attacks. Meanwhile, the Senate, along with the House of Representatives—and, more broadly, the nation—has experienced a political realignment that has polarized both major parties and wiped out the middle ground for the compromises that are fundamental to all constructive lawmaking. In this climate, bipartisanship flickers only in small dark corners—a vast change from the two-party cooperation that approved Social Security in 1935, Medicare in 1964, and the Panama Canal treaties in 1978. These developments, along with an ideological push for smaller government and a pervasive sense that the nation's best days do not lie ahead, raise serious questions about the ability of the Senate—a creation of eighteenth-century political theorists—to respond effectively to the pressing needs of the twenty-first century.

For as long as there has been a Senate, it has lived in the shadow of its yesterdays. Visitors to today's US Capitol Building are guided into the beautifully restored Old Senate Chamber, a monument in crimson and gold to the Senate's nineteenth-century age of grand oratory, when that body prevailed over the House of Representatives and dictated to presidents. A short walk down the hall and around the corner, past the marble portrait busts of former vice presidents, is the richly frescoed Senate Reception Room, a historical pantheon to nine senatorial giants whose images are displayed in hopes of inspiring their modern successors. Each of those senators earned his place in that senatorial hall of fame "for acts of statesmanship transcending party and state lines," with statesmanship defined as "leadership in national thought and constitutional interpretation as well as legislation."[2] Nearby, in various senators-only quarters, are displayed imposing portraits in oil of those who have served as floor leaders over the past fifty years. No modern member is immune to a thorough grounding in the Senate's history, traditions, and culture—and wistfulness about the promises of that past.

Among the Senate's more senior members and observers are those who recall the body in the 1960s and '70s—a time of national turbulence and legislative challenge flowing from the assassination of President John F. Kennedy, Lyndon Johnson's "Great Society," the civil rights revolution, the awfulness of Vietnam, and the forced resignations of a vice president and president. One observer-participant believes that was the era of the "Last Great Senate."[3]

Coming from this concentration on successes of the past is a sense that those who are muddling through the present dangerous and upsetting times are falling short. Reformers have called for fundamental constitutional changes to make the government more responsive to majority opinion. One boldly suggests—and immediately concedes as "extremely unlikely"—"an end to the Electoral College, weighted in favor of the small states; a Senate based on population instead of the present system of representing states rather than people; and simultaneous elections and identical term lengths for president, representatives, and senators, replacing the staggered elections we now have and eliminating the distractions of midterm elections."[4] Others, more simply, look back to the original arrangement of having state legislatures elect senators.[5]

A growing chorus of popular opinion chants with increasing volume that today's Senate has become "dysfunctional." That widely accepted belief puts a burden on the definition of "dysfunctional": "incapable of serving the purpose for which it was devised."[6] What did the framers of the Constitution think they were doing in establishing a bicameral national legislature after their half-dozen years of experience with the single-chambered Congress under the Articles of Confederation? In this, they were following the model of most state legislatures, which had two chambers that could check on and refine or block one another's decisions. The framers also deliberately created a second chamber that represented all states equally, thereby giving the 10 percent of the nation's population that resides in half of those states 50 percent of the Senate's representational clout. Without this "Great Compromise," representing citizens equally in the House and states equally in the Senate, there likely would have been no US Constitution. What we know today as the United States of America could have ended up as the divided states of America, in some loose commercial union not unlike that of modern Europe. To guarantee the permanency of that large state–small state relationship, the framers embedded in Article V the assurance that "no State without its consent shall be deprived of its equal suffrage in the Senate."[7] So the Supreme Court can issue decisions affecting the structure of the nation's other representational bodies to assure "one person one vote," but never for the US Senate. From this inborn mal-apportionment comes the Senate's embedded charter to give full and fair—and extended—expression to minority points of view. And from this arrangement flows the Senate's most distinguishing characteristic—the filibuster.

Perhaps that structure made sense in the late eighteenth century, when it was devised, and possibly for the nineteenth century. But starting in the twentieth century, the United States of America began to be drawn into the world's woes and became vulnerable to the will of its friends and enemies. The necessary responses to these external challenges changed the power relationships between the United States and the rest of the world, and, at home, between the legislative and executive branches. In this age of terrorist-driven states with access to nuclear arsenals, does it still make sense to have as an integral part of the government an eighteenth-century debating society?

Yet the Senate has demonstrated that, with strong winds of national sentiment at its back, it can act quickly and decisively—if not always prudently, as its experience in adopting the Iraqi War Resolution in 2002 by a vote of seventy-seven to twenty-three reminds us. Like any other fallible human institution, the Senate will benefit from constant scrutiny and openness to revision. Over the decades since 1789, such change has come to the Senate at a seemingly glacial pace, with those seeking constructive reform always getting less than they wished. Popular election of senators required a century—more or less—to make its way into the Constitution. Formally elected Senate floor leaders emerged episodically during the first half of the twentieth century, culminating in the strong-armed leadership of Lyndon Johnson. After Johnson, and his Republican counterparts Robert Taft and

Everett Dirksen, principal leadership shifted decisively and permanently from multiple committee chairmen to two floor leaders.

World War II, a watershed in so many other areas of American life, spurred the Senate to provide professional staffs for its members and committees—a profound institutional change that triggered the construction of two additional office buildings and the human resources infrastructure to manage up to seven thousand aides. That expanded universe, including eleven thousand staffers working for the House of Representatives, brought into existence a highly competitive newsgathering environment. Multiple daily newspapers and insatiable online information purveyors now comb Capitol Hill for even the smallest nuggets of legislative intelligence. Staffers, long professionally anonymous, now attract the type of coverage—from gossip columns to feature-length articles—formerly accorded only to prominent Senate members. Legions of reporters and bloggers exponentially quicken the communications flow in this once-provincial world. An otherwise obscure senator who decides to place a hold on nominations to force an executive agency to befriend interests within his or her state suddenly is known to thousands and then millions as the national media pick up the story. Citizens who would otherwise spend little time thinking about the functionality of the Senate rush to conclude that this senator is emblematic of the entire institution. This is particularly so as they receive corroborating information that the Senate failed to pass any of its thirteen annual appropriations bills, or that it has just set a record for the number of cloture petitions filed to cut off debate, or that a senator is obligated to spend every day of his or her six-year term chasing the political contributions necessary to mount a credible reelection campaign likely to cost in the tens of millions of dollars. Candidates seeking to unseat Senate incumbents naturally espouse change, and they never hesitate to point out not only the flaws in the incumbent, but also in the Senate specifically and "Washington" generally.

History moves in cycles and so does the Senate. Where is the Senate of the twenty-first century headed? This volume, while focused squarely on the past from the perspective of this century's second decade, offers some hints. As long as the US Constitution—the world's oldest continuing written charter of government—remains in effect, the fundamental structure of the Senate will stand unchanged. There can be little doubt of that. Yet its history attests loudly to the fact that the Senate is susceptible to change; its way of doing business has been overhauled frequently in the context of an institution that is two-and-one-quarter centuries old. There are two predictable responses to the perennial question (also common a century ago): Would the framers of the US

Constitution recognize today's Senate? The first is, in its fundamentals, yes. The second is, not a chance! The fact that enlightened people can render such opposing judgments suggests that the Senate is a functioning, if awkward, institution in need of regular revision.[8] Scanning the two-plus-century landscape, one will note significant change, coming in episodic and unplanned bursts, and one will note dire frustration. This book seeks to identify the Senate's historical rhythms and place these oscillations in that context.

NOTES

———❦———

For more than thirty years, Richard Baker and Neil MacNeil met periodically over lunch to pursue their mutual fascination with the "how" of the Senate's history and culture. Following MacNeil's death, Baker agreed to bring his seventeen-year project to a conclusion, editing, as well as updating, a much longer manuscript. Following journalistic conventions, MacNeil disdained footnotes. He chose instead to identify his sources "on matters of consequence that I have newly uncovered" by referring to them in the body of his text. To create the endnotes that readers expect in a work such as this, Baker combed MacNeil's massive collection of research materials, as well as the extensive historical literature on Congress, to incorporate citations to significant works of Senate scholarship. In a few instances, documentation for the exact sources of MacNeil's quotations—many of them anecdotal—could not be uncovered. They are included without specific citation as one might find in a book reflecting more than a half century of observation and reporting. Late in 2012, MacNeil's family, noting his 1970 biography of Senate Republican leader Everett Dirksen, donated his papers to the Dirksen Congressional Center in Pekin, Illinois. A state-of-the-art congressional archives, the Dirksen Center was processing those papers at the time of this volume's publication.

Preface

1. Excellent modern-era studies on this point include Burdett A. Loomis, ed., *Esteemed Colleagues: Civility and Deliberation in the U.S. Senate* (Washington, DC: Brookings, 2000); Thomas E. Mann and Norman

J. Ornstein, *It's Even Worse Than It Looks: How the American Constitutional System Collided with the New Politics of Extremism* (New York: Oxford University Press, 2012); Barbara Sinclair, *The Transformation of the U.S. Senate* (Baltimore: Johns Hopkins University Press, 1990); Frances E. Lee and Bruce J. Oppenheimer, *Sizing Up the Senate: The Unequal Consequences of Equal Representation* (Chicago: University of Chicago Press, 1999); and Ross K. Baker, *House and Senate*, 4th ed. (New York: Norton, 2008).

2. William S. White, *Citadel: The Story of the U.S. Senate* (New York: Harper & Brothers, 1957), ix.

Prologue

1. Robert C. Byrd, *The Senate, 1789–1989*, S. Doc. No. 100–20 (1988–1991).
2. 143 Cong. Rec. S21–23 (daily ed. January 7, 1997).
3. Ibid.
4. Ibid.
5. Ibid.
6. Trent Lott, *Herding Cats: A Life in Politics* (New York: Regan Books, 2005), 112–3.
7. John David Dyche, *Republican Leader: Political Biography of Senator Mitch McConnell* (Wilmington, DE: ISI Books, 2009), 62–3.
8. William C. Allen, *History of the United States Capitol*, S. Doc. No. 106–29, 303–5.
9. John Harwood, "For New Congress, Data Shows Why Polarization Abounds," *New York Times*, March 7, 2011; Jennifer E. Manning, *Membership of the 112th Congress: A Profile*, March 1, 2011, Congressional Research Service Report R-41647; Norman J. Ornstein, Thomas J. Mann, and Michael Malbin, *Vital Statistics on Congress* (Washington, DC: American Enterprise Institute, 2008).
10. "Presiding Loses Prestige in the Senate," *Roll Call*, August 2, 2011; U.S. Senate, *Traditions of the United States Senate*, 17–8, http://www.senate.gov/reference/resources/pdf/Traditions/pdf.
11. Presentation to the Bipartisan Policy Center, Washington, DC, January 19, 2012, broadcast on C-SPAN.
12. Ross Baker, *Friend and Foe in the U.S. Senate* (New York: Free Press, 1980).
13. Martha Sherrill, "Snowe and Collins Might Not Like Each Other Much, but They Love Maine and Their Jobs," *Washington Post*, May 6, 2011.
14. 156 Cong. Rec. S8277–79 (daily ed. November 30, 2010). The 1996 election cycle produced an unusually large number of voluntary retirements. Those senators' farewell addresses are collected in *Lessons and Legacies: Farewell Addresses from the Senate*, Norman J. Ornstein, ed. (Reading, MA: Addison-Wesley, 1997). Ornstein, a veteran political analyst, observed, ". . . the notable diversity and high quality of these retirees elevates their collective departure from the status of a footnote in congressional history to an event with more profound consequences. . . .

Their legacy was a 'reputation for fairness, thoughtfulness, and moderation of manner'" (ix–x).

15. John Trumbull to John Adams, March 20, 1791.

Chapter 1

1. 156 Cong. Rec. S8278 (daily ed. November 30, 2010).
2. T. W. Farnham, "At $97 per Vote, Top Spenders Lost," *Washington Post*, November 9, 2010.
3. Edmund Randolph, May 31, 1787, George J. Schulz, ed., *Creation of the Senate: From the Proceedings of the Federal Convention, Philadelphia, May–September, 1787*, S. Doc. No. 100–7, 3 (1987).
4. Philip B. Kurland and Ralph Lerner, eds., *The Founders' Constitution* (Chicago: University of Chicago Press, 1987), 2:183–208.
5. Roy Swanstrom, *The United States Senate 1787–1801*, S. Doc. No. 87–64, at 14–8 (1988).
6. George H. Haynes, *The Election of Senators* (New York: Henry Holt, 1906), 3–14.
7. Richard R. Beeman, *Patrick Henry* (New York: McGraw-Hill, 1974), 167–8.
8. Haynes, *Election of Senators*, chapter 2.
9. Leonard D. White, *The Jacksonians: A Study in Administrative History, 1829–1861* (New York: Macmillan, 1954), 300–324.
10. Robert V. Remini, *Andrew Jackson and the Course of American Freedom, 1822–1832* (New York: Harper & Row, 1981), 198.
11. Robert V. Remini, *Andrew Jackson and the Course of American Democracy, 1833–1845* (Baltimore: Harper & Row, 1998), 347.
12. Ivor D. Spencer, *The Victor and the Spoils: A Life of William L. Marcy* (Providence, RI: Brown University Press, 1959), 60.
13. David Potter, *The Impending Crisis, 1848–1861* (New York: Harper & Row, 1976), 331–55.
14. Robert W. Johannsen, *Stephen A. Douglas* (New York: Oxford University Press, 1973), 663–79.
15. "Speech at Springfield," June 17, 1858, *Writings of Abraham Lincoln* (New York: Lamb Publishing, 1906), 3:16.
16. Anne M. Butler and Wendy Wolff, eds., *Senate Election Expulsion and Censure Cases, 1793–1990*, S. Doc. No. 103–33, at 80–81 (1995).
17. Brooks M. Kelley, "Simon Cameron and the Senatorial Nomination of 1867," *Pennsylvania Magazine of History and Biography* 87 (October 1963): 375–92.
18. Clarence E. Macartney, *Lincoln and His Cabinet* (New York: Charles Scribner's Sons, 1931), 46.
19. James Bryce, *The American Commonwealth* (New York: Macmillan, 1888), 1:158.
20. Oscar Lewis, *Silver Kings: The Lives of McKay, Fair, Flood, and O'Brien, Lords of the Nevada Comstock Lode* (New York: Alfred A. Knopf, 1947), 116.

21. Mark Wahlgren Summers, *The Era of Good Stealings* (New York: Oxford University Press, 1993), 50–54, 226–7, 231–7.
22. *World Almanac*, 1902; Haynes, *Elections*, 86–89; George H. Haynes, *The Senate of the United States* (Boston: Houghton Mifflin, 1938), 1046–8.
23. Butler and Wolff, eds., *Senate Election Cases*, 192.
24. Ibid., 264.
25. David M. Jordan, *Roscoe Conkling of New York* (Ithaca, NY: Cornell University Press, 1971), 87.
26. Butler and Wolff, eds., *Senate Election Cases*, 174–7.
27. Mark Twain and Charles Dudley Warner, *The Gilded Age* (Hartford, CT: American Publishing, 1873).
28. Haynes, *Election of Senators*, 45–6.
29. Richard E. Welch Jr., *George Frisbie Hoar and the Half-Breed Republicans* (Cambridge, MA: Harvard University Press, 1971), 72.
30. James C. Murphy, *L.Q.C. Lamar: Pragmatic Patriot* (Baton Rouge: Louisiana State University Press, 1973), 179–81.
31. Gordon B. McKinney, *Zeb Vance: North Carolina's Civil War Governor and Gilded Age Political Leader* (Chapel Hill: University of North Carolina Press, 2004), chapter 22.
32. Bryce, *American Commonwealth*, 131.
33. Haynes, *Senate of the United States*, 102–3.
34. Ibid., 103.
35. Francis Butler Simkins, *Pitchfork Ben Tillman: South Carolinian* (Baton Rouge: Louisiana State University Press, 1944), chapter 26; Daniel W. Hollis, "'Cotton Ed Smith'—Showman or Statesman?" *South Carolina Historical Magazine* 71 (October 1970): 235–56.
36. C. Vann Woodward, *The Strange Career of Jim Crow* (New York: Oxford University Press, 1955), 86–9.
37. Raymond Arsenault, *The Wild Ass of the Ozarks: Jeff Davis and the Social Bases of Southern Politics* (Knoxville: University of Tennessee Press, 1984).
38. William S. White, *Citadel: The Story of the U.S. Senate* (New York: Harper & Brothers, 1956), 68.
39. David Graham Phillips, *Treason of the Senate* (Chicago: Quadrangle Books, 1964).
40. Ibid., 59.
41. Haynes, *Senate of the United States*, 96–7.
42. Ibid.
43. George Frisbie Hoar, "Election of Senators by Direct Vote of the People," reprinted in S. Doc. No. 59–232 (1906).
44. William F. Holmes, *The White Chief: James Kimble Vardaman* (Baton Rouge: Louisiana State University Press, 1970), 56.
45. William Alexander Percy, *Lanterns on the Levee* (Baton Rouge: Louisiana State University Press, 1993), 149.
46. Butler and Wolff, eds., *Senate Election Cases*, 281–4.

47. Haynes, *Senate of the United States*, 132–5.
48. His formal statement appears in the *New York Times*, February 6, 1910.
49. John F. Kennedy, *Profiles in Courage* (New York: Harper & Brothers, 1956), 183.
50. George Rothwell Brown, *The Leadership of Congress* (Indianapolis: Bobbs-Merrill, 1922), 252–3.
51. Ibid.
52. Charles Willis Thompson, *The New Voter: Things He and She Ought to Know about Politics and Citizenship* (New York: G. P. Putnam's Sons, 1918).
53. Jesse Frederick Essary, *Covering Washington* (Boston: Houghton Mifflin, 1927), 199.
54. Bryon W. Daynes, "The Impact of the Direct Election of Senators on the Political System" (PhD dissertation, University of Chicago, 1972).
55. David I. Walsh, 65 Cong. Rec. 10451–53 (1924).
56. Haynes, *Senate of the United States*, 1071.
57. Ibid., 1082.
58. Ibid.
59. Butler and Wolff, eds., *Senate Election Cases*, 302–5.
60. Ibid., 333.
61. Ibid., 325.
62. Ibid., 328.
63. Haynes, *Senate of the United States*, 1078.
64. Francis Butler Simkins, *Pitchfork Ben Tillman: South Carolinian* (Baton Rouge: Louisiana State University Press, 1944, reprint 1967), 394–6.
65. C. Vann Woodward, *Origins of the New South, 1877–1913* (Baton Rouge: Louisiana State University Press, 1971), 342–3.
66. Ibid., 332–3.
67. Dewey W. Grantham Jr., *Hoke Smith and the Politics of the New South* (Baton Rouge: Louisiana State University Press, 1958), 150.
68. For Turner Catledge's description of race relations in Mississippi, see *My Life and the Times* (New York: Harper & Row, 1971), 6–7, 24–8.
69. Woodward, *Origins*, 340.
70. *New York Times*, March 29, 1908.
71. Woodward, *Origins*, 394–5.
72. For a survey of Bilbo's racial views, see Adwin Wigfall Green, *The Man Bilbo* (Baton Rouge: Louisiana State University Press, 1963), 104–5; Theodore Bilbo, *Take Your Choice: Separation or Mongrelization* (Poplarville, MS: Dream House Publishing, 1947).
73. *New York Times*, June 23, 1946; *Time*, July 1, 1946, 1.
74. Butler and Wolff, eds., *Senate Election Cases*, 376–9.
75. Virginia Hamilton, *Hugo Black: The Alabama Years* (Baton Rouge: Louisiana State University Press, 1972), 128.
76. Richard Lowitt, *George W. Norris: The Persistence of a Progressive* (Urbana: University of Illinois Press, 1971), 472–3, 484–6.

77. Julian M. Pleasants, "'Buncombe Bob' and Red Russian Fish Eggs: The Senatorial Election of 1932 in North Carolina," *Appalachian Journal* 4 (Autumn 1976): 51–62.

78. Robert Griffith, *The Politics of Fear* (Lexington: University Press of Kentucky, 1970), 125–31.

79. Helen Gahagan Douglas, *A Full Life* (Garden City, NY: Doubleday, 1982), 314–5.

80. Ingrid W. Scobie, *Center Stage: Helen Gahagan Douglas* (New York: Oxford University Press, 1992), 286.

81. Claude Denson Pepper with Hays Corey, *Pepper: Eyewitness to a Century* (San Diego: Harcourt Brace Jovanovich, 1987), 197.

82. "Legendary Campaign," *New York Times*, February 24, 1983.

83. "Florida: Anything Goes," *Time*, April 17, 1950, 16; see also George Smathers oral history interview, August 1, 1989, US Senate Historical Office, http://www.Senate.gov/artandhistory/oral_history/George_A_Smathers.htm, 27–8.

84. James T. Patterson, *Mr. Republican* (Boston: Houghton Mifflin, 1972), 177.

85. Paul Douglas, *In the Fullness of Time: The Memoirs of Paul H. Douglas* (New York: Harcourt Brace Jovanovich, 1972), 136–7.

86. Neil MacNeil, *Dirksen* (New York: World, 1970), 90.

87. Edward L. Schapsmeier and Frederick H. Schapsmeier, "Scott W. Lucas of Havana: His Rise and Fall as Majority Leader in the United States Senate," *Journal of the Illinois State Historical Society* 70 (November 1977): 302–20.

88. Thomas J. Whalen, *Kennedy Versus Lodge: The 1952 Massachusetts Senate Race* (Boston: Northeastern University, 2000), 100.

89. Neil MacNeil's notes, 1958 Senate campaign, MacNeil Papers, The Dirksen Congressional Center, Pekin, IL.

90. Ibid.

Chapter 2

1. 2 U.S.C. 241. The 1925 statute, originally enacted in 1910, was superseded in 1971 by the Federal Election Campaign Act, 86 Stat. 3.

2. Dirksen press conference, US Capitol, April 18, 1967, transcript in MacNeil Papers, The Dirksen Congressional Center, Pekin, IL.

3. Ibid.

4. Neil MacNeil's reporting.

5. Robert G. Baker, *Wheeling and Dealing: Confessions of a Capitol Hill Operator* (New York: Norton, 1978), 51.

6. Ibid., 52.

7. Joseph Napolitan, *The Election Game: And How to Win It* (Garden City, NY: Doubleday, 1972), 216, 223, 234.

8. Joe McGinniss, *The Selling of the President, 1968* (New York: Trident, 1969).

9. Gilbert C. Fite, *Richard B. Russell Jr.* (Chapel Hill: University of North Carolina Press, 1991), 371–4.

10. Ibid., 333; Robert A. Caro, *Master of the Senate* (New York: Alfred A. Knopf, 2002), 599.
11. Neil MacNeil's reporting.
12. *Washington Post*, December 22, 1984; Virginia Van der Veer Hamilton, "Lister Hill, Hugo Black, and the Albatross of Race," *Alabama Law Review* 36 (Spring 1985): 845–60.
13. For an evaluation of Fulbright's views on race relations, see Randall Bennett Woods, *Fulbright* (New York: Cambridge University Press, 1995), 114–9.
14. Michael Foley explores this theme in *The New Senate: Liberal Influence on a Conservative Institution, 1959–1972* (New Haven, CT: Yale University Press, 1980).
15. MacNeil papers.
16. "James O. Eastland Is Dead at 81," *New York Times*, February 20, 1986.
17. "Thurmond Kin Acknowledge Black Daughter," *New York Times*, December 16, 2003.
18. Chris Myers Asch, *The Senator and the Sharecropper: The Freedom Struggles of James O. Eastland and Fannie Lou Hamer* (New York: New Press, 2008), 287–8.
19. Neil MacNeil's reporting.
20. Donald R. Matthews, *U.S. Senators and Their World* (Chapel Hill: University of North Carolina Press, 1960), 68–74.
21. Alben Barkley, *That Reminds Me* (Garden City, NY: Doubleday, 1954), 165.
22. Caro, *Means of Ascent*, 4.
23. Ibid., 388.
24. Naval Appropriations Act of 1867, sec. 1546 (March 2, 1867).
25. Pendleton Act of 1883, 22 Stat. 403 (January 16, 1883).
26. Tillman Act of 1907, 34 Stat. 864 (January 26, 1907).
27. Federal Corrupt Practices Act of 1925, 43 Stat. 1070 (February 28, 1925).
28. 1939 Hatch Act (53 Stat. 1147) as amended in 1940, 54 Stat. 657 (July 19, 1940).
29. Labor Management Relations (Taft-Hartley) Act, 1947, 61 Stat. 136 (June 23, 1947).
30. Federal Election Campaign Act of 1971, 86 Stat. 11 (February 7, 1972) (see 2 U.S.C. 431 et seq.).
31. R. Sam Garrett, "The State of Campaign Finance Policy," Congressional Research Service Report R-41542, p. 3.
32. 2 U.S.C. 431 et seq.
33. Eliza Newlin Carney, "Bundling Rules Are in the Picture, but Out of Focus," *National Journal*, March 30, 2009; updated February 16, 2011.
34. Michael M. Franz, "The Devil We Know? Evaluating the Federal Election Commission as Enforcer," *Election Law Journal: Rules, Politics, and Policy* 8 (September 2009): 167–87, doi:10.1089/elj.2008.0025.
35. 424 U.S. 1 (1976).
36. "Exact Words; Concerning the Advantages of Incumbency," *New York Times*, June 8, 1989.

37. Wisconsin Senator William Proxmire's 1976 reelection cost his campaign only $700, while his unsuccessful challenger spent $60,000. See Herbert E. Alexander, *Financing the 1976 Elections* (Washington, DC: Congressional Quarterly, 1979), 193–6.

38. Larry J. Sabato, *PAC Power: Inside the World of Political Action Committees* (New York: Norton, 1985), xiv.

39. Philip M. Stern, *Still the Best Congress Money Can Buy* (Washington, DC: Regnery Gateway, 1992), 55–8.

40. David Kocieniewski, "GE's Strategies Let It Avoid Taxes Altogether," *New York Times*, March 25, 2011.

41. Herbert E. Alexander, *Financing Politics: Money, Elections, and Political Reform*, 4th ed. (Washington, DC: CQ Press, 1992); Congressional Quarterly, *Congressional Campaign Finances: History, Facts, and Controversy* (Washington, DC: CQ Press, 1992), 51–2.

42. Dennis W. Johnson, *No Place for Amateurs: How Political Consultants Are Reshaping American Democracy*, 2d ed. (New York: Routledge, 2007).

43. For summary of Terry Dolan's political career, see Elizabeth Kastor, "The Cautious Closet of the Gay Conservative," *Washington Post*, May 11, 1987; Allan J. Lichtman, *White Protestant Nation: The Rise of the American Conservative Movement* (New York: Atlantic Monthly Press, 2008), 311.

44. For McGovern's attitude on NCPAC's involvement, see Richard M. Marano, *Vote Your Conscience: The Last Campaign of George McGovern* (Westport, CT: Praeger, 2003), 31–2.

45. The ethicist Daniel Callahan explores this notion in "Doing Good and Doing Well," *Hastings Center Report* 31 (March–April 2001): 19–21.

46. Johnson, *No Place for Amateurs*.

47. Jane Mayer, "Wisconsinites Tune In to a Nasty Senate Race, Reflecting Focus on Character in '86 Campaigns," *Wall Street Journal*, October 9, 1986.

48. Paul Taylor, "Consultants Rise Via the Low Road," *Washington Post*, January 17, 1989.

49. Lawrence Lessig, *Republic Lost: How Money Corrupts Congress* (New York: Twelve Books, 2011); Robert G. Kaiser, *So Damn Much Money: The Triumph of Lobbying and the Corrosion of American Government* (New York: Alfred A. Knopf, 2009).

50. "Why Perot Could Pose a Threat with $100 Million: It's His Own," *New York Times*, April 24, 1992.

51. Andrew Jacobs, "Frank Raleigh Lautenberg; A Known Quantity, Ready for One More Senate Race," *New York Times*, October 2, 2002.

52. Tom Diemer, *Fighting the Unbeatable: Howard Metzenbaum of Ohio: The Washington Years* (Kent, OH: Kent State University Press, 2008), 137.

53. *National Journal Almanac*, 2010, www.nationaljournal.com/almanac/2010/person/jayrockefeller.wv/.

54. Edward Kennedy discusses his 1994 campaign financing in his memoir *True Compass* (New York: Twelve Books, 2009), 444.

55. Josh Richman, "Self-funded Candidates Say It's Worth Every Cent," *Oakland Tribune*, June 5, 2006.

56. Center for Responsive Politics, "OpenSecrets.org," December 31, 2010.

57. Peter Applebome, "Personal Cost for 2 Senate Bids: $100 Million," *New York Times*, November 3, 2012.

58. Janie Lorber, "Cantwell Still Owed $20M from Her 2000 Campaign," *Roll Call*, June 30, 2011.

59. Matt Bai, "The Accidental Senator," *New York Times Magazine*, October 27, 2002.

60. Clifford J. Levy, "Lazio Sets Spending Mark in Losing Senate Bid," *New York Times*, December 13, 2000.

61. Maeve Reston, "Boxer Not Only Beat Fiorina, She Outspent Her," *Los Angeles Times*, December 3, 2010.

62. David Broder, "Turning Politics Back to the Pros," *Washington* Post, May 1, 1973. For an incisive account of one prominent "hired gun," see David Broder, "The Powerful Political Legacy of Lee Atwater," *Washington Post*, April 4, 1991.

63. Alan Ehrenhalt, "Candidates' Media Consultants Are Becoming Too Good," *The Ledger* (Lakeland, FL), September 21, 1986.

64. Mark Shields, "One-day Sale on Tuesday," *Reading Eagle*, November 2, 1994.

65. www.fec.gov/disclosurehs/hsnational.do.

66. Public Law 107–55, 116 Stat. 81; Federal Election Commission, "Campaign Finance Law Quick Reference for Reporters," www.fec.gov/press/bkgnd/bcra_overview.shtml.

67. Garrett, *The State of Campaign Finance Policy*, 5.

68. Anthony Corrado, "Party Finance in the Wake of BCRA," in *The Election After Reform: Money, Politics, and the Bipartisan Campaign Reform Act*, ed. Michael J. Malbin (Lanham, MD: Rowman & Littlefield, 2006), 36.

69. 540 U.S. 93 (2003)

70. Eric Lichtblau, "Long Battle by Foes of Campaign Finance Rules Shifts Landscape," *New York Times*, October 15, 2010.

71. Public Law 110–81, 121 Stat. 735.

72. 130 S.Ct. 876 (2010).

73. Garrett, *The State of Campaign Finance Policy*, 7.

74. Adam Liptak, "Supreme Court Blocks Ban on Corporate Political Spending," *New York Times*, January 21, 2010.

75. http://www.law.cornell.edu/supct/html/08-205.ZS.html.

76. Adam Liptak, "Supreme Court Affirms a Ban on Soft Money," *New York Times*, June 29, 2010; *Republican National Committee v. Federal Election Commission* (08–1953), June 29, 2010.

77. The DISCLOSE [Democracy is Strengthened by Casting Light on Spending in Elections] Act, H.R. 5175, 111th Congress; David M. Herszenhorn, "Campaign Finance Bill Grinds to Halt in Senate," *New York Times*, July 28, 2010.

78. T. W. Farnham, "At $97 per Vote, Top Spenders Lost," *Washington Post*, November 9, 2010.

79. Jane Mayer, "Schmooze or Lose," *The New Yorker*, August 27, 2012, 27.

Chapter 3

1. John F. Kennedy, News Conference 37, June 27, 1962, http://www .jfklibrary.org/Research/Ready-Reference/Press-Conferences.aspx.

2. Kenneth R. Bowling and Helen E. Veit, eds., *The Diary of William Maclay and Other Notes on Senate Debates, Documentary History of the First Federal Congress of the United States of America* (Baltimore: Johns Hopkins University Press, 1988), 9:130.

3. Swanstrom, *Senate*, S. Doc. No. 100–31, at 12–4.

4. Richard Bassett (Delaware), Pierce Butler (South Carolina), Oliver Ellsworth (Connecticut), William Few (Georgia), William S. Johnson (Connecticut), Rufus King (New York), John Langdon (New Hampshire), Robert Morris (Pennsylvania), William Paterson (New Jersey), George Read (Delaware), Caleb Strong (Massachusetts).

5. For a discussion of the constitutional convention's consideration of an executive council to the president, see Joseph P. Harris, *The Advice and Consent of the Senate* (Berkeley, CA: Greenwood, 1953), 24–5.

6. Bowling and Veit, eds., *The Diary of William Maclay*, 9:11–2.

7. Swanstrom, *Senate*, 57–60.

8. R. C. Tripathi, *Second Chambers: Bicameralism Today* (New Delhi: Rajya Sabha Secretariat, 2002), 256–72.

9. Swanstrom, *Senate*, 96.

10. Ron Chernow, *Washington: A Life* (New York: Penguin, 2010), 591.

11. Ibid., 592.

12. US Constitution, art 2, sec. 3.

13. Veto message of President George Washington to the US House of Representatives, April 5, 1792. He issued his second veto on February 28, 1797.

14. *Presidential Vetoes, 1789–1988*, S. Pub. No. 102–12, at 2–8.

15. Washington's Farewell Address, 1796, Avalon.law.yale.edu/18th_century/ washing.asp.

16. Ron Chernow, *Alexander Hamilton* (New York: Penguin, 2004), 304.

17. Charles Warren, "How the President's Speech to Congress Was Instituted and Abandoned," *Odd Byways in American History* (Cambridge, MA: Harvard University Press, 1942), 154–8; *Philadelphia Aurora*, December 14, 1801.

18. Charles Francis Adams, ed., *The Memoirs of John Quincy Adams* (Philadelphia: J. B. Lippincott, 1874), 1:524.

19. Leonard White, *The Jeffersonians: A Study in Administrative History, 1801–1829* (New York: Macmillan, 1951), 51–2.

20. Merrill D. Peterson, *Thomas Jefferson and the New Nation* (New York: Oxford University Press, 1970), 729.

21. Dumas Malone, *Jefferson the President, First Term* (Charlottesville: University of Virginia Press, 2005), 110–12.
22. David S. Heidler and Jeanne T. Heidler, *Henry Clay: The Essential American* (New York: Random House, 2010), 101.
23. Bradford Perkins, *Prologue to War: England and the United States, 1805 to 1812* (Berkeley: University of California Press, 1961), 379.
24. Allan Nevins, ed., *The Diary of John Quincy Adams, 1794–1845* (New York: Longmans, Green, 1928), 262.
25. Louis Fisher, "The President, Congress, Military Tribunals, and Guantanamo," in James A. Thurber, *Rivals for Power: Presidential-Congressional Relations* (Lanham, MD: Rowman & Littlefield, 2009), 326.
26. Chernow, *Washington*, 590.
27. Alf J. Mapp, *Thomas Jefferson: Passionate Pilgrim, the Presidency, the Founding of the University, and the Private Battle* (Lanham, MD: Madison Books, 1991), 12.
28. Tenure of Office Act, May 15, 1820, 3 *Stat*, 582.
29. Andrew Jackson's Protest to the Senate, April 15, 1834, avalon.law.yale.edu/19th_century/ajack006.asp; Jon Meacham, *American Lion: Andrew Jackson in the White House* (New York: Random House, 2008), 287–8.
30. Robert V. Remini, *Daniel Webster* (New York: W. W. Norton, 1997), 415–20.
31. H. W. Brands, *Andrew Jackson* (New York: Doubleday, 2005), 418–20.
32. Joseph P. Harris, *Advice and Consent of the Senate*, 54.
33. John C. Fitzpatrick, ed., *The Autobiography of Martin Van Buren* (Washington, DC: Government Printing Office, 1920), 320–2.
34. Meacham, *American Lion*, 138–40.
35. *Presidential Vetoes*, S. Pub. No. 9–12 (1992).
36. Remini, *Daniel Webster*, 408–9.
37. Senate Republicans toyed with the idea in 1999, when they lacked the votes necessary to convict President Bill Clinton on House-passed articles of impeachment.
38. Alexis de Tocqueville, *Democracy in America* (New York: Harper & Row, 1966), 1:204–5.
39. Whigs used this slogan against Van Buren during his unsuccessful 1840 presidential reelection campaign.
40. James Bryce, *American Commonwealth*, abridged and edited by Louis Hacker (New York: G. P. Putnam's Sons, 1959), 1:27.
41. Ibid., 1:34.
42. William H. Harrison, Inaugural Address, March 5, 1841, James D. Richardson, *A Compilation of Messages and Papers* (Washington, DC: Bureau of National Literature and Art, 1904), 4:14–5.
43. Heidler and Heidler, *Henry Clay*, 339–40.
44. John C. Calhoun, *The Papers of John C. Calhoun*, Clyde N. Wilson, ed. (Columbia: University of South Carolina Press, 1984), 15:546.
45. Harris, *Advice and Consent*, 66–8.

46. Charles G. Sellers Jr., *James K. Polk, Jacksonian, 1795–1843* (Princeton, NJ: Princeton University Press, 1957–1966), 2:324–6.

47. Journal entries for February 8 and April 6, 1847, Milo M. Quaife, ed., *The Diary of James K. Polk during his Presidency, 1845–1849* (Chicago: A. C. McClurg, 1910), 2:371, 458.

48. K. Jack Bauer, *Zachary Taylor: Soldier, Planter, Statesman of the Old Southwest* (Baton Rouge: Louisiana State University Press, 1985), 257.

49. Zachary Taylor's Inaugural Address, March 5, 1849, avalon.law.yale.edu/19th_century/taylor.asp

50. Heidler and Heidler, *Henry Clay*, 476–9.

51. Philip S. Klein, *President James Buchanan* (Newtown, CT: American Political Biography Press, 1962), 429.

52. Doris Kearns Goodwin, *Team of Rivals: The Political Genius of Abraham Lincoln* (New York: Simon & Schuster, 2005), 394.

53. Ibid., 341–3.

54. Abraham Lincoln, *The Living Lincoln: The Man, His Mind, His Times, and the Wars He Fought*, Paul M. Angle, ed. (New Brunswick, NJ: Rutgers University Press, 1955), 521.

55. Abraham Lincoln, Address at Pittsburgh, Pennsylvania, February 15, 1861, *Abraham Lincoln: Complete Works*, John G. Nicolay and John Hay, eds. (New York: Century, 1894), 1:679.

56. "Message to Congress Enclosing Draft of Bill to Compensate States that Abolish Slavery, July 14, 1862," *Life and Works of Abraham Lincoln: State Papers, 1861–1865*, Marion Mills Miller, ed. (New York: Current Literature Publishing, 1907), 6:135–6. In a June 27, 1862, address, Charles Sumner reminded his Senate colleagues that the president "is only the instrument of Congress under the Constitution," *The Works of Charles Sumner* (Boston: Lee and Shepard, 1874), 7:139.

57. Wilfred E. Binkley, *President and Congress* (New York: Vintage, 1962), 135.

58. David Herbert Donald, *Lincoln* (New York: Simon & Schuster, 1995), 511.

59. Bruce Tap, *Over Lincoln's Shoulder: The Committee on the Conduct of the War* (Lawrence: University of Kansas Press, 1998).

60. Eric Foner, *The Fiery Trial: Abraham Lincoln and American Slavery* (New York: W. W. Norton, 2010), 271–2.

61. Hans L. Trefousse, *Benjamin Franklin Wade: Radical Republican from Ohio* (New York: Twayne, 1963), 221.

62. Michael Burlingame and John R. Turner Ettlinger, eds., *Inside Lincoln's White House: The Complete Civil War Diary of John Hay* (Carbondale: Southern Illinois Press, 1997), 219.

63. For Wade's opinion of Lincoln, see Trefousse, *Wade*, 219–27; T. Harry Williams, *Lincoln and the Radicals* (Madison: University of Wisconsin Press, 1941), 352–3.

64. Trefousse, *Wade*, 249; Williams, *Lincoln and the Radicals*, 375.

65. Williams, *Lincoln and the Radicals*, 374.

66. Trefousse, *Wade*, 234.

67. Woodrow Wilson, *Congressional Government: A Study in American Politics* (Boston: Houghton Mifflin, 1885).

68. Trefousse, *Wade*, 249.

69. Ibid.

70. Ibid., 250.

71. Michael Les Benedict, *The Impeachment and Trial of Andrew Johnson* (New York: Norton, 1973), 299.

72. Paul H. Bergeron, *Andrew Johnson's Civil War and Reconstruction* (Knoxville: University of Tennessee Press, 2011), 270n.48.

73. Charles A. Jellison, *Fessenden of Maine: Civil War Senator* (Syracuse, NY: Syracuse University Press, 1962), 221, 229–30.

74. For accounts of bribery and spying associated with the Johnson impeachment trial, see David O. Stewart, *Impeached: The Trial of President Andrew Johnson and the Fight for Lincoln's Legacy* (New York: Simon & Schuster, 2009).

75. Ralph J. Roske, "The Seven Martyrs?," *American Historical Review* 64 (January 1959): 323–30.

76. Kennedy, *Profiles*, chapter 6.

77. Stewart, *Impeached*, 424–5.

78. James Ford Rhodes, *History of the United States from the Compromise of 1850* (New York: Macmillan, 1906), 6:388–9.

79. Henry Adams, *The Education of Henry Adams* (Boston: Houghton Mifflin, 1918), 266.

80. The wealthy importer Alexander T. Stewart was disqualified under a provision of the 1789 statute creating the Treasury Department, with its responsibility for customs houses, barring those engaged in trade and commerce from holding this post.

81. H. W. Brands, *The Man Who Saved the Union: Ulysses S. Grant in War and Peace* (New York: Doubleday, 2012), 526.

82. For a survey of the evolution of "personally obnoxious," see Harris, *Advice and Consent*, 217–26. For application to judicial nominees of the doctrine of senatorial courtesy, see Mitchel A. Sollenberger, *The History of the Blue Slip in the Senate Committee on the Judiciary, 1917–Present*, Congressional Research Service Report RL-32013.

83. Thomas C. Reeves, *Gentleman Boss: The Life of Chester Alan Arthur* (New York: Alfred A. Knopf, 1975), 77.

84. George F. Hoar, *Autobiography of Seventy Years* (New York: Scribner's, 1903), 2:45.

85. Mark W. Summers, *The Era of Good Stealings* (New York: Oxford University Press, 1993), 95–100; Brands, *The Man Who Saved the Union*, 545.

86. Ari Arthur Hoogenboom, *Rutherford B. Hayes: Warrior and President* (Lawrence: University Press of Kansas, 1995), 266.

87. C. Vann Woodward, *Reunion and Reaction: The Compromise of 1877 and the End of Reconstruction* (Garden City, NY: Doubleday, 1956), chapter 9.

88. Harris, *Advice and Consent*, 79–84; Hoogenboom, *Rutherford B. Hayes*, 352–5.
89. Hoogenboom, *Rutherford B. Hayes*, 295–6.
90. David M. Jordan, *Roscoe Conkling of New York* (Ithaca, NY: Cornell University Press, 1971), 264–6.
91. Hoogenboom, *Rutherford B. Hayes*, 323; Reeves, *Gentleman Boss*, 118, 324.
92. Margaret Leech and Harry J. Brown, *The Garfield Orbit* (New York: Harper & Row, 1978), 208.
93. Jordan, *Roscoe Conkling*, 382–92.
94. Candice Millard, *Destiny of the Republic* (New York: Doubleday, 2011), 37.
95. Jordan, *Roscoe Conkling*, 390–91.
96. Ibid.
97. Ibid., 385; Allan Peskin, *Garfield* (Kent, OH: Kent State University Press, 1978), 563, 570. Peskin asserts that Garfield's victory over Conkling in securing Senate confirmation of Robertson's nomination halted "that steady drift of power to the Senate that had been such a striking feature of national politics over a generation . . . , the first step towards that steady accretion of presidential power that would in later years transform the whole nature of the office" (564, 565).
98. Thomas Platt, "Senator Platt's Autobiography, Part II: The Garfield-Conkling Feud," *McClure's Magazine* (1910), 35:324.
99. Millard, *Destiny*, 168.
100. Reeves, *Gentleman Boss*, 322–7.
101. Ibid., 280–81.
102. Ibid., 324.
103. Alyn Brodsky, *Grover Cleveland: A Study in Character* (New York: St. Martin's, 2000), 154.
104. Ibid., 136.
105. Grover Cleveland, "On Giving Reasons for Removal from Office," March 1, 1886, *The Writings and Speeches of Grover Cleveland*, George F. Parker, ed. (New York: Cassell, 1892), 474–5.
106. Brodsky, *Grover Cleveland*, 118.
107. Stephen Miller, *Special Interest Groups in American Politics* (New Brunswick, NJ: Transaction, 1983), 89.
108. *The Writings and Speeches of Grover Cleveland*, 86.
109. James A. Kehl, *Boss Rule in the Gilded Age: Matt Quay of Pennsylvania* (Pittsburgh: University of Pittsburgh Press, 1981), 116–7.
110. H. W. Brands, *T.R.: The Last Romantic* (New York: Basic Books, 1997), 219.
111. Harry Joseph Sievers, *Benjamin Harrison: Hoosier Statesman* (Chicago: Regnery, 1957), 63.
112. Theron Clark Crawford, *James G. Blaine* (Philadelphia: Edgewood, 1893), 222–3.
113. Richard E. Welch, *The Presidencies of Grover Cleveland* (Lawrence: University Press of Kansas, 1988), 136.
114. John R. Lambert, *Arthur Pue Gorman* (Baton Rouge: Louisiana State University Press, 1953), 230–32; 26 Cong. Rec. 7801–9 (1894).

115. Grover Cleveland to Ambassador Thomas F. Bayard, February 13, 1895, in Allan Nevins, ed., *Letters of Grover Cleveland, 1850–1908* (Boston: Houghton Mifflin, 1933), 377.

116. Sean Dennis Cashman, *America in the Gilded Age* (New York: New York University Press, 1984), 259.

117. Brodsky, *Grover Cleveland*, 20.

118. Rhodes, *History of the United States from the Compromise of 1850*, 8:458.

119. Arthur Meier Schlesinger Jr. and Fred L. Israel, *My Fellow Citizens: The Inaugural Addresses of the Presidents of the United States* (New York: Facts on File, 2010), 212.

120. "President McKinley in War Times," *McClure's Magazine* (July 1898), 11:222.

121. Henry F. Pringle, *Theodore Roosevelt* (New York: Blue Ribbon Books, 1931), 124.

122. Warren Zimmermann, *First Great Triumph: How Five Americans Made Their Country a World Power* (New York: Farrar, Straus, and Giroux, 2002), 322–3.

123. William Roscoe Thayer, *Life and Letters of John Hay* (Boston: Houghton Mifflin, 1915), 2:254.

124. Hoar, *Autobiography*, 2:313–5.

125. For Senate action on the treaty, see David F. Trask, *The War with Spain in 1898* (New York: Macmillan, 1981), 468–70.

126. H. Wayne Morgan, *William McKinley and His America* (Kent, OH: Kent State University Press, 2003), 320–21.

127. Trask, *The War with Spain*, 468–70.

128. Harold F. Gosnell, *Boss Platt and His New York Machine* (Chicago: University of Chicago Press, 1924), 117–21.

129. Edmund Morris, *The Rise of Theodore Roosevelt* (New York: Coward, McCann & Geoghegan, 1979), 724.

130. Edmund Morris, *Theodore Rex* (New York: Random House, 2001), 30.

Chapter 4

1. Theodore Roosevelt and Will Irwin, *Letters to Kermit from Theodore Roosevelt, 1902 to 1908* (New York: Charles Scribner's Sons, 1946), 24–5.

2. Richard Hofstadter, *The American Political Tradition and the Men Who Made It* (New York: Vintage, 1989), 223.

3. Nathan Miller, *Theodore Roosevelt* (New York: Morrow, 1992), 355–6.

4. Horace Samuel Merrill and Marion Galbraith Merrill offer an insightful account of the group they call the "Senate Four"—the "Big Five" minus Eugene Hale—in *The Republican Command, 1897–1913* (Lexington: University Press of Kentucky, 1971); see also Morris, *Theodore Rex*, 72–5; Charles Willis Thompson, "Out-Ringing the Rings in Senate Circles," *New York Times*, August 22, 1920.

5. Edmund Morris provides an admirable description of this transformation in *Theodore Rex*.

6. *Selections from the Correspondence of Henry Cabot Lodge and Theodore Roosevelt, 1884–1918* (New York: Scribner's, 1925), 1:512.
7. Morris, *Theodore Rex*, 423, 438.
8. Ron Chernow, *The House of Morgan: An American Banking Dynasty and the Rise of Modern Finance* (New York: Atlantic Monthly Press, 1990), 106.
9. Secretary of State John Hay signed the Hay-Herran Treaty on January 22, 1903, and the Senate, by a vote of seventy-three to five, gave consent to its ratification on March 17; David McCullough, *The Path Between the Seas* (New York: Simon & Schuster, 1977), 332.
10. Theodore Roosevelt, *I Took the Isthmus: Ex-President Roosevelt's Confession* (New York: M. B. Brown, 1911), 7, from a speech to students at the University of California, Berkeley, March 23, 1911.
11. Theodore Roosevelt, *Theodore Roosevelt: An Autobiography* (New York: Macmillan, 1913), 357.
12. Roosevelt, *Autobiography*, Wayne Andrews, ed. (New York: Octagon, 1975), 282.
13. Theodore Roosevelt to William Howard Taft, March 13, 1903, quoted in Rhodes, *History of the United States from the Compromise of 1850: The McKinley and Roosevelt Administrations, 1897–1909* (New York: Macmillan, 1922), 8:279.
14. Theodore Roosevelt letter of January 17, 1903, Elting E. Morison and John M. Blum, eds., *Letters [of Theodore Roosevelt]* 8 vols. (Cambridge, MA: Harvard University Press, 1951–54), 3:406.
15. Patricia O'Toole, *When Trumpets Call: Theodore Roosevelt After the White House* (New York: Simon & Schuster, 2005), 33.
16. Louis Arthur Coolidge, *An Old-Fashioned Senator: Orville Platt of Connecticut* (New York: Kennikat, 1910), 572.
17. Joshua David Hawley, *Theodore Roosevelt: Preacher of Righteousness* (New Haven, CT: Yale University Press, 2008), 143.
18. Annual Message of December 5, 1905, see University of California Presidency Project at www.presidency.ucsb.edu/
19. Francis Butler Simkins, *Pitchfork Ben Tillman: South Carolinian* (Baton Rouge: Louisiana State University Press, 1944), 421–3.
20. Ibid., 408–10.
21. The source of MacNeil's quote remains elusive. Elsewhere, Roosevelt was quoted as saying of Tillman that his "blatant radicalism offsets his sturdy honesty and minimizes the power of his brain." Archibald W. Butt, *The Letters of Archie Butt* (Garden City, NY: Doubleday, 1924), 100. For an account of the searing hostility between Roosevelt and Tillman, see Simkins, *Pitchfork Ben Tillman*, chapters 27–9.
22. One eminent scholar concluded, "The Senate, in the end, supplied the federal executive with authority beyond any antecedent definition to mitigate the maladjustments of a growing industrial society." John Morton Blum, *The Republican Roosevelt* (Cambridge, MA: Harvard University Press, 1977), 104.

23. Theodore Roosevelt to James E. Watson, August 18, 1906, Elting E. Morison and John M. Blum, eds., *The Letters of Theodore Roosevelt*, 5:367.
24. Roosevelt, *Autobiography*, 443.
25. Butt, *The Letters of Archie Butt*, 100.
26. Miller, *Theodore Roosevelt*, 218.
27. Theodore Roosevelt, *The Roosevelt Policy: Speeches, Letters and State Papers Relating to Corporate Wealth and Closely Allied Topics* (New York: Current Literature, 1919), 2:570.
28. Henry Wilkinson Bragdon, *Woodrow Wilson: The Academic Years* (Cambridge, MA: Harvard University Press, 1967), 338–9.
29. Woodrow Wilson, *Congressional Government*, 238.
30. Woodrow Wilson, *Constitutional Government in the United States* (New York: Columbia University Press, 1908), 70.
31. Lewis Gould, *The William Howard Taft Presidency* (Lawrence: University Press of Kansas, 2009), 185–99; John Milton Cooper, *The Warrior and the Priest: Woodrow Wilson and Theodore Roosevelt* (Cambridge, MA: Harvard University Press, 1983), 160.
32. "The New Freedom is only the old revived and clothed in the unconquerable strength of modern America." Woodrow Wilson, *The New Freedom: A Call for the Emancipation of the Generous Energies of a People* (New York: Doubleday, Page, 1913), viii.
33. Woodrow Wilson to Ellen Axon, October 30, 1883, in Eleanor Wilson McAdoo, *The Priceless Gift* (New York: McGraw-Hill, 1962), 32.
34. Wilson, *Congressional Government*, 72, 111–2.
35. David J. Rothman, *Politics and Power: The United States Senate, 1869–1901* (Cambridge, MA: Harvard University Press, 1966), 39; Robert V. Remini, *The House* (New York: HarperCollins, 2006), 279.
36. Albert Burleson interviews by Ray Stannard Baker, March 17–19, 1927, Ray Stannard Baker Papers, Library of Congress, Box 103; John Milton Cooper Jr., *Woodrow Wilson* (New York: Alfred A. Knopf, 2009), 214–5.
37. Ibid.
38. Wilson, *Constitutional Government*, 130.
39. Ibid., chapter 3.
40. Quoted in Geoffrey Nunberg, *Going Nuclear: Language, Politics, and Culture in Confrontational Times* (New York: Public Affairs, 2004). 185.
41. Cooper, *Woodrow Wilson*, 214.
42. H. W. Brands, *Woodrow Wilson* (New York: Times Books, 2003), 33.
43. Arthur Link, *Woodrow Wilson and The Progressive Era* (New York: Harper, 1954), 41–2.
44. George Harvey, "Six Months of Wilson," *New York Times*, November 2, 1913.
45. For background on the "Binding Caucus," see Walter Oleszek, "John Worth Kern," in Richard A. Baker and Roger H. Davidson, eds., *First Among Equals: Outstanding Senate Leaders of the Twentieth Century* (Washington, DC: CQ Press, 1991), 28; John R. Lambert, *Arthur Pue Gorman* (Baton Rouge: Louisiana State University Press, 1953), 303.

46. "Federal Leadership," *New York Times*, August 4, 1913.

47. The Revenue Act of 1913, 38 Stat. 114 (October 3, 1913).

48. Cooper, *Woodrow Wilson*, 215 (Ray Stannard Baker interview with Burleson, March 17–19, 1927).

49. Franklin L. Burdette, *Filibustering in the Senate* (Princeton, NJ: Princeton University Press, 1940), 114–5.

50. Woodrow Wilson, statement, March 4, 1917, Cooper, *Woodrow Wilson*, 380.

51. Albert Bushnell Hart, ed., *Selected Addresses and Public Papers of Woodrow Wilson* (New York: Boni and Liveright, 1918), 66.

52. John Milton Cooper Jr., *Breaking the Heart of the World: Woodrow Wilson and the Fight for the League of Nations* (New York: Cambridge University Press, 2001), 17.

53. August Heckscher, *Woodrow Wilson* (New York: Maxwell Macmillan International, 1991).

54. Ibid., 433–7.

55. Burdette, *Filibustering in the Senate*, 119–23.

56. Cooper, *Woodrow Wilson*, 378–80.

57. Burdette, *Filibustering in the Senate*, 127–8.

58. Cooper, *Woodrow Wilson*, 384–8; "President Calls for War Declaration," *New York Times*, April 3, 1917.

59. Cooper, *Woodrow Wilson*, 420–24.

60. Ibid., 445–8; Heckscher, *Woodrow Wilson*, 485.

61. Quoted in Charles W. Eliot, "The Voter's Choice in the Coming Election," *The Atlantic Monthly* 126 (October 1920): 535.

62. Cooper, *Woodrow Wilson*, 436.

63. Cooper, *Breaking the Heart of the World*, 34–5; Cooper, *Woodrow Wilson*, 454–6.

64. Wilson's constitutional qualms are supported in Denna Frank Fleming, *The Treaty Veto of the American Senate* (New York: G. P. Putnam's Sons, 1930), 22–30.

65. Cooper, *Woodrow Wilson*, 479–80; William C. Widenor, *Henry Cabot Lodge and the Search for an American Foreign Policy* (Berkeley: University of California Press, 1980), 315–20.

66. Widenor, *Henry Cabot Lodge*, 308; Henry Cabot Lodge, *The Senate and the League of Nations* (New York: Scribner's, 1925), 147.

67. Cooper, *Woodrow Wilson*, 478.

68. Ibid., 529–32.

69. Ibid., 543.

70. Ibid., 545.

71. Cooper, *Breaking the Heart of the World*, chapter 7.

72. Cooper, *Woodrow Wilson*, 558–9.

73. Senator Knute Nelson quoting Woodrow Wilson on his return from Paris in 1919, in Richard F. Pettigrew, *Imperial Washington* (Chicago: C. H. Kerr, 1922), 211. Pettigrew, who served in the Senate from South Dakota from 1889 to 1901, believed that body was "declining in importance. It can now be ignored by business, whereas, twenty years ago, it had to be reckoned

with. It has become a sort of storage plant for the preservation of mediocre intellects and threadbare reputations" (208).

74. Thomas A. Bailey, *Woodrow Wilson and the Great Betrayal* (New York: Macmillan, 1945), 88; Robert H. Ferrell, *Presidential Leadership from Woodrow Wilson to Harry S. Truman* (Columbia: University of Missouri Press, 2006), 57.

75. Lance Morrow, *Second Drafts of History: Essays* (New York: Basic Books, 2006), 134.

76. Eugene P. Trani and David L. Wilson, *The Presidency of Warren G. Harding* (Lawrence: University Press of Kansas, 1977), 55–9; 61 Cong. Rec. 169–73 (1921).

77. 61 Cong. Rec., 172 (1921).

78. For general assessment of Lodge as majority leader, see George Rothwell Brown, *The Leadership of Congress* (Indianapolis, IN: Bobbs-Merrill, 1922), 254, 256, 259.

79. Clinton Wallace Gilbert, *Behind the Mirrors: The Psychology of Disintegration at Washington* (New York: G. P. Putnam's Sons, 1922), 157.

80. Fleming, *The Treaty Veto of the American Senate*, 31–2; Royden J. Dangerfield, *In Defense of the Senate: A Study in Treaty Making* (Norman: University of Oklahoma Press, 1933), 292.

81. *Address of the President of the United States to the Senate Presenting the Report of the Washington Conference, February 10, 1922*, S. Doc. No. 67–126, at 84.

82. Calvin Coolidge, *The Autobiography of Calvin Coolidge* (New York: Cosmopolitan, 1929), 161–2.

83. Ibid., 160.

84. Robert H. Ferrell, *The Presidency of Calvin Coolidge* (Lawrence: University Press of Kansas, 1998), 195.

85. Herbert Hoover, *The Memoirs of Herbert Hoover: The Cabinet and the Presidency, 1920–1933* (New York: Macmillan, 1952), 223.

86. Ibid., 291–2.

87. William E. Leuchtenburg, *The Perils of Prosperity, 1914–1932* (Chicago: University of Chicago Press, 1958), 251.

88. Hoover, *Memoirs: The Great Depression, 1929–1941* (New York: Macmillan, 1952), 103.

89. Hoover, *Memoirs: The Cabinet and the Presidency*, 217.

90. Ibid.

91. Hoover, *Memoirs: The Great Depression*, 103.

92. Ibid., 101.

93. William E. Leuchtenburg, *Franklin Roosevelt and the New Deal, 1932–1940* (New York: Harper & Row, 1963), 55.

94. Hoover, *Memoirs: The Great Depression*, 113.

95. United States, *Public Papers of the Presidents of the United States: Herbert Hoover, 1930* (Washington, DC: GPO, 1931), 559.

96. Hoover, *Memoirs: The Great Depression*, 36.

97. Donald A. Ritchie, *Electing FDR: The New Deal Campaign of 1932* (Lawrence: University Press of Kansas, 2009).

98. Franklin D. Roosevelt, *Inaugural Address*, March 4, 1933.

99. Henry F. Ashurst, *A Many-Colored Toga: The Diary of Henry Fountain Ashurst*, George F. Sparks, ed. (Tucson: University of Arizona Press, 1962), 333.

100. Richard Hofstadter, *The Age of Reform* (New York: Knopf, 1955), 307.

101. Patrick J. Maney, *The Roosevelt Presence: The Life and Legacy of FDR* (New York: Twayne, 1992), 49–57.

102. Hofstadter, *The Age of Reform*, 307.

103. Mark O. Hatfield, *Vice Presidents of the United States, 1789–1993*, S. Doc. No. 104–26, at 385–95.

104. Donald C. Bacon, "Joseph Taylor Robinson: The Good Soldier," in Baker and Davidson, eds., *First among Equals: Senate Party Leaders*, 93.

105. Jean Edward Smith, *FDR* (New York: Random House, 2007), 317.

106. William E. Leuchtenburg, *The FDR Years* (New York: Columbia University Press, 1995), 16–7.

107. David McKean, *Tommy the Cork: Washington's Ultimate Insider from Roosevelt to Reagan* (Hanover, NH: Steerforth, 2003), 59, 195–6; William Lasser, *Benjamin V. Cohen: Architect of the New Deal* (New Haven, CT: Yale University Press, 2002), 88, 92, 103.

108. For formulation of the Roosevelt administration's "Hundred Days" legislation, see Maney, *The Roosevelt Presence*, 50–5, and James MacGregor Burns, *Roosevelt: The Lion and the Fox, 1882–1940* (New York: Harcourt, Brace & World, 1956), 168–71.

109. Wilfred E. Binkley and Malcolm C. Moos, *A Grammar of American Politics: The National Government* (New York: Knopf, 1949), 455.

110. The House of Representatives at the beginning of that Congress included only eighty-nine Republicans among its 435 members.

111. Maney, *The Roosevelt Presence*, 89–98.

112. James A. Farley, *Jim Farley's Story: The Roosevelt Years* (New York: Whittlesey House, 1948), 73, 75.

113. Burt Solomon, *FDR v. the Constitution: The Court-Packing Fight and the Triumph of Democracy* (New York: Walker, 2009), 250–59.

114. Farley, *Jim Farley's Story*, 146.

115. Haynes, *Senate*, 990–94.

116. Jean Edward Smith, *FDR*, 414. For more on George and Smith, see Susan Dunn, *Roosevelt's Purge: How FDR Fought to Change the Democratic Party* (Cambridge, MA: Harvard University Press, 2010), chapters 7 and 8.

117. For an inspired account of this transition, see James T. Patterson, *Congressional Conservatism and the New Deal: The Growth of the Conservative Coalition in Congress, 1933–1939* (Lexington: University of Kentucky Press, 1967).

118. Charles E. Bohlen, *Witness to History, 1929–1969* (New York: Norton, 1973), 210.

Chapter 5

1. "War Powers Act Doesn't Apply for Libya, Obama Says," *New York Times*, June 16, 2011.

2. Franklin D. Roosevelt, *Message to Congress*, September 7, 1942, in *Senate Journal*, 77th Cong., 2nd Sess., at 377.

3. Sam Rayburn Papers, Dolph Briscoe Center for American History, University of Texas at Austin, Address at Dallas, Texas, December 10, 1940. Rayburn appeared on the cover of the September 27, 1943, *Time* magazine. The accompanying article described him as the greatest "compromiser" since Henry Clay. Rayburn preferred to be known as "the persuader." D. B. Hardeman and Donald C. Bacon, *Rayburn* (Austin: Texas Monthly Press, 1987), 288–9.

4. George B. Galloway, "Congress: Problem, Diagnosis, Proposal," *American Political Science Review* 36 (December 1942): 1091–102.

5. Robert C. Byrd, "Congressional Reform: The Legislative Reorganization Act of 1946," in *The Senate, 1789–1989*, 1: chapter 28.

6. Alonzo L. Hamby, *Man of Principle: A Life of Harry S. Truman* (New York: Oxford University Press, 1995), 295.

7. Arthur H. Vandenberg Jr. and Joe Morris, eds., *The Private Papers of Senator Vandenberg* (Boston: Houghton Mifflin, 1952), 167.

8. Harry S. Truman, *Memoirs: Year of Decisions* (Garden City, NY: Doubleday, 1955–1956), 1:145.

9. Robert H. Ferrell, *Off the Record: The Private Papers of Harry S. Truman* (Columbia: University of Missouri Press, 1997), 201.

10. Harry S. Truman, "Annual Message to the Congress on the State of the Union, January 6, 1947," www.trumanlibrary.org/whistlestop/tap/1647 .htm; 93 Cong. Rec. 136–7 (1947).

11. David McCullough, *Truman* (New York: Simon & Schuster, 1992), 643–4.

12. James T. Patterson, *Mr. Republican* (Boston: Houghton Mifflin, 1972), 422.

13. www.presidency.ucsb.edu/ [January 5, 1949].

14. Donald R. McCoy, "Harry S. Truman: Personality, Politics, and Presidency," *Presidential Studies Quarterly* 12 (Spring 1982): 216.

15. Patterson, *Mr. Republican*, 452–5.

16. Dana D. Nelson, *Bad for Democracy: How the Presidency Undermines the Power of the People* (Minneapolis: University of Minnesota Press, 2008), 124; Dean Acheson, *Present at the Creation* (New York: Norton, 1969), 415.

17. Patterson, *Mr. Republican*, 489.

18. Fite, *Richard B. Russell Jr.*, 264.

19. David McCullough, *Truman*, 744–6.

20. Ibid., 863–4.

21. Patterson, *Mr. Republican*, 584.

22. Stephen Ambrose, *Eisenhower the President* (New York: Simon & Schuster, 1984), 60.

23. Richard M. Fried, *Nightmare in Red: The McCarthy Era in Perspective* (New York: Oxford University Press, 1990), 134.

24. Duane Tananbaum, *The Bricker Amendment Controversy: A Test of Eisenhower's Political Leadership* (Ithaca, NY: Cornell University Press, 1988), 216–9.

25. *Reid v. Covert*, 354 U.S. 1 (1957).

26. Ambrose, *Eisenhower*, 155.

27. Later in 1959, with the admission of Hawaii to the Union, the balance became sixty-five Democrats and thirty-five Republicans.

28. Richard A. Baker, "A Slap at the 'Hidden-Hand Presidency': The Senate and the Lewis Strauss Affair," *Congress and the Presidency* 14 (March 1987): 1–16.

29. "Ev and Charlie: GOP End Men," *Newsweek*, April 24, 1961.

30. Edward L. Schapsmeier and Frederick H. Schapsmeier, *Dirksen of Illinois: Senatorial Statesman* (Urbana: University of Illinois Press, 1985), 131–3.

31. Ibid., 132.

32. (Washington) *Daily News*, September 7, 1961; Schapsmeier and Schapsmeier, *Dirksen*, 134.

33. Congressional Quarterly Inc., *Congressional Quarterly's Guide to the Congress of the United States* (Washington, DC: Congressional Quarterly, 1971), 658.

34. Kenneth E. Collier, *Between the Branches: The White House Office of Legislative Affairs* (Pittsburgh: University of Pittsburgh Press, 1997), 30–35; Richard A. Baker interview with Bryce Harlow, December 13, 1985, Clinton Anderson Papers, Library of Congress, Washington, DC.

35. Shelby Scates, *Warren G. Magnuson*, 192, 197; Theodore C. Sorensen, *Kennedy* (New York: Harper & Row, 1965), 44–5.

36. William Hildenbrand oral history, US Senate Historical Office, 64.

37. Doris Kearns Goodwin, *Lyndon Johnson and the American Dream* (New York: Harper & Row, 1976), 226.

38. Michael R. Beschloss, ed., *Reaching for Glory: Lyndon Johnson's Secret White House Tapes, 1964–1965* (New York: Simon & Schuster, 2001), 373.

39. Neil MacNeil, *Dirksen: Portrait of a Public Man* (New York: World, 1970), 228.

40. Paul K. Conkin, *Big Daddy from the Pedernales: Lyndon Baines Johnson* (Boston: Twayne, 1986), 255–58.

41. Robert A. Caro, *The Passage of Power* (New York: Alfred A. Knopf, 2012), 568–9.

42. MacNeil, *Dirksen*, 213; Caro, *The Passage of Power*, 564–6.

43. 111 Cong. Rec. 5059–61 (1965); millercenter.org/president/speeches/detail/3386.

44. MacNeil, *Dirksen*, 258.

45. Ibid., 258–9.

46. Taylor Branch, *At Canaan's Edge: America in the King Years* (New York: Simon & Schuster, 2006), 530.

47. MacNeil, *Dirksen*, 321.

48. Ibid., 327–8.

49. Laura Kalman, *Abe Fortas* (New Haven, CT: Yale University Press, 1990), 327–58.

50. Louis Baldwin, *Honorable Politician: Mike Mansfield of Montana* (Missoula, MT: Mountain Press, 1979, 36, 351.

51. Ibid., 283–4.

52. Robert C. Byrd, *Losing America: Confronting a Reckless and Arrogant Presidency* (New York: Norton, 2004), chapter 3; Louis Fisher, *Defending Congress and the Constitution* (Lawrence: University Press of Kansas, 2011), 268–72; Louis Fisher, *Constitutional Conflicts between Congress and the President*, 5th edition, revised (Lawrence: University Press of Kansas, 2007), 270–81.

53. Charlie Savage and Mark Lander, "White House Defends Continuing U.S. Role in Libya Operation," *New York Times*, June 16, 2011.

54. James Reichley, *Conservatives in an Age of Change: The Nixon and Ford Administrations* (Washington, DC: Brookings Institution, 1981), 227.

55. Fisher, *Congressional Conflicts*, 202–6.

56. Hildenbrand oral history, US Senate Historical Office, 117.

57. Ibid., 118.

58. Stanley I. Kutler, *The Wars of Watergate: The Last Crisis of Richard Nixon* (New York: Norton, 1994), 404.

59. Fred Emery, *Watergate: The Corruption of American Politics and the Fall of Richard Nixon* (New York: Times Books, 1994).

60. John Herbers, "Nixon Resigns," *New York Times*, August 9, 1974.

61. Neil MacNeil interview with Gerald Ford, MacNeil papers, The Dirksen Congressional Center, Pekin, IL.

62. 120 Cong. Rec. 27, 847–9 (1974); James Cannon, *Time and Chance: Gerald Ford's Appointment with History* (New York: HarperCollins, 1994), 360–62.

63. Richard Reeves, *A Ford, Not a Lincoln* (New York: Harcourt Brace Jovanovich, 1975), 147.

64. Cannon, *Time and Chance*, 407.

65. Ibid., 393.

66. Ibid., 395.

67. Hatfield, *Vice Presidents of the United States, 1789–1993*, 500.

68. Cannon, *Time and Chance*, 415.

69. Byrd, *The Senate*, 1:714.

70. Cannon, *Time and Chance*, 397.

71. Ibid., 399.

72. Gerald R. Ford, *A Time to Heal* (New York: Harper & Row, 1979), 134, 150, 156.

73. Cannon, *Time and Chance*, 409.

74. Ibid., 411.

75. Kennedy, *True Compass*, 353.

76. Jimmy Carter, *Keeping Faith: Memoirs of a President* (New York: Bantam Books, 1982), 37.

77. Thomas P. O'Neill and William Novak, *Man of the House: The Life and Political Memoirs of Speaker Tip O'Neill* (New York: Random House, 1987), 297.

78. Byrd, *The Senate*, 1:716.

79. Carter, *Keeping Faith*, 92.

80. Hildenbrand oral history, 248.

81. Byrd, *The Senate*, 1:716–7; David A. Corbin, *The Last Great Senator: Robert C. Byrd's Encounters with Eleven U.S. Presidents* (Washington, DC: Potomac Books, 2012), 172.

82. *Encyclopedia of the United States Congress*, edited by Robert E. Dewhirst and John David Rausch Jr. (New York: Facts on File, 2007), 307.

83. Donald A. Ritchie, "Presidents Working with Congress from Truman to Obama," *Congress and Harry S. Truman: A Conflicted Legacy* (Kirksville, MO: Truman State University Press, 2011), xxvii–xxx.

84. Byrd, *The Senate*, 1:715–8; Jimmy Carter, *White House Diary* (New York: Farrar, Straus & Giroux, 2010), 85.

85. Robert C. Byrd, *Robert C. Byrd: Child of the Appalachian Coal Fields* (Morgantown: West Virginia University Press, 2005), 381–5.

86. Adam Clymer, *Drawing the Line at the Big Ditch: The Panama Canal Treaties and the Rise of the Right* (Lawrence: University Press of Kansas, 2008), 101–2.

87. Ibid.; Corbin, *The Last Great Senator*, 182–5.

88. Clymer, *Drawing the Line*, chapter 21.

89. Byrd, *Robert C. Byrd*, 396–7, 399–401.

90. Carter, *Keeping Faith*, 271.

91. For a superb explanation of this conclusion, see Ira Shapiro, *The Last Great Senate* (New York: Public Affairs, 2012), x–xii.

92. Trent Lott, *Leading the United States Senate* (Washington, DC: GPO, 2002).

93. Hildenbrand oral history, 222.

94. George C. Edwards III, *At the Margins: Presidential Leadership of Congress* (New Haven, CT: Yale University Press, 1989), 72.

95. Trent Lott, *Herding Cats* (New York: Regan Books, 2005), 89.

96. Marilyn Berger, "Ronald Reagan Dies at 93," *New York Times*, June 6, 2004.

97. Lou Cannon, "Ronald Reagan," *Encyclopedia of the United States Congress* (New York: Simon & Schuster, 1995), 1674–5.

98. Byrd, *The Senate*, 2:592.

99. Ibid.; Corbin, *The Last Great Senator*, 206.

100. Senate amendment 93, 99th Cong., 1st Sess., May 10, 1985.

101. Lott, *Leading the United States Senate*, 107.

102. Lott, *Herding Cats*, 92.

103. G. William Hoagland oral history, US Senate Historical Office, 27–9; *Bowsher v. Synar*, 487 U.S. 714 (1986).

104. For a classic account of the passage of the 1986 Tax Reform Act, see Jeffrey Birnbaum and Alan Murray, *Showdown at Gucci Gulch: Lawmakers, Lobbyists, and the Unlikely Triumph of Tax Reform* (New York: Random House, 1987), 3–22.

105. Mark J. Oleszek and Walter J. Oleszek, "Congress and the President," in James A. Thurber, ed., *Rivals for Power: Presidential-Congressional Relations* (Lanham, MD: Rowman & Littlefield, 2009), 262–5.

106. Julie Johnson, "Democrats Press Meese to Resign," *New York Times*, March 31, 1988.
107. George H. W. Bush inaugural address, January 20, 1989; http://bushlibrary .tamu.edu/research/public_papers.php?id=1&year=1989&month=01.
108. Michael Oreskes, "Senate Rejects Tower, 53–7," *New York Times*, March 10, 1989.
109. Byrd, *The Senate*, 2:42.
110. In the Congress that met during George H. W. Bush's second two years, 1991–1993, the number of cloture motions filed reached sixty for the first time.
111. Tom Daschle, *Like No Other Time* (New York: Crown, 2003), 58.
112. Byrd, *Robert C. Byrd*, 504.
113. Clarence Thomas, *My Grandfather's Son: A Memoir* (New York: Harper, 2007), 198; Kevin Merida and Michael A. Fletcher, *Supreme Discontent: The Divided Soul of Clarence Thomas* (New York: Doubleday, 2007), 398.
114. Neil A. Lewis, "Judiciary Panel Deadlocks, 7–7, On Thomas Nomination to Court," *New York Times*, September 28, 1991.
115. Richard L. Berke, "Thomas Accuser Tells Hearing of Obscene Talk and Advances; Judge Complains of 'Lynching,'" *New York Times*, October 12, 1991.
116. Lott, *Leading the United States Senate*, 64–5.
117. Ibid., 65.
118. Ibid.
119. Sidney Blumenthal, *The Clinton Wars* (New York: Farrar, Straus & Giroux, 2003), 159.
120. Lott, *Herding Cats*, 171–2.
121. Daschle, *Like No Other Time*, 57.
122. Ronald Reagan, State of the Union Address, February 4, 1986, www.reagan .utexas.edu/archives/speeches/1986/20486a.htm.
123. Robert C. Byrd, *The Senate of the Roman Republic: Addresses on the History of Roman Constitutionalism*, S. Doc. No. 103–23 (Washington, DC: GPO, 1995).
124. *Clinton v. City of New York*, 524 U.S. 417 (1998).
125. Ken Gormley, *The Death of American Virtue: Clinton v. Starr* (New York: Crown, 2010), 641–6.
126. Jonathan Schell, "Say What You Will, It's a War in Libya," *Los Angeles Times*, June 21, 2011.

Chapter 6

1. Harry Reid, "Judicial Nominees," 153 Cong. Rec. 11.936-7 (2007).
2. David M. Herszenhorn, "As the House Votes to Cut $60 Billion, Standoff Looms," *New York Times*, February 12, 2011.

3. *Federalist 63*, March 1, 1788; www.constitution.org/fed/federa63.htm.

4. Max Farrand, ed., *The Records of the Federal Convention of 1787* (New Haven, CT: Yale University Press, 1911), 1:48.

5. *Federalist 62*, February 27, 1788; www.constitution.org/fed/federa62.htm.

6. Wilbourn E. Benton, ed., *1787: Drafting the U.S. Constitution* (College Station: Texas A&M University Press, 1986), 1:480–82.

7. The earliest-known documented version of this story appears in an 1871 letter from constitutional law professor Francis Lieber to Representative James Garfield (R-OH). See Thomas Perry, ed., *The Life and Letters of Francis Lieber* (Boston: Osgood, 1882), 416–7.

8. *Federalist 55*, February 6, 1788; www.constitution.org/fed/federa55.htm.

9. U.S. Const., art. I, sec. 3.

10. In the late eighteenth century, a white American could expect to live an average of forty years, although most of the deaths contributing to this figure occurred before the age of thirty, as a consequence of high rates of infant mortality, or after fifty-five.

11. U.S. Const. art. II, sec. 2, cl. 2.

12. U.S. Const. art. I, sec. 7, cl. 1.

13. U.S. Const. art. I, sec. 3, cl. 5, 6.

14. A common joke among House members over the decades boasts that when a House member abandons that chamber for a seat in the Senate, the action raises the cumulative intelligence level of both bodies.

15. Thomas Jefferson, *A Manual of Parliamentary Practice for the Use of the Senate of the United States* (Washington, DC, 1801), published in many editions including one published by the Senate to commemorate the 250th anniversary of Jefferson's birth (S. Doc. No. 103–8, Washington, DC, 1993).

16. "It is a breach of order in debate to notice what has been said on the same subject in the other house, or the particular votes or majorities on it there: because the opinion of each house should be left to its own independency, not to be influenced by the proceedings of the other; and the quoting them might beget reflections leading to a misunderstanding between the two houses." Ibid., sec. 17, pt. 19.

17. "Wants Senate Abolished," *New York Times*, April 28, 1911.

18. Neil MacNeil, *Forge of Democracy: The House of Representatives* (New York: David McKay, 1963), 373.

19. Enoch Knight, "Thomas B. Reed: An Appreciation," *New England Magazine* 30 (April 1904): 217.

20. Samuel Walker McCall, *The Life of Thomas B. Reed* (Boston: Houghton Mifflin, 1914), 252.

21. Linda Greenhouse, "Congress Sworn In, Begins Its Work," *New York Times*, January 7, 1987.

22. William Maclay, *Journal of William Maclay: United States Senator from Pennsylvania, 1789–1791*, Edgar Maclay, ed. (New York: Boni, 1927), 222.

23. Robert V. Remini, *Daniel Webster: The Man and His Time* (New York: Norton, 1997), 279–81.

24. On November 14, 1831, the day the Kentucky governor certified his election, Clay wrote to a friend, "You will see that I am sent to the Senate, whither I shall go with no anticipated satisfaction." *The Papers of Henry Clay* (Lexington: University of Kentucky Press, 1984), 8:424.

25. For a thorough account of the interaction of these three, see Merrill Peterson, *The Great Triumvirate* (New York: Oxford University Press, 1987), 5–6.

26. Remini, *Daniel Webster*, 329–32.

27. Alexis de Tocqueville, *Democracy in America* (New York: Knopf, 1945), 1:202–5.

28. Thomas Hart Benton, *Thirty Years' View* (New York: Appleton, 1871), 1:206–7.

29. MacNeil, *Forge of Democracy*, 7–8.

30. Bryce, *The American Commonwealth* (Philadelphia: Morris, 1906), 63.

31. MacNeil, *Forge of Democracy*, 45–7.

32. Robert V. Remini, *The House* (New York: HarperCollins, 2006), 130.

33. MacNeil, *Forge of Democracy*, 71–2.

34. Remini, *The House*, 235.

35. MacNeil, *Forge of Democracy*, 100–102.

36. James Grant, *Mr. Speaker!: The Life and Times of Thomas B. Reed, the Man Who Broke the Filibuster* (New York: Simon & Schuster, 2011), 133.

37. Harry Thurston Peck, "Twenty Years of the Republic (1885–1905)," *The Bookman: A Magazine of Literature and Life* 21 (May 1905): 298.

38. Asher C. Hinds, *Hinds' Precedents of the House of Representatives of the United States, Including References to Provisions of the Constitution, the Laws, and the Decisions of the United States Senate* (Washington, DC: Government Printing Office, 1907–1908). 1:v.

39. Grant, *Mr. Speaker!*, 259–67.

40. Eric F. Goldman, *The Tragedy of Lyndon Johnson* (New York: Knopf, 1969), 284.

41. O. O. Stealey, *Twenty Years in the Press Gallery: A Concise History of Important Legislation from the 48th to the 58th Congress* (New York: Publishers Printing Co., 1906), 109.

42. Robert S. Allen and Drew Pearson, *Washington Merry-Go-Round* (New York: Horace Liveright, 1931), 221.

43. Ralston Hayden, *The Senate and Treaties, 1789–1817: The Development of the Treaty-making Functions of the United States Senate during Their Formative Period* (New York: Macmillan, 1920), 40–53.

44. Todd Estes, *The Jay Treaty Debate, Public Opinion, and the Evolution of Early American Political Culture* (Amherst: University of Massachusetts Press, 2008), 181–7; Jerald A. Combs, *The Jay Treaty: Political Background of the Founding Fathers* (Berkeley: University of California Press, 1970), chapter 11.

45. For an extended House examination of this issue, see "Power of the Senate to Originate Appropriation Bills," H. Rpt. 46–147, February 2, 1881.

46. Lionel A. Sheldon, "The Cuban Reciprocity Treaty: . . . No Revenue or Appropriation Bill Originating in the Senate Has Ever Been Enacted into Law," *American Economist* 31 (June 19, 1903): 291.

47. The periodically published congressional publication, *Our American Government* [2003 edition], under the heading "48. Must All Appropriations Bills Originate in the House?" offers the following response: "Although the Constitution clearly delegates sole authority to originate tax measures to the House of Representatives, it makes no clear statement regarding the authority to originate appropriations measures. Despite occasional disputes between the House of Representatives and the Senate over such authority, the House customarily initiates such appropriations bills. The Senate from time to time initiates special appropriation measures that provide funds for a single agency or purpose" (21).

48. *Committee on Appropriations, United States Senate, 138th Anniversary, 1867–2005*, S. Doc. 109–5, at 3–5 (2002).

49. Ibid, 4.

50. MacNeil, *Forge of Democracy*, 392–4.

51. Senate Rule 30, adopted on December 19, 1850, was designed to end the practice by which senators attached private claims bills, which they had been unable to pass as free-standing legislation, to public appropriations in the hectic final hours of a congressional session.

52. This rule was proposed by Representative William Holman. For House application of the "Holman Rule," see Wm. Holmes Brown and Charles Johnson, *House Practice: A Guide to the Rules, Precedents, and Procedures of the House*, 2d ed. (Washington, DC: Government Printing Office, 2003), sections 46–9; Asher C. Hinds. *Hinds' Precedents of the House of Representatives of the United States* 4: sections 4797–4806; 4 Cong. Rec. 445 (1876).

53. Paul S. Reinsch, *American Legislatures and Legislative Methods* (New York: Century, 1907), 109–17.

54. Frank William Taussig, *The Tariff History of the United States* (New York: G. P. Putnam's Sons, 1931), 31, 231–2.

55. Ibid., 327–8.

56. Writing of this era, Theodore Roosevelt's biographer Edmund Morris described the frustrations in 1903 of House Speaker Joseph Cannon. ". . . [Cannon] had seen the House's power decline steadily, till it functioned as almost a legislative bureau of supply to the Senate, sending money and parchment down the corridor on demand." Morris, *Theodore Rex*, 212. For a discussion of the Senate's greater influence on tariff legislation, see Taussig, *Tariff History*, 373–7.

57. Senate Rule 27, January 17, 1877.

58. The Senate revised Rule 16 on March 6, 1922, under the provisions of the landmark Budget and Accounting Act of 1921 (42 Stat 20, June 10, 1921), which the 2005 history of the Senate Appropriations Committee (S. Doc. No. 109–105, at 12) assesses to have been the "most far-reaching single fiscal reform measure promulgated since the establishment of the Republic . . ."

59. In recent times, Senate leaders have been reluctant to engage in conferences with the House. As Senate scholar Steven Smith explains, "Objections to the usual unanimous consent requests to go to conference are potentially costly to the majority, particularly near the end of a session, because they can delay the move to conference. Three motions—a motion to disagree with the House, a motion to request a conference, and a motion to authorize the appointment of conferees—are required for the Senate to go to conference, and all three are debatable and subject to filibusters." Steven S. Smith, "The Senate Syndrome," in Burdett A. Loomis, ed., *The U.S. Senate: From Deliberation to Dysfunction* (Washington, DC: CQ Press, 2012), 149.

60. 1 Annals of Cong. 1168 (February 8, 1790); 1233 (February 11, 1790); 1466 (March 9, 1790); 1514–6 (March 19, 1790).

61. Lawrence D. Longley and Walter J. Oleszek, *Bicameral Politics: Conference Committees in Congress* (New Haven, CT: Yale University Press, 1989), 77–87.

62. Gerald Ford, 1999 interview with Neil MacNeil.

63. Longley and Oleszek, *Bicameral Politics*, 91–107; *New York Times Magazine*, May 20, 1962, 93.

64. [J. William Fulbright] 94 Cong. Rec. 9,206 [June 19] (1948).

65. Mark O. Hatfield, 1981 interview with Neil MacNeil.

66. Neil MacNeil's reporting.

67. In *The Politics of Finance* (Boston: Little, Brown, 1970), John Manley reported that senators normally prevailed on tax measures in the twenty years after 1946, primarily "because politically Senate decisions are more in line with the demands of interest groups, lobbyists and constituents" (253–4). In *Unused Power* (Washington, DC: Brookings, 1970), a study of the Senate's Appropriations Committee, Stephen Horn found that on balance senators won out more often on these money bills than representatives. Horn, later elected a member of the House, pointed out that any senator or representative who managed to save a navy yard or veterans' hospital in his state or district "felt like a winner regardless of what happened to the rest of the bill" (160). Richard Fenno's *The Power of the Purse* (Boston: Little, Brown, 1966) offered a mixed verdict: the House had an initial advantage in originating appropriation bills, but the Senate won twice as often when they differed on dollar amounts (676–8). In their study, *Bicameral Politics, Conference Committees in Congress*, 114–8, Lawrence Longley and Walter Oleszek underscored Fenno's findings that while senators scored high in quarrels over specifics, that accomplishment did not lessen the House's great influence in initiating much of Congress's legislation, especially appropriations bills and those dealing with taxes, social security, and finance.

68. George B. Galloway, "The Operation of the Legislative Reorganization Act of 1946," *American Political Science Review* 45 (March 1951): 44–5.

69. Remarks, June 6, 1995, at a gathering in the Capitol's Statuary Hall to honor *Roll Call*'s fortieth anniversary.

70. Conducting the Watergate investigations were the Senate Select Committee on Presidential Campaign Activities and the House Judiciary Committee; Iran-Contra investigations were managed by the Senate Select Committee on Secret Military Assistance to Iran and the Nicaraguan Opposition and the House Select Committee to Investigate Covert Arms Transactions with Iran.

71. Garrison Nelson, "Joint Committees of Congress, 1947–1992," in *Committees of the U.S. Congress, 1947–1992* (Washington, DC: Congressional Quarterly, 1994), 2:1037.

72. George Rothwell Brown, *The Leadership of Congress* (Indianapolis: Bobbs-Merrill, 1922), 290.

Chapter 7

1. Richard A. Baker and Roger H. Davidson, eds., *First among Equals: Outstanding Senate Leaders of the Twentieth Century* (Washington, DC: Congressional Quarterly, 1991), vii.

2. Gordon S. Wood, *Empire of Liberty: A History of the Early Republic* (New York: Oxford University Press, 2009), 53–7.

3. Thomas Jefferson to Edmund Rutledge, June 24, 1797, *The Writings of Thomas Jefferson*, Andrew A. Lipscomb, ed. (Washington, DC: Thomas Jefferson Memorial Association, 1903), 9:411.

4. Chernow, *Alexander Hamilton*, 389–408.

5. Merrill D. Peterson, *The Great Triumvirate* (New York: Oxford University Press, 1987), 5–6.

6. As of 1837, the thirteen states commonly associated with the North, in order of their entrance to the Union, were: Pennsylvania, New Jersey, Connecticut, Massachusetts, New Hampshire, New York, Rhode Island, Vermont, Ohio, Indiana, Illinois, Maine, Michigan; the thirteen states of the South were: Delaware, Georgia, Maryland, South Carolina, Virginia, North Carolina, Kentucky, Tennessee, Louisiana, Mississippi, Alabama, Missouri, and Arkansas.

7. Heidler and Heidler, *Clay*, 334.

8. Ibid., 343–6.

9. Burdette, *Filibustering in the Senate*, 20–24.

10. Elbert B. Smith, *Magnificent Missourian: A Life of Thomas Hart Benton* (Philadelphia: Lippincott, 1958).

11. Heidler and Heidler, *Clay*, 362–3.

12. Both Webster and Calhoun left the Senate for several years but returned in 1845.

13. Henry Clay's Resolution of January 29, 1850; Fergus M. Bordewich, *America's Great Debate: Henry Clay, Stephen A. Douglas, and the Compromise that Preserved the Union* (New York: Simon & Schuster, 2012), 134–9.

14. Heidler and Heidler, *Clay*, 482–3.

15. Bordewich, *America's Great Debate*, 304.

16. Ibid., 303–16.
17. George Lee Robinson, "The Development of the Senate Committee System" (PhD diss., New York University, 1954), 121–31.
18. Ibid., 130–31; Cong. Globe, 29th Cong., 2d Sess., 30 (1846).
19. Cong. Globe, 32nd Cong., 1st Sess., 32 (December 8, 1851).
20. Cong. Globe, 35th Cong., 1st Sess., 39 (December 16, 1857).
21. Chandler made these remarks in his "maiden address" to the Senate on December 16, 1857; Cong. Globe, 35th Cong., 1st Sess., 40 (1857).
22. Wilmer Carlyle Harris, *The Public Life of Zachariah Chandler, 1851–1875* (Lansing: Michigan Historical Commission, 1917), 66.
23. Philip B. Kunhardt and Peter W. Kunhardt, *Lincoln: An Illustrated Biography* (New York: Knopf, 1992), 362.
24. Rothman, *Politics and Power*, 16.
25. Ibid., 73–4, 107–8.
26. George Alfred Townsend, *Washington Outside and Inside: A Picture and Narrative of the Origin, Growth, Excellencies, Abuses, Beauties, and Personages of Our Governing City* (Hartford, CT: J. Betts, 1873), 505.
27. Walter J. Oleszek, *Majority and Minority Whips of the Senate*, S. Doc. No. 98–45; 2 Cong. Rec. 2488 (1874).
28. Donald A. Ritchie and Wendy Wolff, comps., *Minutes of the Senate Republican Conference, 1911–1964*, S. Doc. No. 105–19, at xviii–xix; Haynes, *The Senate*, 475. Haynes determined that the last meeting of Senate Republicans to have been designated a "caucus" took place on January 28, 1913.
29. Rothman, *Politics and Power*, 33.
30. "Congressional Debates and Public Opinion," *New York Times*, December 15, 1878.
31. James Bryce, *American Commonwealth* (New York: Macmillan, 1888), 1:275 (Chapter 19, "General Observations on Congress").
32. Edward Winslow Martin [pseud. of James Dabney McCabe], *Behind the Scenes in Washington: Being a Complete and Graphic Account of the Credit Mobilier Investigation* (New York: Continental, 1873), 148.
33. Bryce, *American Commonwealth*, 1:158 (Chapter 10, "The Senate: Its Working and Influence").
34. Wilson, *Congressional Government* (Boston, 1885), 213.
35. Merrill and Merrill, *Republican Command*, 17–21.
36. John R. Lambert Jr., *Arthur Pue Gorman* (Baton Rouge: Louisiana State University Press, 1953), chapter 7.
37. Ibid., chapter 10.
38. Merrill and Merrill, *Republican Command*, 18–9.
39. Ibid., 43.
40. Congressional Quarterly, *Origins and Development of Congress* (Washington, DC: Congressional Quarterly, 1976), 202.
41. Rothman, 50–51.
42. Merrill and Merrill, *Republican Command*, 32–3.
43. Ibid., 22–6.

44. Chauncey Mitchell Depew, *My Memories of Eighty Years* (New York: Scribner's, 1922), 180.
45. Thomas C. Platt to William B. Allison, July 26, 1899, William B. Allison Papers, Iowa State Department of History and Archives, Des Moines, Iowa.
46. Lewis L. Gould, *The Most Exclusive Club: A History of the Modern United States Senate* (New York: Basic Books, 2005), 25; Marie Heyda, "Senator James McMillan and the Flowering of the Spoils System," *Michigan History* 54 (Fall 1970): 183–200.
47. James Harvey Young, *Pure Food: Securing the Federal Food and Drugs Act of 1906* (Princeton, NJ: Princeton University Press, 1989), 194–6, 205–6.
48. David Graham Phillips, *Treason of the Senate*, edited with an introduction by George E. Mowry and Judson A. Grenier (Chicago: Quadrangle Books, 1964).
49. Donald A. Ritchie, *Press Gallery: Congress and the Washington Correspondents* (Cambridge, MA: Harvard University Press, 1991), 191.
50. Charles Willis Thompson, *Party Leaders of the Time* (New York: Dillingham, 1906), 26–8; Merrill and Merrill, *Republican Command*, 284–5.
51. Ibid., 283–5.
52. Robert M. La Follette, *Robert M. La Follette's Autobiography: A Personal Narrative of Political Experiences* (Madison, WI: Robert M. La Follette Company, 1913), 191.
53. Walter J. Oleszek, "John Worth Kern: Portrait of a Floor Leader," in Baker and Davidson, *First among Equals*, 18–23.
54. Joseph P. Tumulty, *Woodrow Wilson As I Know Him* (Garden City, NY: Doubleday, 1921), 101.
55. "Democrats Agree to Lobby Inquiry," *New York Times*, May 29, 1913.
56. Byrd, *The Senate*, S. Doc. No. 100–20, at 195–8.
57. M. Cullom Shelby, *Fifty Years of Public Service* (New York: McClurg, 1911), 425.
58. Ibid., 425–6.
59. Henry H. Gilfry, *President of the Senate Pro Tempore*, S. Doc. No. 62–104 (Washington, DC, 1911).
60. William C. Widenor, "Henry Cabot Lodge," in Baker and Davidson, *First among Equals*, 38–50.
61. Henry Cabot Lodge to Theodore Roosevelt, November 22, 1918, *Selections from the Correspondence of Theodore Roosevelt and Henry Cabot Lodge, 1884–1918* (New York: Scribner's, 1925), 2:545.
62. Widenor, "Henry Cabot Lodge," 45–6.
63. John A. Garraty, *Henry Cabot Lodge* (New York: Knopf, 1953), 384–7; Claudius O. Johnson, *Borah of Idaho* (New York: Longmans, Green, 1936), 246–8.
64. Charles Willis Thompson, "Out-Ringing the Rings in Senate Circles," *New York Times*, August 22, 1920.
65. Widenor, "Henry Cabot Lodge," 57–8.
66. Harry Hunt, "Borah—A Big Picture," *La Follette's Magazine* 14 (February 1922): 23.

67. Brown, *Leadership of Congress*, 290.
68. Garraty, *Henry Cabot Lodge*, 424.
69. Burdette, *Filibustering in the Senate*, chapter 5.
70. Oscar W. Underwood, *Drifting Sands of Party Politics* (New York: Century, 1931).
71. A resume of Curtis's career appears in Hatfield, *Vice Presidents of the United States*, 371.
72. Leonard Schlup, "Charles Curtis: The Vice President from Kansas," *Manuscripts* 35 (Summer 1983): 183–201.
73. James Eli Watson, *As I Knew Them* (Indianapolis: Bobbs-Merrill, 1936), 264–5.
74. Herbert Hoover, *The Memoirs of Herbert Hoover: The Great Depression, 1929–1941*, 103. Here, Hoover notes that Watson, as Senate leader, "was always a problem . . . he never fully buried his bitterness over my nomination."
75. Watson, *As I Knew Them*, 262.
76. Ibid.
77. This came from Neil MacNeil's father, who had served as editorial director of the Second Hoover Commission on the Organization of the Executive Branch of the Government (1953–55) and as one of Hoover's literary executors.
78. David Burner, *Herbert Hoover: A Public Life* (New York: Knopf, 1979).
79. Donald C. Bacon, "Joseph Taylor Robinson: The Good Soldier," in Baker and Davidson, *First among Equals*, 63–97.
80. Ibid., 82.
81. Bacon, "Joseph Taylor Robinson," 63.
82. For an account of McNary's bipartisanship as Republican leader, see Steve Neal, *McNary of Oregon* (Portland, OR: Western Imprints, 1985), 141–50.
83. Richard L. Neuberger, "McNary of Fir Cone," *Life*, August 12, 1940, 76–8.
84. Neal, *McNary*, 135–8.
85. Burt Solomon, *FDR v. the Constitution: The Court-Packing Fight and the Triumph of Democracy* (New York: Walker, 2009), 184.
86. Jeff Shesol, *Supreme Power: Franklin Roosevelt v. the Supreme Court* (New York: Norton, 2010), 308–9, 448–51.
87. Solomon, *FDR v. the Constitution*, 238–9.
88. Bacon, "Joseph Taylor Robinson," 92–3.
89. Donald A. Ritchie, "Alben W. Barkley: The President's Man," in Baker and Davidson, *First among Equals*, 127–62.
90. Ibid., 128.
91. D. B. Hardeman and Donald C. Bacon, *Rayburn* (Austin: Texas Monthly Press, 1989), 227.
92. Ritchie, "Alben Barkley," 146–8.
93. Ibid., 150.
94. James Patterson, *Mr. Republican: A Biography of Robert A. Taft* (Boston: Houghton Mifflin, 1972), 335–41; William S. White, *The Taft Story* (New York: Harper, 1954), 57–65.

95. "Old Guard Supreme," *New Republic*, January 13, 1947.
96. David McCullough, *Truman* (New York: Simon & Schuster, 1992), 353.
97. Patterson, *Mr. Republican*, 339–41; *Time*, January 20, 1947.
98. Robert W. Merry, "Robert A. Taft," in Baker and Davidson, in *First among Equals*, 177.
99. Patterson, *Mr. Republican*, 592.
100. Harry S. Truman, "The Truman Memoirs," *Life*, September 26, 1955, 106.
101. Edward L. Schapsmeier and Frederick H. Schapsmeier, "Scott W. Lucas of Havana: His Rise and Fall as Majority Leader in the United States Senate," *Journal of the Illinois State Historical Society* 70 (November 1977): 309.
102. Rowland Evans and Robert Novak, *Lyndon B. Johnson: The Exercise of Power* (New York: New American Library, 1966), 40.
103. Schapsmeier and Schapsmeier, "Scott W. Lucas," 309–12.
104. Ibid., 314–9.
105. White, *The Taft Story*, 163–4.
106. Ibid.; Robert Cowley, *The Cold War: A Military History* (New York: Random House, 2005), 97.
107. Patterson, *Mr. Republican*, part 5.
108. Neil MacNeil's reporting.
109. James J. Kiepper, *Styles Bridges: Yankee Senator* (Sugar Hill, NH: Phoenix, 2001); "Styles Bridges Is Dead at 63," *New York Times*, November 27, 1961.
110. Neil MacNeil's anecdote.
111. Byrd, *The Senate*, S.Doc. No. 100–20 at 2:188.
112. Ernest W. McFarland, *Mac: The Autobiography of Ernest W. McFarland* (privately published, 1979), 109.
113. Ibid., 128.
114. Caro, *Master of the Senate*, 207–12.

Chapter 8

1. Kiepper, *Styles Bridges*, 159–60, 166–9.
2. Richard Rovere, "What Course for the Powerful Mr. Taft?" *New York Times Magazine*, March 22, 1953, 34.
3. Haynes, *Senate*, 480–82.
4. 77 Cong. Rec. 4148 (1933).
5. 81 Cong. Rec. 8840 (1937).
6. White, *The Taft Story*, 174–83.
7. Patterson, *Mr. Republican*, 585–6; White, *The Taft Story*, 184–94.
8. Lewis Gould, *The Most Exclusive Club: A History of the Modern United States Senate* (New York: Basic Books, 2005), 211.
9. Merry, "Robert A. Taft," in Baker and Davidson, *First among Equals*, 163–98.
10. Gayle B. Montgomery and James B. Johnson, *One Step from the White House: The Rise and Fall of Senator William F. Knowland* (Berkeley: University of California Press, 1998), 131–2.

11. Caro, *Master of the Senate*, 521–4; Ambrose, *Eisenhower: Soldier and President*, 489.
12. Caro, *Master of the Senate*, 496.
13. Ibid., 502–5.
14. MacNeil, *Dirksen*, 153–4.
15. William Proxmire, *Uncle Sam: The Last of the Big-Time Spenders* (New York: Simon & Schuster, 1972), 243.
16. Evans and Novak, *Lyndon B. Johnson*, 104; Caro, *Master of the Senate*, 591–5.
17. Neil MacNeil's reporting, MacNeil Papers, Dirksen Congressional Research Center.
18. Montgomery and Johnson, *One Step*, 141–2.
19. Evans and Novak, *Lyndon B. Johnson*, 74.
20. Caro, *Master of the Senate*, 546–7.
21. Ibid., 392–4.
22. Bobby Baker, *Wheeling and Dealing: Confessions of a Capitol Hill Operator* (New York: Norton, 1978), 30.
23. For Baker's account of Lyndon Johnson as a "wheeler-dealer," see ibid., 63–72.
24. Kearns, *Lyndon Johnson*, 143.
25. Montgomery and Johnson, *One Step*, 148.
26. Dwight D. Eisenhower, *Mandate for Change, 1953–1956: The White House Years* (Garden City, NY: Doubleday, 1963).
27. Stephen E. Ambrose, *Eisenhower: The President* (New York: Simon & Schuster, 1984), 164.
28. "Ex-Senator Knowland Is Apparent Suicide," *New York Times*, February 25, 1974; Evans and Novak, *Lyndon B. Johnson*, 169.
29. Evans and Novak, *Lyndon B. Johnson*, 96.
30. James L. Sundquist, *The Decline and Resurgence of Congress* (Washington, DC: Brookings Institution, 1981), 186.
31. Howard E. Shuman "Lyndon B. Johnson: The Senate's Powerful Persuader," in Baker and Davidson, eds., *First among Equals*, 218.
32. Evans and Novak, *Lyndon B. Johnson*, 104.
33. Floyd M. Riddick oral history, US Senate Historical Office, August 25, 1978, 251–6.
34. Robert G. Baker oral history, US Senate Historical Office, June 1, 2009, 67–8, 70–1.
35. Neil MacNeil's reporting, MacNeil papers, Dirksen Congressional Research Center.
36. Tristram Coffin, *Senator Fulbright: Portrait of a Public Philosopher* (New York: Dutton, 1966), 204.
37. Caro, *Master of the Senate*, 611; Evans and Novak, *Lyndon B. Johnson*, 150.
38. George Tames, "Lyndon B. Johnson and the Vanities of Famous Men," Oral History Interview, March 8, 1988, US Senate Historical Office.
39. The Senate Committee on the District of Columbia had recently vacated that space for larger quarters in the newly opened structure today known as the Dirksen Senate Office Building.

40. http://www.senate.gov/artandhistory/art/resources/pdf/Lyndon_B._Johnson_ Room.pdf.
41. William Proxmire, 105 Cong. Rec. 2814–20 (1959).
42. Jacqueline Kennedy, *Historic Conversations on Life with John F. Kennedy* (New York: Hyperion, 2011), 85–7 (conversation of March 4, 1964). For a richly detailed account of this phase of Johnson's career, see Robert A. Caro, *The Years of Lyndon Johnson: The Passage of Power* (New York: Alfred A. Knopf, 2012), chapter 6.
43. Kearns, *Lyndon Johnson*, 107, 168, 402; Caro, *The Passage of Power*, 159.
44. Francis R. Valeo, *Mike Mansfield, Majority Leader* (Armonk, NY: M. E. Sharpe, 1999), 10–11; Don Oberdorfer, *Senator Mansfield: The Extraordinary Life of a Great American Statesman and Diplomat* (Washington, DC: Smithsonian Books, 2003), 154–6.
45. Oberdorfer, *Senator Mansfield*, 156; Robert Baker captures the spirit of this comment in *Wheeling and Dealing*, 133–4.
46. Kyle Longley, *Senator Albert Gore Sr.: Tennessee Maverick* (Baton Rouge: Louisiana State University Press, 2004), 159; Clinton P. Anderson, *Outsider in the Senate* (New York: World, 1970), 309.
47. Baker, *Wheeling and Dealing*, 135; Caro, *Master of the Senate*, 1038–9.
48. Evans and Novak, *Lyndon B. Johnson*, 305–8.
49. Oberdorfer, *Senator Mansfield*, 174
50. Neil MacNeil's reporting, MacNeil Papers, Dirksen Congressional Research Center.
51. Mike Mansfield, 109 Cong. Rec. 22,857–66 (1963); Lott, *Leading the United States Senate*, 13–23.
52. Frederic W. Collins, "How to Be a Leader without Leading," *New York Times*, July 30, 1961, 9; 115 Cong. Rec. 14,102–3 (1961).
53. Oberdorfer, *Senator Mansfield*, 148.
54. Carl Solberg, *Hubert Humphrey* (New York: Norton, 1984), 215.
55. Neil MacNeil's reporting, MacNeil Papers, Dirksen Congressional Research Center.
56. MacNeil, *Dirksen*, 161–4.
57. Ibid., 164.
58. Ibid., 164–6.
59. 109 Cong. Rec. 21245–9, 21282–4 (1963).
60. Ibid., 21277, 21283–4 (1963); MacNeil, *Dirksen*, 230.
61. MacNeil, *Dirksen*, 230.
62. Rule 19 provides that "No Senator in debate shall, directly or indirectly, by any form of words impute to another Senator or to other Senators any conduct or motive unworthy or unbecoming a senator."
63. Burdett Loomis, "Everett McKinley Dirksen: The Consummate Minority Leader," in Baker and Davidson, eds., *First among Equals*, 236–63.
64. 109 Cong. Rec. 22,857–66 (1963)
65. Robert Mann, *Legacy to Power: Senator Russell Long of Louisiana* (St. Paul, MN: Paragon House, 1992), 240–41, 291–5.

66. Byrd, *The Senate*, at 2:195–205, 567–68; Kennedy, *True Compass*, 295–6.

67. John Ehrlichman, *Witness to Power: The Nixon Years* (New York: Simon & Schuster, 1982), 198.

68. Thomas M. DeFrank, *Write It When I'm Gone: Remarkable Off-the-Record Conversations with Gerald R. Ford* (New York: G. P. Putnam's Sons, 2007), 95–6; Yanek Mieczkowski, *Gerald Ford and the Challenges of the 1970s* (Lexington: University Press of Kentucky, 2005), 57.

69. At the time of the Senate's two hundredth anniversary in 1989, Byrd commented on the Senate's continuity, "Many new senators come here thinking that they will quickly make their mark on the institution. Soon, however, they learn that it is the institution that makes its mark on them. The Senate goes on like Tennyson's brook, forever, and it is far greater than the sum of its one hundred parts" (*The Senate*, 2:539).

70. Byrd expressed similar ideas in his 1998 "Leader's Lecture" presentation, "The Senate—The Great Forum of Constitutional Liberty"; Lott, *Leading the United States Senate*, 51; David A. Corbin, *The Last Great Senator: Robert C. Byrd's Encounters with Eleven U.S. Presidents* (Washington, DC: Potomac Books, 2012), chapter 8.

71. Howard H. Baker Jr., in Lott, *Leading the United States Senate*, 37.

72. Byrd expressed similar views in Lott, *Leading the United States Senate*, 51–3.

73. Samuel C. Patterson, "Party Leadership in the U.S. Senate," *Legislative Studies Quarterly* 14 (August 1989): 393–413.

74. J. Lee Annis, *Howard Baker: Conciliator in an Age of Crisis* (Lanham, MD: Madison Books, 1995), xxiii; Neil MacNeil's reporting, MacNeil papers, Dirksen Congressional Research Center. For House Speaker Sam Rayburn's use of one of these folksy quotes, see David Broder, "Beware Second Kick of Mule," *Washington Post*, November 13, 2001.

75. Annis, *Howard Baker: Conciliator in an Age of Crisis*, 1–3, 168.

76. Ibid., 167.

77. Walter Isaacson, Neil MacNeil, Evan Thomas, "The Floor Is My Domain," *Time*, April 26, 1982.

78. Lott, *Leading the United States Senate*, 32–8.

79. Ibid., 36.

80. Neil MacNeil, private conversation with Howard Baker; for Baker's thirteen rules for effective leadership, see Lott, *Leading the United States Senate*, 35–8.

81. Michael Specter, "In This Corner Lowell Weicker," *New York Times*, December 15, 1991.

82. Neil MacNeil, private conversation with Howard Baker; James Reston, "Baker's Turning Point," *New York Times*, January 12, 1983.

83. Jake Thompson, *Bob Dole: The Republicans' Man for All Seasons* (New York: D. I. Fine, 1996), 121.

84. Ibid., 145–8.

85. Neil MacNeil's reporting, MacNeil papers, Dirksen Congressional Research Center.

86. 132 Cong. Rec. 19,216 (1986).
87. Jake Thompson, *Bob Dole*, 154.
88. Bob Dole and Elizabeth Dole, *Unlimited Partners* (New York: Simon & Schuster, 1988), 244.
89. Susan F. Rasky, "The Senate; Choosing a Majority Leader: An Arcane and Curious Process," *New York Times*, September 21, 1988.
90. S. Res. 91, 100th Cong., 1st sess. (January 28, 1987).
91. Steven V. Roberts, "Man in the News: George John Mitchell; Thoughtful Competitor," *New York Times*, November 30, 1988.
92. Ibid.
93. Leslie Feldman and Rosanna Perotti, eds., *Honor and Loyalty: Inside the Politics of the George H. W. Bush White House* (Westport, CT: Greenwood, 2002), 260–62.
94. Trent Lott, *Herding Cats: A Life in Politics* (New York: Regan, 2005), 112–3.
95. Adam Clymer, "The Lawmakers—A Periodic Look at the Titans of Capitol Hill," *New York Times*, August 9, 1993.
96. Ibid.
97. Tom Daschle, *Like No Other Time* (New York: Crown, 2003), 78–9.
98. Gallup Poll, September 6, 1994.
99. Michael Wines, "Leadership Race in the Senate Attracting Mainly Spectators," *New York Times*, June 23, 1994.
100. Ibid.; Sheryl Gay Stolberg, "Daschle, Democratic Senate Leader, Is Beaten," *New York Times*, November 3, 2004.
101. Daschle, *Like No Other Time*, 77.
102. Ibid.
103. Lott, *Herding Cats*, 210–11.
104. Ibid., 211.
105. Michael D. Shear, "Lott and Daschle Offer Advice on Getting Along," *New York Times*, November 10, 2010.
106. Daschle, *Like No Other Time*, 6.
107. Ibid.
108. Lott, *Herding Cats*, 119.
109. Ibid., 120–21.
110. Eric Schmitt, "Chester Trent Lott; A Polished and Pragmatic Ideologue," *New York Times*, June 13, 1996.
111. Lott, *Herding Cats*, 113.
112. Lott, *Leading the United States Senate*, 2.
113. Ibid., 5–6.
114. Lott, *Herding Cats*, 2, 246.
115. Daschle, *Like No Other Time*, 35.
116. David Firestone, "Divisive Words: The Successor: Leadership in Recapturing Senate Pushed First into G.O.P. Spotlight," *New York Times*, December 21, 2002.
117. Robin Toner, "Divisive Words: The Successor: New Challenge for a Surgeon Turned Senator," *New York Times*, December 22, 2002; William H. Frist Jr., *Tennessee Senators, 1911–2001* (Lanham, MD: Madison, 1999), 254.

118. David Brooks, "What Makes Bill Frist Run?" *New York Times*, June 19, 2005.
119. Charles Babbington, "Frist Defends Remarks on Schiavo Case," *Washington Post*, June 17, 2005.
120. Sheryl Gay Stolberg, "Frist Is Treading a Perilous Path Leading to 2008," *New York Times*, April 3, 2006.
121. Carl Hulse, "Aspirations Dashed, Frist Says Farewell," *New York Times*, December 8, 2006.
122. April 3, 2006; Harry Reid, *The Good Fight: Hard Lessons from Searchlight to Washington* (New York: G. P. Putnam's Sons, 2008), 204.
123. Adam Nagourney, "G.O.P. Eyes Tough Task: Winning Reid's Seat," *New York Times*, May 25, 2009.
124. Adam Nagourney, "Reid Faces Battles in Washington and at Home," *New York Times*, January 24, 2010.
125. Adam Nagourney and Carl Hulse, "New Democratic Leader in Senate Is Atypical Choice," *New York Times*, November 15, 2004.
126. "Times Topics: Mitch McConnell," *New York Times*, May 11, 2012.
127. Robin Toner, "A Political Partisan with a Zeal for Focus—Addison Mitchell McConnell Jr.," *New York Times*, November 14, 2002.
128. Carl Hulse and Adam Nagourney, "Senate G.O.P. Leader Finds Weapon in Unity," *New York Times*, March 16, 2010.
129. Lott, *Leading the United States Senate*, 34.
130. Ibid., 35–8.

Chapter 9

1. "A History of Notable Senate Investigations," US Senate Historical Office, http://www.senate.gov/artandhistory/history/common/briefing/Investigations.htm#4.
2. Arthur M. Schlesinger Jr., "Introduction to the Previous [1975] Edition," *Congress Investigates: A Critical and Documentary History*, Roger A. Bruns, David L. Hostetter, and Raymond W. Smock, eds. rev. ed. (New York: Facts on File, 2011), xx–xxi.
3. Telford Taylor, *Grand Inquest: The Story of Congressional Investigations* (New York: Ballantine, 1961), 49–50.
4. Asher Crosby Hinds, *Hinds' Precedents of the House of Representatives of the United States Including References to Provisions of the Constitution, the Laws and Decisions of the United States Senate* (Washington, DC: Government Printing Office, 1907), 2:1052–6.
5. 6 Annals of Cong.184 (1800).
6. Robert Remini, *Andrew Jackson and His Indian Wars* (New York: Viking, 2001), 154–7, 166–8.
7. Taylor, *Grand Inquest*, 50.
8. Donald A. Ritchie, *Press Gallery: Congress and the Washington Correspondents* (Cambridge, MA: Harvard University Press, 1991), 27.

9. Senator William Blount, 1799; Judge John Pickering, 1804; Justice Samuel Chase, 1805: Judge James Peck, 1831.

10. Williamjames Hull Hoffer, *The Caning of Charles Sumner: Honor, Idealism, and the Origins of the Civil War* (Baltimore: Johns Hopkins University Press, 2010), 71–7; Roger A. Bruns, "The Assault on Senator Charles Sumner, 1856," in *Congress Investigates*, 91–103.

11. Roger A. Bruns, "John Brown's Raid on Harper's Ferry," in *Congress Investigates*, 124–37.

12. Cong. Globe, 36th Cong., 1st Sess., 3006–7 (1860).

13. Tap, *Over Lincoln's Shoulder*, 22–6.

14. Ibid., 30–32.

15. Hans L. Trefousse, *Benjamin Franklin Wade: Radical Republican from Ohio* (NY: Twayne, 1963), 156–8.

16. Elizabeth Joan Doyle, "The Conduct of the Civil War," *Congress Investigates*, 160–89.

17. 103 U.S. 168.

18. Charles Fairman, "Justice Samuel Miller: A Study of a Judicial Statesman," *Political Science Quarterly* 50 (March 1935): 15–44.

19. Gerald D. Morgan, "Congressional Investigations and Judicial Review: *Kilbourn v. Thompson* Revisited," *California Law Review* (1949): 37 (4), 556–74.

20. Taylor, *Grand Inquest*, 69–71.

21. John D. Macoll, "The Clapp Committee on Campaign Finance Corruption, 1912–3," in *Congress Investigates*, 384–95.

22. "The Tariff Lobby," May 26, 1913 Statement Given to the Press, *Papers of Woodrow Wilson*, 27:473.

23. 50 Cong. Rec. 1758–9, 1802–15 (1913).

24. U.S. Senate, Committee on the Judiciary, *Maintenance of a Lobby to Influence Legislation*, 63rd Cong., 1st Sess. (1913).

25. Hasia Diner, "The Teapot Dome Scandal, 1922–4," *Congress Investigates*, 460–74.

26. David H. Stratton, *Tempest over Teapot Dome: The Story of Albert B. Fall* (Norman: University of Oklahoma Press, 1998), 187–93.

27. Nancy C. Unger, *Fighting Bob La Follette: The Righteous Reformer* (Madison: Wisconsin Historical Society Press, 2008), 277–8.

28. Stratton, *Tempest over Teapot Dome*, 335–9.

29. Taylor, *Grand Inquest*, 86.

30. Donald A. Ritchie, "The Pecora Committee on the Stock Market Crash, 1933–34," *Congress Investigates*, 500–520.

31. Roger K. Newman, *Hugo Black* (New York: Fordham University Press, 1997), 197.

32. William A. Gregory and Rennard Strickland, "Hugo Black's Congressional Investigation of Lobbying and the Public Utilities Holding Company Act: A Historical View of the Power Trust, New Deal Politics, and Regulatory Propaganda," *Oklahoma Law Review* 29 (1976): 543–76; Arnold Markoe, "The Black Committee: A Study of the Senate Investigation of the Public

Utility Holding Company Lobby" (PhD dissertation, New York University, 1972).

33. Newman, *Hugo Black*, 161–6.

34. *Jurney v. MacCracken*, 294 U.S. 125 (1935).

35. More than a generation later, in 1973, President Nixon announced publicly that he would not permit any of his staff aides at the White House to testify before the Senate committee then investigating the Watergate scandal. That committee's chairman, Sam Ervin of North Carolina, turned to the MacCracken decision. He let it be known that he would move to have the Senate order the arrest of these White House aides and bring them before the Senate to testify. Nixon withdrew his order. The testimony of those aides helped destroy Nixon's presidency.

36. John Edward Wiltz, "The Nye Committee on the Munitions Industry," *Congress Investigates*, 540–65; Matthew Ware Coulter, *The Senate Munitions Inquiry of the 1930s: Beyond the Merchants of Death* (Westport, CT: Greenwood Press, 1997), 1–17, 20, 136.

37. Wayne S. Cole, *Roosevelt and the Isolationists, 1932–45* (Lincoln: University of Nebraska Press, 1983), 160–62.

38. Patrick J. Maney, *Young Bob: A Biography of Robert M. La Follette Jr.* (Madison: Wisconsin Historical Society Press, 2003), 222–5.

39. Alfred M. Landon, Speech, October 20, 1936, quoted in "Congressional Investigations during Franklin D. Roosevelt's First Term," *American Political Science Review* 31 (August 1937): 680.

40. Theodore Wilson, "The Truman Committee on War Mobilization, 1941–44," *Congress Investigates*, 636–52; Donald H. Riddle, *The Truman Committee: A Study in Congressional Responsibility* (New Brunswick, NJ: Rutgers University Press, 1963), 32, 46–7.

41. Wilson, "Truman Committee," *Congress Investigates*, 646–8.

42. Former representative Andrew Jackson May (D-KY) was convicted in federal court on July 3, 1947, on charges of using his position as chair of the House Committee on Military Affairs to obtain munitions contracts. He served nine months in a federal prison and was later pardoned by President Truman.

43. Forrest C. Pogue, *George C. Marshall: Organizer of Victory, 1943–1945* (New York: Viking, 1973), 196–7.

Chapter 10

1. Legislative Reorganization Act of 1946, 60 Stat. 812; Byrd, "Congressional Reform: The Legislative Reorganization Act of 1946," in *The Senate*, chapter 28.

2. Wayne Thompson, "The Pearl Harbor Committee, 1945–46," in *Congress Investigates*, 668–91.

3. Michael Wreszin, "The Dies Committee and Un-American Activities, 1938–43," in *Congress Investigates*, 585–614.

4. Robert Griffith, *Politics of Fear: Joseph R. McCarthy and the Senate*, 2d ed. (Amherst: University of Massachusetts Press, 1987), 102.

5. Joseph McCarthy conversation with Neil MacNeil, MacNeil Papers, Dirksen Congressional Center, Pekin, IL.

6. Ibid.

7. David M. Oshinsky, *A Conspiracy So Immense* (New York: Free Press, 1983), 107; Griffith, *Politics of Fear*, 29.

8. 96 Cong. Rec., 1952–81 (1950).

9. Patterson, *Mr. Republican*, 446.

10. Thomas C. Reeves, *The Life and Times of Joe McCarthy* (New York: Stein and Day, 1982), 284–5.

11. Edwin R. Bayley, *Joe McCarthy and the Press* (Madison: University of Wisconsin Press, 1981), 68.

12. John L. Steele of United Press quoted in ibid., 67

13. Evan Thomas, *The Man to See: Edward Bennett William: Ultimate Insider* (New York: Simon & Schuster, 1991), 68.

14. On May 31, 1957, a federal court convicted playwright Arthur Miller of contempt of Congress for his refusal to respond to all questions from the House Un-American Activities Committee. His defense attorney, Joseph Rauh, argued that the committee had no legitimate reason for posing some of its questions other than to "expose" Miller and that "exposure for exposure sake" was illegal, http://news.bbc.co.uk/onthisday/hi/dates/stories/may/31/newsid_4417000/4417523.stm.

15. William Howard Moore, *The Kefauver Committee and the Politics of Crime* (Columbia: University of Missouri Press, 1974), 100–101; Theodore Wilson, "The Kefauver Committee on Organized Crime, 1950–51," *Congress Investigates*, 715–37.

16. Wilson, "The Kefauver Committee," *Congress Investigates*, 729–31.

17. Moore, *The Kefauver Committee*, 225–30.

18. Ibid., 186–92.

19. Wilson, "The Kefauver Committee," 733.

20. Robert M. Cipes, *The Crime War* (New York: New American Library, 1968), 78.

21. William S. White, "Senate Investigations—Bad," *Citadel: The Story of the U.S. Senate* (New York: Harper & Brothers, 1957), 254–5.

22. Wilson, "The Kefauver Committee," 731.

23. Charles L. Fontenay, *Estes Kefauver* (Knoxville: University of Tennessee Press, 1980), 189.

24. Moore, *The Kefauver Committee*, 236.

25. "Investigations: What Would Harry Say?," *Time*, August 29, 1949.

26. General Harry H. Vaughn oral history interview with Charles T. Morrissey, January 16, 1963, Harry Truman Library, 104–7.

27. McCullough, *Truman*, 744–7.

28. R. W. Apple Jr., "J. William Fulbright, Senate Giant, Is Dead at 89," *New York Times*, February 10, 1995.

29. McCullough, *Truman*, 863–4.
30. Fite, *Richard B. Russell*, 256.
31. Ibid., 257; John Edward Wiltz, "The Committee on the Conduct and Firing of General Douglas MacArthur, 1951," *Congress Investigates*, 757–91.
32. Fite, *Richard B. Russell*, 256.
33. Wiltz, "The Committee on the Conduct and Firing of General Douglas MacArthur, 1951," *Congress Investigates*, 796–801.
34. John Lewis Gaddis, *Strategies of Containment* (New York: Oxford University Press, 1982), 116.
35. Richard Rovere, *Senator Joe McCarthy* (New York: Harcourt, Brace, 1959), 3.
36. Oshinsky, *A Conspiracy*, 197.
37. Neil MacNeil interview with Senator J. W. Fulbright.
38. "Joseph McCarthy and William Benton," Butler and Wolff, *Senate Election, Expulsion and Censure Cases*, 394–7.
39. 96 Cong. Rec. 1952–9 (1950)
40. Griffith, *Politics of Fear*, 208.
41. Ibid., 212–3.
42. Roy Cohn, *McCarthy* (New York: New American Library, 1968), 224.
43. Oshinsky, *A Conspiracy*, 260.
44. Ted Sorensen, *Kennedy* (New York: Harper Perennial, 2009), 47.
45. Cohn, *McCarthy*, 110–13.
46. Oshinsky, *A Conspiracy*, 355.
47. Donald A. Ritchie, "The Army-McCarthy Hearings, 1954," *Congress Investigates*, 822.
48. Ibid., 824–7.
49. Ibid., 824–6.
50. Ibid., 838–41.
51. Griffith, *Politics of Fear*, 259.
52. Charles E. Egan, "Flanders' Motion to Curb McCarthy Hit By Knowland," *New York Times*, June 13, 1954.
53. Arthur Herman, *Joseph McCarthy* (New York: Free Press, 2000), 289–92; Oshinsky, *A Conspiracy*, 479–82.
54. Evans and Novak, *Lyndon B. Johnson*, 81–5.
55. MacNeil, *Dirksen*, 126.
56. 100 Cong. Rec. 16,392 (1954).
57. Neil MacNeil's reporting.
58. Michael J. Ybarra, *Washington Gone Crazy: Senator Pat McCarran and the Great Communist Hunt* (Hanover, NH: Steerforth, 2004), 454–5.
59. Neil MacNeil's reporting.
60. Robert Justin Goldstein, *Political Repression in Modern America from 1870 to 1976* (Urbana: University of Illinois Press, 2001), 344.
61. "The Rights of a Witness before a Congressional Committee," *Fordham Law Review* 29, no. 2 (1960): 357.
62. Neil MacNeil's reporting.

63. Laura Kalman, *Abe Fortas* (New Haven, CT: Yale University Press, 1990), 130.
64. Edward R. Murrow, "A Report on Senator Joseph R. McCarthy," *See It Now* (CBS-TV, March 9, 1954), http://www.lib.berkeley.edu/MRC/ murrowmccarthy.html.
65. Randall Bennett Woods, *Fulbright* (New York: Cambridge University Press, 1995), 305–11.
66. Neil MacNeil's reporting.
67. Caro, *Master of the Senate*, 334.
68. Ibid., 315–6, 343–5.
69. Roger A. Bruns, "The Labor Racketeering Investigation, 1957–61," *Congress Investigates*, 849–66.
70. Ibid., 853; see also John L. McClellan, *Crime without Punishment* (New York: Duell, Sloane and Pearce, 1962).
71. Michael O'Brien, *John F. Kennedy: A Biography* (New York: St. Martin's Griffin, 2005), 385.
72. Evans and Novak, *Lyndon B. Johnson*, 190–94.
73. Joseph Bruce Gorman, *Kefauver* (New York: Oxford University Press, 1971), 358–9.
74. Gardiner Harris, "The Public's Quiet Savior from Harmful Medicines," *New York Times*, September 13, 2010.
75. MacNeil, *Dirksen*, 169–70; 200–01; 309–13.
76. *Jurney v. MacCracken*, 294 U.S. 125 (1935).
77. Keith W. Olson, "The Watergate Committee, 1973–74," *Congress Investigates*, 886–904.
78. Anthony Ripley, "Simple Watergate 'Caper' Sends Ripples over U.S.," *New York Times*, April 27, 1973.
79. Francis R. Valeo, Oral History Interview, November 13, 1985, Senate Historical Office, 598–9; Oberdorfer, *Senator Mansfield*, 432.
80. Olson, "The Watergate Committee," *Congress Investigates*, 894–5.
81. Sam J. Ervin Jr., *Preserving the Constitution: The Autobiography of Senator Sam J. Ervin Jr.* (Charlottesville, VA: Michie, 1984).
82. 294 U.S. 125 (1935).
83. Olson, "The Watergate Committee," *Congress Investigates*, 907–13.
84. Ibid., 898.
85. Ibid., 900–902.
86. Ken Gormley, *Archibald Cox: Conscience of a Nation* (Reading, MA: Perseus, 1997), 286–9.
87. Robert Scheer, "A Tale of Glass Houses and Stones," *Los Angeles Times*, October 15, 1996.
88. Jules Witcover, *Very Strange Bedfellows: The Short and Unhappy Marriage of Richard Nixon and Spiro Agnew* (New York: Public Affairs, 2007), 341–3.
89. Emery, *Watergate*, 395–6.
90. Ibid., 472–4.
91. Ibid., 404.
92. Neil MacNeil interview with Ford, December 6, 1973, MacNeil papers.

93. "The Smoking Gun," Richard Nixon and Bob Haldeman, June 23, 1972, whitehousetapes.net/transcript/Nixon/smoking-gun.

94. Carroll Kilpatrick, "Nixon Resigns," *Washington Post*, August 9, 1974.

95. Seymour Hersh, "Huge C.I.A. Operation Reported in U.S. Against Anti-War Forces," *New York Times*, December 22, 1974.

96. David F. Rodgers, "The Church Committee on Intelligence Activities Investigation, 1975–76," *Congress Investigates*, 927–50.

97. Ibid., 933; Loch K. Johnson, *A Season of Inquiry: The Senate Intelligence Investigation* (Lexington: University Press of Kentucky, 1985), 73.

98. Rodgers, "The Church Committee," 944; William Colby, *Honorable Men: My Life in the CIA* (New York: Simon & Schuster, 1978), 440–42.

99. Rodgers, "The Church Committee," *Congress Investigates*, 934.

100. The final reports and committee hearings are available through the Assassination Archives and Research Center, http://www.aarclibrary.org/publib/contents/church/contents.

101. Frank J. Smist Jr., *Congress Oversees the United States Intelligence Community, 1947–1989* (Knoxville: University of Tennessee Press, 1990), 77–81.

102. Jim McGee and Brian Duffy, *Main Justice: The Men and Women Who Enforce the Nation's Criminal Laws and Guard Its Liberties* (New York: Simon & Schuster, 1996), 309.

103. David L. Hostetter, "The Iran-Contra Hearings, 1987," *Congress Investigates*, 968–84.

104. Jane Mayer and Doyle McManus, *Landslide: The Unmaking of the President, 1984–1988* (Boston: Houghton Mifflin, 1988), 386, 437.

105. Theodore Draper, *A Very Thin Line: The Iran-Contra Affairs* (New York: Hill and Wang, 1991), 552, 589–98.

106. "Arthur L. Liman, a Masterly Lawyer, Dies at 64," *New York Times*, July 18, 1997.

107. *Report of the Congressional Committees Investigating the Iran-Contra Affair* (Washington: Government Printing Office, 1987), 11.

108. Gormley, *The Death of American Virtue*, 44–5.

109. Jeff Gerth, "The 1992 Campaign: Personal Finances; Clintons Joined S&L Operator in an Ozark Real-Estate Venture," *New York Times*, March 8, 1992.

110. Gormley, *The Death of American Virtue*, 61.

111. Ibid., 155; Richard L. Berke, "The President and the Prosecutor," *New York Times Sunday Book Review*, February 16, 2010.

112. Stephen Labaton, "Whitewater Hearing Cleared the Clintons, Democrats Say," *New York Times*, June 19, 1996.

113. Raymond W. Smock, "The Whitewater Investigation and Impeachment of President Bill Clinton," *Congress Investigates*, 1051–4.

114. "Senate Panel Releases Whitewater Report," *All Politics*, June 18, 1996, http://www.cnn.com/ALLPOLITICS/1997/gen/resources/infocus/whitewater/senate.hearings.html.

115. "Sparring over Whitewater," *New York Times*, June 19, 1996.

116. David Maraniss, "The Hearings End Much as They Began," *Washington Post*, June 19, 1996.

117. Roger A. Bruns and Raymond W. Smock, "Preface," *Congress Investigates*, xviii, xxviii.

118. Gail Russell Chaddock, "The 9/11 Commission, 2002–04," *Congress Investigates*, 1093–121; Guy Gugliotta and Susan Schmidt, "Congressional Investigations: More Partisan and Less Powerful," *Washington Post*, November 20, 1997.

119. Roger A. Bruns, "The Hurricane Katrina Inquiry, 2005–06," *Congress Investigates*, 1152–69.

Chapter 11

1. For an insightful essay on Senate speeches, see Byrd, *The Senate 1789–1989*, vol. 3, *Classic Speeches, 1830–1993*, xv–xxiii.

2. Ibid., 267.

3. Remini, *The House*, 35–6.

4. Kenneth R. Bowling and Helen E. Veit, eds., *The Diary of William Maclay and Other Notes on Senate Debates* (Baltimore: Johns Hopkins University Press, 1988), 253 (entry of April 26, 1790).

5. Louis Torres, "Federal Hall Revisited," *Journal of the Society of Architectural Historians* 29 (December 1970): 327–8.

6. http//www.nps.gov/inde/congress-hall.htm.

7. Elaine K. Swift, *The Making of an American Senate, Reconstitutive Change in Congress, 1787–1841* (Ann Arbor: University of Michigan Press, 1996), Chapter 1.

8. Swanstrom, *The United States Senate*, 249.

9. Steven E. Siry, *De Witt Clinton and the American Political Economy: Sectionalism, Politics, and Republican Ideology, 1787–1828* (New York: Lang, 1989), 98–9.

10. Samuel Latham Mitchill to Catherine Mitchill, November 26, 1804, in Samuel Mitchill, "Dr. Mitchill's Letters from Washington, 1801–1813," *Harper's New Monthly Magazine* 58 (April 1879): 748.

11. Remini, *Daniel Webster*, 321, 321n.25.

12. Byrd, *The Senate*, 77.

13. Ibid., 39.

14. Carl Schurz, *Life of Henry Clay* (Boston: Houghton Mifflin, 1915), 1:67.

15. Merrill Peterson, *The Great Triumvirate*, 234–6.

16. Daniel Webster on Alexander Hamilton, March 10, 1831, *The Writings and Speeches of Daniel Webster* (Boston: Little, Brown, 1903), 2:50.

17. Peterson, *The Great Triumvirate*, 257.

18. Daniel Webster's comment in 1839 to and about Robert C. Winthrop, Robert Charles Winthrop, *A Memoir of Robert C. Winthrop* (Boston: Little, Brown, 1897), 23.

19. Henry Clay to Francis Brooke, February 14, 1833, Robert Seager II, *The Papers of Henry Clay* (Lexington: University Press of Kentucky, 1959–), 8:623.

20. For comparable language, see Remini, *Henry Clay*, 326.

21. Benton, *Thirty Years' View*, 342.

22. Remini, *Henry Clay*, 578.

23. John Lyde Wilson, *The Code of Honor; or Rules for the Government of Principals and Seconds in Dueling* (Charleston, SC: Eccles, 1838).

24. For Benton's assessment of Randolph's attitude toward dueling, see Benton, *Thirty Years' View*, 1:475.

25. William M. Meigs, *The Life of Thomas Hart Benton* (Philadelphia, 1904; New York: Da Capo, 1970), 452.

26. Oliver Dyer, *Great Senators of the United States Forty Years Ago* (New York, 1889; Freeport, NY: Books for Libraries Press, 1972). Benton's mid-twentieth-century biographers did not repeat this story, but rather they tell of Benton's bitterness toward his deceased colleague; see Elbert B. Smith, *Magnificent Missourian* (Philadelphia: Lippincott, 1958), 269.

27. Richard H. Sewell, *John P. Hale and the Politics of Abolition* (Cambridge, MA: Harvard University Press, 1965), 116–7.

28. Cong. Globe, 31st Cong., 1st sess, 602–4, 609–10, 762–3 (1850).

29. Peter Harvey, *Reminiscences and Anecdotes of Daniel Webster* (Boston, 1878), 119.

30. James B. Coleman, "Two Irascible Antebellum Senators: George Poindexter and Henry S. Foote," *Journal of Mississippi History* 46 (February 1984): 17–27.

31. Inspired by a February 24, 1838, duel in which Rep. William Graves killed Rep. Jonathan Cilley, this February 20, 1839, statute failed to deter future duels on the infamous Bladensburg Dueling Grounds, conveniently located on the District of Columbia–Maryland border.

32. Cong. Globe, 31st Cong., 1st Sess., 476 (1850). Webster drew the "Hear me for my cause" line from Shakespeare's *Julius Caesar*.

33. William H. Seward, *The Works of William H. Seward*, George E. Baker, ed. (Boston: Houghton Mifflin, 1888), 4:85.

34. Robert W. Johannsen, *Stephen A. Douglas* (New York: Oxford University Press, 1973), 297.

35. Ibid., 434.

36. David Donald, *Charles Sumner and the Coming of the Civil War* (New York: Knopf, 1960), 188–9.

37. Ibid., 175.

38. Haynes, *The Senate*, 1003.

39. Donald, *Charles Sumner and the Coming of the Civil War*, 189–90.

40. Cong. Globe, 34th Cong., 1st Sess., Appendix, 529–44 (1856); Charles F. Horner, "The Speaker and the Audience," *Lyceum Magazine* 32 (January 1923), 16.

41. James Chestnut made this attack following Sumner's June 4, 1860, "The Barbarism of Slavery" address to the Senate. See Stephen Puleo, *A City So Grand: The Rise of an American Metropolis, Boston 1850–1900* (Boston: Beacon Press, 2010), 117–8.

42. Cong. Globe, 34th Cong., 1st Sess., Appendix, 529–44 (1856).
43. Williamjames Hull Hoffer, *The Caning of Charles Sumner: Honor, Idealism, and the Origins of the Civil War* (Baltimore: Johns Hopkins University Press, 2010), 7–11, 80.
44. Arthur Quinn, *The Rivals: William Gwinn, David Broderick, and the Birth of California* (New York: Crown, 1994).
45. Cong. Globe, 36th Cong., 2d Sess., 271 (1861).
46. Ibid., 217 (1860).
47. Ibid., 487 (1861).
48. Goodwin, *Team of Rivals*, 503.
49. David Donald, *Charles Sumner and the Rights of Man* (New York: Alfred A. Knopf, 1970), 64.
50. Bryce, *The American Commonwealth, Part One* (New York: Macmillan, 1910), 120.
51. For an inspired novelistic account of Roscoe Conkling, including his ritualized use of the Senate bathtubs, see Thomas Mallon, *Two Moons: A Novel* (New York: Pantheon, 2000). The standard biography of Conkling is David M. Jordan, *Roscoe Conkling of New York: Voice of the Senate* (Ithaca, NY: Cornell University Press, 1971).
52. Charles Willis Thompson, "When the Senate's 'Big Five' Governed," *New York Times*, October 12, 1930.
53. John Quincy Adams, *Memoirs of John Quincy Adams*, Charles Francis Adams, ed. (Philadelphia: Lippincott, 1876), 9:236.
54. Willard Sterne Randall, *Thomas Jefferson* (New York: Holt, 1993), 359.
55. Burdette, *Filibustering in the Senate*, 77; 36 Cong. Rec. 3070 (1903).
56. Joseph A. Fry, *John Tyler Morgan and the Search for Southern Autonomy* (Knoxville: University of Tennessee Press, 1992), 40–41.
57. Mencken explains why he thought the Senate to have been ruined by the US Constitution's Seventeenth and Eighteenth Amendments in H. L. Mencken, "The United States Senate," *Chicago Tribune*, February 7, 1926, reprinted in H. L. Mencken, *The Bathtub Hoax and Other Blasts & Bravos from the Chicago Tribune* (New York: Knopf, 1958), 172–6.
58. "Senatorial Courtesy," Peter Finley Dunne, *The World of Mr. Dooley*, Louis Filler, ed. (New York: Collier, 1962), 54.
59. Edward Boykin, *The Wit and Wisdom of Congress* (New York: Funk and Wagnalls, 1961), 36.
60. On June 12, 1984, Goldwater responded testily to Senate Majority Leader Howard Baker's request that he yield the Senate floor so that Baker could proceed with previously agreed-upon Senate business. Goldwater asserted about the Senate that "This place is getting to be like a cookie factory." Baker replied, "I don't know whose cookie factory the senator is talking about." Goldwater shot back, "Yours!" Quoted in Barry M. Goldwater, *Pure Goldwater*, John Dean and Barry M. Goldwater, Jr., eds. (New York: Palgrave Macmillan, 2008), 95.
61. Jefferson's Manual, sec. 17.9.
62. Burdette, *Filibustering*, 16–9.

63. Haynes, *The Senate*, 221.
64. Huey Long held the Senate floor from June 12–13, 1935, 79 Cong. Rec. 9085–191 (1935).
65. 110 Cong. Rec. 250, 253 (1964).
66. MacNeil, *Dirksen*, 214.
67. Floyd M. Riddick and Alan S. Frumin, *Riddick's Senate Procedure*, S. Doc. No. 101–28, at 742–5 (1992).
68. Allan A. Michie and Frank Rhylick, *Dixie Demagogues* (New York: Vanguard, 1939), 274.
69. US Senate, Committee on the Judiciary, *The Supreme Court of the United States: Hearings and Reports on Successful and Unsuccessful Nominations of Supreme Court Justices by the Senate Judiciary Committee*, compiled by Roy M. Mersky and J. Myron Jacobstein (Buffalo, NY: Hein, 1977–2007), 18:224.
70. Neil MacNeil's reporting.
71. Antonin Scalia, *Scalia Dissents* (Washington, DC: Regnery, 2004), 25.
72. Dean L. Yarwood, *When Congress Makes a Joke: Congressional Humor Then and Now* (Lanham, MD: Rowman & Littlefield, 2004), 47.
73. US Senate Rule 19(2)—http://www.rules.senate.gov/.
74. MacNeil, *Dirksen*, 203.
75. 67 Cong. Rec. 226 (1925).
76. Haynes, *The Senate*, 382; Bertram M. Gross, *The Legislative Struggle* (New York: McGraw-Hill, 1953), 366.
77. Everett S. Brown, ed., *William Plumer's Memorandum of Proceedings in the United States Senate, 1803–1807* (New York: Macmillan, 1923), 483.
78. Co-author Baker's diligent search of Ralph Edward Flanders, *Senator from Vermont* (Boston: Little, Brown, 1961), failed to uncover this statement.
79. MacNeil, *Dirksen*, 127–8.
80. "The Leader," *Time*, September 14, 1962, 27. Although the authorship was unattributed in this article, and in his biography, *Dirksen* (202), this book's coauthor, Neil MacNeil, wrote that description (see Baker and Davidson, *First among Equals*, 261 n.3).
81. William Safire, comp., *Lend Me Your Ears: Great Speeches in History* (New York: Norton, 2004), 566.
82. Irving Bernstein, *Guns or Butter: The Presidency of Lyndon Johnson* (New York: Oxford University Press, 1996), 67.
83. This book's coauthor was unable to identify the source of this quote, which Neil MacNeil had likely committed to memory.
84. Shelby M. Cullom, *Fifty Years of Public Service* (Chicago: McClurg, 1911), 222; 15 Cong. Rec. 354–64 (1884).
85. *Maiden Speeches of U.S. Senators in the 108th Congress of the United States*, S. Doc. No. 108–16 at v–vi, 3 (2005).
86. Oshinsky, *A Conspiracy So Immense*, 499–500; Griffith, *The Politics of Fear*, 318.
87. Margaret Chase Smith, "A Declaration of Conscience," 96 Cong. Rec. 7894–5 (1950).
88. 100 Cong. Rec. 1106 (1954); Woods, *Fulbright*, 190, 192–3.

89. John Braeman, *Albert J. Beveridge: American Nationalist* (Chicago: University of Chicago Press, 1971), 46.

90. Barry M. Goldwater, *With No Apologies* (New York: Morrow, 1979), 94; for a comment in the same vein, see Barry M. Goldwater, *Pure Goldwater*, 95.

91. Mason Drukman, *Wayne Morse* (Portland: Oregon Historical Society, 1997), Neil MacNeil's reporting; Alden Whitman, "Wayne Morse Dies," *New York Times*, July 23, 1974.

92. Karen Tumulty, "Senate Decides to Live with TV," *Los Angeles Times*, July 30, 1986.

93. Neil MacNeil's reporting, MacNeil Papers, Dirksen Congressional Center.

94. Ibid.

95. Evans Witt, "Senate Leader Wants 'Invisible Half of Congress' on Television," *Anchorage Daily News*, January 25, 1985.

96. Stephen Frantzich and John Sullivan, *The C-SPAN Revolution* (Norman: University of Oklahoma Press, 1996), 260–61.

97. Frantzich and Sullivan, *The C-SPAN Revolution*, 251–3, 271–3.

98. Bob and Elizabeth Dole, *Unlimited Partners: Our American Story* (New York: Simon & Schuster, 1996), 259.

99. David Pryor 131 Cong. Rec. 29,989–90 (1985)

100. Adam Clymer, "Extreme Rhetoric Bedevils Congress," *New York Times*, June 25, 1995.

101. For an elaboration of these ideas, see Thomas E. Mann and Norman J. Ornstein, *The Broken Branch: How Congress Is Failing America and How to Get It Back on Track* (New York: Oxford University Press, 2006).

102. Quoted in Barbara A. Perry, *The Priestly Tribe: The Supreme Court's Image in the American Mind* (Westport, CT: Praeger, 1999), 88.

103. Robert C. Byrd, 141 Cong. Rec. 37731–6 (1995). Although Byrd avoided mentioning the name of the offending senator, all knew he was referring to freshman member Rick Santorum (R-PA). Byrd's statement subsequently came to be cited as a primer on proper manners for the Senate of the early twenty-first century.

Chapter 12

1. 67 Cong. Rec. 3–4 (1925).

2. Lindsay Rogers, *The American Senate* (New York: Alfred A. Knopf, 1926), ix.

3. The most informed recent examination of the filibuster is Richard A. Arenberg and Robert B. Dove, *Defending the Filibuster: The Soul of the Senate* (Bloomington: Indiana University Press, 2012). Other studies by political scientists include Franklin L. Burdette, *Filibustering in the Senate* (Princeton, NJ: Princeton University Press, 1940); Sarah A. Binder and Steven S. Smith, *Politics or Principle?: Filibustering in the United States Senate* (Washington, DC: Brookings Institution Press, 1997); Gregory J. Wawro and Eric Schickler, *Filibuster: Obstruction and Lawmaking in the*

U.S. Senate (Princeton, NJ: Princeton University Press, 2006); and Gregory Koger, *Filibustering: A Political History of Obstruction in the House and Senate* (Chicago: University of Chicago Press, 2010). Legal scholars have also thoroughly pursued this issue. One noteworthy example is Catherine Fisk and Erwin Chemerinsky, "The Filibuster," *Stanford Law Review* 49 (January 1997): 181–254.

4. Fite, *Richard B. Russell Jr.*, 413; "The Congress: Everybody's Getting Fat," *Time*, May 18, 1962.

5. Burdette, *Filibustering*, 43.

6. Koger, *Filibustering*, 116–24.

7. Thomas E. Mann and Norman J. Ornstein, *The Broken Branch: How Congress Is Failing America and How to Get It Back on Track* (New York: Oxford University Press, 2008), 162–9. For a more up-to-date and decidedly angry analysis, see Thomas Mann and Norman J. Ornstein, *It's Even Worse Than It Looks: How the American Constitutional System Collided with the New Politics of Extremism* (New York: Basic Books, 2012).

8. Bowling and Veit, eds., *The Diary of William Maclay*, 156 (September 22, 1789).

9. Ibid., 398 (March 2, 1791).

10. Ibid., section 17.9.

11. 1 Annals of Cong. 21 (1789).

12. Bowling and Veit, eds., *The Diary of William Maclay*, (March 2, 1791), section 34.5.

13. For a discussion of this murky issue, see Binder and Smith, *Politics or Principle?*, 37–9, and Joseph Cooper, *The Previous Question: Its Standing as a Precedent for Cloture in the United States Senate*, S. Doc. 87–104, at 1–13 (1962).

14. 22 Annals of Cong. 1091–94 (1811); Cooper, *The Previous Question*, 9–10. The vote actually occurred nearly three hours after midnight, but was included with the proceedings of February 27. The tumult of that milestone occasion prompted the official reporter of debates to append the following note. "During the course of such a session as that of this evening, many circumstances occur of trivial importance, but yet sufficient to produce warmth, which it cannot be expected of a reporter of the deliberations of a Legislative body to report. Such incidents are of course omitted" (22 Annals of Cong. 1095).

15. Paul R. Corts, "Randolph vs. Clay: A Duel of Words and Bullets," *Filson Club History Quarterly* 43 (April 1969): 151–7.

16. Robert Dawidoff, *The Education of John Randolph* (New York: Norton, 1979), 241.

17. "Patrick Henry" apparently was State Department clerk Philip Richard Fendall II, editor of the pro-Adams *National Journal*, who wrote in a caustic style like that of Adams. This article and others by him were published as a pamphlet entitled "An Argument on the Powers, Duties and Conduct of the Hon. John C. Calhoun, Vice President of the United States, and President of the Senate."

18. Patrick Henry [pseud.], *An Argument on the Powers, Duties and Conduct of the Hon. John C. Calhoun, Vice President of the United States, and President of the Senate* (Washington, DC, 1827), 6 (Letter I, May 1, 1826).

19. Ibid., 23 (Letter III, August 4, 1826).

20. Rule 6, 4 Reg. Deb. 328–41 (1828).

21. John Niven, *John C. Calhoun and the Price of Union* (Baton Rouge: Louisiana State University Press, 1988), 197.

22. William Nisbet Chambers, *Old Bullion Benton* (New York: Little, Brown, 1956), 218–9.

23. Thomas Hart Benton, *Thirty Years' View* (New York: Appleton, 1856), 2:249.

24. Cong. Globe, 27th Cong., 1st Sess. 183–4 (1841).

25. Ibid., 203–5.

26. Heidler and Heidler, *Henry Clay*, 337–8.

27. Benton, *Thirty Years' View*, 2:253.

28. Burdette, *Filibustering*, 26.

29. James P. Coleman, "Two Irascible Antebellum Senators: George Poindexter and Henry S. Foote," *Journal of Mississippi History* 46 (February 1984): 17–27.

30. Cong. Globe, 31st Cong., 2nd Sess., 248–9 (1851).

31. Burdette, *Filibustering*, 32.

32. Ibid.

33. Ibid., 5; Bill Bryson, *Made in America: An Informal History of the English Language in the United States* (New York: Morrow, 1994), 289.

34. Burdette, *Filibustering*, 38.

35. Ibid., 47.

36. James Bryce, *The American Commonwealth* (New York: Macmillan, 1889), 100.

37. Ibid.

38. Thomas Adams Upchurch, *Legislating Racism: The Billion Dollar Congress and the Birth of Jim Crow* (Lexington: University Press of Kentucky, 2004), 130–5.

39. Ibid., 160–6.

40. 26 Cong. Rec. 1637 (1893).

41. Burdette, *Filibustering*, 54; 22 Cong. Rec. Appendix 35–46 (1891).

42. Burdette, *Filibustering*, 60; William M. Stewart, *Reminiscences of William M. Stewart of Nevada* (New York: Neale, 1908), 315; 25 Cong. Rec. Appendix 606–705 (delivered on October 14, 16, 21, 23, 24, 27, and 30, 1893).

43. Burdette, *Filibustering*, 68–9; 29 Cong. Rec. 2754–930 (1897).

44. Burdette, *Filibustering*, 69–72; 34 Cong. Rec. 3520–31, 3548–62 (1901).

45. For Tillman's unceasing efforts to secure appropriations for South Carolina, see Francis Butler Simkins, *Pitchfork Ben Tillman* (Baton Rouge: Louisiana State University Press, 1944), 361–70; Burdette, *Filibustering*, 72.

46. David Thelen, *Robert M. La Follette and the Insurgent Spirit* (Madison: University of Wisconsin Press, 1976), 64–5.

47. Burdette, *Filibustering*, 83–90.

48. Ibid., 91.

49. Woodrow Wilson, *The Papers of Woodrow Wilson*, Arthur S. Link et al., eds. (Princeton, NJ: Princeton University Press, 1983), 41:318–20.

50. 55 Cong. Rec. 45 (1917); Thomas Ryley, *A Little Group of Willful Men* (Port Washington, NY: Kennikat, 1975), 147–9.

51. Burdette, *Filibustering*, 127–8.

52. 52 Cong. Rec. 3322–24, 3787–90 (1915).

53. U.S. Congress, Senate, Committee on Rules and Administration, *Senate Cloture Rule*, S. Prt. No. 112–31, at 115–6.

54. "Congress: Silver-Tongued Sunbeam," *Time*, August 7, 1939.

55. Burdette, *Filibustering*, 116–7.

56. 67 Cong. Rec. 3–4.

57. Charles G. Dawes, *Notes as Vice President, 1928–1929* (Boston: Little, Brown, 1935), 70; Hatfield, *Vice Presidents of the United States*, 363–9.

58. Dawes, *Notes as Vice President*, 287.

59. Ibid., 255.

60. George W. Norris, "Mr. Dawes and the Senate Rules," *The Forum* 74 (October 1925): 582–6; George Wharton Pepper, "Senate Cloture," *University of Pennsylvania Law Review and American Law Register* 74 (1925–1926): 131–8.

61. Conrad Black, *Franklin Delano Roosevelt: Champion of Freedom* (New York: Public Affairs, 2003), 345.

62. Hatfield, *Vice Presidents of the United States*, 389.

63. Anthony J. Badger, *New Deal/New South* (Fayetteville: University of Arkansas Press, 2007), 155.

64. Arthur F. Raper, *The Tragedy of Lynching* (Chapel Hill: University of North Carolina Press, 1933), 18, 153, 187.

65. Burdette, *Filibustering*, 135–6.

66. "Congress Ends Extra Session," [New York] *Evening Telegram*, December 4, 1922; Burdette, *Filibustering*, 137.

67. Tom Connally, *My Name Is Tom Connally* (New York: Crowell, 1954), 171.

68. Ibid., 170.

69. Robert Mann, *The Walls of Jericho: Lyndon Johnson, Hubert Humphrey, Richard Russell and the Struggle for Civil Rights* (New York: Harcourt Brace, 1996), 81–9; Caro, *Master of the Senate*, 598–600.

70. Byrd, *The Senate*, 2:285–6 (1991); "Renew Fight Today on Boulder Dam Bill," *New York Times*, February 24, 1927; 68 Cong. Rec. 4454–56 (1927).

71. Dawes, *Notes as Vice President*, 299; Bascom N. Timmons. *Portrait of an American: Charles G. Dawes* (New York: Harper, 1953), 270.

72. Richard L. Riedel, *Halls of the Mighty: My 47 Years at the Senate* (Washington, DC: Luce, 1969), 89–90.

73. Burdette, *Filibustering*, 136.

74. 83 Cong. Rec. 2204 (1938).

75. U.S. Senate, Committee on Rules and Administration, *Senate Cloture Rule*, 20.

76. 95 Cong. Rec. 2175, 2275 (1949).

77. Martin B. Gold and Dimple Gupta offer a richly documented account of the cloture rule's evolution in "The Constitutional Option to Change Senate Rules and Procedures: A Majoritarian Means to Overcome the Filibuster," in *Harvard Journal of Law & Public Policy* (Fall 2004): 228–30.

78. 95 Cong. Rec. 1717–22 (1949).

79. 95 Cong. Rec. 2042–49 (1949).

80. *Senate Cloture Rule*, S. Prt. No. 112–31, at 24; Gold and Gupta "The Constitutional Option," 236–40.

81. For a nuanced survey of Johnson's racial attitudes, see Caro, *Master of the Senate*, 716–8.

82. Jack Bass and Marilyn W. Thompson, *Ol' Strom* (Marietta, GA: Longstreet, 1998), 178–80.

83. Neil MacNeil's reporting.

84. Gold and Gupta, "The Constitutional Option," 231.

85. Fite, *Richard B. Russell Jr.*, 415; 106 Cong. Rec. 2727 (1960).

86. 106 Cong. Rec. 3220 (1960); for a heated discussion between Johnson and Richard Russell on a Russell tactic to further delay proceedings, see 106 Cong. Rec. 3708–10 (1960).

87. Mann, *The Walls of Jericho*, 250–61.

88. Ibid., 259–61.

89. *Senate Rules and the Senate as a Continuing Body*, S. Doc. No. 83–4 (1953).

90. Floyd M. Riddick, oral history, Senate Historical Office, July 27, 1978, 125–38.

91. Paul Douglas, *In the Fullness of Time* (New York: Harcourt Brace Jovanovich, 1972), 219–20.

92. 108 Cong. Rec. 16,442 (1962); *Senate Cloture Rule*, S. Prt. No. 112–31, at 49.

93. Douglas, *In the Fullness of Time*, 214–8.

94. 108 Cong. Rec. 16431 (1962).

95. "The Congress: Silence in the Senate," *Time*, August 24, 1962.

96. Randall B. Woods, *LBJ: Architect of American Ambition* (New York: Free Press, 2006), 408–12; Reeves, *President Kennedy*, 628–31.

97. 110 Cong. Rec. 2804 (1964).

98. Mann, *Walls of Jericho*, 394.

99. Ibid., 396, 400–401; MacNeil, *Dirksen*, 231.

100. Hubert H. Humphrey, *The Education of a Public Man* (Garden City, NY: Doubleday, 1976), 276.

101. The Dirksen Congressional Center, *Major Features of the Civil Rights Act of 1964*, www.dirksencenter.org; Charles W. Whalen and Barbara Whalen, *The Longest Debate: A Legislative History of the 1964 Civil Rights Act* (Cabin John, MD: Seven Locks Press, 1985), 187.

102. Neil MacNeil's reporting.

103. MacNeil, *Dirksen*, 237.

104. Whalen and Whalen, *The Longest Debate*, 182.

105. 110 Cong. Rec. 13,319 (1964).

106. 110 Cong. Rec. 13,327 (1964); Oberdorfer, *Senator Mansfield*, 226–35.

107. Dennis W. Johnson, *The Laws that Shaped America* (New York: Routledge, 2009), 293.

108. 111 Cong. Rec. 5058–61 (1965).
109. Robert Parker with Richard Rashke, *Capitol Hill in Black and White* (New York: Dodd, Mead, 1986), 188.
110. Stephen G. N. Tuck, *We Ain't What We Ought to Be: The Black Freedom Struggle from Emancipation to Obama* (Cambridge, MA: Belknap Press, 2010), 323.
111. MacNeil, *Dirksen*, 258.
112. 112 Cong. Rec. 142–5 (1966).
113. MacNeil, *Dirksen*, 324.
114. 114 Cong. Rec. 4960 (1968).

Chapter 13

1. Byrd, *The Senate, 1789–1989*, 2:158–9.
2. Peter Carlson, "A Short History of the Filibuster," *American History Magazine*. Published Online August 4, 2010. www.historynet.com/a-short-history-of-the-filibuster.htm.
3. Ibid.
4. Arenberg and Dove, *Defending the Filibuster*, 162.
5. 114 Cong. Rec. 20,900–03 (1968).
6. Woods, *LBJ: Architect of American Ambition*, 850.
7. MacNeil, *Dirksen*, 333.
8. Anthony Summers, *Arrogance of Power: The Secret World of Richard Nixon* (New York: Viking, 2000), 294–7.
9. Carl P. Leubsdorf, "Draft Battle Pledged," *The* (New London, CT) *Day*, May 7, 1971; Mike Gravel and Joe Lauria, *A Political Odyssey: The Rise of American Militarism and One Man's Fight to Stop It* (New York: Seven Stories Press, 2008), 179–80.
10. 117 Cong. Rec. 13,912–8 (1971).
11. "Some Filibuster Opponents Decide It's Not a Bad Idea," *Lewiston* (Maine) *Daily Sun*, October 2, 1971; 117 Cong. Rec. 14887–89 (1971).
12. 117 Cong. Rec. 13,912–8 (1971).
13. Francis R. Valco, *Mike Mansfield, Majority Leader: A Different Kind of Senate, 1961–1976* (Armonk, NY: Sharpe, 1999).
14. "Senate Approves New Cambodia Aid Bill," *Pittsburgh Post-Gazette*, December 17, 1970; John W. Finney, "Mansfield Gains in Split on Bills," *New York Times*, December 24, 1970.
15. Gold and Gupta, "The Constitutional Option," 253.
16. Koger, *Filibustering*, 167–71.
17. LeRoy Ashby and Rod Gramer, *Fighting the Odds: The Life of Senator Frank Church* (Pullman: Washington State University Press, 1994), 76–7.
18. John W. Finney, "Mansfield Fears Basic Changes If Filibuster Compromise Fails," *New York Times*, January 28, 1969.
19. 121 Cong. Rec. 5651–52 (1975); for greater detail on the Senate votes that endorsed, temporarily, the right to cut off debate by simple majority vote, see Gold and Gupta, "The Constitutional Option," 252–60.
20. Binder and Smith, *Politics or Principle?*, 6–19.

21. Wawro and Schickler, *Filibuster*, 267–8.
22. Neil MacNeil's reporting.
23. 123 Cong. Rec. 31,428–36ff.
24. 123 Cong. Rec. 31,916–9 (1977).
25. Byrd, *The Senate, 1789–1989*, 2:153–6.
26. 123 Cong. Rec. 31,916–9 (1977).
27. Byrd, *The Senate, 1789–1989*, 2:154–7.
28. 123 Cong. Rec. 31,927 (1977).
29. Gold and Gupta, "The Constitutional Option," 264.
30. 123 Cong. Rec. 31,927–8 (1977).
31. 123 Cong. Rec. 31,929 (1977).
32. 123 Cong. Rec. 31,930–1 (1977).
33. Byrd, *The Senate, 1789–1989*, 2:156; US Senate, Committee on Rules and Administration, *Examining the Filibuster*, S. Hrg. No. 111–706, at 162.
34. US Senate, Committee on Rules and Administration, *Senate Cloture Rule*, 33–4.
35. Alan Ehrenhalt, "The Right in Congress: Seeking a Strategy," *CQ Weekly Report*, August 5, 1978, 2023.
36. For a nuanced and bipartisan discussion of the "hold," see US Senate, Committee on Rules and Administration, *Examining the Filibuster*, at 321–51.
37. 157 Cong. Rec. S326 (daily ed. January 27, 2011).
38. Neil MacNeil's reporting.
39. "Striking Out, Another Defeat for Jesse Helms," *Time*, October 4, 1982, 40.
40. Jean E. Phillips, *Reorganization of Congress: Modern Reform Efforts* (Hauppauge, NY: Nova Science, 2004), 29–31.
41. 129 Cong. Rec. 7535 (1983).
42. Phillips, *Reorganization of Congress*, 32–4.
43. US Senate Committee on Rules and Administration, *Report of the Study Group on Senate Practices and Procedures*, S.Prt 98-242 (Washington, DC: Government Printing Office, 1984), 16.
44. 131 Cong. Rec. 33,453 (1985).
45. For a vigorously stated case in opposition to televising Senate proceedings, see Bennett Johnston's remarks at 132 Cong. Rec. 1560–69, 2508–17, and 3133–40 (1986).
46. Ibid.
47. S. Res. No. 28, February 27, 1986.
48. "Senate GOP Flexes Muscles of the Minority," *Congressional Quarterly Weekly Report* 45 (1987), 1061.
49. Barbara Sinclair, *Unorthodox Lawmaking: New Legislative Processes in the U.S. Congress*, 4th ed. (Washington, DC: CQ Press, 2011), 136.
50. Neil MacNeil's reporting.
51. Byrd, *The Senate, 1789–1989*, 4 vols. (Washington: Government Printing Office, 1988–1994).
52. Ibid., 2:163.
53. Gold and Gupta, "The Constitutional Option," 260.

54. Democrats gained their sixtieth vote on April 30, 2009, when Arlen Specter left the Republican Party. The seating of Massachusetts Republican Scott Brown on February 4, 2010, ended that "filibuster-proof" period.

55. 157 Cong. Rec. S307 (daily ed., January 27, 2011).

56. Tom Harkin, "Fixing the Filibuster: Restoring Real Democracy in the Senate," *Iowa Law Review Bulletin* 95 (2010): 67–79.

57. Joseph J. Schatz, "Looking for Room to Maneuver," *CQ Weekly*, April 19, 2010, 954.

58. US Congress, Senate, Committee on Rules and Administration, *Examining the Filibuster*, 8–10, 141.

59. 157 Cong. Rec. 300–301 (daily ed., January 27, 2011).

60. Ezra Klein, "Reid and McConnell Agree," *Washington Post*, January 28, 2011; 157 Cong. Rec. S296–328 (daily ed., January 27, 2011).

61. 157 Cong. Rec. S325 (daily ed., January 27, 2011).

62. Ibid.

63. 158 Cong. Rec. S3070 (daily ed., May 10, 2012); Humbert Sanchez, "Senate Filibuster Is in No Real Danger," *Roll Call*, May 15, 2012; Alexander Bolton, "Harry Reid Puts Nuclear Option in His Back Pocket," *The Hill*, May 15, 2012; for coverage of filibuster-related rules changes at the start of the 113th Congress, see 159 Cong. Rec. S247–74 (daily ed., January 24, 2013); Ezra Klein, "Let's Talk: The Move to Reform the Filibuster," *The New Yorker*, January 28, 2013, 24–9; Ezra Klein, "Harry Reid: 'I'm Not Personally, at This Stage, Ready to Get Rid of the 60-vote Threshold,'" *Washington Post*, January 25, 2013; Jeremy W. Peters, "New Senate Rules to Curtail the Excesses of a Filibuster," *New York Times*, January 25, 2013.

64. Robert C. Byrd, "The Filibuster and Its Consequences," Statement to the Senate Committee on Rules and Administration, May 19, 2010, in *Examining the Filibuster*, 160–2.

To the Future

1. Paul Solman, "Land of the Free, Home of the Poor," *PBS Newshour*, August 16, 2011.

2. Richard A. Baker, *200 Notable Days* (Washington, DC: Government Printing Office, 2006), 182.

3. Ira Shapiro, *The Last Great Senate* (New York: Public Affairs, 2012), x–xi.

4. Susan Dunn, *Roosevelt's Purge: How FDR Fought to Change the Democratic Party* (Cambridge, MA: Harvard University Press, 2010), 275–6.

5. Rick Perry, *Fed Up: Our Fight to Save America from Washington* (New York: Little, Brown, 2010), 38, 42–3.

6. *The Random House College Dictionary*, rev. ed. (New York: Random House, 1982), 535.

7. US Const. art. V.

8. The *Wall Street Journal*'s Janet Hook noted at a March 14, 2011, Woodrow Wilson Center conference that the Senate is "hard to love," but that journalists have a greater role than "making fun of an awkward institution."

SELECTED BIBLIOGRAPHY

———

Since its establishment in 1975, the US Senate Historical Office has assigned a high priority to compiling comprehensive and up-to-date bibliographical information on the Senate and the careers of many of its members. For citations to works on the Senate's institutional history, see www.senate.gov/reference/resources. For biographical profiles for the nearly two thousand individuals who have served in the Senate since 1789 (as well as US House members), and associated references to books, scholarly articles, and locations of existing research collections, consult the online *Biographical Directory of the United States Congress* (bioguide.congress.gov). The wealth of these finding aids, the easy availability of numerous online library catalogs, and the stunningly rich offerings of public domain books through the Google Books Library Project allow this work's authors to exclude—with an occasional exception—individual members' biographies, which for a balanced listing would consume many dozens of pages, and to focus on the books, articles, and documents that we found to be expressly helpful.

Abraham, Henry Julian. *Justices, Presidents, and Senators: A History of Supreme Court Appointments from Washington to Clinton.* 4th edition. Lanham, MD: Rowman & Littlefield, 1999.

Allen, Robert S., and Drew Pearson. *Washington Merry-Go-Round.* New York: Liveright, 1931.

Allen, William C. *History of the United States Capitol: A Chronicle of Design, Construction, and Politics.* S. Doc. No. 106–29. Washington, DC: Government Printing Office, 2001.

Amar, Akhil Reed. *America's Constitution: A Biography.* New York: Random House, 2005.

Amer, Mildred L. *The First Day of a New Congress: A Guide to Proceedings on the Senate Floor*. Congressional Research Service Report RS20722.

Arenberg, Richard A., and Robert B. Dove. *Defending the Filibuster: The Soul of the Senate*. Bloomington: Indiana University Press, 2012.

Asbell, Bernard. *The Senate Nobody Knows*. Garden City, NY: Doubleday, 1978.

Bacon, Donald C., Roger H. Davidson, and Morton Keller, eds. *The Encyclopedia of the United States Congress*. 4 vols. New York: Simon & Schuster, 1995.

Baker, Richard A. *Conservation Politics: The Senate Career of Clinton P. Anderson*. Albuquerque: University of New Mexico Press, 1985.

———. "Documenting the History of the United States Senate." *Government Publications Review* 10 (1983): 415–26.

———. "Legislative Power over Appointments and Confirmations." In *Encyclopedia of the American Legislative System*, 1605–19. Edited by Joel Silbey. New York: Maxwell Macmillan, 1994.

———. "Ritual and Ceremony in the United States Senate." In *Rituals in Parliaments: Political, Anthropological, and Historical Perspectives on Europe and the United States*. Edited by Emma Crewe and Marion G. Mueller, 111–34. Frankfurt am Main: Peter Lang, 2006.

———. *The Senate of the United States: A Bicentennial History*. Malabar, FL: Krieger, 1988.

———. "The Senate of the United States." In *Second Chambers: Bicameralism Today*, edited by R. C. Tripathi, 256–72. New Delhi: Rajya Sabha Secretariat, 2002.

———. "The Senate of the United States: Supreme Executive Council of the Nation." *Prologue* 21 (Winter 1989): 289–313.

———. "A Slap at the 'Hidden-Hand Presidency': The Senate and the Lewis Strauss Affair." *Congress and the Presidency* 14 (March 1987): 1–16.

———. "Twentieth-Century Senate Reform: Three Views from the Outside." In *The Contentious Senate: Partisanship, Ideology, and the Myth of Cool Judgment*. Edited by Colton C. Campbell and Nicol C. Rae, 147–66. Lanham, MD: Rowman & Littlefield, 2001.

———. "The United States Senate in Philadelphia: An Institutional History of the 1790s." In *The House and Senate in the 1790s*, edited by Kenneth R. Bowling and Donald Kennon, 292–320. Athens: Ohio University Press, 2002.

Baker, Richard A., and Roger H. Davidson, eds. *First among Equals: Outstanding Senate Leaders of the Twentieth Century*. Washington, DC: CQ Press, 1991.

Baker, Robert G. *Wheeling and Dealing: Confessions of a Capitol Hill Operator*. New York: Norton, 1980.

Baker, Ross K. *Friend and Foe in the U.S. Senate*. New York: Free Press, 1980.

———. *House and Senate*. 4th ed. New York: Norton, 2008.

Barry, David S. *Forty Years in Washington*. Boston: Little, Brown, 1924.

Benedict, Michael Les. *The Impeachment and Trial of Andrew Johnson*. New York: Norton, 1973.

Benton, Thomas Hart. *Thirty Years' View*. 2 vols. New York: Appleton, 1854–56.

Benton, Wilbourn E., ed. *1787: Drafting the U.S. Constitution*. College Station: Texas A&M University Press, 1986.

Beth, Richard S., Valerie Heitshusen, and Betsy Palmer. *Filibusters and Cloture in the Senate*. Congressional Research Service Report RL-30360.

Binder, Sarah A. *Minority Rights, Majority Rule: Partisanship and the Development of Congress*. New York: Cambridge University Press, 1997.

————, and Steven S. Smith. *Politics or Principle?: Filibustering in the United States Senate*. Washington, DC: Brookings, 1997.

Biographical Directory of the United States Congress, 1774–2005. H. Doc. 108–222. Washington, DC: Government Printing Office, 2005. For an up-to-date online edition, which includes bibliographical information on members, see bioguide.congress.gov/.

Birnbaum, Jeffrey, and Alan Murray. *Showdown at Gucci Gulch: Lawmakers, Lobbyists and the Unlikely Triumph of Tax Reform*. New York: Random House, 1987.

Bogue, Allan G. "The U.S. Congress: The Era of Party Patronage and Sectional Stress, 1829–1881." In *Encyclopedia of the American Legislative System*, 107–29. Edited by Joel Silbey. New York: Maxwell Macmillan, 1994.

————. *The Earnest Men: Republicans of the Civil War Senate*. Ithaca, NY: Cornell University Press, 1981.

Bolling, Richard. *House Out of Order*. New York: Dutton, 1965.

Bordewich, Fergus. *America's Great Debate: Henry Clay, Stephen A. Douglas and the Compromise That Preserved the Union*. New York: Simon & Schuster, 2012.

Bowling, Kenneth R., and Donald R. Kennon, eds. *Establishing Congress: The Removal to Washington, D.C., and the Election of 1800*. Athens: Ohio University Press, 2005.

————. *Inventing Congress: Origins and Establishment of the First Federal Congress*. Athens: Ohio University Press, 1999.

————. *The House and Senate in the 1790s: Petitioning, Lobbying, and Institutional Development*. Athens: Ohio University Press, 2002.

Bowling, Kenneth R., and Helen E. Veit, eds. *The Diary of William Maclay and Other Notes on Senate Debates*. Baltimore: Johns Hopkins University Press, 1988.

Bronner, Ethan. *Battle for Justice: How the Bork Nomination Shook America*. New York: Anchor, 1990.

Brown, Ernest S., ed. *William Plumer's Memorandum of Proceedings in the United States Senate, 1803–1807*. New York: Macmillan, 1923.

Brown, George Rothwell. *The Leadership of Congress*. Indianapolis: Bobbs-Merrill, 1922.

Brown, William Holmes, and Charles Johnson, comps. *House Practice: A Guide to the Rules, Precedents, and Procedures of the House*. 2d ed. Washington, DC: Government Printing Office, 2003.

Bruns, Roger A., David L. Hostetter, and Raymond W. Smock, eds. *Congress Investigates: A Critical and Documentary History*. Revised edition. 2 vols. New York: Facts on File, 2011.

Bryce, James. *The American Commonwealth*. 2 vols. Philadelphia: Morris, 1906.

Burdette, Franklin L. *Filibustering in the Senate*. Princeton, NJ: Princeton University Press, 1940.

Butler, Anne M., and Wendy Wolff, comps. *United States Senate Election, Expulsion and Censure Cases, 1793–1990*. S. Doc. No. 103–33. Washington, DC: Government Printing Office, 1995.

Butt, Archibald W. *The Letters of Archie Butt*. Garden City, NY: Doubleday, 1924.

Byrd, Robert C. *The Senate, 1789–1989*. 4 vols. Washington, DC: Government Printing Office, 1988–1994.
Volume 1 and 2: *Addresses on the History of the United States Senate*;
Volume 3: *Vital Speeches, 1830–1993*;
Volume 4: *Historical Statistics, 1789–1992*.

———. *The Senate of the Roman Republic: Addresses on the History of Roman Constitutionalism*. S. Doc. No. 103–23. Washington, DC: Government Printing Office, 1995.

The Cannon Centenary Conference: The Changing Nature of the Speakership. November 12, 2003. H. Doc. No. 108–204. Washington, DC: Government Printing Office, 2004.

Caro, Robert A. *The Years of Lyndon Johnson: Master of the Senate*. New York: Alfred A. Knopf, 2002.

———. *The Years of Lyndon Johnson: Means of Ascent*. New York: Alfred A. Knopf, 1990.

———. *The Years of Lyndon Johnson: The Passage of Power*. New York: Alfred A. Knopf, 2012.

Carpenter, Frank G. *Carp's Washington*. New York: McGraw-Hill, 1960.

Chernow, Ron. *Washington: A Life*. New York: Penguin, 2010.

Clark, Champ. *My Quarter Century of American Politics*. New York: Harper & Brothers, 1920.

Clymer, Adam. *Drawing the Line at the Big Ditch: The Panama Canal Treaties and the Rise of the Right*. Lawrence: University Press of Kansas, 2008.

Cole, Wayne S. *Roosevelt and the Isolationists, 1932–45*. Lincoln: University of Nebraska Press, 1983.

Collier, Kenneth E. *Between the Branches: The White House Office of Legislative Affairs*. Pittsburgh: University of Pittsburgh Press, 1997.

Combs, Jerald A. *The Jay Treaty: Political Background of the Founding Fathers*. Berkeley: University of California Press, 1970.

Comiskey, Michael. *Seeking Justices: The Judging of Supreme Court Nominees*. Lawrence: University Press of Kansas, 2004.

Congressional Quarterly. *Congressional Campaign Finances: History, Facts, and Controversy*. Washington, DC: CQ Press, 1992.

———. *Congressional Quarterly's Guide to the Congress of the United States*. 2d ed. Washington, DC: Congressional Quarterly, 1976.

———. *Origins and Development of Congress*. Washington, DC: Congressional Quarterly, 1976.

Cooper, Joseph, and Elizabeth Rybicki. "Analyzing Institutional Change: Bill Introduction in the U.S. Senate, 1789–1800." In *Senate Exceptionalism*, edited by Bruce Oppenheimer, 182–212. Columbus: Ohio State University Press, 2002.

Cooper, Joseph. *The Previous Question: Its Standing as a Precedent for Cloture in the United States Senate*. S. Doc. No. 87–104. Washington, DC: Government Printing Office, 1962.

Corbin, David A. *The Last Great Senator: Robert C. Byrd's Encounters with Eleven U.S. Presidents*. Washington, DC: Potomac Books, 2012.

Corwin, Edward S. *The President: Office and Powers*, 5th rev. ed. New York: New York University Press, 1984.

———. *The President's Control of Foreign Relations*. Princeton, NJ: Princeton University Press, 1917.

Cover, Albert D., and David R. Mayhew. "Congressional Dynamics and the Decline of Competitive Congressional Elections." In *Congress Reconsidered*, edited by Lawrence C. Dodd and Bruce Oppenheimer, 54–72. New York: Praeger, 1977.

Dangerfield, Royden J. *In Defense of the Senate: A Study in Treaty Making*. Norman: University of Oklahoma Press, 1933.

Daschle, Tom. *Like No Other Time: The 107th Congress and the Two Years that Changed America Forever*. New York: Crown, 2003.

Davidson, Roger H. "Senate Leaders: Janitors for an Unruly Chamber?" In *Congress Reconsidered*, edited by Lawrence C. Dodd and Bruce I. Oppenheimer, 225–52. Washington, DC: CQ Press, 1985.

Daynes, Bryon W. "The Impact of the Direct Election of Senators on the Political System." PhD diss., University of Chicago, 1972.

Dewhirst, Robert E., and John David Rausch Jr. *The Encyclopedia of the United States Congress*. New York: Facts on File, 2007.

Dimock, Marshall Edward. *Congressional Investigating Committees*. Baltimore: Johns Hopkins University Press, 1929.

The Dirksen Congressional Center. *Major Features of the Civil Rights Act of 1964*. www.dirksencenter.org.

Documentary History of the First Federal Congress of the United States of America, March 4, 1789–March 3, 1791. Linda Grant De Pauw, Charlene Bangs Bickford, Kenneth R. Bowling, Helen E. Veit, and William Charles diGiacomantonio, eds. 20 vols. Baltimore: Johns Hopkins University Press, 1972–2012.

Dole, Bob. *Historical Almanac of the United States Senate*. Washington, DC: Government Printing Office, 1989.

Draper, Theodore. *A Very Thin Line: The Iran-Contra Affairs*. New York: Hill and Wang, 1991.

Drury, Allen. *A Senate Journal, 1943–1945*. New York: McGraw-Hill, 1963.

Dunn, Susan. *Roosevelt's Purge: How FDR Fought to Change the Democratic Party*. Cambridge, MA: Harvard University Press, 2010.

Dyche, John David. *Republican Leader: A Political Biography of Senator Mitch McConnell*. Wilmington, DE: ISI Books, 2009.

Dyer, Oliver. *Great Senators of the United States Forty Years Ago*. New York: Bonner's, 1889.

Eberling, Ernest J. *Congressional Investigations: A Study of the Origin and Development of the Power of Congress to Investigate and Punish for Contempt.* New York: Octagon, 1973.

Edwards, George C., III. *At the Margins: Presidential Leadership of Congress.* New Haven, CT: Yale University Press, 1989.

Elliot, Jonathan, comp. *The Debates in the Several State Conventions on the Adoption of the Federal Constitution.* 5 vols. Washington, 1836. memory.loc.gov/ammem/amlaw/lwed.html.

Emery, Fred. *Watergate: The Corruption of American Politics and the Fall of Richard Nixon.* New York: Times Books, 1994.

Epstein, Lee, and Jeffrey A. Segal. "Confirming Federal Judges and Justices." Chapter 4. In *Advice and Consent: The Politics of Judicial Appointments.* New York: Oxford University Press, 2005.

Essary, Jesse Frederick. *Covering Washington.* Boston: Houghton Mifflin, 1927.

Estes, Todd. *The Jay Treaty Debate, Public Opinion, and the Evolution of Early American Political Culture.* Amherst: University of Massachusetts Press, 2008.

Evans, Rowland, and Robert Novak. *Lyndon B. Johnson: The Exercise of Power.* New York: New American Library, 1966.

Farrand, Max, ed. *The Records of the Federal Convention of 1787.* New Haven, CT: Yale University Press, 1911.

Fenno, Richard F., Jr. *Learning to Legislate: The Senate Education of Arlen Specter.* Washington: CQ Press, 1991.

———. *The Making of a Senator: Dan Quayle.* Washington, DC: CQ Press, 1989.

———. *The United States Senate: A Bicameral Perspective.* Washington, DC: American Enterprise Institute, 1982.

Ferrell, Robert H. *Presidential Leadership from Woodrow Wilson to Harry S. Truman.* Columbia, MO: University of Missouri Press, 2006.

Finley, Keith M. *Delaying the Dream: Southern Senators and the Fight Against Civil Rights, 1938–1965.* Baton Rouge: Louisiana State University Press, 2008.

Fisher, Louis. *Constitutional Conflicts between Congress and the President.* 5th edition, revised. Lawrence: University Press of Kansas, 2007.

———. *Defending Congress and the Constitution.* Lawrence: University Press of Kansas, 2011.

Fisher, Patrick. "The Filibuster and the Nature of Representation in the United States Senate." *Parliaments, Estates & Representation* 26 (November 2006): 187–95.

Fisk, Catherine, and Erwin Chemerinsky, "The Filibuster." *Stanford Law Review* 49 (January 1997): 181–254.

Fleming, Denna Frank. *The Treaty Veto of the American Senate.* New York: G. P. Putnam's Sons, 1930.

Foley, Michael. *The New Senate: Liberal Influence on a Conservative Institution, 1959–1972.* New Haven, CT: Yale University Press, 1980.

Foner, Eric. *Fiery Trial: Abraham Lincoln and American Slavery.* New York: Norton, 2010.

Frantzich, Stephen, and John Sullivan. *The C-SPAN Revolution.* Norman: University of Oklahoma Press, 1996.

Frist, William H., Jr. *Tennessee Senators, 1911–2001.* Lanham, MD: Madison Books, 1999.

Furber, George P. *Precedents Relating to the Privileges of the Senate of the United States.* S. Doc. No. 52–68. Washington, DC: Government Printing Office, 1893.

Galloway, George B. "Congress' Problem, Diagnosis, Proposal." *American Political Science Review* 36 (December 1942): 1091–1102.

———. *Congress at the Crossroads.* New York: Thomas Y. Crowell, 1946.

———. *History of the United States House of Representatives.* H. Doc. No. 89–250. Washington, DC: Government Printing Office, 1965.

———. *The Legislative Process in Congress.* New York: Crowell, 1953.

———. "The Operation of the Legislative Reorganization Act of 1946." *American Political Science Review* 45 (March 1951): 44–45.

Gamm, Gerald, and Steven S. Smith. "Emergence of Senate Party Leadership." In Bruce I. Oppenheimer, ed. *U.S. Senate Exceptionalism,* 212–39. Columbus: Ohio State University Press, 2002.

———. "Policy Leadership and the Development of the Modern Senate." In *Party, Process, and Political Change in Congress: New Perspectives on the History of Congress.* Edited by David W. Brady and Mathew D. McCubbins, 432–61. Stanford, CA: Stanford University Press, 2002.

Garrett, R. Sam. *The State of Campaign Finance Policy.* Congressional Research Service Report R-41542.

Gilbert, Clinton W. *Behind the Mirrors: The Psychology of Disintegration at Washington.* New York: G. P. Putnam's Sons, 1922.

Gilfry, Henry H., comp. *Precedents: Decisions on Points of Order with Phraseology in the United States Senate from the First to Sixty-Second Congress Inclusive, 1789–1913.* S. Doc. No. 62–1123. Washington, DC: Government Printing Office, 1914. (Supplement, 1913–1919. Washington, DC: Government Printing Office, 1919.)

———. *President of the Senate Pro Tempore: Proceedings in the United States Senate from April 6, 1789 to December 5, 1911, Relating to the Election, Powers, Duties, and Tenure in Office of the President of the Senate Pro Tempore.* S. Doc. No. 62–104. Washington, DC: Government Printing Office, 1911.

Glennon, Michael J. "The Senate Role in Treaty Ratification." *American Journal of International Law* 77 (April 1983): 257–80.

Gold, Martin B. *Senate Procedure and Practice.* Lanham, MD: Rowman & Littlefield, 2004.

———. and Dimple Gupta. "The Constitutional Option to Change Senate Rules and Procedures: A Majoritarian Means to Overcome the Filibuster." *Harvard Journal of Law & Public Policy* 28 (Fall 2004): 205–72.

Gormley, Ken. *The Death of American Virtue: Clinton v. Starr.* New York: Crown, 2010.

Gould, Lewis L. *The Most Exclusive Club: A History of the Modern United States Senate.* New York: Basic Books, 2005.

Grant, James. *Mr. Speaker!: The Life and Times of Thomas B. Reed, the Man Who Broke the Filibuster.* New York: Simon & Schuster, 2011.

Griffith, Robert. *The Politics of Fear: Joseph R. McCarthy and the Senate.* Lexington: University Press of Kentucky, 1970.

Gross, Bertram M. *The Legislative Struggle: A Study in Social Combat.* New York: McGraw-Hill, 1953.

Gugliotta, Guy. *Freedom's Cap: The United States Capitol and the Coming of the Civil War.* New York: Hill and Wang, 2012.

Halperin, Terri Diane. "Dangerous to Liberty: The United States Senate, 1789–1821." PhD diss., University of Virginia, 2000.

———. "The Special Relationship: The Senate and the States, 1789–1801." In *The House and Senate in the 1790s,* edited by Kenneth R. Bowling and Donald Kennon, 267–91. Athens: Ohio University Press, 2002.

Harkin, Tom. "Fixing the Filibuster: Restoring Real Democracy in the Senate." *Iowa Law Review Bulletin* 95 (2010): 67–79.

Harris, Fred R. *Deadlock or Decision: The U.S. Senate and the Rise of National Politics.* New York: Oxford University Press, 1993.

Harris, Joseph P. *The Advice and Consent of the Senate: A Study of the Confirmation of Appointments by the United States Senate.* Berkeley: University of California Press, 1953.

Hatcher, Andrea C. *Majority Leadership in the U.S. Senate: Balancing Constraints.* Amherst, NY: Cambria Press, 2010.

Hatfield, Mark O. *Vice Presidents of the United States.* S. Doc. No. 104–26. Washington, DC: Government Printing Office, 1997.

Hayden, Ralston. *The Senate and Treaties, 1789–1817: The Development of the Treaty-making Functions of the United States Senate during their Formative Period.* New York: Macmillan, 1920.

Haynes, George H. *The Election of Senators.* New York: Henry Holt, 1906.

———. *The Senate of the United States.* 2 vols. New York: Houghton Mifflin, 1938.

Heidler, David, and Jeanne Heidler. *Henry Clay.* New York: Random House, 2010.

Hess, Stephen. "Why Great Men Still Are Not Chosen President." *Brookings Review* 5 (Summer 1987): 34–39.

———. *The Ultimate Insiders: U.S. Senators in the National Media.* Washington, DC: Brookings, 1986.

Hibbing, John, ed. *The Changing World of the U.S. Senate.* Berkeley, CA: IGS Press, 1990.

Hinds, Asher C. *Hinds' Precedents of the House of Representatives of the United States, Including References to Provisions of the Constitution, the Laws, and the Decisions of the United States Senate.* 8 vols. Washington, DC: Government Printing Office, 1907–1908.

Hoar, George Frisbie. *Autobiography of Seventy Years.* 2 vols. New York: Scribner's, 1903.

———. "Election of Senators by Direct Vote of the People." Reprinted in S. Doc. No. 59–232. Washington, DC: Government Printing Office, 1906.

Hoffer, Williamjames Hull. *The Caning of Charles Sumner: Honor, Idealism, and the Origins of the Civil War*. Baltimore: Johns Hopkins University Press, 2010.

Holst, H. Von. "Ought the United States Senate to Be Abolished?" *Monist* 5 (October 1894): 1–21.

Holt, W. Stull. *Treaties Defeated by the Senate*. Baltimore: Johns Hopkins University Press, 1933.

Huitt, Ralph. "Democratic Party Leadership in the Senate." *American Political Science Review* 55 (June 1961): 333–44.

———. "The Outsider in the Senate: An Alternative Role." *American Political Science Review* 55: 566–75.

Jefferson, Thomas. *A Manual of Parliamentary Practice for the Use of the Senate of the United States*. Washington, DC, 1801. (S. Doc. No. 103–8. Washington, DC: Government Printing Office, 1993.)

Johnson, Dennis W. *The Laws that Shaped America*. New York: Routledge, 2009.

———. *No Place for Amateurs: How Political Consultants Are Reshaping American Democracy*, 2d ed. New York: Routledge, 2007.

Johnson, Loch K. *A Season of Inquiry: The Senate Intelligence Investigation*. Lexington: University Press of Kentucky, 1985.

Jones, Charles O. "The New, New Senate." In *The Tide of Discontent: The 1980 Elections and Their Meaning*, edited by Ellis Sandoz and Cecil V. Crabb Jr., 89–111. Washington, DC: Congressional Quarterly Press, 1981.

Josephy, Alvin M., Jr. *The American Heritage History of the Congress of the United States*. New York: American Heritage, 1975.

Kaiser, Robert G. *So Damn Much Money: The Triumph of Lobbying and the Corrosion of American Government*. New York: Alfred A. Knopf, 2009.

Kennedy, John F. *Profiles in Courage*. New York: Harper, 1956.

Kennon, Donald R., ed. *The United States Capitol: Designing and Decorating a National Icon*. Athens: Ohio University Press, 2000.

Kerr, Clara Hannah Stidham. *The Origin and Development of the United States Senate*. Ithaca, NY, 1895.

Kloss, William, and Diane K Skvarla. *United States Senate Catalogue of Fine Art*. S. Doc. No. 107–11. Washington, DC: Government Printing Office, 2002.

Koger, Gregory. *Filibustering: A Political History of Obstruction in the House and Senate*. Chicago: University of Chicago Press, 2010.

Kravitz, Walter. "Evolution of the Senate's Committee System." *Annals of the American Academy of Political and Social Science* 411 (1974): 27–38.

Kutler, Stanley I. *The Wars of Watergate: The Corruption of American Politics and the Fall of Richard Nixon*. New York: Norton, 1994.

Lancaster, Lane W. "The Initiative of the Senate in Legislation, 1789–1809." *Southwestern Political and Social Science Quarterly* 9 (June 1928): 67–75.

Lee, Frances. *Beyond Ideology: Politics, Principles, and Partisanship in the U.S. Senate*. Chicago: University of Chicago Press, 2009.

Lee, Frances E., and Bruce I. Oppenheimer, eds. *Sizing up the Senate: The Unequal Consequences of Equal Representation*. Chicago: University of Chicago Press, 1999.

Lessig, Lawrence. *Republic Lost: How Money Corrupts Congress*. New York: Twelve Books, 2011.

Lodge, Henry Cabot. *The Senate and the League of Nations*. New York: Scribner's, 1925.

Longley, Lawrence D., and Walter J. Oleszek. *Bicameral Politics: Conference Committees in Congress*. New Haven, CT: Yale University Press, 1989.

Loomis, Burdett A., ed. *Esteemed Colleagues: Civility and Deliberation in the U.S. Senate*. Washington, DC: Brookings, 2000.

———. *The U.S. Senate: From Deliberation to Dysfunction*. Washington, DC: Sage, 2012.

Lott, Trent. *Herding Cats: A Life in Politics*. New York: Regan Books, 2005.

———. *Leading the United States Senate*. S. Pub. No. 107–54. Washington, DC: Government Printing Office, 2002.

Mackaman, Frank H., ed. *Understanding Congressional Leadership*. Washington, DC: Congressional Quarterly Press, 1981.

MacNeil, Neil. "The American Congress: Its Troubled Role in the 1980s." *Modern Age* 24 (Fall 1980): 370–8.

———. *Dirksen*. New York: World, 1970.

———. *Forge of Democracy: The House of Representatives*. New York: David McKay, 1963.

Magleby, David, ed. *The Change Election: Money, Mobilization, and Persuasion in the 2008 Federal Elections*. Philadelphia: Temple University Press, 2011.

Maiden Speeches of U.S. Senators in the 108th Congress of the United States. S. Doc. No. 108–16. Washington, DC: Government Printing Office, 2005.

Main, Jackson Turner. *The Upper House in Revolutionary America, 1763–1788*. Madison: University of Wisconsin Press, 1967.

Malbin, Michael J., ed. *The Election after Reform: Money, Politics, and the Bipartisan Campaign Reform Act*. Lanham, MD: Rowman & Littlefield, 2006.

Manley, John. *The Politics of Finance*. Boston: Little, Brown, 1970.

Mann, Robert. *The Walls of Jericho: Lyndon Johnson, Hubert Humphrey, Richard Russell and the Struggle for Civil Rights*. New York: Harcourt Brace, 1996.

Mann, Thomas E., and Norman J. Ornstein. *The Broken Branch: How Congress Is Failing American and How to Get It Back on Track*. New York: Oxford University Press, 2008.

———. *It's Even Worse Than It Looks: How the American Constitutional System Collided with the New Politics of Extremism*. New York: Basic Books, 2012.

Manning, Jennifer E. *Membership of the 112th Congress: A Profile*. March 1, 2011, Congressional Research Service Report R-41647.

Markoe, Arnold. "The Black Committee: A Study of the Senate Investigation of the Public Utility Holding Company Lobby." PhD diss., New York University, 1972.

Martis, Kenneth C. *The Historical Atlas of Political Parties in the United States Congress, 1789–1989*. New York: Collier Macmillan, 1989.

Matthews, Donald R. *U.S. Senators and Their World*. Chapel Hill: University of North Carolina Press, 1960.

McCabe, James Dabney. *Behind the Scenes in Washington: Being a Complete and Graphic Account of the Credit Mobilier Investigation* . . . New York: Continental, 1873.

McCall, Samuel Walker. *The Business of Congress*. New York: Columbia University Press, 1911.

McConachie, Lauros G. *Congressional Committees: A Study of the Origins and Development of Our National and Local Legislative Methods*. New York: Crowell, 1898.

McPherson, Elizabeth Gregory. "The History of Reporting of Debates and Proceedings of Congress." PhD diss., University of North Carolina, 1940.

McPherson, Harry. *A Political Education*. Boston: Little, Brown, 1972.

Merrill, Horace Samuel, and Marion Galbraith Merrill. *The Republican Command, 1897–1913*. Lexington: University Press of Kentucky, 1971.

Mersky, Roy M., and J. Myron Jacobstein. *The Supreme Court of the United States: Hearings and Reports on Successful and Unsuccessful Nominations of Supreme Court Justices by the Senate Judiciary Committee, 1916–2006*. Buffalo, NY: Hein, 1977–2007.

Montgomery, Gayle B., and James W. Johnson. *One Step from the White House: The Rise and Fall of William F. Knowland*. Berkeley: University of California Press, 1998.

Moore, Charles. *Washington Past and Present*. New York: Century, 1929.

Moore, William Howard. *The Kefauver Committee and the Politics of Crime*. Columbia: University of Missouri Press, 1974.

Morgan, Gerald D. "Congressional Investigations and Judicial Review: *Kilbourn v. Thompson* Revisited." *California Law Review* 37 (1949): 556–74.

Munk, Margaret R. "Origin and Development of the Party Floor leadership in the United States Senate." PhD diss., Harvard University, 1970.

Nelson, Garrison. "The Modernizing Congress, 1870–1930." In *Encyclopedia of the American Legislative System*, 131–56. Edited by Joel Silbey. New York: Maxwell Macmillan, 1994.

Oleszek, Walter J. *Majority and Minority Whips of the Senate: History and Development of the Party Whip System in the U.S. Senate*. S. Doc. No. 98–45. Washington, DC: Government Printing Office, 1985.

———. "Party Whips in the United States Senate." *Journal of Politics* 33 (November 1971): 955–79.

———. *Proposals to Reform "Holds" in the Senate*. Congressional Research Service Report RL-31685.

Oppenheimer, Bruce I., ed. *U.S. Senate Exceptionalism*. Columbus: Ohio State University Press, 2002.

Oshinsky, David M. *A Conspiracy So Immense: The World of Joseph McCarthy*. New York: Free Press, 1983.

Packer, George. "The Empty Chamber." *The New Yorker*, August 9, 2010.

Parker, Robert. *Capitol Hill in Black and White*. New York: Dodd, Mead, 1986.

Patterson, James T. *Congressional Conservatism and the New Deal: The Growth of the Conservative Coalition in Congress, 1933–1939*. Lexington: University of Kentucky Press, 1967.

———. *Mr. Republican: A Biography of Robert A. Taft*. Boston: Houghton Mifflin, 1972.

Patterson, Samuel C. "Party Leadership in the U.S. Senate." *Legislative Studies Quarterly* 14 (August 1989): 393–413.

Peck, Harry Thurston. *Twenty Years of the Republic, 1885–1905*. New York: Dodd, Mead, 1907.

Peffer, William A. "The United States Senate: Its Origin, Personnel, and Organization." *North American Review* 167 (July 1898): 48–63.

———. "The United States Senate: Its Privileges, Powers, and Functions; Its Rules and Methods of Doing Business." *North American Review* 167 (August 1898): 176–90.

Peterson, Merrill D. *The Great Triumvirate: Webster, Clay, and Calhoun*. New York: Oxford University Press, 1987.

Phelps, Timothy M., and Helen Witernitz. *Capitol Games: Clarence Thomas, Anita Hill, and the Story of a Supreme Court Nomination*. New York: Hyperion, 1992.

Phillips, David Graham. *Treason of the Senate*. Edited with an introd. by George E. Mowry and Judson A. Grenier. Chicago: Quadrangle, 1964.

Phillips, Jean E. *Reorganization of Congress: Modern Reform Efforts*. Hauppauge, NY: Nova Science, 2004.

Poore, Benjamin Perley. *Perley's Reminiscences of Sixty Years in the National Metropolis*. 2 vols. Philadelphia: Hubbard Brothers, 1886.

Power of the Senate to Originate Appropriation Bills. H. Rpt. No. 46–147. Washington, DC: Government Printing Office, 1881.

Presidential Vetoes, 1789–1988. S. Pub. No. 102–12. Washington, DC: Government Printing Office, 1992.

Pro Tem: Presidents Pro Tempore of the United States Senate since 1789. S. Pub. No. 110–18. Washington, DC: Government Printing Office, 2008.

Quinn, Arthur. *The Rivals: William Gwinn, David Broderick, and the Birth of California*. New York: Crown, 1994.

Rakove, Jack N. "The Origins of Congress." In *Encyclopedia of the American Legislative System*, 55–70. Edited by Joel Silbey. New York: Maxwell Macmillan, 1994.

Rawls, W. Lee. *In Praise of Deadlock: How Partisan Struggle Makes Better Laws*. Baltimore: Johns Hopkins University Press, 2009.

Redman, Eric. *The Dance of Legislation*. New York: Simon & Schuster, 1973.

Reedy, George E. *The U.S. Senate: Paralysis or a Search for Consensus?* New York: Crown, 1986.

Reeves, Richard. *President Nixon: Alone in the White House*. New York: Simon & Schuster, 2001.

Reid, Harry. *The Good Fight: Hard Lessons from Searchlight to Washington*. New York: G. P. Putnam's Sons, 2008.

Reinsch, Paul S. *American Legislatures and Legislative Methods*. New York: Century, 1913.

Remini, Robert V. *Daniel Webster: The Man and His Time*. New York: Norton, 1997.

————. *Henry Clay: Statesman for the Union*. New York: Norton, 1991.

————. *The House*. New York: HarperCollins, 2006.

Rhodes, James Ford. *History of the United States from the Compromise of 1850*. 7 vols. New York: Macmillan, 1902–06.

Riddick, Floyd M. *Majority and Minority Leaders of the Senate: History and Development of the Offices of Floor Leaders*. S. Doc. No. 100–28. Washington, DC: Government Printing Office, 1988.

————, and Robert B. Dove. *Procedure and Guidelines for Impeachment Trials in the United States Senate*. S. Doc. No. 99–13. Washington, DC: Government Printing Office, 1986.

————, and Alan S. Frumin. *Riddick's Senate Procedure*. S. Doc. No. 101–28. Washington, DC: Government Printing Office, 1992.

Riedel, Richard L. *Halls of the Mighty: My 47 Years at the Senate*. Washington, DC: Luce, 1969.

Ripley, Randall B. *Power in the Senate*. New York: St. Martin's, 1969.

Risjord, Norman K. "Congress in the Federalist-Republican Era, 1789–1828." In *Encyclopedia of the American Legislative System*, 89–106. Edited by Joel Silbey. New York: Maxwell Macmillan, 1994.

Ritchie, Donald A. *A History of the United States Senate Republican Policy Committee, 1947–1997*. S. Doc. No. 105–5. Washington, DC: Government Printing Office, 1997.

————. "Introduction: Presidents Working with Congress from Truman to Obama." In *Congress and Harry S. Truman: A Conflicted Legacy*, edited by Donald A. Ritchie, xvii–xlv. Kirksville, MO: Truman State University Press, 2011.

————, comp. *Minutes of the Senate Democratic Conference, 1903–1964*. S. Doc. No. 105–20. Washington, DC: Government Printing Office, 1998.

————. *Press Gallery: Congress and the Washington Correspondents*. Cambridge, MA: Harvard University Press, 1991.

————. *The U.S. Congress: A Very Short Introduction*. New York: Oxford University Press, 2010.

————, and Wendy Wolff, comps. *Minutes of the Senate Republican Conference, 1911–1964*. S. Doc. No. 105–19. Washington, DC: Government Printing Office, 1999.

Robinson, George Lee. "The Development of the Senate Committee System." PhD diss., New York University, 1954.

Rogers, Lindsay. *The American Senate*. New York: Alfred A. Knopf, 1926.

————. "Staffing the Congress." *Political Science Quarterly* 56 (March 1941): 1–22.

Rohde, David W. "The Contemporary Congress, 1930–1992." In *Encyclopedia of the American Legislative System*, 157–73. Edited by Joel Silbey. New York: Maxwell Macmillan, 1994.

Rosenbloom, David Lee. *The Election Men: Professional Campaign Managers and American Democracy*. New York: Quadrangle Books, 1973.

Rosenfeld, Richard N. *American Aurora: A Democratic-Republican Returns: The Suppressed History of Our Nation's Beginnings and the Heroic Newspaper that Tried to Report It*. New York: St. Martin's, 1997.

Rothman, David J. *Politics and Power: The United States Senate, 1869–1901*. Cambridge, MA: Harvard University Press, 1966.

Samuel, Terence. *The Upper House: A Journey behind the Closed Doors of the U.S. Senate*. New York: Palgrave Macmillan, 2010.

Sargent, Nathan. *Public Men and Events* [1817–1853]. 2 vols. Philadelphia: J.B. Lippincott, 1875.

Schiller, Wendy J. *Partners and Rivals: Representation in U.S. Senate Delegations*. Princeton, NJ: Princeton University Press, 2000.

Schneider, Judy. *Minority Rights and Senate Procedures*, August 22, 2005. Congressional Research Service Report, RL30850.

Schulz, George J. *Monograph Relating to the Creation of the Senate of the United States*. S. Doc. No. 75–45. Washington, DC: Government Printing Office, 1937. (Reprinted with new introduction, S. Doc. No. 100–7. Washington, DC: Government Printing Office, 1987.)

The Senate as a Continuing Body: Extracts from the Congressional Globe. 65th Congress, Special Session. S. Prt. [unnumbered]. Washington, DC: Government Printing Office, 1917.

Senate Rules and the Senate as a Continuing Body. S. Doc. No. 83–4. Washington, DC: Government Printing Office, 1953.

Senators of the United States: A Historical Bibliography. S. Doc. No. 103–34. Washington, DC: Government Printing Office, 1995.

Shapiro, Ira. *The Last Great Senate*. New York: Public Affairs, 2012.

Sherrill, Robert. *Why They Call It Politics*. San Diego: Harcourt Brace Jovanovich, 1984.

Shesol, Jeff. *Supreme Power: Franklin Roosevelt v. the Supreme Court*. New York: Norton, 2010.

Silbey, Joel H., ed. *Encyclopedia of the American Legislative System: Studies of the Principal Structures, Processes, and Policies of Congress and the State Legislatures since the Colonial Era*. 4 vols. New York: Maxwell Macmillan, 1994.

Sinclair, Barbara. "Partisan Polarization, Individualism, and Lawmaking in the Senate." In *Party Wars: Polarization and the Politics of National Policy Making*, Chapter 6. Norman: University of Oklahoma Press, 2006.

———. *The Transformation of the U.S. Senate*. Baltimore: Johns Hopkins University Press, 1989.

———. *Unorthodox Lawmaking: New Legislative Processes in the U.S. Congress*, 4th edition. Washington, DC: Sage, 2011.

Smith, Steven S. *The American Congress*. Boston: Houghton Mifflin, 1995.

———. *Call to Order: Floor Politics in the House and Senate*. Washington, DC: Brookings, 1989.

Smist, Frank J., Jr. *Congress Oversees the United States Intelligence Community, 1947–1989*. Knoxville: University of Tennessee Press, 1990.

Sollenberger, Mitchel A. *The History of the Blue Slip in the Senate Committee on the Judiciary, 1917 to Present*. Congressional Research Service Report RL-32013.

Solomon, Burt. *FDR v. the Constitution: The Court-Packing Fight and the Triumph of Democracy*. New York: Walker, 2009.

Stathis, Stephen W. *Landmark Legislation, 1774–2002: Major U.S. Acts and Treaties.* Washington, DC: CQ Press, 2003.

Stealey, O. O. *Twenty Years in the Press Gallery: A Concise History of Important Legislation from the 48th to the 58th Congress.* New York: Publishers Printing Co., 1906.

Stidham, Clara H. Kerr. *The Origin and Development of the United States Senate.* Ithaca, NY: Andrus & Church, 1895.

Sullivan, Mark, *Our Times, 1900–1925.* 6 vols. New York: Scribner, 1936.

Sundquist, James L. *The Decline and Resurgence of Congress.* Washington, DC: Brookings, 1981.

Swanstrom, Roy. *The United States Senate 1787–1801.* S. Doc. No. 87–64. Washington, DC: Government Printing Office, 1988.

Swift, Elaine K. *The Making of an American Senate: Reconstitutive Change in Congress, 1787–1841.* Ann Arbor: University of Michigan Press, 1996.

Tananbaum, Duane. *The Bricker Amendment Controversy: A Test of Eisenhower's Political Leadership.* Ithaca, NY: Cornell University Press, 1988.

Tap, Bruce. *Over Lincoln's Shoulder: The Committee on the Conduct of the War.* Lawrence: University Press of Kansas, 1998.

Taussig, Frank William. *The Tariff History of the United States.* New York: G. P. Putnam's Sons, 1931.

Taylor, Telford. *Grand Inquest: The Story of Congressional Investigations.* New York: Ballantine, 1961.

Theriault, Sean M., and David W. Rohde. "The Gingrich Senators and Party Polarization in the U.S. Senate." Paper accepted for publication in *The Journal of Politics.* users.polisci.wisc.edu/apw/archives/Theriault-Rohde_2011.pdf.

Thompson, Charles Willis. *Party Leaders of the Time.* New York: Dillingham, 1906.

Thurber, James A., ed. *Rivals for Power: Presidential-Congressional Relations.* Lanham, MD: Rowman & Littlefield, 2009.

Tocqueville, Alexis de. *Democracy in America.* 2 vols. New York: Knopf, 1945.

Torres, Louis. "Federal Hall Revisited." *Journal of the Society of Architectural Historians* 29 (December 1970): 327–28.

Toward a Modern Senate: Final Report of the Commission on the Operation of the Senate, December 1976. S. Doc. No. 94–278. Washington, DC: Government Printing Office, 1976.

Townsend, George Alfred. *Washington Outside and Inside: A Picture and Narrative of the Origin, Growth, Excellencies, Abuses, Beauties, and Personages of Our Governing City.* Hartford, CT: Betts, 1873.

Upchurch, Thomas Adams. *Legislating Racism: The Billion Dollar Congress and the Birth of Jim Crow.* Lexington, KY: University Press of Kentucky, 2004.

US Congress. Joint Committee on the Organization of Congress. *Floor Deliberations and Scheduling: Hearings before the Joint Committee on the Organization of Congress,* 103rd Cong., May 18, 20, and 25, 2003.

US Senate. Committee of Appropriations. *Committee on Appropriations, United States Senate, 138th Anniversary, 1867–2005.* S. Doc. No. 109–5. Washington, 2005.

U.S. Senate. Committee on the Judiciary. *Maintenance of a Lobby to Influence Legislation*, 63rd Congress, 1st sess. Washington, DC: Government Printing Office, 1913.

U.S. Senate. Committee on Rules and Administration. *Examining the Filibuster*, S. Hrg. No. 111–706. Washington, DC: Government Printing Office, 2010.

————. *Senate Cloture Rule: Limitation of Debate in the Senate of the United States and Legislative History of Paragraph 2 of Rule XXII of the Standing Rules of the United States Senate (Cloture Rule) prepared by the Congressional Research Service, Library of Congress*. S. Prt. No. 112–31. Washington, DC: Government Printing Office, 2011.

U.S. Senate. Office of Senate Curator. *United States Senate Catalogue of Graphic Art*. With essays by Diane K. Skvarla and Donald A. Ritchie. S. Doc. No. 109–2. Washington, DC: Government Printing Office, 2006.

Valeo, Francis R. *Mike Mansfield, Majority Leader: A Different Kind of Senate, 1961–1976*. Armonk, NY: Sharpe, 1999.

Wawro, Gregory J., and Eric Schickler. *Filibuster: Obstruction and Lawmaking in the U.S. Senate*. Princeton, NJ: Princeton University Press, 2006.

Whalen, Charles W., and Barbara Whalen. *The Longest Debate: A Legislative History of the 1964 Civil Rights Act*. Cabin John, MD: Seven Locks, 1985.

Whalen, Thomas J. *Kennedy vs. Lodge: The 1952 Massachusetts Senate Race*. Boston: Northeastern University Press, 2000.

White, William S. *Citadel: The Story of the U.S. Senate*. New York: Harper & Brothers, 1957.

Wilson, Woodrow. *Congressional Government: A Study in American Politics*. Boston: Houghton, Mifflin, 1885.

————. *Constitutional Government in the United States*. New York: Columbia University Press, 1911.

Wirls, Daniel, and Stephen Wirls. *The Invention of the United States Senate*. Baltimore: Johns Hopkins University Press, 2003.

Wood, Gordon S. *Empire of Liberty: A History of the Early Republic*. New York: Oxford University Press, 2009.

Woodward, C. Vann. *Origins of the New South, 1877–1913*. Baton Rouge: Louisiana State University Press, 1971.

Yarwood, Dean L. *When Congress Makes a Joke: Congressional Humor Then and Now*. Lanham, MD: Rowman & Littlefield, 2004.

Ybarra, Michael J. *Washington Gone Crazy: Senator Pat McCarran and the Great Communist Hunt*. Hanover, NH: Steerforth, 2004.

Young, James Harvey. *Pure Food: Securing the Federal Food and Drugs Act of 1906*. Princeton, NJ: Princeton University Press, 1989.

Zelizer, Julian E. *On Capitol Hill: The Struggle to Reform Congress and Its Consequences, 1948–2000*. New York: Cambridge University Press, 2004.

Index

Abourezk, James, 342–44
Abramoff, Jack, 50
absenteeism, 321–22, 335
Acheson, Dean, 118, 248, 254
Act to Prevent Pernicious Political
    Activities (1939), 41
Adams, Alva, 111
Adams, Henry, 71
Adams, John, 13, 54, 56–57, 150
Adams, John Quincy
    federal positions and, 59
    Jackson and, 59
    on Monroe, 57–58
    J. Randolph and, 305
    on Senate, 288
    Senate and, 56, 57, 58
    Webster and, 280
Afghanistan, 137
African Americans
    lynchings and, 22, 101, 319–321
    Senate elections and, 21–22, 27–29,
      38–40
    See also civil rights
Agnew, Spiro, 131, 263–64, 267
Aiken, George, 9

Ailes, Roger, 37–38
Albany Regency, 16–17
Albert, Carl, 130, 268
Aldrich, Nelson
    filibusters and, 314–15
    La Follette and, 180–81
    Phillips and, 22
    T. Roosevelt and, 85–86, 87,
      88–89
    Senate leadership and, 25, 76,
      176–79, 288
    Spanish-American War and, 82
Alexander, Lamar, 225, 353–54
Alito, Samuel, 352
Allen, James, 340, 341–42
Allen, William, 63, 313
Allison, William B.
    death of, 180
    T. Roosevelt and, 85–86, 89
    Senate leadership and, 25, 76,
      176–78, 179, 288
The American Commonwealth (Bryce),
    21, 175, 311
American Political Science Association,
    115

Americans with Disabilities Act (1990), 144, 221
Anderson, Clinton, 122, 209
Angle, Sharron, 51
Anthony, Henry, 18–19, 173
anti-poll tax bills, 322
appropriations bills
    B. Clinton and, 146
    filibusters and, 309, 353
    Finance Committee and, 173
    House of Representatives and, 158–161
    Nixon and, 129, 230
    Senate and, 158–161
Appropriations Committee (Senate), 6, 176, 200
Armed Services Committee (Senate), 253–54, 259–260, 338
arms reduction, 102
Arthur, Chester A., 72, 74, 76–77
Ashcroft, John, 48
Ashurst, Henry, 107, 317
Aurora (newspaper), 231, 278

Bailey, Theodorus, 278
Baker, Howard
    civil rights and, 127
    filibusters and, 343, 344–45, 347
    Goldwater and, 410n60
    Panama Canal and, 136
    as party leader, 132, 138, 215, 216–17, 229, 343, 344–45, 347
    Reagan and, 138
    Scott and, 214
    on Senate leadership, 168
    Watergate scandal and, 230, 264, 266, 267
Baker, James, 143
Baker, Robert G. (Bobby), 36, 202, 203, 209
Balanced Budget Act (1997), 147
Bank of the United States, 61, 63–64, 169
Bankhead, William, 191
Banking Act (1933), 240
Banking Committee (Senate), 272–73

Barkley, Alben
    campaign for Senate and, 40
    filibusters and, 323
    McKellar and, 322
    as party leader, 190–92, 197, 198, 246, 322
    as party whip, 190
    F. D. Roosevelt and, 108, 190–92
    Rule 19 and, 293
    on Senate, 292–93
    Senate investigations and, 246
    Truman and, 117, 194
    as vice president, 10
Barry, David, 321
Bayard, Thomas, 321
Bayh, Birch, 45, 134
Beck, Dave, 260
Belknap, William, 73
Benjamin, Judah, 287
Bennett, Robert, 228–29
Benton, Thomas Hart
    Calhoun and, 280
    dueling and, 281–82
    filibusters and, 170–71, 307–8
    Foot and, 278–79
    investigations and, 231
    Jackson and, 61, 154, 169–170
    as orator, 58, 283
    on Senate, 285
    Senate leadership and, 65
    Tocqueville and, 155
Benton, William, 254
Bentsen, Lloyd, 134, 142
Ben-Veniste, Richard, 273
Berger, Victor, 152
Berlin Wall, 124, 144
Beveridge, Albert, 180, 296
Bicameral Politics (Longley and Oleszek), 391n67
Bilbo, Theodore, 28–29
Bipartisan Campaign Reform Act (BCRA, 2002), 50–51
Black, Hugo, 29, 106, 240–41
Bladensburg Dueling Grounds, 409n31
Blaine, James G., 74, 75, 77, 156

Blease, Coleman, 28
Blum, John Morton, 378n22
Bohlen, Charles, 112, 120
Boland, Edward, 270
Bolling, Richard, 162
Borah, William, 99, 102, 106, 183–84
Bork, Robert, 141, 267
Boxer, Barbara, 47, 48
Boyle, William, 252
Bradley, Omar, 254
Bradley, Stephen, 57
Breaux, John, 222
Breyer, Stephen, 145
Brezhnev, Leonid, 137
Bricker, John, 120–21
Bridges, Styles, 195, 197, 211, 212
Bright, Jesse, 172
Broder, David, 49
Broderick, David, 286
Brooks, David, 226
Brooks, Preston, 232, 286
Brooks, Wayland, 32
Brown, George Rothwell, 25, 166
Brown, John, 232–33
Brown, Joseph, 311
Brown, Scott, 419n54
Bryce, James
    on filibusters, 311
    on House of Representatives, 155
    on the presidency, 62–63
    on Senate, 19, 21, 175, 287
Buchanan, James, 65
Buckley, James, 42
Buckley v. Valeo, 42
Budget and Accounting Act (1921),
    390n58
Budget Control Act (2011), 148
Bulkley, Robert, 31
Bumpers, Dale, 347
Bunning, Jim, 346
Burleson, Albert, 92, 95
Burr, Aaron, 56
Burton, Theodore, 24
Bush, George H. W., 139, 141–45, 148,
    221, 222–23

Bush, George W., 274, 351
Bush, Prescott, 142
Butler, Andrew, 18, 286, 310
Butler, Benjamin, 70
Butler, Pierce, 54
Butterfield, Alexander, 266
Byrd, Robert C.
    campaign for Senate and, 32–34
    J. Carter and, 135–37
    filibusters and, 216, 335, 340, 341,
        342–45, 349–351, 354
    Line-Item Veto Act and, 147
    on Meese, 141
    Mitchell and, 220
    1996 orientation remarks by, 3–5, 9, 12
    as party leader, 135–37, 214, 215–16,
        219, 335, 342–45
    as party whip, 215
    presidential nomination and, 134
    Reagan and, 139
    on Senate debates, 301
    on Senate's continuity, 399n69
    Sununu and, 143
    on television coverage, 298
    on Tower, 142
    on Watergate, 133
Byrnes, James, 108

Caldwell, Alexander, 20
Calhoun, John C.
    Compromise of 1850 and, 284
    filibusters and, 308
    Great Triumvirate and, 62, 154,
        170–71, 279–283
    Hayne and, 279
    as House member, 277
    Jackson and, 307
    on Madison, 57
    Polk on, 64
    J. Randolph and, 289, 306
    Senate leadership and, 65
Cameron, J. D., 18
Cameron, Simon, 18, 19, 66, 71
Cannon, Howard, 137
Cannon, James, 132–33, 134

Cannon, Joseph, 156, 390n56
Cannon, Lou, 139
Cantwell, Maria, 48
Capezio, Anthony "Tough Tony," 250
Capone, Al, 250
Carlisle, John, 156
Carnahan, Jean, 48
Carnahan, Mel, 48
Carpenter, Matthew, 18–19
Carter, Jimmy, 134–37, 215–16, 342–43
Carter, Thomas, 313–14
Cass, Lewis, 64, 65
Catledge, Turner, 28
Census Committee, 176
Central Intelligence Agency (CIA), 269
Chandler, Zachariah
    on committee assignments, 172–73
    A. Johnson and, 69
    Lincoln and, 68
    Senate investigations and, 233–35
    Senatorial Clique and, 71
    spoils system and, 18–19
Chase, Salmon, 65, 66, 284
Cheney, Dick, 223
Chertoff, Michael, 273
Chestnut, James, 286
China, 128
Church, Frank, 45, 134, 137, 269–270,
    340
Churchill, Winston, 112
Cilley, Jonathan, 409n31
Citizens United v. Federal Election
    Commission, 35, 50–51
civil rights
    Dirksen and, 126–27, 294
    filibusters and, 38, 125–27, 303,
        318–321
    L. Johnson and, 125–27
    J. F. Kennedy and, 125–26
    Truman and, 117
Civil Rights Act (1957), 328
Civil Rights Act (1960), 294, 328
Civil Rights Act (1964), 125–26, 213–14,
    294, 328, 342
Civil Rights Act (1968), 294, 334, 336

Civil Rights Act (1991), 292
civil service reform, 73, 76–77
Clapp, Moses, 180, 236
Clark, William, 20
Clay, Henry
    as House member, 57, 58, 155–56,
        277
    Jackson and, 59, 60–61, 169–170
    J. Randolph and, 305
    on Senate, 279
    as senator: appropriations bills and,
        159; Compromise of 1850 and,
        64–65, 284; filibusters and,
        307–9; Great Triumvirate and,
        62, 153–54, 170–71, 279–283;
        W. H. Harrison and, 63; Senate
        debates and, 288; Senate
        leadership and, 65; spoils system
        and, 17
    Tocqueville and, 155
    Tyler and, 63–64
Clean Air Act (1963), 144, 221
Cleveland, Grover, 77–80, 87, 176
Clinton, Bill
    H. Clinton's campaign for Senate
        and, 48
    impeachment of, 147, 373n37
    Mitchell and, 221
    Senate and, 145–48, 351
    Whitewater case and, 272–74
Clinton, DeWitt, 278
Clinton, Hillary Rodham, 48, 146,
    272–74
Clinton v. City of New York, 147
cloture
    civil rights and, 126–27, 327–29
    Fortas nomination and, 128
    Martin and, 315–16
    Rule 22 and, 97, 100, 185, 317,
        322–24, 325–26
Clymer, Adam, 221, 300
Cochran, Thad, 39, 224, 350
Cochran, Thomas ("Tommy the
    Cork"), 109
The Code of Honor, 281

Cohen, Benjamin, 109
Cohen, William, 301
Cohn, Roy, 255
Colby, William, 269
Colfax, Schuyler, 73, 289
Collins, Susan, 12
Colombia, 86
Committee on Committees (Senate), 177
Committee on Government Operations (Senate), 129, 246, 255
Committee on Privileges (Senate), 231
committees (Senate)
    assigments of, 6, 172, 201–2, 212
    See also conference committees; joint committees; *specific committees*
communications satellite bill, 329
Communism
    HUAC and, 30, 246–47
    McCarthy and, 30, 247–49, 254–59
    Senate elections and, 30–31
Compromise of 1850, 64–65, 171, 283–84
conference committees, 161–63
Congress Hall (Philadelphia), 277–78
Congressional Budget and Impoundment Control Act (1974), 129
Congressional Government (Wilson), 90, 91, 175–76
Congressional Quarterly (CQ), 119
Conkling, Roscoe, 18–20, 71, 72, 73–76, 287
Connally, Thomas, 292, 320
Continental Congress, 56
Cook, Marlow, 228
Coolidge, Calvin, 103–4, 186, 317
Cooper, John Sherman, 228
corruption
    Grant and, 71–73
    B. Harrison's election and, 78
    Senate elections and, 18–20, 24, 26–27, 40–41
Corzine, Jon, 47, 48
Cosmopolitan Magazine, 22–23, 180

Costello, Frank, 250
Couzens, James, 293
Cox, Archibald, 265, 266, 267
Cranston, Alan, 136, 338
Crawford, Theron, 78
Cuban Missile Crisis, 124
Cullom, Shelby, 182, 295
Cummins, Albert, 237
Curtis, Charles, 105, 186, 198
Cushing, Caleb, 72
Czolgosz, Leon, 83

Daily Times (newspaper), 231–32
D'Amato, Alfonse, 219, 273
Daniels, Josephus, 92, 95
Daschle, Tom
    B. Clinton and, 146
    as party leader, 222–23, 224–25, 227
    on weekly party luncheons, 11
Dash, Samuel, 265
Daugherty, Harry, 100–101, 237–38
Davis, Cushman, 82
Davis, Jeff, 22
Davis, Jefferson, 65, 69, 233, 284, 287
Davis, John, 309
Dawes, Charles, 302, 317–18, 321–22
Dawson, Donald, 252
Dayton, Mark, 47–48
Dean, John, 265–66
debates
    House of Representatives and, 153, 155–56, 157–58, 277, 278
    Senate and, 62, 157–58, 175, 278–293
    Senate elections and, 17, 29, 31–32
    See also filibusters; legislative powers
"declining filibuster," 353
DeLay, Tom, 147
Democracy in America (Tocqueville), 154–55
Democratic Party
    Jackson and, 16–17
    party caucuses and, 172–73, 176, 185, 188, 201–2, 209
    Solid South and, 22, 38
    weekly party luncheons and, 11

Democratic Policy Committee, 202
Democratic Steering Committee, 202
Democratic-Republican Party, 16
Denby, Edwin, 238
Depew, Chauncey, 177
Dies, Martin, Jr., 246–47
Dirksen, Everett M.
    campaign for Senate and, 32, 36
    civil rights and, 126–27
    filibusters and, 126–27, 331–33
    L. Johnson and, 124–25, 126–28, 337
    Mansfield and, 211
    McCarthy and, 257
    Nuclear Test Ban Treaty and, 124
    as orator, 291, 294
    as party leader, 207, 211–13, 291,
        331–33
    as party whip, 211
    Republican Congressional Joint
        Leadership Conference and, 122
    Rule 19 and, 293
    Senate investigations and, 262
Dirksen Senate Office Building, 6–7,
    397n39
Disappearing Quorum, 157, 309–12, 315
Dodd, Christopher, 12–13, 14, 222, 273
Dodd, Thomas, 212–13
Dolan, John ("Terry"), 45
Dole, Bob
    B. Clinton and, 145–46
    D'Amato and, 273
    G. Ford and, 132
    line-item vetoes and, 146–47
    memorial space and, 7
    as party leader, 139–140, 142, 217–220,
        221, 223–24, 348, 349, 351
    on Senate debates on television, 297,
        298–99
    Watergate scandal and, 266–67
Dolliver, Jonathan, 88, 180
Domenici, Pete, 139
Douglas, Helen Gahagan, 30
Douglas, Paul, 32, 291, 328, 329
Douglas, Stephen, 17–18, 65, 171,
    284–85, 286

Duane, William, 231
dueling, 56, 281–82, 286, 305, 308
Duffee, Warren, 297
Dukakis, Michael, 141
Dunne, Finley Peter, 288, 296
Durbin, Dick, 353
Durkin, Martin, 120

Eagleton, Thomas, 348–49
Eastland, James, 38–39, 247, 258, 326, 339
Ehrenhalt, Alan, 49
Ehrlichman, John, 129–130, 214, 265,
    266
Eisenhower, Dwight
    Dirksen and, 211–12
    L. Johnson and, 121–22, 138, 201,
        204, 206
    Knowland and, 204
    Lodge and, 32
    McCarthy and, 255, 256
    Senate and, 109, 119–122
    Sputnik and, 261
    Taft and, 199
elections (House of Representatives),
    14, 150–51
elections (Senate)
    campaign financing and, 14, 26–27,
        35–36, 41–44, 46–52
    corruption and, 18–20, 24, 26–27,
        40–41
    party primaries and, 21–23, 166, 180
    Philadelphia Convention and, 14–15
    political consultants and, 34, 44–46
    racism and, 21–22, 23–24, 27–29,
        38–39
    Seventeenth Amendment and,
        23–34, 35, 166, 289–290
    state legislatures and, 15–21, 150–51,
        166
    television and, 14, 34, 36–38, 44–46
Elkins, Stephen, 19
Ellender, Allen, 322, 333, 340
Ellsberg, Daniel, 265
Emancipation Proclamation, 67
Engle, Clair, 332

Ernst, Richard, 293
Ervin, Sam, 41, 264–67, 268, 403n35
Essary, Frederick, 25
Evarts, William, 73

Fair, James, 19
fair employment practices (FEPC)
    legislation, 322
Fair Housing Act (Civil Rights Act,
    1968), 294, 334, 336
Fairbanks, Charles, 314–15
Fall, Albert, 238
Farley, James, 108–9, 110, 111
Faulkner, Charles, 313
Federal Corrupt Practices Act (1925),
    35–36, 41
Federal Election Campaign Act (1971),
    41–42
Federal Election Commission, 42, 50
Federal Hall (New York), 277
The Federalist, 168
Federalist Party, 16, 168–69
Feingold, Russell, 50–51
Feinstein, Dianne, 47
Fendall, Philip Richard II, 413n17
Fenno, Richard, 391n67
Ferguson, Homer, 109
Ferris, Woodbridge, 321
Fessenden, William Pitt, 70, 173, 287
filibusters
    T. H. Benton and, 170–71, 307–8
    Byrd and, 216, 335, 340, 341, 342–45,
        349–351, 354
    civil rights and, 38, 125–27, 303,
        318–321
    Dole and, 145–46
    Fortas nomination and, 128
    Frist and, 226
    Gorman and, 176
    history of, 302–55
    House of Representatives and, 79,
        157, 309–10
    lynchings and, 101
    Mansfield and, 126–28, 210, 330–31,
        333, 339–341

origin of word, 310–11
origins of, 170–71, 290, 301
Wilson and, 95–97, 100, 185, 315–16
See also cloture; Disappearing
    Quorum
Fillmore, Millard, 64–65
Finance Committee (Senate)
    Aldrich and, 177
    Allison and, 176
    assignment of, 6
    Fessenden and, 173
    General Electric and, 44
    L. Johnson and, 125
    Walter and, 200
    Wilson and, 93
Financial Crisis Inquiry Commission,
    274–75
Fiorina, Carly, 47, 48
Fiske, Robert, 272
Flanagan, Francis ("Frip"), 252
Flanders, Ralph, 256–57, 294
Flint, Frank, 24
Foot, Samuel, 278–79
Foot, Solomon, 173
Foote, Henry S., 282, 309
Foraker, Joseph, 89
Ford, Gerald
    Church Committee and, 269–270
    on House of Representatives, 162
    as House Republican leader, 129–130,
        214
    as president, 43, 131–34, 142
    as vice president, 131, 267, 268
Ford, Henry, 26
Ford, Wendell, 297
Foreign Relations Committee (Senate)
    Lodge and, 97, 99, 183
    MacArthur and, 253–54
    Panama Canal and, 136
    Spanish-American War and, 82
    Sumner and, 173
    treaties and, 82
    Versailles Treaty and, 99
    Vietnam War and, 133
Fortas, Abe, 127–28, 258, 337

Foster, Vincent, 272
Four Years Act (1820), 59
Four-Power Treaty, 102–3
Fowler, Henry, 337
Frear, Allen, 204
freshman senators, 294–95
Frist, William, 223, 225–27, 352
Frye, William, 192
Fulbright, J. William
    campaign for Senate and, 38
    conference committees and, 162–63
    L. Johnson and, 206
    McCarthy and, 254, 259, 295–96
    as orator, 296
    Senate investigations and, 119, 252, 259
    Vietnam War and, 125

Gadsden, Philip, 240
Gallinger, Jacob, 95–96, 182–83
Garfield, James, 74–76
Garner, John Nance
    filibusters and, 319
    party leadership and, 198–99, 206
    Robinson and, 190
    F. D. Roosevelt and, 108, 111, 191
General Electric, 44
George, Walter, 111, 116, 200, 294–95
Gilbert, Dan ("Tubbs"), 251
The Gilded Age (Twain), 20
Gingrich, Newt, 147, 165, 223–24
Ginsburg, Ruth Bader, 145
Glass, Carter, 198, 294
Glenn, John, 298
Goldwater, Barry
    H. Baker and, 410n60
    Church Committee and, 269–270
    filibusters and, 331, 332
    on Morse, 296
    as party leader, 196
    on Senate, 288–89
    Watergate scandal and, 130–31
Gorbachev, Mikhail, 141
Gordon, Slade, 48
Gore, Al, 223
Gore, Albert, Sr., 38, 209, 293, 326

Gorman, Arthur, 79, 176
Gramm, Phil, 140
Gramm-Rudman-Hollings Balanced
    Budget and Emergency Deficit
    Control Act (1985), 140
Grant, Ulysses S., 62–63, 71–74
Gravel, Maurice ("Mike"), 37, 338–39
Graves, William, 409n31
Gray, George, 82, 178
Gray, L. Patrick, 268
Griffin, Robert, 127–28, 215, 337–38
Gronna, Asle, 237
Gruening, Ernest, 37
Grunwald, Mandy, 46
Guiteau, Charles, 76
Gunn, James, 55
Guzik, Jacob "Greasy Thumb," 250
Gwin, William, 286

Haig, Alexander, 267–68
Haldeman, H. R., 214, 265, 266, 268
Hale, Eugene
    T. Roosevelt and, 85–86, 89
    Senate leadership and, 25, 176–78,
        180, 181
Hale, John P., 282
Halleck, Charles, 122
Halley, Rudolph, 249
Hamilton, Alexander, 16, 56, 169, 280
Hamilton, Lee, 271
Hamlin, Hannibal, 172–73
Hammond, James, 286
Hampton, Wade, 21
Hanna, Mark, 83, 85, 87
Harding, Warren, 100–103, 184, 237–39
Harlan, James, 19
Harlow, Bryce, 123, 130, 268
Harris, Fred, 134
Harrison, Benjamin, 78–79, 84
Harrison, Byron Patton "Pat," 98,
    107–8, 190, 317, 320
Harrison, William Henry, 62, 63, 170
Hart Senate Office Building, 7, 223
Hatch, Carl, 41
Hatch, Orrin, 345

Hatfield, Mark, 132, 163
Hawkins, Paula, 219
Hay, John, 81, 378n9
Hayden, Carl, 332
Hayes, Rutherford B., 73–74
Hay-Herran Treaty, 378n9
Hayne, Robert, 58, 154, 279
Haynes, George, 26, 197
Hearst, William Randolph, 22–23
Heflin, J. Thomas ("Cotton Tom"), 28
Heinz, John, 46–47
Helms, Jesse, 217, 347
Helms, Richard, 268
Henry, Aaron, 39
Henry, Patrick, 15–16
Hersh, Seymour, 269
Hill, Anita, 144
Hill, Lister, 38
Hinds, Asher, 156
Hoar, George Frisbie, 21, 72, 91, 293,
    312–13
Hobart, Garret, 83
Hobbs, Samuel, 152
Hoblitzell, John, 32–34
Hoey, Clyde, 119, 252
Hoffa, James, 260
Hofstadter, Richard, 107
"hold", 336, 345–47
Holland, Spessard, 206
Hollings, Ernest, 297
Hollis, Henry, 316
Holman, William, 390n52
Honest Leadership and Open
    Government Act (HLOGA,
    2007), 50
Hook, Janet, 419n8
Hoover, Herbert, 103–6, 186–87, 239
Hoover, J. Edgar, 248
Horn, Stephen, 391n67
House Committee on Un-American
    Activities (HUAC), 30, 246–47
House of Representatives
    appropriations bills and, 158–161
    civil rights and, 126
    conference committees and, 161–63

creation of, 149–150
criticism of Senate and, 151–52
debates in, 153, 155–56, 157–58, 277, 278
Disappearing Quorum and, 157,
    309–10
elections and, 14, 150–51, 327
filibusters and, 79, 157, 309–10
investigations and, 147, 231, 232–33,
    235, 243–44, 245–47, 271
Iran-Contra scandal and, 271
joint committees and, 164–66
legislative powers and, 54–55, 58–59,
    63, 151, 156–57, 170
lynchings and, 319
powers of, 151, 230
president and, 54
Previous Question and, 155–56, 305
T. Roosevelt and, 84, 87, 88
Senate elections and, 23, 24
tariff reforms and, 80
Tocqueville on, 154–55
tradition and, 10
women in, 9
Houston, Sam, 65
Hruska, Roman, 214, 262
Huffington, Michael, 47
Hughes, Charles Evans, 102
Hughes, Harold, 338
Hull, Cordell, 107
Humphrey, George, 120
Humphrey, Hubert, 208, 210–11,
    213–14, 330, 331
Humphrey, Murray "The Camel," 250
Hunt, Sam "Golf bag," 250
Hyatt, Thaddeus, 233, 241
Hyde, Henry, 147

immunity, 295–96. See also use
    immunity
impeachment
    B. Clinton and, 147, 373n37
    House of Representatives and, 151
    A. Johnson and, 70–71
    Nixon and, 130–31, 266, 268
    Senate and, 151, 232

Independence Hall (Philadelphia), 277–78
Inouye, Daniel, 144, 149, 271
Intermediate Nuclear Forces (INF) treaty, 141
Internal Revenue Bureau, 231
Interstate Commerce Act (1887), 236
Interstate Commerce Commission (ICC), 88–89
Iran, 137
Iran-Contra scandal, 141, 165–66, 220–21, 270–71
Iraq Wars, 129
Iraqi War Resolution (2002), 359

Jackson, Andrew
  Clay and, 58, 281
  dueling and, 281–82
  political parties and, 16–17
  Seminole War and, 58, 231
  Senate and, 59–62, 153–54, 169, 279–280, 307
  Wilson on, 95–96
Jackson, Henry, 134
Javits, Jacob, 133
Jay Treaty (1794), 158
Jefferson, Thomas
  Democratic-Republican Party and, 16
  on federal positions, 59
  Manual of Parliamentary Practice, 151–52, 224, 304–5
  as Secretary of State, 158, 161, 169
  on Senate, 150, 169, 288
  Senate and, 56–57
  as vice president, 151–52, 288
Jeffords, James, 223
Jenner, William, 247, 255, 258, 295
Jessup, Philip, 259
"Jim Crow" laws, 22
Johnson, Andrew, 68, 69–71, 287
Johnson, Hiram, 289–290
Johnson, Lyndon
  accents and, 297
  campaign for Senate and, 36, 40–41

Eisenhower and, 121–22, 138, 201, 204, 206
  J. F. Kennedy and, 261
  McCarthy and, 257
  as president: filibusters and, 330–31, 333, 337–38; Senate and, 124–28
  as senator: Armed Services Committee and, 259–260; filibusters and, 323–24, 325–27; investigations and, 261–62; as party leader, 38, 121–22, 124, 199, 200–208, 257, 261–62, 299, 325–27; as party whip, 196, 200–201; quorum calls and, 299
  as vice president, 123, 208–9, 328
Johnston, Bennett, 298, 349
Joint Committee on the Conduct of the War, 67, 69, 233–35
Joint Committee on the Organization of Congress, 245
joint committees, 164–66
joint rules, 163–64
Judiciary Committee (House of Representatives), 268, 392n70
Judiciary Committee (Senate), 82, 172–73, 247, 326
The Jungle (Sinclair), 89, 179

Kansas-Nebraska Act (1854), 285
Katrina, Hurricane, 274
Kefauver, Estes, 38, 249–251, 262, 326
Kelsey, Frances Oldham, 262
Kennedy, Anthony, 51, 141
Kennedy, Edward M.
  accent of, 297
  Byrd and, 4
  campaign for Senate and, 47
  on J. Carter, 134
  as party leader, 214
  Watergate scandal and, 264
Kennedy, John F.
  campaign for Senate and, 32, 34
  on Johnson, 202

Kelsey and, 262
as president: civil rights and, 125–26;
   on Congress, 53; filibusters and,
   328–330; Republican
   Congressional Joint Leadership
   Conference and, 122; Senate and,
   122–24
presidential nomination and, 208
on Ross, 70–71
as senator, 260–61, 294–95
Kennedy, Robert F., 331
Kern, John, 181–82, 185
Keyes, Henry, 321
Kilbourn, Hallet, 235
Kilbourn v. Thompson, 235
King, Rufus, 161, 169
King, William, 281, 308
Kleindienst, Richard, 265
Knowland, William
   Eisenhower and, 121, 204
   McCarthy and, 256–57
   as party leader, 121, 200, 202–3, 204,
      211
Knox, Henry, 53
Knox, Philander, 86
Korean War, 118–19, 129, 194–95, 230,
   253
Kuchel, Thomas, 212, 330
Kuwait, 144–45

La Follette, Robert ("Fighting Bob")
   Aldrich and, 180–81
   Fall and, 238
   filibusters and, 96–97, 185, 314–15
   as orator, 289–290
   presidential nomination and, 181, 186
   Senate election of, 21, 180
   Senate investigations and, 237
   Wilson and, 96–97, 185
La Follette, Robert, Jr., 242
labor unions, 41, 260–61
Lamar, Lucius Quintus Cincinnatus, 21
Landon, Alfred, 242
Lansky, Meyer, 250
Lautenberg, Frank, 47

Laxalt, Paul, 43, 136, 345
Lazio, Enrico ("Rick"), 48
League of Nations, 96, 97, 98–99, 183
legislative powers
   J. Carter and, 135, 137
   Cleveland and, 77–80, 87
   conference committees and,
      161–63
   Coolidge and, 103
   Harding and, 101–2
   W. H. Harrison and, 63
   B. Harrison and, 78
   House of Representatives and,
      54–55, 58–59, 63, 151, 156–57, 170
   Jackson and, 154
   Jefferson and, 56–57
   J. F. Kennedy and, 123–24
   Lincoln and, 66–67
   McKinley and, 80–81
   F. D. Roosevelt and, 107–11, 112–13,
      114
   T. Roosevelt and, 87–90
   Senate and, 54–56, 58–59, 63, 151,
      157
   Truman and, 109, 116–18, 119
   Washington and, 54–56
   Wilson and, 91–97
   See also debates; vetoes
Legislative Reorganization Act (1946), 115
Lewis, J. Hamilton, 182
Library of Congress, 165, 166
Libya, 129, 148
Liman, Arthur, 271
Lincoln, Abraham, 17–18, 62–63,
   65–69, 234–35, 287
Line-Item Veto Act, 146–47
line-item vetoes, 146–47
Lippitt, Henry, 237
Lodge, Henry Cabot
   Borah and, 183–84
   filibusters and, 95–96, 313
   Foreign Relations Committee and, 183
   Harding and, 102–3
   T. Roosevelt and, 85, 87, 183
   Wilson and, 97, 98–100

Lodge, Henry Cabot, Jr., 32
Long, Huey Pierce, 188, 289, 318–19
Long, Russell, 214, 323, 340–41
Longley, Lawrence, 391n67
Lorimer, William, 24
Lott, Trent
    B. Clinton and, 146
    Daschle and, 222
    as freshman, 7
    on Mitchell, 221
    as party leader, 224–25, 352
    as party whip, 223–24
    on weekly party luncheons, 11
Lucas, Scott
    campaign for Senate and, 32
    election defeat of, 196, 200
    Kefauver and, 251
    as party leader, 118, 194, 195, 197
Luciano, "Lucky," 250
Lugar, Richard, 345, 350
lynchings, 22, 101, 319–321

MacArthur, Douglas, 119, 253–54
MacCracken, William, 241, 265
Maclay, William, 54, 153, 154, 277, 304
Madison, James, 16, 56, 57, 150, 151
Magnuson, Warren, 123
Manley, John, 391n67
Mansfield, Mike
    filibusters and, 126–28, 210, 330–31,
        333, 339–341
    L. Johnson and, 124–25
    Nixon and, 128
    Nuclear Test Ban Treaty and, 124
    as party leader, 163, 208–11, 212–13,
        215, 264, 328, 339–341
    on Senate leadership, 224
    Vietnam War and, 125
    Watergate scandal and, 130–31, 264
Manual of Parliamentary Practice
        (Jefferson), 151–52, 224, 304–5
Marcy, William, 17
Marshall, George, 244, 254, 255
Marshall, Thurgood, 143
Martin, Joseph, 115, 253

Martin, Thomas, 185, 315–16
Maslin, Paul, 46
Mason, James, 232–33, 285
Mason, William, 288
May, Andrew Jackson, 403n42
Maybank, Burnet Rhett, 297
McCain, John, 50–51
McCarran, Patrick, 111, 247, 258
McCarthy, Joseph R.
    Bohlen and, 120
    Communism and, 30, 247–49,
        254–59
    Dirksen and, 211
    Fulbright and, 295–96
    immunity and, 295–96
    Johnson and, 203
    Senate investigations and, 247–49
    Taft and, 194
McClellan, George, 234, 259, 260–61,
    340
McConnell, Mitch
    filibusters and, 354
    Lott and, 7
    as party leader, 225, 228–29, 354
    as party whip, 227–28
    soft money ban and, 50
McConnell v. Federal Election
        Commission, 50
McCord, James, 264–65
McDougal, Jim, 272
McDougal, Susan, 272
McFarland, Ernest, 195–96, 197, 201
McFarlane, Robert, 270–71
McGinniss, Joe, 37–38
McGovern, George, 45
McGrory, Mary, 222
McKellar, Kenneth, 116, 200, 322
McKinley, William B., 26–27, 80–83,
    85, 98, 176–78
McLaurin, John, 88, 293
McMahon, Linda, 47
McMillan, James, 19, 179
McNary, Charles, 189–190, 192, 198
Meese, Edwin, 141
Mencken, H. L., 288

Metzenbaum, Howard, 47, 342–43
military draft, 338–39
Miller, Arthur, 404n14
Miller, Samuel, 235
Millikin, Eugene, 193
Missouri Compromise (1820), 58, 153
Mitchell, George, 142, 145–46, 220–23, 266, 350–51
Mitchell, John, 265
Mitchill, Samuel, 278
Mondale, Walter, 343–44
Monroe, James, 56, 57–58, 59
Morgan, Edwin, 71
Morgan, J. P., 86, 239
Morgan, John T., 288
Morrill, Justin, 174, 176
Morris, Edmund, 390n56
Morrison, Cameron, 30
Morse, Wayne, 213, 296, 325
Morton, Oliver, 18–19
Moses, George, 105
Moynihan, Daniel Patrick, 218–19
muckrakers, 22–23, 179–180
Mundt, Karl, 256, 332
Murrow, Edward R., 258
Muskie, Edmund, 220, 344
Myers, Francis, 118, 196, 200

Napolitan, Joseph, 37
National Aeronautics and Space
    Administration (NASA),
    261–62
National Commission on Terrorist
    Attacks Upon the United States
    (9/11 Commission), 274
National Conservative Political Action
    Committee (NCPAC), 45
National Organization of Women, 143
national security, 114
Neely, Matthew, 288
Neuberger, Richard, 207
Newberry, Truman, 26
Nixon, Richard M.
    campaign for Senate and, 30
    filibusters and, 324, 327

as president: G. H. W. Bush and,
    142; G. Ford and, 132;
    impeachment of, 130–31, 266, 268;
    Senate and, 128–131, 214; Supreme
    Court nominations and, 228;
    Vietnam War and, 128–29,
    338–39
presidential campaign and, 37–38, 41
television and, 37–38
as vice president, 324, 327
See also Watergate scandal
Norbeck, Peter, 239
Noriega, Manuel, 144
Norris, George W.
    filibusters and, 96–97, 317, 318
    as orator, 289–290
    Senate election of, 21, 29
    Wilson and, 96–97
North, Oliver, 221, 270–71
North American Free Trade Agreement,
    221
Northern Securities Company, 86
Nuclear Test Ban Treaty (1963), 124
Nye, Gerald, 241–42

Obama, Barack, 129, 148, 227, 352–53
O'Brien, Lawrence
    on Dirksen, 126, 333
    L. Johnson and, 125
    J. F. Kennedy and, 34, 122–23
    Watergate scandal and, 264
O'Connor, Sandra Day, 141
O'Daniel, Wilbert Lee, 40
office suites and staff, 6–7, 290, 359
Old Senate Chamber, 358
Oleszek, Walter, 391n67
O'Neill, Thomas P., 134, 266
Open Housing Act (1968), 328
Ornstein, Norman J., 300–301,
    364–65n14
Overman, Lee, 237

PAC (political action committee)
    system, 42–44
Packwood, Robert, 335

Panama, 144
Panama Canal, 86, 136–37, 179
Parker, Alton, 87–88
party caucuses
    Bryce on, 175
    committee assignments and,
        172–74
    Democratic Party and, 172–73, 176,
        185, 188, 201–2, 209
    Republican Party and, 173–75,
        176–77, 182–83
party primaries, 21–23, 166, 180
party whips, 182, 213
Pastore, John, 163, 290–91
Patient Protection and Affordable Care
    Act (2010), 229
"Patrick Henry," 306
Payne, Henry, 19
Peace Corps, 123
Pearson, James, 347–48
Pecora, Ferdinand, 239–240, 274
Peffer, William, 89
Pendleton, George, 76–77
Pendleton Civil Service Reform Act
    (1883), 41, 76–77
Penrose, Boies, 18, 24–25
Pepper, Claude, 30–31
Pepper, George Wharton, 27
Percy, LeRoy, 23–24
Percy, William Alexander, 23–24
Peress, Irving, 255–56
Pershing, John, 97
Persian Gulf War, 144–45
Peskin, Allan, 376n97
Pettigrew, Richard, 179
Pettigrew, Richard F., 380–81n73
Philadelphia Convention, 14–15, 54,
    149–151, 168
Phillips, David Graham, 22–23, 180
Pierce, Franklin, 65
Pinchot, Gifford, 27
Platt, Orville
    death of, 180
    T. Roosevelt and, 85–86, 88
    Senate leadership and, 25, 176–78

Platt, Thomas ("The Easy Boss"), 76,
    78, 82–83, 178
Plumer, William, 294
Poindexter, George, 283
Poindexter, John, 270–71
political action committee (PAC)
    system, 42–44
political consultants, 34, 44–46
political parties, 16–17
The Politics of Finance (Manley), 391n67
Polk, James K., 64, 309
Pomeroy, Samuel, 20
Powell, Lazurus, 310
The Power of the Purse (Fenno), 391n67
Previous Question rule, 155–56, 304–5
Proctor, Redfield, 81
Profiles in Courage (Kennedy), 70–71
Proxmire, William, 207, 338, 370n37
Pryor, David, 299
Public Utilities Holding Company Act
    (1935), 240

el Qaddafi, Muammar, 129
Quay, Matthew ("Matt")
    filibusters and, 313
    B. Harrison and, 78, 79, 84
    T. Roosevelt and, 83, 84
    spoils system and, 18
Quayle, Dan, 45, 348
quorum calls
    filibusters and, 326–27, 335
    House of Representatives and, 309–10
    Senate debates on television and,
        299–300

racism
    Harding and, 101
    Senate elections and, 21–22, 23–24,
        27–29, 38–39
radio, 29, 37, 109–10
Randolph, Edmund, 15
Randolph, Jennings, 32–34, 137
Randolph, John, 282, 283, 289, 305–6
Rauh, Joseph, 404n14
Raushenbush, Stephen, 241–42

Rayburn, Sam, 114, 115, 191, 204
Reagan, Ronald
  H. Baker and, 216
  G. H. W. Bush and, 142
  Dole and, 217–18
  Iran-Contra scandal and, 270–71
  line-item vetoes and, 146–47
  Senate and, 137–141
Reconstruction Finance Corporation
  (RFC), 119, 252
Reed, Thomas B., 85, 152, 156, 157,
  311–12
Reedy, George, 248–49
Rehnquist, William, 141
Reid, Harry, 14, 51, 149, 226–27, 354
Republican Congressional Joint
  Leadership Conference, 122
Republican Party
  party caucuses and, 173–75, 176–77,
  182–83
  weekly party luncheons and, 11
Republican Steering Committee,
  174–75, 177, 184
Revercomb, Chapman, 32–34
Reynolds, Robert ("Buncombe Bob"),
  30
Rhodes, John, 130
Ribicoff, Abraham, 125, 297, 347–48
Richardson, Elliott, 130, 265, 267
Robert's Rules of Order, 305
Robertson, William, 74, 76
Robertson, Willis, 209
Robinson, Arthur, 198
Robinson, Joseph T.
  death of, 111
  on H. Long, 319
  as party leader, 108, 185–86, 187–89,
  197–98
  F. D. Roosevelt and, 107, 108
  on Senate elections, 25–26
Rockefeller, John D. IV ("Jay"), 47, 177
Rockefeller, Nelson Aldrich, 131–32
Roe v. Wade, 143
Rogers, Lindsay, 302
Rogers, William P., 252

Romney, Mitt, 47
Roosevelt, Franklin D.
  Senate and, 106–13, 114, 187–88, 197
  Senate investigations and, 239–240
  Social Security and, 319
  Solid South and, 22
  Supreme Court and, 110–11, 189–190
  Yalta Conference and, 112, 120
Roosevelt, Theodore
  Cleveland and, 80
  Lodge and, 85, 87, 183
  Platt and, 83
  Senate and, 84–90, 179
  Senate investigations and, 236,
  241–43
  Spanish-American War and, 81
Root, Elihu, 24
Ross, Edmund, 70–71
Rovere, Richard, 197, 254
Ruckelshaus, William, 267
Rudman, Warren, 143, 335
Russell, Richard B.
  Armed Services Committee and,
  253–54
  death of, 338
  filibusters and, 303, 320–21, 326, 329,
  330–31
  L. Johnson and, 196, 200–201, 204
  on the Old South, 38
  as party leader, 329
  Truman and, 119
Russell Senate Office Building, 6–7

SALT-II Pact, 137
Saltonstall, Leverett, 200
Santorum, Rick, 412n103
Sarbanes, Paul, 273, 344
Sasser, James, 226
Saturday Night Massacre, 130, 267–68
Saulsbury, Willard, 287
Sawyer, Philetus, 19
Scalia, Antonin, 141, 292
Schiavo, Terri, 226
Schoeppel, Andrew, 295
Schorr, Daniel, 269–270

Schram, Martin, 135
Schuyler, Phillip, 169
Scott, Hugh, 128, 130–31, 214–15, 268, 293
Securities Exchange Act (1934), 240
Seigel, "Bugsy," 250
Select Committee on Presidential Campaign Activities, 392n70. *See also* Watergate scandal
Select Committee on Secret Military Assistance to Iran and the Nicaraguan Opposition (Senate), 271, 392n70. *See also* Iran-Contra scandal
Select Committee to Investigate Covert Arms Transactions with Iran (House of Representatives), 392n70
Select Committee to Study Governmental Operations with Respect to Intelligence Activities (Church Committee), 269–270
The Selling of the President, 1968 (McGinniss), 37–38
Seminole War, 58, 231
Senate
    composition of, 9–10
    as continuing body, 327–28
    creation of, 149–151, 358–59
    criticism of, 151–52, 288–89
    powers of, 151, 230, 276
    presiding officers and, 10–11
    reform of, 358–360
    tradition and, 10
    women in, 9
Senate chamber, 7–9
Senate Reception Room, 358
Sequoia (yacht), 135–36
Seventeenth Amendment, 23–34, 35, 166, 289–290
Seward, William, 65, 66, 67, 68, 284
Sherman, John, 74, 289
Sherman, Roger, 150
Sherman, William Tecumseh, 68
Sherman Antitrust Act (1890), 86

Sherman Silver Purchase Act (1890), 80, 312–13
Shields, Mark, 49
Simmons, Furnifold, 92, 94–95
Simpson, Alan, 223, 335
Sinclair, Harry, 238
Sinclair, Upton, 89, 179
Sirica, John, 264
slavery
    Calhoun on, 280
    Compromise of 1850 and, 64–65, 171, 283–84
    Lincoln and, 66, 67
    Missouri Compromise and, 58, 153
    Senate and, 153, 171–72
    Van Buren and, 62
Smathers, George, 30–31, 204
Smith, Alfred, 187
Smith, Ellison ("Cotton Ed"), 21–22, 111, 291
Smith, Frank L., 26–27
Smith, Hoke, 28
Smith, Margaret Chase, 295
Smith, Steven, 391n59
Smoot, Reed, 186
Smoot-Hawley Act (1930), 104
soft money, 49–50
Solid South, 22, 38
Sourwine, Jay, 258
Souter, David, 143
Spaatz, Carl, 258
Spanish-American War, 81–82
Sparkman, John, 38, 120, 210–11
Special Committee to Investigate the National Defense Program, 242–43
Special Committee to Investigate Whitewater Development Corporation and Related Matters, 273
Specter, Arlen, 419n54
spoils system, 16–19, 58–59, 60, 71–77
Spooner, John, 25, 85–86, 177, 180
Sprague, William, 71
Sputnik, 261

Squier, Robert, 46
Stalin, Joseph, 112, 120
Stanton, Edwin, 70
Starr, Kenneth, 272, 273
state legislatures, 14–21, 150–51, 166,
    358–59
Stealey, O. O., 157
Stennis, John, 204, 267, 338–39
Stephenson, Isaac, 19
Stevens, John Paul, 51
Stevens, Robert, 256
Stevens, Ted, 217
Stevenson, Coke, 41
Stewart, Alexander T., 375n80
Stewart, William, 173
Strauss, Lewis, 121–22
Sullivan, Mark, 102
Sumner, Charles
    Brooks and, 232, 286
    Fessenden on, 287
    Foreign Relations Committee and, 173
    Andrew Johnson and, 69
    on Lincoln, 66
    as orator, 285–86, 287, 289
Sununu, John, 143
Supreme Court
    G. H. W. Bush and, 222–23
    Clinton v. City of New York and, 147
    Gramm-Rudman-Hollings Balanced
        Budget and Emergency Deficit
        Control Act and, 140
    on international agreements, 121
    Kilbourn v. Thompson and, 235
    Line-Item Veto Act and, 146–47
    Nixon and, 230, 268
    nominations: G. H. W. Bush and,
        143; G. W. Bush and, 352; Clinton
        and, 145; Nixon and, 228; Reagan
        and, 141
    F. D. Roosevelt and, 110–11, 189–190
    Senate debates and, 292
    Senate elections and, 26, 35, 42, 50–51
    Senate investigations and, 241, 265
    Senate structure and, 359
Symington, Stuart, 261

Taft, Robert A.
    campaign for Senate and, 31
    Dirksen and, 211
    Eisenhower and, 119–120
    McCarthy and, 194, 248
    party leadership and, 119–120,
        192–95, 199–200
    Senate investigations and, 236
    Truman and, 116, 117, 118, 253
Taft, William Howard, 90–91, 181
Taft-Hartley Labor-Management
        Relations Act (1947), 193
"talking filibuster," 353
tariff reforms
    Cleveland and, 77–78, 79–80
    Hoover and, 104
    Senate and, 160
    Wilson and, 92–93, 94–95,
        236–37
Tax Reform Act (1986), 140
Taxpayer Relief Act (1997), 147
Taylor, Telford, 239
Taylor, Zachary, 64
Teamsters Union, 260–61
television
    House of Representatives debates
        and, 297–98
    Senate chamber and, 8–9
    Senate debates and, 297–301,
        349–350
    Senate elections and, 14, 34, 36–38,
        44–46
    Senate investigations and, 249–250,
        256, 260
    Watergate scandal and, 266–67
Tenure of Office Act (1867), 70
Territories Committee, 176
thalidomide, 262
Thomas, Charles, 316
Thomas, Clarence, 143–44
Thompson, Charles Willis, 25, 184
Thompson, John, 235
Thurman, Allen, 311
Thurmond, Strom, 38–39, 225, 325, 339
Tilden, Samuel, 73

Tillman, Benjamin ("Pitchfork Ben")
   campaign spending and, 41
   filibusters and, 314
   as orator, 289
   racism and, 21–22, 27–28
   T. Roosevelt and, 88–89
   violence and, 88–89, 293
Tillman Act (1907), 43
de Tocqueville, Alexis, 62, 154–55
Toombs, Robert, 286–87
Tower, John, 39, 142, 269–270
Townsend, Charles, 94
Townsend, George Alfred, 174
tracking polls, 46
treaties
   J. Carter and, 136–37
   executive agreements and, 114,
      120–21
   Foreign Relations Committee
      and, 82
   McKinley and, 81–82
   T. Roosevelt and, 86–87
   Senate and, 151
   Washington and, 53–54, 158
   See also specific treaties
Truman, Harry S.
   Kefauver and, 251
   as president: bipartisan foreign
      policy and, 103; HUAC and, 247;
      McCarthy and, 248; Senate and,
      109, 115–19, 192–94; Senate
      investigations and, 119, 252,
      259–260
   on Senate elections, 31
   Senate investigations and, 119,
      242–43, 252, 259–260, 274
   as senator, 31, 115–16, 242–43, 274
   Sparkman and, 38
Truman Committee, 242–43, 274
Trumbull, John, 13
Trumbull, Lyman, 174, 310
Tumulty, Joseph, 99–100
Twain, Mark, 20
Tydings, Millard, 30, 111, 248
Tyler, John, 63–64, 73, 170–71

Underwood, Oscar, 102–3, 185,
   319–320, 322
Underwood Tariff Act, 236–37
Union Party, 68
United Nations, 116, 120
Universal Declaration of Human
   Rights, 120
Unused Power (Horn), 391n67
US Post Office, 231, 241
use immunity, 263, 265, 271

Van Buren, Martin
   Albany Regency and, 16–17
   as president, 61, 62, 170
   as senator, 306
   as vice president, 283
Van Devanter, Willis, 110–11, 190
Vance, Cyrus, 337
Vance, Zebulon, 21
Vandenberg, Arthur, 115, 116, 193, 296,
   322–23
Vardaman, James K., 23–24, 98
Vare, William, 27
Vaughan, Harry, 252
Versailles Treaty, 93, 98–100, 183–84,
   237, 316
vetoes
   J. Q. Adams and, 56
   J. Adams and, 56
   Arthur and, 76
   G. H. W. Bush and, 221
   G. Ford and, 134
   Jackson and, 60–61, 169
   Jefferson and, 56
   A. Johnson and, 70
   Lincoln and, 66–67
   Madison and, 56
   Monroe and, 56
   F. D. Roosevelt and, 191
   Truman and, 117, 193
   Tyler and, 171
   Washington and, 56
   See also line-item vetoes
vice presidents, 10, 168, 172
Vietnam War, 124, 125, 128–29, 133, 338–39

violence
    Senate elections and, 23–24
    Sumner and, 232, 286
    Tillman and, 88–89, 293
    See also dueling
Voorhees, Daniel, 312
Voting Rights Act (1965), 38, 328, 336

Wade, Benjamin, 66, 67–69, 173,
    234–35, 285
Walsh, David, 26
Walsh, Edmund, 247–48
War of 1812, 57
War Powers Resolution (1973), 128–29,
    144, 148
Warren, Earl, 127, 337
Warren, Francis, 186
Washington, George, 53–56, 150, 158
Watergate scandal
    H. Baker and, 230, 264, 266, 267
    committees and, 165–66
    G. Ford and, 131, 267
    House of Representatives and,
        165–66, 263
    MacCracken decision and, 265,
        403n35
    overview, 41, 263–69
    H. Scott and, 130–31
Watkins, Arthur, 257
Watson, James ("Sunny Jim"), 105, 106,
    186–87
Ways and Means Committee (House of
    Representatives), 44, 159
weapons, 286
Webster, Daniel
    as House member, 277
    on the presidency, 59
    presidential bid of, 64
    on Senate, 276
    as senator: appropriations bills and,
        159; Compromise of 1850 and,
        284; Great Triumvirate and, 62,
        153–54, 170–71, 279–283; Jackson

and, 60, 169; as orator, 58, 279;
    Senate leadership and, 65
    Tocqueville and, 155
Weicker, Lowell, 217
Welch, Joseph, 256
Welker, Herman, 295
Wheeler, Burton K., 186
Wherry, Kenneth, 194–95
Whig Party, 16–17, 65, 169
White, Edward, 185
White, Wallace, 192–93, 194
White, William S., 251
Whitewater Development
    Corporation, 272–74
"Why Great Men Are Not Chosen
    Presidents" (Bryce), 62–63
Wicker, Tom, 122
Willey, Waitman, 71
Williams, George Henry, 72
Williams, John Sharp, 93
Wilson, Charles, 256
Wilson, Pete, 140
Wilson, Woodrow
    Cleveland and, 80
    on Congress, 175–76
    filibusters and, 95–97, 100, 185,
        315–16
    on president's role, 90, 93
    Senate and, 91–100, 102, 181–82
    Solid South and, 22
    Underwood Tariff Act and, 236–37
women, 9
World War I, 95–98
World War II, 112, 115–16
Wright, Silas, 283

Yalta Conference (1945), 112,
    120, 121
Yarborough, Ralph, 142
Young, Milton, 332
Yulee, David, 310

Zwicker, Ralph, 256